PLAIN LIVES IN A
GOLDEN AGE

This is an account of the ordinary people of the province of Holland, in the seventeenth century, Holland's 'golden age', and in particular during the eighty years of war with Spain. First published in Dutch as four short volumes, it has been recognised as a pioneering attempt to write a history 'from below', based on a mass of contemporary documentary evidence, much of it previously unexplored.

Professor van Deursen explains first how the common man made his everyday living, as a labourer, for instance, or a peasant, sailor or soldier, and how much he had to spend. The second section answers questions about the way people spent their spare time, in playing, drinking, and (more occasionally) reading. Courtship and marriage are discussed, along with the everyday life of married women, who were nearly always obliged to add to the family income through their own labour. Professor van Deursen then examines the common man as subject and citizen, his relations with the authorities and his grudging attitude towards taxation. The final section deals with religion and popular culture. Although folk were free to make their own choices among a variety of denominations – Calvinist, Catholic, Mennonite among them – every sect was tinged by a strict sense of propriety and sobriety.

Professor Van Deursen is an outstanding and gifted scholar of the seventeenth-century Netherlands. His breadth of coverage over a wide range of questions in social history, such as the family, sex, and working and living conditions, will ensure that this English translation by Dr Maarten Ultee will become a standard work for students. The volume is attractively illustrated throughout with contemporary paintings, engravings and pamphlets.

PLAIN LIVES IN A GOLDEN AGE

Popular culture, religion and society in seventeenth-century Holland

A. T. VAN DEURSEN
Translated by Maarten Ultee

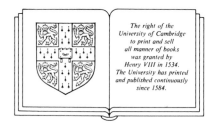

The right of the
University of Cambridge
to print and sell
all manner of books
was granted by
Henry VIII in 1534.
The University has printed
and published continuously
since 1584.

CAMBRIDGE UNIVERSITY PRESS

Cambridge
New York   Port Chester
Melbourne   Sydney

Published by the Press Syndicate of the University of Cambridge
The Pitt Building, Trumpington Street, Cambridge CB2 IRP
40 West 20th Street, New York, NY 10011, USA
10 Stamford Road, Oakleigh, Melbourne 3166, Australia

Originally published in Dutch as *Het kopergeld van de Gouden Eeuw* in four volumes
by Van Gorcum, Assen, 1978, 1979, 1980, 1981
and © 1978, 1979, 1980 and 1981 Van Gorcum & Comp. B.V., Postbus 43, 9400 AA Assen
First published in English by Cambridge University Press 1991 as *Plain Lives in a Golden Age:
popular culture, religion and society in seventeenth-century Holland*
English translation © Cambridge University Press 1991

Printed in Great Britain by Butler & Tanner Ltd, Frome and London

British Library cataloguing in publication data

Deursen, A. T. van
Plain lives in a golden age: popular culture, religion and society in seventeenth-century Holland
1. Netherlands. Social conditions, 1568–1795
I. Title   II. Kopergeld van de Gouden Eeuw. *English* 949.203
ISBN 0 521 36606 2
ISBN 0 521 36785 9 pbk

Library of Congress cataloguing in publication data

Deursen, Arie Theodorus van.
[Kopergeld van de Gouden Eeuw, English]
Plain lives in a golden age: popular culture, religion and society in seventeenth-century Holland
/A. T. Van Deursen; translated by Maarten Ultee.
        p.   cm.
Translation of: Het kopergeld van de Gouden Eeuw.
Includes bibliographical references.
ISBN 0–521–36606–2. – ISBN 0–521–36785–9 (paperback)
1. Netherlands – Social conditions.   2. Netherlands – Economic conditions.   3. Netherlands –
Foreign population – History – 17th century.   4. Working class – Netherlands – History – 17th
century.
I. Title.
HN513.D4813   1991
306'.09492'09032 – dc20   90–1684 CIP

ISBN 0 521 36606 2 hardback
ISBN 0 521 36785 9 paperback

CONTENTS

ILLUSTRATIONS

PREFACE TO THE ENGLISH EDITION

This book has a simple aim: to tell how the common people of Holland lived during war with Spain. That sentence says it all. It speaks of telling, rather than of analysing or exploring in depth. Our goal is both simple and modest. Description must precede explanation; and so long as much of the description remains uncertain or totally obscure, any detailed attempt at explanation must be premature.

The reader will infer from that initial mention of the common people that the book will not discuss the elite, but rather all the other members of society: petty shopkeepers and wage earners, peasants and craftsmen, soldiers and sailors, beggars and vagrants, groups which included both men and women.

In discussing the common people of Holland, i.e. those who lived in the province of that name, the provincial sample is not taken as representative of the whole United Provinces of the Netherlands. The present text may indeed apply to other regions, but not necessarily so. The enclosing dates of the study are 1572 and 1648, the years in which Holland won and established its independence. However, the latter date receives more emphasis than the former because the emphasis has been placed on the 'Golden Age', generally speaking the first half of the seventeenth century.

Finally, the book describes how the common people of Holland *lived*. Of all the words in my opening sentence this one has the most pretensions. It has no limits, and thus cannot be realised. But might we not thus describe all historical writing, which can at best only approach 'the truth'? If the reader comes even a little closer to the reality of everyday life in seventeenth-century Holland, our story will not have been told in vain.

Many people have assisted directly or indirectly in the preparation of this work. In the Dutch edition I mentioned Mesdames Corry van Renselaar and Joke Roelevink, and I should like to repeat their names here. I must also add that of the translator, Dr Maarten Ultee, whose resourcefulness always found a solution for the most impenetrable problems. Despite his efforts, any shortcomings still found in the text remain my responsibility.

PART I

Daily Bread

Chapter 1

PEOPLE OF LITTLE WISDOM AND LIMITED POWER

On Christmas eve, 1593, a severe storm landed three rich Delft brewers in such serious financial difficulties that they were unable to meet their obligations. Soon afterwards their collapse brought down others as well, and the entire Delft brewing industry, once so flourishing, began to decay.[1] This is how the seventeenth-century historian Pieter Bor explains the beginning of the decline of the breweries of Delft. Yet nowadays we are likely to find his explanation unsatisfactory. To our way of thinking, if the major industry of Delft was really flourishing in 1593, it should certainly have withstood a few strong winds. And if Delft brewing still appeared to be declining twenty years later,[2] we are even less inclined to believe that a calm Christmas eve in 1593 could have been its salvation.

Nonetheless, Bor helps us to understand two important points better. First, we see the extreme fragility of seventeenth-century prosperity. One day of bad weather is mentioned in the chronicles of the time as an irreparable blow to the most important industry in one of the largest cities of Holland. Also, we see that even in a period of economic growth in such a small place as the province of Holland, there were all kinds of variations and exceptions. Before we can accept historical accounts of Dutch prosperity, it must be demonstrated specifically for every industrial sector and city. An economy that was so sensitive to small crises frequently had to settle accounts. In an age of great expansion on the one hand and limited governmental control on the other, the bill had to be paid by the economically weakest members of society. We should hardly expect to find prosperity for the mass of the Dutch population in the seventeenth century.

Naturally there were differences among the population. Within the mass we can distinguish three separate groups, in descending order: the small bourgeois, the petty artisans, and the common people. The boundaries were fluid, largely determined by the practically unknowable and highly fluctuating factor of personal prosperity. 'Wherever there is a penny [*stuiver*] to be earned, ten hands try to grab it,' Baudartius declared in 1624.[3] Since the beginning of the sixteenth century, the population of Holland had been growing rapidly, sometimes even explosively.[4] Economic expansion gave the common people some chances to move up, but the population explosion meant that they were more likely to move down in the oversupplied labour market. Therefore we shall not try to divide the people into income groups; rather, we shall attempt a rough sketch of the material conditions of life in various categories, arranged by occupation and profession: the urban craftsmen, small farmers and agricultural workers, sailors and fishermen, and finally soldiers. Those who were no longer able or willing to work for their daily bread will remain beyond the scope of this chapter.

I

Let us begin with the artisans in the cities, for they illustrate immediately how difficult it is to make further divisions of the working population. What could be more natural than to group the independent craftsmen with the petty bourgeoisie, and the apprentices with the poorer community? It may even be true: the ownership of their own little businesses could well have given small bosses a world-view different from that of their wage-earning servants. But there was hardly any material difference between their positions.[5] The Amsterdam capital-tax register of 1585 lists not a single apprentice among the taxpayers, and only a handful of small tradesmen.[6] A great number of masters of guilds could not afford even a single journeyman. Thus in 1581 in Leiden there was no more than one journeyman for every five or six masters.[7] Of the more than fifty pinmakers who worked at Gorinchem in 1597, none was rich enough to carry on independent trade abroad. All of them had to live from day to day, buying new raw materials every week with the profits of their sales, because they had no capital reserves.[8] It may safely be assumed that the standard of living of such masters was barely better than that of an apprentice.

Most of the time we do not know how high the workers' wages were,[9] but it is readily understood that 'high' is not the right word in this context. The playwright who declared that in Holland everything was expensive except labour[10] may have been looking for cheap applause, but he was probably not far from the truth. During the years of the war against Spain, wages always remained rather low despite moderate increases, as table 1 taken from sources relating to workers' wages, shows. Insofar as it is possible to draw a conclusion from these figures, they appear to suggest that the daily wage for a skilled worker around 1600 came to about fourteen st., and had risen half a century later to twenty st.[11] Can we justly call these wages low? There were undoubtedly artisans who had considerable incomes. In this table the shipwrights of Amsterdam stand out sharply, although it must be said that the figures come not from the workers themselves, but from their protesting customers,[12] who wanted to show that Amsterdam rates were extravagantly high. In Amsterdam we encounter other, more formidable incomes: a yearly wage of 400 guilders (in Dutch, 'gulden') with a free place to live for the master journeyman of a cloth-dyer,[13] or a potter's journeyman earning 543 guilders per year.[14] Some cases may involve lucky individuals, but there were certainly entire categories with reasonable to good earnings. At Amsterdam for example these included the certified weighing-scale carriers,[15] the goldsmiths obviously, and to a somewhat lesser degree the building trades.[16]

But many workers were notoriously badly paid. Among them were the glass-blowers, who around 1650 enjoyed only ten st. a day and free beer – probably a limited freedom – and all unskilled labourers in general.[17] Thus the wages of the fourteen st. in 1600 and twenty st. in 1650 should be considered those of a skilled Amsterdam worker. These are two important qualifying terms, because, according to the employers at least Amsterdam wages were comparatively high.[18] In any case the spinners and weavers of Leiden earned substantially less: according to the testimony of their own employers not even enough to live.[19] In 1577 Jan van Hout placed the blame for the great numbers of poor in Leiden squarely on the cloth industry.[20] At the time he may have put too much weight on that sector of the economy, but his view proved prophetic. Sixty years later the workers were so hard-pressed that they were willing, after a sixteen-hour day, to work paid overtime.[21] That happened in May, 1637, thus in a season when there was much sunlight and consequently long working days. From the table it is already apparent that wages fluctuated according to the seasons: the unspecified figures probably refer to summer wages. The working day began at 4 or 5 a.m. in summertime, an hour later in

Table 1. *Wages of artisans in Holland*

Year	Place	Occupation	Daily wage in stuivers
1569	Delft	carpenter[22]	10
1579	Amsterdam	unskilled labourer[23]	8
1581		slater[24]	14
1600	Amsterdam	unskilled labourer[23]	10–11
1603		unskilled labourer[23]	13
1604		slater[24]	14
1609	Amsterdam	cloth-shearer[25]	14
1612	Haarlem	bleacher[26]	12
1617	Amsterdam	cloth-shearer[27]	14
1618	,,	cloth-shearer[27]	15
1620		slater[24]	20
1620		mason[24]	20
1621		carpenter[24]	winter 16, summer 20
1624		mason[24]	winter 12, summer 18
1628	Amsterdam	cloth-shearer[27]	16
1631	,,	cloth-shearer[27]	18
1633	,,	cloth-maker[28]	18
1640	,,	potter[29]	17–18
1641	,,	shipwright[30]	30–40
1641	(elsewhere)	shipwright[30]	20–24
1641	Zaanstreek	shipwright[31]	summer 26
1645		slater[24]	winter 18, summer 20
1646	Amsterdam	soapmaker[32]	30
1646	,,	mason[32]	20
1646		cloth-shearer[33]	20

summer wages. The working day began at 4 or 5 a.m. in summertime, an hour later
in winter; it lasted until 9 p.m. in summer, and in wintertime at least until 7 p.m.
or later if possible.[34] Winter work-time reduced production and thereby wages. The
carpenters and masons of Amsterdam saw their wages reduced by $12\frac{1}{2}$ per cent in
spring and autumn, and in winter by as much as 25 per cent. Calculated over the
entire year, the result was that the average weekly wage came to about 90 per cent
of the summer wage.[35] Workers must have rejoiced at the lengthening days:

> What a comfort it is for the hard-working tradesman, because
> his little daily wage will increase:
> Although he can barely scratch out his daily bread.[36]

Was this poetic licence, to say the wages of labour were minimal? Can the approximate subsistence level be determined?

Complete certainty on this point is not possible, but we do have several ways of
investigating the matter further. We know that in the sixteenth century rye bread
was the most important staple of the workers' diet. The bread consumption of a
married couple with two young children has been estimated at five pounds a day.
Furthermore it has been calculated that expenditure on bread could not exceed 44
per cent of family income. Anyone who exceeded this level fell below the subsistence
line and became a pauper.[37] For Leiden we have a price series of twelve-pound
loaves of rye bread, showing the yearly averages (see table 2).[38]

If we assume for ease of calculation that the above-mentioned standard household
would consume three loaves per week, then during this period the expenditure on
bread would have fluctuated between 28.2 st. and 16.5 st. Those with an income of
fourteen st. per day, or eighty-four st. per week, could afford to spend thirty-seven
st. on bread, according to the 44 per cent rule. Even in the most expensive years they
would not have gone hungry, provided they had regular employment. Unskilled and
low-paid workers with their ten st. per day or sixty st. per week could spend as
much as 26.4 st. on bread. Consequently they would have been in need only in
1597–9. However, these figures should be used with caution. In the first place it is
probable that the poorest people consumed more than 2,500 grammes of bread per
day: for those on marginal incomes, Blockmans and Prevenier estimated the figure
at 3,200 grammes.[39] If so, the totals immediately look quite different: the weekly
bread requirement rises to 44.8 pounds, and the weekly expenditure fluctuates

Table 2. *Prices of Rye bread at Leiden, twelve pound loaves (in stuivers)*

1596 8.1	1601 6.9	1606 5.5	1611 7.4	1616 7.6
1597 9.3	1602 6.8	1607 6.0	1612 7.9	1617 9.3
1598 9.4	1603 7.8	1608 7.8	1613 7.9	1618 7.6
1599 9.2	1604 7.2	1609 7.9	1614 7.2	1619 6.6
1600 8.3	1605 6.4	1610 7.2	1615 6.6	1620 6.4

between 20.5 and 31.1 st. The working people of Leiden would already be facing misery when the bread price exceeded seven st., or in seventeen of the twenty-five years listed in the table. Secondly, it would be simplistic to conclude that a daily wage of 10 st. produced a weekly income of 60 st., for it was exactly those lowest-paid workers who were least certain of regular employment. And thirdly, average figures always flatten out the peaks and valleys. Bread prices depended on imports and supplies available, and were thus subject to great variations. In truly hard times the official price of a twelve-pound loaf could rise to fourteen or fifteen st.[40] On the black market the price could go as high as twenty-four st.,[41] but even a price of fourteen st. put bread beyond the reach of nearly all artisans.

There is yet another method. We can look for examples of incomes that we have reason to believe were cut down to the last penny. It seems likely that the States of Holland in 1577 would not have paid a penny more than necessary when they specified the pensions of two elderly nuns from the former convent in Dordrecht. Each would receive fifty guilders per year.[42] In 1579 a similar sum was earmarked for the orphaned child of the bailiff of Beverwijk. The child itself had nothing, but people hoped 'to educate it to honour and virtue'.[43] Apparently that was still possible for one guilder per week. Perhaps even this was calculated rather generously for the sake of honour and virtue, because in Louris Jansz's farce of 1583, 'Onse Lieven Heers Minnevaer', a father who has fallen on hard times asks for twenty-five guilders for each of his children.[44] This was a modest request, because prices were rising in the 1580s. A nun from Loosduínen asked in 1586 for an increase in her pension, from fifty-five to eighty guilders, and the States of Holland approved.[45] They certainly would not have done so if they thought that a single woman could live on fifty-five guilders. The maintenance costs of prisoners of war in that period came to four st. per day, or about seventy-three guilders per year.[46] In 1602 these costs rose to ten st.,[47] or 182 guilders 10 st. per year. Obviously at that time a profit had to be made on them. But the new tariff probably also reflected a real rise in prices,[48] for the daily maintenance costs for the crew of a Dutch galley amounted to $61\frac{1}{2}$ st. in 1598.[49] A certain Passchier Verdurmen, who asked for complete support from the parish charity of Zwartewaal in 1614, requested a weekly payment of two gld.[50] For children the sums were always lower. The almoners of Amsterdam usually maintained orphaned children for twenty st. per week.[51]

Let us now return to the question: were the workers' wages minimal? Around 1600 the typical wage was fourteen st. per day. That would amount to 218 gld. 10 st. per year, if the wages remained constant. Allowing in most cases a reduction of 10 per cent for seasonal fluctuations would leave an annual income of 196 gld. 13 st. This is, however, assuming continuous work and earnings throughout the year, which was almost certainly not so. Even if someone did have such good luck and earned nearly 200 gld., his problems were by no means over. On the basis of the foregoing data, we are not exaggerating when we set the minimum needs for an adult in 1600 at eighty gld., and for a child at half that sum. Then we must conclude that a young family could not live on the wages of a single healthy adult

1. *The cobbler's workshop*, by David Ryckaert III

breadwinner. Other members of the household also had to work, and large families with many children were condemned to seek help from public charity. Although wages were slowly rising, they could not keep pace with prices.[52]

Thus the women of the working class had to work. Only women above the poverty level could allow themselves the luxury of specialising in the unpaid profession of housewife. For many there was no other choice but suffering hunger or going to work, and this was considered quite normal. Belonging to the working class meant that both husband and wife 'were forced to win their bread by work'.[53] In 1581 the working population at Leiden was nearly 30 per cent female.[54] Normally they worked in traditional female occupations: 'spinning, washing, scouring'.[55] Young girls became servants in wealthy households, housekeepers in their own houses, as for example Maarten Harpertsz. Tromp remembered from his youth: 'his mother washed the sailors' shirts and starched collars for money'.[56] Our playwrights tell us about working women who earned money on the side through sewing and spinning.[57] Unmarried young women were thus probably drawn to the textile towns. Leiden owed its surplus of women over men to the many jobs for combers and spinners in the cloth industry.[58] The Amsterdam silk trade was already bringing the girls and women together in large workshops.[59]

Women also operated small shops,[60] or sold goods door to door.[61] These may have been part-time supplementary occupations, but we also encounter independent businesswomen, who took over the management of firms during the extended absence of their husbands, or when they became widows.[62] Sometimes widows could even remain members of a guild after the death of their husbands.[63] Foreigners found these independent businesswomen one of the noteworthy sights of the country. While the men wasted their time doing nothing, Fynes Moryson said, women took care of all business.[64] Women in Holland were better able to do that, Antonio Carnero judged, because the men were addicted to drink.[65] Indeed, superficial observers could regard Holland as a woman's country, because thousands of men were away

2. *Spinster on her doorstep*, by Adriaen van Ostade

at sea. Nevertheless, women held an inferior position in the working world. Their wages were probably always low, even when they practised their trades well. An experienced bleach-girl of Haarlem in 1601 earned no more than eight stuivers per day,[66] the same as a poorly-paid unskilled labourer. While she was clearly at a disadvantage compared to men, at this time she may have been better off than women later in the seventeenth century, because she was seldom burdened with the roughest manual labour in unhealthy enterprises such as brick-making and salt-boiling works.[67] Those few women who were employed to do this work in the early part of the century were not known for their feminine charm and sweetness.[68] But a girl did not have much choice. Salt-shed or spinning wheel, day or night work, she mostly had to accept what her birthplace happened to offer. She had to endure long days in the Leiden cloth workshops, or long nights in the Wormer biscuit-bakery.[69]

Neither women nor men had much influence on their fate. Did they try to get control of their working conditions? Unions were unknown in the seventeenth century, and other types of workers' organisations were still embryonic. The guilds often had a *gildebos*,[70] or support fund for widows, retired and disabled members, but employees were excluded from it. If they wanted to assure themselves of income in case of illness or disability, they could form *knechtsbossen*, provided that the guild and city authorities approved.[71] During our period such associations already existed,[72] but it is highly unlikely that they were significant.[73] Workers' wages were not high enough to provide great capital injections to a savings fund for mutual aid. Wages would have to rise first, and nearly all attempts to accomplish this end were fruitless. They were not very numerous anyway, and always limited to one sector of the economy. Examples of successful workers' protests, such as that of the Leiden bargemen's mates in 1609, are rare. There the issue was not wages but working conditions, which were changed in the workers' favour.[74]

Sometimes workers tried to make agreements among themselves, for example to declare certain workshops 'dirty', that is to boycott them.[75] Some guilds, in particular the Amsterdam hatmakers, had cause to complain about conspiratorial apprentices.[76] But there were other trades that remained completely quiet: the biscuit-bakers of Wormer and Jisp were never involved in any conflict about wages.[77] Perhaps this point could be established for many more trades if it were researched systematically. We find fairly frequent labour unrest only among the journeymen cloth-shearers.[78] Occasionally they also went on strikes (for example, in Hoorn in 1639[79] and Leiden in 1643)[80] which ended in defeat for the strikers. No wonder, since all conditions for their success were lacking:[81] the factory that brought all the workers together in daily companionship did not yet exist; the authorities always supported the employers, and regarded strikes as revolts plain and simple; and the overpopulation in Holland created an unusually unfavourable climate for demands for wage increases. These factors applied to nearly all trades. What little labour law existed, in the guild privileges, laid practically all obligations on the worker. Even his opportunity to resign voluntarily was sometimes restricted, in order to protect the bosses in busy times.[82]

Yet we should not see the journeyman worker as a docile work-horse deprived of all rights. In his own modest way he too belonged among the privileged members of the community. Employers and workers probably stood shoulder to shoulder in the fight against mechanisation. Both their interests were served by the 1623 declaration of Holland limiting the number of ribbon-mills, which manufactured hair-ribbons and garters 'to the noteworthy damage, even total ruin, of many thousands of people, who make the same ribbons with foot-powered looms'.[83] This 'thousands' certainly did not come from a statistical count. But pressure of the same kind could have slowed down the development of industrial mills in the first decades of the seventeenth century.[84] The council of Rotterdam in 1637 was unable to carry out plans for the building of a large fulling-mill. The gentlemen who were supposed to survey the site were 'placed in evident fear of their lives' by an angry public, and thought the price of technical improvement too high.[85]

Furthermore, the guild was the journeyman's guarantee that he would keep his work and his daily bread, even though Holland was overrun with foreigners. In the guild he sought protection against competition from foreigners, people from other regions of the Republic, Hollanders from other towns and villages, and fellow townsmen who had not passed through the guild apprenticeship. He was quite willing to restrict the number of jobs,[86] or tried to reserve them for native-born inhabitants. According to the guild regulations of 1623, if an Amsterdam carpenter was unemployed, he could always demand the job of a foreign journeyman.[87] Now it is true that the mere existence of legal regulations proves little, even less in the seventeenth century than in the twentieth. Control and enforcement of the regulations were more important, and on just those points the Amsterdam carpenters did have success. In 1640 it appears that the journeymen of the shipwrights' guild were powerful enough to insist on the very high daily wage of 36 st., for a working day of only twelve hours.[88] An earlier attempt by the employers to lengthen the working day had failed: the fourteen-hour day introduced in 1621 had to be reduced in 1625 owing to 'great complaints'.[89] In the shipwrights we encounter a group of workers who knew how to share in the profits of Amsterdam's position as the marketplace of the world. Merchants and ship's captains wanted to reduce idle time in the harbour to an absolute minimum: as soon as their ships were seaworthy again, they sought to take advantage of the first favourable wind. When large ships came in, the shipowners not only paid the shipwrights full wages but also gave them free meals in order to speed up the work. The exploitation of such opportunities assured the Amsterdam journeymen of their abnormally favoured position for that time. They even took along with them the casual labourers, more of whom were hired at busy times. With daily wages of thirty st.,[90] these men also earned considerably more than the average workers.

Such opportunities were more frequently found in Amsterdam. When in the autumn the Baltic fleet sailed in, and everyone wanted his grain unloaded first, the grain-porters raised their demands, and their daily wages sometimes tripled.[91] The same tactic was used by the cloth-shearers in 1628, when they went on strike just at the moment when the ships were lying ready for the voyage to the East, and the owners could not get their cloth-orders on board fast enough.[92] On this occasion, then, the worker found fortune on his side. Yet for most workers a very low standard of living remained their daily lot. It is true that wages in Holland were certainly not bad by the standards of the time, and there is no reason whatsoever to paint an excessively dark picture of the Dutch workers. After all, Holland attracted foreign workers, who found conditions there better than at home; that qualification must nearly always be made when judging social conditions in this region. Conditions in seventeenth-century Holland were not good, but where were they any better?

II

A foreign observer, the above-mentioned English world traveller Fynes Moryson, described the countryside of Holland in 1595 as packed full of an infinite number of villages, built so closely together that he could not tell where one ended and another began.[93] To his mind this mass of people reflected prosperity. Moryson was certainly convinced that the country was full of people because life was good in the Dutch countryside. Without further information we could naturally also draw the opposite conclusion from his observations: population, thus poverty. In which direction should we go?

For their prosperity villages often depended in the first place on their arable lands and pastures. If the population was too great to feed itself from these sources, then it could only achieve a decent standard of living if there was also adequate employment available outside agriculture. Now it is certainly true that arable and grassland farming must have suffered terribly from the misfortunes of the hard times during the early years of the war against Spain. At the beginning there was the All Saints' Day Flood of 1 November 1570, one of the greatest flood disasters in Dutch history. Even before the farmers could recover from the flood damage, civil war broke out in Holland in 1572. From 1573 onward, deliberate flooding during the sieges of Haarlem, Alkmaar and Leiden placed large areas of the countryside under water. And when the military situation again permitted, there was no money to pump the land dry and to repair the dikes.[94] The Alphen region, for example, was still almost completely depopulated in the summer of 1575; about 92 per cent of the land was flooded or abandoned.[95] The Alblasserwaard and the Vijfherenlanden remained under water for four years after the dikes were breached in 1573,[96] and the Alblasserwaard was flooded again in 1579.[97] There is no report of a great flood in that year, but flooding of the land was by no means always the result of a breach in the dikes. The struggle against water was fought with inadequate weapons. Many polders remained flooded all winter,[98] and the lowest fields could be kept dry in summer only with great difficulty. Moryson, who visited

Holland in the summer of 1593, was troubled by the heat, 'farre exceeding the ordinary heat of that clime'.[99] Even so, on his tour he saw that the pastures near Gouda were swamped with water.[100] In the most endangered places, such as Huisduinen,[101] the Schermereiland[102] or the region of Voorne,[103] sixteenth-century technology was not advanced enough to prevent the steady crumbling away of the land.

With a growing population, the loss of land inevitably led to increases in land prices. This can be observed over the entire sixteenth century,[104] and this increase naturally had its effects on leases and rents,[105] although it may be true that rents followed land prices at a somewhat slower pace.[106] The capital increase made arable land and pastures a good investment, and thus brought it into the hands of those who had the most to invest, the wealthy townspeople. This development had already begun early in the sixteenth century. In the first place it was primarily villagers who moved to the city, and retained ownership of their land.[107] But as the wealth of Holland became more and more concentrated in the cities, farmers who needed money owing to a bad harvest or illness sought help in town, and went there to sell or mortgage their land.[108] By this means bourgeois ownership continually expanded. Even before the revolt against Spain, considerably more land was in the hands of burghers than of nobles or the church.[109] In surface area, the share of the land owned by farmers in Holland was indeed not inconsiderable; the great majority of them also owned their own houses.[110] But these buildings were of the most primitive construction – 'old low wooden houses covered with straw'[111] – representing only very limited worth,[112] and the farmers' own properties were mostly found on second-class land.[113]

This relationship would also change over the course of the seventeenth century, ever more in favour of the city landowners. In that period the Hollanders took the initiative in the struggle against water. The great polder projects began in 1597 with the Zijpe, and ended only in 1635 with the Schermer.[114] To build these dikes required far more capital than the farmers could amass. When the Zijpe was pumped dry, many former owners of this flooded and rediked polder had to give up their old lands, because they were no longer able to finance the costs of the works.[115] Prosperous Amsterdam merchants and regents such as Boelesz., Cromhout and Bardesius became the new lords of the Zijpe.[116] In the Noorderkwartier in the first half of the seventeenth century, around fl. 20,000,000 was invested in land reclamation.[117] We can best understand the magnitude of these enormous sums by noting that investment in land far exceeded that in the great trading companies.[118]

The land thus came more and more into urban hands. The farmers became tenants instead of owners. The logical conclusion is that the farmers fell behind. Our doubts disappear when this view is confirmed by the sources, as in this pamphlet of 1608: 'Look at the border areas, how the lands have deteriorated and been flooded on all sides. See also here in Holland and Overmase, how many householders have to leave their homes, or at least sell the same and then rent them again. See also what kinds of people buy them, if many of them have not got rich through this war.'[119] As another author of the time said, the farmers had become tenants of the war profiteers.[120]

Nonetheless let us weigh these words carefully. Neither pamphleteer says that country folk have been reduced to beggary. They say only that the burgher rather than the farmer is making the big profits. When businessmen invested so heavily in land, it was not a form of disinterested development aid. They were not philanthropists who sought to maintain complete villages at the cost of great personal sacrifice. They invested their money in land because they expected a good profit from it. They continued to do so for years, because their expectations were not disappointed. Naturally they had to suffer reverses from time to time. In the Heer Hugowaard the investors' dreams were so far removed from reality that in 1684 people seriously considered allowing the polder to be flooded again, in order to make at least some profit from catching fish.[121] If agriculture had continually run at a loss, the regents and businessmen would probably have sold their land back to the country folk, but in the seventeenth century there is no sign of anything of the kind. We have no indication that the farmers' share of the land increased; rather there is evidence that it declined.[122]

Why was ownership of land so attractive, and why was acreage constantly expanded? In part this was simply the result of the continually increasing prices in our period. No one benefited more from this trend than the seller of agricultural produce,[123] which rose in value more than anything else. But perhaps it was more significant that Dutch agriculture had developed along a new pattern. While in the Middle Ages it had served primarily to feed the local population,[124] by the second half of the sixteenth century it was no longer able to do so. Grain production lagged far behind population growth. Consequently Holland had to live on imports, and became dependent on the grain of eastern Europe for its food. The farmers of Holland specialised in growing flax, hops and linseed,[125] crops that could serve as raw materials for the most important industries. This new orientation can already be observed clearly at the reclamation of the Zijpe: 'cabbage, oats, mustard, peas and grain will be sown'.[126] The great polder projects of the seventeenth century were inspired by the hope that the reclaimed surface area would produce just as much good arable land.[127] And although these hopes were misleading, the reorientation continued all the same. Arable land increasingly became a supplier to industry, and also made even larger areas suited for market gardening. While in the sixteenth century it was limited to the neighbourhood of Leiden, a century later it had a firm foothold in large areas of North Holland.[128]

The new crops changed more than just the appearance of the fields. Anyone who sows wheat or barley, the vegetable growers of Holland said in 1603, can do no more than pray for God's blessing, 'without the farmer doing anything about it for the rest of the year, except to weed it, then in harvest time to be satisfied with what the Lord Almighty has given him'.[129] Market gardening was completely different. Once the vegetable beds had been prepared for their purpose at great

3. *The fishwife*, by Adriaen van Ostade

difficulty and expense, then they would still have to be 'turned over, scraped, clawed and otherwise handled carefully many times before they can be sown'. It was the same for other new crops: they required more work than did grain. Market gardening became increasingly labour-intensive, and thus created more employment. Furthermore, since market gardening found new customers in industry, it could afford to pay reasonable wages.

Around the middle of the seventeenth century agricultural labourers earned fifteen to twenty stuivers per day,[130] a good wage in comparison to the more expensive life in the city. Thus it was possible for the population of the countryside to lead a comfortable existence, despite the increase of urban landownership. The seventeenth-century tenant or labourer probably reached a higher standard of living than the sixteenth-century independent farmer. At Hoorn in 1632 a *morgen* of land (about two acres) was sold for 3,280 guilders. The Enkhuizen chronicle of Brandt and Centen does indeed find this price on the high side, but still sees it as proof that the war had 'strongly blessed and enriched' the inhabitants.[131] Not everyone had received the same share of blessings. No doubt the city burghers were the greatest profiteers, and aroused the jealousy of the villager who worked hard with sweaty hands for a jug of buttermilk and a hunk of cheese.[132]

> He should be grateful to be relieved
> Of this plague, and sit on his ass
> Working in village or city,
> Instead of always wandering on the Zijpe.[133]

So sang the polderboys of the Zijpe, according to Valcooch, and indeed no one could say that they had drawn the long straws of life. Yet all country folk did gain some advantages from the renewal of Dutch agriculture. Perhaps, as Velius said, there was in fact no country in the whole world where 'the wealth and prosperity of the average householder' exceeded that of the country people of Holland.[134]

The same applies in some degree to livestock raising. The rising value of the land was also related to the increasing demand for butter and cheese.[135] But livestock raising was a risky business. The low-lying meadows were the first victims of water, and an extra rainy summer could ruin the hay crop. In the chilly and wet Dutch climate the animals had to stay in their barns a very long time in winter.[136] Therefore we encounter few large livestock farmers. In 1598 the Nieuwlander polder counted seventy tenant farmers who owned considerable flocks of sheep, but only eight cows in all.[137] For the same period in the Zijpe, Valcooch speaks of rich farmers who milked fifteen cows.[138] True, Van Buchell says that in the Waterland the 'mediocres villici' owned twenty-four cows,[139] but was this townsman perhaps mistaken about the correct understanding of landed 'mediocritas'?[140] When Bredero describes the Amsterdam meat market and allows the butchers to sing the praises of their wares, it appears that only mutton is for sale: 'See, there's a Wieringer suckling lamb, that's a Schaeger sheep, that's a year old Longtail'.[141] In any event, in the sixteenth century it was practically impossible for a farmer to live off the produce of his cattle alone.[142] In 1600, the North Holland village of Katwoude cited as proof of its great poverty that the 'inhabitants can barely support themselves, since they can only raise cattle, which they mostly allow to graze on their land'.[143]

Livestock were then still raised for supplementary income and for home use. The Dutch country dweller of the sixteenth century was not yet a specialised livestock or grain farmer who concentrated all his energies on the market where he would sell his produce. His little piece of ground, his two or three cows, were only part of his livelihood, not his only means of income. Villagers earned money through fresh-water fishing and duck-hunting; spinning and weaving; transport of freight by land

and water; digging turf and cutting reeds.[144] At Alphen aan de Rijn, for example, there were 179 households in 1562. Only eighty-seven of them owned land.[145] Moreover, in South Holland especially the villagers' own land often consisted only of a few patches of bog, which were exploited for peat,[146] sometimes so radically that through intensive working, the land changed into water.[147] All these activities were carried out by the same people. When the polder works of Nieuw Beyerland were delayed by continual rains in June 1582, many of the dike-workers got tired of waiting and went to the ports to sign on as sailors. The entrepreneurs then feared the whole project was endangered, because in July even more workers would slip away when the hay and grain had to be harvested.[148]

The countryman had to be a jack of all trades. The overpopulated countryside was enough to make him realise that 'not a tenth of the people could live from the fruits and profits of agriculture'.[149] Now modern people have a universal panacea for overpopulation in agricultural regions, at least if they have no concern about the environment: industrialisation helps cure all ills. As far as they could, country dwellers of the seventeenth century sought the same remedy. The Zaanstreek in particular offers ample evidence. The sailcloth-weaving of Krommenie,[150] the biscuit-bakeries of Wormer and Jisp,[151] and especially the sawmills and shipbuilding yards provided jobs for hundreds of Zaankanters in their own neighbourhood.

The Zaanstreek is the example of a successful breakthrough of industrialisation in the countryside. Zaandam gradually became a centre of shipbuilding at the expense of Edam, which was still flourishing around 1600: Edam was then probably launching a hundred ships a year, but in the course of the seventeenth century it was surpassed by Zaandam.[152] The Zaankanters attributed this to the 'alertness and sobriety of these inhabitants'.[153] I would not underestimate this factor, but Zaandam was certainly helped along by the shortsightedness of the Amsterdam sawyers' guild, which lobbied with great energy and much success against the building of sawmills in their city.[154]

Another contribution to the economic life of this region was provided by the Wormer biscuit-bakers. Evidently they knew how to make themselves indispensable to the economy of Holland, because they benefited from legal protection seldom given to industries in the countryside. The Wormer bakers were specifically allowed 'to transport their biscuit and sell it in all places'.[155] The bakers regarded this freedom as a vital necessity for the populous villages of Wormer and Jisp, 'so heavily burdened with many poor inhabitants'.[156] There was no lack of protests, particularly from Amsterdam.[157] In the second quarter of the seventeenth century the Zaanlandse firms went into decline[158] – perhaps because they had lost the protection they formerly enjoyed?[159]

The trades of the countryside were almost never and nowhere beyond criticism. Time and again the States of Holland heard complaints about industrial activity outside the city walls. The official argument was often that control over production and sales was much harder there than in the cities, with the result that tax collection suffered from the dispersion of industry.[160] The naked truth, however, is that in

Holland the cities held nearly all the political power, and they wanted to use it to get rid of country competition. They feared 'that by the exercise of all trades and crafts in the countryside the cities would be depopulated at one fell swoop'.[161] They did not want Zaandam to become more important than Purmerend, or Vlaardingen to grow larger than Schiedam. According to a report of 1612, the many breweries at the tip of North Holland ought to disappear, in the interests of Alkmaar, because 'now there is no one, thanks to the beer-sellers of the countryside, who cares for the city'.[162] Similarly it was necessary to take action against 'the pedlars who walk about the countryside with cloth and rags in order to sell the same',[163] because they certainly 'divert trade from the cities'.[164]

What the cities actually thought about the matter became clear in 1641, with a proposed general regulation for rural trades:[165] a curious mixture of reasonableness, respect for established rights, and undisguised urban egotism. It was practical and reasonable to allow those industries that were obliged to draw their raw materials directly from the surrounding countryside: tilemakers, brickmakers, and lime-burners were thus free to establish themselves outside the city walls. Established rights were maintained, as for example when breweries were permitted only 'in the same places where they had been before 1594'.[166] All enterprises begun since then would thus have to close their doors, without taking into account any new needs that might have arisen. Yet all the great polder works had taken place after 1594, with the consequence that these newly won lands would have to transport their beer from the cities. In this way, and many others besides, the proposal reveals its origins. It generally draws the line where industrial activity is not strictly necessary in order to maintain the village as a village. Thus it permits tailors to work outside the cities, along with shoemakers, wagon-makers, surgeons and roofers. Blacksmiths are allowed, but not ironworks. Boat-builders for small boats 'with four or fewer lasts' (of cargo, thus to a maximum of eight tons) are permitted, but not shipbuilders. Small fat-merchants, yes; large traders in fats, no. The intention is only too clear: the village market must remain strictly local. Village interests are subordinate to city interests.

The 1641 proposal did not lead to new regulations, and the States did not succeed in setting the Zaanlandse clock back a hundred years. Once rural industry had acquired some substance, it did not allow itself to be suffocated by regulations. But the plan of 1641 was rooted in an old tradition and conformed exactly to the urban way of thinking. In 1601 Delfshaven received from the city of Delft permission to construct shipyards, 'provided that Delfshaven does not grow too much'.[167] It is difficult to find a better illustration of the actual relationship than this unabashed restriction. Prosperity in the countryside must not be greater than the cities are willing to allow. Every city had its 'own' villages, often quite literally, for the cities had acquired the seigneurial rights. Cities such as Leiden and Rotterdam held the lordships of many domains in their surrounding areas, and as such were literally empowered to lay down the law. Such a village was a dependency of the city, but on the other hand enjoyed the advantage of having its interests defended by a corporate body mightier than the village council. By comparison other villages were generally worse off.[168]

On only one occasion was there an attempt to break free of the urban yoke. In 1614 several North Holland villages on the initiative of De Rijp[169] organised a meeting to protest against a newly enacted regulation against rural trade. The Deputised Councils of the Noorderkwartier simply forbade this meeting. The villages then appealed to an old privilege dating from the time of Jacoba van Beieren, but the Deputised Councils answered without further ado 'that the present-day constitution of this entire land does not allow such business, writing or meeting to be done or held'.[170] The only people who would occasionally speak up for the villages in the meetings of the States were the nobles of Holland. They wanted to have the Knighthood recognised as 'representatives of the countryside'.[171] But even if this was not entirely a matter of prestige on their part, such interventions by nobles on behalf of the villages were extremely rare.[172]

The village consequently remained a step-child of the provincial administration of Holland, restricted in its growth, narrowly limited in its possibilities and tasks. But we are obliged to end as we began: compared to the city dweller, the villager might suffer the disadvantages of political discrimination, but in the eyes of foreigners he was an enviable darling of fortune. 'If the islands of paradise lie anywhere on earth, they must be here, because in the whole land we found nothing that smacked of poverty or filth.'[173] This is how the Frenchman Charles Ogier described Holland, while on a journey from Amsterdam to Leiden. Perhaps this only proved that paradise had fled from the earth, because even here human happiness was not absolute. Yet seen in the light of the times and compared to his counterparts in other countries, the rural inhabitant of Holland was indeed a privileged creature.

III

Naturally, in the coastal province of Holland the village could also or primarily have been a fishing village. In this period 'fish' meant chiefly herring. Arend van Buchell finds room in his diary to mention that a proud fisherman of Scheveningen caught 1,700 shellfish in two hours on 2 November 1590,[174] but this achievement belongs under the heading of curiosities. Barrels of herring were the order of the day. In the opinion of contemporaries, the herring fisheries were of extraordinary importance: 'the chief trade of these lands,' as the States of Holland described them in several declarations.[175] Maurice of Nassau supposedly said that the humble herring was the little stone in the slingshot with which the Dutch David brought down the Spanish Goliath.[176] But Maurice himself did not like fish,[177] and probably knew little about the price of herring. In any event, it is certain that with this remark he grossly overstated the significance of the herring fisheries, as indeed did most people in the seventeenth century.[178]

The herring fleet, however, was not small. If we accept Kranenburg's figure that the province of Holland put to sea 450 to 500 herring boats,[179] then every spring a minimum of 6,000 or 7,000 men and boys must have been engaged in herring fishing.[180] The population of the actual fishing villages did not by itself suffice to man this fleet. The Noorderkwartier was always an important recruiting area for the herring fisheries, especially after the beginning of the revolt against Spain, when Enkhuizen had become by far the most important port for herring boats.[181]

Furthermore, many of those who stayed on land were also interested in the results, because the herring trade was very popular among small investors. A taste for financial enterprise was the hallmark of early seventeenth-century people great and small. Behind the Lemaires and Van der Vekens, who entrusted their ten-thousands to the risks of commerce, there stood a whole army of smaller middle-class investors, inspired by their desire for great profits to gamble their limited capital in all sorts of more or less solid speculations.[182] We shall encounter this gambling-crazy multitude several more times in our account,[183] but the herring fishery was positively one of their most cherished objects. At Rotterdam in 1599

4. *The Dutch herring fleet*, by Pieter Vogelaer

nearly the entire herring trade was in the hands of 'bakers, coopers, ropemakers, pulley-makers, shoemakers, fishermen, first mates, butter and cheese-merchants, and other such people, most of whom have very little capital'.[184] They formed partnerships with ten, fifteen or more participants, who joined together to finance one herring boat.

These investors had not chosen a safe haven. A small vessel such as a herring boat was subject to all sorts of dangers, certainly in wartime, when it could easily fall prey to privateers. Thus it was reported in 1625 that Enkhuizen had lost a hundred herring boats to the privateers of Dunkirk.[185] Consequently the fishing industry continually needed new capital, which could be found primarily in the cities: the profits of the herring trade went to Enkhuizen, and to a lesser extent to Delft, Rotterdam, Schiedam and Brill.[186] The villages gained little. If it was thanks to the herring trade the Vlaardingers could boast 'that their place was also greater than a common village',[187] the small fishing villages along the North Sea coast were among the poorest in Holland. In 1623 they all shared the dubious honour of receiving partial remission of the payment of capitation-tax, 'because of a larger number of poor'.[188] That poverty of 1623 was not a temporary crisis phenomenon. Zandvoort was already on the books in 1594 as a 'desolate sea-village'.[189] In 1608 Katwijk aan Zee had a growing number of poor 'owing to the unfortunate and meagre catch'.[190] Egmond aan Zee was inhabited in 1615 by 'very miserable folk … who can barely live, in austere destitution, from what God gives out of the sea, which must be caught with great cost and peril'.[191]

The sea villages never emerged from misery, because they experienced what is technically called 'an abnormal demographic profile'.[192] The death rate for adult men, who 'drowned at sea and otherwise died in storms',[193] was unusually high in fishing villages, with the result that the burden of poor relief for widows and orphans was far above average. Sometimes one-third of the population was dependent on relief.[194] Then there was no money left for the public works necessary to maintain the chief industry. Goeree in 1594 had no means to prevent the silting up of its harbour.[195] The place needed all it could get for its poor, but their number could only increase if the island was no longer able to earn its livelihood through fishing. Similar conditions were chronic along the coast of Holland. Because people had too little money to control nature with good water defences,[196] these sea villages sank deeper and deeper into poverty. It was a hopeless situation: to lift themselves out of their misery, the men of these areas were willing to do any kind of work, no matter how badly paid. Thus van Meteren could write in 1599 that no one was prepared to go into the herring fisheries for wages as low as the Dutch earned from them.[197]

More numerous than fishermen, however, were sailors in the merchant marine. Their number is difficult to determine. For 1636, Van der Woude hesitantly arrives at an estimate of about 1,800 ships, with a capacity of 200,000 lasts.[198] This figure may provide some basis for an estimate of the total number of sailors, if we take as a starting point the Holland declaration of 1607 relating to the manning and armament of merchant ships. From this declaration it appears that the States thought it necessary to have approximately one crew-member for every seven loads of cargo, as shown in table 3.[199] Should we take this relationship as a guide, and thus conclude that for 200,000 cargo-lasts some 28,000 to 29,000 seamen were required? Here some reservations should be noted. There is a possibility that the true figure was somewhat lower. The Dutch merchant marine was certainly known for working as economically as possible because its ships carried very small crews.[200] But it is likely that the declaration takes this dubious habit into account. The greatest ships on this list carried crews of twenty-one. With such crews it was possible to sail to the Levant or to Guinea, though in view of the length of the voyage and dangers from pirates and Spaniards this was a false economy. Such voyages are recorded,[201] and may have happened often. Yet it seems certain that we should increase our estimate of 28,000 to 29,000 sailors, instead of decreasing it. It is well known that the large ships that went on longer voyages had considerably larger crews, often in a ratio of one man for every two lasts of cargo.[202] As a consequence in the first half of the seventeenth century the Dutch East India Company alone already had an annual crew requirement of 2,000 to 3,000 men.[203] In addition, the Dutch war fleet used relatively heavy manning on its ships, in order to board enemy ships successfully. A crew of 80 to 100 or more was normal in the time of Tromp and Piet Hein,[204] and it probably was always thus.[205] Consequently Bruijn and Lucassen arrive at an estimate of 33,000 for all sailors in 1610, and a total of 46,000 for the years 1630–40.[206]

From time to time the sailor was jobless. Then he could seek employment as a dike-worker or polder boy, for example while awaiting the sailing of the herring fleet.[207] But several thousand must always have been at sea. The high population

Table 3. *Crew requirements on Dutch merchant ships, 1607*

Cargo-lasts	Men	Boys	Total
Up to 50	7	1	8
60	8	1	9
70	9	1	10
80	10	2	12
90	11	2	13
100	12	2	14
110	13	2	15
120	14	2	16
130	15	2	17
140	16	2	18
150	17	2	19
160	18	3	21

density and the lack of industrial employment in the countryside served to make the sea one of the most important occupations.[208]

The mariner's rewards were modest. His wages were not high, but perhaps that was not the greatest objection. In 1636 sailors in the war fleet received ten to eleven guilders per month,[209] while those of the merchant marine probably got eleven to thirteen guilders.[210] Taking into account their board, the total approximated to twenty guilders,[211] which cannot be called a magnificent wage, but for a profession with so many youthful practitioners[212] it was not extraordinarily low either. Furthermore, wages were higher toward the end of our period. Tromp thought in 1641 that it was no longer possible to get sailors for eleven guilders per month. At that time they wanted fourteen to seventeen guilders.[213] Apparently that was the least they could expect elsewhere.

But the sailor's trade had other disadvantages besides low pay. First of all, after the Pacification of Ghent in 1576, the sailors were the only Hollanders who were consistently and directly confronted with the enemy; we shall return to this point in another context.[214] In addition seamen ran the extra risk of meeting North African pirate ships, and suffering harsh imprisonment in Tunis and Algiers. This, too, will be considered later.[215] Thirdly, every sailor had to experience all the discomforts that attended sea voyages as long as wind was the principal source of power. Sailing ships were small. The greatest of them did not exceed a thousand tons. They had to make maximum use of their cargo space, with the result that living quarters were extremely cramped. They did not provide their crews with adequate protection against harsh cold or terrible heat. They had to take along several months' worth of provisions, while the only means of preservation were vats of salt; their store of food and drink was kept in unrefrigerated, often sweltering hot areas. Everything brought on deck from below, the future governor-general Reynst wrote in 1613, was so warm that it might have been sitting on a fire.[216] Food spoiled rapidly, and sailors were obliged to share it with rats, worms, spiders and cockroaches – but they could not allow themselves to throw it away. On long voyages it was even necessary to ration the provisions. In particular the East Indiamen with their crews of 200 or more had no choice, and they were required to share out carefully their wormy biscuit and stinking water.

We observe this when we follow a voyage to the Indies closely with the help of a journal kept by one of the crew. We have chosen that of Johan Both Volckertsz, who set sail on one of the Company's vessels in May 1614.[217] On 12 June, the unlimited consumption of beer was halted: each person then received one can per day. On 20 July, that ended entirely. Once the beer-barrels were empty, the ration was set at one can of water and three small measures of French wine. At the end of August, rations were cut back to two measures of wine. Starting in November, each crewman received only half a can of water, but in January, 1615, that was reduced still further to six small measures, and in February that went down to three. To save water, peas were no longer served. Finally in March fresh provisions were taken on board, but in August the ration was back down to six small measures.

The food supply also went from bad to worse. Butter became very scarce in March 1615, and by May it had completely disappeared. Hot food – stew – could not be served after September, 1615. The crew then complained bitterly of hunger, but conditions could not be improved. By October, the crew was subsisting primarily on bread, supplemented on Sundays with a piece of salted meat and on Thursdays with a portion of bacon.

This is only one example, but by comparison with other voyages it does not appear to us that Johan Both was extraordinarily unfortunate. Rotten victuals and bad water doled out by the mouthful were the normal food and drink on long voyages,[218] no matter how many provisions were loaded on board. Jacques l'Hermite's voyage around the world, begun in April, 1623, lasted nearly three and a half years. Halfway through the voyage an inventory was made: 'no more [food] found than 58,660 pounds of bread, the other victuals proportionately scarcer'.[219] Scarce indeed, because what good is 58,000 pounds of bread for more than a thousand men in mid-ocean? The stores might suffice for two more months, but there were still about twenty months to go.

As a result of this diet and the by all accounts cramped living quarters of the seamen,[220] there must have been full-time work for the medical staff. This consisted, however, of only one barber-surgeon and perhaps a barber's mate. The East India Company refused in any case to send along better-qualified medical doctors, saying 'that there are so many villages in Holland that do not have doctors and nonetheless live'.[221] In this regard the situation on board Dutch East Indiamen was probably not abnormally unfavourable, compared to that of other ships. Jacob van Heemskerck set sail in 1601 with twenty-four ships and two yachts. He was allowed to take along five surgeons, and only if – as was the rule, his instructions openly state – they were young and incompetent could a sixth one be added.[222] We should keep in mind that this fleet was destined to engage in a battle that would cost the lives of a hundred men. Anyone who recalls the dramatic description of Tobias Smollett's *Roderick Random* of ships' surgeons in full activity during a sea battle[223] can hardly form a too sombre impression of the medical care enjoyed by Heemskerck's wounded.

It is true that not every sailor went to the East Indies or had to fight at sea. Most stayed in Europe, where shorter voyages and regular replenishment of supplies would have made shipboard life easier to endure. We should not assume that the working conditions of all sailors were comparable to those on the Company ships. Our information about the seafaring life is mostly taken from descriptions of long voyages, and consequently is coloured too darkly. Indeed, many more sailors passed through the Danish Sound and the Straits of Gibraltar than across the Equator or around the Cape of Good Hope. We know less about their situation, but it must have been more pleasant than that of employees of the East India Company.[224] Nevertheless, a pamphleteer of 1631 wrote, as if it were the most ordinary thing in the world, that no sailor in his right mind would choose to undertake a voyage to the Baltic if he had a chance to go to Archangel.[225] At first it is difficult to understand this preference. But if this really is the voice of public opinion as the emphatic tone of voice suggests, then the sailors of the 'mother-trade' to the Baltic must also have had their share of distressing experiences.

In any case the sailor's trade as such had rather low prestige in the seventeenth century.[226] 'If my husband had lived a bit more respectably', sighs the character Joosje in W. D. Hooft's *Jan Saly*, if he had been more often to church and less in the tavern, then he would already have been city beer porter for a long time, 'but now he must tumble along over a tempestuous sea.'[227] Seamen were 'rough mates',[228] 'coarse companions',[229] known for their 'unruliness, disobedience, recklessness, and violence'.[230] The seafaring life, according to *dominee* Westerman, was little else than drinking, fighting and whoring.[231] The worst reputation attached to the men of the navy[232] and the great companies.[233] Baudartius tells us in 1624 that previously unknown species of birds were suddenly seen in this country. This was explained as a sign that the ships of the West India Company had arrived at their destination, and 'our soldiers and sailors raised such a ruckus, that the very birds flew away from there'.[234] The description of the behaviour of the Dutch sailors in Guinea as noted in a declaration of 1614 was indeed well suited to confirm such expectations.[235] Even on shore in Holland itself sailors could become a plague on their surroundings. When they became bands of vagrants, particularly in winter time, areas of high concentration such as Voorne had to be protected by a sort of police regulation.[236] In the Hollands Noorderkwartier it was thought prudent to abandon collection of the hundredth-penny tax in November, 1579, 'because as the season turns to winter, all the seafaring folk have returned from the sea'.[237]

On board ship the men were kept under control by severe discipline. Anyone who wounded another would be pinned to the mast with a knife through his hand, until he tore himself loose. Anyone who killed another would be bound to the dead body and thrown overboard. The old articles of association are swarming with similar punishments.[238] They remained officially on the books for the navy until 1795.[239] It is possible that the heaviest penalty was used sparingly, or at least applied in such a manner as to postpone somewhat the cutting short of human life. Often the ultimate remedy was not execution, but marooning the offender on an island.[240] The ships' logs do not reveal everything about the application of the lighter punishments, for minor infractions were probably not always recorded. Yet some captains must have found it advisable not to rule too harshly. In important situations, we observe the well-known Willem IJsbrandsz. Bontekoe consulting his crew[241] or listening to them.[242] Bontekoe's method was probably used by many others as well. Maurice warned the Venetians who recruited 600 sailors in Holland in 1619 that they must not be too severe with their men. Comradeship and, above all, generous distribution of beer and wine would persuade the Dutch sailors to perform well.[243]

Nonetheless, the seafaring life in the seventeenth century was unthinkable without strict discipline. Discipline was a necessary precondition. When Van Buchell described the shipmates of Olivier van Noort as 'nautas ad quidlibet audendum promptos',[244] he might well have been thinking of an audacity that could also be directed against their superiors. More than once a crew succeeded in making themselves masters of a ship and using it for piracy.[245] Vice-admiral Haultain recommended in 1612 that a sufficient number of soldiers should be stationed on all warships, to keep the sailors in check.[246] But the cure could be worse than the disease if it was a question of maintaining peace and quiet on board, because the presence of soldiers also generated tensions. On board Company ships the soldiers and sailors sometimes lived with each other as deadly enemies.[247]

The other side of the coin of this unruliness was great personal courage.[248] The crewmen of Heemskerck and Willem Barentsz. on their northern voyages repeatedly attacked polar bears and walruses, at great risk to their own lives. It may be true that they did not yet have any sense of the strength and resistance of these animals,[249] but even later they did not shrink from battle with them.[250] The award for bravest representative of this group of sailors must go to a certain Herman Hermansz., whose name deserves to be rescued from obscurity. In 1613 his ship was attacked at Gibraltar by three Turkish frigates. During the battle, the gunpowder caught fire. Of all the Dutchmen, only Herman Hermansz. was able to save his life by holding onto the floating foremast while wrapped in the topsail. When two of the Turkish ships then sailed away, he fearlessly swam towards the third, climbed aboard, and overpowered the few survivors of the battle. Entirely on his own he brought his prize to Malaga harbour.[251]

If one could find any men who, rightly dissatisfied with the low social status they enjoyed, possessed enough daring and energy to take their lives into their own hands, it would have to be among the seamen. Perhaps the government and the merchants should have counted themselves lucky that the potential of a revolutionary-minded proletariat was not realised on dry land. Neither urban worker nor rural labourer was to the same degree as the sailor the victim of an economic system that sought to exploit him at the lowest price.

IV

We still have the soldiers to deal with. They certainly formed the least important of our four categories in Holland. During the first years of the civil war the province was full of warring bands, Spaniards as well as rebels (*geuzen*). But that experience will be discussed later on.[252] At the moment we are concerned with the soldier as employee. Who was he? How much did he receive? What were his prospects and working conditions?

To the first question we can answer that in most cases he was a foreigner. The armies of William the Silent, Maurice and Frederick Henry always consisted for the most part of mercenaries. Germany was the most important reservoir of troops. France, England and Scotland also furnished considerable contingents, Denmark and Switzerland some isolated companies. There were also Dutch regiments, but far too few in number to outweigh the international character of the States army.

It is true that Dutch troops might be added to a regiment recorded as Scottish or German because it needed constant replenishing in wartime, when it was often impossible to get more men from the country of origin. At the end of the Twelve Years' Truce in 1621, when it was necessary to rebuild the companies that had been reduced to 70 percent of their wartime strength, more than twenty fuller's apprentices in Leiden signed up. They were motivated, according to the employers, by their excessively low wages.[253] We know that many Hollanders worked for low daily wages, but reactions such as those of the Leiden fuller's apprentices remained exceptional. There is no question that the army's continuous demand for manpower represented a dangerous competitor for the workshop, the farm, the merchant marine and the herring fisheries. Let us take this as a warning to be careful not to paint the working class of the sixteenth and seventeenth centuries as a hopeless lumpen-proletariat. The Hollanders preferred to leave the profession of war to foreign workers. Captains who formed their companies in Holland in 1604 were specifically told that they must take no 'scoundrels or beggars'.[254] Were these the only recruits who joined voluntarily?

The wages were indeed not high enough to form an attractive alternative to other modestly paid work. In the 1570s they came to seven or eight guilders per month.[255] The normal pay amounted to nine to twelve gld. per month in 1599,[256] and in 1623 it had risen further, to eleven to fifteen gld.;[257] it should be noted, however, that in the military language of the time a 'month' consisted of six weeks. Compared to other workers' wages, the soldier thus received less in cash, yet his pay was not so bad compared with what sailors got. These wages guaranteed a minimal existence, as they should, for it was too dangerous to let armed men go hungry. The pay, together with supplements for room and board while on garrison duty, was sufficient for a frugal style of life. Naturally it was no more than that: the States of Holland decided in the year 1606 to grant an extra payment to five men who had informed them 'that while conducting themselves as men of honour, they had come to the point at which they could not survive on their pay'. Here it was a case of a *déclassé* nobleman and a couple of sons of not inconsiderable functionaries. They received in addition to the ordinary pay supplements varying from 50 to 100 per cent.[258] The thousands of others who made no noise about their honour had to make do with their two guilders a week.

His miserly wage and foreign origins notwithstanding, many a soldier nonetheless found a female partner for life. At any rate, Huygens says, 'The baggage in his train consists of knapsack, wife, and child.'[259] There are no statistics on this point; I know of only one exact figure. In June 1588, the guards of Maurice were ordered to move from Dordrecht to The Hague. These men had explicit orders to leave their women behind: at that time these appeared to be twenty-six in number.[260] Huygens would have led us to expect a higher figure, certainly among an elite unit such as the guards, because the elite soldier of the time was pre-eminently an experienced veteran, who had long ago reached the age of marriage. Perhaps Huygens was misled by appearances. Sixteenth-century armies always had a great train of women and boys.[261] The soldier was responsible for himself. He had to find his own food, and also medical assistance if necessary. For this reason alone it was difficult to do without the women camp-followers, but it may well be asked if more often than not relationships were established for a single campaign rather than for longer. In contrast to civilian society, living together while unmarried was not forbidden in the army.[262] What appears to confirm Huygens' observation, however, is the testimony of the church council of Schoonhoven in 1622 that soldiers were extraordinarily keen to marry, with an express preference for widows. They wanted to marry formally women who had lost their husbands only ten to twelve weeks before.[263] Or perhaps it was the women who exerted the greater pressure? A widow with a young family was well advised to find another breadwinner as soon as possible. For military widows this was also the best solution. It was much more difficult for women who saw their husbands return from battle as permanent invalids, and were thus reduced to beggary with them:

> She half-wishes that he were not still alive to tell the tale,
> Embarrassed with a stump, enriched with a third leg;
> How much more convenient a crippled man than none at all;
> That is the epitaph his nearest and dearest would give him –
> And that is the rotten fruit of risking blood for money.[264]

Do these lines express compassion for the lot of the unfortunate beggar? I fear that for Huygens, contempt here wins out over concern. Anyone low enough to wager his life for money should not complain if fortune turns against him. There is no great awareness here that the soldier had wagered his body because Huygens and his friends would rather not themselves fight for church and fatherland, and that they could permit others to fulfil this duty in exchange for payment. But Huygens was not the only one to keep himself at a distance from his protectors. When in 1600 Maurice sent a soldier suffering from smallpox to the Delft hospital, the city, with an eye to the costs, asked henceforth to be spared from such persons. Once a soldier fell sick, it was better to discharge him immediately.[265] Soldiers were equally unwelcome in the Amsterdam hospital. The regents did not want to bring convalescent burghers in contact with that sort of people.[266]

Soldiers in the Dutch community did indeed form a discriminated-against group. On the other hand, it could also be said that the government took more responsibility for them than for the general population. Pension rights were unknown in seventeenth-century society, even for soldiers. The authorities of the Republic recognised no obligation whatsoever for these. But there was some development in that direction, though not yet at the beginning of the seventeenth century. If the States-General then did grant an annuity to a widow, it was almost always because she still had claims on the arrears of wages of her former husband, or on the wages advanced by a captain to his men. These obligations were then bought off by a pension act.[267] The widows receiving pensions were thus almost without exception wives of officers. Below that rank there was a small group of privileged persons who owed their pensions to their participation in some 'notable exploit' such as the battle of Gibraltar, the surprise attack on Brill, or the peat-barge at the capture of Breda.[268] Devoted service for many years, however, did not convey a pension right. Anyone who had become unfit for military tasks and asked for support from the States-General could count on no more than one grant of ten to twenty gulden, 'out of commiseration', and that only on condition that he never again troubled Their High and Mightynesses.[269]

A few cases from the dossiers will illustrate this. The soldier Willem Thijsz., who had twenty-five years of service, was disabled in 1611 because his right arm had become crippled. He then asked for a sum to support himself, his wife and his children. What he received was a single payment of eighteen gulden.[270] This was in any event more than Samuel d'Erme got: he had lost both of his legs in the service of the nation, and he had to be content with the sum of twelve gulden, granted to him 'out of commiseration as alms'.[271] The widow of Captain Moncrieff was remembered with fifty gulden. She had lost her husband and three sons in the war.[272]

Yet there were some who, for reasons that are unclear, received modest grants. These were the elderly soldiers who were enrolled with the so-called 'appointed ones'. That meant they remained on the payroll at a lower rate than normal pay, mostly with the obligation to do such duty as they could. These 'appointed ones' were preferably assigned to soft jobs, such as guarding the Muiderslot, or the house in Woerden.[273] This exceptional arrangement probably became more common over the course of time. After the Peace of Münster at least, the number of 'appointed ones' had risen to 1,215.[274] They did not receive enough money to live on, because the payment was normally eight or nine guilders per 'month' of six weeks. To supplement their income they were thus in exactly the same position as those who earned less than the minimum necessary income: they had to depend on public or religious charity. They were not allowed to beg,[275] but that nearly always held true for those receiving relief.

Seen in the European context, the soldiers of the States army had rather favourable prospects. They had no right to a pension, but stood a reasonable chance of getting one, which increased as the war against Spain dragged on. In general, the working conditions of soldiers in the Republic were not bad compared to those in other countries. Measured against the standards of the age, officers and subordinates had reason to be satisfied with each other.

The turning point, as is well known, lay in the first years of Maurice's stadholdership. In 1586 and 1587 complaints about the misdeeds of soldiers were still heard rather frequently by the States of Holland. The complaints came particularly from the countryside,[276] but also from small cities[277] such as Naarden, where the garrison behaved as if they were a band of robbers charged with guarding the town gate, demanding that anyone who came in or went out hand over his goods.[278] 'Whoever does good to a peasant, does harm to God, (that) is the soldiers' watchword.'[279] At that time this principle was still applied frequently, fully justifying

Roemer Visscher's reply: whoever calls a soldier a bully and a captain a plunderer is only speaking the simple truth.[280]

To say that all complaints were silenced after 1587 is certainly an overly adventurous statement. It can be disproved quite easily with the help of the sources. At the turn of the century the countryside was still not free of its burdens.[281] Everhard van Reyd ascribed the failure of an attack on Lier in 1595 to the 'laxness of justice and discipline'.[282] But he may also have been voicing resentment that the string of uninterrupted successes since 1590 was not continued in that year. Foreign observers speak quite differently about discipline. The English traveller Fynes Moryson, who was not overflowing with kindness in his judgments on the Dutch, praised the severe military discipline of the States army in roughly the same year as when Reyd expressed his disappointment. Moryson told of a Dutch soldier who was hanged because he had exchanged hats with a prisoner who had been promised amnesty.[283] Moryson's countryman Sir Thomas Overbury spoke in similar fashion again in 1609. The soldiers of the Republic perpetrate fewer misdeeds against civilians and commit fewer thefts than any others in the world.[284] The Dutchman Van Meteren supports his views, and assures us that the States troops were welcome everywhere in the cities and the countryside.[285]

Maurice made the soldiers accustomed to regular wages and decent treatment. In exchange he demanded obedience. The undisciplined soldier was punished severely – Moryson's anecdote is by no means an isolated example[286] – and sometimes outlawed. In 1587 the Dutch peasants were granted permission to use weapons to chase away soldiers who remained in the countryside without marching orders.[287] Soldiers who had given themselves marching orders were regarded as tramps. In 1597 the States of Holland placed them under the jurisdiction of bailiffs,[288] the officers charged with the arrest of beggars and vagabonds. A soldier who had been released from hospital received thirty stuivers as travel money to rejoin his company, so that he need not ask for help from anyone along the way.[289] Demobilised companies were sometimes offered transport back to their land of birth. In 1629 during the siege of 's-Hertogenbosch many extra soldiers were taken on; as winter approached they were discharged, the English and Scots directed to depart via Rotterdam, the Germans via Deventer. Anyone who remained would be regarded as a vagabond.[290]

This policy was successful. The Republic gained control of its army. Discipline could never be relaxed, the soldier must know for certain that he would hang for a swopped hat or a stolen chicken. A soldier of the Gorinchem garrison robbed a woman of her money outside the city in 1623, while pretending to be a *landsknecht* in Spanish service. His trial was held in Gorinchem, but the bailiff received orders to appeal the case if the man was not sentenced to death.[291]

The double security of regular payment and strict punishment for anyone who helped himself kept the soldiery quiet, so much so that during temporary delays in payment the companies did not rob or mutiny, but rather sold their horses and weapons[292] or took their clothes to the pawnbroker.[293] In 1635 the French garrisons in Het Gooi went without payment for a long time, awaiting the subsidies that were supposed to come from France. They lived on the edge of desperation, and some burghers of Muiden and Naarden feared that plunder would be the order of the day. However, the bailiff of Muiden, who was responsible for public order, did not take seriously threats of mutiny and revolt. He told the soldiers that 'those who disobey here in this land can look forward to the gallows'. The men appeared little impressed. They answered that there was not much to choose between hanging and dying of hunger.[294] Nonetheless Het Gooi remained calm. The experience of the soldiers also confirmed that almost all who had to earn their living with their hands accepted the unequal division of portions. There was seldom talk of genuine social unrest. Craftsmen, farm labourers, fishermen, sailors and soldiers accepted the social order as it stood. They certainly knew that others were better off than themselves, but this knowledge did not move them to revolt or revolution.

Chapter 2

THE ATTRACTION OF HOLLAND

It is an historical maxim that immigration stimulates population growth. But in the seventeenth century the connection between the two was even closer, for without immigration a population would not grow at all. Since the population of Holland increased in the late sixteenth and early seventeenth centuries by leaps and bounds, immigration must then also have been of an extraordinary magnitude. Demographic research has clearly established this point for the cities that have been studied most carefully: Rotterdam, Amsterdam and Leiden. We know that between 1581 and 1621 at Leiden the total number of immigrants came to 28,000.[1] The city's population increased in those years from about 12,000[2] to 45,000 inhabitants. Leiden had a very strong foreign influx, particularly of Southern Netherlanders. An account from 1588 stated that the city 'for the most part is inhabited by foreigners, who were driven from Brabant, Flanders and other areas.'[3] In the census of 1622 it appeared that a majority of the population was still of Southern Netherlandish origin.[4] In Amsterdam the situation was similar. In the first half of the seventeenth century, the Bloemstraat and its immediate area was a foreign quarter,[5] where it was easier to make oneself understood in French or Flemish than in Amsterdam dialect. Here too the influx continued. Over the entire seventeenth century the majority of Amsterdam bridegrooms were born outside the city;[6] they were at first Flemings and Walloons, then primarily Germans, who came to seek their fortune in Amsterdam.

Germany and the Southern Netherlands were the primary sources of supply, but other nations played a considerable part as well. In connection with Amsterdam the Jewish immigrants come to mind. A Jewish community already existed there at the end of the sixteenth century,[7] and would increase considerably in the seventeenth, when the Thirty Years' War also encouraged Jewish refugees to find a safer home.[8] Could they find a better haven than Amsterdam, where in 1642 Frederick Henry made an official visit to the synagogue of the Portuguese Jews? Amsterdam remained a unique meeting point for Jews and Netherlanders. But in the seventeenth century the contacts were not immediately very intensive, and they were hardly encouraged by the government. The Jews fell under a sort of little apartheid law. Jews were not supposed to take Christian servants, thought the States of Holland in 1615.[9] A year later an Amsterdam court stated that Jews must not become too familiar 'in frequenting and conversing with the women and daughters of these lands'.[10] At the conquest of Wesel by the States troops in 1629, not only the houses of 'diehard papists' were plundered but also those of the Jews.[11] Was this the work of mercenary soldiers, who had a different attitude from that of Dutchmen? Probably so, for in the minor riots that had taken place earlier in Dutch cities one never heard that the houses of rich Jews were attacked, as did happen in German cities. To the Dutch, the Jew was not the contemptible opponent, the fiercely hated enemy of the Christian faith. But he was alien to that faith. Nor was it possible to make a Christian of him, since the conversion of the Jews could only begin when the signs of the last days were fulfilled, and the second coming of Christ drew near.[12] Thus it was necessary for the Dutch people, even the lower social groups, to keep a certain distance from the Jews. In the seventeenth century the Jewish contribution to popular life and popular culture in Holland could not be, and was not yet allowed to be, very great. Nor were the Jews extraordinarily numerous in comparison with other groups of foreign origin.

The number of Britons was certainly greater. There were quite a few English and Scottish companies in the States army, and sometimes they also resulted in permanent settlements. In a city such as Brill, which had English troops in its garrison for years on end, many men had married local girls.[13] The cloth industry also drew labour from the British Isles. Amsterdam already boasted two English religious communities in 1608; the larger of them had about 300 communicants.[14] The unfriendly religious climate in their own country caused the number of English immigrants to increase significantly in the following decades.[15] By 1632 there were already seventeen English and Scottish religious communities in the Dutch Republic, nine of them in Holland.[16]

The German contingent, however, was already much larger. The Amsterdam church council in 1620 called Otto Badius to their service especially because of his German origin: people had often asked the consistory to hold divine service in German, to meet the needs of the numerous German servant population.[17] The Germans were nearly always found at the lowest levels of society, in the worst-paid occupations. Sometimes they came to do seasonal farm labour[18] – the hand-reapers, as they were later known, 'who seek their livelihood from one area to another, with digging, diking, and such-like houseman's work'.[19] Germans were especially useful in remedying the shortage of sailors.[20] These Germans were 'foreigners' in the country, and they remained such when the concept changed its meaning. At first anyone who was born outside a given city or province was regarded as a foreigner, though later on it became usual in the Republic to term all those born in the United Provinces 'Netherlanders'.[21] This new definition thus also excluded the Germans, but in shipping the German seamen quickly became so numerous and consequently indispensable that they were sometimes placed on the same footing as Nether- landers. The 'Register of all the Netherlandish captives, now slaves in Tunis', made in 1613, also listed men who came from Bremen, Emden, Lübeck and Hamburg.[22] Captain Hillebrant Gerbrantsz. Quast, sent out in 1615 to work for the liberation of these captives, received an instruction prepared by the chief clerk of the States General, which told him to look after the interests of 'all the Netherlanders' in

Tunis and Algiers. Oldenbarnevelt, who had the habit of critically re-reading outgoing mail before it left the office, crossed through these words and changed them to 'all the inhabitants and settlers of the United Netherlands'.[23] No doubt this was an attempt to state more correctly what the chief clerk also had in mind, namely to include the sailors who had served on Dutch ships even though they had not been born in the Netherlands. In any event, on the list of those released we again find German names.[24]

This German immigration would continue for a long time, even beyond the limits of the period discussed here. That was not the case for the largest influx that had taken place during the war against Spain: the Flemings, Brabanters and Walloons. This migration was concentrated in the last decades of the sixteenth century, and reached an estimated total of 60,000 to 80,000.[25] The great majority came to settle in Holland. The peak occurred around 1585, in the two-year period when the Duke of Parma recaptured Brussels, Ghent, Mechelen and Antwerp for the Spanish king. The increase can be seen clearly in the Amsterdam burghership books. In the years 1580–4, 13.2 per cent of the newly registered burghers were of Southern Netherlandish origin; in 1585–9, that figure was 44.2 per cent.[26] With some variation owing to local details, all large cities in Holland displayed the same pattern.[27]

According to contemporary historians Flanders and Brabant were left desolate. If we can believe Van Meteren,[28] towns with 2,000 to 3,000 houses were entirely abandoned in 1587. The best houses had become the lairs of wild animals where wolves settled in the bedsteads. At Ghent in a single year a good hundred people had reportedly been eaten by wolves. Packs of wild dogs roamed the countryside, everywhere overgrown with weeds. While this dramatic sketch may not be entirely free from exaggeration, the colder language of official documents tells us that in Flanders in 1591 vacant building lots were given away free, without rent or lease.[29] An investigation carried out in Brabant in 1587 showed that various villages had been reduced to one-tenth of their previous population, or sometimes even entirely abandoned.[30]

How were these foreigners received in Holland? In part the men from the South successfully avoided the ordinary lot of the foreign worker, who seemed to be created to do the heaviest, most dangerous and worst-paid work.[31] There was a considerable number of skilled craftsmen among the Southern Netherlanders, who gave the Holland textile industry a powerful injection of talent. The Amsterdam silk trade owed its rise entirely to new immigrants.[32] The cloth industries of Amsterdam, Rotterdam and Alkmaar worked with refugees from Aachen and Liège.[33] The city government of Amsterdam also granted loans and subsidies to this sector of the economy.[34] Haarlem's rapidly increasing prosperity in the 1580s rested in a significant way on the 'foreign bleachers and merchants'.[35] In Gouda the cloth industry again took advantage of the situation,[36] while Schoonhoven was able to attract tapestry weavers from Brabant and Flanders.[37] Delft offered bonuses to Flemish traders, and provided housing by rebuilding the former convent of St Ursula.[38] Even the countryside was able to draw some advantage from the new arrivals, despite the opposition of the cities.[39] Southern Netherlandish gardeners brought previously unknown crops into cultivation in the area around Haarlem and Leiden.[40] Indeed, the States of Holland wavered in considering regulations against the rural trade built up by the immigrants. They understood only too well that with their knowledge and skills these contributors to communal prosperity would immediately be welcomed in another province.[41]

The foreigner was received with friendship if he belonged to the better sort, but he could not automatically count on a hearty welcome. The States of Holland in 1629 would rather not give permission for a charitable collection on behalf of German refugees who had been chased out by the Thirty Years' War. Some reserve was necessary, thought the States, 'so as not to attract more of them here'.[42] People did not like to see more of them when they were not foremen and entrepreneurs, but competitors. Foreigners, Montchrétien declared categorically in 1615, cannot get work in Holland.[43] The cloth-weavers of The Hague imposed a double term of apprenticeship on foreigners; most trades in The Hague had similar regulations.[44] The Amsterdam masons' and carpenters' guilds had the right to demand the dismissal of foreign apprentices if they themselves had no work.[45] In 1621 in all Amsterdam guilds the rule was established (although not well observed) that no master could take on a foreign apprentice before he had made an effort to find a jobless burgher.[46] Until 1632 the hatmakers even had an absolute prohibition against taking on foreign apprentices. In other trades the foreign member was required to pay a portion of his wages to the guild.[47] Some immigrants tried to escape guild regulations by avoiding the city and independently taking to the roads as coppersmiths or tinkers. But they were caught out by the declarations of 1608 and 1622, which were specially directed against 'persons and craftsmen from the lands of Liège, Brabant, Flanders, Hainault and others',[48] thus very particularly against the Hollanders' Southern kinsmen.

The foreigner could not expect much else. The cities of Holland did not show much more consideration for one another when their prosperity was in question. In June, 1590, Rotterdam and Delft had such a violent conflict over the bridge at Overschie that fighting would have broken out if the States had not intervened.[49] Alkmaar thought it safer in 1625 to guard the newest locks at the Heer Hugowaard day and night, because the market competition between Alkmaar and Hoorn was such that each begrudged the other good roads and waterways.[50] The feeling of unity with other regions certainly did not extend further than self-interest demanded. Many regions of the country still had local dress, and the non-Hollander could already be recognised as Frisian or Gelderlander by his costume.[51] Anyone who disguised himself as a Hollander would be known by his speech.[52] Roemer Visscher makes fun of the Frisian girl Thiet, who decided to call herself Griet in elegant Hollands fashion.[53] For Samuel Coster the inhabitant of Drente was the model example of bad provincial culture, the 'plump Drenter, a soul so dull and boorish',[54] while Bredero also reminds us that in Holland Twente and Drente were proverbial for their impoverished backwardness.[55] Yet even those who wanted to

5. *The scissors sharpener*, by Adriaen van Ostade

remain within the bounds of respectability were not blind to the differences. Frisian girls are very different from Holland girls, says Arend van Buchell.[56] He does not add a value judgment, perhaps out of politeness to women. The young Simon Episcopius at least had no such qualms about characterising Frisian men frankly as 'crassi homines'.[57]

It was not likely that nobler crops would grow outside the garden of the United Provinces. 'Pious foreigners are better than misbehaving natives,' Van de Venne readily admitted,[58] but the scales were normally better designed for weighing misbehaving foreigners. The people of Emden are called potshitters,[59] those from Bremen are stupid,[60] and the Westphalians are filthy and unclean, so that a decent person would not eat the food they had touched.[61] When the quack-doctor was brought on stage, he almost always spoke German.[62] The English, 'contemptores omnium gentium',[63] were repaid in their own coin, as Moryson at any rate had to experience when he was shown the door at six different inns in Leiden.[64] Thanks to an unhappy experience with the Duke of Anjou, the Dutch attributed to the French a reputation for deceit and fickleness, which they had not entirely lost when the Dutch in their turn abandoned the French ally at the Peace of Münster.[65]

The Southern Netherlanders, who clustered together in their own neighbourhoods in cities such as Delft[66] and Leiden,[67] did not stand a chance of escaping from this discrimination. Even more so, because here it was not just a question of primitive feelings of aversion found among a half-civilised and uneducated rabble: the Holland regents, by their discrimination against Brabanters and Flemings, gave the lead to public opinion. For the most part these immigrants had abandoned their birthplace because they did not want to bow to Spanish rule or once again act like true sons of the Catholic Church. The argument of the declaration issued in 1622 against the tinkers of Liège, Brabant, Flanders and Hainault must have struck them as bitter indeed: the Hollanders, 'who during the troubles had to endure many taxes and other burdens, as they must still do every day, in their trades and crafts truly deserve to be preferred to the aforementioned foreign craftsmen, who do not belong to the guilds of these lands.'[68] Had the Brabanters and Flemings then sacrificed nothing for the common cause, when they abandoned their homes and possessions? The Holland regents were not trying to devalue the real worth of this sacrifice by rewarding it so magnanimously. They simply did not regard the Southerners as their equals. 'People keep us out everywhere,' complained Usselincx; 'in Holland we count for no more than a Frenchman, German or Briton.'[69]

And rightly so, declared the Amsterdam burgemeester Cornelis Pietersz. Hooft. On no account should these people be accepted in the government, because public office requires 'persons of serious, steadfast and peaceful mind. All of the qualities, if I am not mistaken, are more frequently found among the natives of this country than among those who have come from other lands and regions to live here.'[70] Thus it was a thorn in his side that the foreigners did have their say in Church matters.[71] Hooft was not above putting a sour annotation in the margin of his argument, that it certainly was remarkable how many fraudulent bankruptcies had occurred in the small circle of church council members, most of whom were of southern origin.[72] The same mentality could be found in Grevinchoven, who called Doucher not just a troublemaker, but a 'Walloon troublemaker'.[73] The same spirit inspired the Rotterdam regent Maria van Walenburch to protest against a fine imposed after some compromising materials about her were found among the papers of *dominee* Wittius. As a burgher's daughter she surely could not be condemned on the testimony of 'a foreign person'.[74] That mentality probably also played a part in the preference shown by the curators of Leiden University for Professor Jacobus Arminius, who as a Hollander was supposedly better acquainted with the 'humours of these lands'.[75]

The Southern Netherlanders were entitled to hope for better treatment. Marnix van St Aldegonde, the fiery Calvinist, had called them to emigration with burning speeches: 'Do not stay in the pool of idolatry, where people hold daily processions of Baal, and do not infect your conscience any longer!'[76] 'Remember the patriarch Lot, who for temporary gain chose Sodom as his residence, and narrowly escaped a fiery death!'[77] 'Do you still ask yourselves, who will shelter us? O ye of little faith, do you not know that the earth and all its fullness are the Lord's? Do not storks and swallows fly from distant lands without knowing what they will find, and are they not all fed?'[78] If the Southern Netherlanders could have expected a hearty welcome anywhere, then it should certainly have been in the Republic. 'We are bound to them,' a pamphlet writer is still assuring us in 1621, 'because they have stood in union with us, sworn an oath against the king of Spain with us, and borne the burdens of the war as well as we have.'[79] The national synod of Dordrecht in 1578 also declared that Flemish preachers were not required to serve only Flemish communities, 'since all Netherland is our common fatherland'.[80]

The Flemish preachers themselves had a distinct preference for their own region. Willem Baudartius did not want to remain tied to the church of Kampen in 1596, 'because I and many thousands hope that the Lord God will open the door of the Gospel in Flanders, and [I] wish to place my talents, as the Lord has given them to me, in the service of the church of God in my fatherland.'[81] Here Baudartius is speaking in the name of convinced Calvinists, who had left the South as soon as Parma's reconquest interrupted the free exercise of their religion. They became the mainstay and backbone of the reformed church of Holland. They supplied a large proportion of her officers, preachers as well as elders and deacons.[82] In the 1580s, they were responsible for the strong expansion of the urban churches, both Dutch and French-speaking ones.[83] If a city in Holland wanted to encourage its industry, then it would be wise to engage a Walloon preacher.[84] According to the mission-report of the apostolic vicar Rovenius in 1617, most of the heretics in the Dutch Republic were immigrants from Brabant, Flanders, France and Germany.[85]

Naturally this last statement has no statistical basis. It was probably not based on a careful survey made with the help of membership lists of the reformed churches. More likely it was written with the ulterior motive of inspiring Catholic missionary efforts. If the Calvinist church attracted so many exiles, then surely the native population must have been more inclined toward the old faith. A similar intention is certainly found in appraisals by Remonstrant writers and political leaders – Brandt, Wtenbogaert, De Groot, Hooft, Oldenbarnevelt[86] – who wanted to blame Flemish agitation for the religious disturbances during the years of the truce or the Leicester period. Why was it that Leicester had so many friends in Leiden, Brandt asked, that in no other city of Holland 'did the Leicester faction sow more seeds of mutiny among the community, than in Leiden?'[87] Because 'so many thousands of

Brabanters and Flemings' lived there. De Groot explains the trouble in Leiden and Haarlem in 1617 in precisely the same way: after all, those cities contained 'many thousands of foreigners, waiting for the occasion for change'.[88]

Now it is true that the Calvinist Reyd also blamed the disturbances of 1587 on the Southerners.[89] But while Reyd merely stated this as an observed fact, Brandt sought its origin in the southern character. He declared that Brabanters and Flemings were 'generally regarded as restless, troublesome, power-hungry by nature, also more hot-headed than Hollanders'.[90] Their choice of the wrong party in Leicester's time was not an accidental misfortune. Rather, it was a symptom of their doubtful mentality. Their wild religious enthusiasm would throw the whole country into an uproar, just as they had done with their Calvinist fanaticism in Ghent. Then it would come to pass in Holland as in Flanders: internal division would open the door to the enemy.[91]

The train of thought outlined above comes from the Gouda preacher Herman Herbertsz. He did not doubt the good faith of the Calvinists. He was only worried that their 'untimely and mistaken zeal' would be as damaging as deliberately evil designs. Among others, the regents in particular, mistrust may have had deeper roots. There were some rich men among the foreigners who were cut off from political influence,[92] yet the great mass of foreigners were poor, dissatisfied with the religious tolerance of the regents. The standard of living of the average foreigner in Holland was below that of his native counterpart: the danger was that the poor foreigners might be roused to action by their more prominent excluded fellow countrymen. All the pre-conditions for revolution seemed to be fulfilled.

The poverty of the immigrants from Brabant and Flanders was indeed poignant. We are already aware that in Leiden the native Hollanders formed a minority of the population. But according to tax returns in 1599 only 6 per cent of the total taxable capital of the city was owned by foreigners. No more than 169 of this group held property worth 3,000 gulden or more.[93] Many had arrived in Holland without any capital whatsoever. For the benefit of the Flemings and Brabanters the States of Holland declared in 1584 that no one could have them condemned to pay debts, unless the defendants possessed sufficient means.[94] Even people who had formerly owned houses and farms were sometimes reduced to beggary, and forced to seek charity.[95] In the overpopulated cities of Holland such as Leiden these people came to live in expensive and crowded rented houses,[96] without much hope of a better future. As late as 1643, among the 5,000 souls of the Walloon community at Leiden, 'barely one out of a hundred was reasonably well-to-do'.[97]

In other cities there was also great poverty among the Walloons. In 1619 the Holland diaconate of The Hague offered the much smaller Walloon community one-third of its weekly collections, for the benefit of the poor Walloons.[98] There was a generally accepted rule in all Walloon churches that communion could not be denied to a beggar,[99] a clear distinction from the usual Dutch policy. French-speaking people always headed the list of Amsterdam poor,[100] which was certainly no coincidence. But perhaps this happened also because the Dutch-speaking poor could seek alms from the diaconate of the Dutch-speaking church, who were generally somewhat wealthier than the Walloons. According to C. P. Hooft, at the end of the sixteenth century the Amsterdam deacons served a predominantly foreign clientele.[101] Hooft saw this as discrimination against the Dutch poor, but was he correct in this view? The city poor-relief authorities, who gave preference to burghers' children, had 2,511 impoverished families on their lists in 1611, yet barely 200 of them were Hollanders.[102] Immigrants were significantly worse off than the natives, with a result that a much greater percentage of foreigners was dependent on charity. Yet here, too, as Hooft's example shows, another source of envy and jealousy was discovered. Our playwrights were certainly hoping for applause with their tart critiques of 'foreign drones',[103] the beggars' gang of 'krauts, shits, and knouts'[104] who lived on good Amsterdam money, and 'foreign blockheads, or outlanders',[105] who had come to Holland only to live at public expense.

One might see such remarks as an early protest against abuse of the social welfare system. But I think it would be equally just to describe them as expressions of common, narrow-minded jealousy: it makes no difference whether they come from the mouth of burgemeester Cornelis Pietersz. Hooft or from his namesake, Willem Dirckszoon Hooft, a true man of the people. Hollanders did not want the foreigner to enjoy lives as good as their own: they thought the fat of the land should be reserved for natives. Their jealousy was primarily directed against those who did not stay at the bottom of the social ladder, such as the self-conscious Southerners, who absolutely refused to feel inferior. While it was true in the seventeenth-century that Holland set the tone for the Netherlands as a whole, only a short time earlier Brabant and Flanders had fulfilled that role, and to some extent people still lived with that tradition. Now we ourselves often say 'Holland' when we mean the entire Netherlands, but in the seventeenth century the name 'Flanders' was still occasionally used as a similar *pars pro toto*. Sailors from Holland who overpowered a pirate at Nantes in 1619 heard shouts of encouragement from the shore: 'Courage, bon Flamand!'[106] Even far outside Europe this habit was in vogue. Vice-admiral Sebolt de Weert, who visited Ceylon in 1603 in the service of the East India Company, remarked that here, too, under Portuguese influence, people called his homeland 'Flanders'.[107]

In the eyes of the Hollanders it appeared that the old prestige of Flanders had been wiped away by Holland's success against Spain, after the South had failed and was again subjugated. The Dutch political elite regarded this neither as a stupid piece of bad luck, nor as the result of the lack of natural lines of defence. The regents of Holland probably would have had little good to say about Pieter Geyl's well-known theory of the great rivers, which gave better protection to the North. That Parma had been able to conquer Flanders and Brabant, was, in the opinion of the Hollanders, the fault of the southern kinsmen themselves.[108] The Southerners saw it differently. They regarded themselves as old allies, and in their most reckless moments, as the first founders of freedom. 'We relieved you of the tenth-penny tax', boasted notary Danckaert in February 1616 at an inn in The Hague.[109] And what a dubious character this Jan Danckaert was – at least four times in his turbulent life he got into trouble with the authorities for slander![110] Yet even among such persons as Danckaert the pride of Brabant still lived. The southern Netherlanders, and above all the Brabanters, felt that in good taste and manners they were quite superior to the Hollanders.[111] As late as 1642 Tengnagel in his farce about Frick in the Front House has the widow Dieuwertje complain that her son wants to marry a seamstress 'Who sprang from messy Hollanders, while he descended from neat Brabanters'.[112] What she meant by Brabant neatness becomes clear to us, when we read in Leeghwater's memoirs of his youth that in his birthplace, De Rijp, only one woman washed her clothes with soap, and she was a Brabanter. 'The native women washed their shirts and linens, out of sheer destitution, with dove-shit and other filth, everything in order to save money, and also because they didn't know any better'.[113] The Brabanters were conscious of their own smartness, and foreigners saw it too. For the Englishman Moryson the zenith of cleanliness was not the woman of Holland, but the Brabanter: 'Especially the Brabanters excell for white and fine linen, and for general comlinesse of their garments.'[114] Over time the Hollanders had to see for themselves. Claes Kloet, in the farce of the same title by Biestkens, thought an Antwerp bordello was a first-class hotel, because everything was so wonderfully clean in the Brabant style.[115]

It was not merely a question of external appearances. When in 1615 Jean-François Le Petit praised the people of Dordrecht above all other Hollanders because of their politeness and good manners, he could not think of a higher compliment than to say that they appeared to be Brabanters.[116] *Dominee* Sopingius, who in 1591 had not gone farther south from Utrecht than Breda, noticed then already 'that here in Breda the customs of the burghers are different and softer, different too is the politeness of the people.'[117]

The Hollanders defended themselves by exposing the other side of this refinement. As soon as the desire for luxury had appeared on the scene at the end of the sixteenth century,[118] the Brabanters were blamed for it. 'It is most regrettable that those of Brabant and Flanders who fled from the persecution to Holland, to find here a refuge, have brought their haughtiness with them.'[119] The speaker is an unimpeachable witness, Jacobus Trigland, who had studied in Leuven. Brabant girls, said the Haarlem poet Gilles Quintijn, think themselves too grand to walk. If a Holland girl fancies a romp in the green countryside, she walks there herself. The Brabant girl allows herself to be taken there as a princess in a coach or wagon.[120] They are, it's true, more polite and more lovable than their little Dutch girlfriends,[121] but what an excess of clothes!

> These maids you will know, are called
> Eloquent, and cheerful.
> They are, mark it well, very inclined
> To display and great show:
> They are splendid in their clothes, wicked morals!
> Thus they are, nearly all of them.

They attire themselves, beautiful to the eye,
But far above their station in life
Wearing stockings on their legs, as we know,
Which are called *encarnados* [Spanish for flesh-coloured].
Would you ask about the hooded cloaks that they wear?
These are made of very fine silk
Little hats, of velvet cloth, they have made;
Or of whatever, I know not.[122]

In short, Brabant girls could think their trouble well worthwhile. Quintijn had strained his eyes looking them over. The attention with which he observed Brabant fashion already suggested what the normally frank Moryson said in roundabout manner: the Flemish and Brabant women are not only better clothed than the Dutch, but they were also prettier.[123] Holland girls were not blind. They did not need any further encouragement to dress themselves in clothes of the Brabant cut:

The girls of polite society,
Take their fancy in Brabant style:
They wear their bonnet in Brabant style:
Their hood has earflaps in Brabant style:
Their ruffle is set in Brabant style:
Their velvet dress is in Brabant style:
They button their sleeves in Brabant style:
They pleat their petticoats in Brabant style:
They say 'Yes, verily' in Brabant style:
They speak everything all together in Brabant style:
They sing their song in Brabant style:
They make their way in Brabant style:
In Brabant style
In Brabant style
Amsterdam daughters, give me an answer,
Are you ashamed of Holland bluntness?[124]

How distressing for Roemer Visscher, but the answer of the Holland girls was probably affirmative! The old solidity still had some bastions. Le Petit found at Schiedam in 1615 'the old simplicity and sincerity of the old Hollanders, they hate and reject all pride, magnificence, pomp and excess'.[125] But how long could they resist, when Brabant girls were prettier? The Venetian Giustiniano described the Rotterdammers in 1608 as 'people who do not care for vanity, but for their own business'.[126] Fifteen years later Rotterdam also was not what it used to be:

In particular the people, the wearing of their clothes,
Which, just like a cloud, changes and alters.[127]

When even Protestant ministers such as Wtenbogaert in 1602 had to defend themselves against accusations that they dressed 'in the new fashion',[128] the envy of Brabant elegance must have led to imitation among all who were judged less harshly than the preachers[129] on the strict simplicity of their clothes.

Thus of all the foreign influences, the Southern Netherlandish was undoubtedly the strongest. Over time it was precisely the accessibility of Brabant and Flanders manners that would ease the path to assimilation., In the first half of the seventeenth century, however, these kinsmen formed a not yet entirely adapted element, sometimes held in contempt, sometimes secretly admired, but still always experienced as not-Dutch.

Chapter 3

OUTSIDE THE COMMUNITY

What is really the heart of the social problem? If a modern pollster went from door to door with this question, we can imagine what kind of standard answers would be pre-printed on his forms: a decent wage for all; equal pay for all; worker-participation in enterprises; winning the class struggle; making the class struggle unnecessary. Yet in the sixteenth or seventeenth century no one would have given any of these answers, or even understood them. The social problem was then seen as the problem of poverty. As such it was regarded as insoluble, because according to the prevailing ideas, the poor would be with us always. Sometimes it was even said that God had willed it so, but that was not necessarily meant as self-justification, an excuse for the rich to remain rich with a clear conscience. Perhaps it was different later, but in the seventeenth century the concept of a society without the poor was simply unthinkable. Such a society could only exist as a Utopia, not to be realised by human beings on this earth. Thus the central problem was not the elimination of poverty: that was impossible anyway. At most there were attempts to make poverty bearable. The means chosen for this purpose was poor relief, with money that was made available directly or indirectly – via relief agencies or diaconates – by the rich. Then, however, there arose a second problem. Every rich person had an obligation to give alms. That is the blessing of wealth, said Bredero, to be able to distribute bread to the poor, to help widows and orphans, to build hospitals, to support old people and foreigners.[1] But not every poor person had an equal right to claim relief. The poor person might be a victim, but also a guilty party. In the distribution of alms it was necessary to make a distinction between the two. The honest poor deserved and got help. In declarations, memoirs, and reports, however, there is frequent mention of people most commonly described as 'lazy and sturdy beggars'. These were the ones who did not work because they were born children of beggars and never learnt anything else; or those who could have practiced a trade but preferred to beg rather than do hard work.[2]

This, at any rate, was the way the Holland regents understood the problem. It could be hardly called a comprehensive explanation. Begging and vagrancy undoubtedly had other causes besides laziness and wicked habits.[3] The legion of beggars included redundant workers, who had sought in vain any employer for their labour. Among them were discharged soldiers and deserters,[4] side by side with the war-victims they had plundered. Peasants who suffered one bad harvest too many also became beggars, as did weavers dismissed during crises in the cloth industry.[5] Some of the poor were refugees from religious wars, civil wars, wars of succession; others were clients and servants of bankrupt patrons. Anyone might become a beggar or vagrant in various ways; it was not so easy to leave the ranks of the propertyless wanderers. Sixteenth-century descriptions of life on the road, which have a basis in observation, experience, or immersion – *Lazarillo de Tormes*, Thomas Nashe, Adriaen van de Venne – can fill us with disgust at the filth, cruelty, inhumanity, and above all the shameless egotism of this rough anti-society. Yet seldom do they lack an animal but energetic lust for life, which raises necessity to a virtue, and vice to an honour; sometimes they almost or even completely succeed in making a miserable rogue into a hero.

Literary sources can mislead us. Not every beggar was a Lazarillo, and not every vagrant Reynard the Fox in rags. The picaresque tale is silent about the man reduced to begging out of desperation. We do find the prototypes of Barry Lyndon and Jack Dawkins the Artful Dodger, but not John Barton and Smike and Jo. Each of them had his alter ego in the great mass of sixteenth-century homeless. Their lot was generally hard and sometimes gruesome. Probably they would have been better off with even the worst-paid regular work. Nonetheless we can imagine that many, who either never had strong will or had been broken on the wheel of fortune, did not even try to escape from the legion of beggars. A society that does not provide work for all, that keeps wages so low that the incentive to work is weakened, and that offers poor relief only in the form of charity – such a society itself maintains its parasites. The region of Holland had its share.

This share was not extraordinarily large, however. Once again it appears that shortcomings recognised in Dutch society were not noticed by foreign observers, because they were accustomed to so much worse at home. The Englishman Howell and the Venetian Suriano both said that there were few if any beggars in Holland.[6] Van Meteren even asserted in 1590 that in Holland it was safe to travel unarmed and alone at night while carrying money,[7] because there was so little to fear from wandering vagabonds. As a Dutchman familiar with English conditions, he too came to a rather too favourable judgment when making a comparison with the notoriously dangerous English roads. Beggars and vagrants were apparently seen less often in Holland than elsewhere in Europe. But that did not mean that the inhabitants did not regard them as a real plague, especially in the countryside. The sources frequently speak of vagrants and vagabonds: the very names are more reminiscent of wide open spaces than densely packed little cities. Indeed the declarations say as much in so many words, for example that of 1614: begging is increasing in the cities, but especially in the open areas and the countryside.[8] The States of Holland decided in 1601 that there was no need for a general regulation, 'since almost all cities already have orders on the subject of the poor and beggars there that satisfy their needs'.[9] This may also explain the favourable opinion of foreigners, whose observations primarily reflect the urban scene: the cities as a rule had little to complain about.[10] C. P. Hooft noted with satisfaction 'how few weeds of riff-raff from this so populous corner [of the world] come to fall into the hands of justice, compared to others of our neighbours near and far'.[11] Typical Hooft: on every social level the Hollanders are better than foreigners. But if Hooft did not intend hilarity – and there are not many glimpses of humour in his published speeches – then at least his judgment may not have been far from the truth.

The real nuisance must have been found in the countryside. What did it consist of? We seldom hear of gruesome crimes. At Schoonhoven in 1589 a vagrant was executed because he had cut the hands and feet off the child of a peasant woman who had refused to let him in.[12] At Leiden four vagrants who were caught in the act of burglary killed the householder, his wife, and the servant-girl.[13] Perhaps it might be possible to find other bloody dramas besides these two,[14] but in the sixteenth century murders already received a great deal of publicity.[15] It is certain that very serious crimes did not occur frequently.

The same holds true for violent highway robberies. Admittedly Bredero seems to have thought otherwise in his *Praise of Poverty*:[16]

> Comes a merchant in the woods,
> With fine stones and eastern gold,
> He must leave his gold and his life.

But even then Holland was not exactly covered with woods. Bredero was reproducing a literary cliché here, not describing the risks of daily life. When a wagon was robbed in the vicinity of The Hague in 1630, the fact immediately drew the attention of the States, who promptly issued a new declaration.[17] The year was probably not a coincidence: in 1629 the cost of living had been extra high, for months on end,[18] and 1630 was another year of high prices.[19] The beggar who had to live on the reserves of others fell hopelessly into the pit when two bad years followed in succession. His despair was translated into malice. Regions where many vagrant people congregated then had to pay a heavy price. Delft was a victim during the period of high prices in 1595–7: in the third year of famine, fish-baskets in the middle of the city were emptied, and 'travelling folk' around Delft suffered greatly.[20] These were the exceptional consequences of a long period of scarcity, which led to robberies and organised burglaries in some parts of Holland.[21]

Yet even these more serious crimes occurred rather seldom. When beggars and vagrants turned to theft, they did it mostly as light-fingered passers-by, who picked up a chicken or some apples along their way. Here the boundary of pure criminal behaviour is difficult to determine, because the vagabond could take advantage of old rights that were maintained by the village for the benefit of its poor. Thus they were allowed to glean the fields, once the sheaves had been brought in.[22] But how could the farmer defend the rest of his crop, when the poor swarmed on to his land after the grain harvest? If he chased the gleaners from his land,[23] he took the law into his own hands, and official justice would not support him. The fruits of orchard and field could never remain completely protected, especially when they were regarded as free booty by passing soldiers and sailors.[24] The situation with fishing was actually no different. In 1611 the States of Holland ordered Grotebroek to withdraw a new regulation against fishing with the rod, 'as in conflict with the old tradition of these lands, that the use of the rod is always freely allowed'.[25] But did rod-fishermen have access to every property, and were they allowed to toss their lines in any body of water? In the Rijnland these practices did so much harm to field crops that fishing in private waters had to be forbidden.[26] And then there was peat: as bailiff of Muiden, Hooft had experience with the Gooilanders, who took peat for themselves wherever they found it, even in bogs that did not belong to them. Hooft saw that as 'one of the worst sorts of thievery',[27] but local authorities protested against a prohibition of the practice. They asserted that their villages had been owners of these bogs since time immemorial;[28] thus regarding them as communal property, they were unwilling to recognise the claims of private landowners.

In these and similar cases the actual dispute was between the village poor and the property owners, not between homeless and householders in the literal sense of the word. Beggars and vagrants took advantage of this situation by taking instead of asking. But that was not their ordinary modus operandi. They could seek alms with importunate urgency, though in general they did not make demands. Only once do the sources mention vagabonds who stated their request as a command. Indeed that was roughly the style of the group that roamed between Leiden and The Hague in 1625 under the leadership of Jan Jansz. of Leiden, alias Jan of Paris. They were a gang of unemployed youths fortified with provocative nicknames such as Jan with the Long Hair and Susanne the Babylonian. Until they were caught, they formed an independent troop that invited themselves to dinner with the farmers and danced naked on the Vineyard-lane in Voorschoten. For Jan of Paris these adventures ended with a sentence of twenty-five years' exile. The others received lighter punishments.[29]

This affair was handled by the Court of Holland, perhaps a sign that these provocations against public order were taken seriously, and punished accordingly.[30] It was indeed far from the usual routine. While vagabonds often did join together in small bands, true beggars apparently understood that such defiant light-heartedness would endanger their future. They wanted to practise as long as possible the trade they had learnt: that of beggar. Just like every other occupation, professional begging required training and experience. Urban beggars often lived together in groups, in recognised lodging-houses, where the children could learn from an early age 'in what manner they should beg here; how they should escape the provosts, and when after a long time they are arrested, how they should excuse themselves with ignorance of the declarations'.[31] Begging had a centuries-old tradition behind it. Anyone who wanted to know it thoroughly had quite a bit to learn. Adriaen van de Venne in his *Tableau of the Ridiculous World* sums up no less than forty-two kinds of beggars and vagrants, each of whom used a particular system to earn their living.[32] Thus they were 'released hostages', who said they had been held captive by the Turks. *Kammesiers* pretended to be students, *schleppers* Catholic priests. A *dutsbetter* played the part of a young mother, but anyone who looked under the robes would usually find a man. A *grantuer* simulated the falling sickness, a *vopper*

6. *The wretched*, by Adriaen van de Venne

suffered from sham feeble-mindedness, a *swijger* from jaundice. A *veranier* was a so-called converted Jew; a *nachtbehuyler* one who would go lie in front of people's doors at night and shout loudly.

Many of these tricks have proved their usefulness in all countries and ages. In Henry Mayhew's renowned description of the popular classes in London in the middle of the nineteenth century, *London Labour and the London Poor*, we still encounter various numbers from Van de Venne's catalogue, although in Mayhew they were somewhat less primitive. Had the London beggars of the nineteenth century reaped the profit of two hundred years of extra experience, or were the Hollanders too gullible to be worth the trouble of refined techniques? On his trips to Africa Pieter de Marees found incomparably more professionalism among the beggars of Guinea than among his own countrymen: 'they can sham so well, and are so experienced in that knowledge, that they far surpass all the beggars of our countries, even those who have sat for ten or twelve years by the church doors of Holland and Zeeland'.[33]

De Marees and Van de Venne were not the only ones to see through the beggars' tricks. The States of Holland had issued a declaration against simulated lepers in 1586.[34] Quack-doctors, hawkers, travelling shoemakers and similar folk were specifically mentioned in the laws against begging.[35] Fortune-telling and palm-reading, particularly when practised by gypsies[36] or those who pretended to be such,[37] were not specifically named, although in general 'heathens, Egyptians or similar vagrants' were denied permission to stay in Holland.[38] No declaration was issued against pseudo-exiles, so-called refugees for the faith, but they were called to the attention of judicial officers in 1645.[39]

Vagabonds had always drawn administrative attention, even when the struggle against Spain was still in full swing in the province of Holland. In 1572 Gouda employed a man for twenty-one stuivers per week to make sure that the numerous beggars who wandered about outside the city did not enter through the gate.[40] This regulation bears witness to a strongly developed sense of order, but not to great realism. Would it have had any practical effect, an attempt to cleanse a war-torn country of its wandering beggars? 'A step-child of the war', Constantine Huygens called the beggar.[41] There was indeed a very intimate relationship, with long-term consequences. No one should have expected the Pacification of Ghent in 1576 to free the land of vagrants, even if it did end the state of war on Holland's soil. The province then also had special officers, the bailiffs, whose particular task was to track down and arrest vagrants. Thielman van Eynden Cornelisz. at Haarlem,[42] for example, acted as bailiff for the Noorderkwartier, where he had fourteen men in his service.[43] Pieter van Beest became bailiff of the region between Lek and Zuiderzee in 1589; he had twenty-four assistants.[44] In the same period the islands of South Holland had a bailiff who resided in Gorinchem.[45] The division of responsibilities changed somewhat, however, probably according to need, for in 1596 Bartholomeüs van Buren received a commission for Rijnland, Delfland, Schieland, Amstelland, Gooiland, the lands of Woerden and Blois, and the islands of Overmaas and

Overflakkee. He had at his disposal four horsemen, eight foot-soldiers, and a sloop with two cannons.[46] Manpower was rather severely restricted, although here and there he was assisted by the local watch.[47] The stewards co-operated as well,[48] but they did not act outside their own jurisdictions;[49] as a result, bailiffs with more extensive powers were indispensable.

People most likely did not expect that they could keep the country permanently free of nuisances. Their most important work probably consisted of springing into action with their helpers if matters threatened to get out of hand anywhere. Then they organised a 'general visitation'[50] to the area to arrest all 'vagabonds, rapscallions, and idlers'.[51] The results could be astonishing. As a consequence of the action taken in 1595 by Bartholomeüs van Buren as bailiff of Delfland and Vlaardingen, by 1596 the entire area was freed 'of all vagrants, thugs and vagabonds'.[52] Was this campaign therefore a resounding success? At that moment, yes, but in 1597 the area around Delft was again plagued with 'evildoers, thieves, and publicly expelled outlaws'.[53] The service was thus able to organise quick blitzes that momentarily filled the gaols, but for ongoing control it was too small. It was once suggested that the nets could be tightened by giving each village its own beggar-guard.[54] Yet perhaps people thought this method was too expensive, or they may have realised that one man alone could not take action against the vagabonds. In any case the bailiffs and their ordinary helpers continued to fulfil these functions.[55]

What happened to the captured vagrants? The official policy in Holland was guided by two basic principles, which were not always in harmony with each other. On the one hand, beggars were regarded as rabble that had to be whipped, branded, and banished. On the other hand, authorities proceeded from the fiction that the vagabonds were unemployed people looking for work, and thus had to be helped with suitable jobs. The proclamations specifically said so: all healthy beggars must report to the administration, and say what kind of work they want. If they were unsuccessful in finding work locally, then they would receive permission to travel to another, specifically named city.[56] A journey on foot through twenty cities of Holland could take a rather long time, but that was not the intention. In 1589 the States of Holland decided not to tolerate any vagrants who were unemployed longer than one month. Offenders would be put in the pillory for twenty-four hours – if they were strong enough to take it – and then had to cross the border.[57] Anyone who was unable to work could sign up for poor relief, provided he had been born in Holland. Otherwise he had to leave the province.[58]

Banishment could not be an effective penalty for those who had neither house nor hearth. Trijn Pieters from Maassluis was banned ten times between 1606 and 1617, the year of her execution.[59] She may have set a record, but that is by no means certain. Rather, the pattern of her life shows how easy it was for a banned person to return, even a woman who over time carried the marks of four brandings on her body, and from 1612 was recognisable by her cut-off ears. We can understand why in 1623 the Deputised Councils of Holland preferred to ship far away 'soldiers who have deserted from the enemy and other vagrants … even if it is by sea to Calais, Bremen, Hamburg or other places'.[60]

The more difficult it was to keep beggars out of the country, the more important it then became to find them suitable work. When we see the authorities in Holland working on this problem, it becomes crystal clear that the fiction of the vagrant seeking work was not taken literally. It was in fact highly unusual for plans to put beggars to work to be discussed seriously. A report on poor relief in Leiden in 1577 proposed to accumulate a capital sum of 2,000 to 3,000 gulden in order to provide work for the poor. For example, it would have been possible to employ in net-making those women and children who said they could not get work. Also, the authors of the report considered how to attract to Leiden pin-makers and other craftsmen who practised easily learned occupations; they could then take on ex-beggars as employees.[61] It appears that nothing ever came of these proposals. Another unsuccessful plan came up in 1629, when Frederick Henry was besieging Den Bosch and the enemy had marched over the Veluwe as far as Het Gooi. In the month of August, all manpower was welcome. Holland farmers had to do digging, inhabitants of frontier villages were called to guard duty, and the professional army was hastily expanded with a number of companies recruited abroad. At that moment the States-General decided 'to round up all sturdy beggars, and send them all to the army'.[62] The States of Holland agreed with this decision,[63] although by the end of September it had not yet been carried out.[64] The subject was still under discussion, but now that Den Bosch had been taken and the Spaniards had retreated from the Veluwe, there was more interest in reducing the size of the rapidly swollen army than in military training for sturdy vagabonds. The beggars could again breathe freely.

On one later occasion a similar project was discussed. In 1648 in the States of Holland there was a proposal to populate the controversial Brazilian settlement of the West India Company with vagrants and beggars. Yet this idea was rejected, 'in view of the need of the state not to have vagabonds and beggars there, but to be dressed, cultivated, and maintained by upright persons'.[65] In any event, this language is clear. The beggar was no longer regarded as looking for work, but as useless. He could not be trusted with a decent job.

At that time, work for beggars was almost always forced labour, for which the voluntary supply was too small or entirely lacking. Southern European countries, for example, had galleys. Rowing ships were not normally used in the turbulent waters of the North Sea, but, following Spanish examples, at the end of the sixteenth century the Dutch experimented with two galleys, named the red and the black. It may sound unbelievable, but the black galley was manned by volunteers.[66] The red one was built with other purposes in mind, as will appear from the appointment of her captain: no one other than Holland's most effective vagrant-catcher, bailiff Bartholomeüs van Buren.[67] Under his command served 'vagabonds and useless persons', for life or for a limited sentence.[68] Since the benches provided space for only eight-two rowers,[69] we might suppose that there was no shortage of candidates.

7. *The shoemaker*, by Adraien van Ostade

In August, 1600, however, it was necessary to seek reinforcements from Dordrecht gaol, 'the sturdiest and strongest bandits'.[70] No doubt one of the causes was the high death rate. In view of the bleak Dutch climate, the hard regime and minimal feeding,[71] it was a wonder that in 1601 the number of deaths among rowers of the red galley was no more than twenty-eight, while eighteen to twenty others had to be released from the benches owing to illness.[72] It seems not unlikely that the punishment of sending prisoners to the galleys was seldom applied, because people soon realised that it exceeded the bounds of humanity. Although galleys were occasionally used later,[73] this form of job creation for beggars had but little effect.

In the meantime a better solution had been found. Better in the eyes of the Hollanders themselves, but not only that: it drew the admiration of all Europe. In 1615 the Frenchman Montchrétien explained to his king how the Hollanders had succeeded in magically transforming tiny villages into flourishing cities. In Holland no one was allowed to be simultaneously lazy and ignorant. These vices were cured in the school of bees and ants, and anyone who did not learn the lesson himself received his medicine from the government.[74] This panacea was the Amsterdam house of correction – 'Muster von Sauberkeit, Zucht, Ordnung und fleissiger Arbeit',[75] in the words of another enthusiastic foreigner. Naturally forced labour as a punishment had not been unknown previously. In 1579, for example, prisoners were set to work on the fortifications of Amsterdam.[76] By this means the community profited from the criminal, but the originators of the Amsterdam house of correction wanted the guilty party himself to benefit from his treatment. The criminal was not seen as a hopeless case. It was possible to make a better man of him. At the sentencing of a sixteen-year-old Amsterdam burglar in 1589, the aldermen said that his punishment should really also have an educative character, and in such a manner 'that similar burghers' children should be maintained in continuous labour, thus to be weaned from their wicked habits and to exact improvement in life'.[77] These are the same ideas that Dirck Coornhert put forward in his *Boeventucht*: to make criminals and beggars into useful people through work.[78]

The house of correction rested on these principles. It was a house not of discipline, but of education. The inmates were prepared for a return to society, after they had learnt how to make themselves useful to their fellow citizens. The upbringing had two main parts. The detainee would learn hard work, and he would receive religious instruction.[79] When these two salutary means of correction had changed his nature, he could regain his freedom as a useful member of society.

The example of Amsterdam inspired others. Houses of correction were founded in Haarlem, Gouda, Enkhuizen, Alkmaar and Dordrecht.[80] Not all of them appeared viable. In 1648 there were still four of them left, namely Amsterdam, Haarlem, Gouda and Alkmaar, which however were then seen as too few.[81] Inside and outside the province many more were established.[82] For women there was a spinning-house, with the same pedagogical intentions.[83]

In the first years after its founding the men of the Amsterdam house worked on the loom.[84] Later this became the occupation of weaker inmates. The strongest men had to rasp wood,[85] thus the Amsterdam institution was often called the *rasphuis*. In assigning tasks, there was a preference for heavy physical labour because of a shortage of volunteer workers. But the houses of correction should not simply be classed with the galleys, for they never lost sight of the ultimate goal of education. In the Gouda house of correction, the pounding of hemp was the first work chosen. But the regents of this institution reversed their decision when they realised that

8. *Almshouse visitation by an almoner, accompanied by the chief provost* attributed to Werner van den Valckert

dust released by the process in the enclosed space would undermine the men's health too much to give them a reasonable chance for return to society.[86] There were even cases of boys who were placed in the Amsterdam house of correction for the express purpose of learning a particular trade.[87] Indeed, the detention of girls at the spinning-house sometimes happened at the request of their parents, who could take them back home when they had completed their training.[88] The whole style of life in the spinning-houses did have a friendlier aspect than that of the men. 'They sitt like soe many at schoole, very civilly and quietly att their needle', said the Englishman Peter Mundy in 1640, 'wanting nothing but liberty; many off them better in than out'.[89] No such idyll was written about the *rasphuis*. The States of Holland in 1597 had already given far-reaching powers to the management, by excusing in advance from legal prosecution those guards who might, in an emergency, kill inmates.[90] The Gouda house of correction experienced two riots during its first ten years of existence.[91] That others might have occurred elsewhere is certainly not impossible.

If the houses of correction were intended to give the impetus for a total re-education of the begging folk of Holland, then they failed in their purpose. Was this the reason why, in the first half of the seventeenth century, their number and capacity remained relatively small? The Amsterdam *rasphuis* had accommodation for about seventy persons,[92] excluding the secret house of correction, but that was intended for another social category.[93] If the experiment had really produced the hoped-for results, then surely the scale of operations would have been enlarged. Isaäc Beeckman wrote in 1627 in his journal that children were punished for their improvement, pupils for improvement and example, criminals only for example. Punishment did not improve them, for they usually ended their days on the gallows. Therefore it would be better to put anyone who was whipped even once into the house of correction for life.[94] Here the old ideals of Coornhert's *boeventucht* have disappeared completely: the clients of the house of correction cannot be converted or improved. The educative institutions have deteriorated into penal colonies. Perhaps others thought the same as Beeckman. Yet the optimism of the founding fathers never died out entirely. In 1776 the Englishman John Howard was still just as enthusiastic about the Dutch prison system, and in particular the houses of correction,[95] as previous travellers had been early in the seventeenth century.

Coornhert's mental world was certainly not the same as that of the Calvinists, whose voices had become dominant in the reformed church. Yet even such a fiery Calvinist as Willem Baudartius was an enthusiastic admirer of the system.[96] That is not strange: the church was even more strongly opposed to beggars and vagrants than was the government. For the church thought not only that healthy men and women in the prime of life should use their heads and hands to earn their own living, but also that the handicapped, the aged and other guiltless unemployed should not be allowed to beg: rather, they must be able to live on charity from the rich. Religious and secular poor-relief agencies had a duty to provide for the support of all the needy. These institutions should not abdicate their responsibility, and they had to gather the means diligently in order to care for the truly needy. But then the poor always had to apply for aid if they were in need. They were not supposed to try to help themselves by begging. In the eyes of the reformed church, begging was a public sin.

At first there was some hesitation. In 1595 the church council of Assendelft forbade its members to beg without church consent,[97] but thereby did in principle recognise this way of earning a living. In 1587 the synod of the Walloon churches decided to refuse communion to those who begged out of laziness. Anyone who begged out of necessity would be warned, but not excluded, 'in view of the present times'.[98] Individual Walloon communities such as that of The Hague[99] continued to tolerate begging, but similar half-hearted decisions are not often found in the church registers of the period. If begging out of necessity was allowed, then warnings were surely not right. If however the warning was justified, then the churches could not offer communion to wilful sinners. Such strictly logical trains of thought underpinned seventeenth-century religious discipline in general, and it is not surprising that firm rules were applied to the beggars. In 1599 the church council of Monnikendam forbade Willem Jacobsz. to send his daughter out to beg any more, because it led 'to dishonouring the community'.[100] But anyone who dishonoured the community and brought it into disrepute scandalised the communion of saints and would have to be cut off from it if he persisted in his sin. Thus the Walloon church council of Amsterdam presented a certain Peronnel with an ultimatum: if he wanted to remain a member, he would have to give up begging. If the fruits of his labours were too small to meet his needs, then he might apply to the deacons, but first the begging must stop.[101]

This rule applied also to those who could not work. At Heenvliet in 1602 there lived a lame and dumb church-member who had no possibility of earning a living. The *classis* obliged the deacons to support him. If he went begging anyway, however, he must be excluded.[102] When the diaconate was short of money, the poor would just have to make do with less rather than continue with begging. In 1592 the Walloon church of Leiden paid one guilder to Hubert Chevalier for his immediate needs and granted him regular support of one stuiver per week. But they insisted that neither he nor his wife ever go out begging again.[103] We can hardly imagine that this exchange would have been profitable for the couple. Surely it was possible to scrape together more than one stuiver per week through begging. But apparently the church council judged that membership was worth some sacrifice. No matter what the financial consequences, members were forbidden to beg.[104] In 1594 a few poor people who wanted to join the Mijnsherenland community were also refused when it was discovered that their children went begging from house to house.[105]

So matters remained in the reformed church. Beggars lived openly in sin and could not be members. If they wanted merely to attend the church, naturally that was allowed. 'inasmuch as they wish to hear the word of God', stated a regulation of The Hague in 1591, 'they may in all modesty betake themselves to a place apart in the church', provided they did not hold out their hands at the exit.[106] Nevertheless, as long as they did not give up begging, neither the communion table nor the diaconate's relief fund was open to them.

Public opinion, however, differed from the church councils on this point, and the membership went along with it. It was no coincidence that the church door was the favourite place for beggars to stand, although the church councils forbade not only asking for alms, but sometimes even giving them.[107] Indeed, the authorities also sometimes forbade almsgiving. The magistrates of Gouda announced in 1614 that anyone who gave alms at his door would be fined.[108] The public listened just as little to the burgomasters as to the preachers, and paid no attention at all to

Samuel Coster's poetic warning, that excessive generosity would attract work-shy foreigners:

> They see here the people's great mercy
> For the needy, and in particular for the foreign poor;
> Also the kindness of the overseers of the poor,[109] and great gifts of the community,
> Attract a country full of these masses, and engrave on their bones,
> Laziness, the cause of their greatest need.[110]

But the public did not want to see it that way. Coster's friend Pieter Cornelisz. Hooft had also experienced as much. It was impossible to abolish begging, he stated in a letter to his friend Justus Baack in 1630. When it was forbidden by proclamation, it appeared that 'the rabble bore it very badly, opposing it out of godliness'.[111]

The rabble, and godliness: the combination gives pause for thought. Anyone who belonged to the brotherhood of the poor knew he had much in common with the beggar. Perhaps he too had once held out his hand; surely he too had suffered hunger and cold. Those whom Hooft called the rabble did not live so far removed from the beggars. Quite naturally, a feeling of solidarity existed between both groups. Godliness could increase that feeling, but not only among the rabble. Whether or not the church condemned begging a thousand times, for the ordinary church-members, for the entire population of Holland raised in the Christian tradition, refusing to give alms was an all too rational form of love for one's neighbour. In 1614 it so happened that in Brussels, a woman from Holland who had gone begging in Brabant in order to find her husband was expelled from the city by the authorities. Out of despair, she then took the lives of her two children and herself. A Dutch pamphlet that reported this 'true, woeful, and sad history'[112] did not hesitate to contrast Southern Netherlandish heartlessness with Northern Netherlandish compassion. There were also places in the North where begging was forbidden, but not so rigorously as in Brabant. The magistrates of the United Provinces deserved great praise for taking such good care of their poor, needy and sick; yes, even 'the needy foreigners are not separated from their cities without solace, as these desperate Roman antichristians' had done.

For the magistrates in question the compliment could hardly have been acceptable. They were praised because they enforced so poorly their own proclamations against beggars. Public opinion here marked a boundary that the authorities could not cross. They had to continue tolerating the beggar, and then they might share in the praise of mercy. Their care for the truly needy was included in this praise. Whether they deserved it now requires our closer attention.

Chapter 4

HONEST POVERTY

The modern individual feels entitled to independence. He wants to earn wages that he can spend as he wishes, and which make him independent of the favour of others. Thanks to industrialisation society has become rich enough to pay such wages, and thanks to the labour movement the workers have become powerful enough to demand them.

Neither condition held true for the seventeenth century. Society as a whole was poorer and had not yet experienced the unlimited economic growth of the industrial age. There was no question of a labour movement, and in any case it would have had no chance of success in overpopulated Holland. Thus it was difficult to develop the idea that work carried with it the right to a sufficient income. The wages of labour were paid according to the work. They expressed the value of the work done. Whether anyone could live on those wages was another matter entirely. Naturally it did play some role in the formation of wages, and most workers' wages were indeed sufficient for a rather meagre existence. But the minimum wage was not inseparably bound to the minimum needed. There were wage earners who received too little to provide for their existence, as chapter 1 has shown us. The weavers of Leiden were the clearest example,[1] but nearly every place in Holland had its poor in winter, those who had lost their work or could not make do on the reduced winter wages.[2] Frequently, abnormal circumstances also caused a wage that was adequate in ordinary times to fall short of what was needed for the purchase of absolute necessities.

Abnormal circumstances were not so rare in the sixteenth and seventeenth centuries. Sometimes they struck small groups: a crisis in the cloth industry, a prohibition of exports of hay or grain to the Southern Netherlands, a great fire that destroyed a hundred houses, a local flood. Unfavourable weather of long duration affected the whole province: a wet or hot summer, storm and breaching of the dikes, a hard frost lasting several weeks. The sources give us enough examples of this sort of crisis, with two especially bad periods: 1594–7[3] and 1621–4.[4] At the same time these were always periods of excessively high prices.[5] Actual famine did not occur, for the Amsterdam grain trade guaranteed that there would always be something to eat in Holland.[6] In 1581 the synod of Middelburg cited the 'general difficulties' that would require the proclamation of a day of worship or fasting: war, plague, dearth and religious persecution.[7] The synod said nothing about famine, no more than Datheen had done in his poetic version of the Lord's Prayer:

Deliver us, Lord, from quarrels and envy,
From plague and also from dearth.

In Holland, and in the Republic as a whole, people did not die of hunger. A harsh
cold snap might claim some victims. In the worst winters there were always some
who froze to death.[8] A shortage of bread, however, was no longer mentioned in the
chronicles as a direct cause of death, although a period of prolonged dearth must
have undermined the constitutions of the weaker members of society.

Dearth could become quite fearsome. A considerable part of the population was
then unable to support itself, in the cities as well as in the countryside.[9] The
authorities could take some general measures, such as setting maximum prices[10] or
announcing a prohibition of grain exports.[11] But both were difficult to enforce, and
when the enforcement powers of the authorities were not great, price controls
usually led directly to the rise of a flourishing black market. At Enkhuizen in
November, 1622, the official maximum price for one twelve-pound loaf of rye bread
was fourteen stuivers, but there were plenty of takers at twenty-four stuivers.[12]
Nearly every income drawn from manual labour was then too low to guarantee the
worker a minimal existence. For him the time of honest poverty had arrived.

He could try to rescue himself in four ways. Begging was mentioned in the
previous chapter: it was legal only with official permission.[13] Anyone who did not
have such permission was committing a crime if he asked for alms. We have also
noted already that the church refused any form of aid to beggars. A second
possibility was the pawnshop, and then of course there were also the deacons and
civil poor relief.

Naturally the pawnshop did not offer a real solution, and just as obviously
everyone knew that very well. Although the pawnbroker was decried everywhere
as a usurer, it appears that the authorities regarded pawnshops as a social necessity
for the comfort of the poor. In 1595 the magistrate of Oudewater gave Jacques de
Causa a licence to establish such a shop, 'noting that the inhabitants of this
town, and the surrounding areas, and neighbours, owing to the lengthy war and
destruction of the land, are very impoverished and short of money'.[14] This is
remarkable humanity, helping impoverished people out of their embarrassment by
handing them over to known usurers! But while on the one hand the regents
themselves understood that problem, on the other hand they did not see how to
live without these usurers. As long as the pawnshops have not been abolished, said
the magistrate of Leiden, there should be one in this city: because 'many miserable
people' live here, who are obliged to borrow money in Haarlem, Delft or The Hague,
resulting in needless lost time and expense.[15]

Whether the penniless really needed pawnbrokers was still a question for some.
In the archive of the States of Holland there is a noteworthy plan dating from 1606,
with all kinds of proposals for a new tax system, clearly intended to raise money
where it could be found, namely among the rich. But this friend of the poor had
nothing good to say about the customers of pawnbrokers. He thought it was crystal

clear 'that many miserable people and others bring themselves into ruin in order to indulge their inborn faults of pride, greed and otherwise' – that is the only reason why they borrow money.[16] For this writer, anyone who borrows money is simply someone who wants to live above his station. The splendour-loving nobleman, who mortgages land and houses, just as much as the simple peasant, who goes out in the evening and cannot tear himself away from the beer-tap:

> To the last penny I'll guzzle it down,
> Even if all my clothes have to stay here,
> For I can do without the cloak;
> I hope summer weather will stay for a long time yet...
> I must go on enjoying myself heartily,
> Even if I have to leave my cloak and trousers.[17]

For these happy-go-lucky types the innkeeper himself played pawnbroker, and according to Van de Venne the publicans used this method to attract customers:

> Men, if you come empty-handed
> I'll take a pledge from you.[18]

In such cases indeed it was not a question of actual poverty, although one may well ask whether we should join the protesting tax expert in speaking of pride and greed instead of an understandable desire for a one-off break from the monotony and enforced austerity of everyday routine. Public opinion in any case seldom took the side of those who took collateral. Pawnbrokers were regarded as unscrupulous exploiters, who stole bread from the mouths of the poor. 'Usurers who count on thirty-one percent', said Roemer Visscher scornfully.[19] He was not guilty of exaggeration: the percentage legally allowed was even somewhat higher. For every guilder lent, the pawnbroker was permitted to ask one farthing per week. After 52 weeks the interest would have accumulated to $6\frac{1}{2}$ stuivers, or $32\frac{1}{2}$ per cent. It seems an exorbitant amount, but in our own time J. Melles has calculated that on small loans the brokers could not have made a profit at that rate, and certainly not when the interest was reduced from $\frac{5}{8}$ per cent to $\frac{5}{12}$ per cent per week (21.7% p.a.). Their bad reputation must be attributed to the taking of small pledges rather than to their profits, unless they did not adhere to the established tariffs.[20]

The last-mentioned possibility is not unlikely. At Enkhuizen in 1624 there was a pawnbroker who adhered precisely to the conditions – he even reckoned slightly less interest – and he allowed the poor to profit from the balances of pledges that had been sold. In a typical year his profit was 300 to 400 gulden, and in a good year as much as 700 to 800 gulden.[21] It seems to me that since Brandt found this worthy of note in his description of Enkhuizen, we may, firstly, assume that in the eyes of the public an honest pawnbroker was as rare as a white crow. In the second place, it is likely that many pledges were left, and generally for less than their worth. The unredeemed pledges were in any case sold after a year and a day,[22] and then had to fetch 80 to 100 per cent of the sum lent before any extra profit could be made. If this happened year after year, then either the turnover must have been extraordinarily large, or the sums advanced to the borrowers correspondingly much too low. One can only speculate to what end such practices could lead a businessman less virtuous than that man of Enkhuizen.

Be that as it may, the pawnbroker definitely did not enjoy high esteem. It is generally known that the reformed church wanted nothing to do with him.[23] Furthermore, his reputation was certainly influenced negatively by the unlicensed pawnbrokers and usurers:

> There the stuff is hocked,
> Here by a miss Lors [proverbial name for a swindler], or by a miserly skinflint.[24]

At Gorinchem in 1603 such a person, Govert Pietersz., was arrested for being a 'terrible and unspeakably horrible usurer'. Unlike the licensed pawnbrokers, he had reckoned not around 30 per cent, but 300, 400 and even 500 per cent: by this means within a year many householders 'with wives and children were put on the dike without their goods'.[25] The licensed pawnbrokers, of which there could be only one in each city, probably made less use of such techniques, although their caste as a whole was blamed for the series of fraudulent bankruptcies that occurred among the pawnbrokers in Dordrecht, Leiden, Rotterdam and The Hague in 1606.[26] The number of pawnshops was small – fifteen, according to a report, in 1590, eighteen in 1603[27] – and besides some were under the same management. In 1590 Sion Lus had shops in Dordrecht, Leiden, Amsterdam and Schiedam; Margareta de Mufti had them in Gorinchem and Schoonhoven. Jacques Villere, who was a banker in The Hague in 1590, appeared on the scene again in 1603 as a pawnshop keeper at Dordrecht. His son had just then been sent to the galleys,[28] striking proof that this profession might well produce a high income, but no social prestige: sons of solid businessmen were not punished in this manner.

The approximate relative turnover of the various pawnshops can be found in assessments that the province received from all recognised operators, as their compulsory contribution to the common weal (see table 4).[29] There is not much point in comparing these totals with the population figures, in order to discover the relative demand for the pawnbrokers' services. In the first place, not all of the pawnshops functioned simultaneously in the same measure and way as regional centres; in the second place, the wealth of a lender may have been determined by other factors besides how well his business attracted the poor. It might, however, be possible to see which towns had a big business. Moreover it is striking that Enkhuizen is not on the list, at a time when the town had at least as many inhabitants as Rotterdam or Dordrecht. Could this have had something to do with the well-known strict orthodoxy of the regents of Enkhuizen? We already know that the town later came to have a pawn shop that was compared favourably with others. That the States of Holland decided to seek such extra taxes from the pawnbrokers does suggest that they were more inclined to tolerate these businesses than to encourage them. Most of them were obliged to contribute annually a further sum to the poor.[30] In some cities the private operations were superseded by municipal banks. Amsterdam is the best-known example; Rotterdam followed in 1635.[31]

These municipal banks were not really a form of poor relief either. That was accomplished exclusively by the deacons and the 'masters of the Holy Spirit'. Here we shall not discuss in detail the organisation and operation of poor-relief,[32] but these aspects must not go unmentioned. They also do a good deal to illuminate the unusual church structure of the Republic.

The Republic, and in particular the free province of Holland, were born during the revolt against Spain. But as we shall see later,[33] it was impossible to keep the struggle against Spain separate from the struggle against the Catholic Church. The rejection of Philip II and the prohibition of the mass had become inextricably bound together. As an anti-Spanish power, the Republic had to be a Protestant state at the same time. Thus it was freed from the great family of the European Catholic Church. It opted for the Reformation, but in a highly unusual manner. While other Protestant countries allowed the new church to replace the old in all respects, the Republic stopped halfway. The new church was protected, favoured and privileged; but it did not become a state church. It was no longer the religious community of the people as a whole. Although the reformed faith did hold a privileged place, every subject of the Republic had a free choice as to whether or not to join the church. The Catholic Church remained in existence underground; at

Table 4. *Annual assessments of pawnshops in Holland, 1602 and 1603*

	1602	1603
Dordrecht	1800	1800
Haarlem	1300	1600
Delft	1600	1600
Leiden	1800	2200
Amsterdam	4000	4500
Gouda	800	800
Rotterdam	1000	1200
Gorinchem	500	600
Schiedam	300	300
Woerden	200	200
Oudewater	150	150
Den Briel	300	400
The Hague	1600	1600
Naarden	150	150
Alkmaar	1000	1000
Edam/Monnikendam	300	500
Schoonhoven	200	200
Hoorn	1000	1200
Totals	18,000	20,000

the same time Protestant communities such as Mennonites and Lutherans were even officially recognised and tolerated.

This situation had consequences for charity. Previously, when the religious and civil authorities were bound together, there was only one organisation for poor relief. Now each church community had its own poor, and its own diaconate. But there was more. Each parish had had its own welfare provisions during the Middle Ages. As a result of gifts, bequests and funds provided by the authorities, foundations had come into existence. These were usually named after the Holy Spirit, and the directors were thus called masters of the Holy Spirit. Responsibility for the entire relief effort, for all the needs of the parish, rested with these foundations. The reformation created a new institution for poor relief in the form of the diaconate, but the old institutions simultaneously continued to exist and normally still retained control over their own incomes.[34]

The boundaries of mutual authority and tasks differed from place to place. The most rational solution – consolidation of all income, and combined administration – was certainly the least popular, and by popular I mean liked by the people. The continued existence of different relief funds alongside each other offered the possibility of choice to the poor. Perhaps it would dilute the funds a bit, and it is possible that just for that reason the city with the largest number of poor, Leiden, was at the same time one of the few places where all income for poor relief was brought together in one fund, under the supervision of the magistrate. A single administration meant that distribution could follow a clear policy. In the sixteenth century the rule in Leiden was that families who had already lived there before 1572 always enjoyed preference.[35] From a social point of view this was an

9. 'The prosperity of the nation at sea, or general shipping' and 'Methods of agriculture in the county of Holland'

unfortunate solution in a city whose population consisted largely of immigrants. From an economic point of view the policy was equally bad for an industrial centre that had to attract its labour force for expansion from outside the city. Here the concentration of the poor relief in one agency offered very few advantages. It allowed a small group of privileged persons to develop within the great mass of needy.

In this regard the Leiden solution was indeed typical of its time. Sixteenth-century people were little inclined to seek their welfare and security in equal rights for all. They preferred to see privileges granted to the group to which they themselves belonged. The real profiteers from a social order constructed in this fashion were naturally found only among the ruling elite. But if they were unable or unwilling to rule with excessive force, they would find it easiest to maintain their place atop the pyramid by appealing to the self-interest of lower social groups as well in maintaining the established structure. This goal was achieved in Leiden. Even the worst endowed had a privilege to defend against the poorest, the unendowed.

For the poor however the Leiden system meant that they had lost their freedom of choice. Receiving assistance depended on a circumstance over which they themselves could have no influence. Anyone who had not been born a Leidener always remained, in the most fortunate case, a second-class pauper. Somewhat more attractive for the poor were the places where the diaconate was the central agency for poor relief. While it was true that the deacons would show preference to poor members of the reformed church, at least everyone had an equal chance at the outset to share in the bounty, namely by joining the church. Then indeed a devout supporter of the old faith would have to choose which he preferred, suffering hunger or compromising his conscience. This solution was actually no more humane than the preference shown to natives, and it was equally suspect from an ethical viewpoint.

Furthermore, the civil authorities harboured some suspicions against the concentration of poor relief in the hands of reformed deacons. As we shall see later, in the seventeenth century 'to rule' over the masses meant first of all to keep the people quiet. To preserve calm it was necessary to prevent them from being systematically influenced by forces other than the government. But nothing and no one had a better chance of exercising such influences than the reformed church. For this reason, even preaching was always subject to a light repressive censorship. Similarly, the regents were reluctant to give an independent body control of substantial funds, which could be distributed according to the particular norms and subjective preferences of the institution concerned.[36] To all appearances, the number of places where poor relief was a monopoly of the reformed church was rather small,[37] counting a few villages, but no city of any importance.

As a rule the deacons and masters of the Holy Spirit worked alongside each other. Sometimes, then, there was a certain division of labour, especially in the larger cities. In the villages both institutions often regulated their affairs as they wished.

In general this had as a result that the deacons gave preference to church-members, while the masters of the Holy Spirit favoured native inhabitants. Thus as a rule choice existed only for poor people of native Holland origin. Needy foreigners may have sought to join the church quickly. Indeed, many Southern Netherlandish immigrants had long been members of Calvinist communities. Naturally there were also Catholic immigrants, but we should hardly expect them to be reckoned among the most principled members of their faith. If they had been, they would not have chosen the territory of a Protestant nation as their new fatherland.

Consequently there may have existed a connection between the growth of the reformed church and the settlement in Holland of a great many impecunious foreigners. For them, dependency on relief may have lowered the threshold of the church, which was probably never very high for them anyway. The deacons did not play an active role in recruiting. We are more likely to find – again primarily in the large cities – an inclination not to make church-membership too easy for the poorer candidates.[38] Moreover, help was purchased dearly: religious oversight of the poor not infrequently went hand in hand with the withholding of all support.[39] The needy had to hold strictly to the norms of good and evil as the reformed church understood them. If they had joined the church out of pure self-interest without inner conviction, then in order to maintain their membership they would have to keep on practising in hypocrisy. Still, it is likely that the diaconate of the reformed church had a special appeal in the eyes of the immigrant; but this cannot have had great statistical significance.

For native Hollanders the church was ordinarily not the only source of assistance. If the deacons were richer and more generous than the masters of the Holy Spirit, the choice of religion could be influenced by the material factor, in a community such as Haarlem for example.[40] More often, however, the opposite was the case,[41] and the masters of the Holy Spirit had greater means at their disposal. Membership of the reformed church then carried no material advantage whatsoever. Quite the contrary was possible, if the masters of the Holy Spirit were Catholic and arranged their priorities accordingly, 'to the prejudice of the devout'.[42]

The synods did sometimes complain about that, though we should not therefore immediately conclude that the non-religious poor relief system was a propaganda tool of the Catholic Church. Yet it was always true that the masters of the Holy Spirit or civil relief-masters wanted something in exchange for their help. Their rules were less specific than those of the church, but they expected a certain minimum of morality and modesty from the need. In Kudelstaart the masters did not want to receive any women or children, because with 'their importunate complaints' they made inquiry into true needs too difficult. Only men were welcome, provided that they did not try to influence the masters 'with threats, the drawing of knives, hitting, pushing or otherwise forcing to liberal assistance'.[43] Anyone who calls upon the generosity of others must remain polite. Anyone who receives anything must be grateful and not ask why it was not greater. The court of Brill judged Pieter Pietersz. extra harshly just because he had taken another man's property while 'his parents are maintained at the expense of the city and by alms, and ... he was bound to recognise the same with thankfulness'.[44]

It was thus that the masters of poor relief wanted to see their clients. The poet Bredero saw it differently:

> The poor search for quarrels and brawls,
> They bring into great peril
> The soul that in their body rumbles;
> The rich avoid this danger:
> The rich do not fight,
> Their reason can control their wrath.[45]

But it was not only the soul that rumbled in the body. The stomach was heard even more clearly. When daily bread is at stake, reason seldom wins out over wrath. Yet people did expect as much from the poor man who asked for help. His honest poverty must also be virtuous poverty. He should accept not only the money of the deacons and the masters of the Holy Spirit, but also their mentality. Seventeenth-century poor relief could be very generous if the circumstances allowed it. It could arise from honest compassion and deeply felt Christian charity. But it could hardly avoid forcing the poor man to take on the role shown him by the rich. Poor relief was intended so that he would take another view of life, different from what his need alone would have suggested. In large measure it was successful. The history of Holland is not rich in disturbances. Although the poor may have been dissatisfied, they were not rebellious. Nor did they die of hunger. But no one came a step closer to the solution of the problem of poverty.

Chapter 5

PATHS UPWARD

It is possible to go from rags to riches, and that was equally true in the Holland of the seventeenth century. The Leiden miller's son Rembrandt Harmensz. van Rijn married a burgomaster's daughter and lived on a grand scale. Pieter Pietersz. Hein, a sailor of fortune from Delfshaven,[1] rose to be lieutenant-admiral of Holland. The simple office clerk Jan Poppe became a great merchant; his son Jacob was the richest inhabitant of Amsterdam.[2] Extraordinary talent could receive recognition in the arts and sciences. Talent could also develop in the nation's fleet and receive its just reward. Or if talent was directed toward trade and finance, successful development could bring its lucky owner great wealth.

This last road to fortune seemed to be the shortest. In a rapidly growing economy it was above all the envious outsider who readily believed that considerable capital sums could be gathered together in a trice through the fortunate workings of chance. He might think that here wealth was not a product of industry and knowledge, but of coincidence and cheating. It is therefore not surprising that so many seventeenth-century people tried to play this lottery.

We have already met some of them in the herring trade;[3] we shall meet them again in tax farming.[4] The gambling impulse was found in every layer of society, even among those whose choice of calling and profession had removed them from the cares of the world. The renowned Remonstrant leader Wtenbogaert prided himself on not engaging in business affairs, not having any money invested in interest-bearing loans, and not owning any shares in ships sailing to the East or West.[5] But he certainly knew that there were Protestant ministers who did, and they were not necessarily the most obscure ones. It is unlikely that any would have exceeded the Mennonite teacher Hans de Ries in blamelessness of life, but he too had some money invested in the herring trade.[6]

Nearly everyone participated, either within or beyond his means. Willem Usselincx, a businessman who should have known what he was talking about, said that no Netherlander would put his money into an old sock – neither nobleman nor burgher, neither peasant nor servant. All of them tried to make money with money,[7] even the servant with his handful of saved-up guilders. Young Vondel smacked his lips while he sang of the rich profits of shipping:

> Where she comes into fashion, or sticks out her bosom,
> Every village becomes a city, every shipowner a lord.[8]

Vondel wrote more beautiful verses than that, but he was never more emphatic about the hopes that inspired him as a businessman. He too peered over the sales counter of his small sock-shop in search of great profits, and he would do that for years on end,[9] no matter how little success came of his first efforts.[10] Vondel the merchant was the type who would take his modest share in a ship sailing to the Baltic or the Levant, wherein small capitalists could participate by putting their hundred or two hundred gulden in the cargo,[11] and hope to double their little capital.

This enterprise never stopped, and was practised in countless Holland households. Once in the seventeenth century it led to a real explosion of fantastic speculation: the famous tulip-mania of the 1630s. For us the tulip of Holland is such an unquestionable national possession that we find it hard to realise that this familiar tourist attraction has its own history, and did not exist here four hundred years ago. Tulips appeared in Holland only toward the end of the sixteenth century. The tulip was then a costly plant, a luxury article.[12] The prolonged period of war was not entirely unconnected with the coming of the tulip, which was regarded as a highly secure investment. In case of hasty flight, people could leave the already-planted tulip bulbs in the ground, because even the most painstaking plunderer would not disturb them there. Indeed, the dried bulbs could easily be taken along,[13] thereby transporting a considerable sum to safety.

The immediate danger of war was seldom experienced in Holland during the seventeenth century. Nonetheless the tulip maintained its popularity. The hobby of collecting tulips spread widely, especially in the cities.[14] There it was almost unavoidable that the tulip would become an object of speculation. Investments in trade were often made for short periods.[15] The tulip by its nature was particularly well suited to this. Freshly planted bulbs could be sold straight away with the promised delivery of flowers the following summer. Before they were in bloom, they could be resold many times. This happened in the 'colleges' of flower-enthusiasts – the 'florists' – which met in the cities of Holland. While it was still in the field the bulb was bought and sold repeatedly.[16] At first only bulb-growers and true enthusiasts were involved in the trade. But in the 1630s this circle expanded. In particular, Southern Netherlandish weavers were mentioned among the first persons who carried out tulip speculation on a large scale.[17] They certainly did not have much capital. They could only take part in the flower trade if they were successful in rapidly reselling their purchases at a profit.

That, indeed, was precisely the lure of the tulip trade. There was enormous upward potential in tulip prices. It was possible to sell a small lot for double, quintuple, or even ten times the purchase price.[18] As a result tulips had great appeal to small speculators,[19] who wanted to make their killing in two weeks or less. Old and young played along: according to Aitzema,[20] men and women, servant-girls, peasants, postmen, peat-carriers and chimney sweeps – all of them abandoned their work in order to buy and sell tulips. His account unconsciously reminds us of the nearly hysterical enthusiasm for crusades in the eleventh century and pilgrimages

10. Satirical print on the tulip speculation

in the fifteenth, though it differs in that the reward was gained not in heaven but immediately, here on earth. Anyone who previously had to be content with cheap beer and groats now allowed himself to be served warm sugared wine and roast pheasants. Tulips were traded for a coach and horses, for cows, for fur coats and for paintings.[21] Hundreds of people allowed themselves to be led on by the fabulous profits. Who wouldn't want to become a tulip speculator, if he had got a pound of 'yellow crowns' for twenty-four gulden, and could sell them for 1,200?[22] The best evidence that money could be made here was given by the States of Holland in 1636. They seriously considered imposing a new tax on 'a certain new kind of trade, that is in flowers, tulips and bulbs of the same, in which much money is traded daily'.[23] The impossible dream appeared to have come true for the common man:

Tout le bien du monde est á nous,
Tous les honneurs, toutes les femmes.

But for him the experience was the same as for the peasant girl in the fable of La Fontaine. The pot of milk that was supposed to make her rich came crashing to the ground, and the dream ended. In February, 1637, the tulip speculation ended.[24] A few people had become rich, and many poor. The States of Holland gave their inexorable judgment in their resolution of 4 May 1637: the new tax would not go through, 'because of the change and the embarrassment, that have come to the said flower trade'.[25]

One of the probable victims of the tulip mania was the painter Jan van Goyen.[26] Other artists of the seventeenth century also experienced problems.[27] Emmanuel de Witte fell into poverty.[28] Frans Hals received poor relief in the last years of his life. Rembrandt had to sell his possessions in 1658. If we are obliged to mention such famous names in this context, we can understand immediately that the profession of painter was no assured road to riches. Anyone who wanted wealth was better advised to marry a rich widow, as Ferdinand Bol had done: after his marriage he apparently painted no more new paintings.[29] The same was also once said of Meindert Hobbema: he supposedly gave up painting when he became a wine-sampling official. That conclusion now appears incorrect, but it is no wonder that people readily drew it. Seventeenth-century society saw the painter not as a man with a calling, but as a craftsman who had developed the skill of painting to earn his income. And just like other craftsmen, painters belonged to guilds. Holland was rich in painters at that time, but the number of practitioners of the art was not large enough in any single city to make it possible to set up an exclusive painters' guild. The St Luke's Guild of Amsterdam separated in 1579 from the Guild of Our Lady, which remained reserved for masons and stonecutters. In the new organisation there were not only art-painters, but also plate- and figure-engravers, porcelain-makers, embroiderers and tapestry-weavers, sculptors and stained-glass artists.[30] Their artistic brothers in Haarlem were united with bookbinders, coppersmiths, organ-builders, carpet-makers and ironmongers.[31]

The St Luke's Guilds did not differ from the ordinary guild model. Their rules contain the usual specifications of time of apprenticeship and the required masterpiece.[32] Indeed, the purposes were exactly the same: to train good craftsmen, who produced good products, and were able to ask a good price for them.[33] The painter must know his craft in depth, and therefore must pass through a lengthy apprenticeship. At age eight Jan Lievensz. entered the workshop of Joris Verschoten; two years later he went from there to Rembrandt's future teacher Pieter Lastman.[34] Jan Lievensz.'s father was an embroiderer, and thus worked in a related trade, perhaps in the same guild. Naturally this happened often, especially as painters' sons took over the business of their fathers,[35] and kept the shop in the family. In this regard Frans and Dirk Hals, Isaäck and Jacob van Ruisdael, Van der Velde senior and junior all come to mind. Sons had a better chance of being received favourably into the guild, although it was open to others as well. After all, Rembrandt's father was a miller, while Vermeer's father began life as a silkworker and was later an innkeeper.[36] Carel Fabritius had been a carpenter[37] before he studied with Rembrandt. These men came from the petit-bourgeois milieu where the painter's trade was one possible career choice. Adriaen Harmensz. became a shoemaker, Willem Harmensz. a baker, and Rembrandt Harmensz. a painter.[38] Occasionally there was a painter who had started out on a lower step of society. This was true, for example, of Adriaen Brouwer, whose mother went from door to door selling linen decorated by him.[39] But it was not so easy to rise from such a position. The Leiden painter Pieter Deneyn became a stonemason out of poverty, because his father could not pay the costs of artistic training.[40]

Anyone who had made good use of his years of apprenticeship could produce the proof of his skill by making a masterpiece. This was a condition of a career according to the prescribed rules. No one without the title of master was allowed to sign canvases.[41] Naturally he could take part in the work of a studio, and help produce a piece, but only the master put his name on the work and was responsible for the quality.[42] If he took this rule lightly, there was always control by the guild officials. When for example Rembrandt once made a portrait of a girl that according to the disappointed patron did not resemble her in the least, the painter declared himself ready to correct his work if the guild officials found the complaint justified.[43]

This portrait was painted on commission, which was always the safest method for the craftsman. For his voluntary productions, he had to find some way of selling them to buyers, whereby the guild again offered its protection. Only at the annual market were the guild regulations not in force: then anyone might take a chance,[44] but otherwise the St Luke's Guilds continually guarded against competition from outside the trade, and tried to regulate sales as strictly as possible. At Amsterdam in 1623, for example, the open air sale of paintings was forbidden, while in 1635 the Guild prescribed that no one could sell paintings door to door.[45]

Such sales practices were not developed in an ivory tower. They do not testify to artistic pride and grand distance from the *profanum vulgus* that had no notion of inspired and highly developed culture. Rather, they give a picture of simple business sense, knowing that a dime is more than nine cents. When the painter had finished his works, he wanted to sell them. He worked for the market, and actively sought buyers. And if he took his canvases out on the street and displayed them in a public square, he clearly had the expectation that he would find buyers there too.

The Holland painter worked for his own public.[46] He was a tradesman from the petit-bourgeois milieu. He knew the taste of his kind, and he tried to meet their demands. His clients were people like himself. He lived in the middle of their world, which consisted of middlemen: shopkeepers, guild masters, small and medium-sized merchants,[47] farmers who had some extra guilders to spend. They bought paintings just as they bought chairs and tables.[48] They had a bit of money for a landscape or still-life: not much, so the pieces had to remain low-priced, but this public was so large that it was worthwhile for the artist to satisfy their demand.[49] As long as he delivered enough works, he could earn a living in this buyers' market.

He did have to be satisfied with rather modest profits. The price of paintings depended to some extent on the subject – seascapes and genre pictures generally fetched higher prices than animals or landscapes[50] – but in this buyers' market, prices were never particularly high. Of course it is impossible to cite an average sum, if only because the sources are widely dispersed and moreover varied in nature. The assessed value of inheritances[51] cannot be precisely related to selling prices,[52] which differed in turn from the prices fixed in lotteries.[53] If we compare several figures of the three types, then we arrive at the results shown in table 5. It is clear that we cannot do very much with these figures. They represent a fraction of the total production. But the cautious conclusion that paintings were rather low in price does not appear too risky, and agrees with the judgments of contemporaries. Houbraken tells how Adriaen Brouwer, at the urging of others, found the courage to ask 100 *ducatons* for a commissioned painting, i.e. more than 200 gulden. Contrary to his expectations, the purchaser readily paid that sum. When Brouwer came home, he poured out the moneybag over his bed and rolled about in the silver pieces in a delirium of joy.[54] Beyond that Houbraken does not tell us much about art prices. But he did think it a noteworthy point that Michiel van Mierevelt painted around 5,000 portraits, 'including some for which he got 150 gulden'.[55]

Such a statement in a book that is short on figures was intended to astonish the reader. These were indeed extraordinary amounts. In the tax assessment of fifty-five paintings found in 1640 at the Amsterdam artshop of Johannes de Renialme, the three with the highest prices were a Rembrandt for 100 gulden, a Poelenburg for sixty, and a Jan Miense Molenaer, also for sixty gulden.[56] The most expensive painting in the stock of the widow of Cornelis Rutgers was by Hendrik Schut alias Brootsack, valued at 300 gulden. Next came Poelenburg at 250, and Rembrandt followed in third place at 100 gulden.[57] The average assessed value, however, remained considerably less, as we have noted. We get the impression that there were two ways for painters to achieve high incomes. The first was through unequalled craftsmanship: that was the case with Rembrandt. It is not a coincidence that in both of the inventories mentioned the sum of 100 guilders appeared next to his

Table 5. *Prices of paintings in Holland*

	Total worth	*Number*	*Average price*
Assessments	6,546 gld. 6 st.	402	16 gld. 6 st.
Sales	853 gld. 5 st.	356	2 gld. 8 st.
Lotteries	4,252 gld.	62	68 gld. 12 st.
Totals	11,651 gld. 11 st.	820	14 gld. 4 st.

name. Rembrandt Harmensz. van Rijn was not in the least an unappreciated genius. On the contrary, from his earliest years he attracted attention as an extraordinary talent.[58] Even if it may prove untrue that Rembrandt received 1,600 gulden for the *Nightwatch*[59] – though why should we doubt the testimony of a contemporary? – nonetheless the prices achieved by his works were far above the ordinary. Rembrandt was also one of the few Dutch artists who was occasionally allowed to work on commissions for the court of the Stadholder.[60]

That was the second way to fame and fortune: by pleasing the taste of wealthy patrons. The Dutch Republic was not an ideal environment for this purpose. Its churches gave no employment to visual artists, and it lacked a royal court that could have been the centre of patronage. In William of Orange's time, the struggle for bare survival demanded too much attention. His son Maurice chose an austere style of life without princely airs. Frederick Henry was more strongly attached to outward display, and he made more of Honselaarsdijk than Maurice had done of the manor house at Rijswijk; but compared to Vienna and Madrid it was insignificant. The best commissions came directly from abroad.[61] Christian IV of Denmark, for example, had his agent Theodoor Rodenburg send 350 paintings with a total value of 50,000 gulden.[62]

But such extraordinary royal opportunities seldom came to those who stayed at home. Thus already in the sixteenth century we see Dutch artists in the wider world.[63] Above all, the imperial court of Rudolf II drew many of them.[64] During the Thirty Years' War, Prague and Vienna lost a good deal of their attraction, but artists took advantage of other opportunities. To limit ourselves to just a few Hollanders: Monix of The Hague was in the service of the Pope for thirteen years.[65] Hubrecht Jacobsz. of Delft passed the most productive years of his short life in Venice under the name Hubertus Grimani.[66] Ludolf de Jong, a shoemaker's son from Overschie, worked for seven years in Paris.[67] Cornelis Poelenburg spent some time at the court of the English king Charles I.[68] Is it possible that Poelenburg's foreign fame had something to do with the high assessment of his work in the catalogues cited above? Indeed, we also read of Willem van Aelst, whose 'art became greatly appreciated, and sold for high prices' in Holland – while the same van Aelst had wandered abroad for eleven years, and was 'in that time held in esteem by cardinals, monarchs, and great lords'.[69]

That name van Aelst is no longer familiar to us. Yet at least he is better known than Christiaen van Couwenberch. Of the latter, however, Houbraken states that he achieved such great fame with 'many works of art, history-paintings as well as nudes', that he too was allowed to work on Frederick Henry's Huis ten Bosch. This artist of Delft was in his time the most renowned brushworker of his city, and he is the only one from Delft who receives a separate biography in Houbraken's book of Dutch painters. The other 'fellow citizens, contemporaries and artists' are rattled off in a list, without even the simplest explanation: 'Leonard Bramer, Pieter van Asch, Adriaen van Linschoten, Hans Jordaans, Kornelis de Man and Johannes

Vermeer'.[70] Yes, that last name does suddenly sound more familiar. Who would now hit upon the idea of explaining who Vermeer was by saying that he was a fellow citizen and contemporary of Couwenberch? It is clear that entirely different standards are being applied here. Couwenberch and van Aelst were rightly reckoned among the greats, while Vermeer was a minor artist. Anyone who best satisfied the taste of well-to-do connoisseurs received this reward in fame and fortune. This taste is repeatedly reflected in Houbraken's book. For example, concerning Esaias van den Velde, a specialist in battles and cavalry scenes, we are expressly assured that 'the works from his brush were appreciated at that time, and sold for high prices'.[71] It is really not so strange that Huygens allowed himself to be painted by Hanneman, and Jacob Cats by Mytens,[72] nor that Gerard Honthorst decorated Huis ten Bosch for Frederick Henry and was court painter to the exiled Winter King of Bohemia.[73] These men were painters for the elite, and they earned a great deal of money. Anyone who satisfied the demand of middle-class purchasers could earn a decent living if he worked hard, but only in an exceptional case such as Rembrandt would he receive recognition as a star of the first magnitude.

Rembrandt set his own standard and succeeded. His artistic contemporaries who worked for the middle classes had to be content with a reasonable existence and more limited fame. If they wanted more, they had to adjust their work to the wishes of the elite. If they were unable to do that, they remained at the income level of a skilled tradesman. If they were unable – or was it a question of being unwilling?[74] Michiel van Mierevelt received offers from Archduke Albert and from King Charles I, but he stayed in Holland.[75] David Bailii of Leiden declined offers from the Duke of Brunswick.[76] Anthony van Dyck tried in vain to get Frans Hals to go along to England, but Hals preferred his free, independent life to the English court.[77] Emmanuel de Witte once received an honourable commission from the king of Denmark for two paintings. He accepted, but then said nothing more about it. When the delivery date had passed, the Danish consul went to see how matters stood: he received the reply that 'if the ox-king was displeased with the pieces, he would be able to sell the same to others'.[78]

In Hals, and in de Witte, the bohemian desire for independence went hand in hand with the self-consciousness of the renaissance artist. Measured by his training, position in society, and income, the painter was a petit-bourgeois tradesman; but he thought of himself as having outgrown the middle class.[79] He had become the bearer of higher values than the shoemaker or carpenter. The painters of Dordrecht seceded from the guild in 1642 and formed a 'college'. They refused to accept any longer their old place in the social order, as producers of common articles. The painters thought themselves above mere craft and became artists:[80] this was the source of their pride. 'You were born with a moneybag around your neck, and that's all', Willem van Aelst said to a burgomaster of Amsterdam, 'but everything I am, I earned through merit.'[81] Carel van Mander published his book of painters in 1602. This is the best evidence that at the beginning of the seventeenth century the painter was already more than just another craftsman: there was never a sugarbakers' or shipwrights' book afterwards. Thus while the painter might lack financial recognition, his worth as an artist was firmly established.

Consequently it was also possible once in a while for sons of regents to learn the painter's trade: the Leiden burgomaster Isaäc Claesz. Swanenburgh, Dirc van der Lisse of The Hague,[82] the Haarlemmer Aert Jansz. Druivestein[83] and various members of the Nicolai family of Leiden.[84] Their relationship to art was probably different, however. The sources expressly state that Gillis Schagen, son of the Alkmaar councillor Pieter Schagen, did not paint to earn his living.[85] To be able to draw and paint on his own account never became a requirement for a gentleman, in the way that poetic skill did later. Was it perhaps because the regents were unwilling to send their offspring for training in the painters' milieu, always reputed to be somewhat dissolute? Flinck, the steward of Cleves, had destined his son for a business career and refused to hear of an artistic life. 'May God preserve me from raising my son to be a painter, such people are almost all layabouts, living a profligate life.'[86] His son Govert became a painter anyway, and at the same time put to shame his father's fearful expectations. Yet he had little contact with his artistic brethren: 'Avoiding company where people drank to excess, he seldom came to the rendezvous of the painters.'[87]

Their reputation for wild living again set the painters apart. Even if they earned good money they remained in a different category from the well-to-do burgher. A short while ago we noted that Adriaen Brouwer was beside himself with joy when he brought home 100 *ducatons* for the first time. He managed to spend that fortune almost overnight. When it was all gone, he said 'that he had rid himself of that ballast'. So it went always, Houbraken assures us. When Brouwer had money, he could not keep himself from drinking and carousing.[88] Here too he showed himself a pupil of Frans Hals, who was 'ordinarily filled up to his neck with drink every night'.[89] It was primarily for this reason that Hals, Brouwer, de Witte[90] and Adriaen van Linschoten[91] fell into poverty. Their poverty was not a sign of public neglect, although in the estimation of their contemporaries they stood somewhat behind the court painters. Rather, it was due to the manner in which they spent their income: they earned middle-class wages, but had little use for the bourgeois ideal of sound thrift.

For some of them free life simultaneously meant free-thinking. Emmanuel de Witte may have gained lasting fame for his church interiors, yet at the same time he was known as a notorious scoffer.[92] Adriaen van Linschoten depicted the repentance of Peter, but he could not put himself into Peter's state of mind. 'Wasn't it crazy that he began to cry about it? I have so often lied and sworn against my better judgment, and I never cried about it.'[93] There were others like him, but they were still exceptions – and some were at the opposite end of the spectrum. Albert Cuyp was an elder in the reformed church,[94] Philips Bol was a deacon.[95] Jan van Kuik Woutersz. was burnt at Dordrecht in 1572, one of the last martyrs of the Dutch reform.[96] Frans Hals perhaps best typifies his age and his trade in the hybrid but never hypocritical mixture of alcoholism and piety. No matter what his condition, he never ended his day without an evening prayer: 'Lord, take me soon to your high heaven'.[97] There too, spoke a true man of the seventeenth century. His life makes it very clear why only a few found the painter's profession the route to a higher rung on the social ladder.

The most spectacular careers of the seventeenth century remain those of admirals Piet Hein, Maarten Tromp and Michael de Ruyter. The successful speculator gained riches, the accomplished painter fame and honour; but the admiral got them all simultaneously, even if he had begun in an equally low station. The soldiers of the Eighty Years' War did not yet carry the marshal's baton in their knapsacks. But the sailors might well believe that they had an admiral's pennant folded in their sea-chests. Only at sea was it possible to reach the highest rank without prior education or rank at birth. Witte de With, a working-class lad from Brill, had been apprenticed successfully to a ropemaker, buttonmaker, silkworker, plasterer, sailmaker and tailor – all before he signed up for the service of the East India Company in 1616 at the age of seventeen.[98] This model Jack-of-all-trades and master of none was named vice-admiral of Holland in 1637. The first steps on the ladder were within everyone's reach, because Holland was crawling with failed apprentices. Yet one of those boys nonetheless managed to become vice-admiral. People could identify with such a man. Maurice or Frederick Henry could be admired, but not imitated. Most were by no means able to imitate Tromp and De Ruyter, either, but everyone had the chance to try. In a century that lacked international sports competition, the sea-heroes fulfilled the role of modern football and bicycling stars.

Their fame was just as fleeting as that of 'sportsman of the year'. Does anyone today remember who received that honour ten years ago? Commanders of the fleet could also fall into obscurity. Tromp and de With have kept their great fame, but who still recalls Jasper Liefhebber, their failed competitor on the road to the top?[99] Besides, popular taste rewarded only outward success, not objective accomplishments. 'See how the people rave now', Piet Hein said when he brought home the booty from the Spanish treasure fleet, without even having fought a battle. 'And before, when I had to fight for it, and do much greater deeds than these, people hardly paid any attention to me.'[100] If a commander was not successful, he could not plead extenuating circumstances. The public reacted strongly and emotionally to defeats that touched the Hollanders directly. In August, 1635, the pirates of Dunkirk carried out a successful attack on the Holland fishing fleet. Some sixty-five herring boats were lost. Willem Codde van der Burch came to the rescue with twenty ships and joined battle with Dunkirk forces of approximately equal strength, but he was unable to win the day. When vice-admiral Quast arrived with fifteen more ships, the Dunkirkers fled, without however sustaining any noteworthy losses. Van der Burch knew what the consequences would be; he did not return home, but went into exile near Glückstadt on the Elbe. His house in Enkhuizen was indeed plundered by a furious mob. Van der Burch himself was condemned in absentia for dereliction of duty – which Aitzema thought not unjust, particularly in order to satisfy the people.[101]

Thus the captains often had to pay the price when the means available for the defence of the nation's maritime interests did not suffice. If the Dunkirkers had struck a great blow, Aitzema said, then the people immediately blamed the admiral, the vice-admiral and all the ship's captains. No one was in such an unfortunate position as the commanders of the fleet, Frederick Henry declared. 'Their reputation hangs on the meanest fishwife, who cries out and screams, when her husband is captured, that the admiral is not doing his duty.'[102] Witte de With would even have us believe that Tromp feared the rabble of Holland more than the enemy. In 1639 he attacked the Spanish fleet at Duins only because he feared that otherwise he would be 'struck dead by the canaille' at home.[103]

But Tromp did owe something to the people's favour, and on his side he had done the necessary things to increase their obligation to him. Already in 1629 Tromp was reportedly 'loved and respected by all the world ... for his good exploits'.[104] He was especially popular in Rotterdam. When the Rotterdammers heard cannon-fire far away across the water, they said, fully confident of the outcome, 'that's Maerten Harpertsz.'s prize'.[105] His fame was slower to reach the upper orders. Not until 1635 did Nicolaes van Reigersberch write to his brother-in-law Hugo Grotius about 'a certain Maarten Harpertsz.', whose name was mentioned as a future vice-admiral.[106] It appears that the common people were particularly taken with Tromp in the 1630s, when complaints about the audacious activities of the Dunkirkers were growing steadily louder.

The choice was not self-evident. It was long an axiom of the fleet that a sailor should not be commanded by his former mates who had been promoted to higher rank, but by nobles whose birth had given them natural superiority. Actually this was already the rule on the 'sea-beggars'' fleet,[107] and the principle had also generally been maintained by the Holland and Zeeland admiralties since that time. Exceptions did occasionally occur. Cornelis Dircksz., the victor of the battle of the Zuider Zee in 1573, was rewarded with appointment to vice-admiral of Holland in 1579, 'in view of his boldness, industry and good experience'.[108] But the highest commands were mostly reserved for men with impressive names – Warmond, Van der Does, Haultain, Van Dorp – even when the bulk of the actions at sea were carried out by subordinate officers such as Moye Lambert and Hillebrant Quast. Piet Hein's great triumph of 1628 finally turned the tide. But when he was killed in 1629, two months after his promotion, the choice again fell on Van Dorp. His evident shortcomings caused the people to demand the appointment of an experienced sailor to the highest post: 'People clamoured violently for a real sailor, because they didn't trust men of high rank or noblemen at sea.'[109] In Tromp they hoped to find the new Piet Hein. His promotion at the same time as Witte de With – also described as 'a man who has the favour of the people'[110] – was then widely hailed.

A lieutenant-admiral, a vice-admiral, an executive officer ... but there really were not so many flag-officers. True, there were admirals of Holland, Zeeland and

Friesland in the five colleges of admiralty. There were sometimes great fleets of the East and West India Companies. But the path to the top still remained narrow. It was barely possible for two to walk it side by side. Anyone who wanted to get to the top had to press on and push others back. If he was successful, he certainly made enemies. If he was left behind, then he would always be embittered about the successes of those who had surpassed him. While not judging the good ones too harshly, we must say that a powerful jealousy ruled in the world of sea-captains.[111] Wounded pride and mutual jealousy poisoned the lives of the best of them and spoiled the savour of their apparent successes. Witte de With received little joy from his promotion to vice-admiral, because one rank above him served the man who had now twice surpassed him: a man just like himself, an ordinary working-class lad from Brill, of about the same age.[112] When Van Dorp was dismissed in 1637 in favour of Tromp, he regarded his rival as an intriguer. 'I know well the affront you have done me, because when you were still a private captain, you tried to cut the legs from under me.'[113] Their humble origins made the admirals especially sensitive. Every cabin-boy might admire these men and take them as models, but many a captain and even many a quartermaster could recall the days when their fleet-commander was their equal, and they would only recognise his rank spitefully. 'I have known Maarten for a long time', said an old sailor in a venomous pamphlet directed against Tromp in 1640, 'and always found him a fast talker; it was always and has always been his best weapon.' He fell into line with the preachers, so that the Protestant ministers would whip up public enthusiasm for him.[114]

Tromp, de With and Hein had to live with this jealousy. But they remain examples of successful upward mobility: men of the people, who had climbed a whole series of rungs on the social ladder. That possibility existed in seventeenth-century Holland, in commerce, in the painter's studio, in the fleet, and sometimes in other ways as well. The small shopkeeper Joost van den Vondel, the shoemaker's son Gerbrant Adriaensz. Bredero, and the glassmaker Jan Vos, found recognition in their poetry, although none of them became rich from it. Some also found fame on the way to the pulpit: they shone in the lustre of their extraordinary calling, which offered high status though no great income.[115]

Thus there was mobility in the society. Anyone who was born into the petit-bourgeois class or the community of the poor did not have to stay there all his life. It is difficult to measure how great the mobility was in those circles. We should certainly not overestimate it. For most people, the reality was still a life without prospects, and too many factors beyond their control could have a decisive influence on their success. Yet the knowledge that these chances existed could awaken hope and spiritual strength among those whose striving and desire would otherwise have been killed by rigidity and resignation.

PART II

Popular culture

Chapter 6

WOMEN AND GIRLS

Since women of seventeenth-century Holland had not yet been emancipated, we know little about them. The same point could indeed be made about all unemancipated groups: they barely if ever spoke for themselves. The sources often let us see and hear what others saw and heard, but not what they themselves thought. This was the case for seventeenth-century women. Our information about them is based almost exclusively on the stories and statements of men. Even when a woman was allowed to speak in a legal document or minute-book, it was always a man who wrote down the answers she gave to questions of other men. This is particularly true of the lower levels of society. In every generation women from higher social groups did manage to produce some letters or other personal documents, while working-class women remained silent. Thus it is difficult for us to get a picture of them. Perhaps this gap can be filled by others of their sex. A modern woman equipped with great powers of imagination, a taste for historical detective work, and not overly burdened by theoretical constraints will probably be in a better position to complete the picture we now have of unemancipated women in the early modern period. Here a male historian must necessarily admit he is doing only half a job: he will get no further than a description of women's relations with men, and can only report what interested the men of that period.

Thus we do know something about women's appearance. Anyone who reads travellers' accounts and journals of the sixteenth and seventeenth centuries never really knows in advance the questions to which he will find answers. Yet we can be certain of one thing: if anything at all about women is mentioned, it will relate in some way to their outward appearance.

That applies also to Dutch girls and women. All observers of the period tell us whether they were pretty. Opinions are absolutely unanimous on this point: they really were. Already in 1567 Guicciardini praised 'the very beautiful and white women' that could be seen in Leiden.[1] A generation later Arend van Buchell voiced his complete agreement.[2] The Spaniard Carnero saw Dutch women as 'beautiful and with graceful limbs',[3] and Van Meteren described them as 'large, long, white and beautiful, finely made'.[4] White skin and strong posture were the leading charms of the Dutch girl: these are the characteristics for which she is praised. Cats spoke of 'a lively girl of twenty-six, plump, spirited, amply bosomed – the whole neighbourhood talked about her'.[5] When he wanted to paint a verbal picture of a beautiful young woman, he reached for such words as stout, plump, and round.[6]

11. 'Man was first created from the earth, and thus is dignified, steady, and stands his ground. Woman was made from the bone of man, and thus is more willing to rattle her chatterbox.' Adriaen van de Venne, *Tableau of the ridiculous world*, 1635

Perhaps Cats was expressing popular taste; a man of quality might have preferred a lighter step and slender waist. In Roemer Visscher's works only the man of the people likes round forms.[7] Visscher himself poked fun at broad-boned Waterlands peasant girls, 'who [could] fill a barrel with buttocks, and a tub with breasts'.[8] But his own daughter Anna displayed more of the figure Cats admired,[9] and most Hollanders looked favourably upon it.

The eyes were thus satisfied, yet the behaviour of Holland girls reportedly left much to be desired. The same Arend van Buchell who praised the Leiden girls for their beauty wrote that they behaved in an unmannerly fashion,[10] while Amsterdam girls, no matter how attractive, fell short on modesty.[11] As was his custom, the Englishman Fynes Moryson made an even harsher judgment. He reported that from their early youth Holland girls bossed their older brothers around, and treated them as oafs. When these girls grew up, they were accustomed to having their own way. They chose younger men as husbands, preferably manageable and simple-minded, so that they could arrange all domestic matters to their own liking. I am well aware, the well-travelled Moryson added, that it is possible to find such women all over the world, 'but I may boldly say, that the women of these parts, are above all other truly taxed with this unnatural domineering over their husbands'.[12] Nor did these undutiful women remain confined to the home. Women kept shops, made bargains, and took trips as far as Hamburg,[13] while the men had to stay at home and were sent to the cradle and the stove by their meddlesome wives:

> I'll take care of the customers in the shop,
> You go see if the stew is done,
> That child is screaming, now Jan go back there![14]

Now it is certainly not impossible that a man such as Moryson would have been somewhat influenced by traditional notions. Just as the English woman was known in Holland for her great submissiveness,[15] so the English readily saw Dutch women as proud and power-hungry:

> We are ourselves, our own disposers, masters,
> And those that you call husbands, are our servants.[16]

But the English were not the only ones to hold this opinion of Dutch male–female relationships. Carnero also confirmed that Dutch women took care of many affairs that would have been left to men in other countries; he sought an explanation in the men's great desire for drink, which made them unfit for work.[17] Even so Moryson surpasses him, blaming the surplus of women in Holland on the same weakness for drink, 'which may disable them to beget males'.[18]

Was this a literary fiction – the obedient Dutchman, who allowed himself to be ruled by his wife? If so, it also had its place in Netherlandish tradition, and precisely in the poet Jacob Cats, who showed the mirror of truth as a corrective for both spouses, but especially wives. Not only did Cats make the lover bend to every whim of his beloved – 'As she waves, I must turn about'[19] – but also he knew the inconveniences of married life:

> If a glass or porcelain breaks,
> The house is soon too small,
> So violently does the wife rage,
> It seems she wants to give the maid a thrashing,
> Kitchen, parlour, hall and floor,
> Everything is in an uproar,
> It seems she will go into battle
> With a boy, with a servant,
> With her daughter, or her child,
> With whomever she finds first,
> And, in between, the man
> Will certainly get his share.[20]

Not everyone bore his burden patiently. In the minutes of church councils of the period we also encounter men who ruled their households with an iron fist. The schoolteacher Jan Adriaensz. of Edam rejected warnings about his chastisement of his wife. His conscience did not condemn him as long as he did not beat her to death.[21] Michiel Stevensz. in Schipluiden threw a foot-warmer at his wife's head, because she did not want to go with him to the communion service.[22] When such men were members of the reformed church, they undoubtedly came into contact with church discipline.[23] And even if they were not members, they ran the risk of having to answer to a judge, just as church members also did. 'Myselfe did heare the crier summon a man to answer the beating of his wife before a magistrate',[24] is a quotation that will be recognised as coming from the inevitable Moryson. Whether this happened often, I dare not say. But it does appear that in Holland seventeenth-century people generally accepted that the wife was not absolutely subject to the authority of her husband.

Thus the church council of Haarlem in 1623 refused to send Jan Hendricx as visitor of the sick to the Indies until his wife had appeared personally before them and given her consent.[25] Notary Paets of Leiden was caught in 1619 visiting a forbidden Remonstrant gathering, and was in danger of being punished with the loss of his post. 'It is a heavy burden on my heart', wrote Paets, but why? 'Because my wife did not know about it, and I went there without her consent'.[26] The church minute-books of the seventeenth century often suggest that the physically violent wives found in native farces[27] were modelled on real-life examples.[28] Jacob Cats, who had no hesitation at all about showing a woman her proper place, counted it among the advantages of marriage that a man could learn from his moody wife how to tolerate the shortcomings of other people:

> If your wife has such manners,
> That she speaks with gruff noise,
> See then, that you learn at home
> To relish the faults of others!
> It's to your advantage to put up with her
> To learn forbearance free of charge.[29]

If that was indeed one of the blessings of married life, then we ought to regard the Dutch woman of the seventeenth century as a very independent personage who could take care of herself. It was certainly true of working-class women, who were ordinarily required to go out to work themselves,[30] and who sometimes had to do without their seafaring men for months at a time.

Independence did carry obligations. The Dutch woman was regarded as an adult at an early age. The popular novel of *Gilias* makes this passing reference: 'the king of the island Helyce had a wonderfully beautiful daughter named Eulalis, about fifteen years old'.[31] In 1623, the East India Company sent 'a good number of young daughters' to the colonies, in order to help the employees of the company get wives. They were not to be older than twenty-five, and preferably fifteen, sixteen, seventeen, or even a mere twelve years old.[32] Had they considered the effects of a long voyage on girls of twelve? When in 1589 Arend van Buchell had the good fortune to discover a fascinatingly beautiful girl among his fellow passengers on a barge, he closed the summary of her outward charms with the words: 'she was in her first bloom, twelve or thirteen years old'.[33]

A girl of that age was actually not yet marriageable. But apparently the suitable age began quite early, when she could be an object of desire and thus eligible for marriage. Marriage was accepted as her natural purpose in life; consequently we should expect society to favour and ease the achievement of that goal. At a higher social level this could happen, for example, by means of agreements between families. No doubt that also occurred in humbler circles, especially among small property-holders: farmers with a few pieces of land, or tradesmen who tried to protect the future of their little enterprises with marital agreements.

Anyone who could choose his partner freely had to take advantage of the opportunity, because all too soon young people came to work long hours for their bosses. Sundays thus acquired special importance. Reformed young people could meet each other at church services. Morals were somewhat freer there than in the old church, at least according to the Catholic clergy: they decried as scandalous the sensually arousing Calvinistic faith, which allowed boys and girls to sit next to each other in church, and to sing together from one hymnbook, as if the apostle Paul had not taught that in the religious community a woman must be silent.[34] Yet I am not so sure that boys and girls were allowed to sit next to each other in all churches. Roemer Visscher in his poems has a young man anxious to marry choose a seat in church 'where he could cast amorous glances upon his beloved'[35] – thus not by her side. At the celebration of communion men and women often went to the table separately,[36] and at the synod of Dordrecht in 1618 the Dutch professors also advised separate catechetical instruction for adult men and women.[37]

Whether the church had much or little to offer, it did not like to see its prospective members take advantage of the other possibilities for closer acquaintance that city and village life provided. Indeed, it was precisely on the social behaviour of young people that the church was continually in conflict with traditional popular culture. The church waged war against the two most popular sins of Dutch men, drinking and fighting. But it was perhaps never more severe than when it struck against the women's favourite recreation, dancing.[38] The Spaniard Vázquez said that Dutch women were afflicted with a mad lust for dancing. They could keep going for two or three days at a stretch, and when the fiddler's powers failed they sang the dance-tunes themselves, with such fervour 'that the whole time they appear to be mad'.[39] This must have been the fanatical dancing that *dominee* Wassenburgh also has in mind, when he seriously assures us that dancing was very unhealthy according to the testimony of competent physicians. Indeed, especially after meals one should be careful with 'all vehement movements and great shakings of the body, which are done with violence and force'.[40]

At the time, however, not only cities but also small villages had dancing schools or public dance halls,[41] where this art could be practised. Despite all religious prohibitions, people found it hard to think of a wedding feast without dancing. Even reformed patriarchs were often unable to avoid it, and had to allow the musicians into the wedding hall. The church council of Edam had warned the membership in 1598 that they would have to leave the social hall immediately 'whenever music for dancing is played', in order not to give the appearance of

12. *Dancing couple at an inn*, by Adriaen van Ostade

approving such lewdness.[42] If this order brought any change in the style of life in Edam, the results were not long-lasting, because twenty years later the church council of that city had to retreat to a more entrenched position, and had to forbid the members from allowing 'dancing and leaping' at their own weddings.[43] Even the elders occasionally gave way to their dance-crazed wives and daughters. The elder Quirijn Decker at Naaldwijk had to confess publicly to this weakness.[44] His colleague Claes Dircxsz. in 't Woud had still not brought himself to take this step when he died unexpectedly of the plague, three weeks after the marriage of his son. 'So it often happens', *dominee* Fenacolius moralised in the minute-book, 'that after excessive joyfulness, especially when it is worldly, great sadness follows.'[45]

The wickedness of dancing was so absolutely evident to the preachers that they seldom gave their reasoning for the prohibition. If they did add some evidence, then it was usually a simple reference to the seventh commandment, which forbade 'frivolous dancing parties' as a sin of the flesh.[46] This exposition is indeed in complete

agreement with the explanation of the seventh commandment given by the Heidelberg Catechism,[47] and thus received the approval of the reformed churches. For
devout church-members, the dance hall was an anti-church, a synagogue of Satan;
the love of dancing was the *nec plus ultra* of ungodly life. People were dancing and
leaping at Symon de Cramer's house, said the church council of Zevenhuizen, 'as if
no Christians lived there'.[48] 'Pseudo-christiani', the young Arend van Buchell said
contemptuously of his contemporaries, who did not know how to celebrate a
wedding without dancing.[49] At Dordrecht somewhat later all candidates for confession had to promise that they would not dance.[50] If this requirement had been
omitted earlier and elsewhere, it was only because a dancing Christian was regarded
as a contradiction in terms. Jan Pietersz. Glas of Monnikendam, who in 1599
turned away from a church that had become too worldly in his eyes, declared that
henceforth he would never admonish anyone, 'even if he saw the members dancing
in the streets'.[51] He did not mention murder, manslaughter, theft, adultery or
perjury. A public round-dance by members of the reformed church was evidently
the worst horror he could imagine.

   Dance parties and dancing schools were undoubtedly significant as a marriage
market. This was even one of the objections of *dominee* Wassenburgh in his sermon
on the dance party of the daughters of Shiloh described in Judges 21: he remarked,
very aptly, that dancing leads to ill-advised marriages.[52] But the mass rape of the
virgins described there was not an everyday occurrence, and according to the
Spaniard Vázquez, Dutch girls chose their marital partners with such determined
reasonableness that a rash marriage, contracted in an outpouring of heartfelt
emotion, must have been nearly impossible. Vázquez reported that the Dutch
woman did not ask whether a man was sturdily built or intelligent, nor whether he
was courageous or distinguished. She gave her heart to whoever had the thickest
purse. Sometimes she also tested male character in advance. She would give her
lover as much drink as he wanted, and if he then appeared quarrelsome, she dropped
him. As a general rule, these marriages supposedly worked out very well.[53]

   If Vázquez indeed observed these well-planned affairs, we may still question how
typical they were for the loving girls and boys of the working class. If all purses are
empty, reasonable calculations may be thought to play a less significant role. When
Jacobus Scheltema wrote his description of popular customs of love and marriage
among the Netherlanders in 1832, he limited himself 'to the respectable middle
classes in bourgeois society', because among the common people 'all too often
passion excluded the use of reason'.[54] That was exactly what Jacob Cats saw happen
at peasant festivals, which an honourable girl was well advised to avoid:

> There people recklessly make a mixed bed,
> That is, a net for catching virgins.[55]

Indeed these dangers existed not only at peasant weddings and other great special
occasions, because in North Holland the old custom of night-courting had not yet
fallen into obscurity. Van Buchell confirmed the results of his meetings with girls

from Vlieland: 'facillime ad opus naturae condescendant'.[56] Did this happen only on the islands? In 1601 the High Council of Holland and Zeeland concluded that the proclamations against adultery often had little effect, because 'persons of small condition … are not intimidated by penalties of infamy'.[57] It also appears that for simple people public morality put no strong brake on desires of the flesh. The loose morals of servant-girls became proverbial, as in:

> It costs so much to keep your honour, said the maid,
> That I'm glad I'm well rid of mine.[58]

Or:

> Go in and grab the maid, for the wife is at church.[59]

13. *The singer*, by Adriaen van Ostade

As that saying made clear, the responsibility did not lie solely with the maid. Young married men, Roemer Visscher said, have not yet sown all their wild oats. Even if they are married, they don't feel any ties.[60] Cats also urged 'all honourable young men' not to follow the example of loose morals given by those who mocked the virtuous Joseph.[61] More often, nonetheless, the proverbs made the girl the butt of ridicule, probably because the norms and standards of good moral behaviour were defined by men, who judged a promiscuous woman more harshly than a licentious man. 'Women's lust is much more to be condemned than that of men, because nature does not mark men with such recognisable signs as it does women, having held the reins of shame looser in men.'[62] The man could not help it if woman drove him crazy; she would have to learn to control herself.

Indeed she would, out of necessity, because in the seventeenth century, when there was any mention of the means to dispose of the natural consequences of overly free behaviour, it always concerned persons of the better sort. Sometimes bleeding was tried, 'in the mother-vein on the foot'.[63] That method of interrupting pregnancy did not, however, appear effective. Nor did potions achieve the desired result in cases known to me,[64] not even for the regent of Enkhuizen Jan Simonsz. Blaeuhulck, who made the girl take medicines which (according to the testimony of several physicians) 'are principally aimed at the opening of the womb and the provocation of the menses', so that 'in general they should not be used by a woman who is pregnant'.[65] Blaeuhulck had a doctor prepare the drink, and when it did not work he called for aid from 'a godless and infamous scoundrel, to help him with quackery',[66] yet all without success. When as usual the means failed, or were unknown to the girl, she could see no other course than to abandon the child as a foundling – though that could simply have been a consequence of poverty[67] – or to take its life immediately.[68]

Of course we must always take general complaints of moral decay with a grain of salt, and beware of mistaking the exception for the rule. When we do hear rather often of freer contacts between men and women before and during marriage in Holland, it might be explained in part by the enormous number of sailors that went out from the trading and fishing ports. Even the great promoter of the West India Company, Willem Usselincx, admitted it could possibly be raised as an objection to trade, that owing to the lengthy absence of married men 'many women who stayed at home often fall into great difficulties, and much fornication is committed'.[69] The church council of Edam, which must have been familiar with practical aspects of the problem, found it serious enough to raise in the synod of North Holland. Some sailors stayed away nine years, ten years, or longer, and thus furnished 'no small occasion to immorality and lapse into adultery'.[70] The *classis* considered the question, apparently with even stronger evidence, because it spoke of absences of twelve years or more.[71] Although the *classis* sought a remedy, that was aiming high indeed. The 'Cunning Melis' in W. D. Hooft's farce of the same name found it easy to persuade the fisherman's wife Sytien to come to him for consolation: her husband should have been more considerate of his young wife and chosen a different career.[72] And even Jacob Cats, who was always eager to raise his countrymen to a higher moral plane, told the sailor that he must not judge his grass widow too harshly:

> You who leave a young woman all alone to mourn,
> Think of the way of the world, and what can happen;
> When there is trouble, suffer it with patience:
> Can it be that she is wonderfully frail, and you not without guilt?[73]

The verse says a great deal, because seventeenth-century people took marriage extremely seriously. They regarded it as an irrevocable choice. Engagement already had a binding character, and could not be broken unilaterally.[74] Both parties could force each other to live up to their promises. Ordinarily the woman was the one who had to insist, but a formal promise also gave rights to the man. Two Haarlemmers opposed each other in court in 1624, each claiming to have received a formal promise of marriage from the widow Lysbeth Jans,[75] apparently a very attractive or at least a rich woman. Ariaentje Crammers at Hoornaar was only able to marry Imbert Jansz. in 1620 after Adriaen Adriaensz. had declared before the bailiff and the preacher that he was willing to give her up.[76]

There did have to be proof of the engagement, which was sometimes given in writing; mostly, however, it was in the form of a pledge.[77] That might be any object at all – a ring[78] perhaps, but also a glove or a handkerchief,[79] or even a sum of money,[80] or a single coin, the 'troth-penny'. Anyone who returned the pledge gave up his rights.[81]

The engagement must be carefully distinguished from the publication of the banns.[82] An engagement could be terminated by common consent of the parties, but the banns could not.[83] With the promise given at the banns, the marriage was regarded as already begun; afterwards, it was completed by the formal ceremony, but that brought about no more obligation than was already contained in the promise.[84] Breaking of the banns must therefore also be seen as a form of divorce, obtainable only from the magistrate, by means of 'a separation letter and compensation'.[85] The reformed church did not regard it as an acceptable solution. The church saw the banns as irrevocable, 'since as it appears in Holy Scripture, that the promised female person is already the promised housewife'.[86] Nor did the church accept the unwillingness of both parties to go through with the marriage as a reason for stopping it.[87] Only in very exceptional cases did it waver from this rule, for example, if one of the parties appeared of unsound mind.[88] In such cases the church could not apply definitive judgments: the courts had to intervene, by means of a divorce proceeding. Even when the church had decided on its own account to stop the wedding proclamation, it still maintained the validity of the promise of marriage. When in 1608 it appeared that Jan de Driegerie had not been baptised, the church council of Haarlem refused to proceed with his marriage ceremony, 'nonetheless without annulling the promises already made'.[89] The church was no longer willing to confirm his marriage, but still wanted to require him to have it done by the magistrate.

In these matters the church was stricter than the civil authorities, and sometimes conflicts arose as a result. *Dominee* Mercator at Alphen aan de Rijn had registered a couple for a wedding ceremony, when that night the girl ran off with another man. Her father did succeed in bringing her back home, but in the meantime the bridegroom had lost his desire to marry her. The father then found a third candidate willing to fill the vacancy, and requested the publication of banns for this new couple. Naturally Mercator refused. Indeed, according to church norms, the magistrate would have to break the first banns before a second marriage could begin. Yet the States of Holland judged 'that the preacher should not make any difficulties about this marriage, even less about publishing the banns'.[91]

This marriage at Alphen raises another problem. The bride was committed to the original bridegroom by the promise made at the banns, but presumably she had slept with her abductor. Did this situation give rise to an obligation to marry? The question came to the attention of the synod of Middelburg in 1581, when it was asked whether coitus did not require marriage. The synod answered that it should indeed by God's law,[92] but 'since contrary usage has taken the upper hand in polity', the existing laws would have to be accepted.[93] The laws then allowed a man to father a child without being required to marry the mother. Not only among the well-to-do, but also among the poorer population were unmarried men obliged to support children whose mothers they did not wish to marry, for whatever reasons.[94] The church had accepted this situation, and had given preference to the judicially enforceable marriage promise over coitus. Tobias Herkenius, preacher at Zunderdorp, admitted in 1622 to the *classis* of Edam that he had had intercourse with his servant-girl, 'confessing his misdeed to the brothers with great remorse and many tears'. That mournful man did not for a moment think of marrying the girl: that was impossible, for he was already promised to marry a widow. Some members of the *classis* judged that Herkenius was now required to marry the servant-girl on the basis of Exodus 22:16, 'And if a man entices a virgin who is not betrothed, and lies with her, he shall surely pay the bride-price for her to be his wife' (*New King James Version*). The text appeared to be written specially for this case, but the majority ruled that Herkenius would be free of obligation if he could prove to the magistrate that he had made no promise of marriage to the girl. Herkenius was able to establish this point, and he married the widow.[95]

The question was really quite simple: one woman had received a promise of marriage, the other had not. Coitus did nothing to change the situation. At Noordeloos in 1599 a young man had made a promise of marriage to a girl, but he abandoned her when his mother raised objections. He then gave his promise to another girl, and also went to live with her. In this case therefore two conflicting promises had been made, and the second had been confirmed with coitus. Yet the *classis* of Gorinchem declared that the subsequent events had no influence on the validity of the first promise: that alone established a state of marriage between the boy and the first girl.[96] Thus only when there were no marriage promises to third parties was coitus regarded as requiring marriage, even in cases when the man had fulfilled the requirements of the law, and reached an agreement with the woman for the support of his child.[97] When we hear the churches asking the civil authorities about observance of the rule stated in Exodus 22:16,[98] we must therefore suppose that they had a higher regard for the obligations of a marriage promise than for the Mosaic commandment. Nor should we expect the contrary from the government, because the promise, sealed with a pledge and with consent of the parents,[99] offered far greater juridical security than coitus, which was very difficult to control and prove.[100]

The promise thus made the marriage and created an unbreakable tie. This understanding rested on the idea that marriages were decided by higher authority. Louw Molenaer of Schipluiden, who could not live in peace with his wife, was told by the church council 'that he should look to God's providence, who had given him the same and could take it away again'.[101] He himself could not get rid of her. A man was obliged 'to bear the weaknesses of his wife with patience'.[102] Yet a divorce was not absolutely beyond the realm of possibility. The reformed church allowed dissolution of marriage in cases of adultery or wilful desertion.[103] The church itself did not pronounce the divorce, but directed the complaining party to the magistrate.[104] The civil authorities were no more accommodating, although they recognised more grounds for divorce than the church did. In 1592 the Court of Holland dissolved a marriage on the grounds of the husband's impotence.[105] Nonetheless divorce remained an entirely marginal phenomenon, without influence on the marriage statistics.

That was the official theory of church and state regarding marriage and divorce, though perhaps it was not always approved by public opinion. 'By Heaven's lightning', sighed Jan Goedbloed in the farce *de qua Grieten*,

> If there was a church for unmarrying as well as marrying,
> I would go there right away, and I believe I should get followers,
> Who, in order to be the first ones there, would walk so hard they would gasp for breath.[106]

Not everyone entered into marriage with sober consideration and mature steadfastness. Claes Kloet in the eponymous farce by Biestkens might have successfully silenced his passion because he saw the consequences:

> The reason I did not make her my wife
> Was because I should hardly be able to get rid of her.[107]

But this intelligent reasoner would finally succumb, nonetheless, to an Antwerp prostitute. For others marriage was an unavoidable occurrence, which they barely understood beforehand. 'I thought only of happiness then, and did not think of this heavy suffering', complained Teeuwis de Boer's wife, 'no, I must have a man, I said, who would make a wife out of me.'[108] But Jacob Cats taught what would follow the wedding:

The burdens of the house, the will of the man,
And nearly every year a child.[109]

Or did the last point apply more to Cats' own good burghers than to the women of the working class? Households in the less attractive neighbourhoods of the large cities were generally rather small.[110] It is possible that this was deliberate. The comic poet W. D. Hooft has Griet Jans say in the farce of Cunning Melis that in view of the high cost of living she wants no more children, and that her husband will simply have to restrain himself.[111] This play, however, is dated 1623, a year of excessive dearth,[112] which may well have brought temporary changes in normal domestic behaviour. In any case it seems likely that in the sixteenth century the average age of marriage was low in the Noorderkwartier of Holland.[113] It seems most unlikely that people married young with the intention of restraining themselves from all conjugal relations. Van Meteren at least clearly believed the opposite, and said it was characteristic of Dutch women 'that they are much more fertile than those of other countries'.[114] If households nevertheless remained relatively small, that was more likely the result of high infant and child mortality. When David Coornwinder prepared for death in 1623, he could look back on twenty-one years of marriage with twelve children born alive, 'of which nine souls have gone to heavenly glory and only three are still left on this earth'.[115] This figure lacks statistical significance, as does that of the thirty-six children that Janneken Teunis of Hoorn bore Robbert Jansz.[116] Yet in both cases the rule of Cats apparently did apply: nearly every year a child.

In the great majority of cases marriage led to the formation of a family, which in turn held the marriage together and acted as a practical barrier to divorce. Once a marriage was contracted, it was seldom dissolved. It should be noted, however, that men and women living together did not always legalise their relationship. In Holland couples could choose between the church and the town hall. The reformed churches were open to all, and performed weddings for all baptised people no matter what their faith; but no one was required to use their services. If Catholics, Mennonites or Lutherans did not want to make their way to the churches, they were free to have their wedding recognised by the magistrate. By this means they achieved legal recognition for their marriages. For persons who possessed some capital this was indeed necessary, but the ceremony had no religious significance for them. What counted for the Catholic was the sacrament of marriage, which took place within the community of his own church.[117] What the Mennonite thought important was the confirmation of his marriage in his own Mennonite congregation. Anyone who cut a smaller figure in society, who had no handsome inheritance to divide or to expect, and who faced difficulties in paying the high costs of a peasant wedding felt no strong pressure to have the village registrar write down a marriage that he already regarded as an accomplished fact.

For Mennonites there was another factor, their critical relationship toward the authorities, which could make them unwilling to call for co-operation from the magistrate. At Schiedam in the sixteenth century the Mennonites were not accustomed to have their marriages formalised at the town hall, and only after the wedding ceremony had been completed in their congregation did they inform the town registrar that yet another marriage had taken place.[118] The communities of Aalsmeer, Zaandam and Uitgeest felt bold enough not only to ignore the requirements, but also to protest against compulsory marriage registration to the States of Holland.[119] At Brill the Mennonites did allow their marriage banns to be read in front of the town hall, but they forgot about the formal confirmation, or only sent it in much later.[120] Perhaps in some cases the blame also lay with the Calvinists, who decided the fees. At Woerden, in order to force the Lutherans to celebrate their marriages in the reformed church, the fees for marrying at the town hall were raised to the exorbitant sum of sixteen gulden.[121]

Generally speaking, however, the dissenters of Holland decided for themselves whether or not they would go the route of the church or the town hall. This may seem reasonable, but the unavoidable consequence was that their marriages did not rest on as strong a juridical basis as those of the reformed church. As long as the Mennonites remained faithful to their own religious community, their strong internal discipline could help keep these marriages in order, but if they left the community the incomplete character of these marriages could haunt them. Thus it is not so strange that the civil authorities and the reformed church saw little difference between Mennonite marriage and living together in sin, and referred to the two in the same breath.[122] It is also hard to tell in all cases what sort of relationship was involved, whether a principled Mennonite resistance to authority, or Reformed neglect to seek religious sanction. In 1598 the *classis* of Hoorn complained to the synod of North Holland 'that many persons remain for some months, or even years, at a time, in unlawful households including children, and afterwards leave each other in a scandalous manner'.[123]

Such marriages did not always break down, but by all reports casualness about fulfilling requirements was indeed quite common. In the seventeenth century engaged couples often began sexual intercourse before marriage. That occurred primarily in North Holland,[124] probably as a result of night-courting, but it also happened in the Zuiderkwartier.[125] In various cities, this so-called 'premature conversation' was punished with a fine when the marriage was registered.[126] But this means of upholding good morals backfired, namely when the couple was too poor to pay the fine, and thus decided to keep on living together in an unmarried state.[127] The church could do little about it as long as its own members were not involved. But if banns had never been published, the two partners could not be forced into a legal marriage. According to the proclamations they were supposed to separate, but after the birth of their first child this was hard to accomplish. The woman was probably not in a position to support the child on her own: thus it might easily become a public burden, if for example the father went to sea and effected a practical escape from his maintenance obligations. If the child remained with the father, he would probably be able to support it but not care for it. Thus he would take a female servant, and the same game began all over again.[128]

Perfect order was therefore not to be found in matters of love and marriage. But the complaints, particularly from the church, should not mislead us into thinking that concubinage was the rule and legal marriage the exception. In the overall picture, marriage was a respected institution among the great majority of the population, and married couples stayed together. People honoured marriage because the rules of Christian morality insisted so strongly upon it. Civil authority had largely but not entirely adapted its laws to these demands. It is evident that obedience to biblical norms particularly served the interests of weaker members of society. The position of Dutch women was far more favourable than that of other unemancipated groups in early modern times. The protection of marriage gave them the best social security the society of that period could offer. Thus we can understand why literary sources attribute great independence to the Dutch woman. Her position was strong enough to make us believe that this judgment rested on observation. And perhaps it was not so superficial of seventeenth-century observers to praise a woman's beauty, if she owed her self-awareness in part to her charms. Blessed is the woman who lacks beauty, said Lucas D'Heere, because such women have the virtue of humility.[129]

Chapter 7

THE NATURAL LIFE

In 1841 the writer Everhardus J. Potgieter imagined a Dutch household which has become proverbial, that of Jan, Jannetje, and their youngest child. Not all members of that household received the same attention. The mother and her daughters were described on one page, while Potgieter needed about twenty pages for the father and his sons. The daughters in the story resembled each other so much that they were not even given names: they are no more than neat, buxom girls with nice faces. By contrast each of the boys had a distinctive identity, which was expressed in his name, from Jan Jack-tar the first-born to Jan Ninny the smallest.

We should not have expected anything different. Potgieter saw women only from the outside, saw that they were pretty, and knew everything he wanted to know about them. With the men he had to proceed otherwise. History had told so much about men that it was unthinkable to smooth out all differences into one male stereotype character. Therefore he created Jan the Soldier and Jan Company, Jan Cash and Jan Reliable; Jan Ragtag and Jan Riffraff, Jan Critic and Jan the Poet. We shall have to study the men of Holland from all angles. Potgieter needed fourteen names for them, yet he still omitted the typical farmer and worker, not to mention the inevitable preacher in a family so rich in progeny. No, it is clear that a single chapter will not suffice to describe the Dutchman. He will remain constantly in the foreground, and he even stood in the limelight when we were trying to give some picture of the Dutch woman.

While we want to say a great deal about the Dutchman, is it not possible to choose which of the fourteen types was most common? Actually Potgieter did do that: Jan Jack-tar was the ideal, Jan Ninny the reality. Perhaps, in this overcrowded room, we should first look in another direction, to that deliberately darkened corner where drinking and cursing were rife, in the company of Jan Ragtag-and-Bobtail, Jan Riffraff and Jan Gourd-Bottle the showoff. I do not mean to suggest that the Hollander of the seventeenth century was a godless drunkard. He had to spend too much time working to be drunk every day, and he feared God's wrath even if he never went to church. But I will say that these boisterous spirits, whose background music is so muffled by Potgieter every now and then that we practically forget their presence, are occupied precisely with those things that warm the heart of the company as a whole, although the others know how to control themselves. Coercion, need, a sense of duty, love for one's neighbour or other Christian and social virtues might persuade a person to do regular work, to attend church faithfully, and to obey civil authority. None of these motives could lead him to the tobacco-house or the beer-hall. There we find the Dutchman acting as he himself chose. There no boss, burgomaster, preacher or wife could lay down the law. He behaved according to his nature.

What expectations could that arouse? The men of the seventeenth century readily placed natural life in opposition to Christian life, and saw them as two diametrically opposed poles.[1] The Christian submitted to God's laws, while the natural man was a slave of sin. Sin, nature, world and flesh are practically interchangeable ideas in Calvinist moral theology. Natural life was described in the same words that the apostle Paul used to name the works of the flesh: 'fornication, uncleanliness, licentiousness, idolatry, sorcery, hatred, contentions, jealousies, outbursts of wrath, selfish ambitions, dissensions, heresies, envy, drunkenness, revelries, and the like'.[2] These are just the things we are now going to see., We shall leave aside only the seventeenth-century equivalents of what Paul understood as idolatry and sorcery, which will be considered as a separate subject in part IV of our work. They would not really fit thematically into our approach, because anyone who asked for help from a sorcerer sought support from higher powers, and was motivated by fear or hope. He could no longer maintain the illusion of acting as a free agent in his own affairs.

By contrast, the drunkards, fighters and whoremasters could believe they possessed this freedom of action, at least within certain limits set by the law. The laws of the state were sometimes in accord with the moral law of Christianity, but more often allowed a bit of laxity. On crimes of violence the two differed little, but on drunkenness they varied greatly. As far as prostitution was concerned, in theory the first applied, but in practice the second was closer to the truth. The church condemned it unequivocally, in the full knowledge that it had to speak out most clearly on this point because nowhere were natural desires stronger than in sexuality. Satan had no weapon more formidable than woman, said Wassenburgh, following Jean-Paul Perrin; therefore he had chosen Eve to lead Adam astray.[3] The civil authorities were less resolute. Of course they disapproved of prostitution, but seldom went so far as the ultimate logical consequence of absolute prohibition. It was not completely forbidden. In 1595 a by-law of The Hague specified that no one in the town or the jurisdiction could keep a brothel, under penalty of public flogging.[4] Ordinances against brothel-keepers were found in other places as well,[5] and the girls were sometimes prosecuted, but generally they risked no more than temporary banishment,[6] the typical punishment of the *ancien régime* in Holland when embarrassed. Various city governments abandoned the struggle to eliminate prostitution as hopeless, and contented themselves with regulating the trade.[7] In Oudewater, and no doubt in other places as well, tolerated houses were long established, and leases assigned by the city authorities.[8] In Gouda until 1593 the exploitation was in the hands of the servants of the bailiff, whose wages were based on this extra income.[9]

But with or without toleration, it seems highly unlikely that in Holland during this period there was any city without prostitution – it appeared even in the most proper town of Enkhuizen.[10] In various towns people complained in the early seventeenth century about the increase of this phenomenon,[11] although these complaints were probably based on an unjustified idealised view of the past. Also, municipal control could not be very effective, because in many places immediately outside the city walls a very tolerant regime prevailed. Bredero says of Amsterdam

> That there was hardly one respectable inn beyond the gate;
> There were only whore-houses and brothels.[12]

The bad reputation of Haarlem at the beginning of the seventeenth century[13] could be localised to 'the red house outside the gate of the cross'[14] and similar addresses nearby, or to the 'evil, unruly company of whores and scoundrels' in the inns of Overveen.[15] Perhaps The Hague had similar problems with Voorburg,[16] but the city of the prince itself had no shortage of rendezvous where one could meet gentlemen of the highest rank.[17] In this respect, the comic poet Van Santen compared the town with Antwerp.[18]

As for the origins of the girls, in most cases we can only guess. Naturally we think of the legion of beggars, which certainly counted among its ranks many women who sought or took advantage of opportunities that came their way. Systematic research in the criminal archives might well tell us more, in particular how much faith should be placed in literary sources which place the origins of prostitutes elsewhere, viz. among the native working class of Holland. Trijn Jans and Bleecke An in Bredero's *Spanish Brabanter* were originally Dutch servant-girls.[19] An lived day by day and easily fell into ill repute, while Trijn came to prostitution through a sudden need for money. An started on the game at age fourteen, which was certainly possible given the early maturity of seventeenth-century women: there were even younger ones. In 1620 a girl aged eleven was placed in the spinning-house for that very reason.[20] According to the Spaniard Vázquez, it sometimes happened that young girls and women from Holland went to Flanders to work in a brothel in order to gather a dowry.[21] After all, the comic writer W. D. Hooft had Teun the matchmaker say that married women could also sometimes be obliged to earn some additional income, if their husbands turned out to be too lazy.[22] Thus he too thought first of the Holland housewife.

How much money could be earned in this way is another question to which literary sources may give stylised answers. When Bredero's Trijn and Annetje appear on stage, both of them have just received their wages, which, judging by their reactions, they think high: a Spanish piece of eight for An,[23] and half a *pistole* for Trijn.[24] The first thus received somewhat more, the second somewhat less, than two gulden. An later states that she had once received from her first client a French crown, worth about three and a half gulden,[25] but then she did have a preference for well-heeled gentlemen.[26] Trijn tries to persuade Jerolimo the Spanish Brabanter to part with half of a piece of eight,[27] slightly more than one gulden. That sum is approximately comparable to the two shillings that formed the tariff for run-of-the-mill clients of John Marston's *Dutch Courtesan*.[28] Probably these were the normal prices, according to Bredero, because in his *Moortje* he says that these women only put on high airs when they were in contact with rich men, but otherwise had to be satisfied with roasted turnips, onions, garlic, barley groats, mouldy bread and small beer.[29]

The big money was probably earned at the grand festivities of seventeenth-century amusement, such as the Amsterdam carnival, and certainly at the Valkenburg horse fair.[30] There, at least in some years, was a great crowd of 'beautiful women', who appeared under the escort of Amsterdam innkeepers.[31] The show was rather dependent on the indulgence displayed by the forces of justice. Often was it a question of haggling. In 1611 Willem Mouring offered the bailiff of Wassenaar eighty gulden, on behalf of all the Amsterdammers, if they might ply their trade during the Valkenburg horse fair. The bailiff found that sum too small, but the parties nonetheless reached an agreement, and the Amsterdam landlords received

14. Fair (*kermis*) scene, by Adriaen van de Venne

the necessary attestation of good order, the proof of good moral behaviour. In 1612 there was a rumour that the bailiff had received orders from the Court of Holland to act more strictly. Mouring left his Amsterdam girls at home, 'but discovering otherwise afterwards, picked up a few birds along the road to do some business with them'. These opportune birds earned such good money, however, that they would rather pay the landlady double the usual tariff than do their laundry themselves. Those were great days for girls of pleasure. The ordinary publicans, in the numerical majority, raised loud complaints, 'because the people all go to the whore houses, and therefore we get no business'.

That year they did indeed miss the extra profits the horse fair could have given them. Averaged over the whole year, there was enough demand for their services. Yet it is revealing that in the records of church discipline and admonishment the clients of brothels very seldom appear,[32] while the council records are teeming with drinkers.[33] Church and tavern were opposite poles in literature and preaching. In part I we made the acquaintance of Joosje's husband in W. D. Hooft's farce *Jan Saly*, a man who had been obliged to earn his living at sea because he knew the tavern better than the church.[34] By comparison, Elsje's husband had already been chosen foreman of the grain-porters three times,

> Because instead of going to sit in the tavern, he always goes to church.[35]

The contrast was all the more striking in many villages and cities, where churches and taverns were found in each other's immediate vicinity, as for example in Haarlem.

> So Satan tried to build his huts,
> Where God would found his beloved church and holy word,
> What draws you to the tavern? Go rather to the church:
> And be filled with spirit there. That is wholesome work![36]

With all due respect for this good advice from *dominee* Ampzing, if there was any area where the Hollanders achieved European fame, it was not their deep religious faith, but their taste for beer and wine. Hollanders, Moryson said, drank any time and anywhere. Pilots took the wheel in a state of intoxication and barge skippers stood drunk at the rudder, with the result that the tow-ropes of passing barges became entangled.[37] If he had no drinking partner, the Dutchman would choose his own coat or hat as a boon companion, and drink himself so silly that he reached the same level of reason as the hat or coat.[38] Intemperance among the English was known as drinking in the Dutch manner,[39] and drunkenness was regarded as the Hollander's perpetual excuse for all wantonness and disorder.[40] Indeed Dutch lawmakers had shown some consideration for the drunkard. We have seen the strength of promises of marriage, the absolute bond of one's word, once given. Yet no promise of marriage was valid, not even if it was confirmed with a gift and coitus, if the marriage partner was under the influence of drink and had temporarily lost full use of his faculties.[41] This point of law shows clearly that the Hollander knew very well the disadvantages of drinking; nonetheless, according to Carnero, he would never make any decision, great or small, without pouring a generous drink.[42]

The Hollanders themselves also knew that they drank a great deal, but how could they give up beer and wine? It certainly wasn't brewed for the geese, they said – let us therefore use it to our hearts' content.[43] Anyone who goes to pay visits these days, *dominee* Souterius complained, can no longer count on an instructive conversation about 'good topics, which are pleasant to hear': everything comes down to 'pour it in, drink it up'.[44] People used glasses without bases, so that the guests could not put them down, or ones with a bell that rang as soon as the glass was empty. No party could be called a success if the guests did not suffer terribly the next day 'from headache, and from great disturbance in the body, caused by strong drinking'.[45] Nor was anyone embarrassed about it. If one asked a woman whether it was possible to speak to her husband, she would regard it as an honourable excuse that he was sleeping off his hangover.[46] It was Moryson who said so, but no less a personage than Maurice of Nassau had to experience it, when he once desired to consult the Knighthood of Holland on the afternoon following a party.[47]

The Hollander found many opportunities to use alcohol. He drank at parties: even at funerals people guzzled litres of wine.[48] He drank when he received company. Anyone 'who often had the coming and going of friends and other acquaintances', declared Middelhovius, the rector of Haarlem, could not possibly avoid being drunk frequently.[49] He also drank for reasons of health. 'Wine is a better and more suitable drink than water. While it may be true that water slakes the thirst just as well as wine, nevertheless anyone who would take care of his health will hold wine in far greater esteem than water.'[50] This is a doctor speaking, the Dordrecht physician Johan van Beverwijck. Perhaps his advice was influenced by the very low price of wine in his home town, which was the central depot for Rhine wines.[51] The people of Dordrecht were renowned for 'being able to wash away all heavy-headedness with Rhenish wine'.[52] Elsewhere the choice between water and wine was open only to well-to-do patients; for the poor it goes without saying that beer was the alternative. Water was only drunk when there was a shortage of beer, in times of bad harvests.[53] In any case, according to English visitors, the water of Holland was bad.[54] Beer was the drink of the people. We do not have many figures, but there is little reason to regard the annual per-capita consumption of about 250 litres at Haarlem in 1475 as exceptionally high.[55]

While in early seventeenth-century Holland beer had to take the place of coffee, tea, water and soft drinks, serving to quench the most honest thirst, nevertheless it certainly contained some alcohol. Thus it was also used for precisely the reasons that people have reached for alcohol for centuries. Consequently country inns were indispensable: 'the people who feed themselves only by working the land, usually look for relaxation at the inn'.[56] The cities also had a very high density of inns. At Amsterdam in 1613 there were at least 518 tap-rooms,[57] approximately one for every 200 inhabitants. Alcohol was sold and drunk in 'inns, taverns, cellars, many apothecary shops, and retailers' houses',[58] the last not uncommonly illegal ones evading the high beer-tax. It also appeared that in the winter of 1613–14 at Amsterdam no fewer than 105 of the 518 drink-shops had to close for violations of the law. This evil was almost impossible to stamp out because the illicit tapsters were 'mostly light folk, who had insufficient means to pay the financial penalties':[59] thus they risked little for potentially great profits.

The sums involved were sometimes more than the customers could do without, for by drinking they easily plunged deeply into debt. The government did occasionally try to protect its subjects from themselves by setting a maximum credit limit. The regulations at Oudewater allowed a tavern-keeper or baker to declare under oath the sums he had written on the wall with chalk, but they could not exceed sixteen gulden.[60] In Assendelft it was not even allowed to give more than thirty stuivers of credit. If the innkeeper wrote down more, he could not make a valid claim to the judge.[61] No doubt this was a prudent rule, but the authorities did not have any control over innkeepers who poured drinks in exchange for pledges. The retail price of beer – about $1\frac{1}{2}$ to two stuivers per tankard around the turn of the century[62] – was enough to weigh heavily on a small income, at least for heavy drinkers who took time to reach their capacity. In the farce of *Claas Kloet*, the Antwerp lass Mary says of her husband that he lies snoring 'like a grain-porter who has drunk six or seven *vaan*'.[63] A *vaan* was equivalent to a tankard,[64] and if these were Antwerp tankards, that must mean a quantity of eight or nine litres. Not everyone would have needed that much,[65] but it is still clear that the typical drinker would go to some trouble for an evening's pleasure. True, the prices were adjusted somewhat to the clientele. The French traveller Charles Ogier reported that in 1636 the Rotterdam inns had the custom of charging their patrons according to their social station. A soldier or merchant paid the normal price, a captain five times as much, a prince or ambassador a hundred times as much.[66] That probably also made a difference to the price of a tankard of beer. The taverns at Katwijk, for example, were in the habit of making extra heavy charges; 'for the most beer was drunk by those who were out for a good time, and paid for the beer from their gambling winnings'.[67]

For that matter, the pleasure-seekers' preferred drink was wine, which the common man could not easily afford, owing to its high price.[68] Anyone who drank wine from a tankard must have regarded it as beneath his dignity to check whether the tavern-keeper had filled the vessel; he drank from the spout without raising the lid.[69] Those who used glasses did sometimes throw them over their heads against the wall,[70] and they paid extra for broken glassware.[71] Anyone who could not permit himself such extravagances drank beer along with the majority. In Maurice of Nassau's time, Delft beer had the best reputation: it could make you drunk just as easily as wine, Van Buchell said, while the price was lower.[72] Delft long maintained its fame, even when Haarlem and Dordrecht became competitors.[73] Under Frederick Henry, Rotterdam beer enjoyed the greatest reputation,[74] famous as the city then was for its delicious drinking water.

Beer must have been drunk in Holland as long as the coastline had been inhabited.

By contrast, tobacco was new to our period. In 1598 Van Meteren was still describing smoking as a curiosity. You put a bit of dried powder in a small bowl the size of half a hazelnut, light it with a candle or glowing coal, and inhale the smoke through a pipe-stem, then blow it out your nostrils. 'That is what people call drinking a pipe of tobacco.'[75] The physicians, he added, do not yet rightly know what to think of tobacco, but people say that it is unhealthy. Opinions remained divided on this point in the seventeenth century. 'Divine, rare, superexcellent tobacco', Robert Burton said, but in the same breath also 'hellish, devilish and damned tobacco'.[76] With the greater modesty required by his spiritual calling, *dominee* Udemans also set down the pros and cons: Tobacco is good for the brain, but damaging to the stomach. Heavy smokers declare that they can get by with less food, but one might just as well say that illness allows saving on food. Since tobacco is medicine, it can be harmful in excess.[77]

Udemans wrote in 1640, some forty years after Van Meteren. By then the strange English habit had become naturalised in Holland, and Holland also got its tobacco-houses,[78] with similar results. Van Meteren had already told what happened to the true devotees in England. 'These people become addicted to it, just as drunks do to wine and beer, and cannot do without it.' It was precisely what Udemans then saw his countrymen do: 'There are thousands of people, who would call themselves Christians, who are just as besotted with this foul smoke as children are with sugar'. Udemans found smoking unbecoming to the Christian, less because of the nature of the habit itself than because of the addiction; and besides, all that smoking made people dry and thus aroused their desire for drink. Probably for these reasons church councils occasionally warned members about the use of tobacco.[79] Some of them, however, apparently believed that tobacco itself had a titillating effect, even when not accompanied by alcohol:

> Even though a sailor has drunk only a pipe of tobacco,
> He gets a jolly heart just as if wine had been poured for him.[80]

Would Cats have seen this for himself, that smoking had such power to arouse? In any case he definitely believed it. Many years after Cats had written this verse, his former clerk Pieter van Heynsbergen was arrested because, among other reasons, he had threatened his master with murder and arson. Cats then declared that Heynsbergen was a man who was accustomed to carry out his threats, 'being strangely carried away by tobacco and strong drink'.[81]

It seems as if no one quite knew what exactly was wrong with smoking, but people were trying to express their emotional doubts in moral or medical terms, because without being able to provide a rational basis they still regarded tobacco as an evil. Udemans sought the answer in addiction. Cats foresaw audacious reck-lessness for the typical smoker. Furthermore, we learn from Bredero that there was a popular prejudice that tobacco would dessicate vital bodily fluids, and make men unfit to fulfil their conjugal duty. We probably won't have any more children, states Aeltje in the *Miller's Farce*:

I don't believe that my husband's thing will do it anymore.
Because he drinks too much tobacco, and that (so they say) dries [him] out,
Once he had the habit of being a man in the field, but now he is too weak.[82]

All this opposition had little effect, however, because in 1623 the States of Holland imposed a tobacco tax,[83] an unmistakable sign that consumption must have reached a considerable height. At that time also appeared the first warnings against smoking by girls and women:

They then stink
Like a beer-man, on the bench.
Who would want to sleep with her
When she yawns
Because of her foul stench![84]

All these moral and medical objections, however, could not stunt the growth of tobacco consumption. The Gouda-pipe gradually became an internationally known symbol of the Netherlandish nation as famous as the tulip, the cheese, and the tow-barge. At the end of the seventeenth century this development was practically complete. The religious protest was never particularly strong, and the government began to see the matter purely from a financial point of view, certainly when the avowed anti-smokers – Maurice in the army and Piet Heyn in the fleet[85] – had both died. While Piet Heyn wanted to forbid smoking on board his ships, the Admiralty of Amsterdam proposed in 1630 to encourage all privateers by exempting them from tobacco import-duties.[86] Did people somehow perceive an affective relationship between privateering and pipe tobacco? The fact is in any case that privateering flourished in Zeeland, while the tobacco tax there was far lower than in Holland.[87] In 1644 the Deputised Councils of Holland allowed their position on tobacco to be decided by only one argument: namely, their desire not to damage commerce by disproportionately heavy taxes on this product.[88] Thus the development of the smoking habit produced a pure example of human desires that were able to evolve freely, without any church or state interference worthy of mention.

It was also difficult for the government of Holland to see a role for itself in this matter. The authorities were tolerant enough to take little notice of anything that happened behind closed doors, even those of an inn, as long as there were no consequences outside. The free political discussions of the beer-hall, as long as they were limited to mere words, seldom led to judicial action, even if (as the Haarlem preacher Souterius reported) the magistrate was a perpetual scapegoat of the besotted critics:

'They let it be known that if they sat on the [judicial] bench, everything would be governed better and more wisely, although they cannot govern themselves. They would put all matters in better order, although they themselves live in a completely disorderly fashion at home and abroad. They would rule everything better, better support the country's prosperity, and better manage the country's means and moneys, although they as miserable drunkards cannot rule themselves properly.'[89]

Sometimes these talks alternated with communal singing of an aggressive character, for example quite personal attacks on local worthies, 'scandalous ditties, that have no other purpose than to rob many good people of their name and fame', according to the magistrate of Gouda in 1615, these were nonetheless 'sung lustily in the inns'.[90] There were also songs of better quality. The beer-drinkers of Holland sang the Wilhelmus, the southern Netherlandish Catholic Verstegen assures us, even more lustily than Datheen's psalms in church.[91] During the first years of the revolt he was probably correct. Then the Wilhelmus was a battle song, a challenge to the foe who might come at any moment. In the seventeenth century this threat was no longer felt so strongly.[92] National songs were still heard on all occasions, even in 1616 on the redeption of the towns pledged to the English for loans during the Revolt. This uninspiring political success was celebrated in a panegyric on the melody of 'Pots hondert duysent slapperment' (a bastardised version of the oath 'By God's mercy and sacrament'),[93] but one may suppose that the new words had less appeal than the old ones: now only their robust opening lines are still remembered. The innfolk did sing 'rather rowdily and coarsely', as Revius so elegantly put it.[94]

Thus the inn was indeed the place where the common folk sought to relax and pass the time. There people could drink, smoke, sing, talk, and last but not least, satisfy their desire for gambling. The men played with gusto, and always for money. Not only did they put their stakes on card games such as 'thirty-one' (which ended when one player had thirty-one points),[95] but also grander pastimes such as chess were enlivened by betting.[96] Dice were very popular, and used in a game reminiscent of American craps. The French traveller Charles Ogier declared that in Rotterdam it was quite impossible to choose a porter to carry luggage. As soon as a foreigner had chosen one, another arrived on the scene to shoot dice with the first for the client's trade.[97] In any case the game was so widespread that Isaäc Beeckman described at length in his diary the odds a player could expect on all kinds of throws,[98] although as an elder in the reformed church he ought to have known that participating in games of chance was improper for the membership.[99]

Besides actual games of chance, people also made bets, as adventurous and reckless as only a table full of drunken habitués could invent them. During the kermis of Rugge in 1617 a certain Raeff Berry bet two tankards of beer 'that he with his body completely naked would walk through the village of Rugge, and by this means would drive away all the village women and young daughters (who were there in great numbers); the same he also did accomplish'.[100] Barent Bakker in De Burg in 1624 put his life on the line, by betting that he would sail in a kneading-trough from Texel to Wieringen. Luckily for him it appears that the unmanoeuvrable vessel was sufficiently seaworthy.[101] More commonly, a journey under specified conditions decided the stake. At the inn of Bleiswijk, Abraham Michielsz. van der Stain entered into a discussion with the publican on the question of the exact appearance of a certain pillar in Rome. Abraham offered to go to Rome with his wife to see who was right. The publican demanded a certificate from the Pope and a drawing of the pillar. His opponent successfully satisfied all the conditions, and on his return in 1614 won the stake, the innkeeper's house.[102] The record for the longest journey was probably held by Simon Pietersz. Poorter, who on Epiphany night 1614 promised to go from Haringkarspel to Jerusalem and back within twelve months. Before his departure he sold all his cows, reckoning that if he was successful he would receive double the sales price. He won the bet, and furthermore he managed to do outstanding business with the trading goods he took along.[103]

The one went hand in hand with the other. Bets of this nature were inspired by the general desire to gain great profits quickly. At the inns many transactions were conducted, normally of the sort that one finds mentioned in the church council registers as wicked, foolish, silly, trashy businesses.[104] So frequently did drunken people engage in the strangest and most ill-considered business transactions that in all Holland the law allowed that any purchase or sale contracted in an inn or tavern could be cancelled within twenty-four hours.[105]

High points of tavern life took place during carnivals, annual markets and popular festivals. If anyone wants proof of how strongly the great market days were anchored in the life of the people, there is none better than the simple resolution of the States of Holland, dated 13 September 1574, that the horse fair of Valkenburg could be moved to Zwijndrecht that year.[106] At that time it was not possible to go to Valkenburg, for the Spaniards were there, waiting behind their siege works to starve out the population of Leiden. The entire revolt depended on the defence of Leiden. Should we conclude that this siege held friend and foe in breathless tension? The very last thing that comes to mind is that the destitute and plundered country folk of Holland wanted to go to market to buy horses which soldiers could seize as booty the following day. It is strange, almost repulsive, that the horse lovers did not want to do without their annual amusement, even though they had to ride to Zwijndrecht to have it. Apparently for a sixteenth-century Hollander the holding of a horse fair was an almost inexorable duty that had to be fulfilled no matter what the cost, as if it were the Olympic Games. By comparison with Munich in 1972 the Zwijndrecht horse fair of 1574 does not come off so badly. Valkenburg was simply sacrosanct. In 1612 the States of Holland declared that this market, held every September, was once again the annual rendezvous of all kinds of scoundrels, who came only 'to practise thievery and other nuisances'. It was nearly always the rule that when such considerations were mentioned in a resolution or proclamation they formed the prologue to an absolute prohibition. Nearly – but here we are discussing the Valkenburg horse fair. Thus the States decided that as long as the fair lasted the village could impose an extra tax of ten stuivers on every barrel of beer and one stuiver on every flagon of wine, in order to pay for the required security measures.[107]

Was Valkenburg unique? Certainly it was more than *primus inter pares*, but if any popular festival could be compared to it, there was the Amsterdam *kermis*. That took place at the same time of year, and we have already seen that a considerable group of Amsterdam innkeepers chose to set up their tents at

Valkenburg, preferring the earnings of this country market over potential high profits to be gained at home. Nonetheless the Amsterdam *kermis* was also a great event. Cursing my servant-girl has no effect, said Bredero's miller's wife; if I want her to do anything, I have to promise her a *kermis*.[108] In the most distant parts of the Amsterdam region no church council would hold a communion-service as long as the *kermis* lasted, because the members' desire to go to Amsterdam was simply too strong.[109]

The reformed church was not shy about denouncing anything it regarded as sin. Its accommodating attitude towards the Amsterdam revellers thus shows that the church did not condemn the *kermis* as such. The same view appeared at Brill, where the church council in 1624 had to acknowledge 'that at the *kermissen* these days many abuses contrary to good order are creeping in', by which the council specifically meant games of chance, lotteries, tightrope-walking and similar vanities.[110] Therefore they resolved to ask the magistrate to forbid such abuses. But the church council did not speak of a prohibition of *kermissen*, nor did it even consider telling its own membership to stay away from them. At heart it apparently found the *kermis* tolerable, and the church did not close off all avenues for popular enjoyment.

The church would have had difficulty doing that. Many popular festivities were deeply rooted in tradition and indeed had an entirely honourable motive: christenings, weddings, celebrations of victories by the States' army and other days of national remembrance.[111] Even so, these festivities had their dubious aspects. A baptism might be the occasion for a grandiose meal, richly awash with drink. To save costs the parents would sometimes wait until two or three children could be baptised at the same time, in order to celebrate the affair with one festive meal.[112] These joys of the table had little in common with respectful observance of the sacrament. With the deliberate intention of upsetting this style of life, the reformed church forced the parents to organise their festive days differently, by specifying that baptism and marriage ceremonies could take place only at the afternoon service.[113]

This certainly applied to weddings as well, because marriages lent themselves even more readily to all kinds of festive display that was foreign to churchly morals. Sometimes the bride was still being 'preened and groomed' while standing before the pulpit in the church: she was crowned with flowers and led away by the wedding guests.[114] Wedding-feasts had a reputation for extravagance that went far beyond christenings. At the poor folks' wedding that Van Santen described in his *Snappende Sijtgen*, the bride wore a borrowed cloak and a rented dress, while the groom was dressed in a suit that he had just purchased on the instalment plan – but already by the following day it had to go to the pawnshop to help pay the costs of the wedding.[115] Krul reckons in the farce of *Drooge Goosen* that the bill for the wedding will come to 'one or two thousand guilders'.[116] That was in 1632, for a middle-class wedding. While not an exact figure, it is not a wild exaggeration either. In 1592 Arend van Buchell noted in his journal that the wedding of the Stuver girls in Alkmaar had cost 4,000 guilders.[117] Could not a peasant wedding forty years later

15. *Prince Maurice and Frederick Henry of Orange at the Valkenburg Horse Fair*, by Adriaen van de Venne

then come to a thousand guilders? A young couple should have been protected against such excesses. The government did that occasionally to some extent, at least by using stiff penalties to keep away uninvited guests.[118] The church played a leading role here. Its struggle against the consequences of irresponsibility deserves more appreciation than naive admirers of Dutch folk custom have been willing to grant.

That applies also to the inheritance of entirely and partly religious holidays which the Catholic centuries had given to the Dutch people. St John the Baptist's Day, Shrove Tuesday (Mardi Gras), Epiphany and New Year's Day are repeatedly mentioned in the acts and registers of the reformed churches, and never with a favourable connotation. They were all 'frivolity, superstition and idolatry',[119] bringing dishonour to God's church and the Christian Reformation.[120] It would be better

to get rid of all holidays except Sundays and Christmas, or at least if they were maintained to celebrate them only with an extra church service.[121] The government did not entirely satisfy these demands. Norms differed from place to place, so that one village might have more days of leisure than another. But in many respects the magistrates did come to the aid of the church in its struggle against popular festivals. The statute of Nieuwkoop in 1589 was unusually far-reaching in banning Mardi Gras games and New Year's song feasts, removing unauthorised maypoles from premises where a wedding would be celebrated within a year, and forbidding 'bowling, quacks or gambling tables' at *kermissen*.[122] Not every local administration was so favourably inclined to the preachers, but the prohibition of New Year's song feasts and Mardi Gras games was more than localised Nieuwkoop rigorism.[123]

Of course the government also had its own reasons for these prohibitions. 'No one, no matter who he is, will be allowed to ride, to stick, to pull, to hit, or otherwise to cut open any swans, geese, roosters, rabbits, eels, herring, or other animals, without exception, on foot, on horseback, on water, or on land'.[124] This Rijnland ordinance paints a telling picture of the coarseness of the times, but perhaps the primary motive for the ban was the view that such games were unnecessary waste. The States of Holland might quickly decide to levy heavier taxes on such an extravagant district. We must not see the bailiff of Rijnland in the unlikely role of animal protection officer. Such prohibitions were enacted when the folk custom caused a nuisance to others. In the final analysis, this ordinance also comes down to that point: high taxes would hit the thrifty stay-at-home types, too, those who kept a goose only for the feathers and the cooking-pot. Mostly the connection was more direct, as with New Year's song feasts, which could easily take the form of unconcealed aggressive begging. The prohibition of annoying disorderly conduct was such a regular feature of legislative routine that in 1592, true to custom, the magistrate of Amsterdam at the public lottery for the insane asylum forbade not only the throwing of mud and stones, but also the throwing of snowballs,[125] even though the draw took place in August.

It seems, however, that drinking and feasting Hollanders had their heads so full of liberty that they did not bother about the discomfort of others, and would not let anyone tell them to be quiet. During the *kermis*, the surgeons had their busy season.[126] 'A hundred Netherlanders, a hundred knives', went the proverb.[127] Hollanders very quickly came to blows. Just as duelling among soldiers could not be stamped out, despite heavy penalties,[128] and the warrior made known his challenge 'for all manner of petty sayings, that one or another according to the petulance of his humour would immediately interpret as an affront',[129] so did the burghers and peasants of Holland draw their knives at the slightest provocation. In one disturbance at the bowling green of Leiden in 1612, two young men aged eighteen, Frans Joosten Parmentier and Jan Bouwensz., had an argument. It cannot have been very serious, because they 'went outside together in good spirits', though with an understanding that 'each [would] hit or fight the other'. This led to a knife-fight, through which Jan received a stab-wound in the stomach, and Frans lay dead on the field of battle.[130] A game of cards,[131] an accidental bumping on the street,[132] or a mocking greeting[133] could have deadly consequences for those involved.

In such cases at least a motive could be found. In many villages, however, there were hooligans who would, from sheer enjoyment of fighting, offer to take on all comers in single combat. Jan Michielsz. Engelsman in Brill had planted a stick on the street in front of his house: anyone who removed it had to fight him.[134] Gerrit Kooyman went in 1608 to the *kermis* in Noordeloos and deliberately sought to quarrel with the villagers at the inn: 'Let any one of you come out of the heap, and fight with me'.[135] Various villages had their own permanent troublemakers, whose end could be predicted with fairly great certainty. These were men such as Hendrick Claes Adriaensz. of Naarden, known in all the taverns of that little town by the name of 'Harry the Devil'.[136] Gerrit Jansen of Noordeloos died in 1616 in a tavern brawl that no one but himself had wanted.[137] Heinrick Gerritsz. of Huizen was such 'a great troublemaker during his lifetime' that he, too, like most of these champions, lost his life in one-to-one combat.[138] In these men we recognise the 'Surly Arent' of Bredero's Peasant Company, who was always ready to draw his knife first at peasant festivals, which usually had a bloody outcome.[139] Or they resemble Van Buchell's description of the Waterlands peasants with their dangerous drunk,[140] who makes us understand what a blessing the pacifism of the Anabaptists must have been for those parts.

Knife-fights were apparently an acceptable risk of daily life for the general public. Perhaps this was particularly so in the countryside, but it also happened in cities. In The Hague in 1616 it was necessary to forbid the servants and lackeys of all masters to carry rapiers, daggers, guns, pistols, sticks or other weapons, because 'great insolences and wanton mischief have taken place here in The Hague on the public streets'.[141] This was nothing but the truth, because in the heart of the city of the prince's residence, in May, 1616, at eleven o'clock in the morning on the Lange Vijverberg, a man was stabbed ten times by his assailant before anyone came between them.[142] Perhaps the perpetrator had sought out a quiet moment, but the clerks working in government offices who had a view over the Hofvijver apparently did nothing about it, according to their depositions as witnesses, apart from pressing their noses flat against the windows.

Numerous indeed were the legal measures that were supposed to restrain the popular taste for fighting. The States of Holland in their proclamation of 1589 required everyone who came to drink at an inn to leave his knife at home or to deposit it with the innkeeper, under penalty of a fine of three gulden. If the innkeeper poured drinks for those who refused to hand over their weapons, then he himself was liable to a fine of six gulden. Anyone who drew his weapon first 'in wrathful spirit' would have to pay twenty gulden, even if he did not wound anyone. Causing a wound 'other than necessary defence and protection of one's own body' would cost the perpetrator thirty gulden and corporal punishment.[143] Many such ordinances were primarily enacted at the local level,[144] with varying punishments. When large groups of men had to stay together for prolonged periods, precautions went so far as forbidding pouring and tapping altogether, for example at dikeworks[145] and on the herring fleet.[146] The penalties were sometimes not as severe as those of the proclamation of 1589, but it appears that the authorities did not believe moderate penalties were desirable. In the bailiwick of Woerden at least the amounts were increased, because fighting broke out so often 'owing to the smallness of the fines'. The new proposals are detailed in table 6.[147] The list is long enough to suggest that the Woerden regents had thought of everything. Yet they must have known that their ordinance would not bring an end to the combativeness of their subjects. The sources of Holland make clear enough that the crime of homicide occurred frequently. Then of course armed fighting must have been even more common, even if we take into account that owing to minimal hygiene and the lack of medical knowledge many wounds that were not inherently fatal nonetheless had a deadly outcome.[148]

16. *Outdoor scene*, by Adriaen van Ostade

Manslaughter must not be confused with murder.[149] Murder was a sensational event, at least as soon as the ills of civil war in Holland had passed. The robbery and murder of the jeweller Van Wely in The Hague was the talk of all the Netherlands, even in Ghent and Brussels. When the culprits were broken on the wheel, a stream of curious onlookers came from near and far to witness the execution.[150] A murder was written up in pamphlets, and sung in ballads.[151] When the conspirators in the planned attack on Maurice in 1623 landed in an Amsterdam prison, they brought considerable profit to their keepers: many folk were ready to pay six stuivers each 'in order to see these monsters'.[152]

The great difference between murder and manslaughter appears with striking clarity in the fate of the best-known participant in the attack, the ex-preacher Slatius. He was arrested as a fugitive in Drente, without his captors knowing who he was. Slatius then tried to gain his freedom and at the same time to explain his flight by pretending to be a man who had committed manslaughter in Amsterdam. That was not stupidity on his part, but rather careful calculation. Slatius was speculating on the widely held opinion of his contemporaries that manslaughter had nothing in common with murder, and was a private matter between the perpetrator and the blood relations of the victim. A man who wanted to flee after committing manslaughter seldom saw obstacles placed in his path.[153] If, however, he remained in the place where the deed was done, the punishment imposed was generally not very harsh. Pieter Pietersz. of Brill, condemned to serve a year on the galleys for double manslaughter, regained his freedom after twenty weeks of rowing.[154] Frans Abramsz. of Weesp received the usual penalty at the bailiwick of Muiden in 1622: a fine of one hundred gulden and banishment from his place of residence. However, he was quickly considered for a pardon, because he was favourably regarded.[155]

Yet even men of bad reputation did not have to fear too much from the forces of justice. The aforementioned hooligan 'Harry the Devil' of Naarden had in his life committed one homicide, 'which was not favourable at all', and yet he received no harsher penalty than a fine.[156] Bredero may have been accurate when in the *Farce of the Cow* he noted that among the 'experienced spirited fellows who briskly

Table 6. *Penalties for fighting at Woerden, 1611*

	gulden
Hitting with fists?	3
Drawing a knife	6
Spitting	6
Causing superficial wounds	9
Carrying a knife longer than 7 inches	12
Selling such knives	12
Causing serious wounds (one *lid* deep or two long)	12
Threatening knocking on a door or window	20
Breaking windows	20
Throwing stones	20
Breaking and entering with force	40
Attacking innocent bystanders on the street	30 and corporal punishment
Hitting the prosecutor or witness	loss of the right hand
Committing acts of violence after entering by force	loss of life

strike with their knives' there was one who had already committed manslaughter,[157] and nonetheless still lived in the village. Only under aggravating circumstances did manslaughter become a capital offence. Pieter Anthonisz. Deutera in Korter Aar had visited Salomon Willemsz. in his own house and stabbed him, without the victim having drawn a weapon. The premeditated evil intention marked this deed as 'a very enormous ugly fact'. In fact it was no longer manslaughter, but murder, and the perpetrator was executed.[158]

Such an outcome was the exception. The understanding of manslaughter as a private matter did of course imply that the doer had to reach agreement with the victim's relatives. This was chiefly a financial transaction, the payment of compensation to the immediate family,[159] but that had to go hand in hand with reconciliation. In these practices we see the remnants of the old vendetta, which obviously had not disappeared altogether. Occasionally the deceased's next of kin would still be identified as the one to seek revenge.[160] The law, which did not punish blood relations for hiding one who had committed manslaughter – a crime that could carry a fine of 100 gulden for others[161] – also recognised that families had a distinct position in the conflict.

The strictest view, here as elsewhere in this chapter, was held by the church. It repeatedly protested to the authorities against the ease with which homicide was committed and forgiven in Holland.[162] The church took offence when its buildings were used to atone for killing, and regarded that as dishonour to God's house and temple.[163] It was also extremely reserved in its attitude toward penitent killers, and did not readily allow them at the communion table.[164]

Thus the church tried to conquer sin and nature, but without any spectacular success. Yet the civil authorities could do little more than weakly moderate and channel the disorder. Nature showed itself stronger than either of them. Therefore we have good reason for saying that in this chapter we have met the Hollander of the seventeenth century as he actually was. Part I has shown us that social inequality did not pose a serious threat to internal order. In part III it will become clear that political inequality did not bring about excessive tension either. But in the pursuit of their natural desires the popular classes would allow no one to read them the riot act. Here it appears that they had the power to work their own will. With this victory they remained content. They could hardly have chosen a worse field of endeavour if they wished for a lasting improvement in their condition.

Chapter 8

UPBRINGING

When the Amsterdam silk merchant Isaäc Vlamingh took an apprentice in his service in 1636, he had the rights and obligations of both parties specified in a notarial contract. This was not at all unusual. The archives of the notaries of Holland contain hundreds of such contracts. In this agreement, however, we encounter a less common stipulation. The master insisted that his apprentice should not allow his hair to grow longer than his ears. If it exceeded this limit, he was to get it cut at once.[1]

It was a rather strange rule, but it did not breach the norms of law or behaviour for seventeenth-century people. An employer was empowered to hold his apprentices to such conditions. Not only was he charged with giving them satisfactory vocational training, but he also took general responsibility for the education of the boys that were entrusted to him. In 1624 the magistrate of Geertruidenberg, occupied with the task of putting down a tax revolt, announced strict regulations against anyone who would still feed the unrest. Adults had to take responsibility for their own actions. But 'whatever is done by boys, girls or children will be blamed on their parents or masters and punished' [accordingly].[2] The master, in this case not the teacher but the employer, could be held responsible as if he were the child's father, because his duty was not only to train the children for the bakery or the shoemaker's shop, but also to prepare them for state and society.

This preparation could also take place at home with the parents or at school under the master. The three possibilities were roughly equivalent inasmuch as they satisfied the essential purpose of all education. Naturally the parents played the most important role, because they were irreplaceable during the first years of their children's lives. The parents also had to decide which preparation for social life they wished to give their son or daughter. 'To the education of children', says Simon van Leeuwen, 'pertains not only the use of food and drink, but also clothing, housing, comfort, ease, discipline, teaching and learning of various arts and crafts, according to each one's condition and opportunity.'[3] The choice really resided in the last point. Every couple had to provide food, clothing, housing and discipline for their children. But education and vocational training varied according to condition and opportunity.

This did not necessarily mean attendance at school, and in any case education is far more than that. Schools, as the Deputised Councils (Gecommitteerde Raden) of Holland put it in 1623, 'are like gardens, where the love of God and respect for legal authority must be transplanted into the young'.[4] The same philosophy inspired the States of Holland in 1596, when they took steps to hire a schoolmaster in Cilaarshoek because owing to the lack of education many children 'grow up in frivolity and lewdness'.[5] The authorities saw education as more than imparting various skills, for 'education of the young in the fear of God' served in the first place 'to make the same turn away and keep from all rashness and unsuitableness'.[6] That goal could be achieved through education at school, or equally well by 'teaching the youth a trade or making him suited to some other work, that in future times he would be able to earn his keep honestly and dutifully'.[7] People then saw nothing wrong with child labour. Everyone had to learn contentedly how to earn his daily bread in a worthy trade or profession. If for his occupation he did not need to know how to read, write or count, there was no social necessity whatsoever for him to go to school. Perhaps there was some religious reason for it, but that will be considered later. If a resident of Leiden was correct when he stated that 'the working people multiply twice as fast as the people of quality',[8] the domestic interests of most fathers and mothers would also have been better served by children who began earning early instead of spending a long time learning.

While schoolmasters and employers were recognised educators who had to work in accordance with more or less defined norms, a certain amount of control was necessary to ensure they observed them. This was particularly true for the school, which could also count on drawing the attention of the church. In line with tradition, education had always been an affair of the church, and Protestants placed even higher worth on it than Catholics. The purpose of education lay within the religious community itself. It was not a question of helping the people to develop their talents, for writing or counting was not intrinsically more valuable to the church than milking cows or basket-weaving. Indeed, the parents were the ones who decided which of these things each child would learn, according to condition and opportunity. I do not know of any cases where the parents were admonished by their church council or preacher for not sending their children to school. But as the church of the Bible, the reformed church did desire that as many children and adults as possible would be able to read that Bible.

The true purpose of the reformed religious schools was preparation for church membership. How this education was understood becomes crystal clear in the instruction drawn up for schoolmasters in the neighbouring region of Utrecht in 1588.[9] Anyone who wanted to start a school had to take an examination from the *classis* and sign the confession of the reformed church. The master was required to teach the children the catechism and the psalms. He had to take them along to the sermon, and warn them against the errors of the Papists, Anabaptists and other sectaries. In Holland it was not specified that the school had to be so precisely attuned to the service of the church. But a proclamation of 1589 did forbid the use of books 'that contradict the Christian religion',[10] and there we must not interpret the word 'Christian' too widely. No teacher was putting out atheist propaganda: rather, this order was directed against Rome. It was entirely in the spirit of the reformed church, but a regulation on its own did not mean very much. If the way to reformed education were to be opened, two things in particular were necessary.

In the first place continuous control was naturally required. The church would have liked it best if no one was allowed to practise the profession of teacher without its approval. That would, however, have required the unconditional co-operation of all local authorities, and was thus an unattainable ideal.[11] In several communities the church councils did manage to achieve fairly intensive supervision. In villages this probably required little organisational talent. When the schoolmaster of Barendrecht used his classroom for the establishment of a lottery,[12] or when people in Naaldwijk never saw the children appear in church under the guidance of their teacher,[13] no inspection was needed to bring these irregularities to light. In cities, however, the work demanded a more deliberate approach. Perhaps it could still be done casually in smaller towns,[14] but in larger ones a system was needed. At Haarlem for example it was decided in 1621 that all preachers and elders of the Walloon and Holland churches would visit the schools of their quarter every month.[15] In Amsterdam around 1600 control was less frequent but very intensive when it did take place: it then kept the controllers busy for two weeks.[16]

Oversight alone was not sufficient. The church had to have sanctions at its disposal, and exercise real power over the schoolmaster. That was possible if its influence was great enough to procure his dismissal. In the villages the church frequently did have that power.[17] There the schoolmaster had to bow to its wishes. If agreement was impossible, the teacher had to depart, but he did not thereby escape from the control of the reformed church. In most cases he would try to begin another school elsewhere, and then a good reference from his previous post was indispensable. Consequently the schoolmaster who left under a cloud still preferred to bring about a formal reconciliation.[18]

The church was thus able to achieve something, but its possibilities remained limited. Power does not extend very far unless it can count on money. In her book on education in the province of Utrecht, Engelina P. De Booy has rightly noted that schoolmasters could only take the rules of the church seriously if they were no longer financially dependent on the parents.[19] We observe this in Holland, too. The schoolmaster of Grote Lindt complained in 1587 to the *classis* of Dordrecht that 'he had lost his children, because he wanted to teach them the catechism'.[20] As a result of the pluralist nature of religious life in Holland, the schools that did precisely what the reformed church wanted and tailored their instruction according to the reformed religion might be shunned by Catholic or Anabaptist parents. Each child fewer meant lower earnings for the teacher, because tuition was one of his most important sources of income. Thus prominently displaying the Heidelberg catechism and other textbooks approved by the reformed church might have meant sacrifice on his part. In the confessionally divided cities, the result was a flow of students to private schools[21] – as was noted more than once in Haarlem, for example.[22]

For our period it is highly unlikely that the schoolmaster received so much salary from the public purse that he could be indifferent to tuition fees. The point has not yet been as systematically studied in Holland as De Booy has done in neighbouring Utrecht. In particular little is known about tuition fees in Holland, although the quarterly charges at Rotterdam in 1632 have been established. Anyone who was registered only for reading paid twenty stuivers; pupils who also wanted lessons in writing had to pay thirty stuivers, and the combination of reading, writing and arithmetic came to fifty stuivers.[23] These sums appear rather high compared to the figures found at Utrecht, where in the first half of the seventeenth century reading cost three to four stuivers per month, reading and writing four to five stuivers.[24] The comparison is not very sound, however, because it is based on only one city in Holland, and only four villages in Utrecht. We do not know much about the teachers' salaries, either. In Utrecht for our period five statutes are known, namely Lopik 1623 (100 gld.), Kudelstaart 1624 (24 gld.), Kamerik 1631 (48 gld.), Jutphaas 1635 (120 gld.), and Tienhoven 1640 (100 gld.). It is clear that these sums could not have been the entire incomes of the teachers. The best-paid were still earning far less than skilled or even unskilled labourers.[25]

In Holland the situation was probably no different. Heyndrick Lambrechtsen of Klein Ammers, earning six gulden per year in 1622, was an exceptional case.[26] But the schoolmaster of Loosduinen, who enjoyed ten times as much in 1586,[27] was not able to live on that sum either. Church gatherings also complained more than once about 'the austere maintenance of schoolteachers'.[28] Nonetheless no general regulations were enacted at this time. Since 1594 there had been a fixed minimum salary for preachers in Holland,[29] but there was no similar regulation for school-teachers. Apparently the public purse was inadequate. In 1620 the Amsterdam *classis* proposed a tax on the non-reformed schools for the benefit of the ordinary schoolmasters.[30] Jealousy could have played a part in this, as well as intolerance towards these institutions, which were often Catholic; at the same time it is evidence that ordinary funds were inadequate for the payment of decent salaries.

Thus frequently a schoolmaster was not only dependent on tuition fees, but also obliged to seek other kinds of work. Master Valcoogh said that the village authorities had only one requirement for the appointment of a teacher: he must come cheap. If he could satisfy this condition, 'then the game is won with them, even if the interests of the entire community and surrounding area would suffer, and keep their dear children in perpetual ignorance of reading and writing'.[31] Valcoogh thus thought it quite natural that the ill-paid teacher would earn extra money:

> Because an austere regimen is often
> Given to the schoolteachers here in this land,
> For the reason, that their salaries are rather meagre,
> Therefore they must be complainers.
> Yes, they have no stalls with cows either;
> So it should be, that they make do
> With some manual labour [*handtwerck*], to build their houses.[32]

Handwerk can indeed be understood here as work with the hands. The schoolmasters of Utrecht often doubled as gravediggers.[33] That probably happened in Holland,

17. *Schoolmaster with three pupils*, by Adriaen van Ostade

too, because the little jobs around the church and cemetery – sexton, bellringer, lector, choirmaster, gravedigger – easily lent themselves to combination with school teaching. The teachers of Holland also appear as village secretaries, once again in a position analogous to those of their colleagues in Utrecht, although people in both provinces really thought that this job was too burdensome for part-time work.[34]

Many a schoolmaster occupied in this manner would have been unable to give his classes the attention required by the interests of the children. The quality of education positively suffered because of the combinations. But these part-time jobs were also a means for maintaining popular education. The civil war of the 1570s had put a stop to many schools in Holland, and afterwards the transition from Catholicism to Protestantism again led to hitches and interruptions. At the end of the sixteenth century, we can probably say that in nearly every village of reasonable size a school could be found.

In the cities, the supply of education was probably proportionate to size. In 1620 Gouda had in all twenty to twenty-five male and female teachers.[35] We cannot tell how many children they had in their collective charge. We know very little about the size of schools, and it is scarcely possible to find exact figures because school attendance was strongly affected by seasonal influences.[36] For Utrecht, De Booy comes to the hesitant conclusion that in the eighteenth century a prosperous village school had about sixty pupils,[37] but of course this figure is nothing to go by for the cities of Holland in the early seventeenth century. If every teacher in Gouda in 1620 represented sixty children, then the total number of pupils could have been 1,200 to 1,500. Yet that would be a rather high figure for a city of about 14,000 inhabitants, which was certainly not the richest in Holland.

No doubt there were many schools in Holland, and some of them had large enrolments. A man of experience such as Master Valcoogh thought it necessary in any case to develop a sort of Bell–Lancaster method, 'how a teacher could hear daily four hundred children, nonetheless receiving good instruction'.[38] In this period it is completely unbelievable that there could have been any school in Holland with 400 pupils, which could have given the teacher an income from tuition fees higher than those of university professors of the period.

The seventeenth-century teacher did have one thing in common with the professor: there was no professional training for his job, but at the level of elementary education this situation presented almost no advantages. Presumably the only ones who prepared for teaching under expert guidance were the sons of serving teachers. A school could be passed from father to son just like any other business. At least that gave the assurance that the new holder had been able to learn the art from his predecessor. Thus in Graft in 1588 Cornelis Willemszoon took over the school from Willem Corneliszoon, who had been in service for thirty years, also as the successor to his father, whose term as schoolmaster at Graft had begun in 1521. The same probably happened in other places as well. The only reason why we know of this Graft dynasty is that in 1588 Cornelis Willemszoon was still a minor, and therefore not legally entitled to succeed to the post. He received permission from the States of Holland to allow a certain Jacob Laurenszoon to do the actual teaching temporarily.[39]

Thus we see that the public schoolteacher was a licence holder, who received an official appointment and could not establish himself freely. There were minimum requirements of age, and professional qualifications as well. In 1580 the States of Holland refused to appoint Jan Roelofszoon of Woerden, as long as he had given no information about 'the institution and teaching that will be done by him to the children'.[40] This could imply an investigation into the man's ability, although in the partly Lutheran community of Woerden it is no less likely that the question was raised because of suspicions about his orthodoxy.

Insofar as the investigation was in the hands of church councils, one can be sure that religious impurities would have been an insuperable obstacle, although lack of knowledge of the subject was not. The Haarlem *classis* in September, 1619, allowed Josias van de Lanoote to be a teacher, but with the admonition that 'in the meantime he should diligently practise his writing and singing'.[41] A *classis* would not have been so liberal about the signing of the confession of faith, certainly not in September, 1619, when all teachers were firmly held to the educational rules of the Synod of Dordt.[42]

In fairness one should grant that the *classes* did not always have a free hand. They could delay an appointment, but not make one on their own. In Holland at least I have found no signs of the appointment of schoolmasters by church councils.[43] They did as a rule control the teaching, or tried to, but they had no say in the appointment. Church influence on the matter of orthodoxy was accepted; if however it was a matter of judging professional suitability, then it is questionable whether the opinion of a *classis* or church council carried any extra weight. That would certainly have been difficult in those cases where considerations of a personal nature had pushed a particular candidate to the fore. A cooper's son of Gouda was appointed as schoolteacher in 1605, because his 'bad gait and lameness' did not allow him to earn his living any other way.[44] Apparently employment in the schools functioned here as social welfare for unemployed labourers. One might also doubt the qualifications of a teacher at Brill, who had participated in the battle of the Dunes as a drummer on Tromp's flagship.[45] According to Master Valcoogh, the subject knowledge of the schoolteachers of Holland was in a sorry state. 'Those who could barely write their names, and sing a psalm in an unedifying manner, rushed at once to schoolteaching.'[46] But we should not take Valcoogh as an impartial witness; fortunately we have a means of verifying his judgment. We already know that agencies of the reformed church exercised supervision over the schoolmaster. In the first place this had to do with fulfilling his obligations to the religious community. Yet an incompetent schoolteacher would probably also have short-comings as a catechist and religious instructor, so that complaints about the quality of teaching must have left at least some traces in religious archives.

Indeed that is the case. In 1598 Jan Cornelisz. of Schipluiden had to promise to take lessons in writing and spelling from the *dominee*, because 'various complaints arise daily that his writing is not good enough to teach the children well'.[47] Master Leenaert of Assendelft, equally unskilled in writing, used the same reading-booklets for too long a time, by which he 'caused the children to have disgust for learning'; nor did he understand the art of disciplining disorderly elements 'with proper Christian punishment'.[48] While that relates to the pedagogical side of his job, simple complaints about schoolteachers' lack of competence are not very numerous. Besides the two mentioned above, there was one by *dominee* Pieter Seghers of Simonshaven, who once declared at the *classis* meeting of Brill 'that he would like to be in a place where his children would be taught better in the schools'.[49] But there too some reservations are in order. The relationship between schoolmaster and preacher could not be called ideal in all the villages of Holland. We know of some communities where the teachers challenged the position of the local preachers as fellow intellectuals within the church.[50] The distance between the two was really not very great, as long as the universities were not yet in a position to satisfy the demand for new preachers in sufficient numbers. Certainly until the 1620s many ordinands came from the ranks of those who did not have academic training, the so-called Dutch clerics. A not insignificant portion of them were schoolteachers,[51] who had risen to this dignity through practical exercise in preaching. For an eloquent schoolteacher, the road from the classroom lectern to the pulpit was then not so long. But the schoolteacher stood much lower in esteem; in the church he had no official authority whatsoever. If the preacher or the schoolteacher was a singular personality with even a few pronounced human weaknesses, then conflicts were not long in coming. Such a personality, no doubt about it, was the afore-mentioned Pieter Seghers of Simonshaven.[52] It is certainly possible that there was also something lacking in the schoolteacher. Bad teachers were not all that uncommon in the seventeenth century. But in general I think that the limited number of cases involving schoolteachers in the acts of the *classes* justifies a positive conclusion. Among a group that produced so many candidates for the ministry, there should also have been no shortage of men sufficiently gifted to teach children how to read and write properly.

Did the children take advantage of this? We already know that various kinds of education were offered. Education began with reading, and cost more for writing and arithmetic. In Utrecht it took on average three years for children to make satisfactory progress towards reading.[53] Ordinarily they began to learn writing only when they were eight or nine years old.[54] De Booy appears fully justified in her conclusion that this education must have produced a number of alumni who could read but not write.[55] This could have important consequences, particularly as historians have tried to measure the rate of illiteracy by sampling the marriage registers of Amsterdam. There, but not in other places, the bride and groom had to sign their names to the banns.[56] When it appears that in 1630 one out of every three men and two out of every three women were unable to sign, we learn something about the ability to write, but the percentage of pure illiterates should by all accounts have been lower. Unfortunately, we do not have any means of measuring the difference.

The same uncertainty remains present in every other survey of signatures; more-over, it is generally necessary to set separate conditions for each group surveyed. This holds true for the Amsterdam bridegrooms in any case. The majority of them had been born outside Amsterdam, and a large percentage even came from outside the United Provinces;[57] consequently their ability to sign their names tells us little about the efficiency of schools in Holland. We do know that at the end of the seventeenth century over 80 per cent of the sailors of North Holland were able to write.[58] Another category large enough to permit statistical study consists of the witnesses and defendants in criminal trials. Among them, however, the lower elements of society would have been over-represented, and furthermore so would foreign elements. Thus the percentages of such groups who could write would certainly have been below the average of all Hollanders, as was probably also the case with Amsterdam bridegrooms.

Nonetheless further research in criminal records could well be rewarding, not only because of the figures themselves, but also because witnesses generally gave their occupation and age. Thus for example after the Delft tax riot of August, 1616, thirty-nine men and eight women were questioned. All of them gave their ages, and thirty-four of them gave their occupation or quality.[59] A mass of such documentation would allow a sharper focus on illiteracy in various occupations and age-groups. The age-distribution of these Delft witnesses is very suggestive (see table 7). The high percentage of non-writers among the middle-aged witnesses is quite striking. Actually it is certainly imaginable that the disturbed years of the Duke of Alba's rule and the civil war had a lasting influence on the writing ability of the generations that were then pupils at school. A confusing factor, however, is that in this small group of forty-seven persons, in which middle-aged women are over-represented and thus affect the results unfavourably, only one of the female witnesses could sign her name. In most legal cases the number of witnesses examined was much smaller. But this should not present a problem, because sound results can only be gathered by cumulative counting anyway.

If similar quantitative surveys are to confirm the narrative sources, then their results must be positive. Foreign travellers give us the impression that the general educational level in the Netherlands was rather high by European standards. Guicciardini had already reported that in the countryside nearly everyone could read or write;[60] half a century later Scaliger declared that peasant men and women as well as servant-girls were acquainted with writing.[61] Gerrit de Veer related in his journal during a winter's stay at Nova Zembla that there, too, people passed the time with reading.[62] Perhaps he was speaking of himself, or he may have meant reading aloud; but some letters[63] that have been preserved by chance prove that among the sailors, who certainly could not be said to have a high level of cultural development, at least some could be found who knew how to use a pen. In 1616 a

Table 7. *Writing ability among witnesses at Delft, 1616*

age	writers	non-writers
61–65	0	1
51–60	7	2
41–50	6	6
31–40	7	7
21–30	6	3
17–20	2	0

number of sailors who organised a plot to take over the ship *West-Vrieslant* and turn to piracy, took an oath to each other in writing: 'twenty-eight of them had signed in a round circle'.[64] What a pity that we do not know how many *x*'s were in that circle!

Writing ability among these neglected step-children of culture may exceed our expectations, but that is balanced by the lack of writing found among some persons whose position in society would have led us to expect more. Among the Remonstrant-minded civic guards of Oudewater in 1618 there were more than thirty who could not sign their names,[65] although it was customary in selecting civic guards to pass over the lowest classes. Another elite group, church council members, appears in villages to have included a fairly substantial number of non-writers.[66] At Sliedrecht in 1589 the deacons kept no accounts, because none of them could write.[67] It is impossible to say whether the top layer of justice and administration in the villages was better provided. An act of the bailiff, councillors, judges, bookkeepers, Masters of the Holy Spirit and inhabitants of Boskoop carries thirty-eight signatures, of which twenty-two are names and sixteen marks.[68] This was certainly not an amazingly good score, or did the simple inhabitants spoil the statistic? Jacob Jacobsz. of Nieuwpoort was, according to his fellow inhabitants, well suited to the office of councillor, but he positively did not want to do it, 'as knowing neither reading nor writing'.[69] Presumably he feared getting out of his depth, but at the same time it is clear that people in this small town regarded a pure illiterate as quite acceptable for the job. Apart from the administration, village life offered few possibilities for social promotion with the help of knowledge gained at school. In a pamphlet of the 1630s, the peasant Keesje Maet, who had enough of his meagre wages as a farm labourer, decided to leave for the city. 'I mean to go for a stroll to The Hague, and will seek my fortune there; I know some reading and writing, and a bit of arithmetic'.[70] With these qualities he thought to get ahead at The Hague. Apparently he did not see such opportunities in his village.

Finally let us say a word about women and girls. We heard from Scaliger that the peasant women and servant-girls could write. That was said pretty plainly, but Bredero went even further. He allowed his Amsterdam girls of pleasure to try to read a pawn-ticket, although it's true that the writing was too hard for them.[71] Did they try it in order to appear grand, or was their reading a half-learned skill that had atrophied from want of use? Provisionally I should think the former was the case. While court records do show occasional servant-girls who appeared as witnesses and signed their names, thus confirming Scaliger's observation,[72] 'nescit scribere' were still in the overwhelming majority. Even the schoolmaster's wife had to sign with a cross at a hearing held in Zevenhuizen in 1619.[73] It is conceivable that girls were more likely than boys to stay at school only a short time, thus learning to read but not to write. We are told that the daughter of a Haarlem watchmaker went to school specifically in order to learn reading and sewing.[74] Indeed some contemporaries regarding the schooling of girls as somewhat less important. In 1595 Bodegraven had two schoolteachers, Adolf Pietersz. Doen and

Cornelis Harmensz. The latter gave lessons only to girls, 'because he was found otherwise unsuitable'.[75]

Girls went to work in society early, but many boys did, too. They learned a trade and started it young. Their bosses then became their most important educators.

There was a surplus of working children, and of various kinds. The elite consisted of children whose parents paid training fees to the boss for several years. Many of those contracts still exist. We also know something of the fees that were supposed to be paid in Amsterdam. The sums varied between forty-five and 300 gulden.[76] Only reasonably prosperous parents could afford such arrangements. Wage earners, whose annual incomes seldom exceeded 200 gulden,[77] were not in a position to pay such costs for even one child. They had to get the boys and girls earning money for the family as soon as possible. The poorest, or perhaps also the most short-sighted, could be tempted to seek that income from street-selling, probably often nothing more than disguised begging. Child labour of this sort had a bad name. There were grey areas. In 1608 at Overschie an argument arose between two members of the reformed church, 'whose children both walked along the street with biscuits, cause of the dispute'. The preacher, Goris Adriaensz., tried to act as intermediary but failed; he called for help from the *classis*, which responded very cautiously. The *dominee* should 'admonish both of them to peace and unity, nonetheless without trying to lay down the law on their trade'.[78] Apparently the *classis* had no objection to the biscuit trade as such. If these were goods that the parents themselves prepared and sold, we can understand that such help in the family business was regarded as morally acceptable. It was comparable to the work that weavers' children were required to do in their own homes: as a child of five, Paschier de Fyne, who later became a preacher, got up at four in the morning to help his parents with the spinning.[79]

Child labour was condemned, however, when it contained no training element at all. Parents who sent their children out peddling without teaching them some manual skills were guilty of pure exploitation.[80] Child labour should be a preparation for the future. Thus in 1597 the city government of Amsterdam forbade the carrying of fish by children, because 'young girls and others, employed in carrying fish, grow up in all kinds of disorderliness, without learning any trade that could suit them for other work, with which they could in future times honestly and dutifully earn their living'.[81] This regulation shows us where the line was drawn. Child labour in itself was not wrong; but there were objections to work that taught children nothing, and which they would eventually outgrow.

Thus for seventeenth-century people child labour was not a moral issue. They even thought it was good that children should work. In practice, however, two difficult problems arose. Many children were not in a position to pay the apprenticeship fees. No one could reproach the employers for being unwilling to give them training for free. Consequently, the pupils had to pay with their labour. But then the danger was great that the employer would keep them busy with all kinds of menial tasks that were profitable for himself, but taught the children nothing at all – 'in-between work and boy's work'.[82] There were frequent complaints that the bosses used their boys 'more as slaves than as pupils learning trades'.[83] They had to help with housework, take care of small children,[84] runs errands, and perform all kinds of busy-work that contributed nothing to their competence in the trade.

To curb this abuse somewhat, there was often a regulation that a master could only take a limited number of apprentices into his service.[85] Thus a shoemaker at The Hague could take only one apprentice per year, and a tailor only one every two years. The masters of the St Luke's Guild could never have more than one apprentice at a time, the buttonmakers only two. The swordmakers could only allow a second apprentice to begin when their first one had completed four full years.[86] Yet these regulations did not settle the matter. Apprentices still flocked to the masters, and took years to achieve the required craftsmanship. The official periods of apprenticeship for boys who did not pay were already generally longer than the two or three years for the paying pupils[87] – in Amsterdam generally seven years.[88]

Even if a master kept to the regulations and worked with only a few apprentices, giving sufficient care to their training, there was always the second problem. Payment in kind with labour may sound good in theory, but in an oversupplied labour market the value of apprentice labour was not great. For the boss expenses were unavoidable, because the proclamation of 1597 required him to take care of food, clothing and sleeping accommodation.[89] Now we know that around 1600 the cost of maintaining a child must have come to about forty gulden per year.[90] If we add to this figure the cost of raw materials spoilt by a beginning apprentice, then it is clear that the masters of guild, who were not great capitalists themselves, had to pour money into a young beginner for a long time. Furthermore they ran the risk that the boys would first eat their masters out of house and home, and then change masters when they thought they were worth their keep. Naturally this could be forbidden,[91] but it was practically impossible to enforce such a prohibition.

In fact many small independent craftsmen left apprentices to shift for themselves. They did hold them to the work, but the boys had to find their own food and drink. In most cities the proclamation of 1597 remained a dead letter. Earlier, less restrictive proclamations were observed: they allowed craft apprentices to practise begging,[92] or gave them support from local public welfare funds.[93] In 1613 Amsterdam did try to require observance of the 1597 proclamation by an absolute prohibition of begging: 'the masters who take boys into their service will themselves have to maintain and care for them'.[94] But in 1614 the States of Holland returned to the traditional solution, permission to beg for all craft apprentices who were not yet earning money, or earned too little.[95] Some years might pass before their own wages were sufficient. In 1631 the drapers of Delft set the tariff shown in table 8.[96] Since in this case the minimum age for beginning apprenticeship was ten, not until age fourteen would an apprentice be more or less able to support himself without help. In other trades the boys' wages were sometimes higher, for example in the silk industry,[97] but in our period no real solution to the problem of apprenticeship was found.

Later periods brought the realisation that public welfare support was essential. But this notion was still absent in the seventeenth century, even though the problem of training must have been a source of worry and concern to the government. If the apprentices stayed in servitude for a long time and did not advance very far, then the specific purpose of their training was endangered, namely that they must earn their own keep. The general purpose of all education was also threatened: they should learn to fear God and to obey the authorities. An Amsterdam statute of 1597 found it very troubling that 'the craft children grow up in such a disorderly and godless manner that they neither hear sermons, nor learn to fear or honour God or man'.[98]

Against this background it is easier for us to understand why magistrates in the cities took special measures on behalf of those children particularly entrusted to their guardianship: the orphans who were so numerous in the seventeenth century. Their parents had not been able to provide for their care. Judged by the standards and possibilities of the seventeenth century, the masters of the orphanages, poor-relief officers, and other welfare authorities can probably not be faulted for providing the orphans training in larger firms, as conditions and opportunities allowed. These firms were better able than small masters to bear the initial losses that the employment of unskilled children necessarily implied. At least I should hesitate to say that this happened only 'under the cloak of vocational training',[99] as if the real intention had been merciless exploitation of children. The number of welfare-dependent children in seventeenth-century cities was very high.[100] If the authorities wanted to find work for all of them, they had to do so in the most advantageous manner, thus in the service of employers who could pay a relatively high share of the maintenance costs. Anyone who becomes outraged here may show signs of a strongly developed social consciousness, but even moral indignation remains bound to the ground rule of all historical research, an aversion to anachronism.

Let us examine, for example, one of the older agreements made in this area. Daniël de Meijer received permission to establish a weaving-shop in Rotterdam in 1614. The city agreed to put twenty orphan children at his disposal annually. According

Table 8. *Wages of drapers' apprentices at Delft, 1631*

First year	no wages
Second year	5 st. per week
Third year	10 st. per week
Fourth year	15 st. per week
Fifth year	20 st. per week
Sixth year	25 st. per week

to the contract, he would enjoy this help for sixteen years. Each child had to complete an apprenticeship of four years, without receiving wages.[101] Perhaps this would be intolerable if we changed the date to 1914, but in 1614 these contracted souls were not so badly off in comparison with ordinary apprentices. Their care was assured. Whether this sytem continued to exist in Rotterdam we do not know. But we do know that other towns followed this example. The town council of Naarden decided in 1638 to place all orphan boys who did not already have a trade at the disposal of the drapers. After their training was completed, they received a weaving-loom on loan.[102] Thus it is clear that there was a serious intention to make the years of apprenticeship in the weaver's trade the basis of the later occupation. It will not do to call this exploitation and busy-work.

Naturally, three parties were involved in such an agreement. Besides the children and the magistrates, the drapers also had their obligations. They formed the weakest link in the chain. For each employer the temptation was great to use his apprentices for work that had to be done anyway and could most advantageously be assigned to the least experienced workers. According to the regents of Delft, that was precisely what occurred with the orphans who were taken under contract by six drapers. When the magistrate investigated the situation in 1637, after six years had elapsed, he had to note that there were boys of fifteen and even nineteen years of age, who had already spent four years in training, and yet could do nothing more than carding, spinning and winding. They had not yet learned the actual manufacture of cloth, even though they often worked much longer than the agreed time of eleven or twelve hours per day, sometimes all through the night. The drapers had fallen short on their end of the bargain, and missed the purpose of the education. Since the children had not received any true vocational training, they were not suited 'at the appropriate time to earn their living honourably, to pay the costs of their keep and serve their city with their craft-labour'.[103]

In Delft it did indeed appear that child labour on a large scale – the original contract provided for 125 boys to be taken on[104] – had to be officially supervised if it were not to deteriorate into shameless exploitation. Delft itself did not draw that conclusion, because no regulations were enacted there,[105] not even when the government had become convinced that pitiful abuses were not coincidental occupational hazards, but rather a conscious system to extract the maximum amount of work.[106] In Leiden, where the rulers could draw on longer experience, the burgomasters did accept their responsibility in this matter. For the benefit of the children who had come from foreign places, particularly from Liège, Aachen and Jülich, two inspectors were employed in 1636. They had to pay attention to three points in particular. First, they had to check whether the parents of the young immigrants had indeed consented to their move. Then they had to investigate who 'was living in a merciless and un-Christian manner with his working children'. And finally they had to be convinced that the children were truly cared for, and not forced to go begging in the city or the countryside.[107] In this city with its masses of textile workers we find signs of more frequent public intervention on behalf of the apprentices. Diverse contracts specified that the boys had to learn to read at their masters' expense. When in practice this rule amounted to about as much as everyone could have predicted beforehand, the municipal government itself took measures. In 1648 Isaäc Jansz. was named schoolmaster for the Leiden apprentices in the cloth trade.[108] That this one Leiden swallow should have made a summer in all Holland is more than we can expect. The plan does testify to noble purposes, however little good intentions affected the labour policies of the seventeenth-century regents.

The question of the effectiveness of this education in the workplace is hard to answer. With education at school, it is at least possible to try to measure literacy,

18. 'The child goes to learn a trade', from Jan Luyken, *The three ages of man*, 1712

one of the possible results. By contrast, after three hundred years the professional competence of bakers, butchers, shoemakers and dozens of other craftsmen can no longer be evaluated, or can only be measured indirectly. None of them was personally indispensable. Each of them could have trifled away his time, cut his cloth wastefully, or hit his nails crookedly. Yet as a group they were essential to society. The prosperity of Holland did not rest solely on stadholders, regents and merchants. It was supported by a great mass of ordinary people who were not aware of their significance, but whose craftsmanship assured that the region of Holland would flourish.

The question would become even more difficult if we wanted to know whether the general purpose of all education was achieved in the workplace and in schools. Fear God and honour the king, as the Bible has it (1 Peter 2:17); or, as translated into a republican form consistent with the constitution of Holland: honour the regents. The relationship between the people and the government is indeed a theme that will be treated separately in the next part of this work. We should, however, say something now about the short-term effects of education, and the general methods used in trying to accomplish them. Seventeenth-century people wanted children to grow up in submissiveness. They had no objection whatsoever to a forceful approach. 'It is harmful to rule boys with a cheerful countenance', said Master Valcoogh[109] – a stern face and a hard hand were required. The teachers did have to restrain themselves: they could not be 'raging people cruel as bears and horses'.[110] For this aspersion on their character, the horses probably had to thank only the rhyming imperative of Valcoogh's didactic poem. But he must have known some ferocious schoolmasters, for otherwise why would he find it necessary to warn his colleagues that they must not break the children's legs, nor knock them unconscious, nor chastise them till they bled?

> Keep a cool head, be not hot in spirits,
> Your only instruments will be the strap and the rod.[111]

This forceful, sensible advice should indeed have been in harmony with the norms of the time. A child's life did not always have to be joy and cheerfulness. *That* would even have been harmful for bodily health, as Jacob Cats testified:

> It is good for children if they cry moderately,
> For (as learning teaches us) when someone sheds tears,
> So the bad vapours from moist brine disappear;
> The belly is warmed, and all the tough mucuses
> Are then momentarily forced to clear,
> The spleen opens itself, even if it is completely blocked;
> You, make sure that the child does not bottle up his tears.[112]

This advice was firmly anchored in educational theory. It was in agreement with the Bible and science, and Cats was certainly not a man to preach his moral lessons to others in order to make a secret, sneering exception of himself. Yet because he was so friendly and obliging in his relations precisely with those who were dependent on him,[113] we can hardly imagine the popular sage with a strap in one hand and a rod in the other. In everyday practice even Jacob Cats could well have been the kind of father whom Valcoogh complained about – one of those parents who no longer knew what punishment was, with the result that the children would lie and swear freely and wander through the streets like brutes, because their parents always let them do as they liked.[114]

Was this the despondency of a failing schoolteacher? Valcoogh's *Rule of the Dutch Schoolmasters* dates from 1591. A few years later, in 1594, the States of Holland sent a brief to all local authorities in the cities and towns in order to express, among other things, their concern that 'children are committing great disobediences and insolences towards their parents'.[115] Other observers agreed with them on this point. The church council of Voorburg asked the Court of Holland to forbid the Shrove Tuesday (Mardi Gras) games, 'because many parents who see their children do such business … do not have enough authority by themselves to prevent the same (as it so happens in these deplorable times)'.[116] Perhaps the reader will give no credence to this example if he remembers how his own youth or those of his children also showed this mark of deplorable times. Yet in that same year 1620 in Edam 'the recklessness and looseness of youth' and 'the laxity of parents, who are not doing their duty' occasioned a counterattack led from the pulpit and reinforced by home visits, in order to punish the worst sinners with church discipline.[117]

Nonetheless there was not much that church discipline could do about it. Church discipline was only for members of the reformed church. Their children were beyond its bounds as long as they had not yet formally joined the community themselves.[118] Disciplinary proceedings against children who disobeyed their parents were thus very rare.[119] But parents also were seldom admonished for not properly directing their children.[120] Were church-members such exemplary guardians – with the exception of those at Voorburg and Edam of course – or did church councils fail to see what kind of responsibility they could require of parents? It's a pity, really, that the preachers and consistories did not make a greater effort to enforce the fifth commandment. As a consequence, our knowledge of education at home remains somewhat shadowy. The churches did not react to it very much, and the government seldom intervened with regulations or punishments. In practice, family relationships and the boundaries of parental power depended only on natural feelings of justice and the accidental pedagogical talents of fathers and mothers.

If the child was not working in the family business in that period, he was presumably not too often under the watchful eyes of his parents. The small houses cannot have offered much opportunity for indoor play. Even in the households of reasonably well-to-do craftsmen this could only have been possible if there was room for toys in the workshop.[121] Furthermore party games for older children rather quickly took on a suspect character. The board game of fox and geese was probably all right,[122] but Master Valcoogh wanted nothing to do with cards and dice.[123] Children at play, at least the children of the working classes, were often to be found in the street. There they could keep busy with the virtuous entertainments that one finds depicted on prints and tiles of the time, such as trundling hoops, spinning tops, playing knuckle-bones and leapfrog. Here the visual arts provide a useful corrective for the historian, who is more accustomed to mine his image from the past from written documentation. Stage-plays, pamphlets, chronicles and legal archives no doubt pass over in silence the whole world of children sweetly playing marbles; their authors only reached for the pen in cases of striking disorder or outright criminal behaviour. The lives of seventeenth-century children did have such moments. Boys were always present at street riots; sometimes they even took the initiative. In June, 1619, at Voorburg it was small children who dug up Ledenberg's coffin.[124] The religious disturbances at Amsterdam in February, 1617, were largely the work of boys.[125] Frequently adults were behind them, urging the boys on, as many a Catholic priest knew from personal experience. Similar politically tinged demonstrations could take place with the winking connivance of the authorities, and were instigated by adults; naturally among the boys themselves a fighting spirit and disorderliness were the actual mainsprings. In a calm political climate the authorities realised as much: they forbade public jeering, fighting, and throwing rubbish and paving stones, as in an ordinance of The Hague in 1591.[126]

Children also fought each other. With great pleasure Bredero recalled the child-wars of his youth, in which boys hit each other with cudgels and sticks in order to send the enemy 'bloodied to his home', 'with great screaming'.[127] We know that such battles could be fierce, and not only from the romanticised tradition of literary sources. Prior Wouter Jacobsz. noted in his journal for February, 1576, that the boys of Amsterdam – apparently in imitation of the actual events of the war – constructed barricades and threw stones at each other 'very forcefully and mercilessly'.[128] Another, similar child-war has incidentally come to our notice: it took place in April, 1633, between the boys of Delfshaven and Rotterdam. The two parties fought each other on a dike, 'throwing stones very violently at each other, making holes in the head'. The dike had become impassable for ordinary people.[129] Fights between two cities occurred more than once. The boys of The Hague challenged those of Delft in 1575, but the authorities came between them, fearing discord among the burghers.[130] Perhaps other calamities were prevented in this manner, but it is more likely that only a very small number of these sometimes bloody battles among children has been preserved in the written tradition.[131] The weapons normally consisted of sticks and stones, although Master Valcoogh, who knew his customers well, was aware that some pupils carried knives and used them too.[132]

Was this a preamble to juvenile delinquency? Schoolboys with knives in their belts are exactly what we should expect in a country where the defiant shamelessness of peasant fighters did not shrink from homicide. That in such a region it would once be necessary to punish a murderer aged thirteen[133] does not surprise us, any more than the presence of 'very small boys' in the Amsterdam house of correction, noted by a German traveller in 1614.[134] But surely such a youthful criminal was as exceptional as the crime of murder among adults. In 1614 the village authorities of

Bodegraven wanted to make a statute against fighting applicable to all persons aged fourteen and older. The Court of Holland, whose advice they asked, stated that they could safely raise the age to eighteen.[135] Despite all the complaints about 'homicides or heavy woundings of many good persons' children'[136] people apparently still thought there was no question of alarming juvenile delinquency. The afore-mentioned young murderer was not beheaded, but whipped and branded. People took into consideration the 'young foolish years'.[137] Even the Duke of Alba's government, which inexorably sent captured sea-beggars to the gallows, sometimes showed mercy to cabin-boys.[138]

The child certainly did not occupy a central place in the seventeenth century. The 'tender youth' was not surrounded with sentimental care. Adulthood was the norm, and the child was measured according to that norm. If there had been youth crime on a large scale, it would certainly have led to clear-cut official measures. We can safely assume that for the youth of Holland the path to school and workshop was a common experience. And, apart from a few exceptions, they did not resist the society that wanted them to become like adults.

Chapter 9

POPULAR READING AND THE SUPPLY OF NEWS

There were people who could read, and probably a considerable number of them. But did they do it? Inventories of possessions recorded in the sixteenth and seventeenth centuries seldom include books.[1] If they mention any at all, it is almost invariably the Bible or an edifying work. The cooper Thijmen at Medemblik in 1568 had nothing except 'one book with clasps, of the passion of our Lord, printed at Gouwe, anno 1519'.[2] Cors Steffensz., a farmer of Naaldwijk, owned in 1569 one Dutch Bible, printed three years earlier by Plantijn at Antwerp.[3] Mary Gijsbertsdr., widow of an Amsterdam wine-tax collector, left two books behind in 1578: 'the one of the Legends and the other of the Gospels'.[4] The first-mentioned is probably the same book that we find among the possessions of the Leiden miller's widow Maria Dircksdr. around 1580: 'Jacobus de Voragine, *Historia lombardica quae a plerisque Aurea legenda sanctorum appelatur*', in an edition published 1496. In that household there was also a New Testament, and a book by Henricus de Herph, *Dits die groote ende nieuwe spieghel der volcomenheit* (The Great New Mirror of Perfection).[5] In 1581 the Leiden barge-skipper Simon Willemsz. Wassenaer left only a New Testament to his heirs.[6] For that matter, higher up the social ladder we do not always see any substantially greater selection. At the house of the Leiden draper Gerrit Jacobsz. we find a total of four books: one Bible, one chronicle of Holland, and two other unspecified works.[7] The widow of *jonkheer* Johan van der Bouchorst in 1591 did carry matters a bit further: a collection of six items, of which only the Bible, psalter and New Testament are specifically named.[8]

If these were our only sources, then the conclusions would be obvious: Hollanders read little, and when they did read it was not for amusement but for edification. The first could also be true insofar as Hollanders were not much inclined to while away their evenings, the most suitable hours, in reading. When Brill received an English garrison in 1586, the magistrate raised the quartering costs for soldiers, 'since the English nation have a great need for fire and light'.[9] Apparently these English soldiers spent their evenings by candlelight at the hearth, while the Hollanders did not. In the States' College at Leiden, where the young theologians were lodged, the use of fire and light in the evenings was forbidden.[10] Evidently there was a rule that after sunset students could not and must not open books. Albrecht Haller's eighteenth-century statement that Netherlanders of all classes did not make fires in the evening[11] acquires some credibility. The directors of public buildings evidently took it as axiomatic that human beings should go to bed with the sun. Thus they could do without light and warmth in the evenings, in the Leiden hospices as well as in the Amsterdam house of correction, where no traces of heating facilities have been discovered in the inmates' cells.[12]

Yet the overall impression is misleading, if it makes us think that the sleep-inducing reading (or rather spelling-out) lessons at school had caused the pupils to reject books once and for all. There can be no doubt whatsoever that a reading public existed, and not only among the upper classes. 'All the meetings, negotiations, and travels of common people, were they not enlivened with tales of histories, and made appealing?'[13] Some part of the material for stories was certainly found in reading matter. People read in order to edify themselves, to relax, to stay informed about politics and current events, and to improve themselves. Edifying literature held an important position in this parcel of reasons, but we shall postpone our consideration of it until part IV. Nor will self-improvement get much attention here. As a separate genre, popular works of self-improvement barely existed in the sixteenth and seventeenth centuries. Not until the nineteenth century, with its penny magazines and other educational publications, were there conscious efforts to raise the level of knowledge of the unskilled and to broaden their interests. Seventeenth-century publications sought these goals only in limited areas – particularly in religion, and medical self-help – or accomplished them incidentally in travel accounts that were probably read primarily for adventure, yet on the way informed the reader about foreign lands and distant peoples.

Of the most important genres, two remain: the popular book for relaxation, and the pamphlet for information. Neither of them was unique to Holland, certainly not the first. The stream of pamphlets flowed more slowly in countries that had strict state supervision and careful, authoritative religious censorship. In Holland there was thus more liberty than in many a monarchy. But the popular book was international in its themes and distribution. Knights and giants found their admirers all over Western Europe. Thomas Overbury in his character sketches had a chambermaid become so infatuated with the stories of Robert Greene that she half thought about becoming a wandering noblewoman herself.[14] She had a masculine pendant in Ralph, the grocer's boy, who actually fulfilled the role of knight errant in Beaumont's *Knight of the Burning Pestle*. Dutch literature has not preserved such figures for us. Perhaps we lacked a Greene who could turn the heads of Dutch chambermaids with equal facility. The Netherlandish popular book was often a pitiful mass-product, in which typographical errors were preserved from one publication to the next, and even omissions that made the text incomprehensible were repeated from edition to edition.[15] This had no ill effects on the demand for adventure tales. Many were glued to their books

Of Amadis, of Palmerijn,
Of Orssen and of Valentijn,
Of Malegijs, and of Mandeville,
Of Blancefleur and of Virgil,
Of Uilenspiegel's roguish pranks

Or of Marcolphus and his wife,
Of Fortunatus' purse and hat,
All that tastes so wondersweet to these folk,
Everyone who would much rather hear
And read these works, than God's holy word.[16]

The critical distance that appears in the last lines is expressed more explicitly by most contemporary commentators, especially when they evaluate these popular novels for their worth as reading matter for children. Master Valcoogh almost certainly had these popular histories in mind when he pronounced his damning judgment on 'joky and useless books' which children sometimes brought to school: 'put them away at once, or God will take vengeance upon you!'[17] Popular novels were censored and ridiculed by educators of all persuasions, as if ecumenical consciousness in the seventeenth century found expression only in an interconfessional rejection of all forms of recreational literature. The bishop of Antwerp in 1621 forbade an entire series of popular books, such as *Mariken of Nijmegen, Uilenspiegel*, and *Floris and Blancefleur*.[18] Jacob Cats did not want children's brains to be overexcited 'by anything that Faustus does, or Wagenaer tells'.[19] But all these condemnations had so little effect that at the end of the century Balthasar Bekker could still get irritated by the 'popish jokes and novels of Amadis of Gaul, of the knight Malegijs, of Valentijn and Ourson, of Fortunatus, and that kind of quacks'.[20]

The catalogue of works in circulation was considerably larger. In 1837 L. Ph. C. van den Bergh's *Dutch Popular Novels* discussed twenty-eight different stories, and his list is by no means complete. From Van den Bergh's work, however, it is possible to get an idea of the tastes that this literature had to satisfy. Novels about knights clearly stood at the top of the list. This genre produced the most titles and probably also the greatest number of copies, at least for the truly popular items. The *History of the Four Sons of Aymon* was apparently the most beloved and most-read popular book. *Floris and Blancefleur* and the adventures of the wizard Malegijs achieved a high rating.[21] The holy legends probably lost some ground, although they were still reprinted sometimes in the Republic, for example *Mariken of Nijmegen*, published at Utrecht in 1609.[22] Popular books of genuinely Protestant inspiration did not really take their place. Naturally there were the books of martyrs, but these came in folio format as bound volumes, not in the ephemeral pamphlet format of popular books. Some older stories such as *Til Uilenspiegel* did undergo Protestant rewriting.[23]

Perhaps it is possible to find traces of indirect Calvinist influence here, since in the seventeenth century the popular novel sometimes received a moralistic introduction. The 1648 edition of the *Châtelaine of Vergi* warns all readers against the 'sin of adultery'. It may not matter that this flag of convenience covers a highly improper cargo, and that the medieval author intended instead to teach enterprising lovers how to conceal their amorous adventures from the public eye.[24] Several editions of the *History of Amadis of Gaul* were likewise enriched with a religious-didactic introduction; the author could hardly have objected, since it was simply impossible to spice this light dish with moralistic herbs.[25] The moral offered was often of the cheapest kind: the popular book became an instructive example of what not to do. The first Dutch edition of *Faust* recommended itself thus on the title page: to 'all haughty, pompous, wicked and godless people, as a terrible example, and warning'.[26]

Among the folk heroes, Faust was a new phenomenon of the sixteenth century. There were several others as well, who acquired a place in the pantheon alongside the traditional popular inheritance of the Middle Ages. The Spanish picaresque novels fall in this category, with *Lazarillo de Tormes* at the head of the list.[27] The new heroes include the giant Gilias,[28] Ahasverus the wandering Jew,[29] the fable of Jack and the Beanstalk, translated from English,[30] and the pure Netherlandish product, the fortunes of the Zaankant pirate Claes Compaen.[31] Whether new or old, all of them were influenced to some extent by the transformations of the changing times.[32] The knightly novels of the seventeenth century related an almost extinct culture to a broad public that itself had never played any part in courtly culture. The image thus became coarser, cruder and simpler. Exactly how the knightly armour was supposed to look, or whether the countless battles correctly followed the rules of engagement, were questions about which the lower-class reading public did not bother much. Not only in the picaresque novel was the hero sometimes a young man of insignificant origin. In *Gilias*, the giant is not conquered by a nobleman or a prince, but by 'a blacksmith's apprentice of incredible power and strength'.[33] It is true that matters turned out badly after the marriage of the simple Sievreedt and the rescued princess Eulalis. 'Finally the twenty-four brothers, at the instigation of other courtiers, who would not allow a blacksmith's apprentice to be raised to such a state, killed Sievreedt with poison, and not long afterwards Eulalis died of a broken heart.'[34]

The happy ending is missing in other popular novels, too. Did people read them less because of a need for identification than for a desire for suspense and adventure? Sensational adventure was certainly the chief attraction in many popular books, although there was ample room for amusement, as Uilenspiegel and the picaresque novels testify. Seldom was it amusement of the highest sort: popular humour was not so refined as to reject coarse jokes. Thus the story of Jack and the Beanstalk turns on the fulfilment of three wishes that an old wizard had granted to the eponymous hero. The comical point is hidden in the last wish, by which Jack hopes to teach his wicked stepmother a lesson:

> I wish, that if she begins to stare at me,
> She will have to let a fart ·
> Heard everywhere, in all places.[35]

When Jack came home he could immediately test the power of his wish:

> She cast on Jack a harsh glare
> And then let out such a great fart
> That it resounded far and wide.[36]

Every time she became angry with Jack, the woman felt the force of the magic:

> She began to blast with her ass
> And let out many a fart;
> They all laughed far and wide;
> Some said, 'Woman, control your bum!
> Aren't you ashamed to uncork that cask?'[37]

Contemporary readers and hearers found that funny. That they should have bought or borrowed or read such books is easy to understand. Yet at the same time a quick survey is enough to make us understand why no popular books are mentioned in the catalogues of private libraries or inventories of possessions taken at death. These books were disposable articles of no value, and for an evaluation of someone's property they were as insignificant as the loose issues of an illustrated weekly magazine or railway-novel would be today.

The same generally held true for pamphlets. In most cases they were also ephemeral products. Presumably that applied particularly to pamphlets that had no other purpose than reporting current events to a wider circle. Once they had satisfied public curiosity, their worth declined to that of yesterday's newspaper. Longer popularity may have been achieved by the many pamphlets that were also or exclusively oriented toward forming public opinion: in these writings authors gave commentary, took positions, blamed, praised, and judged. No kind has been preserved in its entirety; but enough remains to permit some generalisations, though certainly no definitive judgment. Catalogues of the large collections are available, yet we lack an overview of pamphlets as a whole, which could inform the user about every extant pamphlet known to have been printed or sold in the Netherlands. We can however provide some preliminary impressions. As a starting point we can choose the most important collection, that of the Royal Library at The Hague, described in the catalogue by Knuttel. First of all, we can examine carefully how many pamphlets per year are listed there, as appears in table 9. The first conclusion suggested by this table is the most significant, and at the same time limits the value of all others; we must treat these figures with great suspicion. This is, after all, only the catalogue of a single collection. A particular year may be shortchanged for all sorts of reasons, with the result that the figures do not present the reality of the offering available at that time. Even the view that more pamphlets appeared in 1618 than in 1591 or 1592 thus becomes disputable, although for the present it remains quite likely.

Reasoning thus from similar appearances, we can observe the first peak of production in the years 1576–79. The causes can be read directly in any chronology of Dutch history: the Pacification of Ghent, the Union of Brussels, the Cologne Peace Congress, the Unions of Atrecht and Utrecht. At that time the burning issues for everyone were war and peace, which increased the need for information. This can be confirmed in all phases of the struggle against Spain. Every time there was talk of peace negotiations we see the yearly totals of pamphlets go up, by comparison with the years immediately preceding: 1594, 1598, 1607–9, 1621, 1629–30, 1632–3,

1643–8. These figures are higher, and often much higher, than in times when the events of the war dominated the news. Victories were reported, celebrated in song and rejoicing; but peace negotiations always brought about a discussion of pros and cons. How much the flood of pamphlets increased the exchange of ideas can be seen particularly during the Twelve Years' Truce (1609–21). Beginning in 1610, religion was the most commonly discussed subject. Only after the expiry of the truce was it driven from first place, but the religious question remained of central importance, and on a number of occasions – 1626, 1630 – it regained its leading position in the league table.

Ordinary wartime actions seemed to decline in importance by comparison, particularly at the beginning. The years of Maurice of Nassau's great victories did not produce a rich harvest of pamphlets. Could this be an accident of preservation in the Knuttel collection? Indeed other collections offer a somewhat larger, but still not bountiful harvest. Was enthusiasm inspired only when Maurice proved his military leadership not just in siege warfare but also on the field of battle? In any case, Turnhout (1597) and Nieuwpoort (1600) received considerably more coverage than objectively more significant military events such as the conquest of Nijmegen or Coevorden. It seems as if the two battles brought about a lasting change, because after their time all great military events were always well represented in the reports: such examples include the sieges of Sluis (1604), Bergen op Zoom (1622), Breda

Table 9. *Pamphlets per year listed in the catalogue of the Royal Library*

		1591	2	1611	106	1631	67
1572	7	1592	2	1612	106	1632	103
1573	18	1593	7	1613	156	1633	39
1574	12	1594	27	1614	150	1634	18
1575	12	1595	19	1615	81	1635	51
1576	37	1596	22	1616	96	1636	62
1577	48	1597	37	1617	176	1637	86
1578	72	1598	53	1618	310	1638	40
1579	120	1599	57	1619	204	1639	65
1580	34	1600	43	1620	121	1640	60
1581	28	1601	21	1621	161	1641	74
1582	45	1602	31	1622	100	1642	108
1583	50	1603	33	1623	111	1643	141
1584	45	1604	46	1624	67	1644	110
1585	40	1605	24	1625	64	1645	101
1586	14	1606	38	1626	91	1646	141
1587	48	1607		1627	54	1647	229
1588	36	1608	215	1628	67	1648	192
1589	16	1609	128	1629	133		
1590	14	1610	129	1630	139		

(1625) and 's-Hertogenbosch (1629). Beginning with the Armada of 1588, the high points of the war at sea were always covered generously, in particular the action at the Downs in 1639, and to a somewhat lesser degree, the capture of the silver fleet (1628) and the battle on the Slaak (1631).

There was remarkably great interest in foreign politics. The battle for the throne in France, the accession of James I in England, and later the Gunpowder Plot were the most frequently discussed events in 1589–90, 1603 and 1606, respectively. Disputes about religion temporarily overshadowed all others, but it still appears that in 1615, for example, there was definite interest in the civil war in France and the succession to Jülich. In the 1620's the war in Germany was sometimes better represented than the Netherlands' own struggle against Spain. Beginning in 1638 the same applies to the outbreak and course of the English Civil War.

Naturally one might ask to what extent these matters are relevant to our theme. After all, we are discussing popular culture: with such pamphlets, are we not reaching too high, or was there also a real demand for pamphlets among the popular classes? A first likely approach is through the prices, but little is known about them. A list, dated January 1610, of a number of then-current publications[38] shows that the selling prices varied greatly, from twelve pennies – three-quarters of a stuiver – to eighteen stuivers. That very expensive item costing eighteen stuivers, however, was an exception. The most frequently represented are prices between three and five stuivers – thus a price that neither strongly stimulated sales, nor could be regarded as downright prohibitive.

One thing must not escape our notice in any case: the pamphlet is a primary source for us, from which we can still learn about the events of the past. But for contemporaries pamphlets and printed newsletters formed only the second source of information, surely more exact and more detailed than the first, the oral rumours that preceded them in time. However quickly the printing press could work, it was not yet in a condition to provide immediate coverage of developments, particularly not in wartime. For the latest news people did not go to the bookstores, but to the market and the harbour. Hooft's letters teach us that he, the bailiff of Muiden, did not disdain the news that ferry-captains brought from Amsterdam.[39] Foreigners in Holland could find themselves surrounded by a flock of curious questioners. The Swiss and Palatine delegates to the Synod of Dordt in 1618 had chosen Gorinchem as the last stopping place on their journey, but they quickly rejoined their ship, because the entire population of the little town swarmed around them.[40]

Not every rumour told the unvarnished truth. The message could be garbled in a hundred different ways, and sometimes turned into its opposite. That did not necessarily mean that people always had to doubt the good faith of the reporter. But in wartime news and propaganda easily blended together. The prior Wouter Jacobsz. had already learned this in the early years of the Revolt. We heard that Oudewater, Delft and Dordrecht have been recaptured by the Spanish, he wrote on the first page of his journal in August 1572, 'but alas, no matter how far and wide these tidings are spread, they always remain loose talk and fables'.[41] The news reports about the war are filled with lies, this pro-Spanish cleric repeatedly declared,[42] and he knew why: the rebels were deliberately falsifying the news. If the Spaniards achieved a battlefield success, there were always people who would immediately contradict and belittle the good news. Again and again they would try to rob the Catholics of their consolation, while they exaggerated their own power and congratulated themselves on the strength of their allies.[43] The certain knowledge that rebels were always liars nonetheless allowed the devout to take heart. If they did receive bad news, they could encourage each other by blaming it on the malicious talk of their enemies, 'who always work toward that end, by the telling of wondrous tales to drive fear and anguish into the hearts of good Catholics'.[44]

Wouter Jacobsz. seems to have believed there was a systematic campaign to drum up support on the home front for the military activities of the rebels. He probably overestimated the organisational ability of his arch-enemies, and he may have succumbed to a well-known temptation in sharply ideological conflicts: to blame every circumstance unfavourable to his own side on conspiracies by the opposition. No doubt some false rumours were indeed circulated in his time. In later years Alexander van der Capellen incidentally gives us a peep at Frederick Henry's kitchen, where they were concocted on his orders: 'Spread rumours that the enemy is beginning to gather troops at Wesel and Venlo.'[45] This was only fitting for a captain-general: he had to make the States General believe that military action was necessary in the eastern part of the country. Thus the rumour had to be reported that the enemy was collecting troops there.

Rumours and suggestive reports were most easily spread by word of mouth. But if it was important to make a certain fact or insight known quickly to many people at the same time, other means had to be used as well. The simplest were the distribution of bills[46] and the sticking of lampoons,[47] the latter sometimes written by hand,[48] and secretly stuck on the walls by night.[49] Other instant productions included ballads, which not only gave information about events in one or two pages, but also interpreted them after a fashion. The English envoy complained in 1618 that an account of a sea-battle successfully won by Dutch whalers over their English competitors at Spitzbergen was being sung in the streets with open mouths and self-assured faces, as if it were a glorious victory over the enemies of the country.[50]

Such ballads were perhaps comparable to our top of the pops, since the seventeenth century also had its popular melodies, although at that time they were based not on American but on French musical production. Charles Ogier wrote in 1636 that all the roads and streets of The Hague were overflowing with French songs.[51] It is possible that in courtly The Hague the population right down to the demi-monde carried a French veneer: the hawker Vroechbedurven (Spoil-quickly) in a farce by Biestkens deliberately offered his wares in broken French to passers-by in The Hague.[52] But for the great Dutch public the foreign melodies were then also given a Dutch text. Some of the most beloved – 'Si c'est pour mon pucellage' (If 'tis for my maidenhood), or the Dutch 'O schoonste personagie' (O most beautiful figure) – did yeoman service for countless rhymes. They also sold rather well. 'Comic rhymes were most in demand,' Van de Venne tells us in passing about the sales of seventeenth-century bookstores.[53] The demand for verses was so great that it could make even street-selling by pedlars worthwhile, although this work may have seemed the last remedy of shiftless folk and wastrels, who had landed on rock-bottom and could not find any other way of earning a living. They could still

> Walk around with almanacs, ballads, and sometimes with 'What wonder! What news!':
> There are so many lazy scoundrels who earn their bread in that way.[54]

In those words, 'What wonder! What news!' we hear the cries of the street-vendors, who wanted to persuade the public to buy the news, and thus sold not only ballads, but also pamphlets. After our excursion into the realm of rumour, we return to the question of who really were the readers of pamphlets: quite often these were indeed destined precisely and particularly for the common man. It seldom happened that pamphlet-writers directed themselves only to the political elite. The small group of regents could easily manage common discussions with the help of copied documents. The printing press was seeking a larger public. Proclamations that temporarily limited freedom of the press during a political crisis always tell us that misleading information is so damaging for 'the uninformed and inexperienced people, and the common man', who might be excited to riot by lying propaganda.[55] Seldom did matters get so far out of hand. But it is possible that fear of rebellion could have made the regents sensitive to the wishes of public opinion. Writings for and against can never entirely be suppressed, Aitzema declared, not even in a monarchy. 'But the worst is, that the approval or rejection of the community easily becomes so strong that it carries away the state itself.'[56]

'The worst,' Aitzema said. This is the typical aristocratic style of thinking found in the regent oligarchy of Holland. A government must be independent of public opinion. Don't ask what the people think of your policy. The perceptions of the public must not prevent the administration from doing its duty.[57] The first statement is by Jacob Cats, the second by Johan de Witt. Both of them were Grand Pensionaries of Holland, one a perfect instrument of stadholderly autocracy, the other the incarnation of Loevenstein regentdom.[58] But Cats and De Witt both believed that the aristocracy should not share its power with the people. That was always the feeling of the ruling party in the Republic. The party in power preferred to retain safe custody of its majority, and would be responsible only to itself. Only the minority party had any interest in using the press to bring about discussion of the policies of its political opponents. The chance was thus always great that the opposition would be better represented in every pamphlet war, because it took the initiative and wanted to keep the flames burning brightly. Consequently, the pamphlet as such is not an exact measure of public opinion. A discussion in the press primarily showed that the minority saw no chance of becoming the majority in the regent's colleges through its own means. The reactions must then show whether it had appraised its chances correctly, and whether it would succeed in mobilising public opinion so that resistance to the regents' policies would become too strong.

The classic example of such an action remains the conflict between Remonstrants and Calvinists during the Twelve Years' Truce. Conditions were then so favourable that the organisers of the action achieved a complete success. For an exemplary treatment within the framework of this study, however, this pamphlet war is less suitable because of its enormous magnitude; besides, it has already been described elsewhere.[59] We shall therefore choose another conflict, which was not entirely separate from the one just mentioned: the discussion about war, peace and truce during the years 1607–9. The victory in this case went to the government. The truce came to pass, despite all the militancy of the pamphleteering opponents. It is true that the pamphlet war did have long-term consequences insofar as it helped to raise the climate of suspicion around Oldenbarnevelt, which eventually made his downfall possible.

A glance at the list of titles shows us quickly that the flood of pamphlets that burst out in 1607 was intended to change the peace policy of Holland. There is indeed 'the *farmers' litany, or complaints of the peasants of Kempen about the miseries of this everlasting Netherlandish war*'.[60] But the peasants of Kempen were not subjects of the Republic. Northern Netherlandish productions seldom appear in the list of pleas for peace: the *Testament of the war* was printed a couple of times,[61] and it had a successor in the *Codicil of the Netherlandish war*.[62] In the battle for public opinion, however, perhaps the most striking pamphlet is a rhyming *Small poetic tract concerning the fruits of war and peace*.[63] Here a peace propagandist had his say, one who recognised that the question was winning popular support. It was no longer necessary to convince the regents. His arguments had to be directed toward the common man: they were intended to restrain him from mass protests against the peace. That is why he made the war party consist of profiteers, who wanted to continue the struggle because they made such good profits from it.

> One is *commisaris* or *commis*, and the other I think
> Has an office of more station;
> In time of peace they would sit in poverty!
> They could barely get their living;
> Now they drink from gold and silver vessels,
> Not knowing, from luxury, what to do and endeavour.[64]

This was a typical seventeenth-century manner of playing on popular sentiment: the author did not merely say that the rich were profiting from the war. The terrible thing was that men of low origins had now landed in the lap of luxury. These *nouveaux riches* were neither great businessmen nor war profiteers, but civil servants who were living handsomely on the public purse. Public opinion in this time was much more sensitive to official corruption than to commercial profiteering; it did not regard the big businessman as public enemy number one, but rather despised the selfish judge or administrator, particularly when he was of humble origin, and

19. The farmers' litany, or Complaints of the peasants of Kempen about the miseries of this everlasting Netherlandish war. From a pamphlet of 1608.

BOEREN-LITANIE
Ofte

Klachte der Kempensche
Landt-lieden/over de ellenden van
deze lanck-duerighe Nederlandtsche
Oorlooghe.

Ghedruckt bij Dirck Cornelisz. Troost/
In den Jare onzes HEEREN
IESV CHRISTI
M.D.C.VIII.

thus still had to make his fortune.[65] That sort of person sought only his own profit, and would never care about the ordinary man.

> Disturbers of the peace, very wrong in their nature,
> They are the worst, their particular welfare,
> Which they gladly prefer to the common good.
> Not giving a thought to the damage war causes,
> For the poor community that we see declining.[66]

Such reasoning was the stock in trade of popular pamphlets. They were less likely to seek their persuasive force in reasoned argument than in appeals to popular feeling. The war propagandists were no different. They certainly did not go into the true motives of the supporters and opponents, but preferred to answer with their own demagogy. Naturally there were fortunate exceptions. Several pamphlets, for example, tried to discuss the issue of peace or war as a question of conscience. Should not a Christian always choose in favour of peace? The very word sounds 'completely loving, friendly and Christian' to our ears.[67] But even these writers do not make it very complicated. One simply says that a just war is better than 'a false and evil deceitful peace',[68] without explaining himself further as to what a just war might be, and whether the struggle against Spain in the year 1607 would fall under that definition. Another refers to Luke 22:36, where Jesus advises the disciples to sell their cloaks and buy swords. Nor did John the Baptist condemn the warrior's craft. He did not impose on soldiers a duty to choose another profession. It was enough if they did no violence to anyone and were satisfied with their pay.[69] Here too one can think that the author was quickly satisfied, and that the question did not really depend on the responsibility of the soldiers, but on the government that took those soldiers into its service. Yet it did at least make sense to ask such questions in a discussion among Christians about war and peace.

This theme seldom appears, however. Most authors argued on another level. The core of their thinking was mainly that Spaniards could never be trusted anywhere. Of course they were able to support the point with ample historical evidence, and the best of them placed special emphasis upon the testimony of the past. The supporters of the war, one of the pamphleteers said, 'have not merely dreamed and guessed, but have experienced examples of it themselves in living memory'.[70] The examples did indeed exist, and the pamphlet war gave them their classical expression in the form of a school textbook which has remained famous, the *Mirror of Youth*.[71] But one can frequently notice that the authors were more interested in a purposive use of historical facts than in an exact account. Let us listen for example to the opening words of the *Catechism of the peace negotiations*,[72] stated in question and answer form:

> Q. Is there a monarch?
> A. Yes, there is someone who would gladly become one.
> Q. What is his name?
> A. Io, el Rey.

Q. What kind of animal is that?

A. What? It is a saint.

Q. In which calendar can one find his name?

A. In the Roman one.

Q. In what letters does his name appear?

A. In black letters.

Q. Is he then a saint without a holy day?

A. Not at all, because he does much more than ordinary saints.

Q. Hey, what then?

A. He even makes saints.

Q. In what almanac can one find their names written?

A. In those of this country.

Q. In what letters are they listed?

A. In red letters.

Here we are listening to the true voice of a popular pamphlet. It is not concerned with objective information, but with influence. Events are not weighed in the balance; they are not even mentioned. They are only used, and interpreted in a manner that stays outside the discussion, because the interpretation is completely fixed. Spaniards are domineering and cruel. They lust for the blood of all Netherlands Protestants. That is the way it always has been and always will be. Convicted before the bar of history, the Spanish king has no more right to appeal, and Philip III must be measured by the same standard as his late father Philip II. But haven't the Spaniards changed? They are even offering peace now! Yes, indeed, but such an offer cannot be more sincere than these prophets of peace themselves. Striving for a peace or truce does not mean a change of purpose; it only means a change of tactics. The purpose remains the complete subjugation of the Netherlands and the introduction of the inquisition. Only the means are new. The story that we find in *Respectable Conversations between the Pope and the king of Spain, concerning the peace to be made with us,*[73] achieved great success. In that pamphlet the king played merely a supporting part. He only asks all the stupid questions, while all the answers come from the Pope, who has hatched a devilish plan to bring a hopeless struggle to an unexpected good end. It is impossible to conquer the Netherlands, he states. Spain has no more money for the task, and Rome cannot get any, because the bishops and cardinals would rather keep it for themselves. And even if a military campaign succeeded in pressing the Hollanders hard, the French would certainly come to their aid. Continuing the war would thus serve no useful purpose in any case. Therefore Spain must offer peace. Spain must do it on the most advantageous conditions possible, so that the allies will strongly pressure the Republic to accept. The peace will actually cost the king nothing, because he will not keep his promise. The Pope will grant him absolution in advance for the sin of breaking his word. Once the heretics have been lulled to sleep, 'then we shall come upon them unsuspected, attack them, destroy them, and uproot them from the earth, so that no memory of them remains'.

This pamphlet clearly shows the somewhat suspect contents of many works written to inform the public.[74] It chooses as its starting point the bad faith of the opponent. This was no coincidental misfortune of wartime progaganda, for precisely the same tactic was used in the religious disputes of the Twelve Years' Truce. Then too the mutual casting of suspicion often took the place of pertinent argument.[75] If the opponent cannot be trusted anyway, one need not take the trouble to refute his arguments. So it went in the debate over the truce. A discussion with the supporters of the peace was useless, because they were unable to see the cardinal fact of Spanish duplicity. They were too stupid to see through that falseness, or perhaps they had also been bought by Spanish gold. Spain saw no chance of conquering the Netherlands, we are told by the *True and short story of the great ambition and cruel tyranny of the king of Spain*.[76] Thus the king had received advice 'that he should annually spend two or three hundred thousand guilders in treasure on the pensionaries'. With this sentence the pamphlet ends. The writer was careful enough not to state that Spain actually paid any pensionaries, to say nothing of mentioning names. But he had done enough to set the reader thinking.

The power of Spanish gold was indeed a favourite theme of these writers. The Spaniard leaned on his golden stick, the Indies. Using this stick he could alternately strike or fondle his neighbours so adroitly that everyone would bow to his wishes. Only one person had always remained resistant to this treatment: 'the rarest thing that I ever heard or saw, is that *seignor* [the Spaniard] never knew how to deal with the Dutchman called Sailor'. Sailor had even firmly seized the stick at the eastern end, and now threatened to wrest it away from Spain.[77] The message of this author is clear enough. Sailor could win the war by his own force, and would then acquire the golden stick for himself. As the booty promised to be his prize, could the prophets of peace in Holland honestly mean what they said? Surely they could not offer Sailor anything better?

In this manner the political information in the pamphlets could have poisonous effects, and be much more dangerous than the typical popular book despised by more enlightened spirits. Yet no serious measures were taken against either genre. A prohibition against printing or selling certain pamphlets always remained casual, and was loosely observed. In the Netherlands the rule was simply that everyone could say and write what he pleased, judged the Frenchman Charles Ogier.[78] This fitted in well with the economic policy of the regents of Holland, who did not gladly restrict the free sale of goods if there was any chance of making a profit on them. An English prohibition against the import of books, enacted on the eve of the civil war, raised an official protest from the States-General.[79]

One simply had to accept that not all printed matter was of superior quality. Pamphlets could slander, deceive and indoctrinate with shameless lack of sensitivity for the interests of others. The virtues of modern mass-media, but no less their vices also, were already present in seventeenth-century pamphlet literature. Then too the dregs often remained in the bottom of the sieve of news-distribution. The titles of many pamphlets still cry out to us: *Horrible murder happened at Delft!*[80] *Pitiful*

20. Sailor and Spanish nobleman pulling on a golden stick (the figures looking on may represent Philip of Spain, Henry IV of France and other European powers). From a seventeenth-century pamphlet.

fire at Wilda![81] *Amazing haunting at Brussels!*[82] Come and read how three students in Kloppenburg raped two girls and murdered four![83] See how sixty-four witches killed more than a thousand people and six thousand animals![84] Son murders his mother and father![85] Innocent girl beheaded at Steenwijk![86]

When a new pamphlet appeared three years later about a young daughter at Vlissingen, who met her end in the same sad way,[87] the question does arise whether a clever businessman simply reheated the old stew in a new pot. Sometimes indeed the actual event was so minor, and described so broadly on the title-page, that the publisher simply mixed some leftovers with the main course: 'here is added a case of haunting, which happened earlier at Rotterdam, by which a great murder was caused'.[88] The printer of the sentence against Claes Jeroensz. – 'for the abominable crimes and incest done by him' – had so little to report besides the actual sentence that he brought up one murder case after another, in a general commentary on the wickedness of the times.[89]

21. *A truthful account of sixty-four witches who through their witchcraft killed over a thousand people, old and young, and six thousand animals.* From a pamphlet

The wickedness of the times, indeed ... because the exploiters of sensationalism generally justified themselves with unctuous moralising conclusions. 'This is, dear reader, short but true, what we have wanted to tell you about these two so gruesome murders. Hoping that such will serve as an example for everyone to guard against similar things.' Anyone who had a desire to commit murder, should murder his desires.[90] The three boys from Danzig, robbers and murderers who had endangered the city and surrounding area for seven years, were specially cited to parents as a warning. 'Will you discipline your children when the twig is still green? Because once they begin to wither, it's too late.'[91] Then perhaps it was best to let the children themselves read these pamphlets as lessons in life, just as the reporter of the murder at Heusden in 1609 urged them to buy and read:

Buy me, famous youth
[You'll find] in me the murder is so explained,
[That] I am always well worth the money.[92]

Thus far everything was for consumption. The people read what they received. The lower class did, however, also have its own group of producers, in the chambers of rhetoric or drama companies. Every city had at least one such company, and often there were more. In the villages, particularly in what is now South Holland, this form of active recreation enjoyed great popularity. In Bergsenhoek, Overschie and Bleiswijk; in Ooltgensplaat, Zwartewaal and Goeree; in Kethel, De Lier and Scheveningen; in Hazerswoude, Stompwijk, or Katwijk aan de Rijn – wherever one went, the dramatists were to be found.[93] Their prize questions and performances attracted the attention of hundreds of interested folk. On festive days for the theatre, such as the celebration of the raising of the siege of Leiden, it was possible to rent balconies and windows for then-fabulous sums, even as much as eighteen gulden[94] – the monthly income of a craftsman. But he could not work then anyway, because in a village in Holland an extended feast would stop all work completely:

Who can still think of haying and threshing and milking,
When it's the annual feast of the dramatists in these parts?[95]

In these colourful popular festivals, the dramatists themselves found a reward for their lengthy efforts. Their ambitions, however, extended somewhat further than performing highly coloured spectacles as occasions for public enjoyment. The chamber of Kethel, for example, pretended to find its origin in the circumstance, 'that the youth within the village and surrounding area of Kethel had little or no exercise directed toward any good works or edification'.[96] Their purpose, as they themselves described it, was spiritual education of youth in the broadest sense of the word. Besides the occasional Bible-study groups under church supervision,[97] the chambers of rhetoric were indeed the only organisations that could be compared to present-day church or secular youth-clubs. This purpose was often expressed in ambitious programmes. The seventeenth-century rhetoricians upheld old traditions from the time of the Reformation by setting prize questions and performing plays that treated current religious problems.[98] While the general public attended their performances for the sake of the farce that was offered as an encore,[99] the chambers strove to reach as high as possible:

> What they show is all taken from scripture and antiquity:
> One might just as well go to school or to church.[100]

Disheartened spectators who expressed their disappointment in this fashion did not, however, represent the feelings of preachers and church councils. The provincial synod of South Holland had noted in 1592 that the Leiden players wanted to present a biblical message on the stage. Far from rejoicing, they brought the dramatists under their watchful eye, 'since their profession was not to speak God's word to the people'. Aggravation instead of edification would be the unavoidable result.[101] Thereby the chief objection to such plays was stated. Anyone who would publicly expound and explain the Bible must have a calling from God, and the church must have confirmed this calling.[102] The rhetoricians had received nothing by which they could legitimate themselves as exponents of the scriptures: their Bible plays were a form of false prophecy. Moreover, the players did not shy away from representing sacred things, as if it did not go beyond human theatrical skill to appear on stage in the form of Jesus Christ or even God the Father. Thus in 1605 the Southland players performed the conversion of Paul, whereby the central character baptised several fellow players on stage.[103] In the same village the company had once played the parable of the rich fool, 'in which one [actor] portrayed the person of God our Heavenly Father'. At Oude Tonge a player had taken on the role of Christ, and had himself baptised by the prophet John the Baptist.[104]

That the church most strongly opposed precisely these plays must have given the rhetoricians the feeling that their noble intentions were misunderstood. Thus it may have been out of pure peevishness that in 1606 the chamber of De Lier 'played a very scandalous piece, full of blasphemies against Christ and the teachings of the truth, to the praise of its so-called rhetoric, to the slander of preachers and godly persons'.[105] It was certainly not prudent to express feelings of rancour in this way. The *classis* of Delft brought the case forthwith to the Deputised Councils and the Court of Holland, and these governing institutions generally showed themselves very sympathetic to objections from the church, as long as the matter involved nothing more than rhetoricians. Only a few chambers were so fortunate as the Corenbloem (Cornflower) of The Hague, which enjoyed subsidies from the magistrate for its performances.[106] Much more often it happened that church and government worked hand in glove to fight the rhetoricians, in principle for the same reasons. Thus the Deputised Councils of Holland prohibited a performance at Maassluis at Easter in 1621, 'because we understand that the said days and all feast days should be employed only to serve the Lord God with thanks and praise, and not spent in lewdness, levity and profanation of the same'.[107] In 1608 the Court of Holland prevented plays at Zoetermeer and Zegwaard because 'such plays are mostly directed toward misuse of God's Word, or scandalous abuse of the government of the country'.[108] Naturally the last-mentioned motive carried a great deal of weight with the magistrates. Had not the chamber of Maasland at the *kermis* of 1605 staged a play 'which was condemned not only for offence to morality, but also for harm to the common good of the country'?[109] And had not the demand for this play been so great that shortly afterwards it was performed in Nootdorp as well?[110]

No effective prohibition of all rhetoricians' plays was ever enforced, although there were sometimes general proclamations issued against 'public plays of rhetoric, whether they be interludes, burlesque plays or others'.[111] But to all appearances the public was too strongly attached to this form of amusement: thus restrictions were limited to casual injunctions,[112] or warnings that under no circumstances was the stage to 'introduce the acts of kings and princes'.[113] Indeed the government would certainly not encourage the formation of new chambers, because they caused nothing but aggravation and scandal anyway – according to the official answer given in 1603 to 'some young villagers and other persons ill-disposed to the common good' at Voorschoten.[114] Nevertheless, their evil intentions appear to have received approval, because twelve years later a chamber did exist in the village.[115]

The reformed church thankfully received support from the government,[116] but on its own it went somewhat further. Donteclock, preaching from the pulpit in Delft in 1582, had already branded the rhetoricians' activities as one of the foremost sins for which the United Netherlands were being punished;[117] yet he was not stricter than the overwhelming majority of his colleagues. In 1606 the *classis* of Leiden considered the question of whether a known rhetorician, who after having shown repentance now again wanted to participate in plays, should also be allowed to take communion. The meeting decided that the man would have to choose between the stage and the sacrament.[118] Participation by church members in a chamber of rhetoric was almost entirely ruled out. The shoemaker of Delft in 1578 who tried the combination by becoming emperor of the rhetoricians while maintaining his membership in the church was presented with the same choice – and two years later he decided to leave the religious community.[119] The rector of Naaldwijk, who had translated a piece for the rhetoricians, 'a dishonest comedy of Terence', no less, was only readmitted to the communion after a confession of guilt.[120] The tailor Cornelis Jansz. at Kethel also got into difficulties with the church council in 1606, when he had accepted an order from the chamber of rhetoric and prepared the costumes for the players who would participate in the Haarlem regional drama festival.[121] And naturally it was quite logical that the church council of Schipluiden should also take action against those who had attended even one performance, and thus tasted the forbidden fruit.[122]

Thus here too church and state had their concerns about popular culture. It may appear that the ordinary Hollander must have seen these two institutions as his opponents, who time and again wanted to prevent him from realising his heart's desires. That was indeed so, but it is only a half truth. The other half must now follow.

PART III

People and government

Chapter 10

THE GOVERNMENT

Popular government is the worst form of tyranny, Cicero says. For that reason the wisest men have always judged that even a tyrant is preferable to anarchy, that is, rule by the masses. Holy Scripture agrees. When it desires to show us Israel at its worst, it says that 'There was no king or regent, but everyone did what was right in his own eyes.'[1]

This was the argument of a preacher, the Remonstrant leader Nicholaes Grevinchoven. Perhaps it is not the most inspired piece of reasoning that this master of logic ever produced, but it is extraordinarily instructive as an example of the thinking of the regent-patriciate of Holland and its admirers. Grevinchoven clearly shows his condemnation of a particular form of government, democracy. Between the lines, however, he also keeps his distance from another form, monarchy. Nowhere in Scripture can we actually read 'that there was no king or regent'. The Bible says more tersely, 'In those days there was no king in Israel', and does not speak of regents (Judges 17:6, 18:1, 19:1, 21:25). Grevinchoven paraphrased, and added the regents, because he wanted to avoid giving the impression that Scripture finds kingship the only effective remedy against democratic chaos. By adding the regents, he chose the middle way of aristocracy.

That system existed in only a few European countries at the time, and it did not enjoy a particularly favourable reputation outside the Republic of the United Provinces. Other states did have a ruling elite, which exercised governing power directly at the local level. But the source of all authority was the monarch, the indivisible sovereign. Such a system of government was regarded as normal, natural and Christian.

The Republic formed a deviation from the usual pattern. It was not the result of deliberation: its political organisation was not the outcome of lengthy consultations, leading to carefully considered constitutional reforms. Instead it arose almost by accident, out of a loose federation of regions that had been under the same ruler. This ruler was certainly the personification of authority in the eyes of the masses. His rule was experienced as natural. Although the tradition of lordly authority in the northern regions was certainly not centuries old, many people had the greatest difficulty in overthrowing their hereditary ruler.[2] Nor, in their rejection of Philip II, were people determined to do away with monarchy altogether. The 'Placard of Dismissal' said as much in so many words: the States would now look for another powerful and merciful prince. Yet all attempts to find a replacement failed. Thus the confederation of the United Netherlands became a Republic. But monarchical thinking had not thereby disappeared.

The House of Orange-Nassau partly filled the vacuum. In Holland William of Orange already stood high in popular esteem before the repudiation of the Spanish king. 'All regarded themselves as fortunate if they were able to see him, [for] they held him, next to God, as the only one to deliver them from all their woes, and thought that he had liberated them from slavery to Spaniards and foreigners,' reported Pieter Bor on Orange's famous tour of inspection of North Holland in 1577.[3] Later the prince lost a good deal of his appeal,[4] but his memory was still held in high regard, and with his sons this half-monarchical popularity came into firmer hands. This has been amply studied and demonstrated for Maurice of Nassau.[5] No similar research on Frederick Henry has been done, but this less controversial politician and equally successful general certainly enjoyed no less popular support and respect than his elder brother.[6] For in the public opinion of the seventeenth century Maurice and Frederick Henry were indeed sovereigns of the Netherlands. 'Our lord and father,' one pamphlet-writer called Maurice in 1613.[7] Frederick Henry's position was described thus by Jacob Cats:

> There is the great sovereign, through whom steady blessing
> Is given to the Fatherland and to everyone;
> Under his rule his mighty power and resounding name
> Are carried aloft on the wings of fame.[8]

This verse had an authoritative sound, because Cats, the popular didactic rhymster, was Pensionary of Holland at the same time. If anyone had to take care that the stadholder of Holland should not feel too powerful, then it was surely the pensionary. But Cats represented him to the public as the great sovereign. That was also how he was seen abroad. The Dutch East India Company in its treaties and negotiations always presented Maurice and Frederick Henry as kings of Holland:[9] it was easier than explaining the state organisation of the Republic to the Bandanese and Javans. The same simplification was also used by the common people of Holland. Captured sailors in Tunis appealed for help from 'the high-born lord and sovereign prince Mauritius, our gracious [lord] next to God, and my lords the States of Holland, our gracious lords'.[10]

The last-named gracious lords might feel slighted in this form of address. They wanted recognition as rulers in their own right. They had to prove that their lordship was strong enough to be able to dispense with the unifying force of monarchy. They guarded their power against the stadholder, but also against the people. Two dangers threatened every state that chose the middle way of aristocracy: first, the vacant throne might be reoccupied; and second, there was a chance that a government without an eminent head would not succeed in holding the subjects at a sufficient distance from the rulers. Foreigners often thought that this danger had become a reality. They declared that the Republic was really a democracy.[11] In that case its political organisation was unsatisfactory, because popular rule meant chaos. No region is as far behind in its payments for the common expenses as Friesland, wrote the Venetian Michiel in 1638, 'since this province is suffering from public disturbances, because it is the most democratic of all'.[12] In order to defend the Netherlands against such allegations, Van Meteren added to his history of the Dutch revolt against Spain a description of the system of government, 'so that people will be able to see that the administration of the United Provinces is not a popular [regime], no matter what many people, including its enemies, would say'.[13]

Democracy was indeed regarded as pernicious by all Dutch writers of this century. The world traveller David Pietersz. de Vries reported that among the Indians of New Netherland the wisest men would consult with each other. 'Yet if the common men are displeased with the resolution, the whole is subjected to the judgment of the riff-raff.'[14] That is not proper government: wise counsel and good leadership become impossible. 'The common people have such a nature that they reject what is most useful, and always desire what is useless or forbidden.'[15] The masses are not reasonable. They do not hone their feelings on the stone of judgment, and they have no solid foundation of understanding. Seneca was right to say 'that there is no proof more vile than the sayings and feelings of the common people'.[16] The people should be quiet and allow themselves to be ruled. P. C. Hooft was willing to admit that 'people here in this country have seen the most powerful changes introduced, often instigated or at least firmly supported by the common people', but he still thought that the art of government consisted in large measure of guiding and ruling those people: 'the handling and keeping quiet of the multitude'.[17] As the bailiff of Muiden, Hooft painted his self-portrait as a successful administrator: 'here no passion is preached, besides that of Our Lord: no petitions are written; no stones are gathered to throw at the lords' heads'.[18]

Power had to stay in the hands of the eminent. Rulers and subjects must not be confused with each other. Lords and servants stood in opposition to each other as two sharply distinguished groups. What are these differences? How can we recognise the regent, and what qualities must he possess? There was a whole complex of characteristics that defined the essence of regentdom. These may be summed up in one seventeenth-century term: the regent had to be 'qualified', that is, a person of quality.

What did it actually mean to belong to the people of quality? Above all, it pointed toward good ancestry. For some regents this was certainly a requirement hard to fulfil. 'A man from the Delft patriciate, thus a brewer', wrote Van Buchell contemptuously about one of the regents of Delft.[19] 'Hans Shitpepper, Hans Pedlar, Hans Brewer, Hans Cheese-buyer, Hans Miller' – see there the very grand men who now sit on cushions, mocked a fierce critic of the States of Holland in 1588.[20]

It was not entirely true, and yet not entirely false either. Naturally the revolution of 1572 had brought new people to the top. Also in a time of civil war and sharp polarisation, the victors had to broaden their base of support in order to maintain their position over their defeated but still dangerous rivals. William of Orange realised as much, as is shown by his efforts in those years to give municipal guilds a share in the government, or at least allow them to play an advisory role.[21] The struggle against Spain required dedicated efforts from everyone and demanded great financial sacrifices. Thus it was necessary to count on 'the community, from which all means must proceed'.[22] But this limited power-sharing never meant anything more than consultation, and it did not last very long. The most significant change of 1572 was probably not that formerly undistinguished persons came to the top, but that a number of already comfortably off families were able to break into the patriciate somewhat more quickly and more easily. Thus in 1578 when Amsterdam joined the revolt, the representatives of big business took over power from the old oligarchs.[23] In general, changes were kept to a minimum. At the beginning of the revolt it had often been necessary to call for aid from new people, because the petty-office-holding nobility of Holland was not entirely persuaded of the happy outcome and waited to see if Alba might win after all. Encouraged by the success of the revolt, however, many people quickly resumed their old positions,[24] so that even after the upheaval many a regent could still speak proudly of his 'entirely good family, who from ancient times have been esteemed and renowned among the most notable of this city'.[25] The authentic cheese-buyers and humbler sorts, who had acquired an honourable place next to the old regents, could hope that the mists of time would also come to the aid of their family; or, if they did not have so much patience, they might themselves establish the glory of the House of Cheese-buyer with legendary family trees. This was done, for example, by their most illustrious representative, the pensionary Johan van Oldenbarnevelt.[26]

    In later political crises the symptoms of 1572 were sometimes recalled on a smaller scale. Maurice's violent solution of the Remonstrant conflict in 1618 brought some fresh blood into the magistracy, and on that occasion too not all the newcomers were of the most distinguished origin. According to Nicolaes Reigersberch, the government had declined in quality. It had become 'too popular' because of the invasion of all sorts of inferior persons – 'barbers and apothecaries and similar sorts'.[27] Without taking any great risk we can bet that detailed quantitative research would not discover many barbers among the members of the town councils. At Brill in 1624 several 'vile workmen' were placed on the list of council candidates. The Deputised Councils of Holland, however, immediately voiced their serious concern, and asked for the Court to intervene: they said it would suit such people better 'to continue their work and thereby to earn their living, than to neglect their work and spend their days at the town hall'.[28] Reigersberch's censorious disqualification is primarily an expression of peevish resentment. In times of high political tension it was not uncommon for those dismissed from the government to discover moral shortcomings among the new men of power. Yet the winners of 1618 knew as well as the losers that having workmen on the council benches could only damage the prestige of their government.

    Men of quality had to serve, but at the same time they would continually have to prove that they were still worthy. Oldenbarnevelt once wrote that children had

22. 'The big fish devours the small ones'

GRANDIBVS EXIGVI SVNT PISCES PISCIBVS ESCA·
Siet fone dit hebbe ick zeer langhe gheweten / dat die groote viffen de cleyne eten

a right to the places of their fathers, provided that the sons actually confirmed their worthy descent through 'alliance, profession and service'.[29] Oldenbarnevelt tended to be repetitious, but on this occasion each of these three terms probably had a particular meaning. *Alliance* meant making a good marriage with a girl of social position, or at least one with money. Oldenbarnevelt frankly applied this rule to his own marriage with Maria van Utrecht: although there were deficiencies in her birth, she brought a great deal of property to the marriage and could expect to receive good inheritances.[30]

Profession and *service* were apparently closely related. The idea was to choose a profession that did not decrease one's worth, to uphold the codes of behaviour, and particularly to show a readiness to serve the country in official posts. Thus the famous Leiden burgomaster Pieter Adriaensz. van der Werff clearly acted contrary to the regent ethos in 1585, when he declined a nomination to the college of the Deputised Councils and wanted to pass the responsibility to 'suitable men ... without occupation and enemies of avarice'.[31] It was expected of men of quality that they would set aside their own occupations when called to public service.

If they could permit themselves this sacrifice, and furthermore, if, as Van der Werff wished, they were to be enemies of avarice,[32] then they must have possessed the necessary private means. Sometimes it was explicitly stated,[33] at other times it was silently hoped, that regents would belong to the richest elements of their towns. 'Are not the richest men the best of the city?' Bredero asked, although his tone was clearly ironic when he declared that it was not intelligence but money that made 'state-worthy men'.[34] By contrast, Vondel chose wealth with complete conviction when he asked his readers

> Whether the judge who is amply supplied with goods
> And money, does as much harm to the law,
> As a poor beggar, who will first sort out the case,
> And then devour the poor [by demanding] presents and gifts?[35]

Thus it was rather serious when someone moved out of his former position, and climbed the social ladder from simple burgher to regent. How would a man 'who formerly was a vile and inferior person' be able to maintain himself in high, often unsalaried posts, except by getting rich from 'the sweat of the good people'?[36] This even became an argument for changing the personnel of the governing colleges as little as possible: otherwise, 'in place of the satisfied it would be necessary to take the hungry ones'.[37] Stay with the old, and do not seek change. Let everyone accept that some are born to rule, others to serve. Let people accustom themselves to their lot in life. From their early youth children were told that 'each should be content in his vocation'.[38] Anyone who practises a profession should have very deeply grounded reasons before he may trade it for another.[39] If he earns little in his trade, he must not be embittered, but should rather think

> That a higher power, who lives in heaven
> Has given each what he needs for his fulfilment.[40]

Thus spoke the regent Jacob Cats. Constantijn Huygens, likewise called to high offices, warned:

> Man reaches neither good nor haven by chance.[41]

It was not blind fate that had chosen the rich and given them the power to rule. Possessions and power were distributed by divine providence. God did not only allow the regents to rule; He chose them for it. Jacob Cats, selected as pensionary of Holland in 1636, declared that he had every reason to decline the appointment, 'unless he cast his eye on the help of God Almighty, who was accustomed, in his fatherly mercy, to bestow an office lawfully, and also the talents to perform the said office well'.[42] The regent thus not only had money and power, but had also received the capacity to fulfil his duty. Yet anyone who has received so much must bear heavy responsibility. A popular song of 1624 explained what was expected of him:

> It is a great and lordly good
> That the Lord God already does for us
> If the people live in a time
> That has good regents,
> Who govern with good policy,
> Exercise fair justice,
> Lead the people in doing their duty,
> And fight against the enemy of the land.[43]

Did such fathers of their country exist? The chronicle-writers reported that in 1636 at the burial of the former Amsterdam burgomaster Reinier Pauw 'many uninvited [people] went along out of love'.[44] Apparently that was regarded as noteworthy. Even if Pauw was a remarkable exception, however, that does not prove that less beloved regents fell short of their obligations. Indeed, most of them did not arouse popular enthusiasm, but they did not seek popular favour either. 'Populum nec amo nec negligo; cum plebe nil negotii est'.[45] Regents were independent of the people's will and did not have to make publicity for themselves. The authority of the regents was practically taken for granted, so that at first they did not have any need for external lustre. A regent of the old school was hardly distinguishable from passers-by in the street. In 1587 a visitor encountered the Leiden magistrate Schot while he was 'sitting on the steps in front of his door'.[46] We find it hard to imagine the bewigged regents of the eighteenth century in such circumstances, but in the time of Frederick Henry this characteristic simplicity was noticed by a French traveller. The deputies came to the States-General in their everyday clothes, with hats and coats in the colours they found most becoming. There had even been some – though this was only what he had heard people say – who attended the sessions in their slippers.[47]

These customs disappeared slowly. In the time of William III the supremely powerful Amsterdam burgomaster Gillis Valckenier kept to the old norms. Yet already rather early in the seventeenth century several men were choosing another style of life. Johan van Oldenbarnevelt, the leader of Holland, bought the seigneurial rights of Berkel and Rodenrijs. To his contemporaries and to us he remains known under his own name. But his sons Reinier and Willem began to call themselves after their acquired properties, Groeneveld and Cralingepolder. Later Willem was able to exchange his title, which smelled a bit too much of new wealth, for Stoutenburg. The Oldenbarnevelts were among the first to aggrandise their names, but they had no shortage of followers even in their lifetime: De Graeff van Zuidpolsbroek, Overlander van Purmerend, Huydecoper van Maarseveen.[48]

Titles created distance from the masses, just as grand houses on the canals had already done and clothes would do soon enough. But that did not make it easier for the regents to feel responsible as fellow men for the people that they ruled. They ran a great risk of regarding their offices in the same way as their capital, their residence or their wardrobe: private possessions for the use of the owner and his relations. Life was good in the Republic, where 'the countryside overflowed with money and goods, and all those who were in office and government could become rich, if they wished'.[49] This was Everhard van Reyd's view of the Netherlands in 1600, but it is not what we should have expected. To us it would seem more natural if Reyd had written: 'all those who were in trade and did business...'. The experience of the seventeenth century, however, appears to confirm that governmental office was a surer path to riches. In 1599 the tax-assessment book of Leiden, the most important industrial city of Holland, shows that great capital sums were not invested in the textile industry at that time. The highest amount recorded is 25,000 gulden belonging to a dyer. Among the very richest citizens, with sums in six figures next to their names, we find a burgomaster, a polder-district councillor, a steward and a pensionary.[50] The richest man in The Hague in 1627 was the diplomat Frans van Aerssen van Sommelsdijck. His property was assessed at 800,000 gulden. In Amsterdam there was no one worth as much as that. Other great fortunes at The Hague also came from the office-holding world. Both of Aerssens' brothers were worth a quarter of a million, and Oldenbarnevelt's widow, despite all the blows her family had suffered, still had 150,000 gulden in 1627. The brothers Johan and Philips Doubleth were both listed at 105,000, which may not seem much for the children of a receiver-general; but then it was said of old Philips Doubleth that he had fulfilled his office 'with rare [and] praiseworthy fidelity'.[51] Most men did otherwise, and were not ashamed. Those who occupied such positions freely admitted 'that in France as well as in England, and almost everywhere, those in government benefit themselves and their friends'. But this spokesman thought he could add, 'that meanwhile the state of the country suffers no danger'.[52]

It is difficult to evaluate the worth of that judgment. As soon as parties were formed in each town, and two groups of regents were hauled over the coals in pamphlets and farces, we can always predict two accusations with absolute certainty: extreme drunkenness[53] and corrupt administration of public finances.[54] Since these charges were used against almost everyone, we should be cautious – but they should also give us pause for thought. Drunkenness was so common in the seventeenth century that it would have been hard to find a Hollander who had never been intoxicated. Thus the charge of drunkenness could be applied to almost everyone, without saying anything that was absolutely untrue. Because we find the charge of corruption just as regularly in the pamphlets, the suspicion arises that it was equally widespread. Officials of the 'Grabbelarity', said a pamphlet-writer, parodying 'Generality'.[55] Every person looks out for himself anyway, declared another; no one would take on the burdens of office, if he did not think he would be better off from it. 'Although people try to persuade one other that they are motivated by diligence to serve their country, it would be a great folly to believe them.'[56] Among the natives of North America the rulers give presents to the common man, reported David Pietersz. de Vries; exactly the opposite occurred among the Christians, where those 'who sit in offices enrich themselves'.[57]

There were many opportunities. The regent-merchant could take advantage of his relations with agents of the *convooien en licenten*, the office of import and export duties. In 1616 the Admiralty of Amsterdam complained that in the eastern part of the country the collectors showed such 'great favour' to the burghers and enterprises of their own city that the tax collections were too low to cover the cost of salaries.[58] In view of this problem, Holland wanted to have the controlling officials transferred frequently,[59] so that at least they would not become tied to their surroundings. That these opportunities and dangers also existed in Holland itself was undoubtedly well known. In 1591 Cornelis Pietersz. Hooft, for example, was caught evading export duties on a fully laden ship with seventy-eight lasts of rye. The matter was accidentally discovered because a headwind had forced the captain to enter the harbour of Flushing, where the control office was not in friendly hands.

23. Satirical print against heartless regents

Thanks to the intervention of Maurice of Nassau, Hooft got off with a small fine of fifty gulden.[60]

Apparently this incident did not damage his good name, because Hooft continued to sit on the council as the moralist of Amsterdam. He was the one who protested strongly against another method of misusing official power: taking advantage of public works.[61] The moral norms of today would certainly be opposed to the practices Hooft censured, by which Amsterdam regents earned thousands by speculating in land that they knew was destined for urban expansion. But just as Hooft's shady activities did not cost him his reputation, the honour of the political opponents he pilloried did not suffer much either. The greatest wrong-doer, Oetgens van Waveren, was burgomaster more than once afterwards. Seventeenth-century regents remained true to the Mosaic Law, 'You shall not muzzle an ox while it treads out the grain' (Deuteronomy 25:4; 1 Corinthians 9:9; 1 Timothy 5:18). They even saw a certain justice in this position. In 1631 the broker Samuel Duyn obtained permission for the diking of several polders on very advantageous conditions. The States of Holland put a stop to it in 1648. After all, Duyn had 'never been in any public service of the country, and consequently he never deserved to pretend to such excessive advantages by donation, much less to benefit at the expense of the general state of the country'.[62] Thus the States did not condemn the extraordinarily high profits outright; what was in question here was the social position of the beneficiary. In this case he was just 'a common broker of low condition', and thus he had no right to such advantages. Seldom was the matter stated so baldly. In 1629 the regents of Hoorn clothed their objections to the proposed diking of the Heer Hugowaard with all sorts of arguments that ostensibly rested on the general interest. The poldering would be too damaging to the trade and commerce of Hoorn. The protests stopped when they themselves received a share in the works and the profits.[63]

Another path to quick riches ran through the tax offices. Positions such as collector or *commis* of finances were much in demand.[64] Even if the pamphlet-writer may have been mistaken when he declared that in such a job a rank beginner would be able to maintain a country house of 30,000 to 40,000 gulden,[65] it remains true that this profession offered attractive opportunities for the play of financial genius. A collection-office could function for the payment of all kinds of public charges. If there was no money in the public coffers, then the receiver was allowed to lend to the state at the legally fixed rate of interest, 8 per cent at the beginning of the seventeenth century. If he could get the money for less, he might often regard the difference in rates as his private profit.[66] This too was still a tolerated practice. Outright embezzlement was not, of course, but there was no effective system of controls. If a receiver regularly borrowed money from his coffers for the financing of his own projects,[67] it would generally pass unnoticed for a long time. François Kegheling, receiver of Gouda, allowed his debt to run up to 285,000 gulden before he fled abroad.[68]

Kegheling's behaviour was definitely criminal. There were other such violations that fell beyond the pale of regent-morality at its most generous, but the passage to crime was gradual. A counterfeiter could not go unpunished if he was caught. On that account, Bartholomeüs Munster and Salomon Voerknecht were arrested in 1618. They were, however, related to prominent families of Amsterdam, Voerknecht for example to the Overlander and Hooft families.[69] This did not necessarily imply any complicity. But the Deputised Councils of Holland wrote to all voting cities in 1621 that precisely these proclamations about coinage were badly observed, 'which is a result of nothing else but your lax [performance of] duty, or perhaps because your members are winking an eye or conniving'.[70] Allowing some small irregularities in the course of exchange was not counterfeiting. But here private conscience was as usual a highly unreliable guide, which time and again discovered new passageways in the continually expanding no-man's-land between good and evil.

The exploiters of state secrets found themselves on that same dangerous ground. Here too it was difficult to draw the line between tolerable and criminal behaviour. Pieter van Heynsbergen, clerk to pensionary Cats, enjoyed 'searching and sniffing' through parcels, and to that end he broke the seals on incoming post.[71] Was this simple curiosity? The forces of justice had their doubts, perhaps also because this simple Pieter was such an easy prey. In 1647, the year of Heynsbergen's trial, a pamphlet publicly labelled Cornelis Musch, secretary of the States-General, as a man 'who robs the land of its capital, reveals state secrets, and has all the great [men] in his hands'.[72] Musch did have to thank the great men that he was allowed to remain in office for three more years, until his protector William II passed away and Musch took his own life. He left behind a great fortune: the higher the office, the better the shady services were rewarded. Between Pieter van Heynsbergen and Cornelis Musch stood dozens of men who once in a while (or often) knew something that would find buyers on the diplomatic market. With so many people in the know, nothing could remain secret anyway. Why then should others be the only ones to profit?

Indeed, evil practices existed on every level. Few were able to see themselves as public servants with only their salaries as compensation. The small fry as well as the big fish sought their advantage, even to the extent that those who drew the lotteries insisted on tips from the winners.[73] But there was a difference: the small fry could be held responsible. Actually only the urban regents could exercise unlimited power. Village councillors had to accept higher authority. When Johan van Oldenbarnevelt acquired the seigneurial rights of Berkel and Rodenrijs, he was immediately solicited by persons who wanted to lease the office of bailiff from him. Oldenbarnevelt refused, however, because he had understood from the notables of Berkel 'that they, the people, were satisfied with the officer and lived together in good unity'.[74] Dirkland also had a watchful overlord in 1595: there the properties for the support of the poor were continually let at low rates because the leaseholders were members of the local administration, and no one dared to bid higher. The overlord was the one who called the matter to the attention of the States of Holland.[75]

Their High and Mightinesses could also intervene on their own initiative. More than once their resolutions show that there was control over the quality of justice and police in the countryside. They did as much as possible, considering that shortcomings in village administration in Holland could frequently be traced to the same cause: the circle of candidates for office was too small. Thus defendants in the courts who sought legal counsel sometimes could find it only among the forces of justice itself, the clerk or even the bailiff, who served as both prosecutor and public defender. No wonder that 'thereby the feeling arises among the community that such cases are [handled] unjustly, or that their testimony is improperly hindered'.[76] Rural communities had a shortage of people of quality, even if we adjust our standards to rural conditions. Even in a place as large as Schagen in 1621 the candidature of blood relations of the first and second degree had to be expressly forbidden.[77] Oostzaan, even larger, might have had ample choice, if it had not over the course of time expanded the number of magistrates to forty-two. Seldom did this large group meet together, so that two successive meetings were sometimes attended by entirely different people, who could on occasion rule in exactly opposite senses if need be.[78]

Was there perhaps inadequate meeting-space for so many rulers? The simplicity of village life often meant there were no public buildings of any substance other than the church. Usually, therefore, the administration met at the inn. The objections are so obvious that it really amazes us that they were so seldom stated. In 1617 the States of Holland declared that Haastrecht urgently needed its own council-hall. At the inn the councillors were wasting their time in 'drinking and clinking, with absurd proposals that come out of drink', which naturally had the result that 'the resolutions [passed] in drinking could not be appropriate'.[79] The consequences continued for some time: only in 1622 did it come to light that the bailiff had pocketed a subsidy of 200 gulden voted for a church window, without ever installing the intended embellishment.[80]

But while small misfortunes might happen, at least in the villages control was possible. In the cities, the situation was different. Justice in the Netherlands was sold like meat at the butcher's shop. This devastating judgment comes from a foreigner, whose name became a synonym for rape of the law: none other than the Duke of Alba.[81] The history of the Republic shows that he was not entirely mistaken. Legal proceedings against a regent were generally held to be useless.[82] Persons of quality fell outside the ordinary rules. In 1620 the Amsterdam wine-buyers protested that they were required to take an oath of office that they would not defraud the fisc, 'having in substance announced that it was unjust that the wine-buyers, being generally persons of quality and with honour, should be subject to take the oath'.[83] Such a demand might be laid on the small shopkeeper, but the man of honour and substance stood above it. Such arguments fitted nicely into the thinking of the Amsterdam burgomasters. When the ship *de Vergulde Pauw* (The Golden Peacock) had problems with the Spanish authorities in 1614, the Amsterdam magistrates forcefully represented the interests of its owners to the States-General, 'as the aforesaid shipowners are mostly persons of quality, merchants and burghers of this city'.[84]

Among the public there was also a clear consciousness of these differences. Dutch literary figures – not the regents P. C. Hooft or Constantijn Huygens, but men of the people such as Bredero, W. D. Hooft and Van Santen – regarded the admin-istration of justice in Holland as systematic favouring of the rich and prominent.

> The poor thief who gets caught
> Goes to the hangman, who hangs him;
> The rich rogue is allowed to walk free.
> When a rich man pleads to the tribunal,
> The sentence against him is suspended:
> He can buy his life with money.[85]

Anyone who would accuse the dramatists of exaggeration can see how in denouncing public sins and abuses the preacher and the comedian frequently spoke the same language. The judgment of God, said *dominee* Becius, will not be like the earthly courts: these are but spiders' webs, which the great flies that sting most fiercely can fly through, while the small mosquitoes stick fast.[86]

Becius spoke these words in the pulpit in orthodox Dordrecht, where the earthly judges sat in the front pews of the church. I do not know that they ever punished Becius for inflammatory language or seditious preaching. There was surely no shortage of examples to prove his point. At the Voorpoort of The Hague, prisoners were housed in accordance with the 'quality of their persons'.[87] In the Amsterdam prison 'merchants of importance or quality' could request special treatment.[88] Differences of rank and position were also observed in the courtroom. In 1603 a certain Henrick Lambertsz. van der Horst received letters of pardon for a moral crime he had committed, but he was too ashamed to allow this to be recorded publicly. The Court of Holland, however, refused to hear the case behind closed doors, considering 'that it is not known to us that the quality of the person of the appellant is so illustrious, or of such merit, that we should be obliged on his account to go outside [the bounds] or disrupt the common order of justice in that case'.[89]

This reasoning implies that those who were persons of quality did not lose the privileges of their position in court. It became clear in 1588, when the lord of Warmond committed manslaughter, and despite the opposition of the Court of Holland received a pardon at the request of Maurice of Nassau. While the Court declared that it would be a bad precedent to allow soldiers to take the law into their own hands, Maurice answered that this case could never have consequences for other delinquents, 'since [God willing] few countrymen in these lands are of such quality as the aforesaid lord of Warmond'.[90] This was the same Warmond whose quality was so highly valued by the peasants that they said the 'house of Warmond was no better than a brothel'.[91] Maurice often came forward as the champion of the nobles, and interceded for them at the Court of Holland. Charles van der Noot, Guillaume de Famars, Arthur Winfield and Ernst van Hohenlohe – all belonging to the noble youth of Europe who found employment in Maurice's army – were brought before the Court in 1616, 'having here in The Hague perpetrated very great violence and wantonness by night'.[92] Yet Maurice ordered the Court to stop the trial, in view of the quality of the accused, the services done by their parents, and the intervention of their friends, 'also being of considerable quality'. This was not entirely agreeable to the Court. 'The origin of the parents can be no pretext for doing evil.' Indeed these were not sons who honoured the great names of their families. *Noblesse oblige* was applied in the opposite sense in this case.

Here the Court displayed good will. It would not excuse reckless disorder and deliberate violence because of the position and rank of the perpetrators. The Court tried to apply this principle to nobles, and in practice it was probably successful with serious excesses committed by persons of the regent class. This was made clear, for example, to the bailiff of Oudewater, who had to appear before the Court because of malicious mischief against the civil guard.[93] But the Court generally could not go further. If a regent committed a crime that exposed him to charges as an ordinary citizen, then he ran a risk. Yet the Court ordinarily had no control over typical official misdeeds. It could not build a dam against corruption and intrigue. The regents would have to do that themselves.

A couple of times they did actually try, or at least made a step in that direction. Such an attempt occurred in the 1620s. The crisis during the Twelve Years' Truce had given rise to the idea that the constitution of the Republic was showing serious flaws. People talked about renewal of the Union of Utrecht, and about more decisive leadership that would be strong enough to settle conflicts among the regions. The mood did not hold sway long enough to lead to any lasting results.[94] Perhaps also the winners did not feel strong enough to stand up against a diminished but certainly not destroyed minority. In that short period the idea also surfaced that new brooms would sweep clean the stables of corruption and intrigue. In 1620 the burgomasters of Amsterdam, the representatives of political Calvinism, proposed to the States of Holland that no one should be allowed to accept gifts at the distribution of offices. Also, directly interested parties would no longer participate in the assignment or extension of charters.[95]

No decision was taken in this matter. Consciences did remain troubled by a vague desire for higher official morality. In 1621 it was noted that many colleges still behaved very carelessly with large sums of money.[96] In particular, the admiralties came to mind. The lords of the admiralties knew how to play ball with each other, and in purchasing *matériel* they would favour themselves and their friends at the expense of the country.[97] Questions likewise arose about the bureau of Van Mierop, the receiver-general of Holland. In 1622 a report confirmed dark expectations. Van Mierop's office appeared to be a chaos of debts and irresponsible expenditure. People saw no better solution than requiring the receiver-general and his *commis* to take an oath and receive new instructions. Why was no stronger action taken? The States themselves gave two reasons. If the affair remained a topic of public discussion, it would lead 'to disservice of the common lands and discredit of the receiver'.[98] Disservice of the common lands in such cases was always cited as a reason for sweeping the whole business under the carpet. Discredit of the receiver, however, was likewise more than a personal consideration. A discredited official meant a risk to the community. Two years later, in 1624, Holland went so far as to dismiss Hendrick Aertsz. Doudijns, clerk of finances, 'for various impolitenesses, evil behaviour and sinister dealings'. But the States regarded this decision as risky because 'this person, having pertinent knowledge of the entire finances of this province, out of desperation or otherwise might do considerable disservice'. It was necessary to put him under secure arrest and confiscate his papers.[99]

The arrest of Doudijns was part of the great purge of 1624, which resulted in better regulation of the Generality Accounting Office, and of the Council of State. The admiralties received new instructions for more effective expenditure of the country's money.[100] The Rotterdam Admiralty did not escape harsher measures. In 1626 special judges received orders to conduct a thorough investigation. Some councillors were condemned to imprisonment, and others ordered to pay high fines and quadruple restitution. Then the regents began to fear their own energy. Waste and corruption were disadvantageous to the Republic, but anyone who fought these evils with overly drastic measures did greater damage to the constitution. After all, the main point was and remained to preserve regent rule. Criticism, even the most justified, would lead to disservice of the common lands, 'because it did nothing other than bring the government to the tongues of the community, and give reason for tumult'.[101] Then the administration would fall short on one of its principal duties: handling and keeping quiet the masses.[102] And was it just to condemn only the Rotterdammers according to high ethical norms? 'If all colleges and magistracies were examined in this manner according to these instructions, we might as well say *Domine quis sustinebit*.'[103] In this quotation we recognize the cynical spirit of Lieuwe van Aitzema. But we can hardly call him a scandalmonger. After a great deal of patience the Deputised Councils asked in 1642 whether some measures should be taken against the Delft revenue-collector De Man. The States of Holland cited no facts that could excuse him. For them it was enough that nothing had been done against other revenue-collectors in similar cases. Taking a hard line against De Man would thus be unfair.[104] This was certainly not justice of the best quality, though it may have been the best obtainable. After the purge of 1624, all who entered the regents' colleges had to take an oath to observe the new regulations. Yet quite commonly they added 'that they swore to uphold the same insofar as they were observed. And those who did not say it, meant it.'[105]

The belief in their own fitness to rule remained foremost in the minds of the regents of Holland. Where would more loyalty be found, asked a pamphlet-writer in 1636: among the individuals who had not yet prepared themselves for service so as to be chosen in the council of their city, or among those 'who out of zeal for government have bound themselves with oaths to exercise the service of the lands in all fidelity'?[106] Some questions should be raised about that fidelity. In matters such as corruption, the pursuit of offices and partisanship, the regents' reputation cannot be upheld as spotless, as contemporaries knew. Yet these remarks are not the last word about regent rule. That statesmen profited from their power was not a peculiar feature of oligarchies. 'To the victor belong the spoils' was a party-slogan born not in an aristocratic republic, but in the ultra-democratic America of Andrew Jackson. Even in our own time, ministerial shuffles in The Hague can still herald surprising official appointments. Seventeenth-century people went further than that. But did they do anything other than realise, within the possibilities of their time, the opportunities that power always gives to rulers intent on profit?

Chapter 11

MONEY

The region of Holland in the seventeenth century was well acquainted with a large number of taxes. Pensionary Jacob Cats, a professional expert, testified in 1640 'that the ordinances relating thereto alone have excresced to a large volume, in such a manner that it has become a special subject apart by itself, in which an entire college can always find work enough'.[1] This special subject has not strongly attracted the interest of posterity. True, the great volume has not remained closed with seven seals, but it has seldom found truly dedicated readers. A complete reading of it now would also go beyond the scope of this work. We shall nonetheless have to turn a few of its pages, because we cannot write the history of the common man while remaining silent about his tax obligations. Certainly during the eighty years of war against Spain the burden increased steadily, and yet there was never enough money. 'The princes or regents spend and waste so loosely and lightly what was earned with so much pain by the subjects', sighed Aitzema.[2] 'How many a civil servant must work and sweat from early morning to evening to collect the excises, impositions, and property taxes. And how many a poor widow has to take it out of her spindle and stay up [working] until midnight.'

This has a rather familiar sound, and it is exactly in accord with the tune we would be most inclined to choose: the man in the street always pays the bill. Yet this is a reason to be extra careful. We can easily be misled if we think we know in advance what the past will tell us. The declaration of Aitzema may be true, but precisely because it sounds so believable we are well advised to call more witnesses, and refuse to accept this immediate confirmation of our suppositions.

In two respects the tax system of Holland was undoubtedly fairer than that of other countries. First, it did not hit the farmers so one-sidedly. For Holland we certainly cannot say that the inhabitants of cities were privileged with respect to those in the countryside, as was for example the case in France. Of course in Holland there were proportionately many more city dwellers than in France, and provincial taxes were established by an assembly of city dwellers, the States of Holland, in which the cities had eighteen of the nineteen votes. At least they did not try to impose an extra levy on the agricultural half of the population. A second difference is one of principle. In Holland there existed no legally established fiscal inequality. No privileges of status applied to the tax system. This does not mean that highly placed persons did not find it easier to obtain tax advantages. 'C'est la loi, mon petit, la même loi pour tous les amis', was a saying only for the benefit of the little people. But it still made a difference that there was no legal basis for showing favouritism toward the more substantial members of society.

In later times people thought that a fair system of taxation had to be progressive. This notion was not altogether foreign to seventeenth-century minds. With the levy of chimney-tax in 1606, the principles of progressive taxation were actually applied. First, the owner had to pay three-quarters of the tax, and the tenant only the remaining quarter. Second, local magistrates could exempt the poor and raise the lost money from the rich.[3] Yet we must not place too much weight on this concession, because the total assessment per chimney came to only thirty stuivers per year, of which only $7\frac{1}{2}$ st. was collected from the tenants. Roughly half of a daily wage, and thus not to be sneezed at; but the levelling tendency remained minimal. Somewhat related was the plan offered by the Deputised Councils in 1641 for a salt-tax levied according to ability to pay. Those on poor relief would be exempt. Those who did not live on relief were counted as 'half capitalists', while those who possessed more than 2,000 gulden would be 'full capitalists'. They also considered imposing a new capital threshold at 20,000 or 30,000 gulden for 'double capitalists'.[4] The proposal was admittedly not very significant, and perhaps the entire plan was nothing more than a smokescreen: Delft at least saw it as an increase in the burdens of 'the little people whom people are currently trying to make into half capitalists'.[5]

The notion that the rich were better able to pay than the poor did show signs of life from time to time. We can sometimes hear the States of Holland say that a particular levy might be considered a good tax, because it would strike hardest at the most prosperous. Thus in 1624 they described the wine-tax as 'one of the most notable impositions, and most burdensome to the rich'.[6] In 1622 the two stuivers on each tun of beer were also called a good excise, 'not pressing so hard on the poor'.[7] For a popular beverage such as beer, this view is certainly questionable. The justification in such cases was usually so limited that it may be asked whether the needs of the poor and the ability to pay of the rich were not catch-phrases designed to conceal the actual intentions. In 1642, when tax increases were proposed on grain, wood and wine, several representatives declared 'that [it would be] better to levy higher taxes on other goods, which are not used for necessity but for comfort and pleasure, than on these'.[8] We can agree that grain was a necessity, but was wine then suddenly used only for medicinal purposes? Or did these deputies see any real disadvantages for their particular cities in these tax increases? We do not know which cities were involved, but perhaps Dordrecht, whose prosperity depended in large measure on its role as *dépôt* for German wines, was among them.

Here there is room for all kinds of speculations, and indeed also for malicious ones. But the regents did not have a bad reputation in this regard. We can observe plenty of complaints about taxes in the seventeenth century, yet we seldom hear public opinion charge the regents with setting tariffs to their own advantage.

Indeed, from the point of view of the rulers, the tax system of Holland was skilfully constructed. With the exception of the property-tax, taxes were levied in the form of excise on consumer goods: beer, salt, soap, candles, coal, peat, beef –

there was almost no article that went untaxed. The levy was generally collected from the retailer, who naturally figured the tax into his prices. The government did not itself collect taxes, but leased them in each district, by auction to the highest bidder,[9] normally for periods of six months.[10] The tax farmer was obliged to pay the sum of the lease at regular intervals to the collector. Any excess that he collected was his private profit, or served to cover his costs.

For a government with few means of power – in comparison with our own time, every government of the seventeenth-century – this was a well-chosen system. The administration could distribute the money, and the entire sum came to the offices of the collectors, people of its own sort. But the unpopular job of levying the taxes was the responsibility of a private person, the individual tax farmer. Popular anger would not so easily be directed against the regents themselves. The tax farmers would literally and figuratively take the blows.

In such a system it was better if the tax farmers did not come from the ranks of substantial members of the community, which might lead the public to identify the tax farmers with wealth and ruling power anyway. In contrast to France, for example, tax farming in Holland was not an object of capital investment by great financiers, but pre-eminently the preferred arena of small fry and punters without capital, 'low and vile persons'.[11] Names of great merchants or leading regent families are seldom encountered in this milieu,[12] and even among the reasonably comfortably-off burghers the tax farmer was not a very frequent phenomenon.[13] Instead the normal type of the Dutch tax farmer was a man such as the shoemaker Adriaen Cornelisz. Bredero – father of the poet Gerbrand – who served on several occasions as tax farmer, surety or co-signer.[14] Usually persons from this level of society took on a lease alone or in combination with others. Thus among the tax farmers we meet Symon Ancemsz., carpenter of The Hague;[15] his Leiden fellow craftsman Pieter Dircksz. van Egmond;[16] the 'workman' Henrick Jacobsz. Metser at Heusden;[17] and the cutler Steven Philipsz. at Rotterdam.[18] We are still on the same social level with the surgeons Cornelis Jansz. of Bleiswijk[19] and Thomas Pietersz. of Vlieland.[20] Often lower-level officials were involved, such as city- and regional-council employees, or village secretaries.[21] Tax farming was then one of the many means used to supplement a small job and provide a living: the pen-and-paper functions in a small village community were generally not full-time posts and certainly not sufficient to support a family. That also held true for schoolteachers, who sometimes appeared as tax farmers themselves,[22] and sometimes assisted as collectors in return for a small salary.[23]

Small districts went along with small purses. Outside the cities only a few taxes were farmed for substantial sums. In 1622, the tax on milling at Wormer brought in 70,000 gulden, which was called 'a noteworthy sum',[24] but that is understandable for the centre of the industry for baking ship's biscuit. In such cases the authorities sometimes investigated whether the bidder could be regarded as 'sufficient for such an important lease'.[25] If they could avoid it, the States of Holland would still rather not do it that way. On several occasions they received attractive offers.[26] Wholesale

24. 'Escape from gaol', from Joost de Damhouder, *Practice in civil cases*, 1649

brandy-merchants asked more than once to take over the impositions for all
Holland. They would then pay more and ask less from the community.[27] The States
wisely decided not to accept. In light of later French experiences, we can only agree
with them. Offering a tax farm at 'dumping prices' was attractive for a couple of
years, but then the government would become dependent on the financiers, who
could set the prices to their own liking, because no one would be in a position to
compete against such a powerful combination and take on the lease at a higher
sum. We also get the impression that tax farms were kept as small as possible in
the early seventeenth century, and as a rule did not exceed 10,000 gulden.[28] In
exceptional cases of large sums the lease was sometimes split, 'divided into smaller
pieces', although that was actually forbidden.[29] Maximum or minimum sizes do not
appear to have existed. In 1606 there was talk of required accounting for all leases
greater than 100 Flemish pounds or 600 gulden.[30] Thus there must also have been
leases for smaller sums.[31] We do indeed find them in the sources, in one case even
a lease for sixty gulden.[32]

If the receipts were unsatisfactory, such tax farmers normally had no means to
take on the risk themselves. Thus in the year 1609 three men formed a combination
for the communal lease of the impositions on farm animals and mills in several
villages of Schieland, for a total of 12,033 gulden. This was a rather daring enterprise,
which appeared to exceed their capacity. Each of the tax farmers suffered a loss of
1,000 gulden. When one of them, Adriaen van Dijck, was convicted as a conspirator
in the planned attack on Maurice of Nassau in 1623, he had still not entirely made
up his debt.[33] Therefore it is not surprising that the resolutions of Holland often
speak of tax farmers asking for delay in payments. Shortages of around 200 gulden
were sometimes enough to exceed the reserves of the farmers;[34] indeed, some of
them had to be discharged for sums of even 100 gulden or less.[35] In the beginning
of the seventeenth century the province had to reckon on an annual loss of 80,000
gulden for 'bad debts on leases and remissions'.[36] In view of the small size of the
leases, a considerable number of tax-farmers must have been involved.

The losses were not immediately disastrous for the finances of Holland: the sum
was less than 2 per cent of the total revenue of the time. Yet it could not be
dismissed with a mere shrug of the shoulders, because who could know if it would
always remain at 2 per cent? Therefore the States took security measures. Tax
farmers were required to obtain a surety. This was not an ultra-solid guarantee.
Usually the sureties were in no stronger a financial position than the tax farmers
themselves: a tailor,[37] a bargemaster or an innkeeper, even if he were called Olivier
van Noort,[38] could not answer for a shortage of a couple of thousand gulden. Giving
sureties for the benefit of shaky tax farmers even seems one of the means by which
those who had adequate wit but slim purses tried to gain small advantages. So
dominee Pieter Seghers from Ooltgensplaat was cited in 1604, 'that he lightly stood
surety for excise-collectors, who could get no other surety'.[39] He would probably
not have done that out of pastoral concern, but in the hope of making a small profit,
blind to the future risk. If a tax farmer was granted delay or partial dispensation

from payments – which thus implied that his surety was equally unable to pay – then he was usually required to post new surety for the remaining sum.[40] But what sort of helpers could such a half-destitute tax farmer get? The tax farmers who had once landed in difficulties often went further down the slippery slope by taking on new leases, in the hope of covering the shortages on one with receipts from the others. If they failed, then their careers ended with an absolute prohibition against ever again serving as tax farmer, surety or cosigner.[41]

The evil of insolvency was never remedied in our period. In 1629 the great arrears on the tax farms formed a separate point on the agenda of the meeting of the States of Holland.[42] At the same time to deal with the tax farmers' requests a separate commission was established, consisting of deputies from Amsterdam, Brill and Monnikendam.[43] They handled the groundless requests themselves,[44] while the others came to the attention of the whole body on set days, Mondays.[45] The resolutions report nothing further about how the cases were handled, so that it might appear on the surface that the problems were solved. Not so, as a coincidental declaration about the receiver Wytenbogaert casually mentioned in 1646: in his bureau alone the 'bad remnants' came to 47,000 gulden.[46]

If we hear so frequently of insolvent and bankrupt tax farmers, then we may suppose that their weak financial position was not the only cause of difficulties. Perhaps the lease-sums were also reckoned very closely, so as to leave only a narrow profit margin: a small setback would be immediately fatal. The total revenues from leases did not increase regularly from year to year, but in a somewhat oscillating movement they did go up steadily during the first half of the seventeenth century. In 1608, the total revenue was 4,344,239 gulden.[47] Forty years later it was 8,455,887 gulden, and in the peak year 1645 it had been as much as 9,206,978 gulden and 13 stuivers.[48] This represented nearly a doubling of the tax burden, while in general we know that incomes rose at most only 50 per cent.[49] The results may be guessed. The more the government demanded, the more the subject began to practise evasion. But it also becomes understandable that the threatened tax farmer should have tried to help himself.

It speaks for his ingenuity that he was successful in his efforts. The whole system was stacked against him. Aspiring tax farmers had to bid against each other every six months, which meant that they remained competitors. In their own interest they had to maximise collections, which suggest that a common interest with the taxpayers was impossible. The money that came in had to be handed over to the receivers, who belonged to another social group, which made it difficult to develop solidarity with them. The structure appears perfect. The tax farmer was so isolated that he seemed forced to remain honest. Yet his business sense often triumphed and successfully overcame all these obstacles.

A proclamation of 1615 forbade tax farmers to make agreements with each other as to who would get which taxes.[50] If this practice had to be forbidden, it shows that it must have been happening. The proclamation did little to change the situation. About thirty years later Jacob Cats claimed to know for a fact that regular participants in the tax farms agreed for a small payment not to increase their bids against others, and not to bargain for each other's leases.[51] The States of Holland were partly responsible for this situation by requiring that the leases for the entire province should be made everywhere on the same day. Thus each bidder could take part in the auction in only one place.[52] But changing this rule was not without risk, since then several wealthy capitalists could perhaps seize the chance to exercise an overwhelming influence on the tax farm. Consequently the local participants continued to form their combinations, and how could anyone reproach them for it? Given the system, their behaviour was perfectly natural. In the last analysis the tax farmers did nothing different from the regents, who divided the administrative jobs among themselves with contracts of reciprocal advantage, as they thought best. This form of conspiracy was not seriously opposed in our period.

Fraudulent agreements between tax farmers and taxpayers were another matter entirely. Action was frequently taken against a very common form of fraud, the leasing of taxes by persons with a direct interest – a miller, for example, who took on the impost on milling in his own district. This was regarded as defensible only if it was done collectively. Thus in 1620 the united candlemakers of the Noorderkwartier[53] and in 1622 those of Amstelland[54] were granted the tax farm on wax and candles. This could be regarded as a payoff for the account of the guilds involved. As long as the revenues did not decrease, this method could be just as good as the normal tax farm. It was indeed used more frequently, for example in 1640 with the grocers, whale-oil merchants, and soap-boilers of Amsterdam and Rotterdam for the tax on oil and whale oil; and with the attorneys of Leiden for the fines on unjustified lawsuits. The States were never enthusiastic about it,[55] but they allowed a free hand to the local authorities, if the latter absolutely wished it.[56]

It was expressly forbidden to take a tax farm in one's own economic sphere as an individual rather than as a group. If a butcher wanted to bid on the livestock-tax, or a brewer on the beer-tax, then he would have to give up his old profession at once.[57] Such conditions were frequently promulgated, and what is more telling, they were also actually applied from time to time. In 1615 a baker in Wormerveer was ordered to pay a fine of 300 gulden because he had taken the lease on milling.[58] This was certainly not an extraordinarily heavy punishment, because in Wormer there was quite a bit of grain involved. Perhaps the States did not want to be too strict, having understood that they should not set any major obstacles to the fulfilment of a thankless job with narrow profit margins. At Amsterdam it happened for three years in a row that the livestock-tax was leased by a man of straw, who did his business under commission from the leaders of the butchers' guild.[59] Tax farmers would also sometimes take on so-called collectors, who really operated for their own account. Normally these were people directly connected with the line of business, who were not allowed to take the leases themselves. This was also forbidden, in 1625.[60] But watertight control was impossible. If prominent guild-bosses found an accomplice protégé prepared to lend his name to the lease for their clandestine responsibility, then only mutual disagreement could bring the combination to light.

Such a tax farmer was the creature of the richest taxpayers. The man of straw voluntarily chose his position. But it could also be forced on the tax farmer. We see this primarily in the beer-tax. The small size of the districts gave the taxpayer of ample means in particular opportunities to reduce his assessments. For an innkeeper it was not too difficult to buy his beer in an adjoining district, and to fulfil his obligations to the tax farmer there.[61] For the neighbouring tax farmer, this meant extra profit, because the innkeeper did not actually belong to his constituency. Thus for the occasion he would probably be prepared to lower his tariff somewhat. The injured tax farmer of the home district could only protect himself by coming to his own agreements with the travelling buyers. In this manner it was possible to have agreements that sometimes gave the beer-retailers enormous discounts.[62] Other businessmen also knew how to play this game. In 1622 the bakers of Edam offered to supply grain to the Amsterdam buyer Jan Bayer at half the usual tax rate, or less if necessary.[63] Ultimately, of course, all this resulted in reduced revenues, which no longer reflected the actual consumption.

Such fraudulent agreements were noted from time to time usually with a sort of despondent indignation. The tax farmer could not be trusted. Therefore, control his affairs, give him no rest, haul him before the courts. But we know seventeenth-century justice and its great problem: *quis custodiet ipsos custodes*? The tax farmers and drink-retailers of Alkmaar agreed in 1620 that for every three tuns of beer only two would be taxed. This happened with the foreknowledge of the magistrate.[64] Tax farmers of woollen cloth at Amsterdam found in 1624 that their predecessors 'had made deals with almost all the cloth-merchants', and had deprived the country of great sums. They brought the matter to light, but after more than six months of litigation they lost the belief that the city councillors truly wanted to know what was in the pudding.[65] Conniving judges could expect little from their agents. In 1623 all the garrison commanders of Holland were warned in writing that 'through the fraud and smuggling of soldiers, the tax revenues on beer have fallen by half'. The 'lax observance of duty' by the commandants must therefore have been partly responsible.[66]

It was not a question of isolated incidents. These abuses were chronic, not least because the urban regents themselves were all too glad to make agreements with the tax farmers.[67] And because one good turn deserved another, they would then take the tax farmers under their protection, if they were threatened with seizure by impatient receivers.[68] A proposal of 1627 for the creation of a kind of central investigative service, independent of the city magistrates,[69] had no chance of passage in the States of Holland. They were even less inclined to place the jurisdiction over illicit agreements in the hands of the Deputised Councils.[70] In 1631, after lengthy delays and negotiations, there was a proclamation that required magistrates as well as tax farmers to take an oath against these agreements.[71] But then there was a waiting period before it was enforced. In 1636 some members of the assembly received orders to study 'how best the agreements could be fought, to the end that such might be done not with words but in reality'.[72] It appeared that the oath against agreements had been entirely ignored in Hoorn, Enkhuizen and Purmerend. In The Hague the tax farmers had rejected it. And in seven voting cities – Dordrecht, Delft, Rotterdam, Schoonhoven, Brill, Edam and Medemblik – the tax farmers had co-operated, but the magistrates had refused.[73]

Here was already apparent what the States of Holland would expressly conclude seven years later: the rules were good enough, if people would only obey them. 'It is uniformly understood', they said, 'that the order that has been established for these [cases] is good and right, and all that is lacking is good and uniform practice.'[74] The style strikes us as more direct than is usual in bureaucratic prose. The chancery language of Holland did become more human and more homely in the years that Pensionary Jacob Cats wielded the pen. Yet the greater eloquence of his prose did not reflect stronger rule. True, Cats did not hesitate to point out the real villains. These were the regents themselves, who as burgomasters destroyed in their own towns what they had first built as deputies in the States. By their actions they called down God's wrath on the land, and brought a multitude of evils over the entire state.[75]

Perhaps Cats was still looking too much to the town hall and the courtroom. It would have been more honest to divide the blame among the tax farmers, regents and taxpayers. None of them came off scot-free. Fiscal morality in Holland was undoubtedly low. Now it is true that fiscal morality has this tendency everywhere, in every period. Perhaps the unusual point about Holland, all things considered, was not that taxes were widely evaded, but that to this almost universal rule exceptions could be found. Farmers of the tax on milling in Wormer and Jisp testified in 1614 that the taxes were paid correctly everywhere in their district. If it were only so in Haarlem and Amsterdam, they said, then the revenue in the cities could increase by thousands.[76] Probably this showed the influence of the Mennonites, who at that time had the reputation of strictly upholding the laws of Christian morality.[77] Where the Mennonites were numerous, such as in the Waterland region, they sometimes also inspired the Calvinists, who did not want to appear too backward by comparison.[78]

Naturally the Calvinists themselves knew what was right. The reformed church councils always enforced discipline against frauds, and sometimes also against members who had a bad name as taxpayers, even if no one had proved anything against them.[79] Yet the members themselves held the reins somewhat looser. 'It is a pitiful situation for a country where liars and cheats can become richer than decent people; it becomes even worse as lying and cheating are practised so much that a man cannot earn his living without them. This happens in the tax farms of this land, because a man cannot make ends meet if he gives the tax farmer his due'.[80] So wrote Isaäc Beeckman in the intimacy of his diary. Is this language entirely fitting to a man who has just refreshed his spirit with Willem Teellinck's *Complete Christian*?[81] Beeckman would still, grumbling, choose Teellinck's side. 'The tax farmers make many scoundrels rich, because decent people will not cheat'.[82] Bravo! But how many decent people can be found in a community of normally constituted and thus sinful people? 'You'll get at least something from me, but nothing at all from others', said an Amsterdammer who was caught evading the tax on milling in 1620.[83] The nature of the tax system of Holland made it rather difficult to see fraud as a crime that injured the whole community. The public saw the tax farmer as a private profiteer,[84] whose blood-sucking practices gave no cause for Christian conciliation.

We should not imagine the tax farmer as an administrator who sat behind a desk writing assessment notices and threatening orders. The tax farmer had to go out in public and investigate the houses and cellars of the taxpayers. He was not allowed, at least not in our period, to do this on his own initiative. Depending on local customs, permission was needed from the sheriff or even from the burgomasters.[85] Nor was the tax farmer allowed to make inspections as often as he wished:[86] such an unlimited power was only granted in highly exceptional cases, on the authority of the States of Holland.[87] But when the tax farmer made his rounds, he also counted on real support from the authorities. Literally, for city-servants or bailiffs accompanied him, and gave the visit an official cachet.[88] Proven fraud could be punished very severely. Willem Willemsz. of Voorburg had in 1617 evaded the beer-tax on three half-vats by presenting a forged receipt. He was condemned to a fine of 260 gulden and three months' imprisonment on bread and water, all at his own expense. This was a mild sentence, because the States had chosen 'mercy before rigour in justice',[89] probably because the delinquent had voluntarily confessed. A suspect who did not do that ran the risk of torture on the rack,[90] because defrauding the fisc was a criminal offence.

The strict rules were apparently not always applied with equal force. But the system of justice was required to offer good protection to the tax farmers. House-searches meant that tax collecting was a dangerous occupation. Often it came down to resistance in word and deed.[91] Tax collectors risked serious injuries during their visitations. Barent Willemsz. of Heusden had his left ear bitten off.[92] He could count himself lucky, because now and then tax collectors were killed in the exercise of their duties.[93] To reduce the chances of murder and manslaughter, the authorities wanted the tax farmers to act tactfully and discreetly, and sometimes they refused to accept someone as a tax farmer if he appeared lacking in this regard – 'because he is much too quarrelsome'.[94] Occasionally the tax collectors themselves made things nasty when they violently broke open cellars,[95] smashed tuns of beer,[96] and readily enforced their will with drawn knives. Thus there were sometimes casualties among the objects of their visits. The bailiff of Amstelland fatally wounded two men at Ouderkerk in 1606. He could however prove that he had acted in self-defence.[97]

The system remained practicable because the means of assessment touched only a limited number of persons directly, the shopkeepers and producers. For a tax system that would have made control of any given household possible and necessary, the police apparatus was not available. Amsterdam did not introduce the wagon-tax in 1642, 'out of consideration of the great number of rabble and rough people, who would be required to pay the specified measure'.[98] The many poor and less well-off, Amsterdam could as well have said. That would indeed have sounded more friendly, but would not have reflected the meaning any better. Amsterdam did not protest because it wanted to spare the weaker people; rather, it feared that it would be unable to maintain law and order if 'the rabble and rough people' also had to learn what a house-search meant. At that time they did not experience it themselves. The rabble paid little taxation directly. They did contribute indirectly, as excise taxes raised the prices of all consumer goods.

Nor did the common people directly receive the benefits of taxation: protection against the enemy, maintenance of public safety, and free practice of the reformed religion. Indeed religion was barely supported by taxation, and just as little went to education or poor relief. Since the tasks of the government were limited, taxes could still remain relatively low. If the burden had been heavier, it would have been necessary to strengthen the forces of public order. A welfare state is possible only if the prompt payment of high tax assessments is still a more attractive alternative than the risks of refusal and evasion. The seventeenth century was unable to accomplish that. The caring state lay outside reality, in Utopia. Before it could become a reality, the administration would have to grow considerably in power.

The only members of the population who drew immediate and personal advantage from the tax moneys were those who worked for the state or had carried out a commission for the government. To the first category belonged lower officials such as messengers and caretakers, and, naturally, sailors and soldiers. Under the second heading fell primarily those who had compulsorily or voluntarily contributed to national defence, for example in military transport and in the building of siege-works. All these groups together formed a fairly numerous company. They were in a position to experience personally how the government used tax revenues and paid its servants. Therefore, they deserve to be discussed separately in this chapter on the people and public money.

The administration was accustomed to deliver a so-called 'ordinance of payment' to its creditors. This was a written order to a specifically named receiver to pay the beneficiary the sum stated. The receivers generally had more ordinances presented to them than they could pay in cash. At the higher levels the sequence of payment was a political matter; at the lower ones it depended on bribes and relations. All these factors played a role for our subjects, but we can reconstruct the order of payment only as it depended on political priorities.

At the back of the queue probably stood the burghers who had performed services for the army and the fleet. The labour-foremen, transporters, and suppliers were always paid late. At the beginning of the Twelve Years' Truce, for example, the receiver-general of the Republic was holding approximately one million gulden of

unpaid bills.[99] These were primarily declarations from contractors for the fortifications. In most instances we do not know exactly in which year they carried
out their works. It does give pause for thought, however, when we still find in a
review of 1613[100] a bill for the strengthening of Rijnberk, because Spinola had
conquered that fortress in 1606. But he had also done the like to Ostend in 1604
and even so the contractors who had done the work there still appeared on the 1613
list, when they were owed nearly 8,000 gulden.

Perhaps these nine years were exceptional, and a great deal of the Ostend works
had already been paid by 1613, but it was indeed a chronic evil. This was particularly
so in the 1630s and 1640s, when the obligations of Holland regularly exceeded tax
revenues,[101] and contractors were driven to the limit of their patience, 'because of
the lengthy non-payment'.[102] Actually the States did understand that the 'labour-
foremen had complained loudly, and had expressed their intense disgust with the
administration'.[103] It was also miserliness of the sort that ran counter to good sense.
Not without justice did Cats expect that the contractors and suppliers would
increase their prices sharply.[104] If I take on a job for 5,000 gulden, said a contemporary pamphleteer, and the country pays me within ten days of completion,
then I'd be willing to do it for 3,000.[105] Thus for cash payment there was an
enormous discount, and that in a time without inflationary worries; this suggests a
very sombre picture of the estimated waiting time for payment. The receivers never
gave interest on an ordinance of payment.[106] Anyone who knew his customers would
then factor the loss of interest into the price. If we assume an annual rate of interest
of 8 per cent, a capital sum with a present value of 3,000 gulden would not exceed
5,000 gulden until after seven years. These are only a couple of figures, but they
clearly show how little confidence the contractors had in the administration.

The labour-foremen stood farthest back. Differences between them and other
groups of burghers, however, were only a matter of degree. Transporters who were
taken into service for the campaign of 1635 still had claims of 700,000 gulden in
1638.[107] In 1640 the bills for 1638 were still unpaid,[108] and in 1646 the transporters
of Holland requested payment 'at least for the year sixteen hundred and forty-
three',[109] as if it would then be impolite to wish already for something on account
for 1644 or even 1645. It should be noted that this involved the transporters of
Holland, who were in an enviable position compared to their counterparts in other
provinces. A proclamation of Holland in 1645 had indeed specified that a transporter
who was drafted for an army baggage train had to present a certificate from the
magistrate of his place of residence, because many were unjustly claiming to be
Hollanders in the hope of better payment.[110] There was an added inconvenience for
the transporter from Holland, in that he could long remain in uncertainty about
how much he had actually earned. Only in 1631 were the daily rates determined
for transport services that had been provided in the year 1628.[111] It often happened
that daily rates for services rendered were set long after the date.[112] Then finally
the ordinance of payment could be written, and the wait for payment would begin.

The handling of this sort of business in the States of Holland generally gives the impression that after three years a creditor acquired the moral right to be impatient. The messengers of the Generality became an item on the agenda when their wages and travel expenses had fallen three and a half years in arrears.[113] Evidently they had then exhausted their reserves. It became necessary to maintain them with advances,[114] and then it became cheaper to go ahead and pay their overdue wages. We also note a term of about three years observed with suppliers to the admiralties. In 1628 the States of Holland decided to make full payment to the creditors of the admiralty at Rotterdam for the ordinances dating from 1625 or earlier, and for sums not exceeding 100 gulden.[115] Thus payments began with the weakest, because they found it hardest to overcome their difficulties. The States of Holland themselves said in 1630 that the debts of the admiralties since 1627 – once again a term of three years – would now have to be paid, because 'many of the inhabitants of Holland, having given credit to the aforesaid colleges, have in the meantime been declared insolvent, and reduced to great poverty and misery'.[116] A bit more consciousness of the debt would not have been out of place for Their Noble Great Mightinesses.

The burghers were the most severely defrauded, because nothing was done for them during the waiting period. Sailors and soldiers also might receive no pay for a long time, but at least they were provided with their living by other means. Sailors could always be certain of their board, though not of money: in 1628 the sailors on inland waterways had yet to receive forty-five months' worth of wages from the Admiralty of the Maas.[117] Indeed Rotterdam had paid almost nothing to anyone during 1626 and 1627, and was running arrears of fifty-two months with its least favoured creditors.[118] With this in mind, even the complaints of the inland barge-skippers that they were still owed sixty to ninety months' pay in 1635 no longer sound completely incredible.[119]

The treatment of admiralty personnel confirms once again that the Republic in the time of Frederick Henry was living somewhat beyond its means, and waged war on a wider scale than it could actually afford. For this endless postponement of payments was both costly and risky. It was risky, because the non-payment of the States' sailors, who fell into the hands of the privateers of Dunkirk, made it easier for them to decide to accept more agreeable service with the enemy.[120] It was costly, too, because the administration was often required to keep more people in service than it really needed. The capture of Breda in 1637 simplified the protection of the internal waterways, so that several ships could have been taken out of service and the crews discharged. That would have produced a saving of 420 gulden per day. But simultaneously it would have been necessary to pay back wages of 163,910 gulden.[121] Without their money, these men could certainly not be sent home: they would undoubtedly have mutinied.[122]

Perhaps the sailors knew that this extreme remedy would always succeed. At least, the experience of Frederick Henry's time teaches that the crews got money as soon as they showed signs of indiscipline. Vice-admiral Liefhebber and Captains Tromp and Juynboll could not sail in May 1633, because their crews refused to

25. 'Real citation; in other words, imprisonment', from *Practice in civil cases*

serve unless money was first put on the table. This action produced 12,000 gulden for them.[123] In 1636, the sailors of Captain Gillis de Vries forced their way into the admiralty building and demanded prompt payment. It was decided to supply the money, and then to punish the ringleaders.[124] The States certainly feared that otherwise these men would gather a following. And rightly so: three months later the sailors of Admiral Van Dorp gained entry to the private homes of the lords of the admiralty, and requested two years' back wages.[125] An even more threatening demonstration took place in 1637, when the 'common populace', otherwise known as the country's sailors, used armed force to demand complete payment. On this occasion also the instigators landed in gaol. Yet the forcibly extracted promises were 100 per cent fulfilled by the States.[126] In the last analysis, they needed their sailors too much.

For the soldiers this was at least equally true. We have already discussed in part I how the States' army in the time of Maurice of Nassau could be brought under strict discipline because it was continually paid on time.[127] Under the stadholdership of Frederick Henry this did not change. The soldiers continued to receive their money, and mostly more or less on time. But between the paymaster and the soldier a middleman had appeared, the so-called solicitor, now more clearly visible than before. When the receivers of Holland had too little cash to pay a certain company, the solicitor would advance the sum to the person responsible, thus to the captain, who had to distribute the pay to the men. For his services, the solicitor collected interest from the captain's account. If a company remained without money for a long time, it could be very expensive for its commanding officer, because the interest was calculated at a fairly high rate. In 1635 some companies of Holland had not received anything for a year and a half or even two years. The captains then had to pay the solicitor 150 to 200 gulden interest per month.[128] It is true that a 'month' in the army was six weeks long, but that also applied to the payment of wages. Once every six weeks, then, the captain received his 150-gulden salary.[129] And once every six weeks he had to pay at least the same sum to the solicitor. Thus every month the captain must have lost ... no, of course the captain did not do that. He reached for the proven expedient of creative accounting. He did not seek replacements for men who had deserted or died, but instead kept their names on the roster. The commanders received the full sum in wages, which could then be applied to the interest. Thus it came about that an army with a nominal total of 80,000 men was in reality only 60,000 men strong.[130] During the war against Spain this situation was never really remedied. It helps us understand why after the peace of Münster people expected wonders from the demobilisation. A small army could be paid without advances from the solicitors. The savings lay not only in the actual demobilisation; rather, all of the nominal manpower could be eliminated, for it had only stood on the paylists in order to cover the interest.

As long as the war lasted this reform could not be carried out. The solicitors continued to play a key role. In 1637 they held unpaid ordinances for a total of 3,343,751 gulden and 17 stuivers.[131] That may have been a low point for the administration, but in 1643 the solicitors were still holding about 2,000,000 gulden in paper.[132] In 1637 the commandent of Grave sent two horsemen to The Hague to ask for payment of the wages. The States of Holland answered that they did not approve of this new method: the army should make use of a solicitor.[133] The commandant of Grave was not a mere unknown, but none other than Thomas Stakenbroek, one of the few non-princely officers with the rank of general. But even he was not allowed to bypass the solicitor.

Therein was certainly one of the disadvantages that this system of postponed payment almost inevitably brought: it gave uncontrolled power to persons without public positions. In the seventeenth-century world this was no anomaly, but that did not remove the dangers. It is true that the intervention of the solicitors had the fortunate result for the soldiers that they themselves did not have to wait for their wages. Anyone who did, and who had no other sources of income, was often forced to offer his ordinances for sale. For the crew-members of the navy this seems to have been the rule. In 1629 the Admiralty of Rotterdam recommended special consideration from the States for sailors who were owed fifty-two months' wages. Since these men had received no official written confirmation, they 'had not been able to sell their shares, to pass them along or transfer them to others'.[134] Such a transaction was not entirely advantageous, either. The purchaser knew that he probably would have to wait patiently for several years, and he never paid the face value of the ordinance. In 1646 seven captains' widows asked compensation for the loss they suffered because 'owing to non-payment by the state'[135] they were forced to the 'sale of its ordinances at a vile price'.[136]

It could be that these widows had suffered extreme disadvantages. Concrete complaints of this nature seldom appear in the resolutions of the States of Holland. More frequently we encounter general lamentations about the misery caused by the trade in ordinances.[137] As proof of abuse they are less convincing than the chapter-and-verse examples cited. But they do show us that slow payment with all its consequences gave the administration a bad reputation. A pamphlet from the 1640s proposes the trade in ordinances as a sure road to quick riches. Professional speculators bought up these papers from labour-foremen, barge-skippers and trans-porters, and realised profits of 30 to 40 per cent.[138] Such thieves were also the reason why the government repeatedly had to invent new taxes or raise old ones, 'that we poor farmers all have to pay'.[139] Now of course the Hollanders were not shy about risky financial transactions. A purchaser of ordinances had to reckon on a considerable risk, because payment could easily take several years longer than he had expected. Shouldn't his enterpreneurial spirit be rewarded? Yes, but again according to our pamphlet-writer the risk was in reality not so great. The ordinance-buyers had eliminated the workings of chance, because they worked hand-in-hand with the receivers. The latter first delayed payment so long that the holders sold their paper out of despair, at rock-bottom prices. Immediately afterwards, the receivers paid the money to the new owners and split the profit with them.

Was this foul slander? Such stories were seldom completely unfounded in the seventeenth century. In 1637 it was forbidden for deputies of the States-General, members of the Council of State and committees in other colleges of the generality directly or indirectly 'to purchase or have purchased any ordinances, unpaid claims, or shares of military officers, labour-foremen, and others no matter of what nature they may be'.[140] The Hollanders did not follow that example. They were not required to do so, either. But in their behaviour with public money, appearances were against them.

Chapter 12

THE COMMUNITY

People must be quiet. These four words give the complete text of the role of the masses on the Dutch political stage, as cast by the regents. But the people did not always play the part faithfully. The regents were inclined to attribute this to the agitation of bad counsellors, such as pamphlet-writers, Spanish sympathisers and reformed preachers. Thus they resolved to fight these influences, although never very energetically. Regent rule made little effort to mould public opinion, yet it seemed confident of its mission. Were the regents right to expect their leadership to be recognised as expressing the wishes and interests of the masses?

Generally the regents' rule in the sixteenth and seventeenth centuries was not particularly directed towards the welfare of the popular classes. Law enforcement, defence against the enemy, and protection of the public church were seen as the primary tasks of the government. All subjects might benefit from them, and all were required to contribute to the costs according to their wealth. Government did not readily regard it as its duty to provide the greatest possible prosperity for all. Poverty was an insoluble problem anyway. The regents of Holland gave some consideration to the consequences of poverty: they sponsored poor relief. And to a certain extent they even participated in the prevention of poverty: they tried to encourage everyone to get good vocational training. The former subject was discussed in part I, and the latter in part II.

Yet more remains to be said. To prevent hunger, the rulers of cities[1] and the regions of Holland tried to maintain control over food prices, above all cereal grains. In the regulations of The Hague in 1572 and 1574, we get a fairly complete picture of what a city administration was willing to do to provide an adequate supply at reasonable prices during the first years of the revolt against Spain. The rulers of The Hague established maximum prices.[2] They checked to see whether the bakers and grain merchants were deliberately withholding their supplies.[3] They prohibited the sale of grain to foreigners, and in time of scarcity they did not allow flour to be used for white bread and cake.[4] They were on their guard to prevent bakers from keeping the wheat-flour separate, and mixing bran in the people's bread 'to the great disadvantage and damage of the poor community'.[5] That our contemporary health-food propagandists would regard precisely that bran as a feast takes nothing away from the good intentions of the magistrates of The Hague.

The customary emergency measures of the States of Holland show many similarities to those of The Hague in 1572. The States also resorted frequently to price controls, and thereby they could fall back on a well-established routine. To draw up the proclamation on grain prices in 1630, they consulted earlier orders from the years 1521, 1556, 1565 and 1596.[6] They could easily have extended this list. Yet control of reserves on the provincial level was never achieved. In 1597 the towns were advised to store up their own reserves for lean years,[7] but they would do so only of their own accord.[8] The sale of grain to foreigners residing in Holland was not forbidden; the restriction at The Hague involved a rather selfish wartime regulation. It was related, however, to the prohibition against exporting grain issued in 1576.[9] Perhaps it is no coincidence that we find such an example in exactly those years when Amsterdam was still on the Spanish side and did not form part of the States of Holland, for the grain trade of Amsterdam was not readily inclined to accept such limitations. Everhard van Reyd even wrote straightforwardly that prohibitions against grain exports from the Netherlands were not possible.[10] That was in 1596, although according to his contemporaries in 1595 the dearth was caused by the great exports to Italy.[11] That export trade was indeed also expressly forbidden,[12] apparently without any visible results. Moreover it was not uncommon in a time of scarcity to withhold raw materials from the beer-brewers.[13] In the worst case the authorities even went so far as to prohibit gleaning the fields,[14] although they did this with understandable reluctance. Those modest handfuls of grain would probably have gone to the neediest people anyway.

Now it is true that concern about the price of bread did not rest solely on love for one's neighbour and compassion.[15] A shortage of grain, declared the States of Holland in 1597, was undesirable for many reasons, among others because 'the workers have the bread taken out of their mouths and become unemployed'. And why was that so damaging to the country? Because of the 'great decrease in revenues from indirect taxes':[16] revenues would decline. We discover this worry more often when we examine closely the resolutions and decisions of the regents of Holland: there was concern about the lot of the common man, but no less for the public finances. Thus in 1609 in The Hague the clandestine sale of bread was forbidden because it led to 'fraud and prejudice against the poor community [by the bakers], who under the cover of making bread a farthing or a ha'penny cheaper would not bake the same to its proper weight, nor use good ingredients'.[17] This was certainly possible, but undoubtedly another reason for this ban was that the clandestine bakeries did not pay the impost on flour.

One possibility is as likely as the other. When the States of Holland agreed to devote a portion of the provincial poll-tax on local poor relief in 1623,[18] they may have feared massive begging and hunger-riots in that year of very high prices.[19] Yet that would not preclude their being simultaneously concerned about the fate of the poor.

Under the heading of social policy we should also discuss public housing. Leiden in particular tried as much as possible to encourage the construction of houses: the municipality bought land from owners who were not in a position to build on it themselves.[20] Thus in 1596 the magistrates had built seventy-one workers' houses, which were rented for the very modest price of six stuivers per week.[21] This was completely inadequate to fight the housing shortage,[22] although it is enough to make us question Jan Romein's proposition that the concept of workers' housing is no older than the second half of the nineteenth century.[23] At Naarden the administration also considered 'building several poor little houses there', as we note incidentally in the resolutions of Holland.[24] It is likely that research in local archives might reveal more about such building activities, because the notion of existing need was current in regent circles.[25]

Care for the subjects did exist, although it was sometimes expressed in the typical regent manner. We know their preference for an immobile stratification of society. At the end of the sixteenth century, there was a desire to give this stratification visible expression in clothing. *Dominee* Puppius of Edam received complaints from his community in 1595, that he had approved the wearing of worldly clothes. Puppius answered that people should make a distinction among themselves.[26] What he meant appeared in the records of church discipline. Beautifully adorned regent women were not reproached by the church, but the family of Intgen Pietersz. did receive a warning, because 'she would eat lard-cakes out of poverty, and yet clothe her children as burgomaster's children'.[27] Similar social distinctions were certainly not general in the reformed church at that time. Most preachers pronounced anathema against all excessive clothing and decoration, without regard to the quality of the wearer.[28] Edam was a community where the church council then consisted entirely of regents, and perhaps under their influence Puppius may have come to his accommodating doctrine, which was also preached outside Edam. Holland's budding growth influenced the clothing customs of a lower *burgerij* who gained more financial muscle, and also wanted to dress in silk and velvet. This was reported by Master Valcoogh:

> People see today, that as time goes by,
> Everyone wants to show off
> In his expenses, his clothing, and all manner of decorations,
> So that you don't know how to distinguish rightly
> A burgher from a farmer or a nobleman.[29]

Thus Valcoogh did not condemn worldly clothing as such, but he did object to a manner of dress that collapsed distinctions between social groups. This was undesirable from a social point of view: furthermore – or perhaps exactly for that reason – people saw moral objections. Persons would compete with each other 'to wear frills and starched collar-ruffs and needlework, even though they might have to withhold bread from their mouths and take their clothes to the pawnbroker'. But naturally people had not acquired all their pomp for the sake of the pawnbroker's clothesrack. Would not servants and maids be led astray towards crime and fornication, if only to beautify themselves, no matter what the cost?[30]

If the people were too weak to protect themselves from such temptation, then the government could consider helping the simple folk by forbidding all that dangerous finery. This indeed happened, but in a half-hearted manner. That is, they did not enact an absolute prohibition against the wearing of costly fabric by the lower classes.[31] Such a regulation would have been discriminatory, but not necessarily dishonest. If the regents were really convinced that fur and gold thread were damaging and dangerous for the common man, then they could have forbidden them. But in general they did not. Here and there local regulations were enacted, and then only for very limited groups: in Vlaardingen, for example, for those on poor relief,[32] and in the States' College at Leiden for students in theology.[33] The States of Holland, however, issued a proclamation that summed up all the disadvantages – the presumption, the confusion of classes – but did not lead to the only logical conclusion of general prohibition. Instead the States enacted a tax on the wearing of such clothes, and exempted all 'qualified' persons and members of their households.[34]

26. Satirical print on broad pleated ruffs

No one was impressed by such a policy. It would have been easier to understand and to justify laws that maintained the distinctions between classes in full force, but did not offer them for sale. Law-making of this kind regulated the privilege of hunting. The nobility of Holland was very attached to that privilege and sought to maintain the stock of game at any price.[35] That price was paid by the farmers. They could indeed use ditches to defend their land against rabbits, but the water on the side nearest the dunes could not be so wide that the animals ran any danger of drowning.[36] In accord with the same principles, the farmers of Kennemerland were allowed to surround their fields and meadows with high fences,[37] but they were not free to shoot harts and hinds even when they found them on their own land.[38] In any case, the rules were clear, though we should not be surprised that country folk did not always observe them strictly.[39]

Evidently they could not accept protection of class interests at their expense as justified. They did not regard wild game as another man's exclusive property. This manner of thinking was related to the mentality of villagers in the bogland areas. Even village bailiffs could not or would not adequately guard the interests of landowners against the clandestine digging of peat.[40] Hooft tried as bailiff of Muiden, but he discovered that 'the warnings . . . have no more effect on reckless people than their own consciences'. They never betrayed their fellow villagers, and they warned each other when they heard of Hooft's coming.[41]

Here public authority fell short of the ideal, and encountered resistance that could lead to violence if it nonetheless tried to enforce its will. We could hardly expect anything else, for the legitimacy of legal prescription was not anchored in the popular mind, and people regarded the officers of justice as defenders of private interests. In all such cases, whether they dealt with hunting rabbits, digging peat, evading taxes, or any other activity wherein people thought they knew better than the controlling magistrates,[42] respect for public order did not appear strong enough to encourage natural obedience. Submission could never be assumed in advance. Have we not already seen how tongues wagged about magistrates in taverns and inns? Contentious as the seventeenth-century Hollanders were, drink loosened their bottled-up rancour, which buzzed in the ears of the regents as a warning, 'in vino veritas'. Dirck Arien, a workman from Oostvoorne, was heading home drunk from Brill one evening in 1616. On his way he met a stadholder and vassals of the land of Voorne. His mocking greeting, 'Good evening, chimney sweeps', earned him a sentence of sixteen years' exile. On appeal the judgment was changed to a fine of six gulden, but the sinner was required 'to beg forgiveness from God and justice with folded hands and bended knees'.[43]

Drunkenness, so often a safe-conduct for criminal thoughtlessness, could not excuse ridicule of the authorities. On the contrary, the Deputised Councils of Holland expressly declared in 1591 that it was not permissible 'that such under the cover of some drunkenness or fury would be accepted or allowed', not even 'under the cover of some declaration of regret'. Surely, what happened today in drunkenness would tomorrow be a wicked example for others, and lead 'to the stiffening of evil-intentioned and restless persons'.[44] Sharp criticism of the authorities was described as seditious behaviour,[45] for which 'the adherents of the common enemy' were all too quickly blamed as the true instigators.[46] In 1620 a number of burghers of Delft and some representatives of Rijswijk came to the States of Holland to complain about their respective bailiffs and various other civil servants. Their requests for the removal of these officers, however, were not even considered. The States decided that 'if such were allowed, the same would be practised against magistrates and all others'.[47]

Indeed it did sometimes happen that magistrates were removed because of public opinion, without their having been convicted of a specific offence by the judicial system. The council of Enkhuizen expelled Jan Symonsz. Blaeuhulck in 1615 because he had fathered a child out of wedlock, and furthermore had sought to terminate the pregnancy prematurely.[48] No complete judicial proof was offered, but the council expressly stated that Blaeuhulck's behaviour had caused 'talking, murmurs and discord among the community of our city', by which the entire administration 'had been brought into disdain and contempt, as if we were the ones who neither wished nor dared to punish evil and such scandalous sins and nuisances'.[49] Yet the conclusive force of this example is limited. Practically without exception the regents of Enkhuizen were strict Calvinists who would not tolerate the violation of the moral laws of the church by their fellow magistrates.

Normally the influence of popular opinion was rejected as dangerous laxity, by which 'one would make the common people absolute masters of the government, so that when it pleased them they would time and again lay down the law not only to the respective magistrates, but even to my lords the States themselves'.[50] The regents bore the responsibility, and therefore always wanted to decide matters for themselves. If the nation's affairs went badly, said the States of Holland in 1633, then the government would get the blame, not the common people.[51] So the latter had better keep quiet: in all the towns of Holland the calling of private meetings was forbidden,[52] and every attempt to involve the common people in government was regarded as reprehensible. In 1621 the Amsterdam magistrates reproached the church council for holding a charitable collection for the French Protestants in La Rochelle. The church council understood where the shoe pinched, and hastened to answer that the collection had been carried out only among 'qualified persons'[53] – thus the matters did not touch the common people.

Yet no matter how much effort the regents devoted to silencing the commons, they were not successful in stifling all political activity. Any policy that was found unacceptable by the simple folk could be opposed 'with such energy, and wrath against the States, that, so it seemed, they were no more than a hair's breadth from revolt'.[54] Particularly when the rationale for decisions was not presented, people could only guess at the motives and began to question the government. In 1587 at Leiden, when Valmaer, Maulde and Cosmo de Pascarengis lost their lives on the scaffold for an attempted revolution in favour of the Earl of Leicester, 'many people remained scandalised by this execution, because the States had not brought to light the causes, disputes and discord which had occurred, with the reasons that moved them to the said execution'.[55] Here at least the regents' renowned tendency to disregard public opinion[56] had gone too far.

Mostly, however, the regents could permit themselves that luxury. As long as only political issues were involved, the public normally restricted itself to murmuring,[57] to 'some shouting and screaming'.[58] Only two motives appear to have been strong enough to move the people to real action: concerns about the faith, and fears about money. The first had already appeared to some extent during the time of Leicester, when opposition came particularly from 'many simple folk, most from the reformed religion',[59] who regarded the States as enemies of the Protestant faith.[60] It became clear as the light of day during the controversies of the Twelve Years' Truce, but that conflict will be discussed later.[61]

And then there was money. We do not mean individual tax evasion or personal resistance to house-searches, even though murder and manslaughter might be involved. Rather, we are thinking of cases where the public registered massive protest through direct action against the introduction, levying or increase of a particular tax. Thus in 1610 the entire village of Maassluis was in an uproar when the local administration laid an extra tax on fish. The officer who made the announcement was pelted with rotten apples, and the magistrate had to call soldiers to help restore order. It seemed to make no difference that this new tax was intended for a very humanitarian purpose, namely the ransom of several Maassluis sailors who had been captured by the Turks.[62] As soon as love for the private purse had aroused emotions, the people no longer asked for reasons and motives; instead they turned with blind fury against the entire administration. In the tax revolt at Delft in 1616 the mob did not spare the secretariat where the papers of the city orphans were kept.[63]

These disturbances at Delft are worthy of closer study because they represented more than a simple reaction to increased tax burdens. The seventeenth-century worker did not yet know precisely what he lacked and what he needed. He was not yet able to express his demands and wishes clearly. The only form of protest that he could imagine was the tax revolt. Such disturbances reveal something of latent social unrest, of the smouldering hatred between the poor and the rich. Netherlanders are always so jealous, complained Aerssen van Sommelsdijck, they are always envious of those 'who prosper and possess more than others'.[64] By contrast, Valcooch saw the situation from below. In his poem on dike-building on the Zijpe he allowed the polder boys to have their own say as the universally exploited and exhausted victims of society:

> Here we still sing our old tune:
> Poverty, poverty, how you have bitten us!
> Lice-ridden and wet we crawl into bed,
> We must sleep in miserable little huts
> In our job there is so little to eat ...
> We always walk with torn clothes and empty [pockets]

We can never earn a penny more
Because we are constantly coming too late,
We work like mules, so that our eyes are distorted,
We get stiff and lame limbs in the bargain
We dig and spade, we empty our caps
And wear out socks, shoes and trousers.[65]

Only rarely was that dissatisfaction voiced as a principled condemnation of the established order. Baudartius tells us that in 1624 a band of thieves and vagrants entered an old ruined church on a summer day. One of their leaders made a speech there about the community of goods, 'de communione bonorum ex lege naturae', and declared that people could take from the rich what they did not freely give.[66] Was it Baudartius who thought up this learned Latin phrase, or was the bandit leader a *literatus* who had fallen on hard times? He could have spiced his discourse with a pinch of Plato and who knows, in honour of the church building, even a text or two from the Acts of the Apostles; of these, his audience may have understood nothing except that they were serviceable to his wished-for moral. In any case this vagabond was one of the very few who – and perhaps only in jest – preached redistribution of goods as the foundation of a new social system. Mostly a rebellious word was only an instantaneous reaction of the one who had been provoked to the extreme. 'It would be better to build a barn, and put all the poorest people inside, and set it on fire!' screamed Maria Jans van Brugge to the overseers of the poor in Amsterdam, when she was arrested for begging. But suddenly she became afraid, and dared not repeat that she would summon the overseers before God's judgment seat as exploiters of the poor.[67]

The people could sometimes find such courage when they acted *en masse*, and as mentioned the Delft tax revolt of 1616 was a striking example.[68] That year the magistrates of Delft had raised the excise on grain, in order to get the revenue needed to excavate a new navigation channel. At the same time, however, they reduced the wine-tax, which made an extremely unfavourable impression on the public. If the city needed money, why then did the magistrates lower the price of a luxury article, while the food of the people had to be more expensive? Many persons, mostly women, assembled at the town hall on August 2, and demanded an increase in wine-taxes instead of those on grain. The sheriff and his helpers did not succeed in holding the crowd in check, and even a promise of amnesty failed to calm them. As a last resort the burgomasters then called out the civic guard, which at Delft – and indeed everywhere else[69] – was chosen exclusively from 'the most suitable, peaceable, and best qualified burghers or children of burghers', and did not tolerate any poor in its ranks.[70] Thus these were the right men to put down a revolt against regent rule; they were 480 strong, all armed with firelocks and muskets. Yet on this occasion their intervention was not effective. Several were disarmed by the rabble as soon as they came out of their houses; others, who had been able to assemble and fire some shots against the crowd, were so heavily pelted with paving stones that they had to sound the retreat. Did these events stay in the memory of the poet Westerbaen, when he later declared that the Delft guards were as well-suited to their firelocks as donkeys to a lute?[71]

The success they had achieved gave the people new courage. The rioters began to speak of an attack on the houses of the rich, saying 'that this evening they would be just as rich'. Evidently they regarded the rich and the regents as one. The administration capitulated. They lowered the grain-excise and several other taxes, and announced a general pardon. That temporarily quelled the disturbances. The cry of 'victory, we have won' was heard, although the recklessness of some was not satisfied: 'we'll have yet more to show!' The flames of rebellion instantly went out when Frederick Henry marched into the city with several companies that evening, under commission from the Deputised Councils of Holland, and not without the foreknowledge of the burgomasters of Delft. All talk of a general pardon was ended. The Court of Holland immediately launched an investigation and had the ringleaders punished in an exemplary manner.

If the revolt failed in the end, the course of events still tells us more about seventeenth-century rebelliousness. Delft could be an indication that such popular movements especially broke out not only where the tax burden was increased, but also where the related circumstances – a decrease in the wine-excise – aroused suspicions of class-favouritism. In 1616 that could already have been known anyway. We recall how a new tax on the wearing of velvet and linen was introduced in 1599. In 1596 the States of Holland had already made a fruitless attempt to put that tax into effect. 'Difficulties and wilfulness' had made the realisation of these plans impossible, especially resentment that the legislators had made themselves exempt.[72]

In regard to the Delft tax revolt presumably it should also be considered that for all practical purposes the saturation point had been reached, and any increase in taxes was risky. This was especially evident after the Twelve Years' Truce, when renewal of the war led to a search for new sources of revenue. At Rotterdam in September 1621, the contract for the twenty-four stuiver tax on tuns of beer was postponed for half a year, in order not to bring about unrest in the community.[73] For Rotterdam another factor that certainly entered the picture was the large number of Remonstrants, who made it more difficult to govern the city. Not long before, the arrest of the Remonstrant preacher Simon Lucae was the occasion of lengthy battles. The same motive – fear of Remonstrant disturbances – may have played a part in Leiden when the council raised objections to the introduction of the poll-tax in 1622, because 'the counting and registration of such a poor community was even dangerous'.[74]

Be that as it may, there was no more talk of Remonstrant dangers during the butter riots of 1624, which broke out spontaneously and independently of each other in several towns of Holland. An increase of about 5 per cent in the butter-tax[75] led to more or less serious disturbances in Amsterdam[76] and Geertruidenberg[77] in particular, but also at Haarlem, Delft and The Hague.[78] Naturally the States of

Holland did not want to accept that 'it should be allowed that the common people could, through tumult and sedition, obstruct the measures adopted by common consent'.[79] The States condemned most strenuously the cities of Gouda, Gorinchem and Schoonhoven, because they lacked courage and had not even dared to proceed with the introduction of the tax.[80] The States also had reason to be dissatisfied with Geertruidenberg, where the magistrates had not shown enough energy in repressing the disturbances, even though the city was still occupied by a strong garrison. Would they allow a handful of whores and young children to dictate the laws?[81]

Now it is certainly true that the rulers of Geertruidenberg had only accepted the increase in the butter-tax most reluctantly.[82] The burgomasters greatly feared that the butter trade would move to Breda, outside the province of Holland. They did protect the person of the tax farmer, but left him to his own devices and ingenuity in fulfilling his duties, although he had promised to ask for less than the new tariff allowed. Yet presumably the greatest problem was precisely that strong garrison. While the States had spoken so unkindly of whores, the testimony of less impassioned witnesses referred repeatedly to the soldiers' wives, and occasionally also to the soldiers themselves. The officer-cadet Jan de Coster, who had promised to help the tax farmer with his collection, was heckled on the street by a large crowd, including some soldiers: 'Here comes the butter-man! If you have the heart to go to the town hall, we'll strike you dead!' His company made life so difficult for him that he felt compelled to resign from the service.

With such soldiery it was impossible to quell a revolt. It was not the only time that solidarity appeared between the soldiers and the greater part of the poor community. A captain of the Dordrecht garrison flatly refused to co-operate in 1647 when the burgomasters appealed to his company: 'To set my men against an enraged community, neither I nor any of our officers can or will do.'[83] In 1612 the sheriff of Vlieland could get no co-operation at all from the extra half-company that was sent to him to provide help with arrests: 'saying they are soldiers with honour, and do not want to perform any constables' or servants' work'.[84] Once in the seventeenth century the administration of Holland stubbornly tried to carry out a policy that went against the will of the great majority. On that occasion it did not succeed with (ordinary) soldiers either: special guards had to be called into service.

The voice of the people became abusive toward these guards. This was a normal reaction, because accomplices of legal authority did not enjoy a good reputation among the public. 'Where can I best find the sheriff?' Bredero's character asks in *The Spanish Brabanter*,

> With Anne Klaas in the Hooren Inn?
> Or with that nice fellow in the Monnikendam tower?[85]

This was said in the friendliest manner, compared to the torrent of abuse that Van Santer's *Spijtige Trijn* (Spiteful Kate) hurled against the entire family of *Snappende Sijtgen*: her father was a drunken good-for-nothing, who later became a constable.

Her father-in-law was the executioner's assistant for six or seven years. Her brother-in-law had rowed on the galleys, her son-in-law had been in prison. Her own husband was a thief and a robber.[86] To us it is most striking that she makes no distinction whatsoever between hardened criminals and officers of justice. For this woman, and perhaps also for Van Santen himself, the scoundrels and their pursuers lived on the same moral level. At times the public seems to have had difficulty tolerating the servants of the law in its midst. Was it a coincidence that at a dance held at Lisse on May Day, 1597, it was the bailiff's servant who was thrown out?[87] If we allow Lisse the benefit of the doubt, the inhabitants of Noordeloos leave us no choice at all. There, time and again, sheriffs, jurors, servants of the law and secretaries were received with catcalls of abuse at weddings and parties: boor, blood sucker, law-twister, stool pigeon, bully, bloodhound![88] At Purmerend Allebert Coopsz. did not want to take communion with Mary Claes, because she had called him a snitch.[89] Apparently he did not find it pleasant to be known as a supporter of authority. This was a typical Netherlandish attitude, according to the English traveller Fynes Moryson. No one here helps to capture a suspect or prevent his escape, he wrote.[90] On the contrary, everyone thought it a humanitarian duty to assist the fugitive as much as possible. Only the executioner, and people of low status who were specially assigned to the task, worked together to arrest perpetrators of capital crimes; as a consequence many escaped.

We have not come to know Moryson as a big-hearted judge, but he was seldom completely in the wrong. The Frenchman Charles Ogier expressed approximately the same sentiments forty years later: the corrupt masses of Holland do not respect any officers at all, he declared with horror.[91] Many times one can find in the case records of the Court of Holland evidence of public opposition to the forces of justice. 'Great noise and trouble' was caused in 1611 by the arrest of a certain Jan Claesz. at Gouda.[92] While this case may have involved an attempt to protect a burgher of the town from standing trial at The Hague, that excuse could not apply in 1613 when two officers of the Court of Holland wanted to arrest an English beggar at the market in The Hague, 'but immediately a great number of people attacked them violently'. Go and catch thieves and rascals, they said, or are there not enough of them? A woman offered each officer a sixpence (*schelling*), if they would let the man go.[93] This was surely more money than she would ever have given to the beggar himself. It is no more than an example, indeed, but according to the description of Bredero's Moortje exactly the same feeling toward the guardians of order prevailed at the market in Amsterdam.

> Oh! I thought, ...
> They should catch the thief, and leave the poor folk to get their pennies.[94]

Scribani said of the Netherlanders that they wanted to be ruled by a friendly hand. The Duke of Alba, 'intending to rule these provinces like the lands of an Indian lord', had chosen the least likely road to win over these people. Violence did not lead to obedience, but rather to resistance.[95]

Alba discovered as much. The Hollanders began a war against him and his Spaniards that lasted eighty years. That struggle definitely ousted the old authorities and became the legitimation for the government of Holland. For the inhabitants of this province the war remained part of their daily existence for eighty years, but not always in the same way. The next chapter will show us how.

Chapter 13

THE WAR

Late in 1648 the small town of Schoonhoven petitioned for the right to nominate a permanent representative to the Admiralty of Amsterdam. The States of Holland were unenthusiastic: an expansion of the admiralty boards was not, they thought, in the national interest, and now that the war was over the task of these boards would become lighter.[1]

The States badly misjudged the situation, for within four years the United Provinces were engaged in a naval war with England. Nevertheless, this incident clearly shows that the States saw the peace of Münster as a turning point in the existence of the Republic, which had been at war throughout its entire history. The memories of even the oldest inhabitants did not go back beyond the battles of Brill and Heiligerlee. As for the younger generation, they knew that the enemy had always been encamped on the borders, Dunkirk privateers had always terrorised the sea, and Catholic priests and monks had always been obliged to lead a furtive existence; meanwhile consumer prices had remained at a consistently high level in order to pay for the war.

That was the Eighty Years' War in the experience of ordinary people. In this chapter we shall endeavour to illuminate this experience by concentrating on five facets of the war as it touched Hollanders. First, we examine the character and spirit of the Spanish army fighting in Holland between 1572 and the Pacification of Ghent in 1576. Second, we observe the mood and tactics of the Beggar forces during this period. In the third place we shall consider how the nature of warfare changed in the time of Maurice and Frederick Henry, when the rebels had a secure base from which to launch their attacks. But even after Holland had ceased to be in the forefront of the war on land, Dunkirk privateers waged a ruthless war against Dutch seamen, the subject of our fourth section. Finally, we consider the predicament of Catholic Hollanders, whose religious affiliations made them politically suspect in the opinion of their compatriots.

I

The Dutch army in the struggle against Spain included only a few regiments of Netherlanders, for it was composed predominantly of foreign mercenaries: Scots, English, French and especially Germans. The Spanish army was scarcely less international in composition. It numbered only about eight thousand native Spaniards, according to the guess of the abbé Brantôme, a French contemporary.[2] Not a bad guess either, judging from the results of modern statistical analysis, which have shown that until 1609 at least the Spanish army was made up for the most part of German and Walloon mercenaries, with the latter usually preponderant.[3] Yet it was the Spaniards who gave this motley collection its special identity. It was no coincidence that a chronicler of the opening phase of the Dutch revolt constantly heard Requesens' triumphant soldiers shouting, 'Hispania, Hispania, victoria, victoria!'[4] The Spanish soldiers formed the military elite in the armies of Philip II. They received the highest pay and drew the best quarters; but they were also the most disciplined, and the toughest in the face of deprivation and hardship.[5] Far from home, unable to desert to their native land, and so compelled to make a virtue of necessity, the Spanish soldiers developed into Europe's finest, their courage and technical military prowess every bit a match for the heroes of subsequent swashbuckling legends.[6]

Yet it was not just the professional skill of the Spanish soldiers that stamped the royal force; that spirit which is the fruit of zeal was also of Spanish origin. The Spanish had been at war for generations. Little by little they had wrested the Iberian peninsula from the Arabs. Just when this task was completed in 1492 with the fall of Granada, Columbus had stepped ashore on the American islands, and the Spanish had found themselves privileged, as they believed, to conquer a whole hemisphere for Castile and the holy faith. When the war began in the Netherlands the Spanish were battle-hardened, they had always been victorious, and they always stood as the champions of Catholic Christendom against heathens and Mohammedans. Almost inevitably they saw the struggle in the Netherlands in the same perspective. Spanish chroniclers of the Eighty Years' War, such as Coloma, Lanario and Carnero, never spoke of the Spanish but always of the Catholic army. In the days of Philip II, declared Lanario, the Catholic religion was forced to take up arms.[7] The Spanish army was the instrument of this religion, the weapon of the Catholic church. 'Remember, gentlemen', Requesens told the Spanish troops in Antwerp, 'that you are Spaniards, and that your King and natural lord is today the sole defender of the Catholic religion, which, for our sins, is persecuted and molested throughout most of the world, and you should esteem it highly that God has chosen you to be his instrument to remedy this situation . . .'[8]

Such an army prepared for war in a way peculiar to itself. When Father Gutiérrez mentioned a skirmish between Spanish soldiers and the Dutch sailors of Olivier van Noort, he told how the Spanish girded themselves beforehand 'with the true Spanish weapons' of confession and sacrament.[9] Thus they assured themselves of divine assistance, which they believed might be made directly manifest and revealed in signs and wonders. 'Milagro!' (miracle), the Spanish cried out, if while digging they chanced upon an image that some prudent priest had hidden away from the Beggars' fury.[10] They carried crosses, little paper icons and relics with them as tangible guarantees of God's favour.[11] Even in the opinion of their enemies, the Spanish seemed to have boundless confidence in 'their saints and saintesses'.[12] Indeed, they were a people who selected even their curses and their expletives like good Catholics, swearing 'by the cross and by St Vincent'.[13] Spaniards were ostentatiously and defiantly Catholic. At the battle on the Zuiderzee Bossu's flagship bore a name calculated not only to make its Catholic provenance clear, but also to be as defiant and provocative as possible: *The Inquisition*.[14] This attests not only to their self-assurance, but also to a positive contempt for their opponents. To have used kid-glove tactics would have done them too much honour: these heretics deserved nothing but the naked, iron fist. For as the Spaniards always identified themselves with the Catholic Church, so they always equated revolt with heresy. 'Lutherans' was their common curse,[15] not only for the Beggars, but actually for all Netherlanders. Spanish mutineers in Utrecht, a city loyal to the crown, cursed its citizens in 1574 as 'great Lutherans and traitors to the king'.[16] The term was employed even beyond the borders of Christendom. On Batjan, in the Moluccas, the Spaniards praised themselves to the inhabitants as being far more useful allies than those cowardly Dutchmen: 'one of us is worth more than ten of such dogs and Lutherans'.[17] It was apparently only with considerable effort that the Spaniards could bring themselves to take their enemies seriously. At Heiligerlee in 1568 the Spanish officer Londoño grudgingly conceded that 'Lutherans' might be possessed of a modicum of strategic military insight: 'overlooking their being heretics, they made decent use of the local situation'.[18]

The Netherlanders for their part perceived in the Spanish not only the attributes of good Catholics, but a certain Spanish haughtiness as well. Spanish pride was almost a byword in the sixteenth century, as the rebels, too, were well aware.[19] They characterised their Spanish adversaries by a variety of nicknames, such as *spek*, *maraan*, *Jan Gat*, and even the word *Spanjaard* itself, which was formed in conscious analogy to *veinzaard* (hypocrite) and *snoodaard* (villain), and supplanted the older, neutral *Spanjool*.[20] In the Beggars' songs the Spanish were often called 'seignor'.[21] To unmask the false pretensions of Spanish pomp, the Spanish soldier was referred to most punctiliously as 'seignor' after he had been thoroughly defeated.[22] The Spanish title of 'Don' was used with equal gusto for the sake of a puckish good laugh. Don *Spek* (Lean and Hungry) has sailed forth to master the sea, we are told by a song written to commemorate the Dutch victory at the battle of the Downs in 1639, but the Hollanders are ready for him: Don Turn-the-Cows is awaiting him, Don Jack, Don Wooden-Leg, Don Fig, Don the Mangler, and even Don Waterdrinker, who during the fray would give his own name gratis to many a Spanish Don.[23]

It was an old score that was settled in 1639. The dons and *señores* of 1639 were not identical with their grandfathers and great-grandfathers of 1572. The family resemblance, however, remained, even if only because the men of 1572 had made such an indelible impression. Before then Spanish soldiers had been almost unknown in Holland. Alba had quartered his troops in the great cities of Brabant and Flanders when he arrived in 1567. Indeed, until the capture of Brill, Spanish troops were only occasionally encountered in the province.[24] Only after April 1572 did people come into regular contact with them. Notorious atrocities were committed at Rotterdam and Naarden in 1572, Haarlem in 1573, and Oudewater in 1575. The burning and plundering of Oudewater probably aroused the most revulsion, as women and girls were 'sold as slaves, yes, even for the low price of three or four *reals*'.[25] When the States of Holland in 1579 looked back to the civil war, they declared that there had been nothing to equal the disaster of Oudewater, 'such that more misery and calamities in other cities could not be found within human memory'.[26] But the human carnage of Rotterdam and Oudewater only showed on a larger scale what was, in the years 1572–6, if not a daily experience then at least a daily threat. The diary of Wouter Jacobsz., a prior from Gouda, reports casually that in December 1573, 'almost the whole of Vlaardingen fled to Schiedam to escape the soldiers of the king'.[27] Accounts for Rijnland indicate that in 1575 the village of Alphen was virtually depopulated.[28] In Beverwijk there were only twelve houses standing in May of 1576. Most of the inhabitants lived in shanties or cellars, and Beverwijk was better off than many other villages in the neighbourhood of Haarlem.[29] Nor would it be difficult to extend this catalogue of misery.

By the time a chronicler from Utrecht noted in 1574 that nineteen Spanish companies had decamped towards Holland, 'robbing and plundering as if the peasants were enemies',[30] this phrase had become a refrain. The Spaniards had set to work in the same way in Flanders in 1567: in a land of heretics everything was booty.[31] This was their outlook when they came to Holland in 1572. *Jonkheer* Arend van Dorp virtually attributed the success of the Revolt to their brutal insolence. Matters were critical when the prince of Orange returned from his unsuccessful campaign in 1572. The governing classes no longer had much confidence in him, and they were casting about for the best way to secure their own advantage. Yet the good God bestowed upon them 'a new and steadfast resolve by means of the scandalous slaughter in Naarden'.[32] No one could feel secure from Spanish reprisals, for the Spanish commanders never kept a promise,[33] or they gave it a perfidious interpretation,[34] and Spanish troops campaigned as though there were not a loyal Catholic to be found in the whole of Holland. Indeed, two Catholic authors assure us repeatedly that the Spanish went about their affairs without the slightest regard to religion. 'They were no respecters of persons', claimed Wouter Jacobsz., 'and they were quite indifferent to whether one was good or bad', i.e. Catholic or Beggar. They raped girls and women, they reduced the richest in the land to penury, they respected neither altar nor chapel, and they did not keep the commandments of their church.[35] The chronicler of Utrecht wrote in the same vein. Though a layman, he was a convinced Catholic and had no objection whatsoever to the persecution of heretics.[36] No one could call him a friend of the Revolt, but he knew very well who his enemies were. They were the Spanish soldiers, 'who rob the churches, abbeys and monasteries and attack the peasants as if they were enemies, nay even Turks'.[37]

This Catholic also attested to the Spanish failure to distinguish between Papists and Protestants. What protection had the religious habit afforded the nuns of

Naarden?[38] A woman was a woman, once the Spaniard was over the city wall: he left no one in peace. He even gloried in the battle: Spanish soldiers refused to carry out an advantageous military operation in August 1575 'because they feared that the war would be over too quickly'.[39] The Spanish army was indubitably Catholic, but it made little effort to distinguish Catholic Netherlanders from Protestants.

II

If Arend van Dorp was right, and the Spanish conquerors of Naarden and Haarlem were the best propagandists Orange could muster, then the question arises whether the captains of the Beggars perhaps unwittingly abetted the Counter-Reformation. The Beggars were no strangers to Holland even before they occupied Brill in April 1572. Since 1569 they had made the seas unsafe for Dutch merchants, and since 1571 their raids had been directed especially against the more remote countryside of Holland.[40]

Ooltgensplaat, Huisduinen, Schellingwoude, Petten, Schagen, Schoorl and a string of other villages had already encountered the Beggars before they ensconced themselves in Brill. Nor was Brill the first town to become the target of their attacks. Dokkum had that privilege in 1569, and the raiders had carried out their most daring action to date at Monnikendam in 1571. Many of the inhabitants of Holland were thus well placed to judge if they had reason to greet the conqueror of Brill as 'the noble lord exalted, of Lumey very wise', as the Beggars' song had it.[41] Gouda certainly knew enough, for on receiving in October 1572 the tidings that Lumey was in the neighbourhood and intent upon making the town his winter quarters, they sent out a message in unseemly haste 'that His Grace should be dissuaded from coming here'.[42] His Grace appeared nonetheless, with seven hundred companions. He left again after thirteen days, but following that short visit the town petitioned the States of Holland for a tax reduction of four thousand guilders, on the grounds 'that the men and train of His Grace would hear no reason, and coerced the burghers into serving their every desire in eating and drinking, notwithstanding what they freely offered in food and drink'. Nor does this sum appear excessive, for Alkmaar obtained a remission of eight thousand guilders following various visits by companies of Beggar troops in December 1572, and January 1573.[43]

Generally, the soldiers were received with a marked lack of enthusiasm. Occasionally, the most lawless elements in the ranks were punished,[44] but this did little to improve matters. The States of Holland were obliged to note in November, 1576, that the towns 'show themselves very reluctant' to accept garrisons.[45] Perhaps people thought these were no longer necessary, since, as they believed, the war was over. The Pacification of Ghent had just been proclaimed. In Gouda the news was received with jubilation;[46] and we have no reason to suppose that people elsewhere, especially in the countryside, were any less war-weary. The Spaniard will string us up if we help the Beggars, said an unknown poet, but the Beggar harries us if we turn to the Spaniard. Nowhere can we find peace, though we should like nothing so much as to abide upon our farms and milk our cows in perfect tranquillity.

For such farmers every soldier was an enemy. In many villages the inhabitants refused to take an oath of allegiance to the rebels. In 1574 the States of Holland decided that everyone should indeed be obliged to take the oath and stand watch: anyone who refused should be incarcerated.[48] Apparently these comrades of coercion were considered reliable enough to share in the responsibility for public safety. The farmer wanted peace first and foremost, and he may rarely have felt any personal involvement in the conflict. Yet it is probably fair to say that this disgruntled majority inclined slightly towards the Beggars if forced to a choice. In his memoirs of the 1568 campaign, the Spanish officer Londoño remarked on the attitude of the inhabitants. In Groningen as well as along the Maas, according to this witness, sentiment was uniformly anti-Spanish. When Alba encamped at Slochteren, it was only with the greatest difficulty that his scouts could discover the location of the enemy, 'because the greatest part of this province were heretics, and they had such a strong dislike for us that they endeavoured to keep secret the retreat of the enemy'.[49] In fact the people of Groningen were by no means such wayward heretics at this time,[50] but anti-Spanish they most certainly were. Londoño's experience in the South was no different: William of Orange dared to take a small army across the Maas, because he relied upon 'the affection of these lands'. Nor was William disappointed. When he camped in Tongeren he was lavishly entertained and given all the provisions required. Alba, by contrast, was admitted the following day most reluctantly.[51] Londoño mentioned only one case of Spaniards being received with beer, bread, cheese and sausages. That happened at a village in Groningen, where they were mistaken for soldiers of Count Louis of Nassau.[52]

Was it any different in Holland? In 1571 eight Sea Beggars attacked the small village of Petten. The inhabitants did not think of offering resistance. They bought off the threat of being plundered for eighty guilders. Were there no men in the village at the time? Yes, but these were on the side of the attackers. No fewer than fifty volunteers enlisted with the Beggars.[53] In March 1572 the local population again showed where its sympathies lay. The peasants of Wieringen helped to guard the Beggars' ships when these became trapped in the ice.[54] Perhaps they were not yet sufficiently familiar with the Beggars, and hard reality would later cool their affection. The experiences at Gouda would suggest this, but the voices of anti-Spanish public opinion still resounded through the province. When in March 1574 Wouter Jacobsz. travelled by canal-boat from Amsterdam to Utrecht, two towns still loyal to the Spanish government, his companions made no secret of their sympathies for the Beggars, 'as they spoke of nothing but the progress of the wicked party', and lustily sang the *Wilhelmus*.[55]

The Spanish made little effort to distinguish the good from the bad. They behaved as though they were conquerors in a hostile, heretical land. They did not call themselves Spanish, but rather Catholic soldiers. In this way they obliged their opponents to adopt a similar attitude, *mutatis mutandis*: the Beggars ceased to distinguish between Spanish and Catholic, and waged the struggle with Protestant slogans on their banners.

For the Beggars, that had always been self-evident. Calvinism was intimately associated with the anti-Spanish underground. It was the ideological flag and sometimes the pretext for the resistance against Alba. A boat bound for the market at Antwerp in February 1570 was attacked just outside Dordrecht by a small vessel with a crew of five. The raiders came alongside singing psalms and shouting 'Vive les gueux!' (Long live the Beggars!). They locked up the crew and made off with five hundred *daalders* of tax money.[56] Though these men probably had no commission from William of Orange and surely did not contribute the money to his war-chest, they considered themselves Beggars and presumably would have joined the fleet if they had been forced to flee the country. Orange expressed the pious wish in 1570 that the Sea Beggars should be 'men of good name and fame'.[57] But no one signing on was asked to provide an attestation of good moral conduct. In practice, the Beggars' crews selected themselves.

The composition of the Beggar forces probably differed little from those of other fighting forces. Serving in the Beggar fleet were the unemployed, the uprooted and the adventurers.[58] But as the 'Spanish' army had an elite of native Spaniards, so too among the Beggars there could be found a hard core of religious refugees who gave the army its Protestant and anti-Spanish stamp. In the North Holland regiment raised during the opening phase of the civil war, we find many soldiers whose sobriquets gave the impression of a consciousness of living on the fringe of human existence: Without-Money, Seldom-Rich, Gambled-Away, Spoiled-Early, Big-Thirst, Unwashed. A few, however, bore names in line with their aspirations: Resistance-against-Alba, Enemy-of-the-Breadgod, Pope's-Sorrow, Monks'-Sorrow.[59] Similarly, professed anti-papists were probably more prominent among the real Sea Beggars, especially among the captains.[60] These elements perhaps explain why the mentality of the Beggar army differed from that of the usual professional mercenary force. A German professional officer who enlisted with Orange in 1573 mentioned in his notes a night assault on an enemy watch-post manned by two sentinels. The Spaniard was stabbed immediately, but the German was interrogated and then turned loose.[61] A true Beggar captain would most likely have killed both men. The Beggar did not share the mercenary's sympathy with others of his kind or his professional calculation which declined to make the soldier's trade any more dangerous than necessary. The Beggars fought with far greater self-awareness and bitterness, with the vengeance of the exile and the *élan* of God's elect. In the war at sea they behaved with unrivalled cruelty. At the battle of Reimerswaal in the waters of Zeeland in 1574, important prisoners were simply cast into the sea without even being stripped of their valuables.[62]

On such occasions there did not seem to be much difference in ferocity between the Spaniards and the Beggars. Yet there was a difference. The Spaniards murdered and plundered indiscriminately, while the Beggars made distinctions. They were waging a civil war, and they realised they needed the help of the population. Even before the Beggars surprised Brill, a pattern can be discerned in their terror. The names of six victims murdered and tortured by the Beggars before April 1572 have been recorded. With one exception these were all representatives of the Catholic Church or supporters of Alba's government.[63] The Beggars knew who their enemies were, and the greatest anxiety about their coming was felt by those who could be identified with Alba and especially with Rome. Lumey's arrival at Gouda in 1572 posed a special threat to the Catholic religion, for the magistrates of Gouda knew quite well that Beggars 'were much given to robbing the churches and houses of God'.[64] Not that there was much of value left in the churches of Gouda. Church silver worth 7,347 Flemish pounds, or 44,082 carolus guilders, had been confiscated to finance the Revolt.[65] Even so, religious houses could not escape the Beggars' violence. Two monks were killed and several béguines were raped.[66] Churches and religious houses were always considered fair game. Huisduinen had been able to forestall plundering in March 1571 with a payment of 150 guilders. But the church fell outside the bargain. The attackers refused to leave it 'unmolested and undamaged for all the money in the world'.[67]

In the propaganda the Beggars' cause was identified with the Protestants' interests. One of the most familiar of the Beggars' songs stated it explicitly: exalt the glory of God, make great His praise, for He hath performed a mighty work for His church.[68] Computers may eventually provide an accurate count of the number of anti-Spanish and anti-papist epithets in the songs of the Beggars. But it seems reasonable to suppose that the anti-papist element did predominate.[69] And if the Spaniards were called 'anti-Christen',[70] it was not simply because this rhymes in Dutch with 'papisten'.[71] In the sixteenth century the term always had apocalyptic undertones, the consequence of more than fifty years of anti-papal polemic. Within a short time this type of propaganda set the tone, even in Amsterdam, which remained faithful to Catholicism longer than any other town in Holland. When Amsterdam did accept the government of William of Orange in February 1578, the monopoly of Catholicism was guaranteed. But within two weeks, scabrous slogans scrawled on the walls heralded the end of the Catholic regime: 'eat priests, shit monks, wipe your arse with canons'.[72] Quite apart from such public graffiti, however, it is clear that the tide was turning against Rome. Wouter Jacobsz. wrote that in February 1578 the Beggars had begun to make distinctions.'They called some Catholics, others double Catholics, and still others three- or four-fold Catholics'.[73] This suggests that the Beggars had won the contest for public opinion.

Some ordinary Catholics did not wish to have the Spaniards back either. They can only be called a 'silent majority' in the sense that they took no steps to reopen churches for their own services. When it was a matter of giving vent to their dislike for the Spanish, however, these Catholics were not silent at all. Perhaps the double Catholics were quiet, and from the three- and four-fold Catholics one might expect public protestations of attachment to the old faith. But these were rare. News of Spanish success was only 'surreptitiously related among the good', according to

Wouter Jacobsz. in June 1578.[74] It took exceptional courage for someone to express his Catholic convictions in public and state 'that he would help restore the Roman religion and cut the throats of all the others of the opposing religion'. Dirk Anthonisz., the bailiff of Oegstgeest in 1579, was such a man.[75] He was arrested, and after two months released with the loss of his post. In this way the States of Holland made it clear that they neither regarded even these three-fold Catholics as dangerous, nor took them seriously. Just two months' detention for outbursts which would have struck a more nervous government as tantamount to treason and conspiracy! In that same year the Catholic Paulus van Loo was indeed relieved as commander of the fort of Muiden. But when it became known that his wife was nine months pregnant, he was allowed to stay until after the child was born.[76] Apparently the security of the territory of Holland was not so seriously threatened by a Catholic commander that the happiness of this joyous event should be disturbed. Already by this time it seems highly improbable that, in the words of the Catholic historian Rogier, 'the great majority of the population of Holland'[77] remained true to Church and King. Holland's Catholics, the three- and four-fold excepted, had made their choice. If the throne could not fall while the altar stood, then the altar would have to be pulled down: better a Protestant *dominee* in the pulpit than the Spaniards within the gates.

I I I

After the Pacification of Ghent, military activity gradually subsided in Holland. Only along the borders did the struggle continue. Geertruidenberg, betrayed to Parma in 1588, remained in Spanish hands until 1593. Heusden had to withstand a siege of almost five months in 1589. Yet gradually the war receded. The direct involvement of ordinary burghers and farmers diminished. When the civil war was at its height in 1575, the States had discussed a proposal 'to conscript one in every four men in the towns and the countryside'. At the time it had been considered impractical, since so many were already participating in the war effort.[78] The Union of Utrecht took the matter up again. In Article VIII provision was made for the registration of all male inhabitants between the ages of eighteen and sixty, the transparent purpose being the formation of a militia. No further action was taken in this connection, however, and the impression remains that these plans for a general call to arms were never taken seriously. Holland returned to the subject once more in 1600, when the agenda of the assembled States included a proposal 'to train and use the children of the inhabitants in the service of the country, in the war on sea and on land'. We have only a rough sketch in the resolutions – the document itself has not been preserved – for a general draft aimed at national military training for the Dutch people. The States did little about it: 'it is found to be contrary to the liberties and character of these lands'.[79]

Rightly so, in view of the form in which the initial proposal was cast. Yet congenital distaste for permanent and universal military service did not exclude compulsory co-operation in times of direct emergency. So villagers were called to lookout duty even after 1576. In 1579 everyone living in the land of Overflakkee was obliged to watch the coasts.[80] South of the Maas, such duty became a permanent institution. In 1621 letters were sent out a month before the expiry of the terms of the Twelve Years' Truce to all bailiffs and dike-reeves ordering them to organise householders once more for lookout duty.[81] These peasants may not have remained in a constant state of alert, but they were ready to be called up at any moment, especially when a severe spell of cold weather caused the rivers to freeze over and exposed the province to the enemy.[82]

In the critical year 1629 the peasants of the whole province were mobilised. While Frederick Henry was besieging 's-Hertogenbosch with his main force, Montecuculi's troops looked as though they were about to invade the heart of Holland. Amersfoort was already in their hands, and Hilversum had gone up in flames. For the first time since Requesens' days the security of Holland was directly threatened. In order to prepare the defences of the *Waterlinie*, the population between Texel and the Maas was called out: from every village 'every sixth man, above eighteen and below sixty years, each equipped with a spade and an axe'.[83] For those who lived closer to the front no exceptions were made: they were required to answer the call, and, armed with pike or gun, to protect their own village.[84]

The danger seemed suddenly to have returned to daily life; it was as if the clock had been put back fifty years and the pattern of the 1570s had returned. When Montecuculi marched on Amersfoort, 'his people plundered the villages, imprisoned the householders, extorted money and committed other barbaric atrocities, making some walk on nails, hanging up others to break their will; they also killed some, and cut off ears and noses'.[85] These are the terms in which the seventeenth-century historian Lieuwe van Aitzema described the advance of this triumphant army. His story seems familiar in two respects. It is as though we were reading again about the soldiers of Bossu and Don Frederick, sometimes in almost identical words. 'They talked only of eating and gorging themselves, they slugged and beat the burghers who refused them', says Aitzema of the occupiers of Amersfoort.[86] 'When we have devoured everything in one place, we travel further; we gobble and guzzle, at the farmer's expense.' That is not Aitzema, but a German officer in the Spanish service, in March 1575.[87] War is back in the land again, history repeats itself word for word. In the second place, Aitzema's account is strongly reminiscent of the blood-and-thunder tales from the chronicles of the contemporaneous Thirty Years' War. The same events, yes, and probably the same hyperboles, too. Military propaganda has made use of such means through the centuries. Such stories should not therefore be accepted at face value. According to the States of Holland, the enemy made an effort to mollify the farmers in the Gooi region and promised to harm no one.[88] Though it would be equally rash to suppose that no harm was done, this may not be all that far removed from the truth. For the purposes of propaganda it was not necessary that Montecuculi's troops should kill or torture on a grand scale: a few atrocities were all that would be required to lend verisimilitude to the stories. Plausibility rather than accuracy was necessary. In this respect the reports of violence in 1629 stand comparison with the Spanish barbarities from an earlier period in the Revolt of the Netherlands.

In 1629 moreover the soldiers, like their predecessors in 1572, made no distinctions between Catholics and Calvinists. A priest who wanted to mediate with Montecuculi was told 'that he should stick to his prayer book'. Nor did these Catholic troops restore the church in Hilversum to the local Catholics: instead they burnt it.[89] And it is indeed an author who was in all likelihood Catholic, Lieuwe van Aitzema,[90] who repeatedly noted that the invading army paid no heed to the confessional loyalties of the inhabitants.[91]

The invasion of 1629 therefore served to revive memories of Spanish cruelty. The psychological shock was probably not entirely unwelcome to the regents of Holland. If the inhabitants did not want to make peace, they had to be ready to bear the costs of the war. The population would be willing to accept those costs only if they saw no better alternative than continuation of the war. And it would not be so bad if from time to time the people learned to fear the Spaniards in Holland. In the eastern parts of the Republic the threat of a Spanish invasion had never been lifted. Mendoza's successes of 1598 created a minor panic in Gelderland and Overijssel.[92] Spinola took Oldenzaal in 1605 and Grol in 1606; the Spaniards occupied both towns for more than twenty years. And in 1624 Hendrik van den Berg took advantage of the frozen rivers to plunder and burn in the Betuwe.[93] If Holland were never exposed to such dangers it would grow complacent. For that reason the scare of 1629 could be said to have been salutary. Frederick Henry exploited these anxieties when, in 1636, he resolutely opposed any cuts in the budget. He warned that the enemy intended to gather 20,000 to 25,000 horse, and would 'not be content to amuse himself with besieging towns, but would penetrate to the bowels and marrow of the state'.[94] And that would mean Amsterdam, The Hague, and Leiden.[95]

Yet it is difficult altogether to escape the conclusion that enthusiasm for the war had waned during the stadholdership of Frederick Henry. The resumption of the war in 1621 after the expiry of the Twelve Years' Truce seems to have had popular support. The archducal emissary Pecquius – en route for The Hague in March in a bid to negotiate a lasting peace – was greeted in Delft by local bully boys, who threw stones and dung 'to show their revulsion to Spaniards'.[96] Baudartius, who recorded this incident, wasted little time in explaining why the man in the street was so anti-Spanish; for ministers like himself the answer was obvious. The Reformed ministers had always been fiery propagandists for the war. They knew very well that their church had prospered in the struggle against Spain. The men of Baudartius' generation also viewed the international power struggle from a religious perspective. For them the Eighty Years' War and the Thirty Years' War were exclusively contests of faith, waged between the alliance of the Protestant powers and the mighty forces of the anti-Christ, led by the Spanish. They were anti-Spanish through and through. At the synod of Dordt in 1618 there were lengthy discussions about the proper rendering of the second person in the new translation of the Bible. One argument used by advocates of the archaic second person singular 'du' was that the alternative, the polite plural 'gij', had been borrowed from the Spanish![97] In 1641 we still find the same uncompromising spirit in a lengthy discourse by *dominee* Wassenburgh against the sin of dancing, during which he sniped at the new fashions in dress – English, French, and worst of all, Spanish, 'our traditional enemies'.[98]

The struggle against Spain had to be continued for the freedom of the Reformed Church and the fatherland. Baudartius related with satisfaction how in 1622 the towns of Holland had, at Maurice's request, formed a number of companies 'who have willingly left their work, wives and children to serve and assist their fatherland in time of need'.[99] This was not the first time the towns had had to provide temporary reinforcements for the army. They delivered a fixed quota, though they were permitted to pay volunteers to take the place of the towns' citizens.[100] Thus it could have happened in 1622: love of country could go hand in hand with the readiness of the unemployed and underpaid to accept money for service – they might well have left behind wives and children, but not always jobs or even houses.

In 1622 this pecuniary objective might have carried weight with ordinary people in Holland. The Twelve Years' Truce had been a time of prosperity,[101] but had not seen increased employment. All the dramatists state that the ordinary man could earn little. 'The rabble are walking around with empty stomachs, because there is no sailing to be done', said Samuel Coster.[102] 'All trades are slow, there is no gain to be made', thought Van Santen.[103] 'It almost seems … that trade had died out here', complained Bredero's innkeeper; the tavern clients had nothing more to spend and passed the whole day quibbling over pennies.[104]

In the people's memory the war began to acquire a life of its own as the good old days. This, at any rate, was Aitzema's assessment. 'The ordinary man around here was weary of the truce: *multis utile bellum*. Many recalled that in times of war there had been a good penny to be earned, and they were certain that there had been more trafficking during the war than under the truce.'[105]

The lure of profits could arouse the lust for war. Those who anticipated diminished returns in peacetime could enjoy the thunder of cannon, provided they were well out of range. 'We skippers and carriers used to earn money like mud', a pamphleteer has a barge-skipper complain at the start of the truce.[106] In 1621 it was hoped that the good old days would return, but the promise remained unfulfilled. Trade reacted somewhat uncertainly to the resumption of hostilities, and in Amsterdam the yield from taxes fell sharply during the summer of 1621 as a consequence of 'the great diminution of trade'.[107] That was the experience of the collector of customs at the weigh-house, but it was shared by the bakers of ship's-biscuit[108] and the brewers.[109] The mood was reflected by W. D. Hooft in his farce *Jan Saly* (1622):

And it's a stifling time, for there's nothing to be earned:
With this war I suppose it won't get any better,
Because all trade is slow, as everyone complains,
For there is almost no one who asks for any goods,
And the frugal people hold tightly to their money.[110]

At the time people had just passed through the hard winter of 1622, with three months of continuous frost. By the end of that year prices had risen sharply to extraordinary heights.[111] In 1623 the situation was no better.[112] When there was only slight relief the following year,[113] the growing discontent found its expression in the butter riots of June 1624.

Perhaps the disappointments of the 1620s blunted the enthusiasm for war in the towns of Holland. But on the border of the province the resumption of war had never been welcomed. Here the chief concern was local security. And in 1621 that could not be assured. Spijk near Gorinchem was so troubled by the enemy 'that the poor people slept at night in the bushes or in the hedges, not daring to show themselves at their homes'.[114] They wanted to reach an understanding with the enemy and buy off the pillaging with an annual tribute, following the example set by villages in the border regions of Brabant and Flanders. Perhaps this was an exceptional state of affairs that did not last very long. Nevertheless, confidence in the protective power of the States' army was shaken in the 1620s. Count Hendrik van den Berg, leading the enemy's campaign in the Betuwe, stirred unrest even in Holland. In The Hague, it was reported that even farmers in the Gooi region had attempted to reach a tributary arrangement with the Count.[115] Their example would, it was feared, be followed by others. The Council of State believed in 1627 that a great many, including 'persons of substance from almost all the towns of Holland' had moved to a neutral zone or taken up residence in villages that had agreed to pay tribute to the enemy. The Council did not say whether this was a consequence of the heavy taxes levied in Holland, or done deliberately to harm the country,[116] but that is beside the point: such conduct was quite foreign to the spirit of 1572.

The old conviction that Spain epitomised tyranny gradually faded away. Repeated accords providing for exchanges of prisoners made the war a little more humane.[117] Maurice and Mendoza reached an agreement in 1602 which emphatically prohibited 'attacks on the weaker sex of women and small children'.[118] That made it easier to live with the war, but it also lessened the fear and hatred of the Spaniard. The government in Brussels used to furnish its subjects who wanted to travel to the Republic with passports in which the northern territories were labelled 'rebel provinces'. The States General occasionally forbade the use of these documents,[119] but Frederick Henry never persuaded them to reciprocate by describing the Southern Netherlands as 'tyrannised provinces'.[120] The matter of nomenclature was not regarded as sufficiently important, and no one wanted to hamper trade for the sake of a few insults. Propaganda about Spanish tyranny gradually disappeared from official publications of the Republic. It was employed for the last time in 1632, in a manifesto that cited the 'horrible facts, taking, plundering, murder and burning of towns' since the beginning of the Revolt.[121] This tract was aimed at the Southern Netherlands when there was a short-lived hope for the reunion of North and South in the common cause against Spain. But the old ferocity was gone. After 1629, the land war had lost its terror for Holland: the Spaniard was beyond the borders, the home army under iron discipline. Thousands of Hollanders, however, earned their living at sea, and their relationship with the enemy was completely different from that of the landlubbers. We now turn to them.

IV

A few years after the discovery of America, a monk visited the king of Peru to preach the Christian religion to him. The monk added, however, that the Pope was the head of Christendom, and that he had granted the king of Peru to the Spanish. The monarch declined to accept this message, declaring that 'the Pope must be an ignorant and shameless fellow, so liberally to dispose of what belongs to others'.[122] So runs the story, at least, in the Utrecht edition of the tales of Christoffel Wagenaer, which related the adventures of Faust's famous companion Wagner in Dutch. This edition is a revision, not a faithful translation. Wagenaer's experiences in Spanish America were a windfall for Dutch readers, who thus received a strong dose of anti-Spanish propaganda as well as entertainment. It is the well-known story of Spanish atrocities against the Indians, now reproduced with spurious precision by the publishers, who for the first time gave a plausible account of the position of the Indies on Wagenaer's arrival in order to underline the changes after the coming of the Spaniards. Santo Domingo had been densely populated at the time, but the bloodthirsty Spanish caused such havoc that the population of one and a half million was reduced to five hundred.[123]

It goes almost without saying that in the propaganda put out by the Republic the 'Black Legend' of Spanish wickedness was exploited to the full. Naturally it also stressed the Spanish tyranny in the Netherlands. Since the first appearance of the *Spieghel der Jeught* (Mirror of Youth) in 1615, Dutch schoolchildren had been able to learn all that Spain had done to mistreat their forebears.[124] But the publication of a book about Spanish cruelties in the West Indies was intended to do more than merely arouse repugnance to all things Spanish. In the West Indies there was a score to be settled. The Spaniard had 'by force and murder snatched a land that did not belong to him'.[125] These atrocities demanded retribution.

> The blood of Indian women and children
> Still cries out for vengeance; what tongue can tell
> Of the unprecedented pain of sulphur, fire and sword,
> For which so many men and kings were conquered![126]

The political versifiers knew that the Dutch nation had been chosen by destiny to execute judgment.[127] And as is so often the case when people take upon themselves the role of Providence, the fulfilment of this sacred duty was to be richly rewarded.

27. Title page from *Mirror of youth, or Spanish tyranny . . . latest edition*. Pamphlet of 1687.

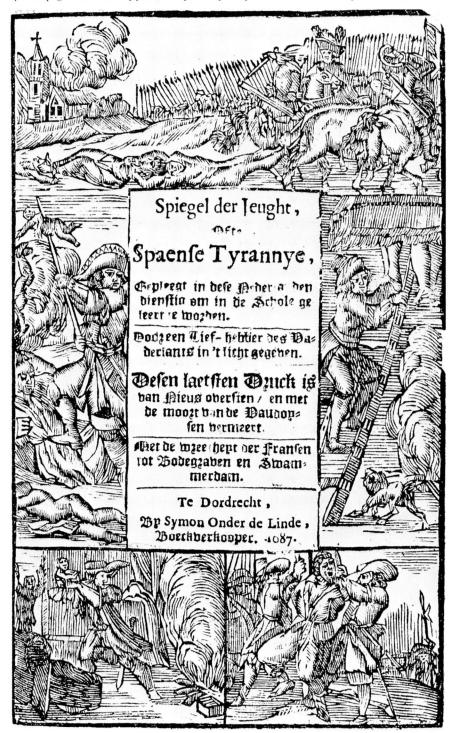

Spiegel der Ieught,
Ofte
Spaense Tyrannye,

Geplreat in dese Neder-a'den
dienstig om in de Schole ge
leert e wozhen.

Doozeen Lief-hebber des Va-
derlants in 't licht gegeben.

Desen laetsten Druck is
ban Nieus obersien / en met
de moozt ban de Vaudop-
sen bermeert.

Met de wzee hept der Fransen
tot Bodegzaben en Swam-
merdam.

Te Dordrecht,
By Symon Onder de Linde,
Boeckberkooper. 1687.

The power of Spain depended on the possession of its American colonies: deprive the Spanish of their American bullion, and the war would be over.[128]

The war at sea, in the Far East and the West Indies, was therefore bound up with the struggle against the Spaniard. He was to be opposed not only in Brabant and Flanders, but also in the Caribbean and the Indian Ocean. And that was the task of the Dutch seamen. The songs glorifying the exploits of Piet Hein were aimed directly at them. They had to have the conviction not only that they could resist the Spaniard anywhere in the world, but also that they might go on the offensive. They should believe that a single sloop manned by Hollanders need not make way for a heavily armed Spanish galleon.[129] Perhaps, too, Dutch mariners bore a personal grudge against the Spaniards, for they continued to encounter the enemy even after the future of the Seven Provinces had been assured. They constantly ran the risk of being killed or imprisoned by a chance encounter with Spanish men-of-war. And many indeed were imprisoned, including the later admiral Piet Hein, who in his youth spent about four years rowing in Spanish galleys.[130]

Such experiences must have strengthened their animosity towards Spain. But some of the blame should also be borne by seventeenth-century shipowners who, in their pursuit of maximum profits, sometimes took irresponsible risks at the expense of their seamen. Instead of waiting for the convoy, they sailed as soon as the wind was favourable. They armed their ships so inadequately that these could be captured by a sloop.[131] They sailed to Guinea with twelve men[132] or to Trinidad with nineteen.[133] The safe return of one of these undermanned vessels was nothing short of miraculous. Dutch merchant ships were not in condition to defend themselves, even against attacks by minor pirates. Thus they offered opportunities that the enemy exploited energetically, and led to the success of the Dunkirk privateers.

Dutch historiography has tended to make light of the Dunkirkers. Japikse, describing how at the end of the sixteenth century Netherlanders swarmed over all the oceans of the world, dismissed them triumphantly: 'Of what significance were Spanish plans to strike at the Republic's trade, the basis of its existence, compared to all these exploits and serious threats? Of what significance was the damage inflicted by the Dunkirkers, even if stronger measures at sea from the Dutch side might have been desirable?'[134]

The damage inflicted by the Dunkirk privateers, however, was not inconsiderable. According to a reasonable estimate, the Republic lost about 3,000 ships to them between 1621 and 1646, when Dunkirk fell.[135] In 1640, a number of Amsterdam traders put the losses in that year at several million guilders;[136] even allowing for some exaggeration the annual figure can seldom have been less than one million guilders, and in the worst years it may have been more than double that. These figures are not excessive. After 1621 the Dunkirkers and other less numerous Southern Netherlandish privateers usually had almost a hundred ships at their disposal,[137] and if each one brought in no more than one or two prizes, the privateers would have realised a million guilders. This state of affairs did have its good side, for it provided employment in the shipbuilding sector in order to offset the losses.[138]

28. *The Dutch privateer 'The Gilded Sun'* by Willem van de Velde the Elder.

But the profits made by Dunkirkers at the expense of the Republic may have roughly equalled the advantages the United Provinces gained from import and export duties.

Dunkirk, wrote a pamphleteer in 1628,[139] is to the Republic what Carthage was to Rome. It is the Algiers of the West, an empty belly that gobbles up everything, a bottomless Danaidean tub. It swallows up in a moment the most precious things that the Hollanders have carried with great effort from far-off lands. It was true: Dunkirk cost the Hollanders a great deal of money. The privateers also exacted another toll, for they were 'the scourge of the seaman's existence at that time'.[140] 'Just add up', urged the pamphleteer, 'how many of your people have been cast overboard into the depths of the sea; yes, frequently with their noses and ears cut off beforehand.'[141] Though more officially slanted sources make no mention of such barbaric practices, they do relate that fro n the beginning of the seventeenth century the Dunkirkers took stern measures against fishermen and sailors who offered resistance. They locked them in their holds and then sank their vessels,[142] or they let prisoners decide by lot which of them should be cast overboard.[143] Between 1601

29. The harbour and city of Dunkirk, print of 1629.

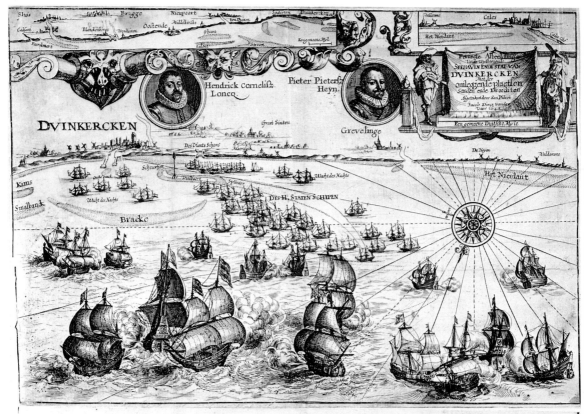

and 1606, the government in Brussels forbade the Dunkirkers to take prisoners.[144] A delicate balance of terror was maintained, for the captains of the admiralties in the Republic also carried orders to cast all Dunkirkers into the sea. Only after 1628 did the practice of killing prisoners cease, when the Dutch sailors refused to be dupes any longer.[145]

But if comparatively few were killed in the struggle with the Dunkirkers, the number of prisoners was very great. Their fate at the beginning of the seventeenth century was uncertain and might depend on their confessional loyalties. In 1609, for example, fifty prisoners were taken on one occasion and brought into Dunkirk. Through the intervention of the Jesuits, the eighteen Catholics were taken aside, but the other thirty-two had to cast lots: ten were allowed to live, while the remaining twenty-two were condemned to the gallows.[146] The execution of prisoners in Dunkirk appears however to have been exceptional. Some even got a chance to serve with the privateers. Those who were not offered the chance or declined it might be put up for ransom. But those too poor to raise the ransom, or those who

30. *The battle between Dutch and Spanish ships at Dunkirk,* by J. Rem.

were not offered the opportunity because they were heretics, would be doomed to row in the galleys or endure imprisonment with no prospect of release.[147] Nor were conditions in the dungeons made more tolerable for those awaiting ransom. If the prisoners were too comfortable – and there was small risk of that in the seventeenth century – they might not try hard enough to raise their ransoms. Descriptions of this accommodation by Southern Netherlanders[148] confirm that the Dutch poet who spoke of 'the filthy jail at Dunkirk'[149] was not guilty of poetic licence.

Until 1609 it was usual to require a ransom of prisoners, but it is not possible to discover how large was the sum demanded for each man. The Archduke Albert wanted its scope to be limited in any case: 'nous faisons la guerre pour chastier les rebelles, et non pour gaigner de l'argent'.[150] That guideline was laid down in 1598, and if the Archduke's exhortation had any effect, the sum raised by ransoms in 1599 should have been low. Possibly it was, but it still amounted to 336,940 guilders. In 1600 the total was 145,650 guilders, and in 1601, 298,950.[151] These were fairly considerable sums, yet they may have been still larger before 1598. In any event the small town of Maassluis complained in March 1579 that it had had to

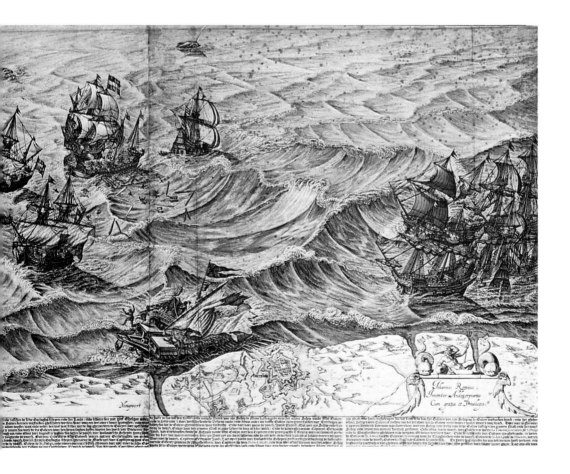

raise some 70,000 guilders in ransoms in two years.[152] At that time the Dunkirkers used to take captive only the captains and other officers of the detained ships. The vessel and goods went free upon the promise of ransom. That was an improvement for the ordinary seaman, since it kept him out of jail. For shipowners, however, this method must have proved crippling in the long run. The privateers no longer had the trouble of running home with their prizes: a single Dunkirk frigate could take a string of hostages on board in a short time and need only sail for home when the holds were filled with captive ship's captains. After the truce, the States-General therefore abolished this convention and captains were forbidden to promise ransom at the expense of their shipowners.[153]

Prisoners continued to be taken as before, but now whole crews were captured. Ransom remained the condition for release, but the seamen could not raise their redemption from the shipowners. Nor should they expect the province to bear the costs, declared the States of Holland.[154] They had to rely on private initiatives. So around 1635, in the Noorderkwartier of Holland and probably elsewhere as well (the matter has not yet been investigated), the so-called seamen's funds were started.[155] These were insurance funds to which participants were required to make a small contribution before each voyage.[156] Occasionally a contributor owed his freedom to such a seamen's fund, but that was apparently the exception rather than the rule. Probably by far the greater part of these funds went to meet the costs of imprisonment, for it was the rule in Dunkirk, as elsewhere in Europe, that prisoners had to pay for their board and lodging. The fund also had to provide relief: every imprisoned contributor from Graft received a daily stipend of eight stuivers.[157] Between 1634 and 1640, a total of 8,440 guilders 5 stuivers 8 pence was invested in that fund. Expenditures for daily support amounted in the same period to 7,875 guilders.[158] Using eight stuivers per day as a basis for calculation, that meant daily support for fifty-three man-years, a figure which does not appear excessive, for in 1635 alone sixty to seventy seamen from Graft were taken prisoner.[159] The expenses of this group for three months – and a shorter imprisonment is hardly likely – would have amounted to between 2,000 and 2,500 guilders. Additional funds for purchasing a prisoner's release were simply not available.

After 1621, however, there were two other ways by which a Dutch seaman might leave the dungeons alive: he could enter the service of the enemy, or be exchanged. The exchange of prisoners raised countless problems during the last twenty years of the struggle against Spain. The practice can be construed as another sign that the terrorism characteristic of the Revolt in its early stages had given way to regular warfare fought by professional armies. Of course neither government was prepared to place the welfare of the prisoners before what it conceived to be the interests of the state. Consequently the procedure of exchange was rarely straightforward and often subject to long delays.

The numerical basis for exchanges presented obvious difficulties. In 1630, for example, the towns of Holland submitted the names of 434 people known to be in enemy hands. The Republic, however, had only 271 hostages in its own prisons to offer in exchange. The States of Holland decided to attempt an exchange on a 'two-for-one' basis,[160] though probably with little hope of success. In 1636, in any case, when the balance was again unfavourable to Holland, the States tried a different tack by offering twenty-five guilders for the capture of each Flemish fisherman who might be included in the exchange.[161] The States also showed interest in the plan of a certain Simon Cornelisz. Doot from Edam, who proposed an expedition to capture prisoners along the Spanish coast, at a price to be agreed upon later.[162] When the numerical advantage lay with the Northern Netherlands, the Republic was usually in no great hurry to agree to an exchange. In 1636 Jan Evertsen brought in the Dunkirk admiral Colaert with two hundred of his men, and it was promptly decided to make no more overtures to the enemy.[163] After the victory off the Downs in 1639, the Republic again had a superabundance of enemy prisoners, so that the Dutch pressed for the exchange to include subjects imprisoned in Spain and the colonies.[164]

A second problem was caused by the constitution of the Republic. The prisoners in Dunkirk were mainly Hollanders, but exchanges were a matter for the United Provinces as a whole. Other provinces may have attempted occasionally to make capital out of this situation. In 1640, at least, the States of Holland believed that the other provinces intended to make their approval of an exchange dependent on Holland's readiness to farm the *convooien en licenten* (export and import duties), instead of having these collected by the admiralties.[165] Holland had always resisted the former arrangement energetically, believing it to be detrimental to commerce. Sometimes exchanges were also held up by problems in the financial arrangements. The States customarily presented an account to those who had been repatriated to the Southern Netherlands for the costs of their imprisonment, and this was then paid by the Spanish government. But in 1641 Brussels had too little money in the exchequer.[166] Nor did the States wish to reward carelessness. In 1629, when the balance of prisoners was in their favour, they decided to exclude from the exchange those unfortunate Dutch seamen who had only themselves to blame for their lot, either because their ships had been inadequately armed or because they had not waited for the convoy.[167]

Much also depended on the quality of the prisoners. In 1629 the States were in no hurry to agree to an exchange because 'among the enemy prisoners in custody here were the boldest, bravest and most enterprising of all their seafaring folk, including those who were guilty of the death of admiral Piet Hein'.[168] Though the motive of revenge played a part, they were chiefly moved by a reluctance to restore to the Dunkirkers the services of some of their best sailors. The States held out against an exchange in 1634 for the same reason. They had only experienced privateers to release, while the imprisoned Hollanders were 'poor and innocent fishermen', so that an exchange would not have been in the interests of the country. There was also a general reluctance to exchange prisoners before the end of the summer, the high season for privateering.[169]

A final and closely related problem hampering exchanges was the insistence that these should not provide the enemy with additional manpower. Spanish seamen incarcerated in Holland were usually included in an exchange only on the understanding that they would return to their native land. This condition was also set for the release of prisoners taken at the Downs,[170] who had been bound for Flanders. Frederick Henry in particular insisted strongly on this condition.[171] Presumably the Spanish prisoners themselves had no objections, for their administration complained in 1641 that those released made off post-haste in any direction, without even reporting back for service.[172]

Such delays and prevarications must have imposed severe strains, not only on the prisoners, who could do little to hasten their release in any case, but also on their wives and loved ones. Sometimes womenfolk and friends campaigned for the seamen's release.[173] Once it even came to a demonstration in front of the home of Jacob Cats, Grand Pensionary of Holland. The protesting women shouted at him that the French and the Zeelanders exchanged their prisoners, and that only the Hollanders were left to stay in the dungeons, 'in stink and filth'.[174]

The regents of Holland may well have felt some sympathy for these prisoners and their anxious families, though this has gone unrecorded in the sources. But another and more persuasive reason why the Republic should care about the prisoners was voiced by Cats, speaking on behalf of Holland in the States-General. Failure to exchange the prisoners might lead them to secure their own liberation by entering the service of the Dunkirkers. And that would certainly have catastrophic consequences, 'granted the prisoners' familiarity with all the inlets and currents of this province'.[175]

The concern was real enough. Many Dutch sailors had a genuine repugnance for the Spanish, and a few may even have been members of the reformed church. Yet they all had one thing in common: they had to sail to earn their living. The war at sea, like the war on land, was fought by professional forces. It is true, nonetheless, that whereas in the army foreigners predominated, the merchant fleet was composed for the most part of seamen from Holland, less so the navy. Though these men would have entered Spanish service far less readily than German mercenaries would have done, it was not impossible. In August, 1579, Parma provided through De La Motte for the fitting-out of several privateering vessels. The States of Holland countered by preparing five or six ships themselves, less to offer resistance than to provide competitive employment and an attractive alternative for profit-conscious Dutch mariners who might otherwise 'offer themselves outside these lands in great numbers, or enlist in the service of the enemy, if not used'.[176]

Competition to attract seamen apparently continued for the duration of the war. In 1589 the strength of the Dunkirkers increased significantly, because 'they enticed the exiles and riffraff from Holland and Zeeland to join them'. The States, however, evidently felt they could ill do without this same riffraff: they responded by making it easier for them to obtain pardon,[177] though with what success is not known. Perhaps the government in Brussels, in its turn, offered attractive terms in a bid to retain the services of these men. Archduke Albert deliberately encouraged defections from the North, and the Rotterdammer Berck was even given a seat in the Dunkirk Admiralty. Dutch turncoats were regarded in Flanders as enterprising and energetic, and as more feared by the rebels than Flemish seamen. They were loyal, too, in the opinion of a Dunkirk clerk, provided they had something to show for it: 'il convient ne les laisser oisifs ny vagabonds'[178] – in other words, given the lure of good booty, their loyalty was assured.

It hardly needs saying that the Dunkirkers recruited their crews from among the prisoners, too. Until the fall of Sluis in 1604, they had an effective means of persuasion in the rowing galleys of Frederico Spinola. Captives who were unable to raise their ransom or who refused the oath of loyalty to the Archduke were chained to the oars.[179] Coercion, promises and expectation of good prizes brought many a sailor to choose the Spanish side,[180] and so it probably continued until the fall of Dunkirk in 1646. Moreover, the government in The Hague treated its seamen as though they were poor relations. Wages were paid well in arrears,[181] compensation for the wounded and crippled was meagre,[182] while the ordinary mariner did not receive his fair share of the spoils.[183] According to Blaeuhulck, a master of naval provisions, many sailors in Holland and Zeeland joined the navy only in order to gain free passage to England. There they jumped ship and embarked for Dunkirk, to join the service they really preferred.[184] The tide could always turn: Tromp's effective blockade of Dunkirk in 1638 prompted many sailors to move north.[185] Nevertheless, the States of Holland had good reason to be anxious about losing experienced seamen to the captains of the Dunkirk privateers.

V

If these defectors were not already Catholic, they had at least to be prepared to become so upon taking up residence in Dunkirk. For the convinced Calvinist, service with Spain was out of the question. But what of Holland's Catholics once the enemy had been expelled from the province? In the seventeenth century Catholics in Holland were no longer exposed to the terrors of civil war. It remained to be seen whether their attachment to their church would undermine their loyalty to the Republic.

Catholics who accepted the new rebel regime suffered certain handicaps. In the seventeenth century the Spanish were still said to be more Catholic than the Pope. In the Beggars' propaganda and victory songs, Spaniards were invariably depicted as devout, bigoted Catholics. When Spaniards surrendered, they allegedly sang the *Miserere*.[186] When they fled, they called upon the Virgin Mary.[187] If they fell overboard, they drowned in holy water.[188] After dying, they were said to travel to a fiery sojourn in purgatory[189] – perhaps in order to find new fireworks to replenish their exhausted stores.[190] Spain was the most faithful paramour of the harlot of Rome,[191] the mainstay and greatest bulwark of the Pope. The battle of the Downs in 1639, the Dutch said ironically, must have occasioned great joy in Rome. Since

31. 'Judgment wanted', from *Practice in civil cases*.

Maarten Tromp had taken so many prisoners, the Pope had finally achieved his heart's desire, for Holland was full of Spaniards. Another feast day should be dedicated to this new St Maarten, for Tromp could assuredly reckon on speedy beatification for his signal success.[192]

The Catholics of the Northern Netherlands shared their faith with these Spaniards, but this aspect received no prominence in the propaganda of the Republic. It preferred to regard the Catholic layman as misguided rather than as a hardened sinner. Instead of identifying him with the Spaniard, it preferred to make him aware of the political peril of his confessional choice. The government, too, approached the matter from this perspective. They regarded the Catholic Church as an organisation closely allied to Spain and dangerous to the state. On these grounds Emanuel van Meteren defended the proscription of Catholic services. 'For political reasons the Catholics were not permitted to hold public worship services. Because of the war, these were suspended for a while.'[193] When in 1644 the French ally urged the States-General to grant Catholics freedom of worship, that body replied that freedom of conscience had always existed in the Republic, but they would not countenance services where people pledged their loyalty and devotion to the king of Spain, 'which nevertheless is known to happen in their official prayers'.[194]

Such prayers were offered by priests. Here the blame was laid upon the shoulders of the clergy, and the flock was separated from its shepherds. In the proclamations and laws, Catholic priests figured not as faithful witnesses who risked their lives to care for souls and administer the sacraments, but as enemy agents, rousing the inhabitants against their legitimate government. For example, an edict of 1594 forbade gatherings 'of those who pretend to be of the Roman religion, on the pretext of worshipping, teaching or reading'. These pretensions, transparent fictions, were merely designed to veil the machinations of the enemy.[195] Priests raised capital for the Spanish army, 'under the guise of confession money'.[196] In Holland itself they were accused of having taken up collections for the relief of 's-Hertogenbosch.[197] Even Frederick Henry could state with certainty that the Catholic clergy 'dare in their sermons and prayers to slander the government of this state as illegitimate, and to pray for the king of Spain in his capacity as count of Holland, to the great detriment of the state and its inhabitants'.[198]

It cannot be denied that the conduct of the clergy gave some substance to these suspicions. Frederick Henry could appeal to recent experiences. In 1635 Catholic priests had refused absolution to French soldiers in the army of the Republic, 'in order to induce them to desert from the service of *Haer Hoogh Mogenden* (Their High Mightinesses, the States-General)'.[199] A few years later the stadholder's position was again corroborated, when confiscated papers revealed that Rovenius, the apostolic vicar, regarded the government of the Republic as heretical and illegitimate.[200] He could hardly have done otherwise, for the Catholic mission in the North fell under the jurisdiction of the nuncio in Brussels. Throughout the war, the apostolic vicars remained in contact with the government in Brussels.[201] When in

1618 twenty Catholics from Holland complained to the Archduke and Archduchess about Rovenius,[202] Albert and Isabella passed the case on to the ecclesiastical authorities, but this incident shows that Catholics in the North also recognised a connection between their church and the Spanish administration in Brussels.

Nor were the clergy content to let the matter rest with formal recognition. Cardinal Bentivoglio believed that Spain deliberately wanted to increase the number of Jesuits in the Republic in order to furnish itself with capable spies.[203] In fact their Father Provincial, Carolus Scribani, did collaborate with professional informers such as Diego López and Sueyro.[204] Correspondence belonging to the English Jesuit Sympson, which was seized in 1598, proves that while he was in Rotterdam he passed on military and naval intelligence to Antwerp.[205] Moreover imprisoned Jesuits were reckoned prisoners of war in 1626, and as such were included in negotiations about the exchange.[206]

There can be no doubt that the leadership of the Catholic Church in the Netherlands inclined towards Spain. But it is less clear what influence they exerted on the political outlook of the faithful. Rogier, the modern historian most knowledgeable about Catholic Holland in the Eighty Years' War, seemed to imply in his commentary on the death of Orange that all Catholics shared the opinion of the priests. He declared that the assassination cannot have cast the people into national mourning, for 'William of Orange, in the eyes of the faithful and loyal Catholics of 1580, was a traitor ... the sentiments with which the majority of Delft's inhabitants watched the Prince's comings and goings in the town must have bordered on hatred'.[207]

But that is to tar all Catholics with the same brush. Most certainly there were Dutch Catholics who would have joined the Spaniard Carnero in describing the execution of Orange's assassin as 'the glorious martyrdom of Balthasar Gerardsz'.[208] In 1610 a certain Roland Lee, who had plans to murder James I of England, considered Balthasar Gerardsz. a holy martyr, who had certainly gone to paradise.[209] Hendrick Achtervelt was a kindred spirit: he took the life of the Protestant minister Franciscus Schorickman at Deventer in 1599 'with premeditation, having sharpened both edges of his knife so that he could better execute that meritorious deed'.[210] Nevertheless, it is quite certain that such zeal was exceptional. Had Catholics everywhere been so fanatical, the Spanish would have put down the Revolt without much difficulty and in far less than eighty years.

Naturally Catholics in Holland did give vent to their strong anti-protestantism. In the neighbourhood of Hoorn, they mocked and jeered at Protestant church-goers.[211] Nearby, at Limmen in Kennemerland, the minister found his pulpit horribly befouled one Sunday morning – the work of papists, everyone believed.[212] At Alkmaar, in a home for elderly women, Trijntge Gerits reportedly 'was so tormented and scorned by the old Papist women', that she attempted to take her own life.[213] On closer investigation it turned out not to be constant pestering that had driven her to take such extreme measures, but her falling under suspicion of having stolen a shirt.[214] This discovery should give us pause for reflection. The words of Jacob Cats come to mind:

> Even when people shout aloud: Diana of Ephesus!
> Go, pay attention to what may be hidden: it will be something else![215]

Religious hatred undoubtedly existed, but it did not usually become serious unless accompanied by other grievances. If Protestant sources tell of Catholics who desired, 'O shameful vindictiveness! That the Spanish banner might wave along the road, and that they might purchase the destruction of the present state and condition of these lands with their own destruction', then the guilt cannot be attributed only to 'their Jesuits, who walk through the land and implant pernicious maxims among the countrymen'.[216] More likely, some unknown provocation stimulated these sharp reactions.

This was the case at Sloten, where in the winter of 1599 the peasants were called out to break the ice to prevent an attack by the enemy. Men who might otherwise have remained indifferent now had to face personal discomfort in the depths of a hard winter for a cause they did not really regard as their own. 'What do these [cursed] sacramental Beggars want to do', they asked, 'harass us into chopping holes and taking arms against our friends? Better to take these rascals who are only ten or twelve strong here, and strike them dead, and then go down to The Hague, and strike the States dead, too.'[217] They challenged their adversaries to strike the first blow, but it never came to a fight. Apparently the provocation had to be very serious before Catholics were willing to take the initiative and resort to arms. 'I wished', said the bailiff of Wassenaar in 1612, 'that I could stoke the fire to burn up the last Beggar.'[218] But a greater threat to the security of Holland might have lain in his readiness to gather the kindling to burn up the first Beggar too.

A latent danger for the Revolt did lurk in Catholicism. Most Catholics could accept Protestant rule without much difficulty, but would not go to the stake for it. Those who had become used to the two faiths living together were startled to see how much passion the Spanish incursion into the Veluwe in 1629 aroused among Catholics.[219] 'I should never have believed it before', wrote Reigersberch to his brother-in-law Hugo Grotius; 'it is a good thing that we have seen it now so clearly.' Reigersberch believed a change of policy would now be unavoidable. Either things would have to be done in such a way that Catholics would be prepared to serve their country, or measures would have to be taken to prevent their endangering the state.[220] Here was a stark choice: the first meant freedom of public worship, the second led to the gallows and the stake. It was precisely the choice that the regents had always successfully avoided. They took care never to deny the Catholics so much that they had to resort to desperate measures instead of unburdening their hearts with verbal abuse.[221] Still less did they ever grant the Catholics so much that the Protestant character of the state was imperilled. The great majority of Catholics seem to have been satisfied with this *modus vivendi*. They strove to conduct them-

32. 'Citation or summons', from *Practice in civil cases*.

selves in such a way that they would not be too closely identified with the Spaniards. The Jesuits, too, displayed great suppleness, allowing considerable room for manoeuvre to those who made their confession,[222] even when they were directly involved in defensive or, still more remarkable, offensive measures against the enemy.[223]

By these means they helped to ensure the continuing existence of their church. They may also have contributed to the passivity of Dutch Catholics, who did not challenge the ban imposed on their public worship even after the war was over. After the Peace of Münster, the Dunkirk menace was eliminated, and the Spaniards soon became allies in the wars against France. But nothing changed for the Catholics. There were occasional lapses of loyalty, most noticeably during the French invasion of 1672. At that time, however, it was again the priests, rather than the laity, whose loyalty to the Republic was most in doubt. During the war the Catholic laity in Holland had freed themselves from the political leadership of their enemy. This wartime influence would have consequences long afterwards.

PART IV

Hell and heaven

INTRODUCTION

Was Johannes Vermeer a Catholic? What was the faith of Rembrandt? Why did Jacob Cats not join the reformed church until he was thirty, and Johan van Oldenbarnevelt not until much later? Just like many others in the early seventeenth century, these men either waited for a long time before they decided their faith, or kept their choice almost hidden from the outside world. Such a phenomenon can have various causes. From a contemporary point of view, the most important was probably that the Hollander could chose his religious community freely. In the Dutch Republic there was no state church to which everyone automatically belonged at birth. Nor did the government exercise any strong pressures. Naturally it did make distinctions. Reformed – Mennonite – Catholic, in descending order, were stages along the way from privilege through tolerance to discrimination, which repeatedly crossed the boundary of outright persecution. The choice of a religious group that stood lower in public esteem could worsen one's social prospects and cut off the roads to advancement. Yet one's life and property were not endangered thereby. Freedom of choice was maintained, and with it the possibility of weighing and considering, postponing a decision until the years of maturity.

It might be a question of careful consideration, because the stakes were high – as a matter of fact, everything. Sixteenth- and seventeenth-century people seldom believed that death marked an end to their existence. On the other side of the grave stood the prospect of eternal life and eternal death, of heaven and hell as an absolute expectation. The consciousness of this inescapable future was not always equally strong. Like people of all ages, the seventeenth-century person was generally busy with the cares and ambitions of the sixty or seventy years of his earthly existence. But he lived in a Christian culture, which continually reminded him that he would one day have to stand before God's judgment seat. Therefore he would still have to choose which way he would go. Postponing and putting off that decision did not arise from doubts about God's existence. People were generally convinced that they would have to put matters to rights with God, and sooner or later most of them went along the path directed by one of the existing religious communities.

Yet certainly on the level of popular culture, religious ideas were not always inspired by the creeds of the churches. Popular belief had very concrete ideas of evil, and was intent on seeking protection against threatening evil forces. In its forms and defence-mechanisms this belief was older than Christianity, but it had been mixed with Christian notions. In discussing popular culture it is always rather artificial to separate the beliefs of the church from the beliefs of the people, because the two were inextricably intertwined. Yet in our account we think it best to make a distinction. If we really want to learn about the practices of religious life, then we should know which norms the church communities presented to that practice. Moreover, every church undoubtedly also had members who were devoted to popular beliefs, and yet observed the rules. It can indeed be illuminating to search for the relationship between those popular beliefs and the churches. After all, it is not unlikely that a church denomination and style of life appealed more strongly to the popular classes insofar as they accorded more closely with popular convictions. From this point of view, we want to study popular belief in general: what did it play upon in Calvinist, Catholic, or Mennonite ideas? Only afterwards shall we try to study beliefs within the churches themselves.

We shall limit ourselves primarily to the three faiths mentioned. The Remonstrants come up only in relation to the conflict of the Twelve Years' Truce, and the Lutherans do not appear at all. This is not meant as disparagement. Popular culture, and church culture as well, must be studied from sources that were created with another purpose in mind, thus providing us with the desired information incidentally. Since the sources do this casually and sporadically at best, we can only make progress if they are numerous. As a result this approach usually cannot be applied to smaller sects in the seventeenth century. Thus it is not to do the smaller churches an injustice that we say little or nothing about them; rather, it is because an account that would do them justice is not within the bounds of possibility.

Chapter 14

POPULAR BELIEF

I

'Let us bow down before the good God.' With these words of introduction to the prayer of thanksgiving that followed, Calvin usually ended his sermons in the pulpits in Geneva. Calvin knew about the good God, and sought Him in every service of worship. Perhaps it is not superfluous to recall this point, because Calvinism is so often identified as belief in the strict God of wrath. Yet if that were the whole truth, Calvinism would have acquired no significant following, for a faith that can only fill the hearts of its followers with fear has no appeal. On the contrary, the believer wants to be freed from fear: he searches for reconciliation. That applies to Calvinists, Catholics and Mennonites. And it is equally true that all three groups desired reconciliation because they feared God's wrath. The old Dutch word *godsvrucht* (fear of God) expresses fear as well as love. Neither one nor the other can be taken away from the belief of seventeenth-century people.

We are referring to the Christian faith as the religious communities saw it and lived it. Consequently we are not speaking of pure popular belief. A characteristic of popular belief is exactly this: it lacks one of the two elements. It is not inspired by love, but driven only by fear: fear of devils, of spirits and of sinister miraculous signs. It is preoccupied with supernatural enemies: above all Satan is the great opponent, the arch-corrupter of the human race. Certainly, there was also attention to Satan in the traditional religious communities of the period; but there people sought protection against diabolic forces, in God's mercy. Popular belief did not do that, because it did not know love. It found protection not in trusting God, but in magic. Thereby it struck out on its own, and none of the religious communities stood further removed from magic than Calvinism.

Yet there was some kinship in that strongly felt fear. In Calvin's teachings the individual counts for nothing. He is unworthy to give, and can only receive. Indeed even that is impossible for him unless he has first been given the will to receive. He is completely dependent and entirely helpless on his own. In their consciousness of human impotence, Calvinism and popular belief could meet each other halfway, without converging. Both saw the individual continually brought into contact with forces that exceeded his own power and made it useless.

Life in the sixteenth and seventeenth centuries, or more generally in the entire pre-industrial period, time and again made people aware of their own lack of power. Their inventions and designs counted for little against the forces of nature. Harsh winters, wet or dry summers, heavy storms, floods, plagues of vermin and animal epidemics are repeatedly mentioned in the chronicles. Sometimes the trouble was violent and general, as in the floods of 1610.[1] Sometimes it lasted a long time and seemed almost endless, as in 1615, when during the winter the rivers were still frozen over in March,[2] and it remained cold in the spring; but in the summer the clay soil cracked from the drought.[3] Occasionally there were real disasters. Everhard van Reyd reported that in 1594 a storm at Texel caused 500 sailors to drown in the Marsdiep.[4] The strength of such reports generally does not lie in the exactness of the figures. Although the true figures may have been only half, or even one-tenth, as great, it was still a disaster. The storm at Texel must have been local, because 1594 is not recorded as a year of dike-breaching and floods.[5] This made human powerlessness all the more evident: even in relatively favourable years, when wind and weather served the farmer and sailor, nature could suddenly strike a small piece of the space of Holland. The villages of Hoge and Lage Zwaluwe, Eethen and Meeuwen received a temporary reduction in taxes in 1602, because of 'the great damage suffered between the tenth and eleventh of July last by hail, thunder, lightning and wrathful weather, which destroyed all their crops in the fields'.[6] Here too misfortune was apparently coincidental, like an unlucky ticket in a lottery: just before the harvest would have begun, and in no more than four villages. But for these four villages it meant suffering months of poverty. This dependence on wind and weather brought uncertainty and raised tensions. The Enkhuizen chronicle of Brandt and Centen not only reports the real accidents, but also notes on one occasion that rising waters had caused great fear among the inhabitants, although the incident ended happily that time.[7] Here we catch the spirit of the age: even if the danger did not become a reality, the mere threat had already reminded the people of their impotence.

In these cases nature was the cause of the calamity. Human negligence hardly played a part: at most in the damming of water, but there too technical ability could not accomplish much.[8] We can say the same about fires in villages and towns. Naturally the origin might lie in culpable carelessness. But once a house had caught fire, people had few means to fight it. The numerous wooden houses with thatched roofs guaranteed that within a short time the entire street would go up in flames. Thus fire at the St Elizabeth convent at The Hague in 1584 destroyed the entire Vlamingstraat.[9] When lightning struck the great church of Edam in 1602, twenty-six houses were burned down.[10] At Vlaardingen in 1606 fire spread so quickly over the Kortedijk that women and children were barely able to save themselves, and all the homes burnt to the ground.[11] In 1627, nearly half of Oostvoorne was destroyed by fire,[12] and a year later Schalkwijk was entirely ruined.[13] Schipluiden was so heavily damaged by fire in 1616 that the village retained its house-tax exemption until 1630.[14] The greatest disasters took place at Naarden in 1615, where 110 houses disappeared in two hours,[15] and especially at Haarlem in 1576, where 449 houses burnt down, along with a church, hospital and convent.[16] Fires were so difficult to put out that prevention was the only defence. At the beginning of the seventeenth century most towns of Holland followed the example of Rotterdam[17] and enacted regulations to cover all roofs with tiles instead of thatch. It was arduous work that took years, and it had to be supported with public subsidies.[18]

In any event people were trying for improvement, although in this period they still had to do without Jan van der Heyden's fire-engine. That prospect of change for the better thanks to technical progress was almost entirely absent from the field of health care. Medical knowledge had not yet made its great leap forward from classical book-learning to experimental research. By the standards of the day, it was probably not bad. In those places where we know the general situation best – at Gouda, thanks to the monograph by Bik – the doctors made a favourable impression despite their bad reputation on the stage, where they were charged with the mistakes of quacks.[19] But Bik covered five centuries, and thus in his long-term study of the sick at Gouda there was movement in the right direction. During our period, the long war against Spain, the changes were generally not very great.

If indeed there was medical care of high quality, it did not extend very far down the social scale. A city such as Haarlem, with more than 40,000 inhabitants, counted nine doctors of medicine in 1628.[20] That is not many, although we should take into account that medical care in the seventeenth century was much less intensive than it is today. Apparently there was little demand for the services of physicians, since Haarlem could make do with nine of them. The reason is not difficult to guess. We have little concrete knowledge of doctors' fees,[21] and the view of the playwrights that they were high is not conclusive.[22] Yet two facts confirm that a private doctor was too dear for many. First, several towns employed a physician who was paid a set salary to treat the poor free of charge,[23] a kind of health insurance for the least prosperous. Second, there was room for medical personnel of lower rank and lesser knowledge. The most prominent among them were the surgeons. In the countryside, for that matter, they often held pride of place, because few villages had their own doctors of medicine. If a village council paid any medical person, it was a surgeon[24] or perhaps also a midwife,[25] who would receive a small salary for community service alongside their private practice. Their abilities varied widely. Some had been trained only by nature. The establishment of surgeons in the countryside was not regulated by law, and in practice was frequently free of all regulation.[26] There may thus have been some good ones. The self-interest of the surgeon did require him to achieve results, because for difficult cases there were often fee-agreements[27] in which the payment depended on success. Thus for example Master Jan in Brill asked the diaconate in Zwartewaal to pay for treating the 'bad hand' of a recipient of poor relief. The church council only granted him a small sum, however, 'since the patient has died'.[28] Such measures did provide some protection against malpractice, but the bills of good surgeons were higher as a result. In Amsterdam a complicated cure might well cost 150 gulden.[29]

The public then sought cheaper help. *Dominees* sometimes provided it,[30] as did cunning women, who had recognised status in a few towns such as Delft.[31] There were also plain quacks who offered their wares in the marketplace or sold them door to door,[32] and finally there were books. The book of secrets by the Dordrecht physician Carolus Battus was expressly intended for the 'common folk'. Its numerous editions seem to confirm the point, but for the modest purses of the most common folk of all there were also watered-down extracts in almanacs and calendars.[33]

Are we straying from our subject? No, because with this medicine for self-treatment we are coming close to magic. 'Eat a little hair of the hare, it's good for stones, says cousin Lieven de Weert'. Isaäc Beeckman, a well-known scientist and doctor of medicine, found that prescription important enough to record in his diary.[34] He did that quite often. Anyone who chews on a piece of oak will get no pain in his side when running.[35] The vapour from sweet milk will cure festering ears.[36] Rubbing with parsley will make swelling disappear.[37] It is quite possible that people found these remedies useful. But their choice and operation rested entirely on faith. They could not help against life-threatening ailments. Medical help, whether learned or not, as yet availed little in the struggle against death: most lives could not be prolonged by it. People were therefore quick to think themselves old. The Bishop of Haarlem Nicolaas van Nieuwland pleaded the weaknesses of his old age when the Duke of Alba reproached him for being so lax in fulfilling his duties. How early for a fifty-eight year old, thought Rogier.[38] Perhaps it was indeed on the early side, but it was not an absurd excuse. Arend van Buchell once spoke in his diaries about an old man of fifty.[39] This may have been an exaggeration coming from his own twenty-six years, but those who had passed sixty attributed advanced old age to themselves,[40] and boasted of their years. In 1641 Jacob Cats thought that he had better not be considered for reappointment as pensionary. After all, he was then by God's grace sixty-three years old, and few members of his family had been suffered to reach that age.[41] Five years later on his next reappointment he was certain he had broken all records. None of his kin had ever become sixty-eight, so that 'therefore he henceforth expected in a short time to move away from here, and go the way of all flesh.'[42]

Cats managed to hold on for another fourteen years. Other seventeenth-century people also attained advanced ages. Constantijn Huygens was able to celebrate his ninetieth birthday, and Joost van den Vondel his ninety-first. Yet they were not typical of their time. If the seventeenth century did not have pensions or superannuation, it was because the aged were not numerous enough to make a general regulation necessary. That probably applies even more strongly as we descend the social ladder. There is no research on the connection between life expectancy and social position in the seventeenth century. But we do know that in the nineteenth century there was a correlation between low wages and short life.

In the seventeenth century it was presumably no different. The standard of medical care, the quality of nutrition, and personal hygiene were indeed low for everyone, but least favourable for the popular classes. The difference appears particularly in the most feared of all diseases, the regularly recurring bubonic plague.[43]

There were no known cures for plague. The treatment was directed more towards preventing further infection than towards the patient's recovery. In fact the spread of the disease was entirely unpreventable, because people believed that it was communicated not only by the victims and their clothes, but also by the air.[44] Then there remained only one remedy, and everyone who had an opportunity had the right

To flee away,
If God plagues the world with unhealthy airs.[45]

But who could escape the air? Plague could vary in intensity from place to place. 'The pest is general over this country, and in some places hot', reported the English diplomat Carleton in 1617.[46] Yet the great epidemics such as those of 1603–1605, 1625 and 1635 struck the entire country. The chronicles of the time wrote mostly about the cities. It is possible that worse housing conditions and excessive concentration of people in poorer urban neighbourhoods did indeed increase mortality rates. But the plague could exist wherever the black rat felt at home. After the first-mentioned epidemic we note that a substantial number of villages received tax reductions, for consistently the same reason: 'owing to the extraordinary deaths there'. This applied to Hardinxveld, Bommenede, Egmond, Schagen, Loosdrecht, Egmond-binnen and Texel.[47]

Epidemics, natural disasters and fires struck people who had no solutions. They did have an idea of the causes. The plague has passed again, wrote Van der Burgh in 1625 to his friend Huygens; if we could only say that with it had also disappeared sin, which had brought about all this![48] That was the general opinion. Sin had aroused God's wrath, which poured out in plague, war, dearth and flood. With disasters that affected the community in its entirety, thoughts indeed seldom turned to ungodly, demonic powers. We do find an example in Isaäc Beeckman of how the plague could be seen as a living being. 'A woman in the ship said that in one house where many people had died of the plague, it glowed at night: and that the plague would fly somewhere in one corner up to the attic by the spiders's-webs, and that there it seemed like a salt-fishbone at night'.[48] This woman evidently regarded the plague as a sort of little devil that made itself visible and (who knows?) perhaps even palpable among people. It is possible that others thought likewise, but few traces of evidence remain.

We do sometimes find the conviction expressed that God gives freedom of action to the devil and sorcerers, when He is resolved to punish humanity with sickness.[50] But the same writer who put this thought into words – the author of the popular book about Christoffel Wagenaer – added expressly that God himself decides on these punishments. We can also easily recognise this, he declared, for 'He does not allow such illnesses to be treated with any medicines, and that is usually the sign or mark thereof, when this illness does not yield or respond to medicine or to the power of herbs'. Thus only one thing can help. People must seek forgiveness in prayer and conversion, 'in the hope that the Lord God might still be moved to mercy, and relieve these lands from the plague'.[51] These words were spoken not by *dominees* or synods, but by the States of Holland in 1624, when the plague was raging and the Spaniards had laid siege to Breda. They saw God's hand in these misfortunes and therefore called for help from the preachers, so that they would inspire their listeners 'to a heartfelt awakening from their great insensitivity in these heavy punishments, to renunciation of their sins, and to improvement of their lives'. It could not be said more clearly than in this official proclamation, that sin aroused God's wrath, and that national disasters could be fought only through national penitence.

The Deputised Councils spoke out in the same spirit at the beginning of that same year 1624: a general day of prayer was proclaimed, 'since it has pleased God Almighty, undoubtedly because of our manifold sins, to visit a great flood of water on this province'.[52] A different punishment, then, but the same cause. Since people knew there was an indissoluble link between sin and punishment, a government that saw the connection could and must carry out a policy that was designed to prevent disasters. It was simply required to root out public sin, to avoid rousing God's wrath. 'We are informed', wrote the Deputised Councils of Holland in 1621 to several sheriffs of South Holland, 'that in your area and jurisdiction the Lord's Sabbath is very crudely profaned, even during the sermons[53] before and after midday, with drinking, bowling, dancing and other unrestricted levity, by which the wrath of God will break out over this country.'[54] Here too there is no talk of suppositions or warnings: God's wrath *might* strike us – no, it is an absolute certainty. Persistence in sin will call down punishment on the land. No one can predict which punishment it will be. In 1625 it appeared to be plague, in 1624 it was a flood, and in 1623 attack by the enemy.[55] But the causes could be tackled. For precisely the same reasons that they had forbidden theatrical performances in 1587, the States condemned disrespect of the Sabbath in 1621. Now that God's anger toward the land was aroused, such idleness could not be tolerated.[56] In 1580 there was a proclamation against adultery. Many thought this was a minor offence. Did they not know that 'nevertheless all such scandalous sins will awaken the wrath of God and [cause it to] break out over land and people, including those who rule and allow them to go unpunished'? Surely history had furnished more than adequate proof![57] Beginning in the 1580s, this motif became increasingly dominant, also in jurisprudence: in discussions of crimes against good morals, it appealed more frequently to the laws of God.[58]

Perhaps Calvinist influence played a role, but in other churches we find an identical consciousness of a link between popular sin and punishment. Human wisdom has no answer any more, wrote the Remonstrant Nicolaes Reigersberch in 1625. 'We see many signs of God's wrath against us. Neither wind nor weather serve us.'[59] We had endured great anxiety in 1572 and 1573, sighed the Haarlem Catholic Verwer in 1574, and hoped better for the future. 'But God better [i.e. thinking they knew better than God], no one wanted to be the least and amend his wicked, loose life. Thus now comes the Lord, whom we have so greatly angered with our evil and ugly sins, and [we] are neither forgiven yet, nor released; [He] can still punish us more every day.'[60] Apparently Verwer saw a balance between adversity and sin. If the old sins were not fully punished yet, and the people were daily accumulating new ones, there could be simply no end to the misery. Even the most pious people could become despondent. The devout Catholic girl Johanna Wouters wrapped the fear around her heart in the evenings when she turned her gaze upwards in the darkness. 'Had a great anxiety when she saw the stars of the heavens, thinking that she had so often angered their Creator'.[61]

Johanna Wouters lived according to the word of the Bible: 'it is a fearful thing to fall into the hands of the living God'.[62] She found her consolation in the old church, but the general spread of this belief in a punishing God must have particularly favoured the growth of Calvinism. A truly Calvinist church can only exercise great attractive power if many people have a deep notion of their own sinfulness. Therein lay the appeal of Calvinism in the early seventeenth century. The churches were never more full than on the days of prayer and atonement.[63] A day of prayer could make such an impression that in 1628 the States of Holland decided, despite the difficult times, that they would rather not proclaim monthly observances, 'in order not to make the dismay among the community and inhabitants greater'.[64]

The timely nature of Calvinist preaching rested in large measure on its repeated call to repentance for one's own corruption. It did not ask questions about the 'why' of suffering. Calvinism let the wrath of God retain all of its fearfulness, but simultaneously gave the believers certainty that they would be protected against that wrath. The shift to Calvinism, to the reformed church, would then have to mean settling accounts with the popular beliefs in magic and exorcism. The widespread fear of unearthly powers undoubtedly increased the attractive power of the reformed church.

II

Calvinism thus appealed to one element present in popular beliefs, but gave an essentially different answer. Did that also hold for the relationship between church teachings and popular beliefs among the Catholics? Here the questions are somewhat more complex. We have already seen in Part III that the discrimination to which the Catholics of Holland were exposed was strongly determined by political factors. Yet not only the reformed church, but also the government offered another motive, that was for example expressed clearly in a proclamation against pilgrimages, issued 23 June 1587: 'the same is notorious superstition, and directly in conflict with the

Lord's Word'.[65] Equally forceful but even more general was the letter announcing the day of prayer in 1621. It revealed that the Spanish war aims were the replacement of the Christian religion by superstition, idolatry and inquisition.[66] Rome stood for superstition and idolatry. Could one really count these Papists among the Christians? *Dominee* Souterius appeared to have doubts when he declared that 'our adversaries' scarcely placed their trust in the King who lived in heaven, but preferred to bow down to 'their saints and saintesses, and wooden and stone idols, that they place in their churches'.[67] Yet if calling for help from the saints was already idolatry, what then was the sacrifice of the mass?

> I have visited countries, hear my tale,
> Where the people present a piece of bread as their God.
> Afterwards they eat him. Are these not strange customs?
> But the greatest wonder above all wonders deep,
> Every day a new God is kneaded there again:
> So that in that land the creature created his creator,
> The common folk came in large numbers,
> And have shown their honour to this baked God.[68]

This jeering description of the eucharist calls to mind the prophet Isaiah: the craftsman chooses a tree and hews it down, he removes the kindling to warm himself, to bake his bread and cook his meat. 'And the rest of it he makes into a god, his carved image. He falls down before it and worships it, prays to it and says, "Deliver me, for you are my god"'.[69] I do not know whether the author had this analogy in mind, but he would probably not have rejected it. The holy mass and the holy virgin were worth just the same to him as the Baäls and Astartes to Isaiah. We find ourselves here in the mental world of the Heidelberg Catechism, which in answer 80 unmasks and brands the popish mass as 'cursed idolatry'. From the point of view of the reformed church, superstition and idolatry were the true marks of the Catholic religion. Not the fringe phenomena, but the core: Catholicism was for the preachers a systematic mixture of religion and superstition.

Therefore they had to be very particular with Rome. They did their work in a country that had undergone the influence of the Catholic faith for centuries. That faith had left deep traces in popular life, which could not be eradicated by decree at the same time as the transfer of all church buildings to the reformers. Inside and outside the church, remnants of the old were long maintained. The new authorities felt obliged to purify Christian life of its Catholic ingredients as well as of elements of folk beliefs. The first could not easily be separated from the second, however, because to the reformed preachers both were manifestations of superstition. Consequently they would not always draw the line, and in a certain sense they were right, even in the eyes of their opponents. Good Catholics, namely the Spaniards, were astonished at the great superstition and the many heathen practices that persisted in the Netherlands.[70] Old, pre-Christian customs indeed still kept their influence on spiritual life and were sometimes intertwined with Catholic folk beliefs. Thus synods, *classes* and church councils joined battle with both of them.

Occasionally in their reaction the brothers took matters all too exactly. Thus the synod of South Holland in 1589 condemned the holding of church services on Good Friday 'at night'.[71] No doubt they wanted to avoid giving any appearance that one time of meeting was holier than another, even if more church-goers would be attracted by the charm of a night service. Even after the establishment of the Reformation, Catholics might desire to visit the old church buildings once again on important festivals. But the Protestant church authorities were not seduced into a policy of concessions. Exactly on those days the sermons had to be specially directed 'to punish the erring and preach the true cross'.[72] Thus the *classis* of Woerden rejected out of hand a proposal to leave the church at Sluipwijk open on St James's eve, or at least to put a collection-box in the churchyard, 'so that by means of the pilgrimage that then happens much money might come into the church'.[73]

This plan was not put forward by the church council, but by the church commissioners, who were responsible for the management of church property. Church commissioners were required to maintain the church building and place it at the disposal of the reformed community. But they were neither named nor controlled by the church council. They did not even have to be members of the reformed

33. Interior of a Protestant church during a service, c. 1650

community: Catholics were not excluded from the church commissions until 1654.[74] Thus it becomes understandable that many a church interior after 1572 still contained strong reminders of the Catholic past. In the Zuiderkerk at Enkhuizen the paintings on the vaults were not covered with yellow paint until 1609.[75] If there it was a question of medieval heritage, elsewhere even at the end of the sixteenth century 'improper paintings' were being placed in the windows, 'that is dance-scenes, *item* that people bring each other crucifixes and other profane things'.[76] At Leiden images of the Trinity remained on the organ-doors of the Pieterskerk. Until 1617, by means of extra lighting these were even called to the attention of the church-goers.[77] In Haarlem in 1622 the consistory still had complaints about 'the public idols' that could be found in various church buildings, namely images of St Bavo, Joseph and Mary, St Nicholas and other saints.[78] In this Catholic stronghold 'vulgar idolatry' had also penetrated the orphanage. Cushions, beakers and other household objects were decorated 'with images of a dove, as representing the Holy Ghost'.[79] The Haarlem church council probably wanted to take advantage of the favourable wind that was blowing in the first years after the synod of Dordt. That was also attempted elsewhere, and with some success.[80] Yet the Englishman John Evelyn, who visited the Republic in 1641, declared that organs, candelabra and monuments here had not been swept away by the impetuous enthusiasm of radical reformers.[81]

It is difficult to say which policy testified to the greater care towards maintaining public order. In Pijnacker there was turmoil when the church commissioners decided in 1608 'to put away a horrible painting'.[82] Elsewhere, however, the people showed themselves averse to images. The Hogerbeets family did not succeed in having the tomb-monument of Petrus Hogerbeets at Hoorn decorated by Hendrik de Keyser, because, Brandt said, 'the uncomprehending people went up in arms'.[83] Maintaining the images in the church primarily satisfied the desires of the Catholics, who could keep on performing their devotions in their own accustomed ways, since God's houses remained open to the public.[84]

The church was also open to everyone in its capacity as general burial-place for all parishioners, regardless of their faith. The reformed church made burial an extremely simple ceremony, without any pomp at all.[85] Even funeral orations were maintained only under pressure.[86] That meant a complete break with the old burial ritual of ringing bells, raising crosses, lighting candles, laying crosses of straw on the doorsteps of the deceased, braiding floral wreaths, etc.[87] Winandus van den Beke, preacher at Zoetermeer, mentioned in one breath 'superstition used by the Papists' and 'heathenish and idolatrous works'.[88] This was a characteristic mixture, in this case entirely correct, too, because the Germanic elements were at least as strongly represented as the Catholic. The oldest church council record-book that has been preserved in Holland reveals that the struggle against these customs was begun immediately. Already in 1573 the church council of Naaldwijk had made an end to bell-ringing at burials, 'to take out of people's hearts the vulgar superstition of the Papists, who declare and teach that ringing is profitable to the deceased'.[89]

34. Service in a Protestant village church, 1634.

The prohibition was intended to be only temporary, until all the inhabitants of Naaldwijk had formed a better understanding of the situation. That is unlikely to have occurred quickly. A short hundred years later Voetius was still warning against superstitious adoration of church bells.[90] Perhaps the preachers could only hope to bring their hearers to different thoughts through preaching and warning, anyway. A prohibition of bell-ringing was generally not within their power, because such things were decided by the church commissioners as managers of buildings and property. Religious bodies could only protest to the government,[91] not arrange matters to their own liking in the church and cemetery. If the church commissioners were Catholic, then even a complete funeral according to the Catholic rites inside the church building was possible in exceptional cases. In Berkhout and Wognum in 1605 priests had been in the church, 'with candles and other external trappings to the scandal and shame of all honourable people'.[92]

Provided that those honourable people belonged to the reformed church: popular beliefs were not on the side of the Calvinists in this matter. In 1625 *dominee* Schevenhusius of Hoornaar was invited to the burial of the daughter of Adriaen Reyersz., who was not really a member of his church; but if he had been a practising Catholic Adriaen would not have invited him. Nonetheless mourners placed crosses on the grave – as Schevenhusius reported, perhaps not without overrating himself – 'in order to defy and provoke him'. With his own hands he broke the crosses, and the following Sunday he preached on Ezekiel 20:18, 'Walk ye not in the statutes of your fathers, neither observe their judgments, nor defile yourselves with their idols.'[93]

In our eyes such behaviour seems somewhat inhumane. Face to face with death, when every word and every action were charged with emotion for the bystanders, Schevenhusius smashed to bits the whole popish caboodle; and then in the pulpit on Sunday he rubbed salt into the wounds. His action was whole-heartedly on the level of seventeenth-century folk culture, where the duty of tolerance was seldom practised, or rather not recognised as a duty at all. Folk culture may have been richly endowed with indifference, but tolerance was alien to its very being. Any believer desired religious freedom for himself and held the confession of others in contempt. Followers of the ruling church could more openly show such feelings without fear of punishment, but the fierceness was common to all. In Stolwijk women came to pray on Sundays at the graves of their relatives, without worrying in the least about the preaching *dominee* and his listening congregation. This custom continued for years, under the terms of at least three preachers[94] – one of whom was Jacobus Trigland, as gifted as he was bold.

We also hear about kneeling women during the services at other places,[95] for example at Enkhuizen in 1625.[96] Not many Catholics lived there, but they were just as rare at Stolwijk. The Counter-Reformation managed to gain no ground in that village.[97] Yet praying for the repose of deceased souls was not so quickly abandoned by the reformed, either. Oldenbarnevelt's servant Jan Francken promised his master that he would always remember him in his prayers. The condemned advocate knew better what it meant to be Protestant. 'No, Jan, that is popish, that is now ended when one is dead. If you want to do something good, do it now, now is the time to pray; after death it doesn't help any more.'[98] Jan Francken was probably a member of the reformed church, for servants often went on Sundays with their master. But on this point he still lived according to the old teaching. As soon as that tradition was again supported by Catholic spiritual care, the Protestant preacher might lose such followers. This pure Catholic conviction formed a permanent threat to the Calvinists.

Here it was a question of what the preachers called popish superstition in unmixed form. The prayer for the dead was not a half-heathen abuse of a Catholicism overrun by folk beliefs. Believers who prayed for the perpetual repose of the souls of friends and relations were faithful children of the mother church. One principle stood opposed to another: quite a different situation from the burial rituals of braiding wreaths and ringing bells. But principles were frequently bound to customs, and the charm of Roman Catholicism lay in the attractive power of both working together. Because of that mixture, the care for the dead has a place in this chapter. Precisely in the combination of these two resided an extra danger to the reformed church.

This applies equally when we traverse the terrain that appears pre-eminently the domain of folk beliefs: the kingdom of good and evil spirits, of witches, sorcerers, fortune-tellers, of exorcism and miraculous cures. Calvinists and Catholics both believed that Satan and his minions exercised power on earth, and both were also convinced that his power could make itself felt in unnatural and horrifying ways in individual persons. Among the great majority of sixteenth- and seventeenth-century people, biblical notions on this matter were entangled with folk beliefs. Also, everyone believed in the possibility of divine intervention for good by means of direct miraculous signs. Yet on these points there were also notable differences.

First, for the Calvinists wonders had all but become history. They did indeed attribute unexpected deliverances or surprising turns in the fortunes of war to divine providence. But in their experience of faith there was actually no room for occurrences that lay beyond the possibilities of nature. If people told stories of miracles worked by the Jesuit fathers in China, they shrugged their shoulders: who had been there to see them?[99]

> *Miracla sic Japanica*
> Must also be believed,
> *Et nulla non deliria,*
> Born in your head.[100]

Yet for the Catholic, miracles were still present in daily life. His church proved the continuity with the apostolic past by continuing the tradition of miracles in its midst. The Catholic priest Cornelis Hendriksz. used that in 1587 as an argument against an apostate, who had chosen to join the heretics: 'Will you then contradict so many holy fathers, enlightened by the Holy Spirit, who shone through miracles, and sealed the Gospel of God with their blood; and then agree with the writings of vagrants, proved by not a single miracle?'[101]

Catholicism in the sixteenth century continued to seek its legitimation through wonders. No Calvinist believer would have expected from even the most pious preacher that he would be able to heal the sick with preaching or sacraments. Catholics, however, did place their hope in the priest. It was said of the Delft priest Maarten Donk that he went to confession and communion in prayer with sick parishioners, in order to ask for their cure. When Donk no longer wanted to go, the sick were supposedly laid on his doorstep.[102] Stalpart van der Wiele once cured a woman of pains in the neck and head, by placing a cross on her forehead.[103] Martinus Regius, a priest who served the hidden Catholic churches of Het Gooi, was not only

35. *The feast of St Nicholas*, by Jan Steen

called a new apostle, but also 'wonderworker'.[104] The Leiden professor Petrus Pauw died a Catholic in 1617. What had led him to the mother church was the miraculous cure of his patient Cornelia Cornelissen. He had pronounced her incurable, whereupon she departed on a pilgrimage to Our Lady of Scherpenheuvel (Montaigu) in the Southern Netherlands. She returned completely cured.[105] In the popular mind, the church could not only cure, but also prevent. People believed that attendance at Sunday mass was a guarantee against calamity in the following week.[106]

That also brings us to the second difference. Catholics and Calvinists both believed in the presence of the devil in everyday life. But while the Protestant had no means of defence other than Bible-reading and prayer, the Catholic also trusted in extraordinary help through exorcism. In the Calvinist church communion was expressly denied to all those 'who bless livestock or people, together with other things, and those who believe in such blessing'. It did occur among the reformed, perhaps even often. 'Blessing and exorcism of animals, casting out fevers and other sicknesses, take place among many of us', admitted the *classis* of Gorinchem in 1589.[107] But such behaviour always gave rise to church discipline. Abraham Jansz. was removed as preacher at Middelharnis in 1597 because he offered his aid to the liberation of the possessed – and for 'foul gain', too.[108] It was an exhausting struggle, which would not be won in one or two generations.[109] In 1616 the Haarlem church council had to take action against several women who had blessed a sick patient.[110] Willemtge Cornelis at Zevenhuizen was excluded from communion in 1620 for the same reason.[111] A former elder of Ottoland cured the sick by means of prayer, but he did not allow any witnesses. That smelled like exorcism, and he too was excommunicated.[112]

Such cases demonstrate how difficult it was for the reformed to do away with the remedy of exorcism. In books of popular medicine, magical prescriptions appeared alongside ordinary ones.[113] Prayer, magic and medicines had sometimes grown into an inextricable whole. Stijntgen Claesdr. of Rotterdam cured by means of drinks and powders, with which she spoke the following words: 'This I give you in the power of the Almighty God, who created and made heaven and earth. Herewith through God's power I tread down everything that may be troublesome or harmful to your flesh or blood. This I give you in the name of the Father, in the name of the Son, and in the name of the Holy Ghost'. Thus she cured what she herself called unnatural illnesses, with the medicine tossed in as an extra; there were some herbs that also helped against unnatural illnesses.[114]

We find such phenomena in all churches. But while Protestant preachers condemned them, it could happen that Catholic priests were even proud of them. At Limmen in 1635 a priest organised a public exorcism which drew such tremendous crowds 'that all in the surrounding places talked about it'. The exorcist did indeed summon the devil, and ask him which persons in Limmen he had led astray. 'Whereupon the devil answered' – how, the report does not say – 'naming two of the reformed, that he had tempted them by making them read the holy scripture'.[115] This is a primitive report about a primitive sort of Catholicism, but these forms of belief were also found among Catholic leaders. No less a person than Franciscus Dusseldorpius tells us about a servant-girl living in Gouda, who was long possessed by the devil. In 1572, in the marketplace, she met a man with a beard, who made himself known as the same devil who had formerly lived in her. Now, however, he had left her, because he had received orders to instruct the heretic preacher. A few days later out of curiosity the girl went into the church. She actually saw the bearded man standing behind the *dominee* in the pulpit.[116]

Dusseldorpius was convinced of the truth of his story, and perhaps the most energetic Calvinists also wanted to believe that the preachers in free-thinking Gouda, in their eyes 'the rats' nest and dung-cart of all heresies',[117] received their inspiration from the devil. But in general they regarded exorcisms more as a dangerous form of Catholic propaganda. If Rogier has calculated correctly, the Northern Netherlands in the period 1580–97 went through the peak of their witch-persecution, 'that is precisely in the years of the strict protestantising policy'.[118] Indeed it is not unlikely: for the reformed church these were practically the same enemy, two variants of superstition. Anne Pieters was placed under censure by her church council in 1620, 'because she had fallen so far as to seek advice from a pope [Catholic priest], who was, she admitted, at the same time a fortune-teller'.[119] Such a woman would not have thought of seeking out her own preacher for the miraculous convergence that she apparently hoped to find among 'popes' and fortune-tellers. Sorcerers, according to the Amsterdam church council in 1597, simultaneously promote 'the kingdom of the devil and the Roman Antichrist'.[120] It was actually the same. Anyone who thought he was bewitched, declared the Leiden *classis*, was quickly tempted to seek help among 'popes and popish believers'.[121] The sorcerer Cornelis Gerritsz. of The Hague was indeed for years a formidable propagandist for the Catholic church in Delfland, Schieland and Rijnland: on occasion he would testify to visions and speaking with angels or spirits, then again he would threaten hellfire against all who appeared indifferent to the old faith.[122] It may have been hard for reformed preachers to see any difference between this self-proclaimed apostle and a Catholic demonstration organised by the church, such as the mass procession of 1,500 men who came to the churchyard of Nibbixwoude in 1624 with cattle and sheep, 'in order to be blessed superstitiously'.[123]

Yet such sorcerers did present a problem to the reformed church. After all, it did not deny the possibility of wonders. The preacher Willem Baudartius clearly wrestled with it in his chronicle. Was the plague of mice in 1617 the result of sorcery, as some people declared? Several witches had indeed admitted that they had changed small birds into mice. But Baudartius warned: let us not ascribe to the devil what God has done. In dry years the vermin multiplied quickly. Since God had now sent three hot summers in succession, followed by winters with little snowfall, it was not strange that there were more and more mice.[124] Thus Baudartius more often tried to find natural explanations in recognition of divine providence. Only seldom in his bulky *Memoryen* did he happen to mention a true wonder and acknowledge it as such. He reports no more than one miraculous cure. One night,

36. Interior of the Nieuwezijdskapel, Amsterdam, during a service, c. 1657, by a follower of E. de Witte

a girl who had been lame and bed-ridden for about twenty-five years saw an apparition, who ordered her to get up in the name of the Lord. The girl obeyed, and feeling was restored in her limbs, 'to the wonder of everyone who heard and saw this wonderwork of the Lord'.[125] I think that Baudartius believed in this story, because the spirit spoke the name of the Lord. A demon would not have dared or been able to do that. Elsewhere he tells of a woman from Berkhout, to whom the devil appeared in the form of her own husband. When he came to lie next to her in bed, she became suspicious, for he was as cold as a block of ice. The woman cried out to God, and thus made this Satan disappear.[126] Nor was Baudartius a peripheral figure of Calvinism. The synod of Dordt chose him as one of the six men who had enough learning to make a new translation of the Bible. If he was prepared to accept without hesitation that the devil in human form could wander through the meadows of Holland, then the same probably held true for nearly all preachers.[127] Besides, the story from Berkhout had come to Baudartius from two *dominees*, David Martensz. of Ursem and Aelbert Jansz. of Berkhout.

A few very careful souls were non-committal, such as the Remonstrant Gerard Brandt on the existence of mermaids: 'As I do not dare to state it with certainty, so do I dare not speak against it'.[128] *Dominee* Westermannus had no doubts whatsoever: in his *Christian seafaring* he treated the question of supernatural powers systematically: 'that spirits exist can be proved from 1. heathen writings. 2. God's Holy Word. 3. church histories. 4. daily experience'.[129] For the author, there could be scarcely any argument on the last point. Westermannus simply called the reader to witness: he would himself certainly sometimes have heard noises in the cemetery such as the nailing of coffins; he would have seen for himself faces in the air and water; he would have known people who had a gift for prophecy.[130] The sources confirm that Westermannus was right. Countless persons were prepared to swear under oath that they had personally met the devil.[131] The velvet-worker David Wardavoir was attacked by Satan for days on end. First the devil promised him immense riches, and offered him a dazzling banquet. When David withstood this temptation, the Evil One had recourse to violence. Devils sprang through his room like mad dogs. The devil also appeared in the form of Christ, but David knew how to confuse him with Bible-texts.[132] Leene Dimmens of Goedereede was less resistant. She had known Satan very well, as a gentleman dressed in red with horses' hooves,[133] who called himself Jacob and lived at Sommelsdijk. From him she had received the power to change herself at will into a spotted cat.[134]

Leene Dimmens was one of the victims of the famous witch-trials of 1586. She escaped from prison, and then committed suicide. Two other women were burnt alive.[135] This was one of the last executions that took place in the province of Holland. It is generally known that the Dutch Republic was one of the first countries to put a stop to the execution of witches. The last death sentence of this type was carried out on Marigje Arriens at Schoonhoven in 1597.[136] After that a few other women were condemned to death, but they were set free on appeal.[137]

This did not mean that persecution became impossible. Sorcery still remained a crime in the seventeenth century. Charles Le Grand, member of the Walloon community of Amsterdam, railed at an old woman for being a witch in 1614. The church council reproached him, not so much on account of his abuse, but because one ought not to speak such a serious accusation without good grounds.[138] If the crime were proved, then a heavy punishment could still follow. In 1619 the court at Schoonhoven condemned Reynier Jansz. to six years' banishment and confiscation of all his goods. He had bought a paper from a 'devil-hunter' that would give him immunity to violence and the law, if he would deny God within twenty-four hours.[139] A witch at Brill was banished for twelve years because her activities led 'to notable sinful misuse of the most worthy name of God'.[140] Dorothé Carstens was gaoled at Weesp in 1619. She had already been convicted twice at Amsterdam; but perhaps she had not always been found guilty of witchcraft. On this occasion, however, aggravating circumstances played a role, since she had received a female client who desired the death of her own husband.[141] There may also have been some connection between fortune-telling and common earthly crimes. It gives pause for thought that fortune-telling women had many contacts with persons who wanted to recover stolen property.[142] Were there specialists who really knew the answers to the questions, so that their fees were actually disguised ransom money? It is one possibility, just as it is also conceivable that girls who came to ask questions about their future husbands[143] hoped to find a successful matchmaker in the supposed fortune-teller.

Many of the cases we cite have been taken from church records. The consultation of witches was a sure road to ecclesiastical censure. It was the preachers' task to denounce from the pulpit all conjuration of devils and fortune-telling, 'so that the perpetrators of such horrible deeds give it up, and that others are taught not to seek help by such God-forbidden means but rather by the Lord God'.[144] 'Forbidden means', said this particular synod of South Holland in its own words; not useless or foolish, because they were not regarded as such. The reformed church did not only object to people wasting their good money fruitlessly on fortune-telling. Its objection was much stronger: that people sought help from dark but very real (for them) anti-christian forces, whose existence is recognised in the Bible, but whose use is repeatedly condemned.[145] When the reformed church spoke of popish superstition, it was more than a crude term of abuse or an emotional cry. It was a judgment upon the Catholic church, that with its superstitious phenomena was placed beyond the pale of the Christian religion. An oversimplified vision of Rome, surely. But insofar as the reformed church had sufficient occasion to bind together continually the concepts of Pope and superstition, for the simple Hollander who had fallen under the charm of folk beliefs or persisted in them the road to Rome was shorter than that to Dordt.

III

The churches naturally had much in common, too, primarily in the means by which they judged the extraordinary. Thus they were unanimous in their recognition that God spoke to humanity by means of omens. With the same regularity as Livy in antiquity, Baudartius and Bockenberg recorded in their chronicles 'prodigia', 'monstra diversa', comets and solar eclipses.[146] Yes, even the States of Holland thought it worthwhile to note in their register of resolutions that in the night of 3 February 1598 at Katwijk a whale was washed ashore.[147] Rumours of sensational omens outside the Netherlands were also spread through Holland, and were made generally known by means of pamphlets: heavy snowfall in Sauerland,[148] terrible thunderstorms at Münster,[149] sudden spouting of a wondrous fountain at Oldenburg.[150] The greater the distance, the more fantastic the description. According to Baudartius, the sea-monster that was washed ashore in 1616 at Kalmar not only carried three halberds on its back, a sword on its forehead, and two elephant's teeth in its mouth, but furthermore had written in great letters on its side, 'Woe, woe, woe, humanity'.[151] That text might apply to most omens, because their meaning was actually always the same: they spurred us to fear the wrath of God.[152] If He showed us any marvellous sight, it was a call to turn away from all the sins by which people angered Him, 'be it idolatry, false religion, whoredom, usury, godless works, or seeking to use wicked financial manipulation and chicanery to steal another's property, or living in contempt and neglect of God's Holy Word'.[153] Whenever a wondrous sign occurs, Baudartius says, it is always a serious warning to us to better our lives.[154]

The direct inspiration for this comment was another marvel from the wonder-rich community of Berkhout, a cow that gave birth to ten calves in April 1623. The writers of chronicles and pamphlets did not scorn these minor remarkable events, but the most sensational were still the changes that became visible in the heavens – and not because people had no understanding of the manner in which they came about. 'Eclipses have ... their natural causes', Van Dam wrote later,[155] but they show no less clearly God's dealings with humanity. *Dominee* Louwijk, who was preacher at Naaldwijk in 1598, wrote that the death of his colleague Pieter Hasaert was a punishment for our sins, and a call to conversion.[156] He would not have found the passing of a seventy-nine-year-old inexplicable, but in this natural occurrence he still distinguished a sign. Then the difference between everyday routine and the extraordinary really disappeared. There was nothing that could not become a sign. Kuchlinus, regent of the Statencollege at Leiden, died on the day after the Bible-reading at table was from Genesis 49, the death of the patriarch Jacob. His funeral orator called that 'presagia' of his approaching death.[157]

If one's entire life, even its normal occurrences, thus became a call to repentance and conversion, the preachers nearly always refused to read a particular message in a special sign alongside the general one. I do not want to go into details about the secrets of the Almighty, wrote Baudartius.[158] 'We must yield to God, what he means by this, and await the outcome', said another author.[159] Even afterwards people could do little more than conjecture. Perhaps Oldenbarnevelt, Grotius, Hogerbeets and Ledenberg were on the beach to see the four whales that had been washed ashore in 1617, and perhaps these beasts were signs of their impending imprisonment. But who could really say for sure?[160] As a result, the reformed church was opposed to those who wanted to announce particular disasters, wars and other events out of the motion of the stars. That would indeed fall under fortune-telling.[161] The preachers did acknowledge that sometimes prophecies came true.[162] Careful astrologers would rather speak of warnings than predictions anyway. The stars, they said, show us how God could act, rather than what must inevitably happen.[163]

> Because we should know anyway
> How to flee from the wrath of God,
> In stars and comets
> God shows us his anger.

At the same time this brings us to the area of the third great religious community, the Mennonites. Just as Calvinism had extra worth in a century that lived in the consciousness of the reality of God's wrath, and just as Catholicism inspired confidence for its help in the struggle against Satan and his thousands of minions, so the lively interest in prophecies, predictions and inspirations worked to the benefit of the Mennonites.[164] The Calvinist Reformation knew only one revelation, the Bible. All those who accepted authority in dreams, visions, or also in reason, along with the Bible, were given the name of fanatics.[165] Yet many had another concept of the Reformation. They thought that the sigh of Moses, 'Oh, that all the Lord's people were prophets and that the Lord would put his Spirit upon them!' (Numbers 11:29), was fulfilled in their own ears. In the seventeenth century this faith did not see such passionate outbursts as in the first half of the sixteenth. Jan van Leyden's holy multitude had been succeeded by the defenceless flock of Menno Simons. But it was all one great family. 'There are now respectable people among the Anabaptists', said Bredero's old Geertruy, 'but Knipperdolling and Jan van Leyden, those were two rogues.'[166] Roguery and respectability sprang from the same roots. The Mennonites remained the spiritual descendants of the Anabaptists of Münster, in that the Spirit spoke directly to them with an inner voice. The Waterlands Mennonites, said a well-known pamphlet of 1627, 'had a primary maxim among themselves, that they taught each other to watch for the speaking and moving of the spirit, and to pay attention to its ideas, in order to adjust themselves accordingly; and that they [should] come closer to what came to them'.[167] The author also informs us that some even declared that the Spirit had revealed to them a new method for the construction of watermills.[168] For such people the inner voice must have become a completely independent power, the private property of a few blessed souls, and the Bible or external word at most another means to call forth the Spirit, like Aladdin's magic lamp. At least, instead of announcing the good news to all, they had asked for a patent on their revelation from the States-General, as if they could regulate the inspiration of the Holy Spirit by means of legal prescriptions.

This pamphlet-writer himself came from Mennonite circles. His example shows that the most extreme conceptions of personal inspiration did not go unchallenged. But that takes nothing away from the fact that for simple spirits with deep religious feeling there could be great fascination in a faith that brought divine inspiration and prophecy within the reach of the entire community, and abolished the tutelage of the layman. Thanks to the gift of the Spirit, he would indeed be able to speak with authority to his brothers, without arduous study. How closely some in the reformed church also still lived by the inner voice appeared after the Synod of Dordt, when for example at Rijnsburg a group of Remonstrant sympathisers broke away to form a sect of 'enthusiasts', whose leaders testified that they themselves had received the Holy Spirit just as the Apostles had once done.[169] At Hazerswoude the Remonstrants simply joined the Mennonites. A young rhetorician, Jacob Gerritsz. Clomp, immediately became their exhorter, without any preparation.[170]

It is probably no coincidence that these two cases involved Remonstrants. Insofar

37. Short and truthful account of the remarkable attack and salvation of David Wardavoir, clothworker, which happened in Utrecht ... From a pamphlet of 1595.

Cort ende warachtich
verhael vande wonderlicke aen-
bechtinge eñ verloſſinge van David Wardavoir,
Trijp·wercker/geſchiet binnen Vtrecht.

In dichte geſtelt tot vertrooſtinghe van alle
aengebochte perſonen.

Gedruckt tot Vtrecht/by Salomon de Roy. 1595.

as the Protestantism of the 'enthusiasts' had entered the river-bed of the reformed church, it later flowed together with the stream of the youth movement, which was set in motion by Arminius. Herman Herbertsz., who contributed much to make Gouda pro-Remonstrant later, taught 'that the certainty of conscience in true faith must come with the spirit, and that without the scriptures'.[171] When he was still a preacher at Dordrecht, Herman Herbertsz. refused to discuss with his colleagues what they would preach about on the following day. 'We do not have the power', he declared, 'because we, in so doing, would prevent or proscribe ... the gift of the Holy Spirit'.[172] These were ideas that came close to accepting the inner voice as the highest authority and source of knowledge.

The great majority of reformed preachers condemned this inspiration. They did call preaching a gift,[173] but at the same time they always used the word 'study' as a synonym for the making and preparing of a sermon. Not only did they reject direct revelations and prophecies, but they considered them as signs of a disturbed mind. At Edam in 1608 lived the prophetess Trijn Gerrits, who received revelations in dreams. The church council did not hesitate for a moment to investigate the worth of her prophecies, and wondered only if they could proceed against her with ecclesiastical censure, in view of the uncertainty whether she 'should be considered mad or of sound mind'.[174] The Leiden church council made even less fuss of the local prophetess in 1597, and concluded at once from her pretension that she was not responsible, and furthermore that she should be excluded from the communion.[175] Denial of prophecy was probably characteristic of Calvinism all over Europe. At the time of the Synod of Dordt, the Swiss Mayer, who made the acquaintance of a Danish prophetess sent by God's way to settle the religious differences, remarked of this woman in his notes: 'redet sunsten von allerhand sachen gantz vernünftig' (she usually spoke about all kinds of matters in a very reasonable way).[176]

Yes, but ... when Baudartius discussed a little book by Matthias Ehingerus that denounced as liars the prophets who had arisen in Germany, he nonetheless thought that some of their prophecies had come true. I can do no better than wonder at it, he wrote, 'allowing others to judge by what spirit, or influence, they foresaw and foretold these things'.[177] *Dominee* Alutarius of Woerden came face to face in 1623 with the orphan boy Evert Willemsz., who had been temporarily deprived of his hearing and speech, and took no food or drink. In this condition he produced written warnings to repent, which an angel supposedly told him. Alutarius showed him – in writing, because the boy was still deaf – that in the dispensation of the New Testament, visions and revelations had disappeared. Evert recovered after several days, but quickly afterwards fell back into his ecstatic state. When Alutarius came into contact with the boy again, and asked why he was plagued anew with deaf-and-dumbness, Evert wrote: 'because it is not proclaimed through the whole world, that God so mercifully cured me with his mighty hand; and that therefore the Lord is so upset, as now appears that [the story] is not being spread'. The prophet took no risks on this occasion. He allowed his second cure to take place in the presence

38. *Witches' sabbath*, by Adriaen van de Venne

of many witnesses, who promised in advance that they would make the miracle known in print. Not only that: the rector of the Latin school undertook the preparation of a pamphlet, and the church council as well as the magistrate confirmed the truth of this history with their printed approbations.[178]

When ecclesiastical and civil authorities in Woerden were no match for such a notorious faker, there was hope for prophesying pamphlet-writers that their dream-visions, committed to paper, would also find credulous readers.[179] These predictions must have been extraordinarily seductive to faithful church-goers when the inspirations were directly related to biblical prophecy. Often the prognosticators took their wisdom from the Revelation of John,[180] occasionally also from the prophets of the Old Testament. For example, a certain Jacobus Brocardus proclaimed – in 1599 – that the St Bartholomew's Day Massacre in Paris (1572) had been foretold in Isaiah 5:24–5, and also in various chapters of Ezekiel (1, 9 and 44). Jeremiah contained many warnings to the faithful not to emigrate from Germany, while

Daniel 11:35 taught us that the Turks would join with the Papists against the Protestants. Yet Isaiah (15 and 16) and Jeremiah (48) revealed that this monstrous alliance would not prevent the definitive defeat of Spain.[181]

There were many more such pamphlets. We do not know much about their influence and distribution, but time and again there were new ones. And since the South Holland Synod of 1623 asked whether there should not be a ban on the publication of dreams and visions,[182] there must have been no shortage of readers.

We are here on the edge of folk beliefs. Predictions such as those of Brocardus could also have a place in ordinary preaching, if separated from their visionary additions. The mixture again makes it clear that folk beliefs and the Catholic, Calvinist or Mennonite faith could not only fight against each other, but also meet halfway.

Chapter 15

CALVINISTS

I

The Reformation had many faces. Its ways varied from country to country and from period to period. The reformers and the reform-minded had fundamental differences about the goals, means, and tempo of the desired changes. Furthermore, it became evident that the Reformation could not establish one great international church organisation that had the same ecumenical breadth and universal pretensions as the old church of Rome. Reformation meant break, diversity and denunciation. Nonetheless in the end it did normally succeed in founding a single religious community on the national level that had a clear form of its own, and made a claim to be the only true church in its area. This effort was most successful in those countries where it enjoyed the complete co-operation of the civil authorities from the beginning, so that it could immediately replace the Catholic Church in all of its functions. The later the break occurred, the harder indeed it was to become a new general church. Then it was not easy to gather all the flock together again. The church had great difficulty restoring the unity of the faith, which had been strained by the poorly organised Protestant life in its multiple variants during the years of persecution.

This surely applies with particular force to the Republic of the Seven United Provinces of the Netherlands, which was the youngest creation in the series of Protestant powers. Church organisation on its territory could only develop after a long period of fifty years of undirected growth. It goes without saying that at the outset of its existence above ground the new reformed church had to deal with its polymorphous past. It was too much to expect that all of its servants would immediately speak with one voice. Yet it cannot be denied that most of its leaders were going in the same direction: they based themselves on the model of Calvin. This did not happen simultaneously in all provinces, nor with the same determination. In some parts of the land, such as Utrecht, the Calvinising really began only after 1618. This was not the case for Holland. There, although the process did take many years, it was begun at once. The primary means were the unity of teaching, unity of leadership, and unity of discipline.

A complete description of this process would be beyond the scope of this book.[1] Besides, we do not want to study the reformed church as such, but only its place in popular life. But it will still be necessary to establish what this reformed church offered. If we start with the three points mentioned, we can confirm that this church had accepted a reformed confession of faith. As the synod of Emden during the years of exile had already decided that every minister on his appointment would sign the *confessio Belgica*, so the North Holland synod of 1573 agreed to accept the same confession for the sake of unity. The synod wanted the personal agreement of all its ministers: anyone who had never read the confession was ordered 'to read [it] with understanding and afterwards to sign the same with ripe understanding'.[2] In South Holland in 1574 there was already talk of requiring the elders and deacons to sign as well.[3]

In the early years not much came of this. The confession was so little known that the synod of North Holland in 1576 had to insist that each *classis* should possess at least 'one correct and uncorrupted exemplar'.[4] This statement points to an irregular signing policy, yet even if there were only ten copies in the entire province it simultaneously shows the will to force it through, so that every preacher would sign that confession 'with understanding'. To what extent such a policy would succeed depended on the manner in which the second means was applied: the unity of leadership. The leaders tried to tie local communities together in the *classes*, thus bringing into being an enclosed net that would place all local churches under the control of the larger gatherings. With a few exceptions, this organisation was accomplished in the entire region of Holland in the 1580s.

Only then was it possible to proceed seriously on the third point, the general introduction of church discipline. Wherever that happened, a church council had to exist; correspondingly there was a need to set down the business of that body in a minute-book. These minute-books and the records of the *classes* are the primary sources for our knowledge of reformed church life in this period. Since *classes* as well as church councils regularly supported the process of Calvinising, however, a judgment based solely on these sources could contain some bias. The communities that remained passive received little mention. Yet the records of the *classes* compensate for that to some degree, because they did generally devote attention to problematic cases. In some *classes* these communities maintained themselves for a fairly long time, particularly around Gorinchem. But a contrary tendency cannot be found in any *classes* records, and acts of resistance become less and less frequent. Therefore anyone who maintains that the Calvinising process within the church of Holland was complete towards the end of the sixteenth century most closely reflects the sources. Their language is very clear: the formerly cherished view of a relatively open church, which only bolted the door at the synod of Dordt in 1618,[5] now has no more than nostalgic value.

This reformed church had to take the place of the old Roman Catholic one. It was a must, for no country or people could do without religion. Governments in the sixteenth century had a limited notion of their tasks, but protection and maintenance of the Christian church was in their eyes a self-evident duty. A community without places where people could worship and honour God was unthinkable. Besides, the government itself felt this need. In January 1579, one week after the signing of the Union of Utrecht, the States of Holland tried to get the renowned Heidelberg theologian Olevianus into their service, 'in order to hold daily services for the States and those of the provincial court'.[6] Olevianus did not come, and in later times we note that less need was felt for daily exhortation in the high colleges of Holland. Nevertheless the rulers still felt bound to the Christian religion, and gave a special place to the reformed religious community of Holland. As a result they celebrated victories with public services of thanksgiving, and attempted to ward off evil with days of fasting and prayer. The church received control of religious teaching in the schools, and its ministers provided spiritual care for soldiers, sailors and prisoners.

In this manner the reformed church was involved in everyday life and influenced the actions of many people who did not belong to it. But what counted most was that from 1572 onward it received exclusive use of all church buildings. The communion service drove out the mass, and the sermon became the most important part of the service. Drastic liturgical retrenchment made the change apparent, and long dogmatic sermons gave a distinctive voice to the new faith. Yet the church remained standing where it had always stood. In the old church building everyone could ask the new faith for the same services that had been provided by the old: baptism, marriage and burial. The Reformation did not simply break with tradition. As the ruling reformed church became settled, it had at the same time become the carrier of continuity in the exercise of all functions that affected the daily life of all Hollanders.

Consequently, from the moment of its definitive settlement the reformed church possessed a wide appeal. In the first place it was there for its own faithful, who had bound themselves to the church as members. But it was also at the disposal of all the inhabitants of a town or village who wanted to baptise children, who would have their marriage confirmed, or who simply did not want to miss church services on Sunday and had no opportunity other than the now-reformed village church. Thus we often find surrounding the still small core of members a wider circle of interested people who were so clearly recognisable as a group that contemporaries had a particular term for them: the adherents of the reformed religion.

That distinction between the actual members and the followers is repeatedly made in the sources. They sometimes use other terms, contrasting the 'community' of members[7] with 'the common folk', or 'the surrounding of the entire people',[8] – all the others who attended church. At times they indicated the followers as persons 'coming to hear the reformed preaching'.[9] The Catholics also made the same distinction between Protestants who did, and did not, take part in the communion service.[10] Thus for example the Haarlem *klopje* Catharina Oly said of the parents of her religious sister Mayke Jans Terwe that not only had they chosen heresy, but furthermore they were 'so zealous, that they have also given themselves over to taking part in the communion'.[11] She seemed to find something excessive in that, the ultimate in heretical folly. From her point of view she was right: in the first years the members were certainly in the minority vis-a-vis the followers.[12] The community of Alkmaar in 1576, for example, had only 160 members but two preachers.[13] Dordrecht also already had two ministers in 1573, but at the first communion service on 5 July no more than 368 members participated.[14] Similar ratios are still found much later. They suggest to us that the congregation was considerably greater than the community of members: for the spiritual service of such a small group of communicants one minister would have been quite adequate. The number of ministerial positions, however, was based on the number of listeners.

Why did these people attend church? Let us begin answering this question by considering external factors, and then attempt to reach the heart of the matter. First we must ask what the reformed church had to offer everyone, and only afterwards what it gave to its members in particular. In the Middle Ages it was always a hallmark of the local parish that it had the right to hold baptisms, marriages and burial ceremonies. The reformed church would now have to provide for these general needs. It did have some reservations, and it definitively rejected one task: it did not want to take on the burial of the dead.[15] It had no provision for funeral and memorial services, at least not in this period. This was also the reason why the consistories maintained registers of births and marriages, but left the registration of the dead to 'the grave-makers or those who are charged with it'.[16] Churchyards and church buildings remained the normal burial places, and as we saw in the previous chapter, they continued to draw the next of kin who wanted to pray at the graves of the dead.[17] The reformed church, however, played no role as such in the burials. Naturally the preacher could say a pious word or two at the grave. But the church no longer offered any funeral ceremonies.

The situation was different for baptisms and marriages. Here the reformed church stayed closer to tradition. At first there was no general agreement on this point. The synod of North Holland decided in August 1572 that it would be preferable if 'the churches could be relieved of these matters of weddings by political authority'.[18] What they then wanted was to abolish church weddings, and to introduce civil marriage generally. Yet they did not succeed. Civil marriage did emerge as a new form, but most people still chose church weddings. The church made itself available to them. Its only pre-condition – other than the normal legal restrictions, of course – was that the bride and bridegroom must both have received baptism. It was not necessary that baptism should be followed by membership in the reformed community, and it mattered even less whether baptism had taken place in the reformed church. Not even the behaviour and reputation of the prospective spouses were regarded as motives for refusal. If necessary, the church would also certify the marriages of 'reckless and uncouth people'.[19] Thus the reformed church reached far beyond its borders. Only those who had quite consciously made another religious choice would avoid going to church for the confirmation of their marriage vows. The indifferent and the wavering still used its services and exposed themselves to its influence, if only for a moment: but perhaps a moment of increased susceptibility.

The church was still more generous with baptism. It proceeded from the view that every child born into Christianity had a personal right to be baptised. The church saw that service as a duty laid upon it, though it would perhaps have preferred to decline. The previously mentioned synod of North Holland declared in 1572 that a minister should limit himself to the baptism of children of members, if at least he 'could separate his service from the service of the Papists'.[20] Apparently the synod assumed that in Holland there would be freedom of religion for both persuasions. All non-members – the great majority of the population – would then have to go to the Catholic priests for the baptism of their children. More often than not we notice this about the Dutch reformed church of the sixteenth century: in its best moments it showed itself averse to an easy winning of members. It wanted to preach and to dispute, and gladly sought comparison with its opponents, even in public. But it rejected any means that would attract members on grounds other than inner conviction. Anyone who was not certain that he belonged with the reformed had better let his child be baptised by the Papists. He would not thereby place the child at a disadvantage, for baptism by a Catholic priest was equally valid as that by a reformed minister.

Freedom of religion did not last long, however, and that fact did not escape the notice of the reformed church. It did not hold to the policy of this first synod of North Holland, and was eager enough to acquire a monopoly of public worship services for itself. Then it also had to accept the consequences and offer baptism to every child born of Christian parents. This principled decision was made at the synod of Dordrecht in 1578. That gathering stated that baptism could not be refused to the children of papists, whoremongers and excommunicated, 'because baptism is the rightful due of children belonging to the covenant, and it is certain, that these children are not outside the covenant'.[21] Thus it was proclaimed that every Dutch child belonged to the people of the covenant, regardless of the faith or moral behaviour of its parents. Sometimes this was accepted with distaste. Not every minister found it so easy to help parents who did not even take the trouble to appear personally, and allowed the midwife to bring the child; or who refused to answer the baptismal questions; or who were known as 'notoriously profane and godless'.[22] But disputes of this kind were always resolved in favour of the parents, or rather in favour of the child. Baptism in the reformed church was a service offered to the entire Dutch people.

The church doors also stood open to all when sermons were preached on Sundays or weekdays. Anyone who came to listen could be reached by the reformed preacher. Now we should not overestimate these *dominees*. Certainly during the sixteenth century their intellectual level was not particularly high. Many of the ministers in the countryside sprang from the group of so-called 'German clerics', who owed their name to the fact that they knew no language other than Low German (Dutch), and had been allowed to enter the ministry without university studies. Over time the number of learned ministers increased, but the exodus of the Remonstrants in 1618 was a tremendous loss of blood for the church of Holland. In the first decades of the seventeenth century there were definitely still many preachers without university education: they did not reach a high level. But they did build their sermons out of the same elements as the learned preachers did. In particular, the preaching of this time was marked by three characteristics: it echoed the Bible, it launched polemics against those who thought differently, and it stressed punishment and repentance. We shall now say a few words about each of these aspects.

Preaching in this period had a definite biblical sound. Not only did it seek its firm foundation in scripture, but also it often used the very words of the Bible, and expressed itself in images and comparisons that were borrowed from the Old and New Testaments. Anyone who wishes to see a good example should read the *Ziekentroost* (*Consolation for the Sick*) by Cornelis van Hille, at present still included in the supplements to the old Dutch psalter. Bible texts were the building stones of the argument. When the author had to connect two texts, he used phrases drawn literally from biblical language. The language of the sermons and the Bible was largely the same. This showed caution. For the preacher the Bible was the highest authority: he could never say anything better himself. For the listener the hearing of such sermons was an introduction to the language and the mental world of the Bible, so that he would become continually more familiar with that book. Even if he did not and could not read for himself, the Bible was presented to him in preaching, continuously and almost literally. When that same preaching repeatedly told him that this book was the infallible revealed word of God, the listener could be brought to the conviction that he should accept and believe this preached word unconditionally.

Preaching was intended to force him to accept the Bible in the reformed spirit. It thus tried to make the choice clear and unavoidable by presenting its own interpretation at every turn in contrast to those of others. Preaching was directed against 'the enemies of the truth'. It continually pointed out how and why the Catholics, the Mennonites, and later also the Remonstrants did not do justice to divine revelation. Church gatherings saw that as a duty, and demanded that the preachers should rebuke the sects, especially 'popery'. Polemical preaching must convince the waverers, since it was clothed in the authority of holy scripture. Against God's own word the insignificant hare-brained schemes of the Papists were futile. The reformed church knew it was in full possession of the truth, and it shared that truth with church-goers, teaching them how they should use scripture to distinguish between lies and truth.

That conviction could make its possessors proud. For that reason alone preaching had to contain a compensating element. Yet quite apart from that, a sermon without admonition to repentance would have been barely thinkable in that age. We saw in the first chapter how deeply ingrained was the notion of sinful human corruption, in contrast to the majesty of the Almighty. Calvinism was strongly based on that consciousness, and pointed people towards their guilt, the necessity of repentance and conversion to avert the wrath of God. It gave protection against God's punishing hand, in preaching that rested on the firm confidence that it was in full harmony with God's infallible word, and thus could unmask the deviations of other religious communities with incontrovertible proofs.

Such was the power that could be unlocked in Calvinist preaching. We learn from an unimpeachable independent witness, the aforementioned Catharina Oly, that it did indeed happen. She reported that the Catholic girl Aechge Baertesdr. allowed herself to be persuaded by her heretical father to accompany him on Sundays. A Catholic friend had advised her to go ahead for the sake of sweet peace: with a closed heart she could allow the sermon to glide over her anyway. Yet the outcome was different. 'Anyone who touches pitch is contaminated by it. She began to hear the heretical sermons and accept them, yes, she became so enthusiastic about them that she almost joined the community or consistory (so they call it).'[23] Only the death of her father prevented that. At the insistence of her friends she agreed to give up these dangerous habits.

Here Catharina Oly shows clearly what the preaching intended: to turn hearers into members. The sermon was the primary means to this end. Preachers or members of church councils seldom exercised pressure on followers in personal conversations, let alone watched over their church attendance and behaviour. For the reformed, choice was voluntary. It is true that external circumstances were very much in favour of this church, so that it became an almost unavoidable destination for everyone who did not expressly seek other possibilities, or was not forcefully exhorted to another choice. In many places initially there was no alternative to the reformed church. But anyone who did not feel attracted to membership was not forced into it. Even indirect pressure by means of poor relief did not influence its growth significantly, or at all, as we saw in part I.[24]

Thus there was freedom of choice. Actually that is saying too much, as if only the candidate had to decide. The choice had to be made mutually. Church councils were not in the habit of recording new members hastily and rubbing their hands with glee. Indeed, they generally did not set very high standards in matters of doctrine. Separate catechism classes for adults who applied for membership were begun only hesitantly after the synod of Dordt. What the confessional candidates knew of theology they had learnt at school long ago, or picked up along with their attendance at church. There was, however, a careful examination of their conduct. Sometimes followers who presented themselves were addressed in a warning manner: had they considered carefully to what they were committing themselves? Members had to bear good witness. Thus enquiries were made in the neighbourhood, if the candidate had a good reputation. Often the church council decided to test the candidate further during a probationary period. The gate to the pasture stood slightly ajar: it was open, but entrance to the flock was strictly controlled.

Why were the church councils so strict? What was implied by their judgment on individual membership in the community? The great distinction between members and followers was that the former could participate in the communion, while the latter could not. The community was equivalent to the total of the communicants, if one wishes to speak mathematically. The growth of the reformed church can only be measured in the reception registers of new members, and by the total number of communicants. Although the influence of the church reached much further than the circle of its members, we have no hard figures for the followers. Thus figures have their value, but a definition based on numbers alone is completely inadequate if we want to bring the community to life. Then it is not the counting of individuals that matters, but one whole. 'We are members of one body', said the old formula for communion. The bread and the wine are signs of it. 'Because just as one flour is milled from many kernels of grain, and one bread baked; and from many fruits pressed together, one wine and drink flows and mixes together; so shall we all, brought to life by the true faith in Christ, through brotherly love ... all be one body, and such not only in words, but also in deeds show that towards each other.'

That is also a definition of the community: it is one body, namely the body of Christ. That description says more than the quantitative one, or perhaps it says too much. The community of Oosterland consisted of sixty-three members in 1597. This is a bald fact, but it is completely correct and verifiable, because we find all the names in the membership register. The community of Oosterland was one, because it belonged to the body of Christ. While we might also accept this statement as true, it is not verifiable. It represents less a condition than a goal. The community wanted to be and had to be one body: it wanted to live and had to live this unity at the communion table. Yet this was at the same time 'the obstacle to which the members were subject', as the church council of Charlois called it in 1613.[25] Unity did not come into being automatically. With good reason, the communion formula was by far the longest in the reformed service-book. It described in particular how each person must prepare for the communion, in order that the celebration may fulfil its purpose. Ultimately, however, it was not concerned with each individual member, but with the community. That is why the community was actively supported in its effort to become the body of Christ around the communion table. We call this support church discipline. Thereby the purpose of church discipline becomes clear: it sought to preserve the unity of the community, in order to give it the form of the body of Christ.

Consequently the exercise of discipline took place in the community as a whole. The community must not be stained by scandal; for its sake, sin had to be banished from its midst. That was a service to the entire community. If anyone had misbehaved, then the community had to be purified. That took place by bringing the sinner to repentance, and thus reconciling him with the community; or if the sinner was obstinate, by casting him out. Yet neither in the first case nor in the second were the interests of the offender paramount. The community had to be protected against God's wrath: they would have every reason to be afraid, if through their own fault the body of Christ was offended and defiled. Therefore we should not expect church discipline procedures to show scrupulous attention to individual rights. It was possible – and also not in the least exceptional – for a member to be suspended without even being heard. If he was called to speak, he could bring no defenders with him. He was not allowed to examine the evidence against him, and he was not told the names of his accusers. He had to regard the whole church council as a court even if it was a question of personal conflict between him and the minister.

If the church council was convinced of his guilt, he had to accept that judgment personally. For serious offences, he even had to confirm that publicly.

Yet it was the rule that the exercise of discipline should end with reconciliation. At least that was the situation in the sixteenth century, and during the first decades of the seventeenth century. It did not remain so,[26] although we do not know precisely when the change occurred. The tempo at which the change took place was not everywhere the same: the great urban communities surely took the lead in this matter. Nonetheless it is probable that for the whole period of the revolt against Spain discipline ended with reconciliation and confession of guilt.

Thus it becomes understandable why the reformed church did not enjoy explosive growth. Membership was precious: the church wished to place a high price on it.[27] The church wanted all guilt to be atoned for, and had a strict concept of sin. It has also been reproached for ordering Christian life primarily under a series of prohibitions, putting more emphasis on what to avoid than on what should be done, as Father Polman has expressed it.[28] Even those who agree that this criticism is just will have to recognise that this emphasis was not entirely misplaced. The life of the people in the sixteenth century was hard and rough. When the church said that members should not 'live like common folk',[29] such an expression testifies to insight into reality. Could we say that the folk we met in the first three parts of this book lived their lives in accord with God's commandments? Occasionally, indeed, that influence appeared. The ordinary Hollander was kind to the poor, as we saw in part I. He honoured marriage, as shown in part II. But he was also unruly and quickly offended. He drank heavily and gambled enthusiastically. He discriminated against foreigners and evaded taxes. All these offences and much else besides were marked in the communion formula as sins that provoked offence and thus stained the body of Christ. These were the sins that church discipline fought systematically. The minute-books of church councils are filled with them, and Calvinists should not be ashamed of that.

Polman's reproach, however, is not thereby laid to rest. Was the positive element indeed lacking? Was there no Calvinist piety that found expressions other than avoidance and prohibition? In this chapter we have already had occasion to mention the Haarlem *klopje* Catharina Oly. We know much about this community of devout women in Haarlem because Catharina wrote down their life stories, and for some of them funeral orations have been preserved. I want to cite here a passage that Father Joost Cats spoke at the burial of Itgen Pieters de Goyer: 'She understood well what a spiritual gathering consisted of, that is: not only for a group of people to live with each other, but also to make one spiritual body out of many people as spiritual members, each to be the other's member.'[30]

These expressions are already familiar to us. They remind us strongly of the communion formula, that we 'are all one body, and not only in words, but also in deeds show that towards each other'. This was not a stray idea in reformed theology, either. The Heidelberg Catechism says 'that the believers each and every one as members of the Lord Christ share all his treasures and gifts in common', and that therefore 'each has an obligation to use his gifts freely for the benefit and blessing of the other members'.[31] The Dutch confession of faith would have all who join the church 'serve to the edification of the brothers, according to the gifts God has given them, as mutual members of one and the same body'.[32] In all three of these writings the life of the believers is described in terms that are clearly related to what Joost Cats in his funeral sermon thought was the characteristic of the cloistered community. A cloister was shut off from the world: likewise the reformed community. Its members had given up the world. Membership in Christ meant, according to the words of the baptismal formula, 'being attached to the Lord God, trusting Him and loving Him with all [one's] heart, with all [one's] soul, with all [one's] mind and with all the powers to forsake the world, to kill our old nature, and walk in a new godly life'. Such a community wanted to take seriously the priesthood of all believers. Thus it exacted of each the full pound of holiness.

That was certainly a positive requirement, but it was fulfilled differently than in the cloister. The Catholic virgins of Haarlem long stood under the leadership of Mother Superior Trijntgen Dirckx Wij. This woman always got up at four-thirty in the morning, 'having her exercises and little prayers while she dressed'. At five a.m. she went to the church, and after the service she remained there in prayer and meditation until nine. From nine to ten 'she practised silence', with the help of the rosary. Then she discussed spiritual matters with others for one hour. At eleven o'clock she turned inward again. While she was at table, she took care that only edifying conversations took place. Occasionally the Mother Superior would seek company after eating, but her conscience was easily troubled, 'as if she had been deprived of her Heavenly Bridegroom, saying: Am I not enough for you, do you still have to find comfort in creatures'?[33] This piety is impressive, but it is Catholic to the bone. Reformed devotion did not seek peace and solitude in specially dedicated places, nor did it use objects that supported sanctification, such as rosaries and crucifixes. Any room would do as long as there was a Bible; with Trijntgen Dirckx Wij the Bible is not even mentioned. Yet it is certain that Calvinist piety was much rarer, for in this form it required time and concentration. Calvinists did not have cloisters any more. They had to stand in the middle of life, and earn their bread with their own hands through long working days. The devotion of the inner room could not flourish. The emphasis had to fall on obedience to God's commandments in daily life, at home and in public.

It is certainly possible that some people's attachment to their faith found expression in ordinary work, and that others could publicly see and hear it. Occasionally this can be confirmed. If Dutch people think of the role of women during the siege of Haarlem in 1572–3, in most cases only the name of the martial Kenau Simonsdr. Hasselaer comes to mind. The Haarlemmer Willem Verwer preserved another impression in his diary. Young girls participated so spiritedly in strengthening the fortifications 'that they went on top of the walls signing psalms and other hymns of praise, to the pleasure of all people who came there or nearby'.[34] Was this a challenge to the enemy encamped outside? Indeed it was, but in other centuries girls would have chosen songs other than the psalms of Datheen. In more normal circumstances as well, we sometimes discover psalm-singing. Constantijn Huygens explained the lack of harmony in church singing from the fact that so many people sang psalms at home while working, and preferred their own variations to the difficult melody.[35] Thijs Jasparts of Purmerend was such a person, who testified in 1626 that he often practised with his children. Catholics had frequently teased them about it, and wanted to know if they had also learned 'Out of the depths O Lord'.[36] Then these Catholics must have heard Psalm 130 so often that they knew the beginning, just as today one would not have to be a pop-music fan in order to know the first line of a hit song. At least in Purmerend, therefore, the Catholics passing by in the street listened to the psalm-singing that rang from the houses. And perhaps there were places when people gathered now and then in the open air in order to sing psalms. In February, 1620, the record-book of the town council of Gouda reported that as an established custom, apparently even during the winter season.[37]

Just as the Catholics inform us about psalm-singing in Purmerend, they were also the ones who much more often gave the impression that Calvinism and Bible-reading went hand in hand. 'All trades and arts have their time, manner, and masters, in order to learn the same', said the Catholic propagandist David. 'Only the holy scripture has now become a trade that everyone dares to take on.'[38] There are those who always carry the Bible with them, Verstegen stated, 'in order to study it in the streets'.[39] According to the Spaniard Vázquez all Dutch women – without any exception, he expressly added – were prepared to discuss religious matters. 'This comes because many books are printed in the local language. The Bible especially is very widespread, and they read it from their early youth and know it by heart.'[40]

Church councils, *classes* and synods did not always agree. They were less impressed by the knowledge of the faith and attachment to the Bible shown by their members. Too many sources speak about weak and inexperienced members for us to ascribe these complaints to excessive pastoral concern. It was undoubtedly true of all church-minded folk in that age – and probably so in other ages as well, though that is not at issue here. The weak formed the majority. We may be more inclined to excuse them than the church councils were. Anyone who had to work for a master all day long for his daily bread had little time left for the Bible and prayer. Religion did not have to disappear from such lives, but the practice of religious exercises had to be limited to Sundays, no matter how warmly the synods spoke of 'house-prayers in the evenings, which each house-father is obliged to do with his household'.[41]

Thus it is not illogical that the reformed churches put a strong emphasis on living the faith in daily work, obeying God's commandments in practice. And perhaps, in the eyes of the Calvinists, the performance of devout deeds all too quickly took on a popish appearance. Johannes Bogerman told Maurice of Nassau on the latter's deathbed that he had spoken with William Louis in the last hours of his life about

Archduke Albert, who went to get an indulgence at Our Lady of Scherpenheuvel. William Louis had laughed about it, and thanked God that he had received other lights. Maurice agreed that 'Count William always had Scherpenheuvel with him'.[42] Such a commentary is thoroughly Protestant. Maurice did not believe that God's mercy was easier to find in Heilo or in Scherpenheuvel: for him one place was no holier than another. So thought all Calvinists: the typical Roman devotion had no value for them. They had learned how to express their belief in daily existence. The true Christian was the one who did his work correctly and faithfully.

The consequence of this attitude could be a far-reaching Christianisation of everyday life: we see the concrete expression in the poetic works of Jacob Cats. It was certainly possible that they could make living the faith somewhat colourless and plain, and form Christians who were always dutiful and good, but never ardent or zealous. Only in a crisis could Calvinism develop the last-mentioned qualities: under persecution, in time of war, or also during religious strife. Then Calvinists became violent and aggressive. It would be tempting to draw lines of continuity, and see these characteristics of early modern Calvinism in later centuries: Abraham Kuyper in the nineteenth century, who consciously roused his fellow believers to struggle; the German occupiers during the Second World War, who did so unwittingly. But let us not give ourselves over to provocative speculations. The ordinary facts are lively enough. The religious struggles of the Twelve Years' Truce can confirm that unequivocally.

II

The disturbances in the church provide us with wonderful material. Unrest always makes the sources flow more freely, and thus increases the chances of good observations. Here all the more so, because the ordinary church people that we want to learn about participated actively in the struggle. It was an embittered internal struggle, in which they were divided into two camps: Calvinists versus Remonstrants.

If I have called one party Calvinists, the other Remonstrants, it is not because I have weighed both tendencies in the theological scale and assigned labels in accord with the expression of dogma. I chose these terms for the simplest reason, that the parties involved did so themselves. One party wanted to be called Calvinist, while the others loathed the name. Some theologians assure us that, from the point of view of the history of dogma, both groups should be seen as Calvinist.[43] Thus they find it clarifying to use the same name for both, and consequently speak of 'an internal Calvinist conflict'.[44] Whatever the foundations of learning on which this conclusion may rest, in the eyes of all early seventeenth-century people it would have caused confusion, and in the ears of Remonstrants it would have sounded offensive. Without any dogmatic or historical pretensions, let us therefore use the names the people themselves preferred to bear, and which, according to their conviction, indicated not agreement but a clear difference.

I shall describe that difference in a few words. Both groups declared that man becomes saved through faith. For Calvinists this meant that God gave faith to the ones that He had chosen for it. Faith is a fruit of election. By contrast, the Remonstrants said that God chose those who He foresaw would believe. Election is thus a fruit of faith.

But what are such formulas worth to us? They come from theology, and have a particular charge and meaning for practitioners of that discipline. Our concern is not with the theologians, however, but with the people of the church. The question then becomes not which theological position both sides adhered to, but how this was reflected on the level of the community. We must try to find out how this teaching was explained to the listeners, and how they themselves were able to assimilate and understand it.

The first is a relatively simple task. While it was true that instruction was for the most part given from the pulpit, and only an infinitesimal percentage of the sermons have been printed, the stream of pamphlets in this period was extraordinarily rich. The authors were normally ministers: undoubtedly they used the same arguments in the pulpit. So often do they reveal on the title pages that their writings are intended for 'simple folk', for 'the common man', that they certainly tried to keep the pulpit style on the most popular level. Two striking characteristics emerge from these pamphlets. First, a great deal of the argument consisted of citing and explaining Biblical texts. No wonder, because we have also seen this characteristic in the preaching. Reformed preachers thought that they should augment their hearers' knowledge of the Bible, and they believed that no person or thing, no fact or reasoning, could go beyond the authority of the Bible. An appeal to the Bible was always conclusive, and thus had to be the foundation for instruction.

We know, however, that as a rule preaching also contained a polemical element. The pamphlet war in the Twelve Years' Truce allows us to see something of the coarsening that explanation of the Gospel had to suffer under the influence of confrontation. We can observe that propagandistic enthusiasm on both sides led the writers astray into demagogic and perfidious arguments.

Among the Remonstrants that process occurred within the framework of theology. Their tactic consisted of taking one point out of context of the whole, and then with inexorable logic driving it home, as the proverb says, to where the road paved with good intentions must lead. Literally, too: Calvinists taught not only election, but also condemnation, and all the condemned would go to hell. That was the favourite subject of the Remonstrants, perhaps their most popular point. They reasoned thus: according to the Calvinists some people – most, as the propaganda would have it – are already before their birth doomed for all eternity. No one knows who these people are. Every new-born child may thus belong to the damned. Calvinists cannot know for certain that the infant who dies will go to heaven. Their God is a tyrant, who sends innocent children to hell. Calvinistic parents must continually be in doubt, when they have laid a young child in his grave: was he damned? Remonstrant propaganda had to admit that this teaching could not be found among the Calvinists. But no wonder, because they themselves were ashamed of it, and thus did not want to talk about it. At the same time, all possibility of answering the charges was eliminated. Denials would not help the Calvinists, since one could indeed be certain that on this point they were not telling the truth.

A second line of attack followed exactly the opposite course. It did not begin with damnation, but rather with election; it reproached Calvinism not for its tormenting uncertainty, but, on the contrary, for its unjustified confidence. Does election exist for eternity? Well then, the so-called elect can sin lustily and mock all God's commandments. Heaven will still remain their sure destination! Calvinism flies in the face of common sense. The most horrible godlessness will have just as little influence on a man's fate as the most touching love for his neighbour. Christian morality becomes senseless.

Counter-Remonstrant propaganda presents no more cheerful vision. It also paints the opinions of opponents in the most unfavourable light. God gives his grace to the people whom He finds worthy. Thus we must do our best to find favour in God's eyes: that is, to earn heaven itself by means of good works. Why then was the Reformation necessary? Remonstrantism in its basic teaching is nothing other than popish error. Yes, but it is even worse than that. The best representatives of this propaganda gladly charge it with other heresies as well. Not only was Remonstrantism actually Roman Catholic, but it was also Socinian, Arian and libertine. It hardly needs saying that the quality of the proofs presented declined as the charges became more serious.

In the most dubious genre, these arguments were also mixed with political aspersions,[45] again following a well-known kind of logic. Remonstrants are really Catholics. Catholics are friends of Spain. Tolerating Remonstrants means opening the gates to the Spanish army. This was an unavoidable conclusion, and, within the limits of such argumentation, irrefutable.

Finally there was another argument of somewhat more worth, that nonetheless gives just as false an image of Remonstrantism as the ones already mentioned: Calvinists willingly appealed to history. They said that their teachings had always been taught in the reformed church. Remonstrantism is new, Calvinism is old. Remonstrants are offering novelties, and thus are in error. Nowadays if anyone is short of arguments, he can do good service to his cause by repeatedly saying that he is seeking change and renewal. Seventeenth-century people thought exactly the opposite. Maintaining, restoring and going back could always count on arousing emotional sympathy. Propaganda simply could not miss such an opportunity.

Consequently, it should be crystal clear that the two parties gave out information at the lowest level. They obviously sought to influence readers and listeners who were susceptible to demagogy. They strove for mass appeal among an uncritical

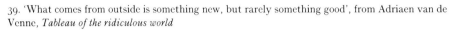

39. 'What comes from outside is something new, but rarely something good', from Adriaen van de Venne, *Tableau of the ridiculous world*

public. Naturally this judgment on both camps is too general. Not all preachers resorted to these dubious methods: perhaps they were only a minority on both sides. After all, we know little more about the sermons than that they frequently discussed points of dispute. We do know about the pamphlets, and we can confirm that in a number of these writings the arguments stated above were used. But even if we combed through the entire collection and established the exact frequency of demagogic polemic as a percentage of the total, it would still be unknown whether good or bad information made the greatest impression.

For we have no right to be unfair toward the church folk. We cannot assume that they were susceptible only to provocation, and did not understand the core of the dispute. Statistics would tell us nothing about that. We can call witnesses, but it is not always easy to decide on what their judgment rests. Three members from Benthuizen heard Calvinist preachers say that God's grace cannot be lost. They were 'scandalised to the utmost about it'.[46] These men were undoubtedly thinking in a Remonstrant way, but it cannot be determined whether biased propaganda against the teaching of irresistible grace had awakened or even stirred up their abhorrence. In any case, Remonstrant members who explain why they made that choice nearly always list the same points as played leading roles in the propaganda. Sometimes it was the perseverance of the saints, such as among the three men of

Benthuizen; sometimes it was pre-ordained eternal condemnation. In one case we can say with certainty that demagogy had achieved complete success: In 1620 a member in Monnikendam was seriously disturbed 'that the synod at Dordrecht would have decided that all young children are damned'.[47] That was his idea of Calvinism: all children will go to hell.

Among the Calvinists there are also examples of highly emotional reactions to propaganda. Remonstrants say 'that there is no God, no resurrection',[48] asserted an Amsterdammer in 1617. We seldom hear it expressed so crassly, and honesty requires us to say that this testimony comes from a hostile source – perhaps it was not true. The slogan that Remonstrantism was equivalent to salvation by good works does appear to have made some impact, and especially the argument that Remonstrantism was new, and not in accord with the confessions of faith of the reformed church. Naturally, conflict with the confessions did indeed exist; in the literature of struggle, hostile and objective elements cannot always be separated so easily.

In the meantime there is no doubt that opinions were formed by the preachers. I would rather speak of preachers than sermons, because the former does not exclude the latter, and furthermore it includes the personal element, the tie between the community and its leader. Early seventeenth-century people wanted harmony to reign between the minister and the community. That was worth a great deal to them. In the first forty years of the existence of the reformed church of Holland, dozens of ministers were released from their churches by discharge or transfer. The reasons varied widely: frequently mentioned are drunkenness, too-free relations with women, an ill-considered marriage, slackness in visiting the sick, disputes with the church council, and lack of preaching ability. Sometimes the blame was divided, and sometimes it was certainly not the *dominee* who had caused the disharmony. Then the *classis* tried to find him another parish, because troubled relations made communion services impossible, and thus hindered the functioning of the community. Yet if keeping the peace was worth so much trouble and so many victims, then in a good relationship the *dominee* must have had great authority in his community. It was normal in the disputes of the Twelve Years' Truce for members to follow the lead of their ministers.

That applies very particularly to the Remonstrants. It is most exceptional to find anything more than incidental Remonstrantism in a community with a Calvinist preacher. The great majority of Remonstrant supporters lived in communities with Remonstrant preachers, and included all social levels of the population. That Remonstrantism appealed only to a social and intellectual elite is by no means confirmed by the evidence – indeed we should not have expected it to be so from the propaganda.

For Calvinists the picture was *mutatis mutandis* the same, though with much greater variation. During the years of the truce the civil authorities and officials often forced the appointment of young Remonstrant ministers to vacant communities, especially in the *classes* of Leiden, Rotterdam and Brill. This was nearly

40. *Fishing for souls* (allegory of the jealousy among the various religious parties during the 'Twelve Years' Truce' between the Dutch Republic and Spain), by Adriaen van de Venne

always contrary to the expressed wishes of the members, who had been brought to anti-Remonstrant views by previous incumbents. It was also a significant influence that the majority of the churches chose against Remonstrantism, so that choosing sides for Calvinism to some extent had the character of a choice for the entire union

of churches. In any event, nearly every Remonstrant minister had part of his own community against him, while that was the exception to the rule for Calvinist ministers. In both cases it was true that a decision that differed from the local majority opinion was more likely to be made on the higher than on the lower social level. This can be observed in both camps. In anti-Remonstrant Amsterdam, for example, we find a small group of Remonstrant notables. On the other hand, in Remonstrant cities such as Gouda and Schoonhoven we find Calvinist minorities, who were under the leadership of relatively well-to-do burghers. Only superficial observation would describe the conflict between Remonstrants and Calvinists as a form of class struggle.

But struggles did occur. In many communities it appeared that the choice led to an active attack on the opposition. The manner varied, and clearly betrays the influence of the preachers. Until the synod of Dordt, the Remonstrants strongly emphasised the need to preserve the unity of the church. Their preachers did not ask for special privileges, but only for the liberty to hold their own views. When there were *dominees* of both groups in one city, such as in Leiden or The Hague, the Remonstrants wanted most of all that both groups would continue to accept each other. Their supporters appear to have followed this pattern also. In Oudewater, for example, the Remonstrant-minded not only attended church with the pliable De Raedt, but also with the strict Calvinist Johannes Lydius. In the first phase of the struggles during the years of the Truce, their behaviour was in general not aggressive. They only went into agitation if, in a place where the minister belonged to the Remonstrants, the Calvinists tried to organise their own services under the leadership of a minister from elsewhere. Then it could happen that Remonstrants would take violent action to prevent the exercise of such an intention. But even then people could maintain that they stayed inside the boundaries drawn by their leaders. The unity of the church would simply have to be maintained: if there was no other way, it would have to be done with violence.

In general, however, before the synod of Dordt there was far more activity among the Calvinists. Their struggle went through two phases, although they sometimes came in quick succession, and the purpose remained the same: they wanted to break off communion with the Remonstrants. In the first place they wanted to hear no sermons by their opponents. Calvinists would stay away from church if a Remonstrant was preaching; they would listen only to their own *dominees*, and they moved to other villages or towns if they found no minister of their persuasion in their home areas. Eventually, however, this was not enough for them. A church building is indeed more than just a place offering the opportunity to hear edifying discourses. It is the gathering place of the community, and the community was one, the body of Christ. The unity with Christ could only be maintained if the community exercised discipline. But that was impossible, if it could not fight heresy. Without discipline the celebration of communion was impossible, and what would a Christian community be without the sacraments? Sometimes necessity was the mother of invention in finding solutions. Calvinists who did not accept their local preacher could take part as guests in the communion services of a nearby community more to their liking. But within the concept of discipline as the Calvinists themselves understood it, that was a perilous decision. In a normal community the church council should make certain that no unworthy persons took part in the communion. The receiving church council, however, was not in a position to place the visitors under the normal control of church discipline. A responsible distribution of the sacraments was only possible in a completely functioning community, with a church council that was recognised by all the members and could enforce discipline; that council would also have to be prepared to exercise it, without making any exceptions on points of theology. Thus it was not simply a question of one or two sermons each Sunday: the opposition between Calvinists and Remonstrants had to tear apart the church organisation. Without communion services and church discipline, the Calvinist communities would not exist.

The regents of Holland with Oldenbarnevelt at their head did not understand Calvinism very well, or they underestimated the attachment of the church folk to existing Calvinist church structures. The massive support for Calvinist views was not the least of the reasons why the conciliatory policy of the regents failed. If the struggles of the Truce proved one thing, it was that the church folk of Holland reacted sharply when they thought their right of free exercise of religion was threatened. The Calvinists showed that already before the synod of Dordt. The Remonstrants showed it even more strongly after the upheaval. They in turn separated themselves from the church that no longer wanted to tolerate them, and here also the simple ones showed the greatest fierceness. They formed the primary audience of the persecuted Remonstrant ministers. They paid the fines, which were equivalent to weeks and months of a worker's salary. In several places such as Nieuwpoort they went to the sermons armed and brought about bloody battles with the forces of justice, which on one occasion at Rotterdam in 1621 caused four deaths.

This heroic Remonstrantism died out fairly quickly. The Remonstrant brotherhood concentrated itself in the towns, and over time found its adherents primarily among the higher social groups. During the persecutions, however, the Remonstrant church folk defended their cause with as much fire as if they had been Calvinists. Or should we say that the right to their own forms of worship was of fundamental importance for all Hollanders, no matter what their faith? Let us now pose that question to the Catholics of Holland.

Chapter 16

CATHOLICS

I

As favourable as the situation of 1572 was for the Calvinists, so it was unfavourable for the Catholics. Within a few months the ruling church had lost all its rights, and was even persecuted by the triumphant heresy. All official support was taken away. Now the Catholic Church of Holland had to rely on its own power to prove its worth. Could it rate its chances for success highly, or would it disappear without a trace, as the Swedish Catholic Church did in the same century?

Undoubtedly the church had a chance, because although it was not flourishing in 1572, neither was it in a state of deep decay. Naturally, during the long centuries of its spiritual monopoly, Catholicism had been somewhat taken for granted, and consequently from time to time and perhaps frequently its services degenerated to routine outward appearances. Frequent communion had become rare,[1] catechisation received little attention,[2] and the widespread popular devotion of around 1500 was past its peak.[3] But anyone who would see here the causes of the Reformation must be rather embarrassed with the development of the young reformed church: on precisely these points practically nothing changed. Calvinism did not arouse a new movement of piety, it did not even offer the opportunity for frequent communion, and only after the synod of Dordt did it begin to take catechesis seriously. Apparently it did not regard these shortcomings as so important that it felt obliged to bring about improvement. Therefore, the picture of Northern Netherlandish Catholicism on the eve of the revolt against Spain should not be painted too darkly. Catholic life was not functioning so badly, and in particular spirituality did not fall short in the care of souls.[4]

In 1572, however, much more was desired. For a short time the Catholic Church was exposed to bloody persecution, that demanded of its servants that they be prepared for martyrdom. The first victim fell quickly after the capture of Brill. He was Hendrik Bogart, priest of Hellevoet, certainly not a model priest: in learning and life he was below average. The year before, in 1571, he had come under suspicion of heresy. He did sometimes hear confessions in taverns. He had fathered three children with his housekeeper. Is this our notion of a man who would seal his faith with the sacrifice of his life? Perhaps, says Opmeer's book of martyrs, he was specially chosen by God for that very reason, 'so that it would appear that to become a martyr for Christ is not the work of human agency, but a gift of divine grace'.[5] It is also dangerous to call conviction 'weak' because it is defective in its foundations, and tolerant of personal shortcomings. Andries Woutersz., the priest of Heinenoord, was equally unedifying and immoral in his life. Yet he too showed, wrote Estius, that it is not difficult for God to enrich a man poor in deeds with the gift of His grace.[6] He was killed along with the famous martyrs of Gorinchem.

Among the religious of Gorinchem there were also men of an entirely different stripe. At processions Claes Poppel tried diligently to search out unworthy spectators, and he never hesitated to use violence to force them to devotion if necessary. Lenaert van Vechel informed the civil authorities about persons who he thought could be dangerous to the church.[7] Jeroen van Weert, assistant superior of the Franciscans, was also strict: he rejected with horror all leniency toward supporters of the new faith.[8] Theirs were strong convictions, fervently avowed and applied in practice. It made no difference whatsoever to Lumey's Beggars. One of the Gorinchem martyrs was ninety years old, and another of infirm spirit. But they were Catholic, and wanted to remain so. That was grounds for martyrdom for all clergy, and the motive for killing for the Beggars. We must make no mistake about either party. Why did the Sea-Beggars lose sight of all humanity toward Rome?

Holy oil served as boot polish, holy vessels for drinking, consecrated hosts were profaned, priests tortured and hanged. The destruction of what was holy – in their eyes as well – became an obsession with them. Because all of this had nothing to do with zeal for the pure gospel. The Sea-Beggars still sang the old church songs, if need be in a twisted way, but no psalms. For this singing and whoring gang, the new faith was only an excuse to wreak vengeance on the Mother Church for their own uprootedness and desperation.[9]

This long quotation sounds convincing, and it is taken from a book that was one of the high points of Catholic popular historiography: De Lange's history of the martyrs of Gorinchem. Yet I think he was mistaken here about the Sea-Beggars. Their hatred of Rome was more than personal revenge. The Beggars did indeed sing psalms, as we have already heard in part III.[10] In their ranks we do find common criminals and all sorts of miserable riffraff. Yet the pacesetters of Catholic persecution were religious fanatics, whom we have also met. They wanted to annihilate everything Roman, just because they took their opponents seriously. For them Catholicism was not merely folly, but primarily corruption. Their conviction was too radical to respect what was holy to others. It was precisely that holiness that they wanted to attack. Therefore they drank from the chalice, decked themselves out in monks' habits and hoods, and set plates of meat in front of their defenceless captives on Friday evenings after long fasts.[11] This was the heartlessness of the fanatic, who would arbitrarily sacrifice his fellow man for his own good cause. His behaviour remains just as contemptible. But the Beggars were no whoring gang of drunks, who thought every faith equally worthwhile for the price of booty and a good show. They did not hate the church in general, but rather the Roman Catholic Church in particular. That is why they hanged priests, and opened church doors to the Calvinists wherever they went.

The Catholic clergy were able to respond accordingly. The great majority emigrated. A minority remained behind, and only some of them crossed over to the reformed church.[12] Perhaps we should agree with Rogier in seeing this as proof that most were firm enough to be able to choose between the teachings of the church and heresy. This makes an even stronger impression when we recall that in 1572 it was a question of life or death. On the other hand, such an absolute choice may have eased the decision: no compromises were needed to help waverers cross the threshold. Anyone who had to give up his all and could keep nothing old may have found the inspiration to persevere, even if it meant risking his own life.

The situation was different for the Catholic church folk. They now had to refrain from traditional expressions of devotion, and found the church buildings occupied by preaching *dominees* and their listening communities. But they were not forced to choose. Soul and salvation were not immediately at risk. If they had to make such a decision at once, the old church would probably have won a comfortable majority of the population. Since the ultimate choice was expected only of priests and monks, the masses could remain aloof. Although Catholicism was still the only faith on the horizon for most of them, it came just as naturally to them to regard the Spaniards as their enemies. They would rather be popish than Turkish, yet at the same time rather rebels than Spaniards. Many who had little to win or lose stayed what they were, and did not agitate to bring the priest back to the village church. They were not equipped for religious strife.[13]

Devout Catholics certainly did exist. Catharina Oly told of a certain Dirk

41. 'A man without faith is like a ship without a captain', from J. de Brune, *Emblemata, or moral Symbols*, 1624

Areiaensz. who emigrated to Cologne when Dordrecht joined the rebels: he 'could not tolerate it because of the godly zeal that was inside him'.[14] In 1573 Claesge Jans left her home town of Hoorn, 'because through sin, heresy gained the upper hand there'.[15] She landed in Amsterdam, where there was a great increase in refugee Catholics at that time.[16] This was only a temporary refuge, however, since Amsterdam also changed faiths in 1578; then the Catholics no longer had a single place of refuge on Holland soil. The Calvinists were on the march: if they encountered no priests on their way, they would win. So it happened elsewhere, for example on South Beveland. There is little reason to suppose that Catholicism would have been maintained in Holland if it had been left completely to its own devices.

Naturally Catholicism could remain alive for a number of years without priestly support. Local traditions frequently relate that immediately after the banishment of their leaders the faithful organised clandestine gatherings. These traditions are probably not very reliable.[17] It is true that there was great demand for the services of those priests who remained behind,[18] enough even to attract religious orders from outside the province, mendicants who came offering their help to the orphaned Catholics.[19] But anyone who sought more than occasional services from the church was short-changed. When the above-mentioned girl Claesge Jans returned to Hoorn after all sorts of wanderings, she missed her daily personal contact with the clergy. 'Found herself desolate, because she had no guide for her spirit.'[20] For the devout the olden days remained a precious memory, which moved them to tears when they considered,

how much and how greatly the Holy Secrets were honoured; how great honour was shown in God's house by nobles as well as common people, town dwellers as well as country folk; what zeal in prayer; what love in the giving of alms; what exactness in fasting; what glory on the feast-days; what remorse of the heart in the confessional; what attention in hearing the mass and in prayer; what improvement in morals and life through the hearing of God's word.[21]

No one will judge the writer of this paean of praise harshly for having malformed the past into a paradisiacal idyll. We should be even less surprised that he paid less attention to what in retrospect demands the most respect in that century: the reorganisation of Catholicism in Holland under the leadership of Sasbout Vosmeer. As vicar-general from 1583 and apostolic vicar from 1592, this priest of Delft took over responsibility for the leadership of the archbishopric of Utrecht. He had to work secretly, wandered around the country in all sorts of disguises, and ended his life in exile. He had few collaborators. In 1602 he could only count on about seventy priests, half of whom worked in the bishopric of Haarlem.[22] Under his successor, Rovenius, more gradually joined the fold, although their numbers remained below those of the reformed ministers, while the official duties of a priest demanded much more time than those of a *dominee*.

These leaders did however find helpers among the so-called *klopjes*, devout women who did not take vows, but lived a celibate life in communities. We also encounter male assistants: the priest of Berkel in 1637, for example, had at his disposal more than twenty *klopbroeders*,[23] and perhaps that was the case elsewhere as well. But the majority consisted of unmarried women, who would have chosen the life of the cloister if the times had permitted. They supplied the needs of the altar, formed the choir, catechised and visited members of the parish.[24] Sometimes they lived together in groups, the best-known example being the Haarlem virgins of den Hoek. They were probably quite numerous in Holland as a whole, not only in the towns – in 1643 Gouda had a couple of hundred of them[25] – but also in the countryside. The priest of Noordwijk declared in that same year 1643 that he had 'no more than nine of such who allow themselves to be employed in the service of the priest and those things relating to the altar'.[26] If that was truly a small number, and if we assume that everywhere there were nine of these women for each priest, then in the 1640s in Holland there must have been three thousand of them. But that is a risky way of making statistics.

It is noted of several *klopjes* in particular that they accomplished a great deal for their faith. The village of Akersloot, at the end of the sixteenth century still 'a savage heretical place', reportedly became an ornament of the Catholic Church under the influence of three of these women.[27] But perhaps another factor should be taken into account: at the beginning of the seventeenth century Akersloot had a *dominee* who had no talent at all for preaching, and with 'his smallness of gifts'[28] he had alienated the adherents. Still, it might have had something to do with the women. With naive rectitude Catharina Oly reported how the Franciscan Arnoldus ab Isca at Amsterdam after 1578 used the services of the then-young Maria Wouters:

seeing that she had a delightful disposition and could strongly attract the affection of worldly people, and since the times were very dangerous because of the heresy by which the Calvinists had first gained the upper hand there, so he found himself prepared to use her as a helper in awakening hearts to divine love.[29]

A real darling, equipped with all the powers of persuasion that nature has been pleased to give pretty young girls! Maria and her sister Johanna 'were both beautiful in appearance, fine and great of stature, very friendly and delightful in conversation, lively and alert in manner, true as gold in the service of their neighbours, diligent and industrious in their handiwork'.[30] Does it surprise us 'that they sweetly won people to the faith, to the knowledge of their faults, and brought them to their duty, often even before they themselves knew it'?[31]

That the women of Holland could be pretty we have already noted in Part II. It also appeared that they were not lacking in self-consciousness. Among all the good that we must say of the *klopjes*, it strikes us that the first characteristic fell victim to mortification[32] sooner than the second. Catharina Oly, the leader of the Haarlem community of virgins who so endearingly described the lives of her religious sisters, was definitely the assertive type, 'small in figure, nonetheless alert and swift in her limbs, quick and fast in all her emotions, and powerful in her actions'.[33] She was accustomed to make her presence known emphatically, because 'she also cast a diligent watchful eye over the shortcomings of those nearest to her, that is her underlings, who were commended to her, and whom she had to improve'.[34] Thus she limited herself to correcting her subordinates. But we are citing from a necrology, and perhaps the author of Catharina's life had to pay the usual toll to that genre.

The spiritual guide of the virgins, Joost Cats, gives in one of his sermons a picture of how, among the women, there were some who did not hesitate to involve him in their striving to improve their fellow men. As he noted, 'Now they do not have enough use of the Holy Sacraments. Now their superior does not preach spiritually enough. Now he has too much to do, so that he cannot take care of them. Now he is too lax when they are in sorrow, because he does not console them immediately.'[35] And Catharina herself told of several *klopjes* who had helped the Jesuit mission, yet presently taken on the leadership themselves:

When there was a change in the fathers, which did not please them or the community, they went to the Father General, [and] stated their reasons; often when there was something to do in the community, it was done by these maidens; yes, so much so that the father did not regulate them and in external matters they almost ruled more than the fathers.[36]

Only in external matters? In the last analysis they often gave catechism and brought many young Catholics to their first understanding of the teachings of the church. The Carmelite Petrus Bertius thought that they were completely unsuited to the task.[37] It is questionable if they possessed less training and didactic talent than the schoolmasters who taught the Heidelberg Catechism. It appears likely that the *klopjes* were more determined than the teachers, and that something of their greater fervour was expressed in the lessons as well. The councillor Sebastiaen Francken found on an official visit to Gouda in 1643 'that the same *kloppen* are unbelievably daring and cause more damage to the country and the religion than the popes'. They said that the Protestants were damned for all time. They said that Calvinists had stolen the churches, and raised their pulpits 'on the devil's head'.[38] We cannot call this hate-filled exaggeration: it bears too much resemblance to what the Delft *klopje* W. D. Reeck said in her biography of Stalpart van der Wiele. With strictly logical exclusiveness, she described the Catholics as 'Christians', and Catholicism as 'the Christian faith'.[39]

II

The *klopjes* and the fathers working together did invaluable service to the progress of their church in Holland. They were not able to make the entire province Catholic as formerly, but they were successful in achieving a strong and lasting restoration. This growth occurred in the face of repression. Thus it was not equally strong everywhere, and alongside considerable gains there were small losses here and there. But broadly speaking, the number of active Catholics certainly increased over the whole of this period. We can, however, say the same of the number of members of the reformed church. Both churches were expanding, and each tried in its own way to conquer the people in between for itself. It was a complicated process, with many interdependent factors influencing each other. In order to see it more clearly, we shall study it from two different sides. First we shall note the growth of the Catholic Church, and the circumstances that favoured this growth. Subsequently we shall direct our attention to the regulations against Catholicism. Finally, we shall ask how we can best characterise these phenomena in their entirety.

The growth of Catholicism in Holland is undeniable. It was almost a phenomenon characteristic of the province. Around 1700 we find that about half of the Catholic communities in the seven northern provinces were in Holland.[40] Naturally all the towns of Holland figure on the list, and we know that many Catholics lived in some of them. Gouda already had that reputation in the late sixteenth century,[41] and in later times this was increasingly confirmed.[42] At Haarlem, the most important centre of Catholic activity in Holland, a report in 1628 stated that half of the population was attached to the old faith.[43] Yet Rome seldom had overwhelming influence in the cities. At Leiden the Catholics had about thirty meeting places in 1641.[44] This may sound considerable, but the clandestine Catholic churches were necessarily small: altogether they served about 3,000 people, not a strikingly large number in a city of 50,000 inhabitants. Catholicism in Holland was primarily a religion of country folk, with the core areas in Westfriesland, Kennemerland, and the boglands between Utrecht and Leiden, south of the Haarlemmermeer. In that region, according to the sources, there were assembly places for more than a thousand persons.[45] Now it may be true that in the seventeenth century round figures are more reflective of enthusiasm or worry than exactness, but in this case they do show clearly that Catholics were present. Thus far their language is unambiguous.

What was the appeal of the Catholic Church? We already know one motif. Liturgy and sacraments according to the Catholic rite satisfied a centuries-old need. People did not readily abandon this tradition, certainly not if no alternative was offered. At Wijk aan Zee, for example, the Reformation never gained entry during the sixteenth century. In 1600 there was no reformed community yet; about half a century later, of the 500 inhabitants only twenty-five were enrolled as reformed members.[46] In the villages of Kennemerland such as Limmen, Castricum and Heemskerk the situation was no different.[47] They had always remained Catholic, and thus did not need to be won back for the faith. When *dominees* finally established themselves there, it was too late. The revival of the Catholic Church, begun in the 1580s, preceded the arrival of Calvinism. It is possible that this applies to other parts of Catholic Holland as well. In 1588 the States of the province issued a declaration against 'the wickedness of popery' and 'indecent [sexual] intercourse'. They sent it to the courts of Kennemerland, Brederode, Beverwijk, Assendelft, Egmond, Nieuwburg, Hoorn, Hoogwoud, Opmeer, Veenhuizen, Sint Maarten, Schagen, Nieuwe Niedorp, Abbekerk, Sijbekarspel, Grootebroek, Westwoud, Wijdenes, Schellinkhout, Amstelland, Waterland and Zeevang, Oosthuizen and Etersheim, Texel, Wieringen, Vlieland, Terschelling, Haarlem, Alkmaar, Bergen,

Spanbroek, Enkhuizen, Zybelhuizen, Monnikendam and Callantsoog.[48] This is a long list, but by no means an exhaustive one, not even for the Noorderkwartier. The places must have been specially chosen. Not all of them had a reputation for Catholic sympathies – the opposite is true of Monnikendam[49] – but then the declaration did have a double purpose. In any event we find a goodly number of the future Catholic communities on this list. Apparently in 1588 Catholicism was already a fearsome power in these places. Presumably there was barely an hiatus in the Catholic cure of souls, and the Protestant preachers could only begin their work after the priests had already returned. As yet we can only state this in a hypothetical manner, while awaiting further research. But for the time being there is much to suggest that many villages in North Holland only came into contact with Calvinism rather late, and that it never enjoyed a monopoly.

A second factor that could favour keeping Catholicism on the local level may seem peculiar, and its influence is difficult to judge: I mean the somewhat half-hearted way in which foundations and institutions around the church and charitable services were modified to suit the changed conditions. Before the Reformation, public worship and poor relief were intended for all, without distinctions. The necessary buildings and other properties belonged to the entire parish. No change took place in these arrangements in 1572, at least not for the church buildings and properties to support the poor.[50] The directors of these foundations, the church-wardens and masters of the Holy Spirit, were always chosen from the most notable members of the village community, and not only from the reformed. Catholic churchwardens were certainly not exceptional.[51] They could do little for their co-religionists, because they were required to place the church building at the disposal of the reformed group. Yet in the area of charity there were sometimes possibilities. In 1623 the *classis* of The Hague in 1623 cited Rijswijk in particular as a village where 'the masters of the Holy Spirit, as they are called, lure away the poor folk who are not satisfied with the distributions of the diaconate, and promise to maintain them, on the condition that they promise that they will not go to the Christian reformed church'.[52] This complaint does not stand in isolation,[53] and had already inspired a remonstrance from both Holland synods to the States in 1619.[54] In 1634, Catholics were excluded from the administration of poor relief,[55] yet one may doubt whether this order was carried out.

The persistence of Catholic influences also appears from time to time in the orphanages. Naturally the official policy changed. Henceforth these institutions would have to offer the children a reformed upbringing. Thus the Bible was read aloud at meals,[56] and the orphans were required to attend church with the Calvinists. These changes were not brought about quietly and silently, as became apparent in Haarlem in 1580: 'Thomas Thomisz. Goudsmit, master of the Holy Spirit in Haarlem, forced the children of the Holy Spirit to attend the rebel church, and the children went weeping and crying to that church.'[57]

Why did the children cry? Perhaps some of them still remembered what they had learnt from their parents. Surely others were upset because until that time a Catholic spirit had ruled in that orphanage. In the last decade of the sixteenth century we find a Catholic house-mother of an orphanage at Texel, who did take the children along to the Protestant sermon, and also allowed them to work on Catholic holidays. But when she had fulfilled these external obligations, she supplemented them at home with Catholic instruction.[58] Did Texel's isolated location favour this procedure? It is possible, but we get exactly the same information about the orphanage in the oldest city in Holland. When the three-year-old Claertgen Heyndriksdr. became an orphan, Catharina Oly reported, she was fortunate to land in the Dordrecht orphanage. Both the house-father and house-mother were Catholic, and raised the children in that faith, 'paying particular attention that they would say their prayers mornings and evenings, teaching them many pious little prayers, persuading the children to this end with small images and other gifts'.[59] I do not know if other orphanages engaged in such Catholic illegality, or whether they followed the same ingenious sytem of child-rearing. Gradually the chances for Catholics must have decreased, because orphanages did not function outside all controls.

Catholic customs could well have been maintained longer in institutions for adults. The *classis* of The Hague spoke of their concern in 1619, 'that in some poor-houses and hospitals some superstitions and idolatry are still practised, as a result of a lack of oversight'. They did not see it as a disappearing remnant, but on the contrary confirmed that here and there these practices were just coming into use.[60] Besides, new Catholic institutions were also founded. The Buytewech family founded a court of almshouses exclusively for Catholic widows at Gouda in 1614;[61] the slightly later almshouses of Cool were also Catholic.[62] The Rotterdam merchant Van der Veken did not set any religious conditions in his letter of foundation. He did ask his children to ensure that the direction remained in the hands of Catholic persons. If the government were to interfere in the matter, his heirs were told to sell the houses, and take the money to found new almshouses in Mechelen, in the Catholic Southern Netherlands.[63]

In general it was natural in charitable foundations for the reformed element to predominate, at least in leadership and oversight. But the doors stood open to visitors, thus also to the Catholic clergy, who made use of this facility. This brings us to the third factor: the great effort of the Catholic clerics. Calvinist ministers were in the first place servants of the word. They found their chief duty in preaching.[64] They generally visited the members of their community only in the week preceding the communion service, and they almost never went to the houses of non-members, not even if followers lived there.[65] Visiting the sick was among their duties, but in the cities there were often special helpers, the so-called comforters of the sick.[66] The priests of the Counter-Reformation in Holland showed a broader understanding of their profession. They visited the sick not only at home, but also in the hospitals and prisons.[67] Even during plague epidemics they did not fear the danger.[68] Thus the Rotterdam priest Sebastiaen Hoochkamer himself fell victim to the plague in 1642.[69] All were motivated by the reason cited by Stalpart van der

Wiele's biographer: he went everywhere he was called, even among the most dangerous illnesses, 'in the hope of being able to win a soul'.[70]

So the priests were taught. Sasbout Vosmeer, the apostolic vicar, deliberately chose a wandering existence in order to know the people better and win their respect, 'through work, through suffering hunger and thirst'.[71] The Haarlemmer Cornelis Has was surely a priest after his own heart, industrious not only in his care for the Haarlem poor, 'not sparing any foul or fierce illness', but also regularly to be found among the fishermen of Zandvoort. When strong winds and heavy rain struck, Has saw his opportunity and went to Zandvoort, for then the bad weather had kept the seamen at home. Dripping with water and shivering from the cold, he went to work at once, 'to give these people their share of the divine word, and the use of the holy sacraments'.[72] This dedication by itself must have found receptive hearts.[73] 'It is unbelievable with how much diligence and how much fervour of the heart they come [to the faith],' testified Father Assendelft after a visit to Langendijk in the 1590s. 'You see in them the zeal of the first Christians.'[74]

This clergy repeatedly gave new succour to that zeal. If we had always had such priests, people in the Catholic communities said, then the Reformation would never have won, let alone gained a solid foothold.[75] This devout lamentation did not stop to consider that it was precisely those barren times that had made such priests. The dead branches have blown off in the wind, thought Vosmeer; the green ones remain unscathed.[76] I think that even the green ones acquired a fresher colour. Anyone who would become acquainted with clerics at their worst should see them triumph. A suffering church succeeds in bringing them back to their duty.

Many Catholic clergy were able to rediscover that duty, and some of them sacrificed their lives for it. That was not required of laymen in the time of the Beggars, and became even less likely under the moderate rule of the States of Holland. But the newly awakened zeal for the faith of their priests did present the choice more forcefully to the laity. Could one still find salvation in the old church building, where the *dominees* were preaching now, or was the one and indivisible truth vested in the old faith? To my mind, there lay the fourth reason for Hollanders to choose in favour of the Catholic Church. That reason is closely related to the first, the habit that had been rooted for centuries. But it goes deeper, because it rests not only on familiarity, but also on conviction. Rome's power lay in its impersonal, timeless certainty, independent of failing priests and tottering structures: the unshaken possession of an eternal truth, supported by the tradition of fifteen centuries. It was this certainty by which Catharina Oly dares to assure us how matters ended for the wife of a Haarlem burgomaster, who harboured indestructible hatred for all *klopjes*: 'But praise God, the same have remained, and even greatly increased; but she was destroyed, her name taken out of the book of life, remaining and dying obstinately in heresy.'[77] For her there was no middle way. Anyone who wanted to go to heaven had to go through Rome; otherwise he would go to hell. Geertruidt van Veen, a future Haarlem *klopje*, reawakened the old faith in her heretic father, when she once sat in a corner crying, and he asked her why she wept. 'Answered, that it was because she saw that the one whom she loved most of all, that is her father, dying in the state that he was then in, would in all eternity never see the countenance of God.'[78]

The fervour of this little scene should not conceal that in mixed religious households shocking tableaux could be played out around a deathbed, in the struggle for a human soul. Cors Jansse of Voorburg, Calvinist father of a Catholic household, received frequent visits from his minister in his last days. The family looked on with suffering eyes. After much urging by his children, the father also allowed a priest to come on one occasion. However, the dying man gave no sign of conversion, 'which caused such great sadness in the house that not a dry eye was to be seen'. Should we attribute it to those tears, that by a last-minute confession the man departed this life as a Catholic? It seems to have been one of Stalpart van der Wiele's least enviable triumphs. Yet more such histories were told about him.[79] That was how Catholic priests saw their duty: often they could appeal successfully to the feeling, which never totally died out among many people, that no salvation could be found outside the old church. In 1622 at Dunkirk, in revenge for the execution of captured pirates in Holland, twenty-two prisoners were put to death. One was Catholic, two were Mennonites, the rest Reformed. But nineteen died as Catholics.[80] The same story is told about the Sea-Beggars. No matter how fanatical they were, still at the foot of the scaffold they frequently converted back to the Catholic faith.[81]

III

Consequently Rome had a chance in the struggle against Calvin. On the other hand, it was exposed to dangerous attacks. In 1573, Catholic worship in Holland was suspended.[82] The Pacification of Ghent in 1576 had for a short time raised the possibility of mutual toleration, but that carefully measured freedom in a few cities did not last long. The proclamation of December 1581, forbade Catholic religious services and instruction, even in private, on penalty of fines.[83]

Between sanction and prohibition, it seems there was inconsistency. If a religion was so dangerous that it had to be forbidden, then it would require regulations other than penalties to the purse. But this strange combination is characteristic of the policy of the Holland regents. The limit where the States of Holland stopped was freedom of conscience. They were proud 'that all the inhabitants of the United Provinces are allowed freedom of their conscience'.[84] It has always been pointed out by Catholic historians, rightly so, that this was an empty form.[85] The Catholic faith requires the mediation of the priest. The Catholic who does not search for this mediation remains guilty in his conscience. The regents gave him less than the minimum he needed: they gave only what would suffice for a libertine Protestant, and regarded Catholicism only as a way of thinking, not as a way of living. If their 'toleration' was nothing more than a haughty claim for their own limited norms of freedom, it did not deserve the name.

In practice they went further, and winked at the exercise of Catholic worship. That concession was necessary to prevent civil war and the shedding of blood: an active policy of persecution against a considerable part of their own population would have led to failure or to mass murder, and probably to both. But it remained a concession to necessity. Secret toleration of the Catholics was a necessary evil. I think that the proclamations were serious when they complained so frequently about popish insolence. If the regents themselves had been able to create the world, then they probably would have made it moderate Protestant. Presumably most of them were unsympathetic towards Catholicism. Their resentful mood appeared from time to time, when popish iniquities were forbidden along with other forms of deviant behaviour. Thus we have the proclamation of 1588, already cited, against Roman recklessness and sexual intercourse outside of marriage, or that of 1640 against swearing, 'and the Jesuits and other popish clergy'.[86]

But what could a government do, when it knew that a large group of its subjects did not want to abandon the Catholic faith? Official recognition was unthinkable, for Catholicism was an element of political disorder, it was filled with superstition, and it was highly offensive to the ruling church. Harsh repression and execution were even less worthy of consideration, for Catholics were numerous and reasonably obedient as long as they were not provoked to extremes. Thus policy had to find a path between the two poles, in clandestine recognition that must never give offence. The Catholics were allowed to have what they could not possibly do without, but at the same time, by means of incidental police measures, they were warned of the limits of their underground freedom.

Sometimes this policy got out of hand. The Rijnland priest Martinus van Velde was handled so roughly on his arrest in 1639 that he died a month later from the injuries.[87] It might be called a marvel that no more such misfortunes occurred, because among the servants of justice there were certainly some harsh zealots with a yen for chasing papists. The government did not wish it, and mostly it was successful in keeping the hunters under control. Most priests caught in the act escaped with a short prison term and banishment.[88] Occasionally one would suffer longer captivity. Albert Eggius was detained for two and a half years,[89] but then he was vicar-general of the diocese of Haarlem, and substitute for Sasbout Vosmeer. The apostolic vicar himself was arrested once, when he was surprised during a house search and found the exits blocked by armed men, with two burgomasters in command. The leaders asked Vosmeer who he was. He said his name. The burgomasters exchanged a glance, and let Vosmeer out through the front door.[90] For both parties this was the best solution; also for the regents. Anyone who persecuted Catholics, and then caught an apostolic vicar, would have to hang him. But the political goal was not to wipe out Catholics, but to keep them quiet. Martyrdom for Sasbout Vosmeer was the last thing that the States would wish.

The system rested on mutual understanding among the local agents of justice

42. 'The unfortunate events in the life of Pastor Maarten van Velde', engraving after a design by Pieter de Grebber, 1639

and the Catholic leadership. In exchange for payments, bailiffs and sheriffs were prepared to tolerate clandestine churches, and raid them only after giving advance warning, '*pro forma* sometimes to disturb the mass', as the *classis* of Dordrecht wrote scornfully.[91] For the Catholic subjects that amounted to an extra tax for the private benefit of the sheriffs. But official tariffs did not exist. The size of the payments depended primarily on leniency or capriciousness. The sheriff of Hilversum offered freedom for twenty gulden per year in 1638.[92] His counterpart at Berkel, however, demanded no less than 250 gulden in 1646, to be paid by fifty parishioners in Berkel and Pijnacker.[93] In large places these so-called recognition monies brought in considerable additional income. At Gouda the Catholics paid 400 gulden per year in 1594,[94] at Delft about twenty years later even 1,000 gulden was requested.[95] The negotiating position of the Catholics was not particularly strong.

A sheriff who absolutely refused to come to terms could make Catholic worship impossible. Purmerend experienced that in the 1620s, under the incorruptible Cornelis van der Nieuwstadt.[96] The Catholics then had to go to surrounding villages on Sundays and holidays.

At the same time flight could be a remedy against excessive profiteering. In 1633 the Catholics of Huisduinen had their own priest, but the sheriff asked for more than they wanted to pay. On the following (extortion) attempt, they by-passed their own officer: they tried to establish the priest's residence in nearby Abbestede.[97] As a rule the parties managed to agree, and the sheriffs showed themselves sensitive to the persuasive power of money.[98] But it was never a risk-free assurance. There was always a chance that local rulers, and naturally also Protestant ministers, would make complaints to higher authorities, if they wanted their sheriff or bailiff to execute the proclamations to the letter of the law.[99] If any deeper investigation came of it, there could be great discomfort. In 1634 Gideon van Geesdorp, as substitute for the general prosecutor of the Court of Holland, carried out a very strict check in Aarlanderveen.[100] Perhaps he did that primarily in order to raise the market value of his own co-operation: in the 1650s he was undoubtedly well paid as protector of the Catholic communities in The Hague and Wassenaar.[101]

The Catholics were best served when the sheriff or the councillors or even both also belonged to their religion. That was certainly not out of the question. In the countryside local authorities and courts might very well be in Catholic hands, because governmental power was preferably conferred on men of standing and wealth. In predominantly Catholic villages it was normal for the well-to-do also to be of that faith, and from their circle came the sheriffs, councillors, members of the polder board, and other officials. In 1622 the synods of Holland assured the States that village authorities quite often consisted of 'Papists or people without any religion'.[102] True, this is not unbiased testimony, but it is not difficult to list a series of places where it applied unconditionally.[103]

We do get the impression that, if possible, people would rather not entrust the office of sheriff to a Catholic. In any case examples can be found of Papist sheriffs being reported to their superiors.[104] At Hoogwoud in 1614 a bailiff was named: his wife was Catholic, and before his appointment he too had always attended mass. The Court of Holland then gave his predecessor special authority to guard against clandestine meetings in this area.[105] But success was not assured if the councillors did not lend their co-operation. On more than one occasion P. C. Hooft as bailiff of Muiden found that proceeding against Catholic meetings was pointless. First, there were hardly any persons of unimpeachable character ready to serve as witnesses. Second, the councillors always rejected the testimony of court officials on the grounds of prejudice.[106] All this was possible in Het Gooi, in cities such as Weesp, for example, where in 1622 the Catholics held all the offices, high and low.[107] It was probably the rule that a preponderance of legal power was exploited in this manner. We know this was certainly true for the area around Hoorn,[108] and undoubtedly in Kennermerland or the bog region matters followed the same course.

Consequently there were villages where the Catholics could follow their convictions without fear and without toleration as the good and true faith, with nothing but contempt for the heresies of Calvin. Places such as Aarlanderveen, Langer Aar, Zevenhoven, Amstelveen and Aalsmeer seemed to find it quite normal that 'besides their ordinary minister, [they] also have an idolatrous pope',[109] as the ordinaries involved confirmed bitterly. Around Hoorn the Catholics even dared to ridicule Protestant church-goers[110] as 'bread-eaters and consistory scoundrels'.[111] In Reewijk the ringing of the bells on Sunday was the signal for both parties to come to church, but as the Catholics were ordinarily the first ones finished, they waited outside for the Calvinists, 'ridiculing and mocking them'.[112] In Berkel the Catholics swarmed together on the path to the church, so that the reformed were continually 'obliged to yield, so that they are not pushed along by the crowd and elbowed aside'.[113] Names cannot hurt you, says the proverb. But this behaviour did increase the group consciousness of the Catholics, and it spoiled church attendance for the Protestant minority. Anyone who did not hold firmly to his beliefs might well ask himself if the reformed communion was worth the weekly annoyance. And would not the great supply of Catholic marriage partners in these overzealous Papist communities quickly catholicise mixed marriages?

For the government this aggressive attitude was presumably an incentive to act with care. The sheriff of Grootebroek wrote to the Court in 1610 that he really could do nothing against the Catholics. He could be somewhat harsher, but he judged this imprudent: 'the nature of the people could take it badly'.[114] The substitute prosecutor Gideon van Geesdorp did dare to take such risks during his tour of the Catholic communities of Holland in the winter of 1634–5. Several times he encountered passive resistance. At Berkel the Catholics Geesdorp caught refused to give their names when he came to disturb their meeting.[115] In Aarlanderveen the 300 persons present wanted to force their way outside. Geesdorp, who had brought along three henchmen, warned them 'not to resist justice'. Then they stayed, but Geesdorp could not record which ones were guilty: 'Said, that they did not know their names and were not required to tell me.'[116] In Kudelstaart matters came to blows. Geesdorp had almost grabbed the priest, but he was torn away by the church-goers and threatened with knives.[117] A few did say that they did not want to obstruct him if he came from the Court. But his servants heard people shout, 'that they had enough of the prince and the Court', while some even 'stuck out their backsides, saying: I wipe my ass with the Court'.[118]

The balance of numbers and local power relations could inspire other villages of Holland to great frankness. Yet it did not happen often. At Nibbixwoude in 1624, Mattheüs de Clerck, bailiff of Westfriesland and the Noorderkwartier, by no means a minor person, was disarmed and put out in the street together with his servant.[119] In 1616 the Catholics on Texel also chased away the bailiff's steward, 'beating him bloody and blue'. The bailiff was not successful in a subsequent attempt to command more respect, and was driven away with pitchforks.[120] Indeed there were several cases of a more or less serious nature – usually less – that we have already described in part III.[121] The leaders of Catholicism in Holland, Vosmeer and his successor Rovenius, regarded the government of the States as illegal.[122] Therefore, on grounds of principle, Catholics did not condemn resistance against this authority. Nor did they use the Catholic Church as an underground organisation to collect and systematically arouse such resistance: the ties between Rome and Spain were exploited barely if at all. The fact of those ties did work to their disadvantage, because they played into the hands of Protestant propaganda. Spanish support for the Catholic cause did not have any positive consequences for the co-religionists in Holland, however much they continued to hope even after the Peace of Münster.[123]

Our conclusion could be that while the government was indeed opposed to the Catholic Church, this opposition produced no extraordinary results. The proclamations made the exercise of the Catholic religion somewhat costlier, and for the clergy they meant real discomfort and personal risk. They did not form a serious obstacle.

Naturally coercion by the authorities would seldom be able to force important changes, even if the proclamations had been applied more strictly. Generally the government would not have taken such measures if the impression had not been given that there was a need for strict policy. In the society of the sixteenth and seventeenth centuries such a wish could come from three sources: the protected church, organised corporations such as guilds, and public opinion.

The reformed church was undoubtedly behind the proclamations. In several cases anti-Catholic legislation can be traced back to preceding complaints by *classes* or synods.[124] Popish superstition did come under discussion at such gatherings from time to time, even with a certain regularity, but not excessively so. Synods gave it more attention than the *classes* did, and these in turn more than church councils. The historian who found that 'in the acts of the urban church councils . . . there was no point that appeared on the agenda so regularly as that of popish mischief'[125] must have been unlucky in his sample, and I can hardly imagine that this statement is based on material from Holland. The local struggle against Rome was carried out more in the pulpit[126] than in the council chamber. In the pulpits the attacks were indeed hard and sharp, as can be seen directly from the printed sermons,[127] and indirectly from theological writings for study and popular use. Sometimes such booklets were worthy of refutation,[128] but the standard over time was dubiously low, and sank even deeper than in the controversy between Remonstrants and Calvinists. The worst reached a scatological level,[129] and, if the names had been changed, could have been used to equal effect by both parties: they contain no arguments, only terms of abuse and other humourless expressions of contempt.

Publications of this sort were intended for the masses. They could have led to increasing religious hatred. The propaganda war of the Twelve Years' Truce achieved that result on a certain level. The sources do not give the same impression for the struggle between Rome and Reformation; or rather, they give it in a surprisingly one-sided manner. In this chapter as well as in part III we have seen examples of outbursts of rage and aggressive behaviour. Catholics were always the challengers: almost never do we see Protestants answering the challenges. True, sometimes street urchins would follow a priest in the street,[130] but that was all there was to it. In 1633, when the Spanish negotiators made their residence in The Hague available to priests for mass, the States saw 'that the community began to murmur against it, and make threats'.[131] But no direct action occurred as a consequence. It is possible that local archives here and there may still bring some Protestant aggression to light, but a rich harvest seems improbable. Perhaps because Catholics were often in the majority in the countryside, Protestants chose the wiser course of discretion. But did the urban rabble ever break the windows at the clandestine Catholic Church of Our Lord in the Attic in Amsterdam? No, never. If people thought that the authorities would not tolerate it, then their conclusion was presumably correct. Yet it is difficult to see how that judgment could have been grounded in experience.

Provisionally we can only confirm that the masses in Holland had little or no inclination to anti-catholic action, in contrast to their counterparts in other countries. We cannot yet explain why. Did they not feel threatened by Rome? Did the urban populations contain too many Roman-minded people in their ranks to allow themselves to be hitched to the wagon of Calvin? We do not know, and perhaps will never know. But if I had to choose, my vote would go for the latter of the two hypotheses mentioned. Although it is difficult to base conclusions on purely negative evidence, in this case the gaps in the material perchance complement each other. Yet I do not know of any cases in which the guilds of Holland considered excluding, or took measures to exclude, their Catholic brothers. In France, Catholic majorities did attempt that with Protestant minorities; in Holland the opposite did not take place. Could it be for the simple reason that the opposite case itself did not occur, and that Catholics formed the majority of the craftsmen of Holland?

If anyone were applying for a position with the government, membership of the right faith could help his chances. 'Hear, young man, I give you good advice; you must go to church, and not neglect one sermon, then you will come to the notice of the lords.'[132] We must not overestimate this statement, because there were also some lords who did not show themselves in church every Sunday. The regents maintained their influence over their clients more by living in the same towns than through religion. If a Catholic had 'very faithfully' fulfilled the office of postman, then his son might expect a good word on his account.[133] Yet anyone who did not want to miss a single opportunity would do well to place himself among the Calvinists. Perhaps it did happen in some places that a hopeful guild-master suddenly became a zealous church-goer, especially if he had hopes of winning the hand of the daughter of his Reformed employer. No such cases are known to me from the sources, however. They do tell us that household servants sometimes had to go to church with their employers.[134] Those were private agreements, not always made, although regular contact with household members of another faith could naturally lead to conversions.[135]

Probably the direct confrontation between the two faiths took place primarily in the household. In her biographies of the Haarlem *klopjes* Catharina Oly recounted several cases of religious strife among members of a household.[136] Note how two sisters fought over the faith of their mother: on Sunday morning Aefgen Claes had talked her into going so far as putting her hood on her head and having her folding chair ready under her arm, in order to attend the Protestant sermon. But then sister Geertgen came in, and fell about her neck weeping: 'Mother, what are you going to do? What will become of all of us, because once the tree falls, are not all the fruits lost?'[137]

These conversations take us into private rooms and let us hear something about the experience of the Catholic faith in the community. In a moment we shall examine this more closely. But first we must settle the question of what terms best describe the vicissitudes of the rival churches during this period. The Catholics rediscovered their power, but on the other hand the Reformed were also in full swing. Would it be just to acknowledge a positive inspiration in only one of the two, and explain the growth of the other by means of coercion, stupidity, mass delusion and other signs of human corruption? Naturally all of those played some part. That the church buildings fell to the Reformed did not rest on free choice, but on coercion. That popular beliefs helped to maintain the Christian faith testified to the inability of the message of the gospel to catch on to its full extent. But if we wish to do justice to Catholics and Protestants in the early seventeenth century, our starting point must be that both appealed to the believers in their own manner.

In my opinion that is also what the historian Fruin meant by his famous saying that the Reformation cannot be explained as a result of decay in Catholicism. 'Even if the Roman church had stayed as pure as in its prime, Protestantism would still, in the ripe fullness of time, have arisen and broken with the mother church and gone its own way.'[138] Rogier called this an axiom that thwarted the posing of the problem:[139] we now have to admit that the growth of the reformed church should be attributed to the process of Protestantisation supported by force. But did Fruin deny the existence of coercive measures? He only wanted to oppose the notion that the Reformation must be understood as the parasite of a temporarily decrepit Catholicism. Even though the Reformation was favoured by the civil authorities, it possessed a life of its own, which might not have found its rightful place even in a Catholic Church that was healthy to the core; the reformers might still have had to seek their salvation outside Rome.

IV

Two churches, with differing forms of piety and religious experience: so sharply distinguished, too, that anyone who has grown up in one of them has difficulty describing and appreciating the spirituality of the other community in a just manner.

Perhaps that distinction will appear most clearly, if we turn back for a moment to the early sixteenth century in as yet undivided Catholic Holland. On Sundays the believers went to mass, and during the week they would occasionally attend a service of praise as well. They probably did not follow matins and other hours, thinks R. R. Post, and indeed it was not expected of them. 'It was the divine service, *divinum officium*, to offer God praise and thanks, which was the task of the clergy appointed for that purpose. The believers could unite themselves with it whenever they had time and desire to do so. It was not their task.'[140] This was an enormous difference from the Protestant service. The priest could chant his hours in an empty building. The *dominee* preached and prayed and baptised in the midst of the community. He did not recognise *divinum officium* that sought to honour God in the isolation of a purely clerical duty.

Our task is thereby made more difficult. Among the Calvinists every official duty was directed toward the community. Even though they may have remained largely passive, they had to be there: without a community there could be no service of worship. By contrast the priest had a function clearly separate from that of the laity; though partly done for their sake, that function was not completed by their presence. We are thus less able to observe the Catholic church-goer, and that drawback was intensified in the time of clandestine churches. Then whatever occurred in the presence of the laity was surrounded by secrecy besides, and written down only in exceptional cases. The meeting places were changed, and meetings were held at night. The bailiff of Rotterdam wanted to disturb a gathering in 1643, but came too late: 'They had already finished early in the morning, before five o'clock.'[141]

This was not the only adjustment to the conditions of the times. The Catholic worship service and the entire experience of piety in the sixteenth century were strongly directed toward the visual, and had an ostentatious character. The underground clandestine church could give only incomplete expression to these inclinations. An investigation in 1644 did reveal that most interiors used as church halls were decorated with various images or decorative plates.[142] The Virgin Mary was found nearly everywhere, and often the crucifix as well. But by that time people had dared to furnish their surroundings somewhat more grandly. In the late sixteenth century, when services took place mostly in barns or in the open air, there could be no question yet of such decoration. The Catholic service was initially only incidental in nature. If there is an opportunity, said Eggius, the South Holland villagers receive the sacraments, and if a faithful and energetic celebrant comes, then they also hear the word of God.[143]

Presumably the frequency of preaching and administration of the sacraments increased quickly in the seventeenth century. For the beginning of the century, Catharina Oly reported that Aafgen Jacobs, born at Bovenkarspel around 1600, was baptised late. 'It was then a very desolate time for the exercise of the Catholic religion, because priests were hardly available.'[144] But the girl did not have to wait more than twelve days, and the story makes it sound as if Catharina regarded such

times as past. We get an incidental view of the Catholic community of Gorinchem
in 1628. In the course of research for the canonisation of the martyrs a number of
aged Catholics were questioned, persons who still had their own memories of the
events. At the same time they had to tell how often they were accustomed to confess
and take communion. Six witnesses came forward.[145] One went once or twice a year.
Another went four times, because he held a public function, and did not want to
lose it: therefore he took communion only outside his place of residence. Two went
at least twenty times a year, and one of them attributed it to the persecution that
he did not have more frequent opportunity. One had become old, and thus went
only five or six times; formerly he went every Sunday. And finally one went on 'all
Sundays and principal holy days'. This is certainly not a low frequency for a
community under pressure, at least among those such as these six, who were among
the most devout.

The same was probably true of preaching. It is likely that preaching formed an
important part of the service at that time. Anthoenis Pietersz. of Leiden invited
his neighbour to attend a Catholic religious service in 1608, with these words: 'we
come together at my house in order to hear something good',[146] although on this
occasion the mass was celebrated, and thus there was something good to do and to
behold. Cornelis Hendricksz., a priest of Alkmaar, told his flock in 1593 that
'the proclamation of God's word far surpasses all other services, even the most
outstanding'. He also said why: there is no better means than pure apostolic teaching
to distinguish the true church from the heretical synagogue.[147] Some of his papers
have been preserved and show how he did it. Among them is a series of fourteen
sermons that refute just as many pretexts by which apostates seek to excuse their
abandonment of the faith.[148]

It was logical for preaching to sound these notes. People were involved in a daily
struggle with a religious group that presented listeners with a choice primarily by
means of preaching. The answer had to consist of polemical and manifold use of the
word on the Catholic side as well. For the meeting at Leiden in 1608 mentioned
above, there is a report prepared by councillor François de Coninck, who devoted
extra attention to 'seditious preaching'. 'The aforesaid mass-pope in his sermon
moreover, speaking about the persons and teachings of the late Maerten Luter [sic]
and Johannis Calvinus, warned the people that they should stay faithful to the
teaching of the holy church that could not fail, or they could not be saved.'[149]

The councillor should not have expected anything different, because such preaching was topical. 'Mass-popes' and ministers both sacrificed at the altar of polemic,
just as both of them followed the taste of the times in their sincere tone, which
sought to move the church-goers to tears.[150] The great orators could do it. Stalpart
van der Wiele, praised as a second Chrysostom, aroused 'such great emotion in
himself and his listeners, that people seldom left the church with dry eyes'.[151] In
The Hague, if people knew that Master Stalpart was going to preach, there was 'a
great swarming in the streets'.[152] Just as among the Calvinists, however, talent was
not apportioned equally, so that even in the rules for virgins an exhortation to

listen truly was not thought superfluous: they 'will take all care not to sleep through the preaching'.[153]

We hear little about other components of the liturgy. There must have been believers who found consolation and edification in them, too. The future *klopje* Maria Cornelisdr. de Hes dated her vocation from the moment that she had heard the Jesuit Willem de Leeuw sing 'Gloria Patri et Filio et Spiritu Sancto'. It sounded so heartfelt and beautiful that she had prayed every day since that God would put her in a place where she could serve Him to the full. 'And the sweetness of the song lay always in her spirit, wherever she went or stayed.'[154] This single story isn't much. Nonetheless it is more than we have about the beauty of Calvinist or Mennonite liturgies. The Catholic Church was in any event the only one that gave a place to the aesthetic element in worship.

Was it a fortunate coincidence? An advantage of experience? Certainly not the former: the Catholic Church formed its members in a way that differed from the Protestant Church. Calvin said that belief did not rest on ignorance, but on knowledge.[155] That determined the way of life of the Calvinist. He wanted to know and understand what he believed. By contrast, the Catholics of the Counter-Reformation were not primarily interested in knowledge. The young Maria Wouters as a girl of twelve often had a rough time of it. She did not always understand the teachings of the church, and then thought she was disbelieving. A chaplain reminded her of Mary's question on hearing the news that she would be the mother of God: 'How can this be, since I do not know a man?' (Luke 1:34). Mary did not understand it at all. How much less would a sinful being! If Maria felt doubt rising, then she should make the sign of the cross and say, 'God, have a care to help me!'[156] The chaplain thus did not try to take away her doubt by clarification and explanation, but by acceptance of the mystery and blind faith in the church.

From this point of view, Bible study was more dangerous than praiseworthy. The mother of Ida Govaerts, as Catharina Oly noted, was a devout Catholic, but after the death of her husband she was subject to religious temptations. Her heretical son gave her a Bible. She set about reading it industriously, and indeed, Satan left her in peace.[157] Yes, no wonder! She had actually given herself over to the devil! 'Began to rely on herself, and separated herself completely from the Holy Church.' If we understand scripture correctly, said Cornelis Hendriksz. in one of his sermons, then it warns us precisely 'on points of dispute not to go to the dead letter, but to the High Priest, that he may give judgement as to the truth, Deut. 17 . . . And Christ bids us listen not to the silent scriptures, but to the church, Matt. 18'.[158] The silent scriptures, the dead letter – can the rejection of personal use of the Bible be expressed more sharply?

In direct confrontation with Protestant friends and relations the Catholics could stand somewhat helpless. Magdaleentgen Lucas came as an orphan child to live with her Mennonite sister, and was immediately pressed to change her faith. When the elders came to visit to talk with her, she could do nothing better than leave the house, 'not being able to resist them with disputing'. When people said to her, 'listen at least once; you can accept the good and reject the evil', she replied, 'I am not wise enough to distinguish them.'[159] Sometimes a Catholic felt ashamed. Herke Gerritsz. began to regret that he was shy and continually lacked resistance. He went to study with friends. He limited himself to one point, the apostolic succession, and became so familiar with the problem that he himself took initiatives to hold public discussions.[160] But this reaction was not typical of the Catholic layman. Herke Gerritsz. later entered the religious life.

Over time more attention was paid to the education of members of the community. In 1613 Wachelaer reported to Vosmeer that in the Gooiland and the bogland region there were many 'who know the catechism and the fundamentals of the faith by heart, so that they can confound the Brabanters and Flemings'.[161] The ideal of Catholic education, however, was presumably best embodied by the Haarlem Virgins, who taught the girls in their sewing-school verses and prayers with the lessons, and did 'pious, educational games' with them. They enjoyed great success. Protestant daughters of prominent regents also came to attend handiwork lessons.[162] The Catholicism was accepted by the parents as part of the bargain: on Sundays in the Protestant church the balance would be redressed.

The churches were now for the Calvinists. But they made far less intensive use of them than the previous owners had done. Calvinists came only for public meetings, while Catholics also practised their private devotion in the church building. Some of them continued to do so after 1572 as well. The mother of Angnietgen Francen came often to the church of Alkmaar, even when it had been transformed into 'a cave of murderers', as Catharina Oly called it. In a quiet corner she would then say her prayers, but often she brought the heretics to mockery.[163] That people still came to pray in the churches has already been mentioned,[164] and Catholics were not against the idea of having to find their last resting place there. Father Petrus den Hollander cried out with joy, when he heard on his deathbed that he would be buried in the church at Rhoon: 'My dry bones will shout that the church occupied by the uncatholics belongs to the Catholics!'[165] But a true Catholic use of the buildings was impossible. The Haarlem klopje Lysbet Pauels learnt the stations of the cross in Ghent, and wanted to practise that devotion at home as well. She had to make do with an old barn, where the images were painted on the walls. This devotion became widespread in Holland, Catharina Oly assures us.[166] That would surprise me, but if she was right she could hardly have meant among the laity.

The veneration of saints of the fatherland was intended for all, and strongly supported by Sasbout Vosmeer.[167] In the repressive mood of the present, the church had to find support in the past. A confraternity in honour of Willibrord and Boniface was founded. Anyone who joined had to read the litany every day, fast once a week, and give alms once a month.[168] The duties were compatible with every occupation in society. The future klopje Claertgen Heyndriksdr., for example, had already joined the confraternity[169] when she was still a servant-girl, working in the midst of the world. In Rovenius' time the traditions of the fatherland were continued in any event. At Leiden in 1628 hopeful people completed the process of canonisation for the Gorinchem martyrs.[170] Papal confirmation was delayed until much later, but that did not disturb the veneration; the suffering church of Holland sought recognition for her own martyrs. Shortly after their death, wondrous stories about the martyrs were already doing the rounds.[171]

The sources say little about the intercession or apparition of saints that were already recognised by the church. In 1592 the confessor of the Haarlem Virgins saw first an apparition of St. Bernard, and immediately afterwards one of the Blessed Virgin.[172] But little further attention was given to it. This was not because the church of those days denied the possibility of direct contact with angels or saints. Many biographies of the Haarlem Virgins give us the impression that devout Catholics strove to lead a life practically detached from the world; their real existence was in the spirit. Thus Trijn Ariaens felt she was actually an inhabitant of heaven, who briefly stayed on earth in a mortal body to convey a message, yet would soon return home.[173] Naturally we find this primarily among members of the religious community, but also sometimes among those who lived in the world. When Giertge Dirksdr., later a virgin of Haarlem, still lived on her parents' farm in Rijswijk, 'the fire of God and His sweet influence were sometimes so great that they came down to her body'. It could happen to her while she stood by the churn. It seemed as if she was dead, without consciousness of the things about her.[174]

A life of denial and strong self-discipline, tied with continuous prayer, would be a means of reaching that state of spiritual ecstasy. When Claertgen Heyndriks was a servant-girl in Dordrecht, she got up every morning at two-thirty and stayed in prayer until seven o'clock.[175] In the long run she landed in the community of virgins. Jannetge Pieters did not. She finally chose marriage, but she remained active in the spiritual life. 'She would rather sit on her mat in silent devotions than busy herself much with outward things.' Not much came of her housekeeping. Catharina also judged 'that she was better suited for the spiritual than the worldly'.[176] Jannetge had lost her sense of perspective. Within reasonable bounds, however, the Catholic mission welcomed lay piety. In 1620 Rovenius gave the faithful his 'Golden Incense-burner', a handbook for lay piety written in Dutch. Rovenius wanted the good Catholic to turn inward three times a day, to consider the question of whether he had gone forward or backward. Progress and decline could best be noted on a small piece of paper.[177]

Rovenius' Catholicism displays a definite puritanical streak: no dancing, no fashionable clothes, no loose reading. Anyone who could bear celibacy would do better not to marry. Chastity for married people was unattainable, as Aegidius the Minorite said: a man can also drink himself drunk from his own jug. And sexual satisfaction could not be found: 'Post coitum omne aminal triste est.'[178] Once again, among the clergy and the virgins, we can find these rules most strictly maintained. But Rovenius also wrote for the laity, and the choice of the religious life must often have been the fruit of an education in these teachings. Various *klopjes* already felt themselves called to the religious life as children. Giertge Dirks was four or five years old when she developed the habit of saying 'that she desired a Bridegroom who had one mother and no father'. It was because the Holy Spirit was already working in her, Catharina Oly declared most definitely,[179] although that does not appear entirely sound theologically. Maria Dob at the age of ten made a vow of perpetual chastity;[180] Anna Barents did likewise at age twelve.[181] Catharina Oly herself had 'said farewell to the idleness of the world and the pleasures of nature' when she was eleven or twelve years old.[182] Neeltgen Isbrants Dob did so when she was thirteen.[183]

The Dob family of Amsterdam raised three *klopjes*, the almost predictable result of an upbringing that taught the girls to seek recreation 'in making little altars and playing with religious games, learning many little prayers and exercises, moving each other to fasting, giving alms, and other good exercises'.[184] In every detail the puritanically minded Catholics strove for soberness and moderation. Father Elbert Jacobse Speijer determined in his testament of 1580 that his two poorest blood relations would be maintained from his inheritance free of charge in the hospital of Oudewater. They did have to be content with the simple meals, because food serves only as relief from destitution as long as we serve God in our earthly bodies. Only once a year, on Epiphany, would either receive 'a little bowl or plate of rice-pudding with which to celebrate a cheerful evening in honour of our truly glorious king Jesus Christ'.[185]

This life must have been strict and hard, but without regrets that for the sake of the heavenly bridegroom people had turned away from earthly delights. Undoubtedly this was only the style of life of an elite, in the spiritual sense. Our most important source, the lives of the Haarlem Virgins, has exactly the same disadvantage as the church-council minute-books, but in exactly the opposite direction: if in the exercise of church discipline the Protestant ministers indicated only the faults, so Catharina Oly preferred to describe the virtues. The missionaries also knew the other side of Catholic life,[186] which inspires less jealousy, and even Catharina Oly was aware of the existence of 'weak Catholics'.[187] Yet the great number of priestly vocations[188] still shows that the Catholics of Holland had found a true spiritual home in the church of the Counter-Reformation. No less than the Calvinists, the Catholics can take comfort from the history of the seventeenth century.

Chapter 17

MENNONITES

I

Life almost ended badly for Heindrik Verwer of Amsterdam. He had always been a good Catholic, until he started to keep too much company with the Mennonites in his neighbourhood. 'That easy life attracted him, so that he left the Catholic religion.' He had already decided to have himself baptised again. But fortunately he had regrets a few days before his death.[1] Readers of Chapter 16 can guess the source of this story. It was indeed Catharina Oly, casting her diligently watchful eye over the faults of her neighbours. When she wrote about her co-religionists, she used her critical talents primarily in a positive way, so that the most colourless life of a Haarlem Virgin still praises God's name in deeds that only a loving eye can discover. When she spoke of those who thought differently, however, everything was precisely the opposite. For the impure, everything was impure. In this respect Trijn Oly was very much a child of her time, coupling a fervent piety with brusque contempt for every faith different from her own. She knew nothing about them. Is it not outrageous, what she asserted about the Mennonites? 'That easy life attracted him.' It is hardly possible to think of a more nonsensical view of late sixteenth-century Anabaptism. If such an opinion tells us anything, it is that beyond the barricades of their own church walls the believers could see only heretics, and never fellow Christians of another confession. Besides, for the Mennonites the situation was exactly the same, as this chapter will show.

The Anabaptist variant of the Reformation is older than the Calvinist. It was spread all over Europe, and before Calvin had written his *Institutes* it had become the mainstream of the Reformation in the Netherlands. Yet it did not win the day there. Indeed, it failed everywhere. The movement that seemed to form a revolutionary force around 1530 was not able to leave a lasting impression on the Reformation in any country. In part the decline of Anabaptism was an example of successful repression: nearly everywhere it was exposed to harsh persecution. In the Northern Netherlands, however, the Anabaptists won freedom of worship. For a short time it appeared that they would be able to take advantage of it,[2] but presently it became clear that here they were also unable to compete equally with the Calvinists and Catholics. Now it is true that the Anabaptists were in a much more unfavourable position than the Calvinists. They lacked the active support of the government, and they did not have political power. But the Catholic Church certainly stood in an even worse position, and nonetheless seized the chance not only to maintain itself but also to win back lapsed members. Why then did Anabaptism fail?

In comparison with the Catholic Church the Anabaptists suffered from two serious disadvantages. The appeal of Rome had its roots in the past, in the centuries-old established conviction that outside this church no salvation could be found. The Anabaptist past was so young that even for its own adherents the faith had not yet become an historically based inevitability. The past did give the Anabaptists power, as will appear presently, but it was not an attractive power that could bring outsiders across the threshold. At first the Anabaptist movement had chosen blood, violence and revolution, and it had achieved nothing by them. To its enemies it remained suspect as a symbol of chaos and disruption, the mother of anarchy and immorality. To its followers it was unable to offer success, the sole justification of revolutions. Anabaptism had a past burdened with the senseless shedding of blood. It lacked an antiquity worthy of respect, which could hallow the peculiarities of a sect with many years of tradition. But it no longer offered the prospect of the brilliant future for God's kingdom on earth, either. Such a movement could hardly possess great attractive power.

The second disadvantage was also connected with the past. The Anabaptists did not draw their real inspiration from the rejection of infant baptism. Their use of adult baptism exclusively was merely a consequence of their view that this sacrament should be reserved to believers alone, and could only be received by those who have made a conscious choice for the Christian life. But the abolition of infant baptism was a very radical and far-reaching change for people who had always believed in the power of the sacrament.[3] In the lives of believers it changed much more than the loss of pilgrimages and images of the saints, even more than the taking of communion in both kinds. Baptism was always regarded as a necessary precondition of salvation. If a child died unbaptised, it could not enter heaven. This tradition was so strong that Calvinist preachers in the early seventeenth century found it hard enough to convince parents that a baptismal service could and must await the coming together of the community.[4] To leave a child unbaptised was, in the eyes of all traditionally minded Christians, to take an extraordinary and inhuman risk. Perhaps we can compare it to the refusal to allow children to be inoculated against common infectious diseases. Such a decision can only be justified by someone who believes that God asks it of him: to endure the horror and ridicule of public opinion by choosing for his child what no one else would dare. The central position of the doctrine of adult baptism formed a barrier to outsiders. This problem may have counted for less in the tempestuous early years of Anabaptism, because the enthusiasm for this doctrine was also encouraged by belief in the certainty of Christ's speedy return. If heaven on earth would dawn shortly, then concern about entry to heavenly paradise would lose its significance. Yet when that perspective was postponed, and the fiery eschatological expectation faded, infant baptism reasserted its claims: delaying baptism for many years became a frivolous provocation of God's providence.

In any case it is certain that during our period, the revolt against Spain, the Mennonites were on the losing side, and continually had to yield ground, particularly to the Reformed.[5] In the course of the sixteenth century they had split into three groups: Waterlanders, Frisians and Flemings. We have some vague data about the numbers of the first group in 1647. At that time there were thirty Waterland communities in the province of Holland.[6] They were found in all the large cities excepting Dordrecht, and also particularly in the Zaanstreek, a centre of Anabaptist activity since the earliest times.[7] Kühler estimates their numbers at 10,000, which would certainly not be low for thirty communities. Naturally some of them were large, such as Amsterdam. In that city about 750 members attended the communion service of the Waterlanders in 1614.[8] But even if this represented 2,000 souls, and if the Frisian following was equally numerous, and that of the Flemings twice as great, the total of all Mennonites in Amsterdam would still come to no more than 7 per cent of the population. We would gladly have more solid figures, yet they would be unlikely to give us a completely different impression. Taking into account all their variants, the Mennonites in Holland as a whole formed a small minority.

We can describe the Mennonite communities as very democratic, and at the same time as extremely authoritarian. This paradox requires further explanation. The Mennonites started from the priesthood of all believers. Every member was a witness to the gospel, individually and directly responsible to God for all his thoughts and deeds. The clergy did not play an intermediary role. Everyone had personal access to the throne of God.[9] They did, however, recognise leaders of different ranks. Anyone who was an exhorter could perform the service of the word. For baptism and communion more was required: only the elders were so empowered, and that dignity could only be acquired by the laying-on of hands by others who already held it.[10] Among the stricter sects in the sixteenth century the elders ruled with an iron hand,[11] and in the seventeenth century their authority remained considerable.[12]

In general the intellectual level of these men was not high. The leader of the community of De Rijp, Jan Willemsz., was a doctor of medicine.[13] Among the older teachers this combination was frequent. But many came from the manual trades and lacked learned schooling.[14] That made them vulnerable to criticism from two directions. First, they could fall under suspicion of self-interest. When they come, mocked Caspar Grevinchoven (Grevinghovius), the collection-plate for the needy is passed round and a rich meal is served. Living on alms suits them well. No one knows how much they earn, but once they have held office for a while, their affairs appear to flourish wonderfully.[15] The evidential value of such arguments is not great, and they could be used against any religious community. But the salaries of ministers of the Reformed Church were neither secret nor very high.[16] Propaganda could say what it liked about the incomes of Catholic priests, but the priests of the early seventeenth century were generally of higher birth than the ministers. Vulgar suspicions would be less likely to strike them than the materially worse-off Mennonites.

The second line of criticism, however, was more important. The tailors and weavers who were called to the office of leader might possess an amazing knowledge of scripture. But they were not immune to the uncritical enthusiasm of the autodidact, and the excessive spiritualisation of the biblical text.[17] Not much was done about theology in their circles.[18] Basic Mennonite writings did exist and were republished in the seventeenth century. The works of Menno Simons and his colleague Dirk Philips were reprinted, as were those of pure fanatics such as David Joris.[19] 'In that which we seek, we fear no one's books, but sample everything and preserve the best,' declared three Waterland teachers in 1626, when they were reproached with having studied Papist works.[20] But did they have sufficient critical judgment for such ecleticism, which ranged from Menno Simons through David Joris to popery?

The reformed church council of Haarlem thought that Mennonite learning was substandard. It issued a sharp warning against the new Mennonite edition of the Bible, because 'the Anabaptists, who appear altogether unlearned, when in the printing of this Bible they came to any doubtful, mysterious or weighty passages (as we understand it to have happened), they were positively unable to understand them, but had to interpret them in accord with their own limited gifts, and thus actually falsified Holy Scripture'.[21] Over time indeed the Mennonites themselves exchanged their own Biestkens Bible for the States' translation.[22] Yet the plan of that edition in 1624 at least testified to some sense of study. There were also sects such as the Frisians, who condemned every attempt at training ministers as sinful pride. Was not the wisdom of this world foolishness with God (1 Corinthians 3:19)? Had the apostles and prophets studied theology?[23]

To some extent, then, Caspar Grevinchoven was right when he accused the Mennonites of having contempt for learning and the study of languages.[24] This was also in accordance with international Anabaptist tradition, which had long harboured suspicions of the university and of theology: Christ himself had chosen shepherds, fishermen and tentmakers to preach the gospel.[25] The Mennonite leader Jacob Jansz. Scheedemaker was willing to allow his colleague Hans Doornaert to hold exhortations, but denied him the right of leading prayer, on the grounds that this was reserved for ordained teachers alone.[26] An exhortation from Scheedemaker himself was, according to one unsympathetic critic, 'an extremely long-winded speech, repeating itself ten times over, about love, friendliness, unity, repentance and conversion', with everything chewed over so often that on leaving the listener knew the entire speech by heart.[27]

Yet there was more to Mennonite explication of the Bible, besides that they did not know how to use learning effectively. In chapter 14 we recalled that the Mennonites still recognised the inspiration of the Spirit. It was no longer a spirit that had laid aside every restriction. Hans de Ries, the Waterlands leader, taught that the Christian knew a twofold word: Christ and the Bible. The book by itself was a dead letter. Christ had to work along with it to enlighten the heart. No one has a natural power to understand the scriptures; Jesus must teach him. What he taught the believers through his Spirit was always consistent with the Bible. 'There is no danger whatsoever that such divine inspiration will ever be in conflict with the written word.'[28] This view appears different from how Maronier tried to describe the work of the Spirit – the inner word – according to the Mennonites: 'an internal revelation of God, alongside the external, so that one does not look only outside oneself for the knowledge of God and His will, in the writings of the Old and New Testaments, as Luther and his followers wanted, but also and primarily within oneself'.[29] If we must regard it in this way, then the inner word has withdrawn itself from the discipline of external revelation.

From this it will be clear that Hans de Ries and his supporters stood on a rather dangerous frontier. Internal and external word cannot conflict, said the Waterlanders. 'What we receive from Him is not dreams or visions, which lead to enthusiasm; [rather,] it is the confirmation of the written word by the Holy Spirit.'[30] In a free-thinking community such as the Waterlanders this could still lead to as many variations as there were members. According to them it came down to what the Bible had to say personally to each. That was all that mattered. 'We are bound to no one's interpretations, but to Holy Scripture. Anyone who wants to raise up his explanations as God's word would place himself on Christ's throne. No one can do that.'[31] But just when no one is allowed to do it, the chances are greatest that everyone will do it.

Therefore one can well understand why precisely those free Mennonites of the sixteenth century saw the rise of the dominant elders in their midst. At least there was someone who could give clarity and make decisions. In the heat of battle some made the word of the elders equivalent to the word of God: 'everything that is ordered by teachers and officers is by their declaration scriptural; those who still dare to rebel are worthy of punishment.'[32] Theologians have sometimes done much damage to their churches. But anyone who would see how a church can be derailed without theological learning will find much instruction in the history of the Mennonites of the sixteenth and seventeenth centuries. Their method of theologising opened the way to boundless freedom as well as to complete subjection to personal authority.

The last danger was perhaps the greatest. After the upheavals of Münster and Amsterdam, Anabaptism had to find a new way. It distanced itself from violence, and remained free from the extraordinary excesses that marked its appearance to the outside world during the revolutionary period. Menno's followers no longer practised nudism or polygamy; nor did they rob churches or hold to the community of property. Yet in its essentials Anabaptism remained the same, although its emphases were different. Mennonites never spoke of 'the church', for they had left it; now they formed a community.[33] Here was the continuity: a special view of community was characteristic of the Anabaptists from the beginning.[34] All Anabaptists wanted an apostolic community that consisted of the true disciples of

Jesus Christ, separated from the world. This view was common to all streams and sects. They differed only in their expectations and attempts to achieve that purity on earth.[35]

We find these same views in Menno Simons. He too envisaged a community of all those who were enlightened by God's Spirit. They had fled from Babel, that is not only from Rome, but from everything that lay outside the bounds of the brotherhood.[36] In the true community Menno saw pure, unadulterated doctrine, upright brotherly love, heartfelt readiness to endure sorrow and oppression, complete obedience to the word – in short, behaviour that was beyond reproach.[37] If a community displayed these characteristics, it might adorn itself with the honourable name of 'community without spot or wrinkle'. No, let us express it better. Community is not an ideal for which human beings can strive. Community has always existed, since the beginning of time, because it was created by God. It found its beginnings in heaven, said the Flemings; on earth Adam and Eve formed the first community, which has continued to exist to the present day.[38] People wanted to make that community, formed by all the children of God, visible in the brotherhood.

Keeping the community pure required religious discipline. All religious communities practised it. By means of discipline the Calvinists also wanted to protect their community from God's wrath, and avoid disrepute in the world. In their exercise of discipline the Mennonites as well as the Calvinists thought first of the community, which must not become infected with sin. Yet among the Calvinists it remained easier to see that the purpose of discipline was only achieved in the reconciliation of the sinner with God and the community. Ordinarily they were successful, and discipline ended with a confession of guilt and renewed acceptance of the repentant sinner. Among the Mennonites, however, the idea of community was often so strong that it seemed as if the disciplinary procedure was already regarded as complete as soon as the sinner was banished. Reconciliation as the goal of discipline faded into the background. Menno Simons would rather die than eat or drink with a banished person. One was not supposed to greet him or to speak to him. Ancient Israel had exterminated violators of God's law. Only under Roman rule was that penalty changed to exclusion.[39] We should not see this as a veiled plea for the restoration of Mosaic law in all its rigour, but from such comments a horrifying view of discipline becomes clear: it has taken the place of physical annihilation. While the community no longer applied the death penalty, in their eyes the offender was as good as dead.

These are conclusions that Menno himself did not draw. He left the door open for repentance. Yet harder attitudes gained the upper hand during the time of persecution. A violator should not first be warned, in the hope of improvement. The ban should strike him immediately, without advance warning. If he then came suddenly to repentance, it was too late. 'No matter what deep remorse the sinner showed, even if he wrung his hands and tore hair out of his head, or cried out what he could do – he had to get out.'[40] Which sin he had committed made no difference. Every offence cost the same high price.[41] No one was allowed to have any contact with the banished person. If he was married, his wife would even have to refuse him marital relations: the notorious *echtmijding*, or enforced marital avoidance, was inexorably applied by the strict sects.

Not all groups followed this doctrine. The Waterlanders thought that the ban applied only to those who remained separated from God by their sin. Repentance and punishment thus meant that one could have the ban lifted.[42] Among other groups, however, the strict customs were maintained, although in the course of the seventeenth century their application became more moderate.[43]

This unique mixture of spiritual freedom and unlimited theologising, with strict discipline and great personal authority of the leaders, made it inevitable that the Mennonites would be especially susceptible to schism and discord. Mennonite divisions in the early seventeenth century were almost proverbial.[44] The Anabaptists were so attached to their own opinions that divisions occurred even in places where their numbers did not exceed five or six families, because 'they were divided among themselves on doctrine',[45] and then they did not want to seek the support of each other's company.[46] The story was the same all across Europe. In other countries Anabaptists called each other heretics even when they were sitting in the same death-cell. There too it was sometimes a question of petty-minded and trivial differences of opinion about minor points of order, or the stubborn pride of two strong personalities. Holland was no different. The Mennonites did not want to bind themselves to anyone else's views[47] and never stepped aside for another: anyone who forces his opinion on me is a sinner, and must be banished. Sometimes the differences would narrow and reconciliation would be tried. But how could it succeed if no one was wrong? The Flemish and Frisian Mennonites once decided to bury the hatchet. Both parties knelt and confessed their guilt to God. Then they arose, and immediately all the trouble was in vain: the Frisians had wanted the Flemings to allow themselves to be lifted up by their hands.[48] Even in a common mortification before God it had to be clear who was really right in the end.

The Flemings formed the largest group,[49] with centres in Haarlem and Amsterdam.[50] Thinking of the community first was their outstanding spiritual characteristic. The community, of course, meant themselves. Reunion of the Mennonites then meant that the others would have to join with them.[51] The Frisians were not far behind them in harshness. They were purest in holding to the views of Menno, but to the strict Menno in the last years of his life.[52] The Waterlanders were the most tolerant, to the Mennonite way of thinking. Their party arose because they wanted to apply banishment only after warnings had been repeated three times.[53] Yet their group was not free of discord either. All three groups had their own factions,[54] and from time to time all were exposed to violent internal strains.

II

It must have been difficult to live in this divided brotherhood, with its excess of freedom, which apparently the members could only use to their own disadvantage time and again, and with its lengthy list of commandments, whose unthinking violation might lead to banishment. We should now examine life at the level of the community to see whether the Mennonites did indeed live in the climate that we have come to expect, namely that of nervous tension and merciless denunciation. It seems it cannot be otherwise, but the sources show us another side of Anabaptism. Let us try to get more insight on both.

Anyone who speaks about Mennonite rules and commandments naturally thinks first of the specific views that so clearly separated the brotherhood from other churches. Not so much the purely theological ones, such as adult baptism and incarnation, but rather the prescriptions that had a direct effect on daily life and forced the Mennonites to show their colours: non-resistance, refusal to swear oaths, rejection of governmental offices, and avoidance of marital relations with banned persons.

Probably none of these rules has more deeply influenced Mennonite life than of non-resistance. No one could avoid this point, for even children were asked to make a decision. There was a boy in Brill who was so often pestered by his playmates, 'having held him in contempt, he being Mennonite, for not being allowed to fight and hit back', that without the knowledge of his parents he walked to Nieuwenhoorn, and had himself baptised in the reformed church.[55] We know this story because it was the beginning of the career of Admiral Witte de With, who during the last forty years of his life took his revenge on his non-resisting youth by fighting and privateering. But was his boyish suffering unique? The Mennonite church elders had warned against the bad influence of playing in the street with 'useless children, that they [Mennonite children] do not thus learn lying, cursing, swearing, fighting and villainy'.[56]

The same temptations, however, troubled adult Mennonites. They were most numerous in the Noorderkwartier of Holland, where many people chose the seafaring life, including Mennonites. If they then wanted to live according to their faith, they were not allowed to defend themselves against attacks by privateers or pirates. The enemy might take advantage of this, and did not miss the opportunity. In 1600 for example the Dunkirk privateers caused heavy damage to the herring fleet because 'the fishermen did not carry guns, and a great number were Mennonites, who do not use weapons anyway'.[57] Mennonite sailors to the Levant might perhaps benefit from a dubious advantage of their non-resistance, because the Algerian pirates declared that they would not make the crew slaves if the captain surrendered his ship and cargo without a fight. Several Mennonite captains discovered to their disadvantage that this agreement was none too strictly observed.[58] Besides, it could be applied only if the ship was sailing under Mennonite command. If the captain was reformed, then at most his sailors might refuse to take part in battles. From a complaint made by Governor-General Pieter Both we know that this did actually happen.[59]

For a tender conscience, however, it must have been barely permissible to set sail in an armed ship, since one knew that in case of need the cannons would be used. The Waterlands teachers thus declared in 1619 that not only owners and captains of armed vessels but also all who sailed on them must be excluded from the communion table.[60] In 1647 they still maintained that members should get rid of shares in ventures that armed their ships.[61] It was not easy to obey the commandment of non-resistance in a country that experienced eighty years of war as the normal situation, so that the struggle against Spain was interwoven with life itself. Where were the boundaries of what was permissible? Among the Amsterdam Mennonites there was a powdermaker. The Waterlanders had no objection to him, but did make serious objections when he wanted to go to the Indies in 1614 in order to ply his trade there. It is difficult to understand their policy. Was it not allowed to shoot at Muslims in the East, and yet permissible to kill Catholics in Europe? Despite the objections of their leaders, the Waterlanders at least probably went their own way. It became more and more customary for them to equip their trading and fishing vessels with weapons,[62] although it was done surreptitiously: no cannons on deck, but muskets in the pilot's cabin.[63]

Less important for most Mennonites was the question of governmental office. In the towns they generally did not come under consideration. Menno had not actually condemned office-holding absolutely, although he did regard it as dangerous.[64] A community that wanted to preserve itself pure from the world would certainly act in the most careful manner possible if it remained hesitant about the exercise of political power. That was indeed the course that most Anabaptists had chosen after the adventure of Münster.[65] In Holland the Waterlanders normally enjoyed the space that Menno had left open to them. They made no objection to an appointment as councillor or any other office, as long as there was no personal involvement with condemnation to corporal punishment.[66] The States of Holland accepted this view, with a somewhat broader interpretation. They allowed the Mennonites to purchase exemption from the obligation to serve in offices, if these were offices and dignities 'having attachment to judicature'. Mennonites were not exempt from other functions if they were chosen for them.[67] This did sometimes cause minor difficulties with Frisians and Flemings, because they kept to strict non-involvement.[68]

With one voice all the sects maintained the prohibition against taking oaths. Neither Frisians nor Flemings nor Waterlanders would swear, and in this they were tolerated by the civil authorities. The reformed church was less generous. The *classis* of Dordrecht once asked if in Holland at least as much could be demanded as in Friesland: namely, there people sought to know of Mennonites who testified to the human truth if they did not think they deserved punishment from God if they had lied.[69] The States of Holland, however, found strengthening of the affirmation unnecessary,[70] and appear to have given that privilege to the Mennonites because of their unconditional reliability. 'Aequi justique tenaces sunt,' explained Van Buchell, 'quorum verba plus ponderis quam aliorum habere dicuntur juramenta.'[71]

Such testimony implies more than we might first think. The seventeenth-century person avoided swearing as much as possible. Anyone who had taken an oath of office and then had to testify before a judge did not make a new oath, but testified on his official oath. That had enough power to require him to love the truth at every subsequent opportunity. The meaning that oaths held for people was illustrated in 1643, when the wine-buyers of The Hague did not want to take the required oath of office that they had not committed tax fraud. The tax farmers explained that this refusal was very disadvantageous for the country. In the region of The Hague alone the wine-tax would have brought in another 20,000 gulden if the oath had been done properly.[72] Here the value of an oath is expressed in quantitative terms. Then we can rightly see how much confidence was expressed in accepting the Mennonite affirmation. This is one of those rare cases in which deviation from the generally accepted norm enhanced the reputation of a minority.

There remains the question of enforced marital avoidance. Particularly in the sixteenth century it separated married couples and tore apart families, all for the sake of a community without spot or wrinkle. The length of this marital avoidance was set by the term of banishment. It could last for years. Caspar Grevinchoven told of Dionijs van de Walle of Leiden, whose wife Mayken Rebays had to promise in 1587 to stay away from her husband as long as she was fertile.[73] Now perhaps Grevinchoven had no hesitation about blaming the entire brotherhood for the rule applied in one exceptionally sad case. But more sympathetic hearts saw the same faults more than twenty years later. A Mennonite text from 1613 shows that marital avoidance and banishment could still bring the offender to the edge of annihilation. Over long terms of banishment women sought out other men and abandoned their children. The banished men lost not only their wives, but also their income, if the brothers no longer did business with them.[74] At its best enforced marital avoidance in such cases was a barbaric means of exacting obedience under duress.

By then milder attitudes already prevailed in the Waterlands communities. It was enough if no one had friendly contact with the banished person; he was no longer declared dead for the brothers and sisters. Over time and as occasions presented themselves, they were allowed to eat, drink, and do business with him.[75] These attitudes would triumph, and put an end to the forms of discipline that gave little chance of true spiritual repentance, and brought the community into external disrepute – precisely the effect that discipline in general sought to prevent.[76]

Apart from the refusal to take oaths it thus appears that the typical Mennonite customs very gradually lost their force. That does not mean that Mennonite behaviour became less striking. After all, the extraordinary rules were not uniquely sectarian ideas, but the expression of an honest attempt to take all the commandments of the gospel seriously. This attitude remained characteristic of the brotherhood. It required members to practise modest life and exact mutual love.

Other churches did that also. Yet, more than the Calvinist or Catholic, the Mennonite of the early seventeenth century emphasised doing good over thinking good or confession, although the norms were the same. Anyone who reads in Kühler what the Mennonites regarded as sin will find nothing that ministers or priests would not gladly endorse: they condemned drunkenness, fighting, dancing, idleness, pride, miserliness, frivolity, dishonesty and extravagance.[77] This was the generally shared view of Christian life, not a singular sectarian ethos.

Nonetheless the South Holland synod had already decided in 1589 that the Anabaptists should be fought on two fronts: first by refutation of their deviations in word and writings, and second through a way of life that was faithful and godly.[78] The latter was apparently necessary in order to be better protected against Mennonite criticism. Here was an acknowledgment that the Mennonites had made more progress than the Calvinists in simple obedience to God's commandments, and that they could rightfully claim the lead. In that spirit Trigland also preached against luxury and extravagance among his own church members. 'The Anabaptists use practically no other argument to draw members away from us than this one. See, they say, how beautifully they have preened themselves! How they are adorned! Would that be the community of God? Would that be God's people?'[79]

In practice it appeared that these arguments occasionally did make an impression. A woman in Monnikendam, who joined the Mennonites in 1615, gave as her only motive that her new brothers and sisters were more godly and better than the Calvinists.[80] Above all the poor showed themselves sensitive to that change of climate. In the early seventeenth century in various communities there are incidental reports of destitute members of the reformed church transferring to the Mennonites.[81] A sensible person will not clothe one part of his body and leave the rest naked, Menno had said; so also the body of the Lord, the community. They should not be partly naked, and therefore God's children should serve each other with their gifts and goods.[82] 'Let him labour, working with his hands what is good, that he may have something to give to him who has need.'[83] These words of the apostle Paul spoke to the heart of the Mennonites: work without ceasing, so that no one has to ask for anything and can share with others.

To this the Mennonites owed their reputation for solidity and reliability, but they presently aroused irritation as well. Perhaps because few people could tolerate daily contact with sober, solemn neighbours who were visibly more advanced in virtue than themselves. But the irritation also had better motives. A community that demands a great deal of obedience runs the danger of transforming the service of God into the service of commandments. For some, that obedience truly represented a wish to be one with the body of Christ. For others, the rules became the be-all and end-all. God's commandments were collected in a table like the rubric of a formulary, and the art consisted of achieving a satisfactory score on each part. This could still happen with the best intentions, although such a well-organised faith would yield but little warmth. In the worst cases, observing the rules was replaced by preserving appearances. This does not mean that all Mennonites were hypocritical,

43. Adult baptism, engraving of 1624

44. The burning of Jan W. van Kuyk and Adriaenken Jens van Molenaarsgraaf at Dordrecht, 1572.

but rather that this sin appeared the greatest temptation to them. Later in the seventeenth century their reputation did suffer somewhat as a result.[84]

It was primarily on their social behaviour that the Mennonites were judged in their own time. For us there are few other possibilities. Mennonite devotion remained enclosed,[85] even in public worship. The reformed preacher Lansbergen once attended a Mennonite gathering and was much struck – unfavourably, of course, because he had come for that very reason – by the way in which this meeting prayed. Here there was no leader who spoke aloud, as in other churches. No, everyone prayed for himself, so that he heard sighing and moaning, but no intelligible words.[86] The custom later disappeared, first among the Waterlanders. As long as it existed, it was perhaps the must typical liturgical expression of the old Anabaptist individualism. If

45. The hanging of Jan Smit of Monnikendam, 1572. Engravings by T. J. van Braght in *The bloody stage, or martyrs' mirror of Anabaptists or non-resisting Christians*, 1685.

the heart was full of desire for God, and tried to find Him in prayer, would the voice of the leader not be disturbing? Does not everyone have his own cares and requests, so that he alone knows the right words for his personal prayer?

Mennonite piety is the piety of prayer. 'How do we know if we stand in God's grace?' some Waterlanders once asked their leader Hans de Ries. He answered: through prayer. Our relationship with God is good, if our prayer goes up to heaven, and we feel that He enlightens our conscience.[87] Direct, personal communion with the Lord: a prayer that will not stop until it is answered. It is true that the Heidelberg Catechism speaks in almost the same language, when it states the necessity of prayer 'in order that God will give his mercy and the Holy Spirit only to those who pray to Him with heartfelt yearning without ceasing and thank him for it'.[88] But the catechism still placed prayer more in the context of thankfulness than as a sacrifice owed to God. By contrast the Anabaptist carried out a dialogue. In his prayers he sought hidden contact with God. He wanted to follow the voice of the inner word.[89]

Thus it becomes clear once again, why the community without spot or wrinkle had so much difficulty preserving unity, even under the regime of inexorable discipline. Mysticism and spiritualism so strongly individualise the faith that only a church with powerful doctrinal authority could hope to hold them under the control of dogma. The Mennonites were least likely to succeed. Even at the time when all the religious communities of Europe acquired their basis in clear-cut doctrine, expressed in their own confessions, the Mennonites did not manage to produce a confession of faith for their followers. They did find another means of putting together their common spiritual inheritance, however, in the History of the Martyrs edited by Hans de Ries.[90] It appeared in 1615, and was then sold for three gulden.[91] This was a remarkably low price for a book of a thousand pages,[92] which made clear the intention to give the entire community the possibility of strengthening themselves through history.

For that purpose the price had to be low indeed. We do not have much information about the social status of Mennonites in that period, but we should probably find them on the lower rungs of the social ladder. Anabaptism from its earliest days had primarily found support among those groups, and had not undergone any evolution since then that would have made it more attractive to the higher classes.[93] The intellectual level of the leaders was low, the true Anabaptist teachings went against the grain of the age, and career interests were not advanced in any way by joining the community. From a social point of view, the brotherhood had the characteristics of a sect: that by itself hindered its growth. Between the privileges of the reformed church and the rich traditions of the Catholic Church, it remained stuck as a curious variation, harmless to the larger religious communities.

AFTERWORD

For seventeen chapters we have followed the seventeenth-century Hollanders in their daily comings and goings. If this work has served its purpose, our knowledge of these Hollanders must have increased. This should apply in particular to the themes of each individual chapter. There the richest harvest should be found, in view of the limited aims we have chosen. It was always a matter of observation, not of analysis. Thus we shall have to remain modest in making the final settlement of accounts.

This is also because our subject was necessarily unlimited. We have focused our attention on the non-elite, an elusive mass. Indeed, limiting our study to peasants, textile-workers, or herring fishermen, for example, would have served little purpose, for our questions were generally not limited to one particular social group. Furthermore, without wishing to pursue such an intellectual concept as the typical Hollander, it can still safely be said that precisely this lack of specificity most accords with the experience of most people who lived in Holland in the seventeenth century.

For our first conclusion can be: all relationships were unstable. It was not that the structures of society were not fixed, but rather that the place of each individual was undefined, and nearly every position was interchangeable. The villager could decide from one day to the next to try his luck in the city. The seaman could without difficulty change himself into a miller's servant, or alternate summer and winter between one occupation and the other. This changing of roles applied not only to manual labour with its low level of schooling. The boundaries between the churches could also move, in one place to the benefit of the Catholics, in another to the advantage of the Calvinists. Only toward the middle of the seventeenth century did this motion finally begin to come to rest.

The life of the ordinary Hollander in this period was consequently difficult to predict. Now it is indeed true that much uncertainty also attended life on the other side of the frontier, but it was of an entirely different nature. First of all, a simple peasant in France or Germany never knew when a bad harvest might strike him so hard that he had no subsistence at all. Yet he knew that if good fortune prevailed, he would always remain a peasant, as would his sons after him, on the same land and in the same village. By contrast, a Hollander often did not know and could not know in which occupation he would end his career, let alone those of his sons.

Secondly, there was also this difference, that elsewhere changes in status usually meant falling down the scale. In Holland, with its higher standard of living the little man may have had only small chances of climbing the social ladder, but change was not necessarily for the worse. Naturally the prosperity of the Golden Age was not evenly distributed. Life was hard at the bottom of society, but the crying poverty encountered in other European countries was not found in Holland.

This does not mean that there were no poor. Their numbers ran into the thousands. But they were not left to their fate. At the local level public money was primarily devoted to two causes: support of the church and poor relief. In this respect these two causes are comparable only to defence, which also fell on the public purse albeit on a national level. There, too, people believed that in order to win the war, sacrifices would be required from everyone.

At first glance the connection between these three is not evident, but it was present. This hardly needs to be demonstrated for the church and poor relief. Although opinions might differ as to who should bear primary responsibility, poor relief was in any case a logical consequence of simple Christian duty. The tie between church and waging war was not equally clear to everyone. The Dutch Revolt would never have succeeded if the Catholics had not tolerated its success. But the States of Holland always saw themselves as the protectors of the public church, and the preachers knew better than anyone that the continued existence of their church was dependent on the outcome of the struggle. No such direct connection exists between war and poor relief. On the contrary, war by its very nature caused poverty. But when the struggle had been displaced to other regions, it was war that strongly supported the prosperity of Holland. Thanks to the economic success it was generally possible to find the means to provide the poor with at least the minimum necessary for survival.

We cannot yet say this with great certainty, however, because the sources used for this book provide inadequate confirmation. Our survey has applied to the entire region of Holland. It gave us a global overview, yet not the detailed specific information that can only be collected by good research in local archives. Consequently there is a pressing need for such research in all the subjects we have surveyed. We hope that anyone who undertakes it will be able to find in this book hypotheses worthy of further testing.

NOTES

ABBREVIATED JOURNAL TITLES USED IN THE NOTES AND BIBLIOGRAPHY:
BGBH   *Bijdragen voor de geschiedenis van het bisdom Haarlem*
BMGN   *Bijdragen en Mededelingen betreffende de Geschiedenis der Nederlanden*
BMHG   *Bijdragen en Mededelingen van het Historisch Genootschap*
BTLV   *Bijdragen tot de Taal- Land- en Volkenkunde van Nederlandsch-Indië*
BVGO   *Bijdragen voor Vaderlandsche Geschiedenis en Oudheidkunde*
JA   *Jaarboek Amstelodamum*
RB   *Rotterdamsch Jaarboekje*
TvG   *Tijdschrift voor Geschiedenis*

1. PEOPLE OF LITTLE WISDOM AND LIMITED POWER

1 *Oorsprongk, begin en vervolgh der Nederlandsche oorlogen*, 4 vols. (Amsterdam, 1679–84), III, book 3, f.78.
2 The Delft tax assessment was reduced in 1612, because the breweries had declined (*Resolutiën van Holland*, 1612, p. 127). In 1615 Ian François Le Petit, *Nederlandsche republycke* (Amsterdam, 1615), p. 88, also thought that the great age of Delft beer had passed: 'the city of Delft, formerly very renowned (but not so much now) for the good beer that was brewed there'.
3 G. Baudartius, *Memoryen*, 2 vols., second edition (Arnhem/Zutphen, 1624), II, book 16, p. 63.
4 A. M. van der Woude, *Het Noorderkwartier*, 3 vols. (Wageningen, 1972), I, pp. 48 and 99.
5 W. van Ravensteyn, *Onderzoekingen over de economische en sociale ontwikkeling van Amsterdam* (Amsterdam, 1906), p. 166.
6 J. G. van Dillen, *Amsterdam in 1585* (Amsterdam, 1941), p. xxxiii.
7 N. W. Posthumus, *De geschiedenis van de Leidsche lakenindustrie*, II (The Hague, 1939); F. Daelemans, 'Leiden 1581: Een socio-demografisch onderzoek', *AAG Bijdragen*, (1975), p. 181.
8 *Res. Holland*, 1597, p. 9 (16 Jan. 1597).
9 Van der Woude, *Het Noorderkwartier*, II, p. 465. For the evolution of wages in Holland, see L. Noordegraaf, *Hollands welvaren?* (Bergen, 1985), pp. 66–95.
10 P. H. van Moerkerken, *Het Nederlandsch kluchtspel in de 17de eeuw*, 2 vols. (Sneek, n.d.) I, p. 101: 'Everything is expensive, while there is nothing cheaper than labour' (Van Santen).
11 Van Dillen, *Rijkdom*, p. 295, estimated the weekly wages of skilled workers at Amsterdam around 1650 at six to eight gulden. There were twenty stuivers in a gulden.
12 The leaders of the great internal navigation guild: Van Dillen, *Bronnen*, III, p. 289.
13 Ibid., III, p. 76 (1643).

14 Ibid., III, p. 497 (1647).

15 Van Dillen, *Rijkdom*, p. 300.

16 J. W. Van Dillen, 'Amsterdam in Bredero's tijd,' *De Gids* 2 (1935), p. 322.

17 Van Dillen, *Rijkdom*, p. 295.

18 This was said by the cloth-shearers in 1628, when wages came to 16 stuivers: ibid., p. 297.

19 Ibid., p. 299 (1638).

20 C. Ligtenberg, *De armezorg te Leiden tot het einde van de 16e eeuw* (The Hague, 1908), p. 300.

21 Posthumus, *Bronnen*, IV, p. 322.

22 J. H. van Dijk, 'De geldelijke druk op de Delftsche burgerij in de jaren 1572–1576', *BVGO*, seventh series, 5 (1935); p. 170.

23 Van Ravensteyn, *Onderzoekingen*, p. 249.

24 O. Pringsheim, *Beiträge zur wirtschaftlichen Entwicklungsgeschichte*, p. 51.

25 J. G. Van Dillen, *Van Rijkdom en Regenten* (The Hague, 1970), p. 296.

26 S. C. Regtdoorzee Greup-Roldanus, *Geschiedenis der Haarlemmer bleekerijen* (The Hague, 1936), p. 163.

27 Van Dillen, *Rijkdom*, p. 297.

28 Van Dillen, *Bronnen tot de Geschiednis van het bedrijfsleven en gildewezen van Amsterdam*, 3 vols. (The Hague, 1929–74), III, p. 29.

29 Ibid., III, p. 282. This man received 40–50 gulden annually in addition to daily wages.

30 Ibid., III, p. 289.

31 Lootsma, *Historische studiën over de Zaanstreek*, 2 vols. (Koog aan de Zaan, 1939–50), I, p. 182.

32 Van Dillen, *Bronnen*, III, p. 437.

33 N. W. Posthumus, *Bronnen tot de geschiedenis van de Leidse textielnijverheid*, IV, 1611–1650, p. 451.

34 See for example *Gouda zeven eeuwen stad* (Gouda, 1972), p. 158 (hacklers in 1585 working from sunrise to sunset in the summer, and from 6 a.m. to 7 p.m. in the winter); Pringsheim, *Beiträge*, p. 49 (weavers at Amsterdam in 1589 working from 4 a.m. to 9 p.m. in the summer, from 5 a.m. to 8 p.m. in the winter); A. C. J. de Vrankrijker, *Geschiedenis van het Gooiland* (Amsterdam, 1940–1), II, p. 119 (same trade at Naarden, 1603, same working hours); E. M. A. Timmer, *Knechtsgilden en knechtsbossen in Nederland* (Haarlem, 1913), p. 7 (tailors at Haarlem in 1609 working summers from 6 a.m. to 9 p.m. or later if there was light, winters from 7 a.m. until 9 p.m.); ARA, Hof 5230, information at Haarlem, 23 March 1625 (watchmakers, summers from 5 a.m. to 9 p.m., winters from daybreak or an hour earlier); Van Dillen, *Bronnen*, III, p. 30 (cloth-finishers at Amsterdam, 1633, 5 a.m. to 7 p.m.); Posthumus, *Bronnen*, IV, p. 451 (cloth shearers at Leiden, 1646, 5 a.m. to 7 p.m.).

35 A. J. M. Brouwer Ancher, *De gilden* (The Hague, 1895), p. 35 (1593). The schedule was as follows: summer ran from mid-March until mid-September, autumn until November 1, winter until February 1, and spring until mid-March.

36 W. D. Hooft, *Verloren soon* (1630), in J. F. Haverman, *W. D. Hooft en zijne kluchten* (The Hague, 1895), p. 111.

37 W. P. Blockmans and W. Prevenier, 'Armoede in de Nedelanden van de 14e tot het midden van de 16e eeuw: Bronnen en problemen', *TvG*, 88 (1975), p. 502.

38 Posthumus, *De geschiedenis van de Leidsche lakenindustrie*, II, (The Hague, 1939), p. 205.

39 Blockmans and Prevenier, 'Armoede', p. 503. In 1635, French soldiers in Het Gooi who had no wages received one and a half pounds of bread daily for sustenance (P. C. Hooft, *Brieven* (Haarlem, 1750), p. 364).

40 T. Velius, *Chronyk van Hoorn* (Hoorn, 1740), p. 499 (1597), p. 499 (1597); Baudartius, *Memoryen*, II, book 15, p. 182 (1623); S. Ampzing, *Beschryvinge ende lof der stad Haarlem in Holland* (Haarlem, 1628), p. 415 (1623).

41 G. Brandt and S. Centen, *Historie der vermaarde zee – en koopstadt Enkhuisen*, 2 vols. (Hoorn, 1747), II, p. 42 (1622); Velius, *Chronyk*, p. 611 (1623).

42 *Res. Holland*, 1577, p. 130 (2 July 1577).

43 *Res. Holland*, 1579, p. 2 (2 Jan. 1579).

44 J. van Vloten, *Het Nederlandsche Kluchtspel van de 14e tot de 18e eeuw*, 3 vols. (Haarlem, n.d.), I, pp. 158 and 159.

45 *Res. Holland*, 1586, p. 258.

46 Ibid., 1588, p. 308 (15 Aug. 1588). Sailors got 4–5 stuivers, p. 122.

47 L. van Aitzema, *Saken van staet en oorlogh* (The Hague, 1669), I, p. 128.

48 Posthumus, *Bronnen*, II, gives five-year averages for the prices of 33 items, using an index of 1580–84 = 100:

1580–1584 100
1585–1589 119
1590–1594 133
1595–1599 148
1600–1604 145

49 *Res. Holland*, 1598, p. 244.

50 Notulen van de kerkeraden, Zwartewaal, 16 March 1614.

51 W. F. H. Oldewelt, 'Het aalmoezeniersweeshuis,' *JA*, 61 (1969), p. 127.

52 Van Dillen, *Rijkdom*, p. 295; cf. J. de Vries, *The Dutch rural economy in the golden age* (New Haven, 1974), p. 183; with the exception of the wages for unskilled labour, all of the wage figures cited there for 1625–49, compared to those for 1580–4, lagged behind the cost-of-living index.

53 Knuttel Pamphlet 1057.

54 Posthumus, *Bronnen*, II, p. 29. Independent working women, 9.8 per cent, women in paid employment, 20.1 per cent.

55 ARA, Hof 385, f. 242, request of Geertge Jansdr., Sept. 1601.

56 Knuttel Pamphlet 4682, p. 21.

57 Van Moerkerken, *Kluchtspel*, I, p. 131 (W. D. Hooft, *Styve Piet*): 'I did my best, with sewing and with spinning'; Van Vloten, *Kluchtspel*, II, p. 107 (G. H. van Breughel): 'Can't I earn [money] with spinning too?'

58 Posthumus, *Bronnen*, II, p. 1596 (figures from 1581 and 1622). Perhaps also Haarlem; see F. Moryson, *An itinerary containing his ten yeeres travell*, 4 vols. (Glasgow, 1907–8), I, p. 95 (1592).

59 J. Z. Kannegieter, 'De Bloemstraat en haar zijstraten ± 1613–1625', *JA*, 54 (1962), p. 88.

60 Haverman, *W. D. Hooft*, p. 112 (W. D. Hooft, *Verloren soon*); Van Moerkerken, *Kluchtspel*, I, p. 103 (Van Santen, *Snappende Sijtgen*); Van Deursen, 'Werkende vrouwen in een Hollands dorp', *De Zeventiende Eeuw*, 4 (1988), p. 11.

61 J. Cats, *Al de werken* (Scheidam, n.d.), p. 232 (*Howelick, Vrouwe*): 'She calls one of the women who walk through the cities / and carry this and that to sell to everyone.'

62 H. A. Enno van Gelder, 'Recente gegevens omtrent de 16e eeuwse koopman', *TvG*, 35 (1920), p. 358.

63 A. C. J. de Vrankrijker, 'De textielindustrie van Naarden', *TvG*, 51, (1936), p. 176 (Naarden, 1603).

64 Moryson, *Itinerary*, IV, p. 58.

65 A. Carnero, *Historia de las guerras civiles que ha avido en Flandes* (Brussels, 1625), p. 4.

66 Regtdoorzee Greup-Roldanus, *Geschiedenis*, p. 160. Other women's wages found in Lootsma, *Historische studiën*, I, p. 81: 75 gulden (for one year); 65 gulden (from Lady's Day, i.e. the Annunciation, until Christmas); and 45 gld. (from May until Christmas); Van Dillen, *Bronnen*, III, p. 126 (1636, 39 gld. per year). All these cases involved young girls.

67 Pringsheim, *Beiträge*, p. 54.

68 S. Coster, *Teeuwis de Boer*, in *Werken*, ed. R. A. Kollewijn (Haarlem, 1883), II. 355–6, where Krijn speaks to the girl Bely: 'You ugly vegetable, people could use you to chase children into their beds, / You had better go to Enkhuizen, to hire yourself out as boilery girl' (in the salt works: see Brandt and Centen, *Historie*, I, p. 290).

69 Lootsma, *Historische studiën*, I, p. 80: in 1634 the night work of the 'bread girls' began at midnight.

70 De Vrankrijker, 'Textielindustrie', p. 276; Brouwer Ancher, *De gilden*, p. 100; Van Dillen, *Bronnen*, III, p. 47; J. de Bosch Kemper, *Geschiedkundig onderzoek naar de armoede in ons vaderland* (Haarlem, 1851), p. 86.

71 Pringsheim, *Beiträge*, p. 57.

72 In Gouda from 1647: *Gouda*, p. 72.

73 I. H. van Eeghen, *De gilden. Theorie en praktijk* (Bussum, 1965), p. 26.

74 Timmer, *Knechtsgilden*, p. 4.

75 The Amsterdam cloth-shearers in 1609: Van Dillen, *Rijkdom*, p. 297.

76 Van Eeghen, *Gilden*, p. 47; Van Dillen, *Bronnen*, III, p. 24 (1633).

77 Lootsma, *Historische studiën*, I, p. 82.

78 Van Dillen, *Rijkdom*, p. 297.

79 Posthumus, *Bescheiden betreffende de provinciale organisatie der Hollandsche lakenbereiders* (Amsterdam, 1917), pp. 8 and 10.

80 Van Dillen, *Rijkdom*, p. 294.

81 Van Dillen, *Rijkdom*, p. 294.

82 *Gouda*, p. 204 (1614, for all workers); Pringsheim, *Beiträge*, p. 44 (Leiden cloth-finishers, 1585); Van Eeghen, *Gilden*, p. 47 (Amsterdam tailors, 1587, 1597, 1599).

83 Baudartius, *Memoryen*, II, book 15, p. 147.

84 Van der Woude, *Het Noorderkwartier*, II, pp. 317 and 464. It is not known when the great expansion began. The ribbon-workers complained in 1648 about the uneven enforcement of the declaration: *Res. Holland*, 1648, p. 124 (20 April 1648).

85 C. te Lintum, 'De Textielindustrie in oud-Rotterdam', *Rotterdamsch Jaarboekje*, 7 (1900), p. 25.

86 Van Dillen, *Rijkdom*, p. 300 (hatmakers of Amsterdam, 1632, maximum 6); Van Eeghen, *Gilden*, p. 47 (clothmakers of Amsterdam, maximum 10).

87 S. J. van Geuns, *Proeve eener geschiedenis van de toelating* (Schoonhoven, 1853), p. 243.

88 Van Dillen, *Bronnen*, III, p. 284.

89 Léonie van Nierop, 'Bijdragen tot de geschiedenis van de Amsterdamse scheepsbouw', *JA*, 48 (1956), p. 38.

90 Van Dillen, *Bronnen*, III, p. 291.

91 Ibid., p. 282 (1640).

92 Van Dillen, *Rijkdom*, p. 297.

93 Moryson, *Itinerary*, I, p. 431, and IV, p. 49.

94 D. A. Valcooch, *Chronycke van Leeuwenhorn* (Amsterdam, 1740), p. 69; H. J. J. Scholtens, *Uit het verleden van Midden-Kennemerland* (The Hague, 1947), p. 165.

95 Posthumus, 'Gegevens betreffende landbouwtoestanden in Rijnland in het jaar 1575', *BMHG*, 25 (1914), p. 170.

96 Fockema Andreae, *Schets van Zuid-Hollandse watersnoden in vroeger tijd* (Voorburg, 1953), p. 16.

97 *Het geestelijk Kantoor te Delft* (Arnhem, 1870), p. 53.

98 Van der Woude, *Het Noorderkwartier*, I, p. 56.

99 Moryson, *Itinerary*, IV, p. 52.

100 Ibid., I, p. 112.

101 H. Schoorl, *Zeshanderd jaar water en land* (Groningen, 1973), p. 102.

102 Van der Woude, *Het Noorderkwartier*, I, p. 43.

103 De Vries, *Dutch rural economy*, p. 31.

104 Van der Woude, *Het Noorderkwartier*, I, p. 44; II, p. 530.

105 Liesker, p. 73; de Vries, *Dutch rural economy*, p. 186.

106 In 1594 the States of Holland twice gave permission for the sale of church property, because the rental income had fallen far below the actual worth. *Res. Holland*, 1594, pp. 129 (De Lier) and 340 (Voorschoten).

107 H. A. Enno van Gelder, *Nederlandse dorpen in de 16e eeuw* (Amsterdam, 1953), p. 26.

108 Ibid., p. 76.

109 De Vries, *Dutch rural economy*, p. 44; Enno van Gelder, *Nederlandse dorpen*, p. 19.

110 De Vries, *Dutch rural economy*, p. 53.

111 This was said of the villages below Edam in 1579 (van der Woude, *Het Noorderkwartier*, II, p. 250). Van Buchell also saw only wooden houses in the Waterland area: the ground was too weak, people said, to bear the weight of stone houses (S. Muller Fzn., *Schetsen uit de middeleeuwen. Nieuwe bundel* (Amsterdam, 1914), p. 408). Leeghwater testifies that most houses in Schermer had no chimneys, attics or floors (*Een klein kronyke omtrent den oorsprong en de vergrooting der dorpen van Graft en De Ryp*, ed. J. A. van Lennep (Haarlem, n.d.), p. 10). Note also that a foreigner had a more favourable judgement. Moryson says categorically, 'in the United Provinces, the houses are most of bricke, as well in cities as in villages' (*Itinerary*, III, p. 491).

112 *Res. Holland*, 1594, p. 437: an inhabitant of Dussen asked for 250 gld. for his house, which had been burned by soldiers; he received 100 gld. P. C. Hooft, *Brieven* (Haarlem, 1750), p. 23: the house and farmstead of a fugitive convicted of manslaughter were sold at Huizen in 1613 for 400 gld.

113 De Vries, *Dutch rural economy*, p. 53.

114 Van der Woude, *Het Noorderkwartier*, I, p. 51.

115 *Res. Holland*, 1596, p. 91; Valcooch, *Chronycke*, p. 92.

116 Belonje, 'Amsterdamsch grondbezit in de Zijpe omstreeks 1600', *JA*, 33 (1936), p. 37.

117 Van der Woude, *Het Noorderkwartier*, I, p. 50.

118 Ibid., III, p. 682.

119 Knuttel Pamphlet 1478.

120 Knuttel Pamphlet 1450.

121 H. A. Enno van Gelder, 'De bedijking van de Heer Hugowaard' (1624–1631), *BVGO*, fourth series, 5 (1906), p. 266.

122 Calculated for the Beijerland polders: C. Baars, *De geschiedenis van de landbouw in de Beijerlanden* (Wageningen, 1973), p. 107.

123 Van der Woude, *Het Noorderkwartier*, I, p. 48; Baars, *Geschiedenis*, p. 199.

124 De Vries, *Dutch rural economy*, p. 71.

125 Ibid., p. 153.

126 Valcooch, *Chronycke*, p. 75.

127 Van der Woude, *Het Noorderkwartier*, II, p. 511.

128 De Vries, *Dutch rural economy*, p. 153.

129 W. J. Sangers, *De ontwikkeling van de Nederlandse tuinbouw* (Zwolle, 1952), p. 122.

130 De Vries, *Dutch rural economy*, p. 183.

131 Brandt and Centen, *Historie*, p. 70.

132 Knuttel Pamphlet 4638, p. 3.

133 Valcooch, *Chronycke*, p. 103.

134 Velius, *Chronyk van Hoorn*, p. 337.

135 De Vries, *Dutch rural economy*, p. 192.

136 Van der Woude, *Het Noorderkwartier*, I, p. 57.

137 Schoorl, *Zeshonderd jaar*, p. 100.

138 Valcooch, *Chronycke*, p. 55.

139 A. van Buchell, *Diarium*, ed. G. Brom and L. A. van Langeraad (Amsterdam, 1907), p. 310.

140 In summing up everything that she expects to inherit, the rich farmer's daughter Lijsje Teunis also speaks of thirty cows (A. van de Venne, *Tafereel van sinne-mal*, Middelburg, 1623, p. 41).

141 Bredero, *Moortje*, l. 644, in *Werken*, ed. J. A. N. Knuttel, 3 vols. (Amsterdam, 1921–9).

142 De Vries, *Dutch rural economy*, p. 71.

143 *Res. Holland*, 1600, p. 315.

144 De Vries, *Dutch rural economy*, p. 68.

145 Ibid., p. 64.

146 ARA, Holland 2600 d, *Doleantie* to the States of Holland, from Hazerswoude, Benthuizen, Zoetermeer, Zegwaard, Stompwijk, Aalsmeer and Rijnsaterwoude.

147 W. J. Diepeveen, *De vervening in Delfland en Schieland tot het einde der zestiende eeuw* (Leiden, n.d.), p. 43.

148 Baars, *Geschiedenis*, p. 45.

149 *Res. Holland*, 1614, p. 58.

150 Lootsma, *Historische studiën*, II, p. 38.

151 Van der Woude, *Het Noorderkwartier*, II, p. 497.

152 Ibid., II, p. 459.

153 Ibid., III, p. 726.

154 Ibid., II, p. 475.

155 ARA, Holland 1384, f. 98 vo.

156 Lootsma, *Historische studiën*, I, p. 51.

157 ARA, Part not. Amsterdam 1, 14 July and 16 Sept. 1615; Lootsma, *Historische studiën*, I, pp. 60–3 (1604, 1612, 1617, 1621).

158 Van der Woude, *Het Noorderkwartier*, II, p. 497.

159 In 1603 the States of Holland had written 'to the bailiff and officer of Saerdam and along the Saerdijck, Wormer, Gisp and Wormer Veer' forbidding the sale of foreign grain in the villages. *Res. Holland*, 1603, p. 7 (10 Jan.).

160 E.g. ARA, Part. not. Amsterdam, 1, 14 July and 16 Sept. 1615; *Res. Holland*, 1577, p. 66, and 1623, p. 96.

161 *Res. Holland*, 1641, p. 38 (2 Feb.).

162 ARA, Holland 2600 e, 'Reasons why the request of those from Hoorn to have a reduction in their assessment should be denied, and those of Alkmaar requesting a reduction in their assessment should be approved.'

163 At the request of Woerden: *Res. Holland*, 1623, p. 96 (16 Sept).

164 Ibid., 1637, p. 197, bill of particulars, November, 1637. See also Posthumus, *De nationale organisatie der lakenkoopers tijdens de Republiek* (Utrecht, 1927), p. xv.

165 *Res. Holland*, 1641, p. 39 (2 Feb.).

166 The choice of that year is not explained in the proposal.

167 R. Fruin, 'Naar aanleiding der vereeniging van Delfshaven met Rotterdam', in *Verspreide geschriften*, VI, p. 133.

168 Cf. H. Blink, *Geschiedenis van den boerenstand en den landbouw in Nederland*, 2 vols. (Groningen, 1902–4), II, p. 14.

169 ARA, Part. not. Amsterdam 1, 8 March 1614.

170 *Res. Holland*, 1614, p. 58.

171 Thus they expressly called themselves in the act by which Frederick Henry was invited to accept the dignity of first noble. Ibid., 1637, p. 28 (5 Feb.). The States had some reservations: apparently they were no longer aware that nobles in the sixteenth century were always regarded in this fashion.

172 In 1629 the nobles protested, apparently without success, against the rules for reimbursement of the cost of excavations carried out when fortifications were built, with the rationale that 'the said resolution is very harsh, and works to the disadvantage of the inhabitants of the countryside'. *Res. Holland*, 1629, p. 194 (28 Sept.). See also ibid., 1630, p. 13 (21 Jan.).

173 K. Schottmüller, 'Reise-eindrücke aus Danzig, Lübeck, Hamburg und Holland 1636', *Zeitschrift des Westpreussischen Geschichtsvereins*, 52 (1910), p. 265.

174 Van Buchell, *Diarium*, p. 249.

175 Brandt and Centen, *Historie*, I, p. 289.

176 R. H. Tawney, *Business and politics under James I* (Cambridge, 1958), p. 25.

177 A. T. van Deursen, *Honni soit qui mal y pense? De Republiek tussen de mogendheden (1610–1612)* (Amsterdam, 1965), p. 54.

178 H. A. H. Kranenburg, *De zeevisscherij van Holland in den tijd der Republiek* (Amsterdam, 1946), p. 26.

179 Ibid., p. 38.

180 Van der Woude, *Het Noorderkwartier*, II, p. 401, reckons that there were twelve to fourteen members in the crew of a herring-bus. Kranenburg figured on twenty men during the season (p. 85).

181 Van der Woude, *Het Noorderkwartier*, II, p. 404. Cf Brandt and Centen, *Historie*, I, p. 287, and R. Bylsma, *Rotterdams welvaren 1550–1650* (The Hague, 1918), p. 92.

182 P. A. Leupe, 'Zeezaken', *BMHG* 2 (1879), p. 107; P. C. Hooft, *Warenar* (Amsterdam, 1616) ll. 1268–9; J. Jacobs, *Epistolae Ho-elianae. The familiar letters of James Howell*, I (London, 1890), p. 29.

183 See p. 67.

184 Bylsma, *Rotterdams welvaren*, p. 41.

185 Kranenburg, *Zeevisscherij*, p. 35.

186 Brandt and Centen, *Historie*, I, p. 287.

187 Acta Delft, 21 May 1609.

188 *Res. Holland*, 1623, p. 53 (30 June).

189 Ibid., 1594, p. 35.

190 Ibid., 1608, p. 572.

191 G. A. Fokker, *Geschiedenis der loterijen in de Nederlanden* (Amsterdam, 1862), p. 261.

192 Van der Woude, *Het Noorderkwartier*, I, p. 38.

193 Fokker, *Geschiedenis der loterijen*, p. 261.

194 Van der Woude, *Het Noorderkwartier*, I, p. 38.

195 *Res. Holland*, 1594, p. 44.

196 Van der Woude, *Het Noorderkwartier*, I, p. 38.

197 C. R. Boxer, *The Dutch seaborne empire* (London, 1965), p. 67.

198 Van der Woude, *Het Noorderkwartier*, II, p. 395.

199 *Res. Holland*, 1607, p. 86.

200 Boxer, *Dutch seaborne empire*, p. 67.

201 E.g. ARA, Hof 5217, testimony of Lambert Pieter Frans, 30 May 1613 (with nineteen men to Trinidad); ARA, Holland 2609 f, testimony of Heyn Claesz., 14 June 1611 (with twelve men to Guinea).

202 Pieter Verhoeff's fleet on his last voyage numbered thirteen ships with a carrying capacity of 4,000 lasts. The number of crewmen was 1,800 to 1,900 (M. E. van Opstall, *De reis van de vloot van Pieter Willemsz* (The Hague, 1972), p. 198). Piet Hein went to the West Indies in 1626 with fourteen ships, capacity of 2,470 lasts, and a crew of 1,336 (Aitzema, *Saken*, I, p. 554); in 1628 he sailed with thirty ships, total capacity 5,555 lasts, and a crew of 2,537, not including an unreported number of sailors on one ship of 250 lasts (ibid., p. 720).

203 J. R. Bruijn, 'De personeelsbehoefte van de VOC overzee en aan boord, bezien in Aziatisch en Nederlands perspectief', *BMGN*, 91 (1976), p. 220.

204 According to the instruction of 1630, warships were required to have on board eighty-five sailors and thirty musketeers (F. Graefe, *De kapiteinsjaren van Maerten Harpertszoon Tromp*, ed. M. Simon Thomas (The Hague, 1938, p. 143). On his appointment as lieutenant-admiral in 1629, Piet Hein wanted the crews reduced from 100 to eighty sailors (Aitzema, *Saken*, I, p. 821). In 1639 the minimum was 110–140 men (J. C. de Jonge, *Geschiedenis van het Nederlandsche zeewezen*, second edition, I (Haarlem, 1858, p. 289).

205 Three warships in 1617 had 82, 90, and 94 men on board, respectively. ARA, St. Gen. Loketkas Admiraliteit 29. De Jonge (p. 288) gives figures of 50–80 men for ships with 24–26 guns, and 90 men for those with 30–36 guns.

206 J. R. Bruijn and J. Lucassen, *Op de schepen der Oost-Indische Compagnie: Vijf artikelen van J. de Hullu* (Groningen, 1980), p. 14. See also P. C. van Royen, *Zeevarenden op de koopvardijvloot omstreeks 1700* (Amsterdam, 1987), p. 25.

207 Baars, *Geschiedenis*, p. 38.

208 Van der Woude, *Het Noorderkwartier*, II, p. 371.

209 Aitzema, *Saken*, II, p. 347.

210 Knuttel Pamphlet 4426, p. 19.

211 In 1588 the food allowance on warships came to $4\frac{1}{2}$ st. (*Res. Holland*, 1588, p. 122). In 1618 it was $5\frac{1}{2}$ st. The captains found that too small, and requested an increase to $6\frac{1}{2}$ st. F. Graefe, 'Beiträge zur Geschichte der See-Expeditionen von 1606 und 1607', *Bijdragen voor Vaderlandsche Geschiedenis en Oudheidkunde*, seventh series, 3 (1933), 201–30.

212 Geyl, *Christofforo Suriano* (The Hague, 1913), p. 269; Aitzema, *Saken*, I, p. 799; Knuttel Pamphlet 4426, p. 19.

213 *Res. Holland*, 1641, p. 249 (19 Sept.).

214 See part III.

215 See part III.

216 J. de Hullu, 'Ziekten en dokters op de schepen der Oost-Indische Compagnie', *BTLV*, 67 (1913), p. 254.

217 ARA, Kol. arch. 971, f. 27ff.

218 De Hullu, 'Ziekten', p. 252.

219 S. P. l'Honoré Naber, "t Leven en bedrijff van vice-admirael De With, zaliger', *BMHG*, 47 (1926), p. 92.

220 *Res. Holland*, 1595, p. 220; De Hullu, 'Ziekten', p. 254.

221 Ibid., p. 260.

222 F. Graefe, 'Beiträge zur Geschichte der See-Expeditionen von 1606 und 1607', *BVGO*, seventh series, 3 (1933), p. 216.

223 Tobias Smollett, *The Adventures of Roderick Random*, I, Ch. 32.

224 For the end of the century, see Van Royen, *Zeevarenden*, pp. 70–5.

225 Knuttel Pamphlet 4155, p. 8.

226 Van der Woude, *Het Noorderkwartier*, II, p. 390.

227 Van Moerkerken, *Kluchtspel*, I, p. 124.

228 Velius, *Chronyk van Hoorn*, cited by Kranenburg, *Zeevisscherij*, p. 89.

229 E. van Meteren, book 13, *Commentarien ofte memorien van den Nederlandtschen staet* (?Amsterdam, 1608), f. viii vo.

230 *Res. Holland*, 1592, p. 77.

231 A. Westermannus, *Christelijcke zee-vaert*, seventh edition (Amsterdam, 1630), p. 211.

232 R. E. J. Weber, *De beveiliging van de zee tegen Europeesche en Barbarijsche zee roovers 1609–1621* (Amsterdam, 1936), pp. 33 and 191.

233 J. de Hullu, 'De handhaving der orde en tucht op de schepen der Oost-Indische Compagnie', *BTLV* 67 (1913), p. 534.

234 Baudartius, *Memoryen*, II, book 16, p. 53.

235 *Groot Placaetboek*, 9 vols. (The Hague, 1658–1796), II, p. 1234 (21 July 1614). On conditions there see also F. L. Rutgers, *Het kerkverband der Nederlandsche Gereformeerde kerken* (Amsterdam, 1882), p. 187.

236 For the region of Voorne, ARA, Holland 1384, f. 196 (26 Nov. 1622); *Res. Holland*, 1636, p. 300 (2 Oct.).

237 Ibid., 1579, p. 163.

238 These were derived from the articles for ships that would sail northward: ibid., 1595, p. 217 (16 June).

239 De Jonge, *Geschiedenis*, I, p. 80.

240 Van Opstall, *De reis*, p. 107; J. C. Mollema, *De eerste schipvaart der Hollanders naar Oost-Indië 1595–1597* (The Hague, 1935), p. 68; A. T. Van Deursen, *Bavianen en slijkgeuzen* (Assen, 1974), p. 17.

241 G. J. Hogewerff, *Journalen van de gedenckwaerdige reijsen van Willem IJsbrantsz. Bontekoe 1618–1625* (The Hague, 1952), pp. 39 and 187.

242 Ibid., p. 17, 24, 145.

243 Geyl, *Suriano*, p. 246.

244 Van Buchell, *Diarium*, p. 473.

245 L'Honoré Naber, 'De With', p. 67; Elias, *Schetsen uit de geschiedenis van ons zeewezen*, I (The Hague, 1916) p. 61.

246 Ibid., p. 61.

247 De Hullu, 'Handhaving', p. 534.

248 See also, e.g., Mollema, *Schipvaart*, p. 302.

249 S. P. l'Honoré Naber, *Reizen van Willem Barents ... en anderen naar het Noorden (1594–1597)*, 2 vols. (s-Gravenhage, 1917), I, pp. 10, 18.

250 Ibid., p. 30: the description of a fight with a polar bear, that lasted 'four glasses long'. Axes and halberds broke on the animal, until the men finally succeeded in shattering its head.

251 ARA, St. Gen. 4928, States-General to the Hoge Raad at Malaga, 3 March 1614.

252 See part III.

253 Posthumus, *Bronnen*, IV, p. 100 (18 March 1621).

254 *Res. Holland*, 1604, p. 107.

255 Wijn, 'Het Noordhollandse regiment in de eerste jaaren van de opstand tegen Spanje', *TvG*, 62 (1949), p. 244.

256 *Groot Placaetboek*, II, p. 257.

257 Aitzema, *Saken*, I, p. 265.

258 *Res. Holland*, 1606, p. 137.

259 C. Huygens, *Gedichten*, ed. J. A. Worp (Groningen, 1892), II, p. 7, 'Een gemeen soldaet'.

260 *Res. Holland*, 1588, p. 227.

261 J. W. Wijn, *Het krijgswezen in den tijd van Maurits* (Utrecht, 1934), p. 14.

262 Ibid., p. 108.

263 Not. Schoonhoven, 22 Feb. 1622.

264 Huygens, *Gedichten*, II, p. 7.

265 *Res. Holland*, 1600, p. 139. Leiden and other towns supported this proposal.

266 A. E. Leuftink, *De geneeskunde bij 's lands oorlogsvloot in de 17e eeuw* (Assen, 1952), p. 17 (1586).

267 E.g. A. T. Van Deursen, *Resolutiën der Staten-General 1610–1670* (The Hague, 1971), *Resolutiën*, I, p. 39.

268 ARA, St. Gen. 40, 3 Jan. 1615, and Van Deursen, *Resolutiën*, I, pp. 3, 56. On the peat-barge, in which some heroic young Dutchmen entered the town of Breda on 4 March 1590 and took it by surprise, see H. P. H. Jansen, *Prisma Kalendarium* (Utrecht, 1988), p. 93.

269 E.g. ibid., pp. 34, 248.

270 ARA, St. Gen. 7475, request of Willem Thijsz., 28 Feb. 1611.

271 ARA, St. Gen. 40, 3 Jan. 1615.

272 Ibid., 2 March 1615.

273 E.g. *Res. Holland*, 1626, p. 66; 1588, p. 352; Hooft, *Brieven*, pp. 25 (1613) and 37 (1615).

274 *Res. Holland*, 1648, p. 451.

275 ARA, Holland 1385, f. 33, to the lord of Woerden, 16 Sept. 1624.

276 *Res. Holland*, 1586, pp. 203 (Gorinchem), 382 (Voorschoten) and 520 (Sassenheim).

277 For Oudewater see W. C. van Zyll, *Oudewater ... geschetst* (Oudewater, 1861), p. 487.

278 *Res. Holland*, 1587, p. 162.

279 H. de Jager, 'Verweerschrift van den contra-remonstrantschen predikant Willem Crijnsze, door de Brielsche regeering afgezet en verbannen', *BMGH*, 17 (1896), p. 166.

280 N. van der Laan, *Uit Roemer Visschers brabbeling*, 2 vols. (Utrecht, 1918–23), I, p. 31.

281 *Res. Holland*, 1596, p. 9; 1597, p. 23; 1600, p. 292; 1603, p. 167.

282 E. van Reyd, *Historie der Nederlantsche oorlogen begin ende voortganck tot den jaere 1601* (Leeuwaarden, 1650), p. 271.

283 Moryson, *Itinerary*, IV, p. 472.

284 Thomas Overbury, *The miscellaneous works in prose and verse* (London, 1856), p. 229.

285 Van Meteren, *Commentarien*, book 16, f. 71.

286 Van Buchell, *Diarium*, p. 255 (7 Jan. 1591): 'duo in patibulo suspensi periere ex praetoriana Nassovii cohorte, qui villicos aliquandiu vexaverant'.

287 *Res. Holland*, 1587, p. 51.

288 Ibid., 1597, p. 23.

289 Ibid., 1594, p. 133.

290 Ibid., 1629, p. 221.

291 ARA, Holland, 1384, f. 287.

292 ARA, St. Gen. 4927, Deventer to the States-General, 2 Feb. 1613, old style.

293 *Res. Holland*, 1598, p. 172 (Nijmegen).

294 Hooft, *Brieven*, p. 364.

2. THE ATTRACTION OF HOLLAND

1 Posthumus, *Lakenindustrie*, II, p. 154.

2 J. L. Eggen, *De invloed door Zuid-Nederland op Noord-Nederland* (Ghent, 1908), p. 24.

3 J. W. Pont, *Geschiedenis van het Lutheranisme in de Nederlanden tot 1618* (Haarlem, 1911), p. 507.

4 A. A. van Schelven, *Omvang en invloed der Zuid-Nederlandsche immigratie van het laatste kwart der 16e eeuw* (The Hague, 1919), p. 13.

5 Kannegieter, 'De Bloemstraat', p. 92.

6 Van der Woude, *Het Noorderkwartier*, II, p. 391.

7 M. Wolff, 'De eerste vestiging der Joden in Amsterdam, hun politieke en economische toestand', *BVGO*, fourth series, 9, p. 373.

8 J. Soetendorp, *Ontmoetingen in ballingschap, II: 1250–1700* (Hilversum, 1965), p. 132.

9 ARA, Part. not. Amsterdam 1, 18 March 1615.

10 Wolff, 'Eerste vestiging', 9, p. 391.

11 D. Souterius, *Seer uytmuntenden Nederlandtsche victoriën*, 2 vols. (Haarlem, 1630) p. 63.

12 Not. Assendelft, Tuesday after 1 June 1608.

13 F. van Vervou, *Enige aenteekeningen van 't gepasseerde vergadering van de Staten-Generael anno 1616–1620* (Leeuwaarden, 1874), p. 2.

14 D. Campbell, *The Puritan in Holland, England, and America*, 2 vols., fourth edition (New York, 1920), II, p. 371.

15 In 1637–8, 339 passengers with passports for Holland left the harbour of Yarmouth: J. W. Stoye, *English travellers abroad 1604–1667* (London, 1952), p. 240.

16 Campbell, *The Puritan*, II, p. 372.

17 R. B. Evenhuis, *Ook dat was Amsterdam*, II (Amsterdam, 1965), p. 274.

18 Van der Woude, *Het Noorderkwartier*, I, p. 224; Valcooch, *Chronycke*, pp. 67, 76.

19 Hooft, *Brieven*, p. 233 (1631).

20 Van Dillen, *Rijkdom*, p. 301.

21 Van Geuns, *Proeve eener geschiedenis*, p. 172.

22 ARA, St. Gen. 6889, Register etc. without date.

23 ARA, St. Gen. 5479, instruction of 26 May 1615.

24 Ibid., appendix to a letter from the Admiralty of Amsterdam to the States-General, 17 Nov. 1615.

25 De Vries, *Dutch rural economy*, p. 95.

26 J. G. van Dillen, 'Amsterdam in Bredero's tijd', *De Gids*, 2 (1935), p. 310.

27 Bylsma, *Rotterdams welvaren*, p. 37 (Rotterdam); Pont, *Geschiedenis*, p. 512 (Haarlem); C. J. de Lange van Wijngaarden, *Geschiedenis en beschrijving der stad van der Goude*, 3 vols. (Gouda, 1813–79), III, p. 96 (Gouda); p. 147.

28 Van Meteren, *Commentarien*, book 14, f. xxxi.

29 Eggen, *Invloed*, p. 12.

30 Ibid., p. 18.

31 J. Tack, *Die Hollandsgänger in Hannover und Oldenburg* (Leipzig, 1902), p. 36.

32 Léonie van Nierop, 'De zijdenijverheid van Amsterdam historisch geschetst', *TvG*, 45 (1930), p. 32.

33 D. Carleton, *Letters during his embassy in Holland 1615–1620*, third edition (London, 1780), p. 56.

34 Van Geuns, *Proeve eener geschiedenis*, p. 241.

35 Z. W. Sneller, 'De tijkweverij te Rotterdam en te Schiedam in de eerste helft der 17e eeuw', *TvG*, 45 (1930), p. 242.

36 *Gouda*, p. 136.

37 Le Petit, *Nederlandsche republycke*, p. 138.

38 Van Geuns, *Proeve eener geschiedenis*, p. 176.

39 Van Schelven, *Omvang en invloed*, p. 8.

40 Eggen, *Invloed*, p. 17.

41 *Res. Holland*, 1613, p. 43.

42 Ibid., 1629, p. 139.

43 A. de Montchrétien, *Traicté de l'oeconomie politique* (Paris, n.d.), pp. 105, 114.

44 C. Plomp, 'Het leerlingwezen in den Haag van de 15e tot de 18e eeuw', *Die Haghe, Jaarboek* (1936), p. 11.

45 Van Eeghen, *Gilden*, p. 28.

46 Brouwer Ancher, *De Gilden*, p. 22.

47 Ibid., p. 24.

48 *Res. Holland*, 1608, p. 753, and 1622, p. 57.

49 Van Buchell, *Diarium*, p. 238.

50 Enno van Gelder, 'Bedijking van de Heer Hugowaard', p. 260.

51 Cf. Van Dillen, *Bronnen*, II, p. 18: 'whom she, the witness, by the speech and clothing took to be a woman from Gelderland'.

52 Van der Laan, *Roemer Visscher*, I, p. 33.

53 Ibid., p. 14.

54 Coster, *Teeuwis de Boer*, l. 186.

55 Bredero, *Spaanse Brabander*, l. 1014.

56 Van Buchell, *Diarium*, p. 320.

57 C. van der Woude, *Sibrandus Lubbertus* (Kampen, 1963), p. 182.

58 A. van de Venne, *Tafereel van de belacchende werelt* (The Hague, 1635), p. 171.

59 Bredero, *Spaanse Brabander*, l. 67.

60 Van der Laan, *Roemer Visscher*, I, p. 29.

61 Bredero, *Klucht van den meulenaer*, ll. 173–6.

62 J. B. F. van Gils, *De dokter in de oude Nederlandsche tooneellitteratuur* (Haarlem, 1917), p. 16.

63 Van Buchell, *Diarium*, cited by S. Muller Fzn., *Schetsen*, p. 408.

64 Moryson, *Itinerary*, IV, p. 61. See also Van Deursen, *Honni soit*, p. 70. In 1581, after the revolt against Philip of Spain, Anjou was offered the sovereignty of the Netherlands by the States-General.

65 In Knuttel Pamphlet 5596, p. 4, the Frenchman says, 'I know that I am from another nation, in which some of you have little faith.'

66 Van Geuns, *Proeve eener geschiedenis*, p. 176.

67 W. J. J. C. Bijleveld, 'Leiden, stad der réfugiés', *Jaarboekje voor de Geschiedenis en Oudheidkunde van Leiden en Rijnland*, 35 (1948), p. 105.

68 *Res. Holland*, 1622, p. 57.

69 Van Schelven, *Omvang en invloed*, p. 39.

70 C. P. Hooft, *Memoriën en adviezen*, 2 vols. (Utrecht, 1871–1925), II, p. 42.

71 Ibid., I, p. 202.

72 Ibid., I, p. 2.

73 Knuttel Pamphlet 3688, p. 57.

74 Bibliotheek Rotterdam 362, request of Maria van Walenburgh, 25 April 1622.

75 G. P. van Itterzon, *Franciscus Gomarus* (The Hague, 1929), p. 86.

76 P. van Marnix van St Aldegonde, *Godsdienstige en kerkelijke geschriften*, I–II (The Hague, 1871–3), I, p. 512 ('Trouwe vermaninge').

77 Ibid., p. 514.

78 Ibid., p. 522.

79 Cited by J. J. Poelhekke, *'t Uytgaen van den treves* (Groningen, 1960), p. 9. This feeling was sometimes shared by the other side, as in Sabbe, p. 129, a song on the devastation of Brabant by Frederick Henry: 'Netherlandish Huguenots violate their own land'.

80 F. L. Rutgers, *Acta van de Nederlandsche synoden der zestiende eeuw* (Utrecht, 1889), p. 264.

81 O. C. Broek Roelofs, *Wilhelmus Baudartius* (Kampen, 1947), p. 213.

82 Van Deursen, *Bavianen en slijkgeuzen*, pp. 90ff.

83 H. J. Jaanus, *Hervormd Delft ten tijde van Arent Cornelisz. (1573–1605)* (Amsterdam, 1950), p. 86 (Delft); J. Uytenbogaert, *Kerckelicke historie* (Rotterdam, 1647), p. 887 (Leiden).

84 D. F. Poujol, *Histoire et influence des églisesz. wallonnes dans les Pays-Bas* (Paris, 1902), p. 75, states that the Walloon workers left Naarden because no French-speaking religious community was established there.

85 J. A. de Kok, *Nederland op de breuklijn Rome-reformatie* (Assen, 1964), p. 10.

86 For Oldenbarnevelt, see Van Deursen, *Bavianen en slijkgeuzen*, p. 268.

87 Brandt, *Historie der reformatie en andere kerkelijke geschiedenissen in en ontrent de Nederlanden*, 4 vols. (Amsterdam, 1660–1704), I, p. 737.

88 Ibid., II, p. 560.

89 Reyd, *Historie*, p. 133.

90 G. Brandt, *Historie der reformatie*, I, p. 709.

91 J. Wtenbogaert, *Brieven en onuitgegeven stukken verzameld met aanteekeningen*, ed. H. C. Rogge, I (Utrecht, 1868), p. 33, Herman Herbertsz. to Wtenbogaert, 11 Nov. 1595.

92 Van Deursen, *Bavianen en slijkgeuzen*, p. 92.

93 Posthumus, *Lakenindustrie*, p. 186.

94 Van Geuns, *Proeve eener Geschiedenis*, p. 176.

95 Note diverse arrangements made by the States-General at the request of immigrants, e.g. ARA, St. Gen. 38, 7 March and 30 Nov. 1613; St. Gen. 4927, the States to the Archdukes, 7 Sept. 1613.

96 Posthumus, *Lakenindustrie*, II, p. 186.

97 P. J. Blok, *Geschiedenis eener Hollandsche stad* (The Hague, 1916), p. 314.

98 ARA, WK Haag 1, 27 June 1619.

99 *Livre synodal contenant les articles résolus dans les synodes des églises wallonnes des Pays-Bas*, I, *1563–1685* (The Hague, 1896), p. 127.

100 Eggen, *Invloed*, p. 27; Van Dillen, 'Bredero', p. 328.

101 Hooft, *Memoriën en adviezen*, II, p. 45.

102 Van Dillen, 'Bredero', p. 325.

103 Bredero, *Spaanse Brabander*, l. 1177.

104 Ibid., l. 1169.

105 W. D. Hooft, *Andrea de Piere*, cited by Haverman, *W. D. Hooft*, p. 75 (1628).

106 Scheurleer, I, p. 130: 'Aen de kant vant water claer / Sachmen daer al comen / Groot en cleyn, te voet, te paert, / Vrouwen, kinders, mee vergaert, / Riepen, courais, bon Flaman.' (On the shore of the water / All came together there / Great and small, on foot, on horse, / Women, children, gathered together, / Shouting, courage, good Fleming.'

107 Tiele, 'Documenten voor de geschiedenis der Nederlanders in het Oosten', *BMHG*, 6 (1883), p. 253.

108 See also J. den Tex, *Oldenbarnevelt*, 5 vols. (Haarlem, 1960–70), I, pp. 301, 310; Brandt, *Historie*, I, p. 736.

109 ARA, Holland 1363 c, testimony of Willem van Veen, 12 Feb. 1616.

110 See J. Wagenaar, *Vaderlandsche historie*, 21 vols. (Amsterdam, 1749–59), X, p. 201; Van Deursen, *Bavianen en slijkgeuzen*, p. 291.

111 Muller Fzn., *Schetsen*, p. 372.

112 Van Vloten, *Kluchtspel*, II, p. 103.

113 Leeghwater, *Klein kronykje*, p. 9.

114 Moryson, *Itinerary*, III, p. 452; cf. P. Mundy, *Travels in Europe and Asia 1608–1667* IV (London, 1925) p. 79.

115 N. Biestkens, *De drie delen van de klucht van Claas Kloet*, ed. G. R. W. Dibbets (Zwolle, n.d.), p. 93.

116 Le Petit, *Nederlandsche republycke*, p. 81.

117 H. Edema van der Tuuk, *Johannes Bogerman* (Groningen, 1868), p. 11.

118 At least that was how Reyd saw it: *Historie*, p. 351.

119 H. C. Rogge, 'Een preek van Jacobus Trigland', in *Godgeleerde Bijdragen voor 1865* (Amsterdam), p. 794. Cf. Coster, *Rijcke-man*, l. 554.

120 G. J. Quintijn, *De Hollandsche Lijs, met de Brabandsche Bely* (The Hague, 1629), p. 222.

121 Ibid., p. 189.

122 Ibid., p. 187.

123 Moryson, *Itinerary*, IV, p. 214.

124 Van der Laan, *Roemer Visscher*, I, p. 76.

125 Le Petit, *Nederlandsche republycke*, p. 134.

126 P. J. Blok, ed., *Relazioni veneziane. Venetiaansche berichten over de Vereenigde Nederlanden van 1600–1795*, Rijks Geschiedkundige Publicatiën, groote serie, 7 (The Hague, 1909), p. 14.

127 *Beschrijvinghe der stadt Rotterdam* (Leiden, 1942), p. 4.

128 Wtenbogaert, *Brieven*, I, p. 54, to Helmichius and Arent Cornelisz., 26 Feb. 1602.

129 Van Deursen, *Bavianen en slijkgeuzen*, p. 71.

3. OUTSIDE THE COMMUNITY

1 Bredero, *Angeniet*, ll. 251–84.

2 Ligtenberg, *De armezorg*, p. 299, a report on poor relief at Leiden in 1577. A third group is also mentioned: those who work, but have nothing left over for the winter, because they spend everything.

3 Cf. E. Chill, 'Religion and mendicity in seventeenth-century France', *International Review of Social History*, 7 (1962), p. 400; G. Salgado, *Cony-catchers and bawdy baskets: an anthology of Elizabethan low life* (Harmondsworth, 1972), p. 12; A. Hallema, *Geschiedenis van het gevangeniswezen hoofdzakelijk in Nederland* (The Hague, 1958), p. 147.

4 Discharged soldiers as beggars, *Res. Holland*, 1602, p. 57; cf. 1635, p. 159.

5 It was precisely at Leiden that the great number of beggars in the late sixteenth century was proverbial. A. Hallema, 'Jan van Houts rapporten en adviezen betreffende het Amsterdamsche tuchthuis uit de jaren 1597 en '98', *BMHG*, 48 (1927), p. 71.

6 Pringsheim, *Beiträge*, p. 61.

7 Van Meteren, *Commentarien*, book 16, f. 71.

8 ARA, St. Gen. 12.163, proclamation of 19 March 1614.

9 *Res. Holland*, 1601, p. 321.

10 Apart from exceptions such as Enkhuizen in 1618: Brandt and Centen, *Historie*, II, p. 26.

11 C. P. Hooft, *Memoriën*, I, p. 179.

12 S. Muller Fzn., *Schetsen*, p. 397.

13 Van Buchell, *Diarium*, p. 260.

14 Van Buchell described these events on the day that he was told about them in that area, 25 January 1591. But it seems to me not unlikely that he was referring to the same 'horrible murder' mentioned in the Resolutions of Holland in 1587: p. 297.

15 See part II.

16 Bredero, *Werken*, ed. Knuttel, III, p. 393.

17 *Res. Holland*, 1630, p. 23 (21 Feb.).

18 Velius, *Chronyk van Hoorn*, p. 333; Brandt and Centen, *Historie*, p. 62.

19 J. van Vloten, *Paschier de Fyne* ('s-Hertogenbosch, 1853), p. 260; *Korte schets der Nederlandsche historiën*, (Amsterdam n.d.), p. 45.

20 *Res. Holland*, 1597, p. 371.

21 Ibid., 1596, pp. 1, 5.

22 Ibid., 1597, p. 350.

23 Rijsoord 1598 (C. A. Tukker, *De classis Dordrecht van 1573 tot 1609*. Leiden, 1965, p. 83).

24 *Res. Holland*, 1598, p. 281, and 1608, p. 625; G. Udemans, *'t Geestelyck roer van 't coopmansschip*, second edition (Dordrecht, 1640), f. 51 vo.

25 *Res. Holland*, 1611, p. 271.

26 S. van Leeuwen, *Costumen, keuren ende ordonnantien van het baljuschap ende lande van Rijnland* (Leiden, 1667), p. 496 (1613).

27 P. C. Hooft, *Brieven*, p. 10 (1612).

28 Ibid., p. 13.

29 ARA, Hof 5655, ff. 79–81.

30 Léonie van Nierop, 'De bruidegoms van Amsterdam van 1578 tot 1601', *TvG*, 52 (1937), p. 263.

31 Baudartius, *Memoryen*, I, book 5, p. 38.

32 Van de Venne, *Belacchende werelt*, pp. 145–54. Examples are also found in Baudartius, *Memoryen*, I, book 5, p. 40, on miraculous cures in the Amsterdam house of discipline.

33 S. P. l'Honoré Naber, *Beschrijvinghe ende historisch verhael van het Gout-Koninckrijck van Guinea . . . door* P. de Marees (The Hague, 1912), p. 100.

34 *Groot Placaetboek*, I, p. 477.

35 *Res. Holland*, 1586, p. 456, and 1596, p. 3.

36 Bredero, *Klucht van de koe*, ll. 5–6: 'One of those heathens, who promise people good fortune / Which they saw in my hand.'

37 I. H. van Eeghen, 'Zigeuners in Amsterdam in 1554, 1592, 1595, 1725', *Amstelodamum*, 52 (1965), p. 53: Jacob Cornelisz. of Dordrecht, aged 24, from early youth, with his mother, 'walked through the land with heathens'.

38 *Res. Holland*, 1596, p. 4.

39 Ibid., 1645, p. 190.

40 J. Tersteeg, 'Vijf bange jaren (Gouda 1572–1576)', *BVGO*, fourth series, 5 (1906), p. 9.

41 Huygens, *Gedichten*, II, p. 3.

42 *Res. Holland*, 1579, p. 128.

43 *Res. Holland*, 1587, p. 329.

44 Ibid., 1589, p. 422. At least one of these men was later his lieutenant: 1617, p. 6.

45 Ibid., 1589, p. 136.

46 Ibid., 1596, p. 172.

47 Ibid., 1612, p. 129 (Goudriaan).

48 Ibid., 1578, p. 18 (Woerden) and 1586, p. 258 (three stewards in Delfland). General remarks in the instruction for *landdrost* Causaert, 1612, p. 295.

49 Cf. ibid., p. 372: the sheriff of Delft had jurisdiction over only a small area, so that all kinds of criminals could escape very close to Delft itself.

50 Ibid., 1595, p. 97 (Rijnland and Delfland): also Van Buchell, *Diarium*, p. 341 (1593, Rijnland); *Res. Holland*, 1603, p. 263 (Rijnland).

51 Ibid., 1595, p. 97.

52 A. Hallema, 'Vlaardingen en Dordrecht als oudste Nederlandse galeiendepots', *TvG*, 66 (1953).

53 *Res. Holland*, 1597, p. 371.

54 Ibid., 1628, p. 47.

55 Ibid., 1636, p. 180.

56 ARA, St. Gen. 12.163 (19 March 1614); *Res. Holland*, 1647, p. 182. In the same spirit, but somewhat less severe, was the proclamation of 1 January 1596: *Res. Holland*, 1596, p. 2.

57 Ibid., 1589, p. 324.

58 Ibid., 1647, p. 183.

59 J. Koning, *Geschiedkundige aanteekeningen betrekkelijk de lijfstraffelijke regtoefening te Amsterdam* (Amsterdam, 1828), p. 123.

60 ARA, Holland 1384, f. 290 (19 Sept. 1623).

61 Ligtenberg, *De armezorg*, p. 302.

62 *Res. Holland*, 1629, p. 140 (10 Aug.).

63 Ibid., p. 151 (16 Aug.).

64 Ibid., p. 190 (24. Sept.).

65 Ibid., 1648, p. 97 (18 March).

66 Hallema, 'Vlaardingen', p. 86.

67 *Res. Holland*, 1600, p. 137.

68 Ibid., p. 227.

69 Hallema, 'Vlaardingen', p. 84.

70 *Res. Holland*, 1600, p. 283.

71 According to Reyd, *Historie*, p. 435, one pound of bread per day. The ordinance of 1598, however, prescribed two pounds of rye bread and a half-pound of cheese. *Res. Holland*, 1598, p. 242.

72 P. J. Sprenger van Eyck, *Geschiedenis en merkwaardigheden der stad Vlaardingen*, I (Rotterdam, 1831), p. 42.

73 In 1635 Machteltge Arentsdr. van Lodenstein of Rotterdam bequeathed 200 gld. to 'the poor who come out of the galley under the college of admiralty of this place'. *Rotterdamsch Jaarboekje*, second series, I (1913), p. 81.

74 Montchrétien, *Traicté*, p. 101.

75 Hallema, 'Jan van Houts rapporten', p. 72. 'A model of cleanliness, discipline, order and diligent work', p. 72.

76 Koning, *Geschiedkundige aanteekening*, p. 73. That was still possible even in the seventeenth century; see, e.g., Amsterdam ordinance of 1613 (Baudartius, *Memoryen*, I, book 5, p. 27).

77 Koning, *Geschiedkundige aanteekening*, p. 33.

78 Hallema, *Geschiedenis gevangeniswezen*, p. 107.

79 Van Deursen, *Bavianen en slijkgeuzen*, p. 20.

80 A. Hallema, *Haarlemse gevangenissen*, (Haarlem, 1928), p. 75.

81 *Res. Holland*, 1648, p. 97.

82 W. Bezemer, 'Het tucht- en werkhuis te Rotterdam', *Rotterdamsch Jaarboekje* 6 (1899), p. 161; T. Sellin, *Pioneering in penology: the Amsterdam houses of correction in the sixteenth and seventeenth centuries* (Philadelphia, 1944), p. 102.

83 Ibid., p. 90.

84 Ibid., p. 49.

85 Hallema, *Geschiedenis gevangeniswezen*, p. 154.

86 *Gouda*, p. 166.

87 Koning, *Geschiedkundige aanteekening*, p. 34.

88 H. Q. Janssen and J. J. van Toorenenbergen, *Brieven uit onderscheidene kerkelijke archieven*, Werken der Marnixvereeniging, third series, IV (Utrecht, 1880), p. 221: Helmichius to Arent Cornelisz., 6 Aug. 1604.

89 Mundy, *Travels*, IV, p. 73.

90 *Res. Holland*, 1597, p. 104.

91 Hallema, *Geschiedenis gevangeniswezen*, p. 154.

92 Sellin, *Pioneering*, p. 47.

93 Brandt, *Historie*, IV, p. 245; Hallema, 'Jan van Houts rapporten', p. 80.

94 I. Beeckman, *Journal tenu par Isaac Beeckman de 1604 à 1634*, ed. C. de Waard, 4 vols. (The Hague, 1937–52), III, p. 32.

95 John Howard, *The state of the prisons in England and Wales . . .*, 2 parts (Warrington, 1777–80), section IV, 'An account of foreign prisons: Holland'.

96 Van Deursen, *Bavianen en slijkgeuzen*, p. 20.

97 Not. Assendelft, 9 Nov. 1595.

98 *Livre synodal*, p. 127.

99 *Res. Holland*, 1640, p. 264: the deacons of the Walloon community in The Hague request subsidy for their beggars.

100 Not. Monnikendam, 5 Dec. 1599.

101 Not. Waalse kerkeraden Amsterdam, 10 Oct. 1611.

102 Veltenaar, *Het kerkelijk leven*, p. 108.

103 Not. Waalse kerkeraden Leiden, 30 Jan. 1592.

104 E.g. Not. Waalse kerkeraden Amsterdam, 26 July 1587; Not. Naaldwijk, 27 April 1586.

105 Tukker, *De classis Dordrecht*, p. 85.

106 Bor, *Oorsprongk*, III, book 28, f. 44.

107 Acta Edam, 17 Aug. 1620, answer to a gravamen from the *classis* Enkhuizen: 'it is understood that to reduce begging people will not give [alms]'.

108 J. G. W. F. Bik, *Vijf eeuwen medisch leven in een Hollandse stad* (Assen, 1955), p. 57.

109 These were the overseers who took care of poor who lived at home.

110 Coster, *Teeuwis de Boer*, ll. 1183–7.

111 P. C. Hooft, *Brieven*, p. 195.

112 Knuttel Pamphlet 2138.

4. HONEST POVERTY

1 The professions of 706 begging families in 1597 are known: 398 of them worked in the textile industry. Posthumus, *Lakenindustrie*, II, p. 188.

2 Jaanus, *Hervormd Delft*, p. 78.

3 *Res. Holland*, 1594, p. 347; 1595, pp. 46, 100, 103, 157; 1596, pp. 10, 45, 46, 435; 1597, p. 62; Fockema Andreae, *Watersnoden*, p. 16; Reyd, *Historie*, pp. 223, 298.

4 Baudartius, *Memoryen*, II, book 13, pp. 1, 123; book 16, pp. 2, 8; Aitzema, *Saken*, I, p. 269; J. van den Sande, *Nederlandsche historie* (Leeuwaarden, 1650), p. 107; Fockema Andreae, *Watersnoden*, p. 17.

5 For 1594: *Res. Holland*, 1594, p. 128. For 1595: Jaanus, *Hervormd Delft*, p. 80; Posthumus, *Lakenindustrie*, II, p. 134; N. C. Kist, *Neerlands bededagen en biddagsbrieven*, 2 vols. (Leiden, 1848–9), II, p. 73; Velius, *Chronyk van Hoorn*, p. 495; *Res. Holland*, 1595, p. 486; Bor, *Oorsprongk*, IV, book 32, f. 122. For 1596: Reyd, *Historie*, p. 298; *Res. Holland*, 1596, p. 377. For 1597: Velius, *Chronyk van Hoorn*, p. 499; *Res. Holland*, 1597, p. 269. For 1621: Brandt and Centen, *Historie*, II, p. 38; Geyl, *Suriano*, p. 366. For 1622: Brandt and Centen, *Historie*, II, p. 42; Baudartius, *Memoryen*, II, book 14, p. 222. For 1623: Velius, *Chronyk van Hoorn*, p. 611; *Res. Holland*, 1623, p. 169; Ampzing, *Beschryvinge*, p. 415; Baudartius, *Memoryen*, II, book 15, p. 182. For 1624: Baudartius, *Memoryen*, II, book 16, p. 124.

6 G. J. Liesker, *Die staatwissenschaftlichten Anschauungen Dirck Graswinckels* (Freiburg, 1901), p. 83; Van der Woude, *Het Noorderkwartier*, I, p. 203.

7 *Kerkelijk handboekje*, p. 129.

8 Velius, *Chronyk van Hoorn*, p. 533 (1608); Baudartius, *Memoryen*, I, book 18, p. 35 (1616); Brandt, *Historie*, IV, p. 463 (1621).

9 In 1514, 31 per cent of the rural households south of the IJ could be classified as poor, while north of the IJ the comparable figure was 23 per cent. De Vries, *Dutch rural economy*, p. 66.

10 E.g. J. Smit, *Den Haag in den geuzentijd* (n.p., 1922), p. 269.

11 As in *Res. Holland*, 1576, p. 182; Knuttel Pamphlet 4155, p. 16.

12 Brandt and Centen, *Historie*, II, p. 42.

13 Cf. Oldewelt, 'Het aalmoezeniersweeshuis', p. 141.

14 G. R. van Kinschot, *Beschryving der stad Oudewater* (Delft, 1907), p. 441.

15 F. van Mieris, *Handvesten der stad Leyden* (Leiden, 1759), p. 362.

16 ARA, Holland 2619 l.

17 Van Vloten, *Kluchtspel*, II, pp. 13, 14.

18 Van de Venne, *Belacchende werelt*, p. 184.

19 Van der Laan, *Roemer Visscher*, II, p. 39.

20 J. Melles, *Het huys van leeninge. Geschiedenis van de oude lombarden en de stedelijke bank van lening te Rotterdam 1325–1950* (The Hague, 1950), p. 39.

21 Brandt and Centen, *Historie*, II, p. 44.

22 Moryson, *Itinerary*, IV, p. 467.

23 J. Reitsma and S. D. van Veen, *Acta . . . gehouden in de Noordelijke Nederlanden gedurende de jaren 1572–1620*, III (Groningen, 1892), pp. 155, 252, 284.

24 Bredero, *Moortje*, ll. 2746–7.

25 ARA, Hof 385, f. 53 vo.

26 Ibid., esp. f. 151 vo.

27 *Res. Holland*, 1590, p. 246; 1603, p. 254.

28 Ibid., 1603, p. 22.

29 Ibid., 1602, p. 364; 1603, p. 254.

30 De Lange van Wijngaerden, *Geschiedenis . . . van der Goude*, III, p. 30 (Gouda 1606, 300 gld. per year); De Vrankrijker, *Geschiedenis van het Gooiland*, II, p. 201 (Naarden 1626, 25 gld. to the poor, 55 gld. to the town).

31 *Res. Holland*, 1635, p. 75.

32 See Van Deursen, *Bavianen en slijkgeuzen*, Ch. 6.

33 See part III.

34 Van Deursen, 'Kerk of parochie?', p. 532.

35 Ligtenberg, *De armezorg*, p. 230.

36 Van Deursen, *Bavianen en slijkgeuzen*, p. 107.

37 Ibid., p. 109.

38 Ibid., p. 117.

39 Ibid., p. 126.

40 Ibid., p. 417.

41 Ibid., p. 109.

42 Vos Azn., p. 66 (Kudelstaart).

43 Van Leeuwen, *Costumen*, p. 542, regulation of 1637.

44 ARA, RAZH Brielle 1, f. 11 (1614).

45 Bredero, *Angeniet*, ll. 287–92.

5. PATHS UPWARD

1 According to Aitzema, *Saken*, I, p. 720.

2 J. G. van Dillen, *Het oudste aandeelhoudersregister van de kamer Amsterdam der Oost-Indische Compagnie* (The Hague, 1958), p. 108.

3 See above, p. 20.

4 See part III.

5 Wtenbogaert, *Brieven*, I, p. 55 (1602).

6 W. J. Kühler, *Geschiedenis van de doopsgezinden in Nederland*, I (Haarlem, 1940), p. 455.

7 E. Beins, 'Die Wirtschaftsethik der calvinistischen Kirche 1565–1650', *Nederlandsch Archief voor Kerkgeschiedenis*, n. s. 24 (1931), p. 147.

8 J. van den Vondel, *Werken*, ed. J. van Lennep, rev. J. H. W. Unger (Leiden, n.d.), II, p. 289.

9 Melles, *Huys van leeninge*, p. 81.

10 Van Deursen, *Resolutiën*, I, p. 791.

11 Leupe, 'Zeezaken', p. 107. Cf. Hooft and Coster, *Warenar*, ll. 1268–9: 'Will you each put in something and venture together / Like all the little vessels on the great voyages?'

12 E. H. Krelage, *Bloemenspeculatie in Nederland* (Amsterdam, 1942), p. 24.

13 Ibid., p. 32.

14 Ibid., p. 42.

15 Van der Woude, *Het Noorderkwartier*, I, p. 48.

16 Van Dillen, *Rijkdom*, p. 219.

17 Krelage, *Bloemenspeculatie*, p. 41.

18 Aitzema, *Saken*, II, p. 504.

19 Krelage, *Bloemenspeculatie*, p. 45.

20 Aitzema, *Saken*, II, p. 503.

21 Krelage, *Bloemenspeculatie*, p. 64.

22 Aitzema, *Saken*, II, p. 504.

23 *Res. Holland*, 1636, p. 183; also p. 150.

24 Krelage, *Bloemenspeculatie*, p. 83; Van Dillen, *Rijkdom*, p. 219.

25 *Res. Holland*, 1637, 84.

26 J. L. Price, *Culture and society in the Dutch republic during the 17th century* (London, 1974), p. 160.

27 Ibid., p. 134.

28 A. Houbraken, *De groote schouburgh der Nederlantsche konstschilders en schilderessen*, ed. P. T. A. Swillens, 3 vols. (Maastricht, 1943–4), I, p. 224.

29 Price, *Culture and society*, p. 135.

30 G. J. Hoogewerff, *De geschiedenis van de St. Lucasgilden in Nederland* (Amsterdam, 1947), p. 142.

31 Ibid., p. 130.

32 Price, *Culture and society*, p. 120.

33 Hoogewerff, *St. Lucasgilden*, p. 81.

34 Houbraken, *Groote schouburgh*, I, p. 233.

35 G. Brom, *Schilderkunst en litteratuur in de 16e en 17e eeuw* (Utrecht, 1957), p. 178; Hoogewerff, *St. Lucasgilden*, p. 26; Houbraken, *Groote schouburgh*, I, p. 48.

36 A. Blankert, *Johannes Vermeer van Delft 1632–1675* (Utrecht, 1975), p. 7.

37 Price, *Culture and society*, p. 137.

38 Ibid., p. 149.

39 Houbraken, *Groote schouburgh*, I, p. 251.

40 Ibid., p. 137.

41 Hoogewerff, *St Lucasgilden*, p. 26.

42 Ibid., p. 28.

43 C. Hofstede de Groot, *Die Urkunden über Rembrandt* (The Hague, 1906), p. 174.

44 Hoogewerff, *Groote schouburgh*, p. 31.

45 H. Floerke, *Studien zur niederländischen Kunst- und Kulturgeschichte* (Munich, 1905), p. 12.

46 On this subject see the excellent chapter in Price, *Culture and society*: 'Painting – The artist as craftsman', pp. 119–69.

47 Price, *Culture and society*, p. 121.

48 Ibid., p. 134.

49 Ibid., p. 122.

50 Floerke, *Studien*, p. 181.

51 Data found in Hofstede de Groot, *Urkunden*, pp. 80, 84, 139; Van Dillen, *Bronnen*, III, p. 389.

52 Selling prices found in Floerke, *Studien*, p. 21; A. van der Willigen, *Les artistes de Harlem*, p. 69; Price, *Culture and society*, p. 121. A. Chong, 'The market for landscape painting in seventeenth-century Holland', in *Masterpieces of Dutch landscape painting*, ed. P. C. Sutton (Boston and London, 1987); J. M. Montias, *Artists and artisans in Delft: A socio-economic study of the seventeenth century* (Princeton, 1982).

53 Lotteries cited in Van der Willigen, *Artistes de Harlem*, pp. 11, 13.

54 Houbraken, *Groote schouburgh*, I, p. 255.

55 Ibid., p. 39.

56 Hofstede de Groot, *Urkunden*, p. 84.

57 Ibid., p. 80.

58 Ibid., pp. 9, 15.

59 S. Slive, *Rembrandt and his critics 1636–1730* (The Hague, 1953), p. 7.

60 Hofstede de Groot, *Urkunden*, p. 75.

61 Hoogewerff, *St. Lucasgilden*, p. 97.

62 Kernkamp, 'Memoriën van ridder Theodorus Rodenburg ...', *BMHG*, 23 (1902), p. 227.

63 Houbraken, *Groote schouburgh*, I, pp. 31, 96.

64 N. Mout, *Bohemen en de Nederlanden in de zestiende eeuw* (Leiden, 1975), p. 70.

65 Houbraken, *Groote schouburgh*, I, p. 216.

66 Ibid., p. 140.

67 Ibid., II, p. 26.

68 Ibid., I, p. 101.

69 Ibid., p. 179.

70 Ibid., p. 186.

71 Ibid., p. 217.

72 Brom, *Johannes Vermeer*, p. 182.

73 Houbraken, *Groote schouburgh*, I, p. 118; Mout, *Bohemen*, p. 93.

74 Cf. Price, *Culture and society*, p. 133.

75 Houbraken, *Groote schouburgh*, I, p. 38.

76 Ibid., p. 93.

77 Ibid., p. 72.

78 Ibid., p. 223.

79 Hoogewerff, *St. Lucasgilden*, pp. 82, 93.

80 Ibid., p. 185.

81 Houbraken, *Groote schouburgh*, I, p. 180.

82 Hoogewerff, *St Lucasgilden*, p. 83.

83 Houbraken, *Groote schouburgh*, I, p. 48.

84 Ibid., p. 29.

85 Ibid., II, p. 25.

86 Ibid., p. 15.

87 Ibid., p. 18.

88 Ibid., I, p. 256.

89 Ibid., p. 73.

90 Ibid., p. 224.

91 Ibid., p. 114.

92 Ibid., p. 222.

93 Ibid., p. 115.

94 Ibid., p. 196.

95 Van der Willigen, *Artistes de Harlem*, p. 85.

96 Houbraken, *Groote schouburgh*, I, p. 41.

97 Ibid., p. 74.

98 L'Honoré Naber, 'De With', p. 65.

99 J. C. M. Warnsinck, *Drie zeventiende-eeuwse admiraals* (Amsterdam, 1943), cited by Graefe, *Tromp*, p. xiv.

100 Warnsinck, *Admiraals*, p. 47.

101 Grafe, *Tromp*, p. 87.

102 Aitzema, *Saken*, II, p. 342.

103 Warnsinck, *Admiraals*, p. 68.

104 Graefe, *Tromp*, p. 45.

105 Ibid., p. 51.

106 H. C. Rogge, *Brieven van Nicolaes van Reigersberch aan Hugo de Groot* (Amsterdam, 1901), p. 208.

107 J. C. A. de Meij, *De watergeuzen en de Nederlanden 1568–1572* (Amsterdam, 1972), pp. 43, 154.

108 *Res. Holland*, 2 April 1579.

109 Knuttel Pamphlet 4682, p. 17.

110 Graefe, *Tromp*, p. 130.

111 Warnsinck, *Admiraals*, p. 8.

112 Ibid., p. 63. In 1629, Tromp had already been promoted over the head of De With to flag-captain under Piet Hein; Hein himself showed a preference for De With, p. 62.

113 Graefe, *Tromp*, p. 53.

114 Knuttel Pamphlet 4682, p. 3.

115 Van Deursen, *Bavianen en slijkgeuzen*, pp. 69ff.

6. WOMEN AND GIRLS

1 Guicciardini (Guicciardijn), *Beschryvinghe van alle de Nederlanden*, tr. Cornelius Kilianius, revised by Petrus Montanus (Amsterdam, 1912), p. 206.

2 S. Muller Fzn., *Schetsen*, p. 455.

3 Carnero, *Historia*, p. 4.

4 Van Meteren, *Commentarien*, book 16, f. 72.

5 J. Cats, *Al de werken* (Schiedam, n.d.), p. 292.

6 Ibid., p. 287.

7 Van der Laan, *Roemer Visscher*, II, p. 51: 'For you I scorned the widow of Jan Cuyf, / Although she was round of breasts and buttocks.'

8 Ibid., I, p. 69.

9 C. Busken Huet, *Het land van Rembrand*, third edition, II (Haarlem, 1898), 2e stuk, p. 318.

10 S. Muller Fzn., *Schetsen*, p. 455.

11 Van Buchell, *Diarium*, p. 228.

12 Moryson, *Itinerary*, IV, p. 469.

13 Ibid., III, p. 350. Cf. Van Buchell, *Diarium*, p. 228, on the women of Amsterdam: 'mulieres mercaturae deditas, sed viris imperantes'.

14 Van der Laan, *Roemer Visscher*, II, p. 44 (Roemer Visscher).

15 Cats, p. 235 ('Houwelick, Vrouwe'); Acta Den Briel, 23 Aug. 1621 and 26 April 1622.

16 W. P. Frijlinck, *The Tragedy of Sir John van Olden Barnevelt* (Amsterdam, 1922), p. 22. Cf. p. CL, from Fletcher's *The little French lawyer*: 'Nor would I be a Dutchman / To have my wife, my sovereign, to command me.'

17 Carnero, *Historia*, p. 4.

18 Moryson, *Itinerary*, IV, p. 468.

19 Cats, *Werken*, p. 10 ('Sinne- en minnebeelden').

20 Ibid., p. 31 ('Galathea ofte hardersminneklachte').

21 Not. Edam, 21 Dec. 1597.

22 Not. Schipluiden, 21 May 1595.
23 See also Not. Charlois, 7 Sept. 1607; Not. Purmerend, 29 June 1613; Not. Schipluiden, 2 Oct. 1594.
24 Moryson, *Itinerary*, IV, p. 468.
25 Not. Haarlem, 3 Oct. 1623.
26 UB Amsterdam, III H 4, f. 14 vo.
27 Haverman, *W. D. Hooft*, p. 42 (*Doortrapte Melis*); Van Moerkerken, *Kluchtspel*, I, p. 105 (Van Santen, *Snappende Sijtgen*).
28 Not. Edam, 17 March 1596; Not. Schipluiden, 6 Dec. 1598; M. W. Schakel, *Geschiedenis van de hoge en vrije heerlijkheden van Noordeloos en Over Slingeland* (Gorinchem, 1955), p. 60; ARA, W. K. Haag 30, verklaring van Yvo Borel. A non-churchly source in P. A. Tiele, 'Steven van der Haghen's avonturen van 1575 tot 1597 door hem zelven verhaald', *BMHG*, 6 (1883), p. 3820.
29 Cats, *Werken*, p. 52 ('Tegenliedt van een trouw-gesinde vrijster het houwelijken aen-radende').
30 See part I, p. 9.
31 Boekenoogen, *Genoechlijcke history vanden schricklijcken ende onvervaerden reus Gilias* (Leiden, 1903), p. 3.
32 Baudartius, *Memoryen*, II, book 15, p. 174.
33 Van Buchell, *Diarium*, p. 211.
34 W. J. C. Buitendijk, *Het calvinisme in de spiegel van de Zuid-Nederlandse literatuur der contra-reformatie* (Groningen, 1942), p. 122.
35 Van der Laan, *Roemer Visscher*, I, p. 29.
36 Van Deursen, *Bavianen en slijkgeuzen*, p. 135.
37 H. Kaajan, *De pro-acta der Dordtsche synode in 1618* (Rotterdam, 1914), p. 337.
38 At least in the sixteenth and early seventeenth century. Wassenburgh confirms that by 1641 freer attitudes were coming into vogue; see Wassenburgh, *Dans-feest der dochteren te Silo* (Dordrecht, 1641), pp. 34, 183, 203, and especially the preface.
39 Vázquez, cited by J. Brouwer, *Kronieken van Spaansche soldaten uit het begin van den tachtigjarigen oorlog* (Zutphen, 1933), p. 106.
40 Wassenburgh, *Dans-feest*, p. 128.
41 Not. Berkel, 24 March 1595 (dance hall at Bleiswijk); Acta Gorinchem, 18 April 1589 (Hoornaar); Not. Berkel, 6 March 1622.
42 Not. Edam, 17 Dec. 1598.
43 Ibid., 3 Feb. 1619.
44 Not. Naaldwijk, 21 Oct. 1590.
45 Not. 't Woud, 23 Nov. 1603.
46 G. Udemans, *Practyke, dat is werckelijcke oeffeninge van de christelijcke hooftdeughden*, second edition (Dordrecht, 1640), p. 279.
47 *Heidelberg Catechism*, answer 109. An attempt at supplying further written evidence appears in C. Grevinghovius, *Onveranderde uitgave van fondamentboek van de ware christelijke ghereformeerde religie* (Lemmer, 1871), p. 364; also on p. 313: at the marriage at Cana, Christ did not dance.
48 Not. Zevenhuizen, 18 Sept. 1605.
49 Van Buchell, *Diarium*, p. 188.
50 G. D. J. Schotel, *Kerkelijk Dordrecht*, I (Utrecht, 1841), p. 168.
51 Not. Monnikendam, 9 Sept. 1599.
52 Wassenburgh, *Dans-feest*, p. 192.
53 Brouwer, *Kronieken*, p. 107.
54 J. Scheltema, *Volksgebruiken der Nederlanders bij het vrijen en trouwen* (Utrecht, 1832), p. 12.

55 Cats, *Werken*, p. 291 ('Spiegel, bedencklijcke gevallen').
56 Van Buchell, *Diarium*, p. 288.
57 Brandt, *Historie der reformatie*, II, p. 18.
58 Van Moerkerken, *Kluchtspel*, I, p. 67, and II, p. 600 (Van Santen, *Lichte Wigger*).
59 Biestkens, *Claas Kloet*, p. 79. On servant-girls see also Bredero, *Griane*, ll. 1548–9, and Haverman, *W. D. Hooft*, p. 77 (*Andrea de Piere*).
60 Van der Laan, *Roemer Visscher*, II, p. 48.
61 Cats, *Werken*, p. 116 ('Velt-teycken'). For similar reactions to Joseph in another country and another century, see Juan Valera, *Juanita la larga*, cap. xxxvii.
62 J. Cos, *Rechts-geleerde verhandelinge over de troubeloften en het daerop volgende huwelyk* (Hoorn, 1738), p. 69.
63 Acta Edam, 2 Oct. 1606.
64 Acta Woerden, 18 June 1620; ARA, W. K. Haag 30 (ca. 1629). In both cases the guilty party was a preacher.
65 ARA, Hof 5219, arrest of several medical doctors. The prescriptions are found in the dossier.
66 ARA, Hof 386, f. 30.
67 De Bosch Kemper, *Geschiedkundig onderzoek*, pp. 84, 90.
68 Quintijn, *Hollandsche Lijs*, p. 174, examples from Haarlem, 1627. In general, Bredero, *Griane*, l. 1551: 'this means that a child could fall into the privy, or the water'.
69 Knuttel Pamphlet 1442, A4.
70 Not. Edam, 6 June 1621.
71 Acta Edam, 7 June 1621.
72 Haverman, *W. D. Hooft*, p. 40.
73 Cats, *Werken*, p. 238 ('Houwelick, Vrouwe').
74 L. J. van Apeldoorn, *Geschiedenis van het Nederlandsche Huwelijksrecht voor de invoering van de franse wetgeving* (Amsterdam, 1925), pp. 45, 79.
75 Not. Haarlem, 2 July 1624.
76 ARA, DTB Hoornaar Ia, f. 90 vo. For other cases of the man as plaintiff, see Acta Delft, 13 Jan. 1609 (Zoetermeer), and Not. Monnikendam, 4 May 1617.
77 Van Apeldoorn, *Huwelijksrecht*, p. 78.
78 Ibid., p. 115; Van der Laan, *Roemer Visscher*, I, p. 56.
79 W. van Engelenburgh, *Geschiedenis van Broek in Waterland van de 16e tot het begin der 19e eeuw* (Haarlem, 1907), p. 127 (1608).
80 Not. Oudewater, 10 Nov. 1610.
81 Not. Edam, 31 Dec. 1606.
82 Thus Van Apeldoorn, *Huwelijksrecht*, p. 116, is correct, in opposition to Fockema Andreae, who regarded all promises of marriage in the Republic as *sponsalia de futuro*. Cf. Acta Delft, 13 Jan. 1609, where the *classis* established that there 'is no small difference between promises *de futuro* and promises *de praesenti*'.
83 J. van Apeldoorn, 'De historische ontwikkeling van het recht omtrent de huwelijkssluiting in Nederland', in *Christendom en historie* … (Amsterdam, 1925), p. 179.
84 Van Apeldoorn, *Huwelijksrecht*, pp. 91, 115.
85 Not. Monnikendam, 4 May 1617.
86 Acta Dordrecht, 1–3 July 1625.
87 Not. Naaldwijk, 15 Feb. 1575; Acta Delft, 26 June 1603; Acta Den Briel, 23 Oct. 1619.
88 The bride: Not. Haarlem, 30 May 1610; the bridegroom: *Livre synodal*, p. 109.
89 For this rule, see Van Deursen, *Bavianen en slijkgeuzen*, p. 142.
90 Not. Haarlem, Easter 1608.
91 *Res. Holland*, 1608, p. 530.

92 Exodus 22:16, and Deuteronomy 22:28.

93 *Kerkelijk handboekje uitgegeven door de synode der Afgescheiden Gereformeerde Gemeente* (Kampen, 1861), p. 158.

94 A. C. Crena de Iongh, *G. C. van Santen's Lichte Wigger en Snappende Sijtgen* (Assen, 1959), p. 309; *Res. Holland*, 1603, p. 326.

95 Acta Edam, 23 May and 23 June 1622, 23 Feb. 1623, 5 Feb. 1624.

96 Acta Gorinchem, 8 June 1599. Thus Carolus Petri, preacher at Purmerend, also said that he had intercourse with his wife before the banns had been announced, but 'this ... was not in whoredom, but living with her lawfully, since between them they had made mutual promises, and this was a secret marriage'. Acta Edam, 2 Oct. 1606.

97 Not. Haarlem, 14 and 17 April 1620.

98 Ibid., 26 July 1620; Acta Alkmaar, 10 Aug. 1620.

99 Secret marriage vows held invalid: Not. Monnikendam, 16 May 1602; *Livre synodal*, p. 129.

100 By refusing to accept coitus as grounds for requiring marriage, the community also prevented minors from marrying against the wishes of their parents: cf. ARA, Hof 5215 (request from the sheriff of Grotebroek, regarding a young man aged seventeen who had run away with a public whore, to force his parents to consent).

101 Not. Schipluiden, 18 Oct. 1606.

102 Not. Haarlem, 25 May 1621.

103 Van Apeldoorn, *Huwelijksrecht*, p. 184.

104 Acta Leiden, 20 Feb. 1585 and 16 Nov. 1599; Acta Den Briel, 12 Oct. 1598.

105 Bor, *Oorsprongk*, III, book 29, f. 15.

106 Van Vloten, *Kluchtspel*, II, p. 252.

107 Biestkens, *Claas Kloet*, p. 42.

108 Coster, *Teeuwis de Boer*, ll. 207–8.

109 Cats, *Werken*, p. 152 ('Houwelick, Maeght').

110 Daelemans, 'Leiden', p. 199.

111 Haverman, *W. D. Hooft*, p. 41.

112 Velius, *Chronyk van Hoorn*, p. 611; *Res. Holland*, 1623, p. 169; Ampzing, *Beschryvinge*, p. 415; Baudartius, *Memoryen*, II, book 15, p. 182.

113 Van der Woude, *Het Noorderkwartier*, I, p. 253.

114 Van Meteren, *Commentarien*, book 16, f. 72.

115 *Kronijk van het Historisch Genootschap*, 22 (1866), p. 123

116 Baudartius, *Memoryen*, I, book 5, p. 37 (1613).

117 On the scruples of Catholics in the Rijnland in 1580, see Van Leeuwen, *Costumen*, p. 414.

118 *Res. Holland*, 1589, p. 727.

119 Ibid., 1597, p. 58.

120 Not. Den Briel, 4 April 1625.

121 N. Plomp, *Woerden 600 jaar stad* (Woerden, 1972), p. 113.

122 *Res. Holland*, 1589, p. 121.

123 Reitsma and Van Veen, *Acta*, I, p. 252.

124 Ibid., I, p. 216 (1596, *classis* Hoorn); Not. Hem, 13 Jan. 1613; Not. Purmerend, 19 July 1622; *Res. Holland*, 1589, p. 121.

125 Not. Oudewater, 15 Jan. 1606; Not. Zevenhuizen, 12 March 1625.

126 Evenhuis, *Amsterdam*, II, p. 103.

127 Not. Edam, 6 May 1607.

128 Hooft, *Brieven*, p. 50 (1617).

129 L. d'Heere, *Den hof en boorngaard der poësien*, ed. W. Waterschoot (Zwolle, 1962), p. 14.

7. THE NATURAL LIFE

1 Van Deursen, *Bavianen en slijkgeuzen*, p. 193.

2 Galatians 5:19–20.

3 Wassenburgh, *Dans-feest*, p. 32.

4 N. Wiltens and P. Scheltus, *Kerkelyk Plakaatboek*, 2 vols. (The Hague, 1722–35), I, p. 720.

5 A. Hallema, 'Rechterlijke maatstaven ten aanzien van de morele integriteit in het verleden', *Verslagen en mededeelingen van de vereeniging tot uitgaaf der bronnen van het Oud-Vaderladsche recht*, 12 (Utrecht, 1962), p. 410 (Amsterdam, 1580); Bik, *Medisch leven*, p. 436.

6 Koning, *Geschiedkundige aanteekeningen*, p. 40.

7 For example, for Amsterdam, ibid., p. 103.

8 A. C. van Aelst, *Schets der staatkundige en kerkelijke geschiedenis … der stad Oudewater* (Gouda, n.d.), p. 502.

9 Bik, *Medisch leven*, p. 56. Cf. Jaanus, *Hervormd Delft*, p. 109, for Delft 1584.

10 Knuttel Pamphlet 2090 (1613).

11 Dordrecht, 1610 (Schotel, *Dordrecht*, p. 169), and especially Haarlem (Reitsma and Van Veen, *Acta*, II, p. 21, and Not. Haarlem, 25 March 1622.

12 Bredero, *Klucht van den Meulenaer*, ll. 14–15. See also his *Klucht van de Koe*, ll. 207–8.

13 Hallema, *Haarlemse gevangenissen*, p. 74.

14 Uytenbogaert, *Historie*, p. 819 (1618).

15 P. Hoekstra, *Bloemendaal* (Wormerveer, 1947), p. 102.

16 ARA, Admiraliteit 646, 25 April 1602, on prostitution at Voorburg.

17 ARA, Hof 5240, testimony of Havius, 16 April 1647 (Zuylesteyn); J. J. Poelhekke, *Frederik Hendrik* (Nijmegen, 1978), p. 219 (the French ambassador).

18 Crena de Iongh, *G. C. van Santen*, p. 165.

19 Bredero, *Spaanse Brabander*, ll. 731–819.

20 Koning, *Geschiedkundige aanteekeningen*, p. 28.

21 Brouwer, *Kronieken*, p. 111.

22 Haverman, *W. D. Hooft*, p. 86.

23 Bredero, *Spaanse Brabander*, l. 575.

24 Ibid., l. 580.

25 Ibid., l. 815.

26 Ibid., ll. 818–19.

27 Ibid. l. 694.

28 Cf. John Marston, *The Dutch Courtesan*, II.II. See also L. C. van de Pol, 'Beeld en werkelijkheid van de prostitutie in de zeventiende eeuw', in G. Hekma and H. Roodenburg, *Soete minne en helsche boosheit. Seksuele voorstellingen in Nederland 1300–1850* (Nijmegen, 1988), p. 136.

29 Bredero, *Moortje*, ll. 2779ff.

30 S. Muller Fzn., *Schetsen*, p. 452.

31 For this and what follows, ARA, Hof 5215, investigation carried out by the sheriff and councillors, 20 Sept. 1612.

32 I know only of the schoolmaster Mieus Claessen, Not. Krommenie, 28 May 1625.

33 Not. Zevenhuizen, 18 Dec. 1605, 15 March, 20 Aug. and 20 Dec. 1606, 8 March 1609; Not. Krommenie, 25 Dec. 1605; Not. Oudewater, 18 March 1605 and 6 March 1611; Not. Naaldwijk, 23 April and 7 May 1617; Not. Assendelft, 30 June 1619; Acta Edam, 29 July 1619 (Ransdorp) and 19 April 1621 (Edam); Not. Purmerend, 31 Dec. 1619; *Livre synodal*, p. 202 (Amsterdam); Jaanus, *Hervormd Delft*, p. 75 (Delft).

34 Part I, p. 25.

35 Van Moerkerken, *Kluchtspel*, I, p. 123.

36 Ampzing, *Beschryvinge*, p. 48.

37 Moryson, *Itinerary*, III, p. 469. On the skippers, see also Knuttel Pamphlet 1450 ('Let the skippers save a bit on beer; they will be better able to earn their bread') and on pilots Cats, *Werken*, p. 343 ('what moves him the most is a full tankard').

38 Moryson, *Itinerary*, IV, p. 63.

39 Lord Herbert of Cherbury, *Autobiography*, ed. S. L. Lee (London, 1886), p. 117.

40 Carleton, *Letters*, p. 225.

41 Cos, *Rechts-geleerde verhandelinge*, p. 36.

42 Carnero, *Historia*, p. 3.

43 Westermannus, *Christelijke zee-vaert*, p. 220.

44 D. Souterius, *Nuchteren Loth* (Haarlem, 1623), p. 19.

45 Ibid., p. 9.

46 Moryson, *Itinerary*, IV, p. 63.

47 Wagenaar, *Vaderlandsche historie*, X, p. 334.

48 Van Moerkerken, *Kluchtspel*, I, p. 136 (W. D. Hooft, *Andrea de Piere*). At the burial of the Hague surgeon Gangelof in 1612 nearly 73 litres of French wine were drunk: R. Krul, *Haagsche doctoren, chirurgen en apothekers in den ouden tijd* (The Hague, 1891), p. 70.

49 Not. Haarlem, 14 July 1628.

50 J. van Beverwijck, *Schat der gesondheydt* (Amsterdam, 1652), p. 145.

51 Moryson, *Itinerary*, I, p. 102.

52 Knuttel Pamphlet 5596, p. 30.

53 Brandt and Centen, *Historie*, II, p. 24.

54 Mundy, *Travels*, IV, p. 66 (Amsterdam).

55 Bik, *Medisch leven*, p. 52.

56 Van Leeuwen, *Costumen*, p. 360.

57 ARA, Part. Not. Amsterdam 1, memorial on the *doleantie* of the leaseholders, March 1614.

58 Westermannus, *Christelijke zee-vaert*, p. 217.

59 *Res. Holland*, 1605, p. 125.

60 *Keuren der stede van Oudewater des graefschaps van Hollant* (Oudewater, 1605), p. 74 (1605).

61 A. Beels, *Handvesten en privilegiën mitsgaders keuren en ordonnantiën van Assendelft* (Amsterdam, 1768), p. 160 (1614).

62 According to *Res. Holland*, 1599, p. 198, at that time the price of a can of beer in the village of De Lier was $1\frac{1}{2}$ stuivers. Moryson reported that guests in the Leiden inns who drank a great deal of beer with their meals paid fifteen stuivers, while more moderate drinkers paid ten stuivers (Moryson, *Itinerary*, I, p. 97). In the seventeenth century the prices were probably somewhat higher.

63 Biestkens, *Claas Kloet*, p. 100.

64 Ibid., p. 127.

65 Although Bredero in his drinking songs also mentions staggering quantities: *Werken*, ed. Knuttel, III, p. 103.

66 Schotmüller, 'Reise-eindrücke', p. 271.

67 *Res. Holland*, 1609, p. 790.

68 Moryson, *Itinerary*, I, pp. 97, 102, speaks in 1592 and 1593 of eighteen to twenty stuivers for a pot of Rhenish wine.

69 ARA, Holland 2619 l.

70 Quintijn, *Hollandsche Lijs*, p. 134: 'Clink, clink, clink – they throw the glasses / Just like fools / Against the wall and partition.'

71 Crena de Iongh, *G. C. Van Santen*, pp. 163, 210, 211.

72 S. Muller Fzn., p. 420; Van Vloten, *Kluchtspel*, II, p. 14; Moryson, *Itinerary*, I, p. 99.

73 H. van Bleiswijck, *Vervolg van de beschryvinge der stad Delft* (Delft, n.d.), II, p. 732; Ampzing, *Beschryvinge*, p. 337.

74 Bylsma, *Rotterdams welvaren*, p. 103.

75 Van Meteren, *Commentarien*, book 19, f. 168 vo.

76 Robert Burton, *The anatomy of Melancholy*, partition II, section IV, member II, sub-section I.

77 Udemans, *Geestelyck roer*, f. 49.

78 Bredero, *Griane*, ll. 7–11.

79 Not. Graft, 24 March 1623.

80 Cats, *Werken*, p. 5 ('Sinne- en minnebeelden').

81 *Res. Holland*, 1647, p. 130.

82 Bredero, *Klucht van den meulenaer*, ll. 73–5.

83 P. H. Engels, *De belastingen en geldmiddelen van den aanvang der Republiek tot op heden* (Utrecht, 1862), p. 89.

84 Quintijn, *Hollandsche Lijs*, p. 196. Cf. Van de Venne, *Belacchende werelt*, p. 70.

85 P. Zumthor, *La vie quotidienne en Hollande au temps de Rembrandt* (Paris, 1959), p. 201.

86 *Res. Holland*, 1630, p. 125.

87 Ibid., 1644, p. 120.

88 Ibid., p. 90.

89 Souterius, *Nuchteren Loth*, p. 129. On political discussions at the inns, see also Knuttel Pamphlet 2698; ARA, Hof 384, f. 151; Schakel, *Noordeloos*, p. 75.

90 Bik, *Medisch leven*, p. 437.

91 Buitendijk, 'Wilhelmus', p. 241.

92 See part III, chapter 13.

93 D. F. Scheurleer, *Van varen en vechten*, I (The Hague, 1914), p. 110.

94 Ibid., p. 212.

95 Cited in Bredero, *Moortje*, l. 3151. On card games, see Knuttel Pamphlet 1397.

96 Beeckman, *Journal*, III, p. 248, proposed introducing time-clocks in chess matches to arrive at a more just division of the stakes.

97 Schottmüller, 'Reise-eindrücke', p. 270 (1636).

98 Beeckman, *Journal*, I, p. 40. People would bet on reaching a certain total in a specified number of throws, or on the number of spots on one die.

99 A case of discipline, e.g. Not. Monnikendam, 12 Nov. 1617.

100 ARA, RAZH Brielle l, f. 27.

101 D. Burger van Schoorel, *Chronyk van de stad Medemblik* (Hoorn, 1767), p. 249.

102 W. Bezemer, 'Een weddenschap om een huis', *Rotterdamsch Jaarboekje*, 3 (1892), p. 224.

103 Burger van Schoorel, *Chronyk*, p. 116.

104 Not. Barendrecht, n.d. 1592; Not. Osterland, n.d. 1602; Not. Naaldwijk, 23 May 1604; Not. Monnikendam, 27 July 1608; Not. Hem, 12 May 1613.

105 Van Leeuwen, *Costumen*, p. 360. Compare, however, *Res. Holland*, 1612, p. 298, where a purchase made in drunkenness was annulled 'as a special favour, and not as a matter of law'. Perhaps the term had not been taken into account.

106 *Res. Holland*, 1574, p. 89.

107 *Res. Holland*, 1612, p. 45.

108 Bredero, *Klucht van den meulenaer*, l. 224.

109 Not. Edam, 5 Sept. 1599; Not. Uitgeest, visitatieregister, 28 Sept. 1625.

110 Not. Den Briel, 11 June 1624.

111 A. C. Duker, *Gisbertus Voetius*, 3 vols. (Leiden, 1897–1914), I, p. 20; J. L. van der

Gouw, 'Voorschoten tijdens het twaalfjarig bestand', *Mededelingenblad van de Historische Vereniging vor de Provincie Zuid-Holland*, 1:2 (1948), p. 5.

112 Reitsma and Van Veen, *Acta*, II, pp. 399, 426; Jaanus, *Hervormd Delft*, p. 135.

113 Van Deursen, *Bavianen en slijkgeuzen*, p. 141.

114 Acta Delft, 2 Oct. 1606.

115 Van Moerkerken, *Kluchtspel*, I, p. 104.

116 Van Vloten, *Kluchtspel*, II, p. 129.

117 Van Buchell, *Diarium*, p. 315.

118 Van Leeuwen, *Costumen*, p. 487 (Rijnland 1575); J. van der Eyck, *Corte beschrijvinghe mitsgaders hantvesten ... van den lande van Zuyt-Hollandt* (Dordrecht, 1628), p. 446 (bailiwick of South Holland, 1621).

119 Not. Alkamaar, 25 June 1606.

120 Acta Dordrecht, 16–17 April 1624.

121 *Kerkelijk handboekje*, p. 110 (synod of Dordrecht, 1578).

122 *Res. Holland*, 1589, p. 437.

123 E.g. Van Leeuwen, *Costumen*, p. 486 (1585); Van der Eyck, *Corte beschrijvinghe*, p. 446 (1620); ARA, Holland 1384, f. 4 (1621).

124 Van Leeuwen, *Costumen*, p. 484 (1584).

125 Fokker, *Geschiedenis der loterijen*, p. 68.

126 Van Gils, *Dokter*, p. 123.

127 Cats, *Werken*, p. 301 ('Spiegel').

128 Souterius, *Nuchteren Loth*, p. 145: 'Whoever refuses to take part is thought to be a scary cat.'

129 ARA, Hof 386, f. 85 vo. (1616).

130 ARA, Hof 5215, examination of Jan Bouwensz.

131 W. G. D. Murray, 'Oud-Rotterdamsch kroegleven', *Rotterdamsch Jaarboekje*, fifth series, 2 (1944), p. 64.

132 'Gemengd nieuws van de Roosandse Kermis', *Rotterdamsch Jaarboekje*, sixth series, 2 (1954), p. 73.

133 Hooft, *Brieven*, p. 233.

134 ARA, RAZH Brielle I, f. 31.

135 Schakel, *Noordeloos*, p. 63.

136 Hooft, *Brieven*, p. 20 (1612).

137 Schakel, *Noordeloos*, p. 68.

138 Hooft, *Brieven*, p. 53 (1617).

139 Bredero, *Werken*, ed. Knuttel, III, p. 115.

140 S. Muller Fzn., *Schetsen*, p. 396.

141 *Groot Placaetboek*, I, p. 523.

142 ARA, Hof 5221, *informatie* regarding Henrick Claire.

143 Wiltens and Scheltus, *Kerkelyk Plakaatboek*, I, p. 716.

144 E.g., *Keuren Oudewater*, pp. 114, 123; *Res. Holland*, 1606, p. 92 (Nieuwkoop).

145 *Res. Holland*, 1600, p. 33 (Oude Tonge). Cf. Baars, *Landbouw*, p. 38: workers on the dikes of the Nieuw-Beyerland polder were forbidden to possess weapons (1582).

146 Kranenburg, *Zeevisscherij*, p. 94.

147 *Groot Placaetboek*, I, p. 523.

148 Note that death within one day could result from wounds to the leg (Brandt, *Historie*, IV, p. 546); to the shoulder (ibid.); to the left arm (Hooft, *Brieven*, p. 97). Death within several days after a wound to the stomach: ibid., p. 211, and Baudartius, *Memoryen*, I, book 9, p. 22.

149 As Den Tex does: *Oldenbarnevelt*, I, p. 40.

150 Carleton, *Letters*, pp. 11, 22.
151 E.g. Scheurleer, *Varen en vechten*, I, p. 160.
152 Baudartius, *Memoryen*, II, book 15, p. 37.
153 Brandt, *Historie*, II, p. 19. In 1601 the Hoge Raad proposed to make all persons present at a manslaughter pay a fine of 12 gld., unless they brought the perpetrator to the sheriff.
154 ARA, Admiraliteit 646, 25 April 1602.
155 Hooft, *Brieven*, p. 91.
156 Ibid., p. 20.
157 Bredero, *Klucht van de koe*, ll. 274–6.
158 ARA, Hof 387, f. 177 vo. (16 March 1624).
159 *Livre synodal*, pp. 137, 141 (1589).
160 Reitsma and Van Veen, *Acta*, III, p. 44.
161 Wiltens, and Scheltus, *Kerkelyk Plakaatboek*, I, p. 718.
162 E.g., Reitsma and Van Veen, *Acta*, I, pp. 208, 215, 219; III, p. 249.
163 Not. Nieuwkoop, 5 July 1620; Acta Woerden, 20 July 1620; W. P. C. Knuttel, *Acta der particuliere synoden van Zuid-Holland 1621–1700*, I, p. 69.
164 *Livre synodal*, p. 238 (Delft 1613); Acta Den Briel, 6 April 1622.

8. UPBRINGING

1 Van Dillen, *Bronnen*, III, p. 120.
2 ARA, Hof 5229, publication of 4 June 1624.
3 Van Leeuwen, *Costumen*, p. 403.
4 ARA, Holland 1384, 11 May 1623.
5 *Res. Holland*, 1596, p. 337.
6 Ibid., 1599, p. 350, *oktrooi* for 's-Gravendeel.
7 Van Dillen, *Bronnen*, I, p. 537.
8 Posthumus, 'Kinderarbeid in de 17e eeuw in Delft', *Economisch Historisch Jaarboek*, 22 (1943), p. 52. If he meant the growth of families he was probably mistaken. Naturally, it would be quite different to say that the growth of the working population was relatively greater.
9 E. P. de Booy, *De weldaet der scholen* (Utrecht, 1977), p. 249.
10 *Res. Holland*, 1589, p. 157.
11 In 1604 the synod of North Holland declared that the hiring of a teacher 'with the approval of the churches' was indeed necessary, but not possible. Reitsma and Van Veen, *Acta*, I, p. 353.
12 Not. Barendrecht, 1593.
13 Not. Naaldwijk, 28 Oct. 1607.
14 Not. Purmerend, 7 May 1620.
15 Not. Haarlem, 13 Aug. 1621.
16 Evenhuis, *Amsterdam*, I, p. 196.
17 Van Deursen, *Bavianen en slijkgeuzen*, p. 166.
18 Not. Krommenie, 7 Sept. 1625; Not. Edam, 26 April and 3 May 1610 (Middelie).
19 De Booy, *Weldaet der scholen*, p. 17.
20 Tukker, *Dordrecht*, p. 97.
21 Private schools 'were all schools undertaken at the risk and initiative of the schoolmaster, who had not received an [official] appointment'. De Booy, *Weldaet der scholen*, p. 104.
22 Van Deursen, *Bavianen en slijkgeuzen*, p. 166.
23 'Een schoolreglement van 1632', *Rotterdamsch Jaarboekje*, 6 (1899), p. 203.

24 De Booy, *Weldaet der scholen*, p. 261.

25 Part I, p. 5.

26 Acta Gouda, 14 Feb. 1622.

27 *Res. Holland*, 1586, p. 75.

28 Reitsma and Van Veen, *Acta*, I, pp. 186 (1594), 213 (1596).

29 Van Deursen, *Bavianen en slijkgeuzen*, p. 72.

30 Acta Alkmaar, 10 Aug. 1620.

31 D. A. Valcoogh, *Regel der Duytsche schoolmeesters*, ed. G. D. J. Schotel (The Hague, 1875), p. III.

32 Ibid., p. 37.

33 De Booy, *Weldaet der scholen*, p. 95.

34 For complaints from Holland about this combination, see Acta Den Briel, 7 Aug. 1600.

35 *Gouda*, p. 366; Not. Oudewater, 1 March 1620.

36 De Booy, *Weldaet der scholen*, p. 73.

37 Ibid., p. 76.

38 Valcoogh, *Regel*, p. 31.

39 *Res. Holland*, 1588, p. 104.

40 Ibid., 1580, p. 115.

41 Acta Haarlem, 25 Sept. 1619.

42 Van Deursen, *Bavianen en slijkgeuzen*, p. 277.

43 In many villages of Utrecht the church council was involved in the appointment process from the beginning. De Booy, *Weldaet der scholen*, p. 87.

44 *Gouda*, p. 366.

45 L'Honoré Naber, 'De With', p. 114.

46 Valcoogh, *Regel*, p. III.

47 Not. Schipluiden, 15 Nov. 1598.

48 Not. Assendelft, 18 Nov. 1595.

49 Acta Den Briel, 13 Nov. 1600.

50 For conflicts of this nature, see e.g. Acta Leiden, 5 March 1599 (Leiderdorp); *Res. Holland*, 1599, p. 206 (Woerden); Acta Haarlem, 5 Nov. 1607 (Master Cornelis Jacobsz.); Van Deursen, *Bavianen en slijkgeuzen*, p. 164 (Hoornaar 1625).

51 Ibid., p. 36.

52 Ibid., pp. 7, 69, 74.

53 De Booy, *Weldaet der scholen*, p. 49.

54 Ibid., p. 54.

55 Ibid., p. 136.

56 Van Dillen, *Rijkdom*, p. 464; De Vries, *Dutch rural economy*, p. 212.

57 See part I, p. 32.

58 Van Royen, *Zeevarenden*, pp. 130–1.

59 ARA, Hof 5222, *informatie* of 2 Aug. 1616.

60 R. Murris, *La Hollande et les Hollandais au XVIIe et au XVIIIe siècle, vus par les Français* (Paris, 1925), p. 113.

61 W. Hollweg, *Heinrich Bullingers Hausbuch* (Giessen, 1956), p. 83.

62 L'Honoré Naber, 'De With', p. 106.

63 Van Deursen, *Bavianen en slijkgeuzen*, pp. 387, 388, 392.

64 L'Honoré Naber, 'De With', p. 67.

65 ARA, Holland 2590 f, request from the civic guards of Oudewater, 1618.

66 E.g. Not. Assendelft, 16 March 1597 (2 of 6); Not. De Lier, 1628 (2 of 11); Not. Stolwijk, 1 March and 31 May 1620 (5 of 8); ARA, D.T.B. Heinenoord 1, p. 48 (3 of 4).

67 Tukker, p. 79.

68 Acta Leiden, 26 Aug. 1612.
69 ARA, Hof 5226, *informatie* regarding Nieuwpoort, 23 Nov. 1621.
70 Knuttel Pamphlet 4638, p. 3.
71 Bredero, *Spaanse Brabander*, ll. 582–5.
72 ARA, Hof 5218, testimony of Bely Claesdr.; Hof 5220, testimony of Fijtgen Reyers.
73 ARA, Hof 5223, *informatie* at Zevenhuizen, 19 April 1619.
74 ARA, Hof 5230, *informatie* at Haarlem, 23 March 1625.
75 *Res. Holland*, 1595, p. 209.
76 Van Nierop, 'De zijdenijverheid van Amsterdam historisch geschetst', *TvG*, 45 (1930), p. 162; Van Dillen, *Bronnen*, III, pp. 9, 33, 34, 36, 56, 61, 109, 125, 155, 209, etc.
77 Part I, p. 7.
78 Acta Delft, 26 June 1608.
79 Van Vloten, *Paschier*, p. 3.
80 Not. Haarlem (Waals), 29 Sept. 1588.
81 Van Dillen, *Bronnen*, I, p. 537.
82 Ibid., III, p. 416.
83 Ibid., I, p. 551 (regulation of 11 Nov. 1597).
84 Van Bleiswijk, *Delft*, II, p. 505.
85 Brouwer Ancher, *De gilden*, p. 48.
86 Plomp, *Woerden*, p. 12.
87 Ibid., p. 11.
88 *Res. Holland*, 1597, p. 381.
89 Wiltens and Scheltus, *Kerkelyk Plakaatboek*, I, p. 240.
90 Part I, p. 7.
91 *Res. Holland*, 1597, p. 381; Van Dillen, *Bronnen*, III, p. 33 (1642).
92 *Res. Holland*, 1596, p. 4.
93 Bik, *Medisch leven*, p. 437 (Gouda 1610).
94 Baudartius, *Memoryen*, I, book 5, p. 38.
95 ARA, St. Gen. 12.163, proclamation of 19 March 1614.
96 Posthumus, 'Kinderarbeid', p. 57.
97 In Amsterdam, ten to fourteen-year-old boys had weekly wages of fourteen to eighteen st. (Van Nierop, 'Zijdenijverheid', p. 163). A silk-ribbon maker in Amsterdam paid girls aged eight to ten in their first year eight st. per week, in their second ten st., and in the third year fourteen and fifteen st. respectively. In addition they received one st. per week as 'play-money' (Van Dillen, *Bronnen*, III, p. 382).
98 Van Dillen, *Bronnen*, I, p. 551.
99 Van Dillen, *Rijkdom*, p. 302.
100 Posthumus, 'Kinderarbeid', p. 52.
101 Te Lintum, 'Textielindustrie', p. 26.
102 De Vrankrijker, 'Textielindustrie', p. 273.
103 Posthumus, 'Kinderarbeid', p. 66.
104 Ibid., p. 57.
105 Ibid., p. 51.
106 Ibid., p. 65.
107 Posthumus, *Bronnen*, IV, pp. 37, 40.
108 Ibid., p. 479.
109 Valcoogh, *Regel*, p. 113.
110 Ibid., p. 7.
111 Ibid., p. 10.
112 Cats, *Werken*, p. 259 ('Houwelick, Moeder'). Cf. Knuttel Pamphlet 1478: 'By crying the

inner conduits are opened, and the members are spread out, which makes people corpulent and lively. In contrast laughing makes people large-mouthed, wrinkle-faced and old.'

113 ARA, Hof 5240, dossier regarding Pieter van Heynsbergen.
114 Valcoogh, *Regel*, pp. 64, 108.
115 *Res. Holland*, 1594, p. 95.
116 ARA, Hof 5225, request of the church council of Voorburg.
117 Not. Edam, 1 March 1620.
118 Van Deursen, *Bavianen en slijkgeuzen*, p. 135.
119 I know of only one case, that of Adryaen Pieter Gerritsz. at Berkel: Not. Berkel, 4 Jan. 1589, 22 Dec. 1591 and 28 Sept. 1592.
120 But they were in the Walloon communities: Not. Leiden (Waals), 21 Jan. 1585, and Not. Amsterdam (Waals), 8 Feb. 1610.
121 ARA, Hof 5230, *informatie* regarding the watchmaker Jan Jansz., 23 March 1625.
122 The preacher's wife of Monster once gave the wife of the sheriff a game of fox and geese as a gift. Acta Den Haag, 27 July 1620. This was the occasion for the latter to break off all contact, but it is unclear whether she found the game so offensive.
123 Valcoogh, *Regel*, p. 28.
124 Van Deursen, *Bavianen en slijkgeuzen*, p. 337. Ledenberg was secretary of the States of Utrecht. He was arrested in August 1618, along with other Remonstrant leaders, and subsequently committed suicide. Jansen, *Prisma kalendarium*, pp. 102, 103.
125 Ibid., p. 338.
126 Bor, *Oorsprongk*, III, book 28, f. 44.
127 Bredero, *Rodderick ende Alphonsus*, ll. 119–22.
128 Broeder Wouter Jacobsz., *Dagboek*, ed. I. H. van Eeghen, 2 vols. (Groningen, 1959–60), II, p. 559.
129 'Burgeroorlog tusschen Rotterdam en Delfshaven', *Rotterdamsch Jaarboekje*, fourth series, 2 (1934), p. 64.
130 J. W. P. Drost, *Het Nederlandsch kinderspel vóór de zeventiende eeuw* (The Hague, 1914), p. 126.
131 A case from Utrecht is cited by Van Buchell, *Diarium*, p. 332 (1592).
132 Valcoogh, *Regel*, p. 24.
133 Koning, *Geschiedkundige aanteekeningen*, p. 29, and Sellin, *Pioneering in penology*, p. 43.
134 E. W. Moes, 'Amsterdamsche vondelingen v', *Amsterdamsch Jaarboekje* (4), p. 96.
135 ARA, Hof 386, f. 11 vo.
136 ARA, Holland 1384, f. 336 vo. (14 Feb. 1624).
137 That is how the former pirate Jacob Sybrantsz. Moll described his own youth: ARA, St. Gen. 7400.
138 De Meij, p. 203.

9. POPULAR READING AND THE SUPPLY OF NEWS

1 In twenty-one inventories for Woerden and vicinity, 1651–61, De Vries found ownership of books mentioned only twice: *Dutch rural economy*, p. 219.
2 H. A. Enno van Gelder, *Gegevens betreffende roerend en onroerend bezit in de Nederlanden in de 16e eeuw*, 2 vols. (The Hague, 1972–3), II, p. 179.
3 Ibid., I, p. 339.
4 Ibid., I, p. 475.
5 Ibid., II, p. 91.
6 Ibid., I, p. 628.
7 Ibid., II, p. 10.

8 Ibid., I, p. 237.

9 *Res. Holland*, 1596, p. 42.

10 Duker, *Gisbertus Voetius*, I, p. 47.

11 Busken Huet, *Rembrand*, II, 2nd part, p. 206.

12 Sellin, *Pioneering in penology*, p. 35: the rooms in the house of discipline could not be heated.

13 C. Wassenaer, *Historisch verhael alder gedenckweerdichste geschiedenissen die hier en daer in Europa … voorgevallen zyn* (Amsterdam, 1622), I, p. 2.

14 Overbury, *Works*, p. 101.

15 E. T. Kuiper, ed. *Die schoone hystorie van Malegijs* (Leiden, 1903), p. 360; G. J. Boekenoogen, *Verspreide geschriften*, ed. A. A. van Rijnbach (Leiden, 1949), p. 246.

16 *Hoejewilt*, cited by B. H. Van 't Hooft, *Das holländische Volksbuch vom Doktor Faust* (The Hague, 1926), p. 89.

17 Valcoogh, *Regel*, p. 12.

18 F. J. Mone, *Übersicht der niederländischen Volks-Literatur älterer Zeit* (Tübingen, 1838), p. 17.

19 Cats, *Werken*, p. 260 ('Houwelick, Moeder').

20 Van 't Hooft, *Volksbuch*, p. 90.

21 Boekenoogen, *Verspreide geschriften*, p. 229.

22 G. D. J. Schotel, *Vaderlandsche volksboeken en volkssprookjes*, 2 vols. (Haarlem, 1873–4), II, p. 116.

23 Ibid., II, p. 132.

24 Boeknoogen, *Verspreide geschriften*, p. 236.

25 W. Davids, *Verslag van een onderzoek betreffende de betrekkingen tusschen de Nederlandsche en de Spaansche letterkunde in de 16e–18e eeuw* (The Hague, 1918), p. 11.

26 Van 't Hooft, *Volksbuch*, pp. 122, 61.

27 Davids, *Verslag*, p. 23.

28 G. J. Boekenoogen, ed. *Genoechlijcke history van den schricklijcken ende onvervaerden reus Gilias* (Leiden, 1903), p.15.

29 L. Debaene, *De Nederlandse volksboeken* (Antwerp, 1951), p. 320.

30 G. J. Boekenoogen, *Vanden jongen geheeten Jacke* (Leiden, 1905), p. 69.

31 Schotel, *Volksboeken*, II, p. 150.

32 See Boekenoogen, *Verspreide geschriften*, p. 237.

33 Boekenoogen, *Gilias*, pp. 3, 18.

34 Ibid., p. 12.

35 Boekenoogen, *Jacke*, p. 24.

36 Ibid., p. 26.

37 Ibid., p. 33.

38 W. P. C. Knuttel, *Catalogus van de pamfletten verzameling berustende in de Koninklijke Bibliotheek*, 8 vols. (The Hague, 1889–1916), part I, p. 340.

39 Hooft, *Brieven*, p. 351. Rumours and news by word of mouth, pp. 271, 272, 276, 277, 279, 297.

40 Kaajan, *De groote synode van Dordrecht in 1618–1619* (Amsterdam, n.d.), p. 64.

41 Jacobsz., *Dagboek*, I, p. 1.

42 Ibid., I, pp. 25, 37.

43 Ibid., I, pp. 221, 222.

44 Ibid., II, p. 451.

45 R. J. van der Capellen, *Gedenkschriften van jhr. Alexander van der Capellen*, I (Utrecht, 1777), p. 403.

46 E.g. ARA, St. Gen. 4927, States-General to the Raad van State, 2 Nov. 1613, on handbills regarding illegal recruitment of soldiers.

47 E.g. Aitzema, *Saken*, I, p. 656; *Provisionele openinghe* (1637), A2 vo.; *Res. Holland*, 1643, p. 66.

48 Van Deursen, *Bavianen en slijkgeuzen*, p. 360.

49 Bredero, *Werken*, ed. Knuttel, III, p. 12: 'At night Envy / Shows with diligence / Its wanton whim / Sticking up mocking posters'.

50 C. de Jong, *Geschiedenis van de oude Nederlandse walvisvaart*, I (Pretoria, 1972), p. 206.

51 Schotmüller, 'Reise-eindrücke', p. 270.

52 Biestkens, *Claas Kloet*, p. 43.

53 Van de Venne, *Belacchende werelt*, p. 118.

54 Crena de Iongh, *G. C. Van Santen*, p. 271. See also Biestkens, *Claas Kloet*, p. 88, the reaction of the hawker Vroechbedurven (Spoil-quickly) when he lost his pack: 'Now I can go walk with my songs, and sing the sad song.'

55 *Groot Placaetboek*, I, p. 211 (20 Dec. 1581); also ARA, St. Gen. 4930, proclamation of 7 July 1615; cf. ARA, Holland 1384, f. 205 vo. (29 Dec. 1622).

56 Aitzema, *Saken*, II, p. 305.

57 Cats, *Werken*, p. 589; A. Kluit, *Historie der Hollandsche staatsregering tot aan het jaar 1795*, 5 vols. (Amsterdam, 1802–5), III, p. 284.

58 In July 1650, Stadholder William II had six of his urban opponents, including Jacob de Witt, arrested and imprisoned at Loevenstein. Their supporters in the regents' party became known as the Loevenstein faction. Jansen, *Prisma Kalendarium*, pp. 103, 114.

59 Van Deursen, *Bavianen en slijkgeuzen*, chapter 13.

60 Knuttel Pamphlet 1395.

61 Knuttel Pamphlet 1409 and 1581.

62 Knuttel Pamphlet 1584.

63 Knuttel Pamphlet 1412.

64 Knuttel Pamphlet 1412, AII vo.

65 See part III.

66 Knuttel Pamphlet 1412, AIII.

67 Knuttel Pamphlet 1424, A2.

68 Ibid., A2 vo.

69 Knuttel Pamphlet 1478, AIV.

70 Knuttel Pamphlet 1456.

71 De Booy, *Weldaet der scholen*, p. 278.

72 Knuttel Pamphlet 1414.

73 Knuttel Pamphlet 1398.

74 In the same spirit, Knuttel Pamphlets 1418 and 1461.

75 Van Deursen, *Bavianen en slijkgeuzen*, pp. 283, 290.

76 Knuttel Pamphlet 1480.

77 Knuttel Pamphlet 1466, AII vo.

78 Schotmüller, 'Reise-eindrücke', p. 263 (1636).

79 *Res. Holland*, 1637, p. 168 (22 Sept.).

80 Knuttel Pamphlet 3008.

81 Knuttel Pamphlet 1821.

82 Knuttel Pamphlet 2088.

83 Knuttel Pamphlet 1822.

84 Knuttel Pamphlet 2087.

85 Knuttel Pamphlet 2090.

86 Knuttel Pamphlet 1819.

87 Knuttel Pamphlet 2089.

88 Knuttel Pamphlet 2088.

89 Knuttel Pamphlet 2218.

90 Knuttel Pamphlet 3008.

91 Knuttel Pamphlet 1687.

92 Knuttel Pamphlet 1688.

93 These places and others are cited by G. D. J. Schotel, *Geschiedenis der Rederijkers in Nederland*, 2 vols. (Rotterdam, 1871), I, p. 64.

94 This number (3 p. VI.) is mentioned in the 1620 celebration of the relief of Leiden; see Van Vloten, *Paschier*, remarks, p. 25.

95 Schotel, *Rederijkers*, II, p. 34.

96 *Reden-ryckers aenwijsinghe*, preface.

97 Van Deursen, *Bavianen en slijkgeuzen*, p. 185.

98 See Fokker, *Geschiedenis der loterijen*, p. 76, Not. Voorschoten, 1615.

99 Schotel, *Rederijkers*, I, p. 136.

100 Ibid., II, p. 33.

101 Reitsma and Van Veen, *Acta*, II, p. 455.

102 Van Deursen, *Bavianen en slijkgeuzen*, p. 56.

103 Acta Den Briel, 10 May 1605.

104 Ibid., 16 Oct. 1607.

105 Acta Delft, 25 May 1606.

106 N. J. Pabon, 'Bijdragen over het godsdienstig, zedelijk en maatschappelijk leven in Den Haag tot het einde der 16e eeuw', *Die Haghe, Jaarboek* (1936), p. 118.

107 ARA, Holland 1384, f. 8 vo.

108 ARA, Hof 385, f. 176.

109 Acta Delft, 28 July 1605.

110 Ibid., 3 Oct. 1605.

111 *Groot Placaetboek*, I, p. 465 (1587).

112 See also e.g., Wittens and Scheltus, *Kerkelyk Plakaatboek*, II, p. 186; Not. Schipluiden, 24 June 1607.

113 ARA, Holland 1384, f. 232. Here it was not a question of a chamber of rhetoric, but of a travelling company of English actors, who wanted to represent the marriage negotiations between Spain and England.

114 *Res. Holland*, 1603, p. 199. See also *Gouda*, p. 137.

115 Not. Voorschoten, 1615.

116 Requests to disallow the refounding of chambers: Not. Schoonhoven, 1 Oct. 1619, and Not. Zevenhuizen, 21 Aug. 1622; regulations against meetings on Sundays during church services: Not. Naaldwijk, 24 June 1601; regulations against performances: ARA, Waalse Kerk Haag 1, 8 March 1623.

117 Jaanus, *Hervormd Delft*, p. 121.

118 Acta Leiden, 26 Sept. 1606.

119 Jaanus, *Hervormd Delft*, p. 120.

120 Not. Naaldwijk, 14 July 1613.

121 Acta Delft, 22 Sept. 1606.

122 Not. Schipluiden, 28 April 1619.

10. THE GOVERNMENT

1 Knuttel Pamphlet 3688, p. 55.

2 A. A. van Schelven, *Willem van Oranje* (Amsterdam, 1948), p. 263.

3 Bor, *Oorsprongk*, I, book 10, f. 254.

4 Van Schelven, *Willem van Oranje*, p. 264.

5 J. Bax, *Prins Maurits in de volksmeening der 16e en 17e eeuw* (Amsterdam, 1940).

6 See Poelhekke, *Frederik Hendrik*, p. 507.

7 Van Deursen, *Honni soit*, p. 119.

8 Cats, *Werken*: preface to the 'Trou-ringh'.

9 E.g. Van Opstall, *De reis*, pp. 228, 250; Tiele, 'Documenten', pp. 250, 254.

10 K. Heeringa, *Bronnen tot de geschiedenis van den Levantschen handel*, I, *1590–1660* (The Hague, 1910), p. 644.

11 Poelhekke, *Frederik Hendrik*, p. 507.

12 'Verslag van den ambassadeur in Den Haag, Francesco Michiel, aan doge en senaat, 27 mei 1638', *BMHG*, 7 (1884), p. 71.

13 Van Meteren, *Commentarien*, book 20, f. 197 vo.

14 H. T. Colenbrander (ed.), *Korte historiael … van verscheyden voyagiens … door d. David Pietersz. De Vries* (The Hague, 1911), p. 244.

15 Knuttel Pamphlet 5596, p. 17 (1647).

16 Knuttel Pamphlet 4426, p. 4.

17 Cited by Van Vloten, *Kluchtspel*, I, p. 5.

18 Hooft to Justus Baeck, 8 April 1619: *Brieven*, p. 134.

19 Van Buchell, *Diarium*, p. 464.

20 Bor, *Oorsprongk*, III, book 24, f. 42.

21 Kluit, *Hollandsche staatsregering*, I, p. 131 ff.

22 Ibid., p. 305; see also II, p. 33.

23 J. E. Elias, *De vroedschap van Amsterdam 1578–1795*, I (Haarlem, 1903), p. xxxix.

24 J. C. Boogman, 'De overgang van Gouda, Dordrecht, Leiden en Delft in de zomer van het jaar 1572', *TvG*, 57 (1942), p. 111.

25 ARA, St. Gen. Loketkas particuliere stukken 52, Blaeuhulck to the magistrate of Schoonhoven, 1 March 1616.

26 A. J. Veenendaal, *Johan van Oldenbarnevelt*, III (The Hague, 1967), p. 390.

27 B. Meulenbroek, *Briefwisseling van Hugo Grotius*, III (The Hague, 1964), p. 99.'

28 ARA, Holland 1385, f. 36 vo., Deputised Councils to Court of Holland, 23 Sept. 1624.

29 Veenendaal, *Oldenbarnevelt*, II (The Hague, 1962), p. 541.

30 Ibid., III, p. 392.

31 Kluit, *Hollandsche staatsregering*, III, p. 435. Several similar cases in N. J. J. de Voogd, *De doelistenbeweging te Amsterdam in 1748* (Utrecht, 1914), p. 18.

32 His words probably echo Exodus 18:21: 'men of truth, hating covetousness'. The standard was upheld on other occasions as well: see Grevinghovius, *Fondamentboeck*, p. 280.

33 *Keuren Oudewater*, p. 4 (1605); *Res. Holland*, 1580, p. 6 (Edam).

34 Bredero, *Angeniet*, ll. 91–4.

35 Vondel, *Werken*, II, p. 185.

36 *Provisionele openinghe*, p. B3 bis vo.

37 Knuttel Pamphlet 4426, p. 26.

38 E. Knuttel-Fabius, *Oude kinderboeken* (The Hague, 1906), p. 8.

39 Beins, 'Wirtschaftsethik', p. 118.

40 Cats, *Werken*, p. 237 ('Houwelick, Vrouwe').

41 Huygens, *Gedichten*, I, p. 158.

42 *Res. Holland*, 1636, p. 128.

43 Scheurleer, *Varen en vechten*, I, p. 145.

44 Elias, *Schetsen*, I, p. lxxx.

45 Huygens, *Gedichten*, III, p. 190.

46 W. Bisschop, *De woelingen der Leicestersche partij binnen Leiden, 1586 en 1587* (Leiden, 1867), p. 103, confession of Valmaer.

47 A. Waddington, 'Sommaire de la forme du régime des Provinces-Unies des Pays-Bas 1647', *BMHG*, 15 (1894), p. 163.

48 Elias, *De Vroedschap van Amsterdam 1578–1795*, I (Haarlem, 1903), p. lxxxi.

49 Reyd, *Oorlogen*, p. 412.

50 Posthumus, *Lakenindustrie*, II, p. 178.

51 Wagenaar, *Vaderlandschen historie*, VIII, p. 183.

52 ARA, Hof 5228, interrogation of Swerius in the case of Stoutenburg's servant Lucq Meusnier.

53 E.g. B. Dwinglo, *Grouwel der verwoestinghe staende in de heylighe plaetse*, 2 vols. (Enkhuizen, 1622), I, p. 43; De Jager, 'Verweerschrift,' pp. 255, 260.

54 E.g. W. Bezemer, 'De magistraatsverandering te Utrecht in 1618', *BMHG*, 17 (1896), pp. 77–96; *Provisionele openinghe*, p. B3 bis vo.; Knuttel Pamphlet 5596, p. 6.

55 Knuttel Pamphlet 4638, p. 7.

56 Knuttel Pamphlet 4426, p. 27.

57 Colenbrander, *De Vries*, p. 245.

58 Veenendaal, *Oldenbarnevelt*, III, p. 713.

59 ARA, St. Gen. 3174, 11 Aug. 1615 (consent of Holland). Also found earlier, *Res. Holland*, 1579, p. 274 (14 Nov.).

60 H. A. Enno van Gelder, *De levensbeschouwing van Corn. Pietersz. Hooft*, (Amsterdam, 1918), p. 30.

61 Ibid., pp. 13–15.

62 *Res. Holland*, 1648, p. 114 (26 March).

63 Van Gelder, 'Bedijking van de Heer Hugowaard', p. 262.

64 Knuttel Pamphlet 4638, p. 7.

65 Ibid., p. 4.

66 ARA, Holland 2619 l.

67 A similar case: ARA, Hof 386, f. 18 vo., 31 Dec. 1614 (Medemblik).

68 Veenendaal, *Oldenbarnevelt*, II, p. 153.

69 J. E. Elias, *Geschiedenis van het Amsterdamsche Regentenpatriciaat*, (The Hague, 1923), p. 39.

70 ARA, Holland 1384, f. 18 vo. (19 May 1621).

71 ARA, Hof 5240, *informatie* regarding Pieter van Heynsbergen, 16 April 1647.

72. Knuttel Pamphlet 5596, p. 8.

73 Fokker, *Loterijen*, p. 80.

74 Veenendaal, *Oldenbarnevelt*, II, p. 144 (21 June 1606).

75 *Res. Holland*, 1595, p. 202 (8 June).

76 *Groot Placaetboek*, II, p. 1451 (Holland proclamation of 1 Aug. 1603).

77 ARA, Holland 1384, f. 93 (27 Dec. 1621).

78 *Res. Holland*, 1617, p. 52 (8 March).

79 Ibid., p. 159 (23 June).

80 ARA, Holland 1384, f. 136 (6 June 1622).

81 R. Fruin, *Geschiedenis der staatsinstellingen in Nederland tot den val der Republiek*, ed. H. T. Colenbrander (The Hague, 1901), p. 119.

82 D. J. Roorda, *Partij en factie* (Groningen, 1961), p. 49.

83 *Res. Holland*, 1620, p. 261 (14 Dec.).

84 ARA, St. Gen. 4929, the magistrate of Amsterdam to the States-General, 9 Oct. 1614.

85 Bredero, *Werken*, ed. Knuttel, III, p. 385 (*Lof van de rijckdom*). See also Van Moerkerken, *Kluchtspel*, I, p. 68 (Van Santen, *Lichte Wigger*), and Haverman, *W. D. Hooft*, p. 110 (*Verloren Soon*).

86 J. Becius, *Het ghesette exemplaar der godloosen, ofte historie Sodomae ende Gomorrae* (Arnhem, 1638), I, p. 81.

87 *Groot Placaetboek*, II, p. 1507 (1610, instruction to the gaoler).

88 Oldewelt, *Amsterdamsche archiefvondsten* (Amsterdam, 1942), p. 37 (1605), instruction to the gaoler).

89 ARA, Hof 385, f. 29 vo.

90 ARA, Hof 384, f. 18 vo.

91 J. Prinsen, 'Een paar "seltsame trou-gevallen",' *Oud-Holland*, 35 (1917), p. 186.

92 ARA, Hof 386, f. 64 vo.

93 ARA, Hof 5224.

94 Fruin, *Staatsinstellingen*, p. 393ff.

95 Evenhuis, *Amsterdam*, I, p. 283.

96 *Res. Holland*, 1621, p. 90 (May 1621).

97 Ibid., p. 36, no date. Also ARA, Holland 1384, f. 116 vo. (25 March 1622): 'the great excesses which are committed by the respective colleges of the admiralties, to turn to their own profit as part of their emoluments'.

98 Engels, *Belastingen*, p. 35ff.

99 *Res. Holland*, 1624, p. 94 (2 Aug.).

100 Aitzema, *Saken*, I, p. 298.

101 Ibid., I, p. 530.

102 See above, p. 142, and below, p. 188.

103 Aitzema, *Saken*, I, p. 530.

104 *Res. Holland*, 1642, p. 69 (19 March).

105 Aitzema, *Saken*, I, p. 317.

106 Knuttel Pamphlet 4426, p. 26.

11. MONEY

1 *Res. Holland*, 1640, p. 133 (13 July).

2 Aitzema, *Saken*, I, p. 680.

3 *Res. Holland*, 1606, p. 104 (April).

4 Ibid., 1641, p. 264 (27 Sept.).

5 Ibid., p. 278 (8 Oct.).

6 ARA, Holland 1385, f. 3 vo.

7 *Res. Holland*, 1622, p. 144 (20 Sept.).

8 Ibid., 1642, p. 147 (3 July).

9 Auction according to ibid., 1611, p. 253 (26 Nov.).

10 Ibid., 1626, p. 75 (25 June).

11 ARA, Holland 2600 d, proposal for redress on the beer ordinance.

12 Schilperoort may be an exception (*Res. Holland*, 1619, p. 166, 6 July), if the persons mentioned are indeed Delft regent-families.

13 Mostly in the towns. Some established burghers were involved in tax-farming in The Hague: H. E. Enno van Gelder, 'Haagsche cohieren, I (1627)', *Die Haghe Jaarboek* (1913), pp. 37, 54, 56, 58.

14 J. ten Brink, *Gerbrand Adriaensz. Bredero* (Leiden, 1859), II, p. 485.

15 *Res. Holland*, 1612, p. 92 (29 March).

16 Ibid., 1617, p. 189 (7 Sept.).

17 Ibid., 1618, p. 327 (30 Oct.).

18 ARA, Holland 2590 a, request of Steven Philipsz. (1608).

19 *Res. Holland*, 1597, p. 605 (23 Dec.).

20 Ibid., 1611, p. 259 (29 Nov.).

21 Ibid., 1612, p. 67 (20 March, city employee, Dordrecht); 1618, p. 108 (12 May, secretary, Aalsmeer), and 273 (14 Sept., dike-council employee, Rijnland); 1619, p. 149 (7 Nov.).

22 Acta Haarlem, 19 Sept. 1618; *Res. Holland*, 1612, p. 108 (10 April).

23 ARA, Part. Not. Amst. I, 7 March 1615.

24 ARA, Holland 1384, f. 98 vo. (25 Jan. 1622).

25 ARA, Holland 1385, f. 42 vo. (3 Oct. 1624, wine tax Amsterdam).

26 ARA, Part. Not. Amst. I, 5 and 8 March 1616 (great leases demanded in Dordrecht and Delft); *Res. Holland*, 1629, p. 171 (23 Aug., sugar-tax).

27 Ibid., 1639, p. 168 (8 Sept.), and 1636, p. 65 (19 March).

28 In Leiden e.g., in 1622, 6,450 pounds for the tax on woollen cloth (ARA, Holland 1384, f. 106); Delft, 1580, for the peat-tax, 8,524 gld. (*Res. Holland*, 1580, p. 53, 5 April); Geertruidenberg, 1579, same tax, 4,000 gld. (ibid., 1579, p. 192, 21 Aug.).

29 Division of the salt-tax at Haarlem: ibid., 1612, p. 99 (3 April); at Goeree and Overflakkee: ibid., 1648, p. 264 (29 July).

30 ARA, Holland 2619 l.

31 A proclamation of 1 October 1604 speaks of tax farms below 100 golden *reals*, i.e. 600 gulden (*Groot Placaetboek*, I, p. 1633).

32 On the butter-tax at Geertruidenberg in 1624, see ARA, Hof 5229, *informatie* on the butter revolt, 9 June 1624.

33 ARA, Hof 5228, no. 3, Van Dijck: tax-farm contract for Adriaen van Dijck c.s., and request to the States of Holland, 12 Dec. 1616.

34 See e.g. *Res. Holland*, 1580, p. 140 (9 July, 296 gld. 10 st.); 1597, p. 57 (1 March, 600 gld.); 1611, pp. 252 (25 Nov.) and 259 (260 gld.); 1612, pp. 67 (348 gld.) and 92 (1,650 gld.); 1617, p. 29 (15 Feb., 224 gld.); 1618, p. 10 (400 gld.); 1619, p. 149 (126 gld. 10 st.) and 164 (1,000 gld.); ARA, Holland 2590 a, request of Steven Philipsz., 1608 (243 gld.).

35 *Res. Holland*, 1618, p. 273 (44 gld.) and 327 (54 gld.).

36 'Inkomen van Holland en West-Friesland (1622)', *Kronijk van het Historisch Genootschap Gevestigd te Utrecht*, 28e jaargang, 1872, sixth series, 3 (1873), 1872, p. 409.

37 *Res. Holland*, 1611, p. 123 (30 May).

38 J. W. IJzerman, *De reis om de wereld van Olivier van Noort 1598–1601*, 2 vols. (The Hague, 1926), II, p. III. Van Noort circumnavigated the globe in 1598–1604. His Rotterdam privateers hoped thereby to seize ships of the Spanish treasure fleet. His route to the spice islands proved too lengthy for commercial purposes. Jansen, *Prisma Kalendarium*, p. 98.

39 Acta Den Briel, 6 April 1604.

40 *Res. Holland*, 1617, p. 219 (31 Oct.), one example out of many.

41 Ibid., 1618, pp. 19 (22 Jan.), 50 (6 March), 357 (13 Nov.), and 393 (21 Dec.).

42 Ibid., 1629, pp. 35 (14 March), 52 (22 March), 112 (20 June).

43 Ibid., 1629, p. 98 (11 July). The same three towns in 1641, p. 268 (30 Sept.), thus apparently a fixed combination.

44 Ibid., 1636, p. 241 (11 Dec.).

45 Ibid., 1641, p. 268 (30 Sept.).

46 Ibid., 1646, p. 358 (6 Dec.).

47 ARA, Holland 2599 c, 'Staet in 't cort van 'tgeene de gemeene middelen over Hollandt ende Westvrieslant verpacht in den jare 1608' (Brief overview of the general revenues leased in Holland and West-Friesland in 1608 ...).

48 ARA, Financiën van Holland 826, 'Staet van 't beloop der verpagte gemene landsmiddelen zedert der. jare 1624 tot 1649 incluys' (Survey of the evolution of leased general revenues from 1624 to 1649 inclusive).

49 See part I, p. 4.

50 *Groot Placaetboek*, I, p. 1633.

51 *Res. Holland*, 1648, p. 201 (4 July).

52 Ibid., 1641, p. 246 (17 Sept.).

53 Ibid., 1620, p. 54 (17 March).

54 Ibid., 1622, p. 39 (10 March) and 1627, p. 43 (5 March).

55 Ibid., 1641, p. 246 (17 Sept.) and 1629, p. 116 (25 July).

56 Ibid., 1618, p. 183 (12 July) and 1605, p. 251 (14 Sept.).

57 *Groot Placaetboek*, I, p. 1633 (proclamation of 1 Oct. 1604).

58 ARA, Part. Not. Amst., 16 Sept. 1615.

59 Van Dillen, *Bronnen*, III, p. 239 (8 Sept. 1639).

60 *Groot Placaetboek*, I, p. 1633 (1 April 1625).

61 ARA, Holland 2600 d, proposal for redress on the beer ordinance.

62 *Res. Holland*, 1620, p. 91.

63 Van Dillen, *Bronnen*, II, p. 465.

64 *Res. Holland*, 1620, p. 91 (20 May).

65 ARA, Holland 1385, f. 6, Deputised Councils to Amsterdam, 25 July 1624.

66 ARA, Holland 1384, f. 225 vo. (10 March 1623).

67 W. F. H. Oldewelt, 'De Hollandse imposten en ons beeld van de conjunctuur tijdens de Republiek', *JA* (1955), p. 54.

68 *Res. Holland*, 1627, p. 102 (6 May) and 1647, p. 60 (14 Feb.).

69 Ibid., 1627, p. 60 (17 March). Something similar already noted in ARA, Part. Not. Amst. I, 10 March 1615.

70 *Res. Holland*, 1629, pp. 110 (19 July); 121 (27 July).

71 Ibid., 1629, p. 176 (25 Aug.); 1631, pp. 34 (19 March), 52 (3 and 4 April); 1633, p. 13 (session of 16 Feb. to 26 March).

72 Ibid., 1636, p. 44 (5 March).

73 Ibid., 1636, p. 74 (4 April).

74 Ibid., 1643, p. 78 (18 March).

75 Ibid., 1640, p. 140 (12 July).

76 Lootsma, *Zaanstreek*, I, p. 108.

77 Van Deursen, *Bavianen en slijkgeuzen*, p. 152.

78 Ibid., p. 205.

79 Ibid., p. 32.

80 Beeckman, *Journal*, II, p. 302.

81 Ibid., p. 301.

82 Ibid., p. 356.

83 Van Dillen, *Bronnen*, II, p. 377.

84 Oldewelt, 'Hollandse imposten,' p. 55.

85 ARA, Part Not. Amst. I, 7 March 1615.

86 Cf. *Res. Holland*, 1608, p. 514 (21 March).

87 Ibid., 1598, p. 146 (7 April).

88 A. C. Kersbergen, 'Adrianen van Oringen, "pachtersse en collectrice" van imposten', *Rotterdamsch Jaarboekje* (1934), p. 92.

89 *Res. Holland*, 1617, p. 2 (6 Jan.).

90 ARA, Holland 1384, f. 35 vo. (13 July 1621).

91 Oldewelt, 'Hollandse imposten', p. 55; Schakel, *Nordeloos*, p. 94; *Res. Holland*, 1588, p. 229 (1 July); ARA, Part. Not. Amst. I, 17 March 1615; ARA, Holland 1384, f. 82 vo. (9 Nov. 1621); Kersbergen, 'Adrianen van Oringen', p. 95.

92 ARA, Holland 1385, f. 23.

93 ARA, Hof 384, 3 Dec. 1591 (Adriaen Louwen, Polsbroek); ARA, Hof 385, 1 Nov. 1611 (Gerrit Adriaensz., Texel); Hooft to an unknown tax collector, *Brieven*, p. 43; *Res. Holland*, 1618, p. 134 (30 May, Gijsbrecht van Teylingen, Zandvoort).

94 Ibid., 1591, p. 68.
95 Van Dillen, *Bronnen*, II, p. 297 (1618, Amsterdam).
96 Ibid., p. 156 (1616, Amsterdam).
97 *Res. Holland*, 1606, p. 353 (22 Dec.), and 1607, pp. 15, 16.
98 Ibid., 1642, p. 201 (2 Aug.).
99 Van Deursen, *Honni soit*, p. 61.
100 ARA, Holland 2592 b III, 'Staet van schulden tot laste an de Generaliteyt, tot betalinge van dewelcke voor alsnoch geen ordre is genomen' (State of debts of the Generality, for the payment of which no order has yet been made).
101 ARA, Holland 2641.
102 *Res. Holland*, 1635, p. 142 (27 July).
103 Ibid., 1635, p. 128 (12 and 13 July).
104 Ibid., 1642, p. 82.
105 Knuttel Pamphlet 4368, p. 6.
106 Knuttel Pamphlet 4519, p. A 1 vo.
107 *Res. Holland*, 1638, p. 13 (17 Feb.).
108 Ibid., 1640, p. 20.
109 Ibid., 1646, pp. 90 (13 March), 209 (9 June).
110 *Groot Placaetboek*, II, p. 445 (22 March 1645).
111 *Res. Holland*, 1631, p. 70 (16 April).
112 E.g. ibid., 1629, p. 172 (23 Aug.).
113 Ibid., 1648, p. 418 (10 Dec.).
114 Ibid., 1648, p. 124 (20 April).
115 Ibid., 1628, p. 158 (21 Aug.).
116 Aitzema, *Saken*, I, p. 1012.
117 *Res. Holland*, 1628, p. 103 (14 July).
118 Ibid., 1629, p. 211 (30 Nov.).
119 Ibid., 1635, p. 13 (16 Feb.).
120 L. C. Vrijman, *Kaapvaart en zeeroverij* (Amsterdam, 1938), p. 134.
121 *Res. Holland*, 1637, p. 226 (Nov.).
122 Ibid., 1636, p. 65 (19 March).
123 Graefe, *Tromp*, p. 75.
124 *Res. Holland*, 1636, p. 85 (15 April).
125 Graefe, *Tromp*, p. 102.
126 Ibid., p. 124; *Res. Holland*, 1637, pp. 190 (13 and 14 Oct.), 210 (12 Nov.).
127 Part I, p. 30.
128 *Res. Holland*, 1635, p. 145 (points of description, Sept. 1635).
129 For the salaries in 1635, see Aitzema, *Saken*, I, p. 265.
130 *Res. Holland*, 1635, p. 226 (20 Dec.).
131 Ibid., 1637, p. 7 (16 Jan.).
132 Ibid., 1643, p. 164 (8 May).
133 Ibid., 1637, p. 225 (16 Dec.).
134 Ibid., 1629, p. 212 (30 Nov.).
135 Ibid., 1646, p. 354 (6 Dec.).
136 Ibid., 1647, p. 27 (25 Jan.).
137 E.g. ibid., 1632, pp. 62, 63 (23 June–7 Aug.).
138 Knuttel Pamphlet 4638, p. 5.
139 Ibid., p. 6.
140 Aitzema, *Saken*, II, p. 490.

12. THE COMMUNITY

1 R. van Schaïk, 'Prijs- en levensmiddelenpolitiek in de noordelijke Nederlanden van de 14e tot de 17e eeuw: bronnen en problemen', *TvG*, 91 (1978), p. 215.
2 J. Smit, 'De levensmiddelenpolitiek in Den Haag gedurende de jaren 1572–1574', *BVGO*, fifth series, 6 (1919), p. 269.
3 Ibid., p. 270.
4 Ibid., p. 264.
5 Ibid., p. 268.
6 *Res. Holland*, 1630, p. 135 (15 Nov.).
7 Ibid., 1597, p. 279 (3–13 June).
8 Van Schaïk, 'Prijs- en levensmiddelenpolitiek', p. 228.
9 *Res. Holland*, 1576, p. 182 (24 Oct.).
10 Reyd, *Oorlogen*, p. 298.
11 Velius, *Chronyk van Hoorn*, p. 495.
12 *Res. Holland*, 1595, p. 486.
13 Ibid., and Ampzing, *Beschryvinge*, p. 415.
14 *Res. Holland*, 1597, p. 269 (10 June).
15 See also Van Schaïk, 'Prijs- en levensmiddelenpolitiek', p. 228.
16 *Res. Holland*, 1597, p. 279 (3–13 June).
17 *Groot Placaetboek*, VIII, p. 453.
18 *Res. Holland*, 1623, p. 147.
19 On high prices in 1623 see Baudartius, *Memoryen*, II, book 15, p. 182; Ampzing, *Beschryvinge*, p. 415; *Res. Holland*, 1623, p. 169; Velius, *Chronyk van Hoorn*, p. 611; Van Deursen, *Bavianen en slijkgeuzen*, p. 122. On the fear of disorders aroused by new taxes in December, 1623, see *Res. Holland*, 1623, p. 187.
20 Van Buchell, *Diarium*, p. 338 (1593).
21 Posthumus, *Lakenindustrie*, II, p. 170.
22 In 1608 the situation in Leiden was still very bad: Not. Alkmaar, 31 Aug. 1608.
23 J. Romein, *De lage landen bij de zee* (Utrecht, 1934), p. 336.
24 *Res. Holland*, 1617, p. 3.
25 Ibid., 1604, p. 302.
26 Not. Edam, 17 Sept. 1595.
27 Ibid., 1 Jan. 1598.
28 Van Deursen, *Bavianen en slijkgeuzen*, p. 222.
29 Valcoogh, *Regel*, p. 107.
30 ARA, Holland 2619 l.
31 As Romein thought: *Lage landen*, p. 345.
32 J. H. van Linden van den Heuvell, *Uit de geschiedenis van het weeshuis te Vlaardingen* (Vlaardingen, 1955), p. 22 (1596).
33 Duker, *Voetius*, I, p. 44.
34 ARA, Holland 2600 d, proposal for sumptuary tax.
35 Hoekstra, *Bloemendaal*, p. 105.
36 J. B. van Loenen, *Beschrijving en kleine kroniek van de gemeente Hillegom* (Hillegom, 1916), p. 136 (1597).
37 *Res. Holland*, 1605, p. 230.
38 S. Ampzing says that harts and hinds were still plentiful there in 1628: *Beschryvinge*, p. 73.
39 Hooft, *Brieven*, pp. 43 (1616), 67 (1619).
40 ARA, Hof 384, f. 31 (1588).
41 Hooft, *Brieven*, p. 52 (1617).

42 Thus it appears that time and again herring fishermen would break the laws, when these were in conflict with customs they regarded as established and appropriate. A. Beaujon, *Overzicht der geschiedenis van de Nederlandsche zeevisserrijen* (Leiden, 1885), p. 35.

43 ARA, RAZH Brielle l, f. 17.

44 ARA, Hof 384, f. 151.

45 ARA, Hof 385, f. 157 vo. (1607).

46 *Res. Holland*, 1606, p. 310.

47 Ibid., 1620, p. 215.

48 See part II, p. 89.

49 ARA, Hof 386, f. 29 vo.

50 ARA, Holland, 1384, f. 81 (1621).

51 *Res. Holland*, 1633, p. 1 (descriptive letter).

52 Knuttel Pamphlet 5596, p. 18.

53 Evenhuis, *Amsterdam*, I, p. 288.

54 Reyd, *Oorlogen*, p. 100, speaking of the time of Leicester. Cf. Bisschop, *Leicestersche partij*, p. 5, Leicester to Walsingham, 26 Dec. 1585: 'the States dare not be but queen Elyzabethes, for, by the living God, yf ther shuld fall but the least unkindness, thorow ther default, the people wold kyll them'.

55 Van Meteren, *Commentarien*, book 14, f. 41 vo.

56 See part II, p. 142.

57 Reyd, *Oorlogen*, p. 268.

58 Den Tex, *Oldenbarnevelt*, II, p. 27.

59 Reyd, *Oorlogen*, p. 100.

60 Bisschop, *Leicestersche partij*, p. 30.

61 Van Deursen, *Bavianen en slijkgeuzen*, chaps. 11–17.

62 S. Blom, *Geschiedenis van Maassluis* (Utrecht, 1948), p. 116.

63 ARA, Hof 5222, preliminary *informatie* of 10 Aug. 1616.

64 *Res. Holland*, 1637, p. 40 (12 March).

65 Valcooch, *Chronycke*, pp. 101, 99, 100.

66 Baudartius, *Memoryen*, II, book 16, p. 1624.

67 *Maandblad Amstelodamum*, 1966, p. 59.

68 On the Delft riot, see Baudartius, *Memoryen*, I, book 8, p. 53; ARA, Holland 2590 e, sentence of the Hof van Holland; ARA, Hof 5222, preliminary *informatie* of 10 Aug. 1616; G. B. Rotterdam 2182, Deputised Councils of Holland to Deputised Councils of Westfriesland, 2 Aug. 1616.

69 G. J. Sikesz, *De schutterijen in Nederland* (Utrecht, 1864), p. 24.

70 Ordinance of the civic guard and watch of the city of Delft, 12 May 1580, Delft, 1616, art. V. Art. VI says that anyone who fell into poverty was discharged. The last rule also applied at Gouda: see e.g. De Lange van Wijngaarden, *Goude*, III, p. 44.

71 Crena de Iongh, *G. C. Van Santen*, p. 25.

72 Bor, *Oorsprongk*, IV, book 33, f. 76.

73 ARA, Holland, 1384, f. 64 vo.

74 *Res. Holland*, 1622, p. 120.

75 ARA, Holland, 1384, f. 379 vo. The butter cost 5 st. and one penny (*oortje*) per pound, and 80 gld. per vat. The excise tax amounted to one penny (*oortje*) per pound, and 4 gld. per vat.

76 Van Dillen, *Bronnen*, II, p. 536.

77 ARA, Hof 5229, *informatie* of 9 June 1624.

78 ARA, Holland 1384, f. 379.

79 Ibid., f. 379 vo.

80 Ibid., f. 385.

81 Ibid., f. 382.

82 See also ARA, Hof 5229, *informatie* of 9 June 1624.

83 Knuttel Pamphlet 5996, p. 25.

84 ARA, Hof 5215, request of Gerrit Jacobsz. Achtman (1612).

85 Bredero, *Spaanse Brabander*, ll. 1966–7.

86 Crena de Iongh, *G. C. Van Santen*, p. 349.

87 A. M. Hulkenberg, *De Aagtenkerk van Lisse* (Lisse, 1960), p. 44.

88 Schakel, *Noordeloos*, p. 75.

89 Not. Purmerend, 23 Oct. 1616.

90 Moryson, *Itinerary*, IV, p. 471.

91 Schottmüller, 'Reise-eindrücke', p. 270.

92 ARA, Hof 385, f. 213 vo.

93 ARA, Hof 5217, *informatie* of 15 Jan. 1613.

94 Bredero, *Moortje*, ll. 719–20. Other cases of resistance to arrest in ARA, Hof 5219, articles for Maritgen Jacobs Laediegat (1615); ARA, Hof 5665, f. 72 (1622).

95 L. Brouwers, S. J., *Carolus Scribani 1561–1629* (Antwerp, 1961), p. 487.

13 THE WAR

 1 *Res. Holland*, 1648, p. 442 (18 Dec.).

 2 Abbé Brantôme, cited by E. Gossart, *L'établissement du régime espagnol dans les Pays-Bas et l'insurrection* (Brussels, 1905), p. 15.

 3 G. Parker, *The Army of Flanders and the Spanish Road 1567–1659* (Cambridge, 1972), p. 271.

 4 H. Brugmans, 'Utrechtse kroniek over 1566–1576', *BMHG*, 25 (1904), pp. 175, 178.

 5 Parker, *Army of Flanders*, p. 32.

 6 Cf. Parker, *Army of Flanders*, p. 13.

 7 'Coligese manifestamente de todos los autores que han escrito de la historia del rey don Felipe Segundo deste nombre, que por sustentar dentro de sus Estados de los Paises Baxos, y en las tierras que son sugetas, la religion catolica fue forçado a tomar las armas.' F. Lanario, *Las guerras de Flandes desde el año de 1559 hasta el de 1609* (Madrid, 1623), f. 1.

 8 Parker, *Army of Flanders*, p. 178 (1574).

 9 I Jzerman, *Olivier van Noort*, I, p. 254.

10 Brouwer, *Spaansche soldaten*, p. 76.

11 Parker, *Army of Flanders*, p. 179.

12 Souterius, *Victoriën*, I, p. 81.

13 Scheurleer, *Varen en vechten*, I, p. 68.

14 Cf. Calderón de la Barca, *El sitio de Bredá*, cited by J. R. Schrek, *El sitio de Bredá* (The Hague, 1957), p. 120, where a Spanish captain says to the defenders: 'perros erejes, ministro soy de la ynquisición santa'. (Dogs of heretics, I am a minister of the Holy Inquisition.)

15 Scheurleer, *Varen en vechten*, I, p. 24 (1574): 'Vene vous canaille, Luthranen ende rapaille'.

16 Brugmans, 'Utrechtse kroniek', p. 236.

17 Van Opstall, *De reis*, p. 278.

18 R. Fruin, 'Gedenkschrift van Don Sancho de Londoño', *BMHG*, 13 (1892), p. 30.

29 Gossart, *Régime espagnol*, p. 15. G. Parker, 'Francisco de Lixalde and the Spanish Netherlands (1576–1577): some new evidence', *TvG*, 89 (1976), pp. 7 ff.

20 S. A. Vosters, *Spanje in de Nederlandse litteratuur* (Amsterdam, 1955), p. 10.

21 E.g. Scheurleer, *Varen en vechten*, I, pp. 64, 75, 184.

22 See also the apparently ironical summing up of the names of Spanish ships at the battle of Gibraltar, in Scheurleer, *Varen en vechten*, I, p. 77:

> d'Admiraelsschip St. Augustijn,
> d'Vies-Admiraelsschip hiet divijn,
> Delvega Nostra Dona:
> Madre de Dios, St Anna,
> Met Nostra Dona del Regia,
> Oock la Conceptiona:
> St Christoffel, S. Nicolaes,
> El Dona de Rosaros dwaes,
> El Dona des Doloros,
> Met Nostra Dona de la O,
> Het twaalfste hiet St Pedro,
> Al Galioens vol Seignoros.

23 Scheurleer, *Varen en vechten*, I, p. 293.

24 De Meij, *Watergeuzen*, p. 209.

25 Brugmans, 'Utrechtse kroniek', p. 236.

26 *Res. Holland*, 1579, p. 28.

27 Jacobsz., *Dagboek*, I, p. 347.

28 Posthumus, 'Landbouwtoestanden', p. 170.

29 *Res. Holland*, 1576, p. 75.

30 Brugmans, 'Utrechtse kroniek', p. 141.

31 Parker, *Army of Flanders*, p. 179.

32 A. van Dorp, *Brieven en onuitgegeven stukken*, ed. J. B. J. N. Ridder de van der Schueren, 2 vols. (Utrecht, 1887–8), I, p. 116.

33 C. M. Schulten, 'Het beleg van Alkmaar', in *Alkmaar ontzet 1573–1973*, ed. I. Schöffer (1973), p. 61; Parker, *Army of Flanders*, p. 203.

34 See W. J. Verwer, *Memoriaelbouck*, ed. J. J. Temminck (Haarlem, 1973), p. 83: at the siege of Haarlem the garrison of a fort surrendered on the condition that their lives be spared. 'Don Frederico seijde: ic het u het leven toegeseijt, maer niet het eten. Interim Perierunt miserii.' (Don Frederico said, I granted you life, but not [the right to] eat. Meanwhile they died of wretchedness.')

35 Jacobsz., *Dagboek*, I, p. 166. See also I, pp. 120, 122; and II, p. 550.

36 Brugmans, 'Utrechtse kroniek', p. 10.

37 Ibid., p. 136.

38 Ibid., p. 122.

39 Ibid., p. 241.

40 De Meij, *Watergeuzen*, p. 311.

41 Scheurleer, *Varen en vechten*, I, p. 3.

42 Tersteeg, 'Vijf bange jaren', p. 8.

43 N. J. M. Dresch, 'Rekening van Maerten Ruychaver, thesaurier in het Noorderkwartier, 1572/73', *BMHG*, 49 (1928), p. 75.

44 *Res. Holland*, 1574, pp. 67, 98: two cases of forced dismissal from service.

45 Ibid., 1576, p. 195 (17 Nov.).

46 Tersteeg, 'Vijf bange jaren', p. 15.

47 Schulten, 'Beleg van Alkmaar', p. 63.

48 *Res. Holland*, 1574, p. 191 (12 Nov.).

49 Fruin, 'Londoño', p. 43. See also p. 32: 'los paysanos, apasionados del conde Ludovico'. ('The peasants, enthusiastic supporters of Count Louis [of Nassau].')

50 J. J. Woltjer, 'Van Katholiek tot protestant', in *Historie van Groningen, Stad en Land*, ed. W. J. Formsma, p. 207.
51 Fruin, 'Londoño', p. 69.
52 Ibid., p. 43.
53 De Meij, *Watergeuzen*, p. 57.
54 Ibid., p. 177.
55 Jacobsz., *Dagboek*, I, p. 389. On the popularity of the *Wilhelmus*, a Beggar song which later became the national anthem, see also Verwer, *Memoriaelbouck*, p. 86.
56 De Meij, *Watergeuzen*, p. 139.
57 Ibid., p. 44.
58 Ibid., pp. 172, 179.
59 Wijn, 'Regiment', p. 248.
60 De Meij, *Watergeuzen*, p. 179.
61 F. De Witt Huberts, 'Een tot nu toe niet gebruikt dagverhaal van Haarlem's beleg, geschreven door een ooggetuige', *BMHG*, 47 (1926), p. 10.
62 De Jonge, *Nederlandsche zeewezen*, I, p. 113.
63 De Meij, *Watergeuzen*, p. 113.
64 L. A. Kesper, 'De Goudsche vroedschap en de religie', *BVGO*, fourth series, 2 (1902), p. 404.
65 Ibid., p. 403.
66 Ibid., p. 405.
67 De Meij, *Watergeuzen*, p. 57.
68 Scheurleer, *Varen en vechten*, I, p. 5.
69 Ibid., pp. 11, 15, 19, 21, 25, 27, 29.
70 Ibid., p. 33.
71 Ibid., p. 27: 'Dees papisten, dees wreede antichristen'.
72 Jacobsz., *Dagboek*, II, p. 709.
73 Ibid., p. 703.
74 Ibid., p. 732.
75 *Res. Holland*, 1579, pp. 143 (25 June), 186 (18 Aug.).
76 Ibid., p. 161 (13 July).
77 As L. J. Rogier thought: *Geschiedenis van het Katholicisme in Noord-Nederland in de 16de en 17de eeuw*, 5 vols., third edition (n.p., 1964), II, p. 336.
78 *Res. Holland*, 1575, p. 165 (20 Aug.).
79 Ibid., 1600, p. 436 (4 Dec.).
80 Ibid., 1579, p. 237. At that time people were afraid of landings, as appears from p. 206.
81 ARA, Holland 1384, f. 7 (10 March 1621), to the bailiffs, dike-reeves, etc. of Voorne, Putten, de Lage Waard, Strijen, de Krimpenerwaard, Zuid-Holland, Middelharnis, de Arkelse Waard, Oude en Nieuwe Tonge, De Lopikerwaard and Beijerland.
82 E.g. *Res. Holland*, 1599, p. 29; Wassenaer, *Historisch verhael*, II, p. 71 (Jan. 1622).
83 *Res. Holland*, 1629, p. 123 (29 July).
84 Ibid., 1629, p. 145 (14 Aug.).
85 Aitzema, *Saken*, I, p. 866.
86 Ibid., p. 867.
87 K. Obser, 'Aus dem Freiheitskampf der Niederlande. Briefe eines badischen Kriegsmans', *BMHG*, 47 (1926), p. 46.
88 *Res. Holland*, 1629, p. 154 (17 Aug.).
89 Aitzema, *Saken*, I, p. 867.
90 J. J. Poelhekke, *Met pen, tongriem en rapier* (Amsterdam, 1976), p. 85.
91 Aitzema, *Saken*, I, p. 868.

92 Reyd, *Oorlogen*, p. 353.

93 Aitzema, *Saken*, I, p. 271.

94 *Res. Holland*, 1636, p. 36.

95 The same purpose may have been served by rumours of threatened landings by the Dunkirkers (ibid., 1632, p. 99; 1635, p. 47), or even of attacks 'on the island of Schouwen, of Goederede, or on the lands of Voorne, or yes even on the city of Brill' (ibid., 1637, p. 61).

96 Baudartius, *Memoryen*, II, book 13, p. 44.

97 Kaajan, *Pro-acta*, p. 116.

98 Wassenburg, *Dans-feest*, prefaces.

99 Baudartius, *Memoryen*, II, book 14, p. 154.

100 *Res. Holland*, 1599, pp. 181, 227.

101 Van Dillen, *Rijkdom*, p. 19.

102 Coster, 'Tiisken van der schilden', l. 1579 (1613).

103 Van Moerkerken, *Kluchtspel*, I, p. 103 (Van Santen, *Snappende Sijtgen*).

104 Bredero, *Klucht van de koe*, ll. 110–15.

105 Aitzema, *Saken*, I, p. 5.

106 Knuttel Pamphlet 1450.

107 ARA, Holland 1384, f. 27 (23 June 1621).

108 Van Dillen, *Bronnen*, II, p. 405.

109 Ibid., 471.

110 Van Moerkerken, *Kluchtspel*, I, p. 116 (W. D. Hooft, *Jan Saly*).

111 Baudartius, *Memoryen*, II, book 14, p. 222; Brand and Centen, *Historie*, II, pp. 38, 42.

112 Ampzing, *Beschryvinge*, p. 415; Velius, *Chronyk van Hoorn*, p. 611; Baudartius, *Memoryen*, II, book 15, p. 182.

113 Baudartius, *Memoryen*, II, book 16, p. 124.

114 ARA, Holland 1384, f. 72 (14 Oct. 1621).

115 Ibid., f. 340 vo. (Deputised Councils to P. C. Hooft, 22 Feb. 1624).

116 *Res. Holland*, 1627, p. 246.

117 In 1602, 1622, 1623, and 1638 (Aitzema, *Saken*, I, p. 126).

118 Ibid., p. 128.

119 *Groot Placaetboek*, II, p. 85 (19 April 1633 and 6 July 1633).

120 Aitzema, *Saken*, II, p. 450 (1637).

121 *Groot Placaetboek*, II, p. 13 (22 May 1632).

122 J. Fritz, *Die historie van Christoffel Wagenaer, discipel van D. Johannes Faustus* (Leiden, 1913), p. 144.

123 Ibid., p. 127.

124 D. L. Daalder, *Wormcruyt met suycker. Historisch-critisch overzicht van de Nederlandse kinderliteratuur* (Amsterdam, 1950), p. 39.

125 Scheurleer, *Varen en vechten*, I, p. 180: triumphal song of Samuel Ampzing on the capture of the treasure-fleet.

126 Ibid., p. 139, on the sailing of the fleet of Willekens to the West Indies, January 1624.

127 Ibid., p. 134, on the founding of the West India Company.

128 Ibid., p. 142, on the sailing of Willekens.

129 According to Warnsinck, *Drie zeventiende-eeuwse admiraals*, p. 41.

130 Ibid., p. 15.

131 *Res. Holland*, 1624, p. 15.

132 ARA, Holland 2609 f, testimony of Heyn Claesz., 14 June 1611.

133 ARA, Hof 5217, testimony of Pieter Frans, 30 May 1613.

134 I. H. Gosses and N. Japikse, *Handboek tot de staatkundige geschiedenis van Nederland* (The Hague, 1920), p. 96.

135 For 1626–34, R. Baetens, 'Organisatie en resultaten van de Vlaamse kaapvaart in de 17e eeuw', *Mededelingen Academie voor Marine van België*, 21 (1969–70), p. 106, gives a total of 336 ships sunk and 1,499 captured, with a value of 11,383,492 gld. The share of the Northern Netherlanders came to around 80 per cent. The prizes for 1642–6 came to 4,674,515 gld. for Northern Netherlandish ships, and those for 1641 to 2,000,000 gld. Baetens estimates the total for 1635–40 to 7,000,000, certainly not too high for a period that began with the disastrous year 1635. (*Res. Holland*, 1635, p. 135; H. Malo, *Les corsaires: les corsaires dunkerquois et Jean Bart*, 1 (Paris, 1913), p. 318). The grand total for 1626–46 thus comes to 22,781,308 gld. (Baetens, 'Kaapvaart', p. 109). This does not include the ships sunk. Also, public sale of prizes in Dunkirk brought in less than the normal market prices.

136 *Res. Holland*, 1641, p. 4.

137 Baetens, 'Kaapvaart', p. 98.

138 Van der Woude, *Het Noorderkwartier*, II, p. 467.

139 Knuttel Pamphlet 3804, A 1.

140 Van der Woude, *Het Noorderkwartier*, III, p. 713.

141 Knuttel Pamphlet 3804, A 3.

142 Malo, *Corsaires*, p. 225. Van Meteren says that fishermen were nailed to their ship: *Commentarien*, book 22, f. 36 vo.

143 *Res. Holland*, 1626, p. 129.

144 Malo, *Corsaires*, pp. 254, 256.

145 Aitzema, *Saken*, I, p. 775.

146 Malo, *Corsaires*, p. 296.

147 Ibid., p. 250.

148 Ibid., p. 251.

149 Scheurleer, *Varen en vechten*, I, p. 227, 'Lof des Vryen Vaerts'.

150 Malo, *Corsaires*, p. 250.

151 Baetens, 'Kaapvaart', p. 106.

152 *Res. Holland*, 1597, p. 70.

153 *Groot Placaetboek*, I, p. 1072 (3 May 1621); Brandt and Centen, *Historie*, II, p. 37.

154 *Res. Holland*, 1631, p. 131.

155 S. Lootsma, '"Draecht elckanders lasten." Bijdrage tot de geschiedenis der "Zeevarende Beurzen" in Noord Holland', *West-Friesland's 'Oud en Nieuw'*, 3 (1929), p. 21; Van der Woude, *Het Noorderkwartier*, II, p. 372.

156 Lootsma, 'Draecht elckanders lasten', p. 25. The sum was not the same everywhere. Contributions varied from several stuivers to 3 gld. 12 st.

157 Ibid., p. 22.

158 Ibid., p. 25.

159 Van der Woude, *Het Noorderkwartier*, III, p. 713.

160 *Res. Holland*, 1630, p. 37.

161 Ibid., 1636, p. 29 (20 Feb.).

162 Ibid., 1636, p. 82 (11 April).

163 Ibid., 1636, p. 46 (7 March).

164 Ibid., 1639, p. 236 (10 Dec.).

165 Ibid., 1640, p. 223 (12 Oct.).

166 Ibid., 1641, p. 268 (1 Oct.).

167 Ibid., 1629, p. 226 (22 Dec.).

168 Ibid.

169 Ibid., 1640, p. 115 (28 June).

170 Ibid., 1639, p. 218 (3 Nov.).

171 Ibid., 1640, pp. 189 (20 Sept.), 199 (1 Oct.).

172 Ibid., 1641, p. 268.

173 E.g. ibid., 1641, p. 260 (25 Sept.).

174 Ibid., 1640, p. 148 (19 July).

175 Ibid., 1640, p. 22 (12 Oct.); see also p. 123 (4 July).

176 Ibid., 1579, p. 196 (24 Aug.).

177 Van Meteren, *Commentarien*, book 15, f. 68.

178 Malo, *Corsaires*, p. 248.

179 Ibid., p. 250.

180 Reyd, *Oorlagen*, p. 321.

181 See above, p. 183, and De Jonge, *Nederlandsche zeewezen*, I, p. 229.

182 According to the turncoat Van der Dussen in 1628 (De Jong, *Nederlandse walvisvaart*, I, p. 188). In the proclamation of 8 Feb. 1645 the amounts varied from 800 gld. (for the loss of two eyes or two arms) to 120 gld. (for the loss of one foot): *Groot Placaetboek*, II, p. 2381.

183 De Jonge, *Nederlandsche zeewezen*, I, p. 243.

184 Graefe, *Tromp*, p. 111 (1637).

185 Malo, *Corsaires*, p. 345.

186 Scheurleer, *Varen en vechten*, I, p. 87 (battle of Gibraltar, 1607).

187 Ibid., p. 243 (battle on het Slaak, 1631).

188 Knuttel Pamphlet 1397 (battle of Gibraltar, 1607).

189 Scheurleer, *Varen en vechten*, I, p. 120 (battle of Malacca, 1615).

190 Ibid., p. 257 (battle on het Slaak, 1631).

191 Ibid., p. 179 (treasure fleet, 1628).

192 Ibid., p. 307.

193 Van Meteren, *Commentarien*, book 16, f. 70 vo.

194 *Res. Holland*, 1644, p. 55 (9 March).

195 *Groot Placaetboek*, I, p. 218 (1 July 1594).

196 ARA, Holland 1384, f. 25 vo., Deputised Councils of Holland to the bailiff of Rijnland, 18 July 1621.

197 *Res. Holland*, 1629, p. 119 (27 July).

198 Ibid., 1636, p. 12 (31 Jan.).

199 Ibid., 1635, p. 99 (18 May).

200 Rogier, *Katholicisme*, III, p. 539.

201 Ibid., p. 496.

202 J. D. M. Cornelissen, *Romeinsche bronnen voor den kerkelijke toestand der Nederlanden onder de apostolische vicarissen 1596–1727*, I, *1592–1651*, p. 242.

203 Ibid., p. 146.

204 Brouwers, *Carolus Scribani*, p. 474.

205 ARA, Holland 1363, Sympson to Vestingham, 4 Feb. 1598.

206 *Res. Holland*, 1626, p. 128 (23 and 24 Sept.).

207 Rogier, *Katholicisme*, III, p. 509.

208 Carnero, *Historia*, p. 182. The relevant chapter is headed 'De la muerte del príncipe de Orange y del glorioso martirio de Balthasar Gerardo Borgoñón'.

209 ARA, Hof 5213, testimony of Heyndrick Doessen, 27 Dec. 1610.

210 Van Meteren, *Commentarien*, book 21, f. 3 vo.

211 ARA, Hof 387, f. 192 (1624). See also F. S. Knipscheer, 'De vestiging der gereformeerde kerk in Noord-Holland 1572–1608', *Nederlandsch Archief voor Kerkgeschiedenis*, n.s., 5 (1907), p. 143.

212 ARA, Hof 387, f. 190 vo. The incident took place on 22 Oct. 1622.

213 Not. Alkmaar, 27 Nov. 1605. Among this generation a strong attachment to the old ways was more common: see e.g. Acta Den Haag, 7 July 1619: 'we understand that in some poorhouses and hospices several superstitions and idolatry are still practised'.

214 Not. Alkmaar, 4 Dec. 1605.

215 Cats, 'Sinne- en minnebeelden', *Werken*, p. xxxiv.

216 Not. Haarlem, 20 July 1621.

217 *Res. Holland*, 1599, p. 29.

218 ARA, Hof 5215, Jacob van Banchem to Hugo de Groot, 24 Sept. 1612.

219 F. S. Knipscheer, 'Abdias Widmarius, predikant te Uitgeest, en het kerkelijke leven eener gereformeerde gemeente in de XVIIe eeuw', *Nederlandsch Archief voor Kerk-geschiedenis*, n.s., 3 (1905), p. 315.

220 Meulenbroek, *Hugo Grotius*, IV, p. 90.

221 See also e.g. ARA, Hof 385, f. 134, 21 July 1605 (Berkhout and Wognum); Hooft, *Brieven*, p. 372, 17 Jan. 1636 (Weesp).

222 F. van Hoeck, *Schets van de geschiedenis der Jezuïeten in Nederland* (Nijmegen, 1940), p. 131.

223 J. Andriessen, S. J., *De Jezuïeten en het saamhorigheidsbesef der Nederlanden 1585–1648* (Antwerp, 1957), p. 54. They did believe that in general Catholic soldiers in the army of the States-General should be denied absolution. Ibid., p. 58.

14. POPULAR BELIEF

1 Veenendaal, *Oldenbarnevelt*, II, p. 405.

2 ARA, St. Gen. 40, res. 7, 12, and 20 March 1615.

3 Baudartius, *Memoryen*, I, book 7, p. 81. A harsh winter followed by a rainy summer in 1621: II, book 13, p. 123.

4 Reyd, *Oorlogen*, p. 223.

5 Van der Woude, *Het Noorderkwartier*, I, p. 55.

6 *Res. Holland*, 1602, p. 327 (17 Oct.).

7 Brandt and Centen, *Historie*, p. 101.

8 See part I, p. 12.

9 Smit, *Den Haag*, p. 334.

10 Burger van Schoorel, *Chronyk*, p. 211.

11 Sprenger van Eijk, *Vlaardingen*, p. 42.

12 A. A. Arkenhout, 'De kerkbrand te Oostvoorne', *Zuid-Holland*, 5 (1959), p. 50.

13 Ampzing, *Beschryvinge*, p. 501.

14 *Res. Holland*, 1616, p. 74 (25 June). Comparable cases are Zandvoort, ibid., 1597, p. 88 (13 March), and Werkendam, ibid., 1619, p. 137 (26 June).

15 De Vrankrijker, *Geschiedenis*, II, p. 189. Baudartius, *Memoryen*, I, book 7, p. 19, speaks of 'two hundred and fifty houses and barns'.

16 Ampzing, *Beschryvinge*, p. 282.

17 H. C. Hazewinkel, 'De rode haan kraaide in Rotterdam', *Rotterdams Jaarboekje* (1963), p. 252.

18 Velius, *Chronyk van Hoorn*, p. 536 (Hoorn, 1608: twenty-five to thirty thatched roofs had to be replaced annually); Pabon, 'Bijdragen', p. 178 (The Hague, subsidies for roofing with tiles); Brandt and Centen, *Historie*, II, p. 24 (Enkhuizen, 1618: prohibition against making new thatched roofs, or repairing old ones); Lootsma, *Historische studiën*, I, p. 67 (prohibition of thatched roofs).

19 Bik, *Medisch leven*, p. 231. Cf. Coster, *Rijcke-man*, ll. 1502ff., and Huygens, *Gedichten*, II, p. 18.

20 Ampzing, *Beschryvinge*, p. 147.

21 The city physician of Gouda could charge a fee of three st. per day-visit, six st. per night-visit, and $1\frac{1}{2}$ st. for examination of urine. He also received a fixed salary of 204 gld. per year.

22 Haverman, *W. D. Hooft*, p. 50.

23 Pabon, *Bijdragen*, p. 107 (The Hague, 1592); Bik, *Medisch leven*, pp. 563 (Gouda, 1582) and 565 (Gouda, 1617).

24 J. D. B. Ringoir, *Plattelandschirurgijns in de 17e en 18e eeuw* (Bunnik, 1977), p. 55; *Res. Holland*, 1596, p. 37 (23 Feb., Ooltgensplaat).

25 J. L. van der Gouw, *Het ambacht Voorschoten* (Voorburg, 1956), p. 35.

26 Ringoir, *Plattelandschirurgijns*, p. 53.

27 Schakel, *Noordeloos*, p. 62; Van Dillen, *Bronnen*, III, pp. 297–301.

28 Not. Zwartewaal, 15 May 1622 and 12 March 1623.

29 Van Dillen, *Bronnen*, III, pp. 297, 301.

30 Reitsma and Van Veen, *Acta*, III, p. 42 (South Holland, 1595); Van Deursen, *Bavianen en slijkgeuzen*, p. 74.

31 E. D. Baumann, *Uit drie eeuwen Nederlandse geneeskunde* (Amsterdam, n.d.), p. 42.

32 Krul, *Haagsche doctoren*, p. 7; Bik, *Medisch leven*, p. 581; Beeckman, *Journal*, II, p. 321; see also Bredero, *Stommen Ridder*, ll. 1931–40.

33 Van 't Hooft, *Volksbuch*, p. 51; Schotel, *Volksboeken*, I, pp. 19, 163.

34 Beeckman, *Journal*, I, p. 22.

35 Ibid., I, p. 60.

36 Ibid., III, p. 312.

37 Ibid., I, p. 87.

38 Rogier, *Katholicisme*, I, p. 223.

39 Van Buchell, *Diarium*, p. 284.

40 Broek Roelofs, *Baudartius*, p. 201; Van Vloten, *Kluchtspel*, I, p. 184.

41 *Res. Holland*, 1641, p. 67 (15 March).

42 Ibid., 1646, p. 161 (5 May).

43 De Bosch Kemper, *Geschiedkundig onderzoek*, p. 83.

44 J. G. Dijkstra, *Een epidemiologische beschouwing van de Nederlandsche pest-epidemieën der XVIIe eeuw* (Amsterdam, 1621), p. 43.

45 Cats, *Werken*, p. 202 ('Houwelick, Vrouwe').

46 Carleton, *Letters*, p. 163.

47 *Res. Holland*, 1603, p. 228 (8 Sept.); 1604, p. 330 (28 Dec.); 1605, pp. 62 (9 March), 236 (4 Sept.), 238 (6 Sept.), 332 (16 Dec.).

48 Huygens, *Gedichten*, II, p. 107.

49 Beeckman, *Journal*, II, p. 307.

50 Fritz, *Wagenaer*, p. 27.

51 *Res. Holland*, 1624, p. 138 (29 Nov.).

52 ARA, Holland 1384, f. 341 vo., 28 Feb. 1624.

53 Here the manuscript reads *predicanten* (preachers).

54 Ibid., f. 37 vo. (15 July 1621).

55 Ibid., f. 214 vo. (21 Jan. 1623, letter for a day of prayer).

56 *Groot Placaetboek*, I, p. 465 (9 Aug. 1587).

57 Ibid., III, p. 502 (1 April 1580).

58 Hallema, 'Rechterlijke maatstaven', p. 420.

59 Rogge, *Reigersberch*, p. 27.

60 Verwer, *Memoriaelbouck*, p. 157.

61 *Bijdragen voor de geschiedenis van het bisdom Haarlem (BGBH)*, vol. XVIII, p. 124.

62 Hebrews 10:31.

63 Evenhuis, *Amsterdam*, I, p. 191.
64 *Res. Holland*, 1628, p. 38 (14 March).
65 *Groot Placaetboek*, I, p. 219.
66 ARA, Holland 1384, f. 38 vo.
67 Souterius, *Victoriën*, I, p. 81.
68 Knuttel Pamphlet 1675 (1609).
69 Isaiah 44:17.
70 Vázquez, cited by Brouwer, *Kronieken*, pp. 96 and 122.
71 Reitsma and Van Veen, *Acta*, II, p. 345.
72 Acta Leiden, 25 July 1601 (Valkenburg).
73 Acta Woerden, 20 July 1620.
74 Van Deursen, 'Kerk of parochie?', p. 532.
75 Brandt and Centen, *Historie*, I, p. 278.
76 Reitsma and Van Veen, *Acta*, III, p. 43.
77 Acta Leiden, 7 Nov. 1622.
78 Not. Haarlem, 6 May 1622.
79 Ibid., 23 July 1624.
80 P. D. Muylwijk, 'Aanteekeningen over Gouda', *Bijdragen van de Oudheidkundige Kring 'die Goude'*, 2 (1940), p. 119 (Gouda, 1621 and 1622); Acta Dordrecht, 20–22 April 1621 (Giessen-Nieuwkerk); Not. Schoonhoven, 7 June 1621.
81 Stoye, *English travellers*, p. 247.
82 Acta Delft, 11 Sept. 1608.
83 Brandt, *Historie*, II, p. 29.
84 See below, p. 301.
85 Mundy, *Travels*, IV, p. 67.
86 Acta Woerden, 4 March 1621 and 21 Oct. 1625 (Bodegraven); Duker, *Gisbertus Voetius*, I, p. 150 (Vlijmen); Not. Berkel, 13 Nov. 1588 and 1 Jan 1592.
87 J. J. Woldendorp, 'Flitsen uit de kerkelijke geschiedenis van Zoetermeer-Zeegwaart na de reformatie', *Jaarboekje voor geschiedenis en oudheidkunde van Leiden en omstreken* (1956), p. 90 (Zoetermeer, 1586); ARA, Holland 1384, f. 242 (Rijnsaterwoude, Zeven-hoven, Langerak and Nieuwkoop, 1623); Reitsma and Van Veen, *Acta*, II, p. 93 (*classis* Amsterdam, 1619); Not. Purmerend, 28 July 1624 (*classis* Haarlem); ARA, Hof 385, f. 16 (Voorburg, 1602).
88 Woldendorp, 'Flitsen', p. 91.
89 Not. Naaldwijk, 27 Sept. 1573.
90 G. D. J. Schotel, *De openbare eeredienst der Nederlandsch hervormde kerk in de zestiende, zeventiende en achttiende eeuw*, second edition, ed. H. C. Rogge (Leiden, n.d.), p. 44.
91 Van Deursen, 'Kerk of parochie?' p. 533.
92 *BGBH*, vol. VI, p. 150 (Hof van Holland to the sheriff of Hoorn, 21 June 1621).
93 ARA, DTB Hoornaar Ia, 12 Jan. 1625.
94 Van Deursen, *Bavianen en slijkgeuzen*, p. 394.
95 *BGBH*, VI, p. 173 (Purmerend, 1626); J. I. J. M. Velthuyse, *Katholiek Berkel en Rodenrijs in de loop der eeuwen* (Rotterdam, 1948), p. 35 (Berkel, ca. 1640).
96 Brandt and Centen, *Historie*, II, p. 51.
97 *BGBH*, VIII, p. 433: in 1643 only two or three Catholics were living in Stolwijk.
98 Fruin, 'Verhaal der gevangenschap van Oldebarnevelt, beschreven door zijn knecht Jan Francken', *Kroniek van het Historisch Genootschap*, 30 (1874), p. 773.
99 Van Deursen, 'Het oordeel van François van Aerssen over de moord op Hendrik IV van Frankrijk', *TvG*, 76, p. 298.
100 Andriessen, *Jezuïeten*, p. 218.

101 *BGBH*, XV, p. 425 (Cornelis Hendricksz. to Nicolaes Ruich, 13 July 1587).

102 P. Noordeloos, *Pastoor Maarten Donk*, 2 vols. (Utrecht, 1948), II, p. 25.

103 B. A. Mensink, *Jan Baptist Stalpart van der Wiele* (Bussum, 1958), p. 212.

104 L. J. van der Heyden, *Katholiek Hilversum voorheen en thans* (Hilversum, 1917), p. 21.

105 O. F. M. Sloots, ed. Cunibertus, *De minderbroeders te Leiden* (Rotterdam, 1947), p. 172.

106 R. R. Post, *Kerkelijke verhoudingen in Nederland vóór de reformatie van ± 1500 tot ± 1580* (Utrecht, 1954), p. 402.

107 Acta Gorinchem, 18 April 1589.

108 Acta Den Briel, 24 April 1597. A similar charge was made against Rodolphus Uuyterwijc of Zuidland, 27 April 1599.

109 E.g. Reitsma and Van Veen, *Acta*, III, pp. 173, 206; Acta Leiden, 3 Nov. 1610.

110 Not. Haarlem, 9 Oct. 1616. A similar case, 24 May 1622.

111 Not. Zevenhuizen, 12 April 1620.

112 Acta Dordrecht, 1 Aug. 1617.

113 Schotel, *Volksboeken*, I, pp. 163ff.

114 ARA, Hof 5222, *informatie* regarding Hestertgen Pietersdr. at Rotterdam (1617).

115 *BGBH*, III, p. 435.

116 R. Fruin, *Verspreide geschriften*, 10 vols. (The Hague, 1900–5), VII, p. 291. Other reports of exorcism: Sloots, *Minderbroeders*, p. 191, and *Gouda*, p. 308. Dusseldorpius was an advocate at the Court of Holland. His Catholic devotion led him to flee to Utrecht (1597); he took holy orders in 1609 and worked as a popular preacher with Sasbout Vosmeer, the apostolic Vicar. He wrote annals of his times. R. Fruin, *Uittreksel uit Francisci Dusseldorpii Annales 1566–1616*, Werken van het Historisch Genootschap Gevestigd te Utrecht, third series, 1 (The Hague, 1893).

117 Van Deursen, *Bavianen en slijkgeuzen*, p. 53.

118 Rogier, *Katholicisme*, I, p. 70.

119 Not. Hillegersberg, 6 Dec. 1620.

120 Brandt, *Historie*, I, p. 816.

121 Acta Leiden, 21 Sept. 1586.

122 Reitsma and Van Veen, *Acta*, III, pp. 87 (1597), 107 (1598), 219 (1604).

123 *BGBH*, VI, p. 165 (Hof van Holland to the sheriff of Hoorn, 1 June 1624).

124 Baudartius, *Memoryen*, I, book 9, p. 126.

125 Ibid., I, book 11, p. 95.

126 Ibid., I, book 8, p. 54 (1616).

127 At the end of the seventeenth century, Balthasar Bekker (*De betoverde wereld*, 4 vols., Deventer, 1739, I, p. 124), was still writing that most people had not entirely rejected magical beliefs.

128 Brandt and Centen, *Historie*, I, p. 278. See also the cautious description of the unnatural plague of 1619 in the orphanage of Enkhuizen, II, p. 33.

129 Westermannus, *Christelijcke zee-vaert*, p. 267.

130 Ibid., p. 274.

131 Besides the examples already cited in the text, and those to follow, see also Post, *Kerkelijke verhoudingen*, p. 438; J. de Vries Azn, 'Adolphus Tectander Venator', *Oud-Holland*, 40 (1922), p. 159; Fritz, *Wagenaer*, p. 7; Knuttel Pamphlet 1247; De Hullu, 'Ziekten'.

132 Knuttel Pamphlet 945.

133 When the devil changed himself into human form, there was always something visibly lacking, 'because he can never make himself a complete person': Biestkens, *Claas Kloet*, p. 77.

134 Rollin Couquerque, 'Heksenprocessen te Goedereede', *Tijdschrift voor Strafrecht*, 12 (1897), p. 139.

135 H. van Dam, *Korte beschrijvinge van het eylandt Westvoorn, ende de geschiedenissen van de stadt Goederede* (Rotterdam, 1680), p. 98.
136 J. Scheltema, *Geschiedenis der heksenprocessen* (Haarlem, 1828), p. 258.
137 Baschwitz, p. 296.
138 Not. Amsterdam (Waals), 26 May 1614.
139 ARA, RAZH Schoonhoven 2322, 3 Dec. 1619.
140 Not. Den Briel, 13 Sept. 1622. For the sentence, see ARA, RAZH Brielle, 16 Sept. 1622.
141 Hooft, *Brieven*, p. 70.
142 Not. Edam, 22 Feb. 1598; Not. Zevenhuizen, 21 July 1613; Not. Ridderkerk, 1616 (p. 64); Crena de Iongh, *G. C. Van Santen*, pp. 341; Not. Haarlem, 23 March 1622; Acta Gouda, 30 May 1622; Acta Dordrecht, 27–28 June 1623.
143 Cats, *Werken*, p. 162; Crena de Iongh, *G. C. Van Santen*, p. 347.
144 Reitsma and Van Veen, *Acta*, II, p. 346 (1589).
145 'Which is condemned in God's word': Schotel, *Dordrecht*, p. 169 (1606).
146 E.g. KB, MS 131 A 2 IX, ff. 460, 470, 477; Baudartius, *Memoryen*, I, book 6, p. 8; book 7, p. 60; book 9, pp. 97, 102; book 10, p. 103; II, book 12, p. 113; book 15, p. 178.
147 *Res. Holland*, 1598, p. 46 (3 Feb.).
148 Knuttel Pamphlet 2220.
149 Knuttel Pamphlet 2315.
150 Knuttel Pamphlet 3007. Other examples of wonder-pamphlets: 1057, 1820.
151 Baudartius, *Memoryen*, I, book 7, p. 60.
152 Knuttel Pamphlet 3737.
153 Westermannus, *Christelijke zee-vaert*, p. 283.
154 Baudartius, *Memoryen*, II, book 15, p. 179 (1623).
155 H. van Dam, *Historisch verhaal van alle de schrickelijcke hoge watervloeden, tempeesten, etc.* (Rotterdam, 1680), p. 179. This view was already current before the period discussed here, as shown by Beeckman, *Journal*, I, p. 261 (1618).
156 A. Pijnacker Hordijk, *Kerkelijk Naaldwijk* (Nijmegen, 1898), p. 34.
157 Duker, *Gibertius Voetius*, I, p. 63.
158 Baudartius, *Memoryen*, I, book 6, p. 8.
159 Knuttel Pamphlet 1692.
160 Baudartius, *Memoryen*, I, book 9, p. 202.
161 Grevinghovius, *Fondamentboeck*, p. 77. Specific cases of stargazers who received warnings: Not. Oudewater, 28 Nov. 1604; Not. Haarlem, 24 March 1617.
162 Baudartius, *Memoryen*, II, book 15, p. 99. In the same spirit, Aitzema, *Saken*, II, p. 898.
163 Knuttel Pamphlet 2492, A ii.
164 Knuttel Pamphlet 972.
165 Thus Marnix calls the libertines 'geestdrijvers' (fanatics), because they gauged the Bible according to the lights of their own understanding. Cf. J. H. Maronier, *Het inwendig woord* (Amsterdam, 1890), p. 226.
166 Bredero, *Moortje*, ll. 2598–9. Berndt Knipperdollinck was an early Anabaptist leader from Münster, radical and iconoclast. He became one of the visionary 'prophets' of the sect and was executed after the recapture of Münster in 1536.
167 Knuttel Pamphlet 3773, p. 7.
168 Ibid., p. 6.
169 Brandt, *Historie*, IV, pp. 107, 115; Van Vloten, *Paschier*, p. 75.
170 ARA, Hof 5229, *Informatie* regarding Hazerswoude, 13 Oct. 1623.
171 J. Hania, *Wernerus Helmichius* (Utrecht, 1895), p. 198.
172 Schotel, *Dordrecht*, p. 130.
173 Van Deursen, *Bavianen en slijkgeuzen*, p. 55.

174 Acta Edam, 12 May 1608.

175 Dozy, 'Kerk en staat te Leiden, in het laatst der 16e en begin der 17e eeuw', *Mededeelingen van de Maatschappij der Nederlandsche Letterkunde te Leiden over 1897–1898* (Leiden, 1898), p. 32.

176 Kaajan, *Pro-acta*, p. 14. Also: 'war wol bekleidet und redete vernünftig' (she was well dressed and spoke reasonably).

177 Baudartius, *Memoryen*, II, book 16, p. 51. See also his report of a conversation with a prophet from Gelderland, I, book 7, p. 20.

178 Knuttel Pamphlet 3500.

179 Outward signs, which were discussed earlier, sometimes went together with the messages of prophets, who appeared as interpreters of scripture: e.g. Knuttel Pamphlet 972.

180 Schotel, *Volksboeken*, I, p. 103.

181 Knuttel Pamphlet 1111.

182 Knuttel, *Acta*, I, p. 83.

15. CALVINISTS

1 This chapter is generally based on my *Bavianen en slijkgeuzen*. Thus the only references to that book will be for direct quotations.

2 Reitsma and Van Veen, *Acta*, I, p. 7 (31 March 1573).

3 Ibid., II, p. 129 (16 June 1574).

4 Ibid., I, p. 39.

5 As e.g., I. Schöffer, review of A. T. van Deursen, *Bavianen en slijkgeuzen*, TvG, 91 (1978), p. 302.

6 *Res. Holland*, 1579, 30 Jan.

7 Van Deursen, *Bavianen en slijkgeuzen*, p. 128.

8 Reitsma and Van Veen, *Acta*, I, p. 79 (1580).

9 *BGBH*, VII, p. 80 (P. C. Hooft to the Hof van Holland, 3 Feb. 1636).

10 E.g. *BGBH*, XX, pp. 385, 388.

11 Ibid., XIX, p. 289.

12 A. Duke and R. Jones, 'Towards a reformed polity in Holland 1572–1578', TvG, 89 (1976), p. 383.

13 H. E. Enno van Gelder, *Revolutionnaire reformatie* (Amsterdam, 1943), p. 20.

14 Ibid., p. 25.

15 Van Deursen, 'Kerk of parochie?', p. 534.

16 Reitsma and Van Veen, *Acta*, II, p. 132 (17 June 1574, South Holland).

17 See above, p. 246.

18 Reitsma and Van Veen, *Acta*, I, p. 4.

19 Van Deursen, *Bavianen en slijkgeuzen*, p. 142.

20 Reitsma and Van Veen, *Acta*, I, p. 2.

21 Van Deursen, *Bavianen en slijkgeuzen*, p. 136.

22 Ibid., p. 138.

23 *BGBH*, XX, p. 385.

24 Part I, pp. 63–5.

25 Van Deursen, *Bavianen en slijkgeuzen*, p. 195.

26 A. T. Van Deursen, 'Amsterdams hervormde gemeente in 1678', in *1578–1978. 400 jaar hervormd Amsterdam*, special issue of *Present* (May 1978).

27 Duke and Jones, 'Reformed polity', p. 383.

28 P. Polman, OFM, *Godsdienst in de gouden eeuw* (Utrecht, 1947) p. 23.

29 Van Deursen, *Bavianen en slijkgeuzen*, p. 193.

30 *BGBH*, XXXIV, p. 321.

31 Answer 55.

32 Article 28.

33 *BGBH*, XXXII, pp. 299–301.

34 Verwer, *Memoriaelbouck*, p. 29.

35 C. Huygens, *Ghebruik en onghebruik van 't orgel in de kerken der Vereenighde Nederlanden*, second edition (Amsterdam, 1659), p. 113.

36 *BGBH*, VI, p. 180.

37 P. D. Muylwijk, *Vervolgd en toch overwinnars. Historisch verhaal uit de zeventiende eeuw* (Gouda, n.d.), p. 172.

38 Divoda Jansen, p. 8.

39 Buitendijk, 'Wilhelmus', p. 185. According to Overbury (*Works*, p. 56), in England some men had a Bible hanging from their belts. He states this specifically of a button-maker from Amsterdam who lived in England.

40 Brouwer, *Kronieken*, p. 92.

41 Reitsma and Van Veen, *Acta*, II, p. 133 (Zuid-Holland, 17 June 1574).

42 Aitzema, *Beschryvinge*, I, p. 378.

43 W. Nijenhuis, 'Varianten binnen het Nederlandse calvinisme in de zestiende eeuw', *TvG*, 89 (1976), p. 358.

44 *Algemene geschiedenis der Nederlanden*, 6 (1979), p. 340.

45 See part II, p. 147.

46 Van Deursen, *Bavianen en slijkgeuzen*, p. 296.

47 Ibid., p. 295.

48 Ibid., p. 294.

16. CATHOLICS

1 Post, *Kerkelijke verhoudingen*, p. 409.

2 Ibid., p. 419.

3 Ibid., p. 437.

4 Ibid., p. 425.

5 J. de Lange, *De martelaren van Gorcum* (Utrecht, 1954), p. 114.

6 H. A. van der Valk, *Kerkelijk Oud-Beijerland* (Oud-Beijerland, 1907), p. 145.

7 De Lange, *Martelaren*, p. 91.

8 T. van Vugt, *De gehangenen in de turfschuur. Brielse julinacht 1572* (Hilversum, 1972), p. 20.

9 De Lange, *Martelaren*, p. 117.

10 Part III, p. 205.

11 Fruin, *Verspreide geschriften*, II, p. 302.

12 Rogier, *Katholicisme*, II, p. 336, and especially for Holland, p. 383.

13 Duke and Jones, 'Reformed polity', p. 377.

14 *BGBH*, XIX, p. 150.

15 Ibid., 10, p. 295.

16 Noordeloos, *Maarten Donk*, II, p. 55.

17 L. J. Rogier, *Geschiedenis van katholiek Delfshaven* (Haarlem, p. 27. There are examples from a later period: *BGBH*, XXXV, p. 112 (Korter Aar, 1594); ibid., XLIV, p. 329 (Gorinchem, ca. 1600); K. Verhoofstad, *Katholiek Purmerend* (Purmerend, 1943), p. 55 (Purmerend, 1606).

18 *BGBH*, XVIII, p. 429; Rogier, *Katholicisme*, II, p. 372.

19 Fruin, *Verspreide geschriften*, III, p. 289.

20 *BGBH*, XVII, p. 243.

21 Ibid., xv, p. 443 (Father Cornelius Hendriksz., end 16th century). See also ibid., xvii, p. 262 (Trijntgen Dirks Wij).

22 Rogier, *Katholicisme*, iii, p. 513.

23 Velthuyse, *Katholiek Berkel*, p. 34.

24 Ibid., p. 33.

25 *BGBH*, vii, p. 353 (report of councillor Seb. Francken, July 1643).

26 Ibid., p. 387.

27 Ibid., iii, p. 300.

28 Van Deursen, *Bavianen en slijkgeuzen*, pp. 80, 130.

29 *BGBH*, xviii, p. 118.

30 Ibid., p. 120.

31 Ibid., p. 121.

32 Clothing regulations, ibid., 42, p. 37.

33 Ibid., xvii, p. 235.

34 Ibid., xvii, p. 238.

35 Ibid., xxxi, p. 108.

36 Ibid., xviii, p. 88.

37 Rogier, *Katholicisme*, iv, p. 761.

38 *BGBH*, vii, p. 353.

39 Ibid., xlvi, p. 346.

40 Rogier, *Katholicisme*, v, p. 1100.

41 Moryson, *Itinerary*, iii, p. 455.

42 *Gouda*, p. 292.

43 Van Hoeck, *Jezuïeten*, p. 44.

44 Sloots, *Minderbroeders*, p. 196.

45 *BGBH*, vii, p. 347; *Bijdragen voor de geschiedenis van de roomsch-katholieke kerk in Nederland*, 2 vols. (Rotterdam, 1888–92), i, p. 113.

46 Scholtens, *Midden-Kennemerland*, p. 172.

47 Ibid., p. 177.

48 *Res. Holland*, 1588, p. 227 (29 June).

49 *BGBH*, xvii, p. 298.

50 Van Deursen, 'Kerk of parochie?', p. 532.

51 Van Deursen, *Bavianen en slijkgeuzen*, p. 22.

52 Acta Den Haag, 4 Dec. 1623.

53 Part i, p. 65.

54 Van Deursen, *Bavianen en slijkgeuzen*, p. 106.

55 *BGBH*, lvii, p. 332.

56 Van Deursen, *Bavianen en slijkgeuzen*, p. 181.

57 Verwer, *Memoriaelbouck*, p. 214.

58 *Bijdragen*, i, p. 19.

59 *BGBH*, xvii, p. 276 (similar to xix, p. 141).

60 Acta Den Haag, 7 July 1619.

61 *Gouda*, p. 222.

62 Ibid., p. 228. It dated from 1637.

63 A. J. M. Alkemade and B. Woelderink, 'Het hofje van Johan van der Veeken', *Rotterdams Jaarboekje* (1968), p. 255.

64 Van Deursen, *Bavianen en slijkgeuzen*, p. 56.

65 Ibid., p. 129.

66 Ibid., p. 98.

67 H. J. W. Verhey, *Soli Deo Gloria. Geschiedenis van de oud-katholieke parochie van de Heilige Laurentius en Maria Magdalena te Rotterdam* (De Bilt, 1950), p. 29.

68 Sloots, *Minderbroeders*, p. 183; *Bijdragen*, I, p. 142.
69 Verhey, *Soli Deo Gloria*, p. 26.
70 *BGBH*, XLVI, p. 332.
71 *Bijdragen*, I, p. 57.
72 *BGBH*, XVIII, p. 89.
73 Something similar in Fruin, *Verspreide geschriften*, III, p. 320. There such an action did indeed result in a conversion.
74 *Bijdragen*, I, p. 21.
75 Fruin, *Verspreide geschriften*, III, p. 314.
76 Ibid., p. 316.
77 *BGBH*, XVIII, p. 104.
78 Ibid., XIX, p. 307.
79 Ibid., XLVI, p. 342.
80 Vrijman, *Kaapvaart*, p. 131. Cf. Van Deursen, *Bavianen en slijkgeuzen*, p. 150.
81 De Meij, *Watergeuzen*, p. 165.
82 Enno van Gelder, *Revolutionnaire reformatie*, p. 179.
83 Rogier, *Katholicisme*, II, p. 349.
84 *Res. Holland*, 1630, p. 9 (17 Jan.).
85 Polman, *Godsdienst*, p. 50; Rogier, *Katholicisme*, II, p. 351.
86 *Res. Holland*, 1640, p. 164 (2 Aug.).
87 *BGBH*, XXVI, p. 148.
88 E.g. *Bijdragen*, I, pp. 22, 110.
89 Rogier, *Katholicisme*, III, p. 505.
90 Fruin, *Verspreide geschriften*, III, p. 300.
91 Acta Dordrecht, 1–3 July 1625.
92 Van der Heyden, *Katholiek Hilversum*, p. 24.
93 Velthuyse, *Katholiek Berkel*, p. 38.
94 Rogier, *Katholicisme*, II, p. 354.
95 Fruin, *Verspreide geschriften*, II, p. 380.
96 Verhoofstad, *Katholiek Purmerend*, p. 55.
97 M. M. J. Hoogenbosch, *12 eeuwen katholicisme aan het Marsdiep* (Heiloo, 1966), p. 27.
98 *BGBH*, VII, p. 60 (the ministers of Kudelstaart, Kalslagen, and Aalsmeer to the Hof van Holland, 25 March 1635).
99 E.g. ARA, Holland, 1384, f. 25 vo., Hof van Holland to the bailiff of Rijnland, 18 June 1621; *BGBH*, II, p. 174 (the magistrate of Oudewater to the Hof, 17 Jan. 1636); ibid., VII, p. 60 (see previous note).
100 Ibid., 3, p. 125.
101 Rogier, *Katholicisme*, II, p. 355.
102 Brandt, *Historie*, IV, p. 787.
103 E.g. Schottmüller, 'Reise-eindrucke', p. 264; Noordeloos, *De Streek*, p. 7; Tukker, *De classis Dordrecht*, p. 74; *Res. Holland*, 1622, p. 3 (6 Jan.); Not. Hillegersberg, f. 32 vo.; ARA, Holland 1384, ff. 45, 92, 98, 137.
104 Ibid., ff. 45 (Veen), 98 (Waasbeek).
105 ARA, Hof 386, f. 9, 18 April 1614.
106 *BGBH*, VI, p. 167 (21 July 1624); 7, p. 81 (27 Jan. 1643).
107 *Res. Holland*, 1622, p. 3 (6 Jan.).
108 Rogier, *Katholicisme*, II, p. 387.
109 *BGBH*, VII, p. 59 (1635).
110 ARA, Hof 387, f. 192, Hof to the sheriff of Hoorn, 11 June 1624.
111 Knipscheer, 'Vestiging', p. 143.

112 *BGBH*, VII, p. 364 (July 1943).

113 Velthuyse, *Katholiek Berkel*, p. 35, probably c. 1640.

114 *BGBH*, VI, p. 152 (the sheriff to the Hof, 28 Aug. 1610).

115 *BGBH*, VII, p. 71 (13 Jan. 1635).

116 *BGBH*, III, p. 125 (17 Nov. 1634).

117 Ibid., VII, p. 54 (9 Jan. 1635).

118 Ibid., VII, p. 57.

119 Ibid., VI, p. 168.

120 Ibid., VI, p. 157.

121 Part III, pp. 226ff. Also *BGBH*, VI, pp. 173, 178; XVII, p. 285.

122 On Vosmeer, e.g., see Rogier, *Katholicisme*, III, p. 508; on Rovenius, J. Visser, *Rovenius und seine Werke* (Assen, 1966), p. 158.

123 J. J. Poelhekke, *Geen blijder maer in tachtigh jaer. Verspreide studiën over de crisisperiode 1648–1651* (Zutphen, 1973), p. 110.

124 Van Deursen, *Bavianen en slijkgeuzen*, p. 145.

125 Rogier, *Katholicisme*, II, p. 343.

126 Van Deursen, *Bavianen en slijkgeuzen*, pp. 51ff.

127 See above, p. 265.

128 Reitsma and Van Veen, *Acta*, I, p. 252 (North Holland, 1598).

129 As an example for the Catholic side, see Noordeloos, *Maarten Donk*, II, p. 49; for the Protestants, Knuttel Pamphlet 1414 A III.

130 Van Deursen, *Bavianen en slijkgeuzen*, p. 337.

131 *Res. Holland*, 1633, p. 47.

132 Knuttel Pamphlet 4682, p. 22. See also part I, p. 25.

133 *BGBH*, XVIII, p. 101.

134 Ibid., XVII, p. 276.

135 To the Calvinists, ibid., p. 280; to the Catholics, Not. Haarlem, 5 Nov. 1619.

136 E.g. *BGBH*, XXXV, p. 284; also above, p. 289.

137 *BGBH*, XVII, p. 281.

138 Fruin, *Verspreide geschriften*, III, p. 260.

139 Rogier, *Katholicisme*, II, p. 329.

140 Post, *Kerkelijke verhoudingen*, p. 436.

141 *BGBH*, VII, p. 84.

142 Ibid., VIII, pp. 210–19.

143 *Bijdragen*, I, p. 24.

144 *BGBH*, XVII, p. 297.

145 *BGBH*, XLIV, pp. 321–335.

146 *BGBH*, I, p. 25.

147 Ibid., XV, p. 453.

148 Ibid., XV, p. 401.

149 Ibid., I, p. 65.

150 Van Deursen, *Bavianen en slijkgeuzen*, p. 65.

151 *BGBH*, XLVI, p. 328.

152 Ibid., XLVI, p. 326.

153 Ibid., XLII, p. 46.

154 Ibid., XVIII, p. 445.

155 Van Deursen, *Bavianen en slijkgeuzen*, p. 161.

156 *BGBH*, XVIII, p. 123.

157 Ibid., XVII, p. 278.

158 Ibid., XV, p. 432. See also Velthuyse, *Katholiek Berkel*, p. 32.

159 *BGBH*, XVIII, p. 245.
160 Ibid., LV, p. 135.
161 *Bijdragen*, I, p. 71.
162 *BGBH*, XXXV, p. 289.
163 Ibid., XVIII, p. 61 (also X, p. 295).
164 See above, p. 246.
165 *BGBH*, X, p. 61.
166 Ibid., XVIII, p. 108.
167 Rogier, *Katholicisme*, V, p. 1051.
168 *BGBH*, XXXV, p. 402.
169 *BGBH*, XIX, p. 142.
170 Sloots, *Minderbroeders*, p. 168.
171 Fruin, *Verspreide geschriften*, II, p. 314.
172 *BGBH*, XXIX, p. 295.
173 Ibid., XX, p. 380.
174 Ibid., XX, p. 346.
175 Ibid., XIX, p. 143.
176 Ibid., XVIII, p. 112.
177 Visser, *Rovenius*, p. 30.
178 Ibid., p. 72.
179 *BGBH*, XX, p. 345.
180 Ibid., XVIII, p. 99.
181 Ibid., XVII, p. 261.
182 Ibid., XVII, p. 235.
183 Ibid., XVIII, p. 92.
184 Ibid., XVIII, p. 94.
185 Ibid., II, p. 121.
186 *Bijdragen*, I, p. 18.
187 *BGBH*, XXXIV, p. 331.
188 Velthuyse, *Katholiek Berkel*, p. 39.

17. MENNONITES

1 *BGBH*, XVII, p. 270.
2 Duke and Jones, 'Reformed polity', p. 383.
3 C.-P. Clasen, *Anabaptism, a social history 1525–1618* (Ithaca, 1972), p. 98.
4 Van Deursen, *Bavianen en slijkgeuzen*, p. 140.
5 Edema van der Tuuk, *Johannes Bogerman*, p. 47; G. J. Vos Azn., *Voor den spiegel der historie!! Amstels kerkelijk leven van de eerste zestig jaren der vrijheid* (Amsterdam, 1903), p. 94.
6 Kühler, *Doopsgezinden*, II, p. 65.
7 Van der Woude, *Het Noorderkwartier*, I, p. 134.
8 Kühler, *Doopsgezinden*, II, p. 66.
9 C. Krahn, *Dutch anabaptism: origin, spread, life and thought (1450–1608)* (The Hague, 1968), p. 256.
10 Kühler, *Doopsgezinden*, I, p. 300.
11 Ibid., I, p. 347.
12 Ibid., II, p. 75.
13 G. Fopma, 'Uit de geschiedenis der doopsgezinde gemeente in de Rijp', *Doopsgezinde Bijdragen*, 54 (1917), p. 32.
14 Kühler, *Doopsgezinden*, II, pp. 108, 114, 143, 144.

15 Grevinghovius, *Fondamentboek*, p. 124.
16 Van Deursen, *Bavianen en slijkgeuzen*, p. 72.
17 J. H. Wessel, *De leerstellige strijd tusschen Nederlandsche gereformeerden en doopsgezinden in de zestiende eeuw* (Assen, 1945), p. 116.
18 Kühler, *Doopsgezinden*, II, p. 15.
19 Ibid., II, p. 2.
20 Ibid., II, p. 45.
21 Not. Haarlem, 5 March 1624.
22 Kühler, II, p. 10.
23 W. J. van Douwen, *Socinianen en doopsgezinden. Doopsgezinde historiën uit de jaren 1559–1626* (Leiden, 1898), p. 49.
24 Grevinghovius, *Fondamentboek*, p. 173.
25 Clasen, *Anabaptism*, p. 79.
26 S. Blaupot ten Cate, *Geschiedenis der doopsgezinden in Holland, Zeeland, Utrecht en Gelderland*, I (Amsterdam, 1847), p. 123.
27 Kühler, *Doopsgezinden*, I, p. 373.
28 De Ries, cited by Kühler, *Doopsgezinden*, I, p. 376. See also H. W. Meihuizen, *Menno Simons, IJveraar voor het hersel van de nieuwtestamentische gemeente 1496–1561* (Haarlem, 1961), p. 80.
29 Maronier, *Het inwendig woord*, p. 133.
30 Kühler, *Doopsgezinden*, II, p. 146.
31 Ibid., II, p. 4.
32 Ibid., I, p. 399.
33 Krahn, *Dutch anabaptism*, p. 255.
34 J. Decavele, *De dageraad van de reformatie in Vlaanderen (1520–1565)*, 2 vols. (Brussels, 1975), I, p. 620.
35 Krahn, *Dutch anabaptism*, p. 258.
36 Meihuizen, *Menno Simons*, p. 109.
37 Ibid., p. 114.
38 Kühler, *Doopsgezinden*, II, p. 119.
39 Meihuizen, *Menno Simons*, p. 137.
40 Kühler, *Doopsgezinden*, I, p. 312.
41 Meihuizen, *Menno Simons*, p. 137.
42 Kühler, *Doopsgezinden*, II, p. 34.
43 Ibid., II, p. 10.
44 Van Douwen, *Socinianen*, pp. 47, 64.
45 ARA, Hof 5229, *informatie* regarding Hazerswoude, 29 Aug. 1623.
46 Knuttel, *Acta*, I, p. 111.
47 Kühler, *Doopsgezinden*, II, p. 71.
48 Blaupot ten Cate, *Doopsgezinden in Holland*, I, p. 128.
49 Kühler, *Doopsgezinden*, II, p. 76.
50 Ibid., II, p. 125.
51 Ibid., II, p. 116.
52 Ibid., II, p. 106.
53 Krahn, *Dutch anabaptism*, p. 234.
54 Kühler, *Doopsgezinden*, II, p. 5.
55 L'Honoré Naber, 'De With', p. 65.
56 Kühler, *Doopsgezinden*, II, p. 292.
57 Brandt and Centen, *Historie*, I, p. 272.
58 ARA, St. Gen. 6899, request from several prisoners in Algiers to Maurice and the States of Holland and Zeeland, 18 July 1615.

59 Van Deursen, *Honni soit*, p. 29.
60 Kühler, *Doopsgezinden*, II, p. 37.
61 Ibid., II, p. 38.
62 Ibid., II, p. 37.
63 Van Deursen, *Bavianen en slijkgeuzen*, p. 152.
64 Blaupot ten Cate, *Doopsgezinden in Holland*, I, p. 157.
65 Krahn, *Dutch anabaptism*, p. 238.
66 Kühler, *Doopsgezinden*, I, p. 342.
67 *Res. Holland*, 1612, p. 298 (14 Dec.).
68 Kühler, *Doopsgezinden*, II, p. 36.
69 Acta Dordrecht, 28–9 July 1622.
70 E.g. *Res. Holland*, 1628, p. 50 (21 March).
71 Van Buchell, *Diarium*, p. 310.
72 *Res. Holland*, 1643, p. 278 (17 Sept.).
73 Grevinghovius, *Fondamentboek*, p. 325.
74 Kühler, *Doopsgezinden*, II, p. 35.
75 Ibid., II, p. 34.
76 Cf. Van Deursen, *Bavianen en slijkgeuzen*, pp. 203ff.
77 Kühler, *Doopsgezinden*, II, p. 57.
78 Reitsma and Van Veen, *Acta*, II, p. 348.
79 J. Hartog, *Geschiedenis van de predikkunde in de protestantsche kerk van Nederland* (Utrecht, 1887), p. 42.
80 Van Deursen, *Bavianen en slijkgeuzen*, p. 152.
81 Ibid., pp. 124–6.
82 Krahn, *Dutch anabaptism*, p. 241.
83 Ephesians 4:28.
84 Kühler, *Doopsgezinden*, I, p. 344.
85 Ibid., II, p. 39.
86 Ibid., I, p. 374.
87 Ibid., II, p. 39.
88 *Heidelberg Catechism*, answer 116.
89 Kühler, II, p. 41.
90 Ibid., II, p. 1
91 Ibid., II, p. 102.
92 Also compared to the price of a Bible: Van Deursen, *Bavianen en slijkgeuzen*, p. 182.
93 For what follows, see also Clasen, *Dutch anabaptism*, p. 341 and others.

BIBLIOGRAPHY

MANUSCRIPT SOURCES

ALGEMEEN RIJKSARCHIEF, THE HAGUE (ARA)
Admiraliteit 646.
Collectie doop-, trouw- en begraafboeken Heinenoord 1 en Hoornaar 1a.
Financiën van Holland 826.
Hof van Holland (Court of Holland) 384–7, 5213, 5215, 5217–25, 5226, 5228, 5229, 5230, 5240, 5655, 5665.
Koloniaal archief 971.
Particuliere notulen Amsterdam 1.
Rechterlijke archieven Zuid-Holland (RAZH) Brielle 1, Schoonhoven 2322.
Staten van Holland, 1363, 1384, 1385, 2590, 2592, 2599, 2600, 2609, 2619, 2641.
Staten-Generaal (States-General) 38, 40, 3174, 4927–4930, 5479, 6889, 6899, 7475, 7574, 12163, Loketkas Admiraliteit 26; Loketkas particuliere stukken 52.
Waals hervormde gemeente Den Haag, 1, 30.

UNIVERSITEITSBIBLIOTHEEK, AMSTERDAM (UB)
    III H 4 (Paets).

KONINKLIJKE BIBLIOTHEEK, 'S-GRAVENHAGE (KB)
    MSS 131 A–2 IX (Centuriae van Bockenberg).

GEMEENTE BIBLIOTHEEK, ROTTERDAM
    Handschriftenverzameling van de remonstrantse gemeente 362, 2182.

CHURCH ARCHIVES
Acta van de classes:
    Den Briel (no. E2, 1594–1609; no. 3a, 1609–23).
    Delft (Classis 's-Gravenhage no. 137, 1603–21).
    Edam (no. 96, 1605–28).
    Gorinchem (classis Heusden no. 2, 1588–1618).
    Gouda (no. 1, 1617–23, and 1625–38).
    's-Gravenhage (no. 2, 1607–1636).
    Haarlem (no. 2, 1603–20).
    Leiden (no. 3, 1585–1618).
    Woerden (no. 7, 1617–26).

Notulen van de kerkeraden:
    Alkmaar (no. 1, 1604–9).
    Assendelft (1594–1703).
    Berkel en Rodenrijs (1588–1709).

Edam (no. 1, 1594–1611; no. 2, 1611–54).
Haarlem (no. 3, 1608–21).
Hillegersberg (no. 3, 1605–25).
Monnikendam.
Naaldwijk (no. 8, 1572–1709).
Oudewater (1586–1621).
Purmerend (no. 1, 1611–40).
Ridderkerk (no. 2, 1603–45).
Schoonhoven (no. 1a, 1614/1618–60).
Stolwijk (no. 14).
Uitgeest (no. 2, 1624–68).
Voorschoten (no. 1, 1615–1782).
't Woud (1587–1682).
Zevenhuizen (no. 1, 1603–40).
Zwartewaal (no. 11, 1611–1711).

Notulen van de Waalse kerkeraden van Amsterdam (no. 1a–1c, 1585–1625) en Leiden (no. 40, 1584–1611, and 41, 1611–48).

KNUTTEL PAMPHLET COLLECTION

945, 972, 1057, 1111, 1247, 1395, 1397, 1398, 1409, 1412, 1414, 1418, 1424, 1442, 1450, 1456, 1461, 1466, 1478, 1480, 1581, 1584, 1675, 1687, 1688, 1692, 1819, 1820, 1821, 1822, 2087, 2088, 2089, 2090, 2138, 2218, 2220, 2315, 2492, 2698, 3007, 3008, 3500, 3688, 3737, 3773, 3804, 4147, 4155, 4368, 4426, 4519, 4638, 4682, 5596.

BOOKS AND ARTICLES

For articles, the number of the first page is given.

Aalst, A. C. van, *Schets der staatkundige en kerkelijke geschiedenis en van de maatschappelijken toestand der stad Oudewater tot hare inneming en gedeeltelijke verwoesting in 1575*, Gouda, n.d. [1892–3].

Aitzema, L. van, *Saken van staet en oorlogh*, I–III, The Hague, 1669.

Alkemade, A. J. M., and B. Woelderink, 'Het hofje van Johan van der Veeken', *Rotterdams Jaarboekje*, seventh series, 6 (1968): 247.

Ampzing, Samuel, *Beschryvinge ende lof der stad Haerlem in Holland*, Haarlem, 1628.

Andriessen, SJ, J., *De Jezuïeten en het saamhorigheidsbesef der Nederlanden 1585–1648*, Antwerp, 1957.

Apeldoorn, L. J. van, *Geschiedenis van het Nederlandsche huwelijksrecht voor de invoering van de franse wetgeving*, Amsterdam, 1925.

Apeldoorn, L. J. van, 'De historische ontwikkeling van het recht omtrent de huwelijkssluiting in Nederland', in *Christendom en historie, lustrumbundel van het Gezelschap van Christelijke Historici* (Amsterdam, 1925), p. 67.

Arkenhout, A. A., 'De kerkbrand te Oostvoorne', *Zuid-Holland*, 5 (1959): 50.

Arnoldsson, Sverker, *La leyenda negra. Estudios sobre sus origines*, Göteborg, 1960.

Baars, C., *De geschiedenis van de landbouw in de Beijerlanden*, Wageningen, 1973.

Baetens, R., 'Organisatie en resultaten van de Vlaamse kaapvaart in de 17e eeuw', *Mededelingen Academie voor Marine van België*, 21 (1969–70): 89.

Baschwitz, Kurt, *De strijd met den duivel*, Amsterdam, 1948.

Baudartius, G., *Memoryen*, 2 vols., second edition, Arnhem/Zutphen, 1624.

Baumann, Evert Dirk, *Uit drie eeuwen Nederlandse geneeskunde*, Amsterdam, n.d. [1951].

Bax, J., *Prins Maurits in de volksmeening der 16e en 17e eeuw*, Amsterdam, 1940.

Beaujon, A., *Overzicht der geschiedenis van de Nederlandsche zeevisserrijen*, Leiden, 1885.

Becius, Johannes, *Het ghesette exemplaar der godloosen, ofte historie Sodomae ende Gomorrae, eertijts verclaert in XXV. predicatiën uyt Genes. cap. XVIII ende XIX, 't samenghestelt door Aegidius Joh. fil. Becius*, Arnhem, 1638.

Beeckman, Isaäc, *Journal tenu par Isaac Beeckman de 1604 à 1634*, ed. C. de Waard, 4 vols., The Hague, 1939–52.

Beels, A., *Handvesten en privilegiën mitsgaders keuren en ordonnantiën van Assendelft*, Amsterdam, 1768.

Beins, Ernst, 'Die Wirtschaftsethik der calvinistischen Kirche 1565–1650', *Nederlandsch Archief voor Kerkgeschiedenis*, n.s. 24 (1931): 81.

Bekker, Balthasar, *De betoverde wereld*, 4 vols., Deventer, 1739.

Belonje, J., 'Amsterdamsch grondbezit in de Zijpe omstreeks 1600', *JA*, 33 (1936): 37.

Bergen, Edward van, *Geschiedenis van Loosduinen*, Loosduinen, 1927.

Beschrijvinghe der stadt Rotterdam, Leiden, 1942.

Beuningen, W. van, *Het geestelijk kantoor te Delft*, Arnhem, 1870.

Beverwijck, J. van, *Schat der gesondheydt*, Amsterdam, 1652.

Bezemer, W., 'Een weddenschap om een huis', *RB*, 3 (1892): 221.

Bezemer, W., 'De magistraatsverandering te Utrecht in 1618', *BMHG*, 17 (1896): 71.

Bezemer, W., 'Het tucht- en werkhuis te Rotterdam', *RB*, 6 (1899): 149.

Biestkens, Nicolaes, *De drie delen van de klucht van Claas Kloet*, ed. G. R. W. Dibbets, Zwolle, n.d.

Bijdragen voor de geschiedenis van de roomsch-katholieke kerk in Nederland, 2 vols., Rotterdam, 1888–92.

Bijdragen voor de geschiedenis van het bisdom Haarlem (BGBH), 65 vols., 1873–1958.

Bijleveld, W. J. J. C., 'Leiden, stad der réfugiés', *Jaarboekje voor de Geschiedenis en Oudheidkunde van Leiden en Rijnland*, 35 (1948): 104.

Bik, J. G. W. F., *Vijf eeuwen medisch leven in een Hollandse stad*, Assen, 1955.

Bisschop, W., *De woelingen der Leicestersche partij binnen Leiden, 1586 en 1587*, Leiden, 1867.

Blankert, Albert, *Johannes Vermeer van Delft 1632–1675*, Utrecht, 1975.

Blaupot ten Cate, S., *Geschiedenis der doopsgezinden in Holland, Zeeland, Utrecht en Gelderland*, 1, Amsterdam, 1847.

Bleiswijck, H. van, *Vervolg van de beschryvinge der stad Delft*, Delft, n.d.

Blink, H., *Geschiedenis van den boerenstand en den landbouw in Nederland*, 2 vols., Groningen, 1902–4

Blockmans, W. P., and W. Prevenier, 'Armoede in de Nederlanden van de 14e tot het midden van de 16e eeuw: bronnen en problemen', *TvG*, 88 (1975): 502.

Blok, P. J., *Geschiedenis eener Hollandsche stad. Eene Hollandsche stad onder de Republiek*, The Hague, 1916.

Blok, P. J., *Geschiedenis van het Nederlandsche volk*, 4 vols., Leiden, n.d. [1912–15; 1923].
ed., *Relazioni veneziane. Venetiaansche berichten over de Vereenigde Nederlanden van 1600–1795*, Rijks Geschiedkundige Publicatiën, groote serie, 7, The Hague, 1909.

Blom, S., *Geschiedenis van Maassluis*, Utrecht, 1948.

Boekenoogen, G. J., ed., *Genoechlijcke history vanden schricklijcken ende onvervaerden reus Gilias*, Leiden, 1903.

Boekenoogen, G. J., ed., *Vanden jongen geheeten Jacke*, Leiden, 1905 ('The Friar and the Boy').

Verspreide geschriften, ed. A. A. van Rijnbach, Leiden, 1949.

Boogman, J. C., 'De overgang van Gouda, Dordrecht, Leiden en Delft in de zomer van het jaar 1572', *TvG*, 57 (1942): 81.

Booy, Engelina P. de, *De weldaet der scholen. Het plattelandsonderwijs in de provincie Utrecht van 1580 tot het begin der 19de eeuw*, Utrecht, 1977.

Bor, Pieter, *Oorsprongk, begin en vervolgh der Nederlandsche oorlogen*, 4 vols., Amsterdam, 1679–84.

Bosch Kemper, J. de, *Geschiedkundig onderzoek naar de armoede in ons vaderland*, Haarlem, 1851.

Boxer, C. R., *The Dutch seaborne empire*, London, 1965.

Brandt, G., *Historie der reformatie en andere kerkelijke geschiedenissen in en ontrent de Nederlanden*, 4 vols., Amsterdam, 1660–1704.

Brandt, G., and Sebastiaan Centen, *Historie der vermaarde zee- en koopstadt Enkhuisen*, 2 vols., Hoorn, 1747.

Bredero, G. A., *Werken*, ed. J. A. N. Knuttel, 3 vols., Amsterdam, 1921–9.

Briels, J. G. C. A., *Zuidnederlandse immigratie in Amsterdam en Haarlem omstreeks 1572–1630*, 1976.

Brink, J. ten, *Gerbrand Adriaensz. Bredero*, Leiden, 1859.

Broek Roelofs, O. C., *Wilhelmus Baudartius*, Kampen, 1947.

Brom, G., *Schilderkunst en litteratuur in de 16e en 17e eeuw*, Utrecht, 1957.

Brouwer, J., *Kronieken van Spaansche soldaten uit het begin van den tachtigjarigen oorlog*, Zutphen, 1933.

Brouwer Ancher, A. J. M., *De gilden*, The Hague, 1895.

Brouwers, SJ, L., *Carolus Scribani 1561–1629*, Antwerpen, 1961.

Brugmans, H., 'Utrechtse kroniek over 1566–1576', *BMHG*, 25 (1904): 1.

Bruijn, J. R., 'De personeelsbehoefte van de voc overzee en aan boord, bezien in Aziatsch en Nederlands perspectief', *BMGN*, 91 (1976): 218.

Bruijn, J. R., and J. Lucassen, *Op de schepen der Oost-Indische Compagnie: Vijf artikelen van J. de Hullu*, Groningen, 1980.

Buchell, Arend van, *Diarium*, ed. G. Brom and L. A. van Langeraad, Amsterdam, 1907.

Buitendijk, W. J. C., *Het calvinisme in de spiegel van de Zuid-Nederlandse literatuur der contra-reformatie*, Groningen, 1942.

Buitendijk, W. J. C., 'De dichter van het Wilhelmus', *Nieuwe Taalgids*, 33: 241.

Burger van Schoorel, Dirk, *Chronyk van de stad Medemblik*, Hoorn, 1767.

Busken Huet, C., *Het land van Rembrand*, third edition, II, Haarlem, 1898.

Bylsma, R., *Rotterdams welvaren 1550–1650*, The Hague, 1918.

Campbell, Douglas, *The Puritan in Holland, England, and America*, 2 vols., fourth edition, New York, 1920.

Capellen, Robert Jaspar van der, *Gedenkschriften van jhr. Alexander van der Capellen*, I, Utrecht, 1777.

Carleton, Dudley, *Letters during his embassy in Holland 1615–1620*, third edition, London, 1780.

Carnero, Antonio, *Historia de las guerras civiles que ha avido en los estados de Flandes desdel año 1559 hasta el de 1609*, Brussels, 1625.

Cats, Jacob, *Al de werken*, Schiedam, n.d.

Chill, Emmanuel, 'Religion and mendicity in seventeenth-century France', *International Review of Social History*, 7 (1962): 400–25.

Chong, A., 'The market for landscape painting in seventeenth-century Holland', in *Masterpieces of Dutch Landscape painting*, ed. P. C. Sutton, Boston and London, 1987.

Clasen, Claus-Peter, *Anabaptism, a social history 1525–1618: Switzerland, Austria, Moravia, South and Central Germany*, Ithaca, 1972.

Colenbrander, H. T., ed., *Korte historiael ende journaels aenteykening van verscheyden voyagiens in de vier deelen des wereldt-ronde, als Europa, Africa, Asia ende America gedaen door d. David Pietersz. De Vries*, The Hague, 1911.

Cornelissen, J. D. M., *Romeinsche bronnen voor den kerkelijke toestand der Nederlanden onder de apostolische vicarissen 1596–1727*, I, *1592–1651*, Rijks Geschiedkundige Publicatiën, Groote serie, 77, The Hague, 1932.

Cos, Jan, *Rechts-geleerde verhandelinge over de troubeloften en het daerop volgende huwelyk*, Hoorn, 1738.

Coster, Samuel, *Werken*, ed. R. A. Kollewijn, Haarlem, 1883.

Crena de Iongh, A. C., *G. C. van Santen's Lichte Wigger en Snappende Sijtgen*, Assen, 1959.

Daalder, D. L., *Wormcruyt met suycker. Historisch-critisch overzicht van de Nederlandse kinderliteratuur*, Amsterdam, 1950.

Daelemans, F., 'Leiden 1581: Een socio-demografisch onderzoek', *AAG Bijdragen*, 1975.

Dam, H. van, *Historisch verhaal van alle de schrickelijcke hoge watervloeden, tempeesten, etc.*, Rotterdam, 1680.

Dam, H. van, *Korte beschrijvinge van het eylandt Westvoorn, ende de geschiedenissen van de stadt Goederede*, Rotterdam, 1680.

Davids, W., *Verslag van een onderzoek betreffende de betrekkingen tusschen de Nederlandsche en de Spaansche letterkunde in de 16e–18e eeuw*, The Hague, 1918.

Debaene, L., *De Nederlandse volksboeken. Ontstaan en geschiedenis van de Nederlandse prozaromans, gedrukt tussen 1475 en 1540*, Antwerp, 1951.

Decavele, Johan, *De dageraad van de reformatie in Vlaanderen (1520–1565)*, 2 vols., Brussels, 1975.

Deursen, A. T. van, 'Amsterdams hervormde gemeente in 1678', in *1578–1978. 400 jaar hervormd Amsterdam*, special issue of *Present*, May 1978.

 Bavianen en slijkgeuzen. Kerk en kerkvolk ten tijde van Maurits en Oldenbarnevelt, Assen, 1974.

 Honni soit qui mal y pense? De Republiek tussen de mogendheden (1610–1612), Amsterdam, 1965.

 'Kerk of parochie? De kerkmeesters en de dood ten tijde van de Republiek', *TvG*, 89 (1976): 531.

 'Het oordeel van François van Aerssen over de moord op Hendrik IV van Frankrijk', *TvG*, 76 (1963): 284.

 Resolutiën der Staten-Generaal 1610–1670, The Hague, 1971.

 'Werkende vrouwen in een Hollands dorp', *De Zeventiende Eeuw*, 4 (1988): 3.

Diepeveen, W. J., *De vervening in Delfland en Schieland tot het einde der zestiende eeuw*, Leiden, n.d.

Dijk, H. J. van, 'De geldelijke druk op de Delftsche burgerij in de jaren 1572–1576', *BVGO*, seventh series, 5 (1935): 169.

Dijkstra, J. G., *Een epidemiologische beschouwing van de Nederlandsche pest-epidemieën der XVIIe eeuw*, Amsterdam, 1921.

Dillen, J. G. van, 'Amsterdam in Bredero's tijd', *De Gids* (1935) II: 308.

 Amsterdam in 1585: Het kohier der capitale impositie van 1585, Amsterdam, 1941.

 Bronnen tot de geschiedenis van het bedrijfsleven en gildewezen van Amsterdam, 3 vols., The Hague, 1929–74.

 Het oudste aandeelhoudersregister van de kamer Amsterdam der Oost-Indische Compagnie, The Hague, 1958.

 Van rijkdom en regenten. Handboek tot de economische en sociale geschiedenis van Nederland tijdens de Republiek, The Hague, 1970.

Dorp, Arend van, *Brieven en onuitgegeven stukken*, ed. J. B. J. N. Ridder de van der Schueren, 2 vols., Utrecht, 1887–8.

Douwen, W. J. van, *Socinianen en doopsgezinden. Doopsgezinde historiën uit de jaren 1559–1626*, Leiden, 1898.

Dozy, 'Kerk en staat te Leiden, in het laatst der 16e en begin der 17e eeuw', *Mededeelingen van de Maatschappij der Nederlandsche Letterkunde te Leiden over 1897–1898*, Leiden, 1898.

Dresch, N. J. M., 'Rekening van Maerten Ruychaver, thesaurier in het Noorderkwartier, 1572/73', *BMHG*, 49 (1928): 45.

Drost, Johanna W. P., *Het Nederlandsch kinderspel vóór de zeventiende eeuw*, The Hague, 1914.

Duke, Alastair, and Rosemary Jones, 'Towards a reformed polity in Holland 1572–1578', *TvG*, 89 (1976): 373.

Duker, A. C., *Gisbertus Voetius*, 3 vols., Leiden, 1897–1914.

Dwinglo, B., *Grouwel der verwoestinghe staende in de heylighe plaetse*, 2 vols., Enkhuizen, 1622.

Edema van der Tuuk, H., *Johannes Bogerman*, Groningen, 1868.

Eeghen, I. H. van, *De gilden. Theorie en praktijk*, Bussum, 1965.
    'Zigeuners in Amsterdam in 1554, 1592, 1595, 1725', *Amstelodamum*, 52 (1965): 53.

Eggen, J. L. M., *De invloed door Zuid-Nederland op Noord-Nederland uitgeoefend op het einde der XVIe en het begin der XVIIe eeuw*, Ghent, 1908.

Elias, J. E., *Geschiedenis van het Amsterdamsche regentenpatriciaat*, The Hague, 1923.
    Schetsen uit de geschiedenis van ons zeewezen, I, The Hague, 1916.
    De vroedschap van Amsterdam 1578–1795, I, Haarlem, 1903.

Engelenburg, W. van, *Geschiedenis van Broek in Waterland van de 163 tot het begin der 19e eeuw*, Haarlem, 1907.

Engels, P. H., *De belastingen en geldmiddelen van den aanvang der Republiek tot op heden*, Utrecht, 1862.

Evenhuis, R. B., *Ook dat was Amsterdam*, I, II, Amsterdam, 1965–7.

Eyck, J. van der, *Corte beschrijvinghe mitsgaders hantvesten, privilegien, costumen ende ordonnantien van den lande van Zuyt-Hollandt*, Dordrecht, 1628.

Floerke, Hanns, *Studien zur niederländischen Kunst- und Kulturgeschichte. Die Formen des Kunsthandels, das Atelier und die Sammler in den Niederlanden vom 15.–18. Jahrhundert*, Munich, 1905.

Fockema Andreae, *Schets van Zuid-Hollandse watersnoden in vroeger tijd*, Voorburg, 1953.

Fokker, G. A., *Geschiedenis der loterijen in de Nederlanden*, Amsterdam, 1862.

Fopma, G., 'Uit de geschiedenis der doopsgezinde gemeente in de Rijp', *Doopsgezinde Bijdragen*, 54 (1917): 9.

Frederiks, J. G., and P. J. Frederiks, *Kohier van den tweehonderdsten penning voor Amsterdam en onderhoorige plaatsen over 1631*, Amsterdam, 1890.

Frijlinck, W. P., *The tragedy of Sir John van Olden Barnevelt*, Amsterdam, 1922.

Fritz, Josef, *Die historie van Christoffel Wagenaer, discipel van D. Johannes Faustus*, Leiden, 1913.

Fruin, R., 'Gedenkschrift van Don Sancho de Londoño', *BMHG*, 13 (1892): 1.
    Geschiedenis der staatsinstellingen in Nederland tot den val der Republiek, ed. H. T. Colenbrander, The Hague, 1901.
    'Verhaal der gevangenschap van Oldenbarnevelt, beschreven door zijn knecht Jan Francken', *Kroniek van het Historisch Genootschap*, 30 (1874): 734.
    Verspreide geschriften, 10 vols., The Hague, 1900–1905.
    (ed.), *Uittreksel uit Francisci Dusseldorpii Annales 1566–1616*, Werken van het Historisch Genootschap Gevestigd te Utrecht, third series, I, The Hague, 1893.

Gelder, H. A. Enno van, 'De bedijking van de Heer Hugowaard (1624–1631)', *BVGO*, fourth series, 5 (1906): 231.

Gegevens betreffende roerend en onroerend bezit in de Nederlanden in de 16e eeuw, 2 vols., The Hague, 1972–3.

De levensbeschouwing van Corn. Pietersz. Hooft, Amsterdam, 1918.

Nederlandse dorpen in de 16e eeuw, Amsterdam, 1953.

'Recente gegevens omtrent de 16e eeuwse koopman', *TvG*, 35 (1920): 199, 344.

Revolutionnaire reformatie, Amsterdam, 1943.

Gelder, H. E. van, 'Haagsche cohieren, 1 (1627)', *Die Haghe Jaarboek* (1913): 9.

'Een loterij in 1605', *Die Haghe Jaarboek* (1916): 161.

Geuns, S. J. van, *Proeve eener geschiedenis van de toelating en vestiging van vreemdelingen in Nederland tot het jaar 1795*, Schoonhoven, 1853.

Geyl, P., *Christofforo Suriano*, The Hague, 1913.

Gils, J. B. F., *De dokter in de oude Nederlandsche tooneellitteratuur*, Haarlem, 1917.

Glas, P. J., 'Nicolaas Cornelisz. de Wit, gen. Scapecaes', *BVGO*, fourth series, 6 (1907): 67.

Gossart, E., *L'établissement du régime espagnol dans les Pays-Bas et l'insurrection*, Brussels, 1905.

Gosses, I. H., and N. Japikse, *Handboek tot de staatkundige geschiedenis van Nederland*, The Hague, 1920.

Gouda zeven eeuwen stad. Hoofdstukken uit de geschiedenis van Gouda, Gouda, 1972.

Gouw, J. L. van der, *Het ambacht Voorschoten*, Voorburg, 1956.

'Voorschoten tijdens het twaalfjarig bestand', *Mededelingenblad van de Historische Vereniging voor de Provincie Zuid-Holland*, 1:2 (1948).

Graefe, F., 'Beiträge zur Geschichte der See-Expeditionen von 1606 und 1607', *BVGO*, seventh series, 3 (1933): 201.

De kapiteinsjaren van Maerten Harpertszoon Tromp, ed. M. Simon Thomas, The Hague, 1938.

'Piet Heyn als Leutnant-admiral von Holland', *BVGO*, seventh series, 6 (1935): 174.

'Beiträge zur Geschichte der See-Expeditionen von 1606 und 1607', *Bijdragen voor Vaderlandsche Geschiedenis en Oudheidkunde*, seventh series, 3 (1933): 201.

Grevinghovius, C., *Onveranderde uitgave van fondamentboeck van de ware christelijke ghereformeerde religie, met uytlegginghe over de woorden Jesu Christi Matth. 7 vers 15 door Christianus à Porta*, Lemmer, 1871.

Groot Placaetboek, 9 vols., The Hague, 1658–1796.

Guicciardijn, Lowijs, *Beschryvinghe van alle de Nederlanden*, Cornelius Kilianus, tr., revised by Petrus Montanus, Amsterdam, 1612.

Hallema, A., *Geschiedenis van het gevangeniswezen hoofdzakelijk in Nederland*, The Hague, 1958.

Haarlemse gevangenissen, Haarlem, 1928.

'Jan van Houts rapporten en adviezen betreffende het Amsterdamsche tuchthuis uit de jaren 1597 en '98', *BMHG*, 48 (1927): 69.

'Rechterlijke maatstaven ten aanzien van de morele integriteit in het verleden', *Verslagen en mededeelingen van de vereeniging tot uitgaaf der bronnen van het Oud-Vaderlandsche recht*, 12, Utrecht, 1962.

'Vlaardingen en Dordrecht als oudste Nederlandse galeiendepots', *TvG*, 66 (1953): 69.

Hania, J. *Wernerus Helmichius*, Utrecht, 1895.

Hartog, J., *Geschiedenis van de predikkunde in de protestantsche kerk van Nederland*, Utrecht, 1887.

Haverman, J. F., *W. D. Hooft en zijne kluchten*, The Hague, 1895.

Hazewinkel, H. C., 'De rode haan kraaide in Rotterdam', *Rotterdams Jaarboekje*, seventh series, 1 (1963): 251.

D'Heere, Lucas, *Den hof en boomgaard der poësien*, ed. W. Waterschoot, Zwolle, 1962.

Heeringa, K., *Bronnen tot de geschiedenis van den Levantschen handel*, 1, *1590–1660*, The Hague, 1910.

Heidelberg Catechism (Calvinist), revised by the synod of Dordt, 1619.

Herbert of Cherbury, Edward, Lord, *Autobiography*, ed. S. L. Lee, ed., London, 1886.

Heyden, L. J. van der, *Katholiek Hilversum voorheen en thans*, Hilversum, 1917.

Hinsbergen, P. J. C. G. van, *Bijdrage tot de geschiedenis van de gemeente Nieuwkoop en haar onderdelen*, n.p., 1962.

Hoeck, F. van, *Schets van de geschiedenis der Jezuïeten in Nederland*, Nijmegen, 1940.

Hoekstra, P., *Bloemendaal*, Wormerveer, 1947.

Hofstede de Groot, C., *Die Urkunden über Rembrandt*, The Hague, 1906.

Hollweg, Walter, *Heinrich Bullingers Hausbuch*, Giessen, 1956.

L'Honoré Naber, S. P., *Beschrijvinghe ende historisch verhael van het Gout-Koninckrijck van Guinea anders de Gout-Custe de Mina genaemt, liggende in het deel van Africa, door P. de Marees*, The Hague, 1912.

''t Leven en bedrijff van vice-admirael De With, zaliger', *BMHG*, 47 (1926): 47.

Reizen van Willem Barents, Jacob van Heemskerck, Jan Cornelisz. Rijp en anderen naar het Noorden (1594–1597), 2 vols., The Hague, 1917.

Hooft, B. H. van 't, *Das holländische Volksbuch vom Doktor Faust*, The Hague, 1926.

Hooft, C. P., *Memoriën en adviezen*, 2 vols., Utrecht, 1871–1925.

Hooft, P. C., *Brieven*, Haarlem, 1750.

Warenar, dat is Aulularia van Plautus, Amsterdam, 1616.

Hooft, W. D., *Jan Saly*, second edition, Amsterdam, 1633.

Hoogenbosch, M. M. J., *12 eeuwen katholicisme aan het Marsdiep. De r.k.-kerk van Huisduinen en Den Helder in de loop dekr tijden*, Heiloo, 1966.

Hoogewerff, G. J., *De geschiedenis van de St. Lucasgilden in Nederland*, Amsterdam, 1947.

Journalen van de gedenckwaerdige reijsen van Willem IJsbrantsz. Bontekoe 1618–1625, The Hague, 1952.

Houbraken, A., *De groote schouburgh der Nederlantsche konstschilders en schilderessen*, ed. P. T. A. Swillens, 3 vols., Maastricht, 1943–4.

Howard, J., *The state of the prisons in England and Wales...*, 2 parts, Warrington, 1777–80.

Hulkenberg, A. M., *De Aagtenkerk van Lisse*, Lisse, 1960.

Hullu, J. de, 'De handhaving der orde en tucht op de schepen der Oost-Indische Compagnie', *BTLV*, 67 (1913): 516.

Hullu, J. de, 'Ziekten en dokters op de schepen der Oost-Indische Compagnie', *BTLV*, 67 (1913): 245.

Huygens, Constantijn, *Gedichten*, ed. J. A. Worp, I–IV, Groningen, 1892–4.

Ghebruik en onghebruik van 't orgel in de kerken der Vereenighde Nederlanden, second edition, Amsterdam, 1659.

IJzerman, J. W., *De reis om de wereld van Olivier van Noort 1598–1601*, 2 vols., The Hague, 1926.

'Inkomen van Holland en West-Friesland (1622)', *Kroniek van het Historisch Genootschap Gevestigd te Utrecht*, 28. jaargang, 1872, sixth series, 3 (Utrecht, 1873): 402.

Itterzon, G. P. van, *Franciscus Gomarus*, The Hague, 1929.

Jaanus, H. J., *Hervormd Delft ten tijde van Arent Cornelisz. (1573–1605)*, Amsterdam, 1950.

Jacobs, Joseph, *Epistolae Ho-elianae. The familiar letters of James Howell*, I, London, 1890.

Jacobsz., Broeder Wouter, *Dagboek*, ed. I. H. van Eeghen, 2 vols., Groningen, 1959–60.

Jager, H. de, 'Verweerschrift van den contra-remonstrantschen predikant Willem Crijnsze, door de Brielsche regeering afgezet en verbannen', *BMGH*, 17 (1896): 107.

Jansen, H. P. H., *Prisma Kalendarium*, Utrecht, 1988.

Janssen, H. Q., and J. J. van Toorenenbergen, *Brieven uit onderscheidene kerkelijke archieven*, Werken der Marnixvereeniging, third series, parts IV and V, Utrecht, 1880–5.

Jong, C. de., *Geschiedenis van de oude Nederlandse walvisvaart*, I, Pretoria, 1972.

Jonge, J. C. de, *Geschiedenis van het Nederlandsche zeewezen*, second edition, I, Haarlem, 1858.

Kaajan, H., *De groote synode van Dordrecht in 1618–19*, Amsterdam, n.d.
De pro-acta der Dordtsche synode in 1618, Rotterdam, 1914.

Kannegieter, J. Z., 'De Bloemstraat en haar zijstraten ± 1613–1625', *JA*, 54 (1962): 82.

Kerkelijk handboekje uitgegeven door de synode der Afgescheiden Gereformeerde Gemeente, gehouden te Hoogeveen anno MDCCCCLX, Kampen, 1861.

Kernkamp, G. W., 'Memoriën van ridder Theodorus Rodenburg, betreffende het verplaatsen van verschillende industrieën uit Nederland naar Denemarken met daarop gewonnen resolutiën van koning Christiaan IV (1621)', *BMHG*, 23 (1902): 189.

Kersbergen, A. C., 'Adriana van Oringen, "pachtersse en collectrice" van imposten', *Rotterdamsch Jaarboekje*, fourth series, 2 (1934): 86.

Kesper, L. A., 'De Goudsche vroedschap en de religie', *BVGO*, fourth series, 2 (1902): 391.

Keuren der stede van Oudewater des graefschaps van Hollant, Oudewater, 1605.

Keuren en ordonnantien ter Nieuwer-Amstel 't zeedert den jaare 1599, Amsterdam, 1727.

Keuren en ordonnantien van 's-Gravenhage, I, The Hague, 1735.

Kinschot, G. R. van, *Beschryving der stad Oudewater*, Delft, 1907.

Kist, N. C., *Neerlands bededagen en biddagsbrieven*, 2 vols., Leiden, 1848–9.

Kluit, A., *Historie der Hollandsche staatsregering tot aan het jaar 1795*, 5 vols., Amsterdam, 1802–5.

Knipscheer, F. S., 'Abdias Widmarius, predikant te Uitgeest, en het kerkelijke leven eener gereformeerde gemeente in de XVIIe eeuw', *Nederlandsch Archief voor Kerkgeschiedenis*, new series, 3 (1905): 291 and 396.
'De vestiging der gereformeerde kerk in Noord-Holland 1572–1608', *Nederlandsch Archief voor Kerkgeschiedenis*, n.s., 5 (1907): 137.

Knuttel, W. P. C., *Acta der particuliere synoden van Zuid-Holland 1621–1700*, I, The Hague, 1908.
Catalogus van de pamfletten verzameling berustende in de Koninklijke Bibliotheek, 8 vols., The Hague, 1889–1916.
De toestand der Nederlandsche katholieken ten tijde der Republiek, The Hague, 1892.

Knuttel-Fabius, Elize, *Oude kinderboeken*, The Hague, 1906.

Kok, OFM, J. A. de, *Nederland op de breuklijn Rome-reformatie*, Assen, 1964.

Koning, J., *Geschiedkundige aanteekeningen betrekkelijk de lijfstraffelijke regtoefening te Amsterdam, voornamelijk in de zestiende eeuw*, Amsterdam, 1828.

Korte schets der Nederlandsche historiën, Amsterdam, n.d.

Krahn, Cornelius, *Dutch anabaptism: origin, spread, life and thought (1450–1608)*, The Hague, 1968.

Kranenburg, H. A. H., *De zeevisscherij van Holland in den tijd der Republiek*, Amsterdam, 1946.

Krelage, E. H., *Bloemenspeculatie in Nederland. De tulpomanie van 1636–37 en de hyacintenhandel 1720–36*, Amsterdam, 1942.

Krul, R., *Haagsche doctoren, chirurgen en apothekers in den ouden tijd*, The Hague, 1891.

Kühler, W. J., *Geschiedenis van de doopsgezinden in Nederland*, I–II, Haarlem, 1940.

Kuiper, E. T., ed., *Die schoone hystorie van Malegijs*, Leiden, 1903.

Laan, N. van der, *Uit Roemer Visschers brabbeling*, 2 vols., Utrecht, 1918–23.

Lanario, Francisco, *Las guerras de Flandes desde el año de 1559 hasta el de 1609*, Madrid, 1623.

Lange, D. de, *De martelaren van Gorcum*, Utrecht, 1954.

Lange van Wijngaerden, C. J. de, *Geschiedenis en beschrijving der stad van der Goude*, 3 vols., Gouda, 1813–79.

Leeghwater, Jan Adriaensz., *Een klein kronykje omtrent den oorsprong en de vergrooting der dorpen van Graft en De Ryp*, ed. J. H. van Lennep, Haarlem, n.d.

Leeuwen, Simon van, *Costumen, keuren ende ordonnantien van het baljuschap ende lande van Rijnland*, Leiden, 1667.

Leuftink, A. E., *De geneeskunde bij 's lands oorlogsvloot in de 17e eeuw*, Assen, 1952.

Leupe, P. A., *Reize van Maarten Gerritsz. de Vries in 1643 naar het noorden en oosten van Japan volgens het journal gehouden door C. J. Coen*, The Hague, 1858.

Leupe, P. A., 'Zeezaken', *BMHG*, 2 (1879): 95.

Liesker, G. J., *Die staatswissenschaftlichten Anschauungen Dirck Graswinckels*, Freiburg, 1901.

Ligtenberg, Christina, *De armezorg te Leiden tot het einde van de 16e eeuw*, The Hague, 1908.

Linden van den Heuvell, J. H. van, *Uit de geschiedenis van het weeshuis te Vlaardingen*, Vlaardingen, 1955.

Lintum, C. te, 'De textielindustrie in oud-Rotterdam', *Rotterdamsch Jaarboekje*, 7 (1900): 1.

Livre synodal contenant les articles résolus dans les synodes des églises wallonnes des Pays-Bas, I, *1563–1685*, The Hague, 1896.

Loenen, J. B. van, *Beschrijving en kleine kroniek van de gemeente Hillegom*, Hillegom, 1916.

Lootsma, S., '"Draecht elckanders lasten." Bijdrage tot de geschiedenis der "Zeevarende Beurzen" in Noord Holland', *West-Friesland's 'Oud en Nieuw'*, 3 (1929): 12.

Historische studiën over de Zaanstreek, 2 vols., Koog aan de Zaan, 1939–50.

Malo, H., *Les corsaires: les corsaires dunkerquois et Jean Bart*, I, Paris, 1913.

Marnix van St Aldegonde, Philips van, *Godsdienstige en kerkelijke geschriften*, I and II, The Hague, 1871–73.

Maronier, J. H., *Het inwendig woord*, Amsterdam, 1890.

Meihuizen, H. W., *Menno Simons, IJveraar voor het hersel van de nieuwtestamentische gemeente 1496–1561*, Haarlem, 1961.

Meij, J. C. A. de, *De watergeuzen en de Nederlanden 1568–72*, Amsterdam, 1972.

Meilink, P. A., 'Rekening van Dirk van Kessel voor diensten aan den prins van Oranje over de jaren 1571–1574', *BMHG*, 47 (1926): 332.

Melles, J., *Het huys van leeninge. Geschiedenis van de oude lombarden en de stedelijke bank van lening te Rotterdam 1325–1950*, The Hague, 1950.

Mensink, B. A., *Jan Baptist Stalpart van der Wiele*, Bussum, 1958.

Meteren, Emanuel van, *Commentarien ofte memorien van den Nederlandtschen staet, handel, oorloghen ende gheschiedenissen*, Amsterdam, 1608.

Meulenbroek, B., *Briefwisseling van Hugo Grotius*, III–IV, The Hague, 1961–4.

Mieris, Frans van, *Handvesten der stad Leyden*, Leiden, 1759.

Moerkerken, P. H. van, *Het Nederlandsch kluchtspel in de 17de eeuw*, 2 vols., Sneek, n.d.

Moes, E. W., 'Amsterdamsche vondelingen v', Eene Beschrijving van Amsterdam in het jaar 1614, *Amsterdamsch Jaarboekje*, 4 (1891): 96.

Mollema, J. C., *De eerste schipvaart der Hollanders naar Oost-Indië 1595–1597*, The Hague, 1935.

Mone, Franz Joseph, *Übersicht der niederländischen Volks-Literatur älterer Zeit*, Tübingen, 1838.

Montias, J. M., *Artists and artisans in Delft: A socio-economic study of the seventeenth century*, Princeton, 1982.

Montchrétien, Antoyne de, *Traicté de l'oeconomie politique dedié en 1615 au roy et à la reine mère du roy*, Paris, n.d.

Moryson, Fynes, *An itinerary containing his ten yeeres travell*, 4 vols., Glasgow, 1907–8.

Mout, Nicolette, *Bohemen en de Nederlanden in de zestiende eeuw*, Leiden, 1975.

Muller Fzn., S., *Schetsen uit de middeleeuwen. Nieuwe bundel*, Amsterdam, 1914.

Mundy, Peter, *Travels in Europe and Asia 1608–1667*, IV, London, 1925.

Murray, W. G. D., 'Oud-Rotterdamsch kroegleven', *Rotterdamsch Jaarboekje*, fifth series, 2 (1944): 41; 3 (1945): 1.

Murris, R., *La Hollande et les Hollandais au XVIIe et au XVIIIe siècle, vus par les Français*, Paris, 1925.

Muylwijk, P. D., 'Aanteekeningen over Gouda', *Biujdragen van de Oudheidkundige Kring 'die Goude'*, 2 (1940): 119.

Vervolgd en toch overwinnars. Historisch verhaal uit de zeventiende eeuw, Gouda, n.d.

Nierop, Léonie van, 'Bijdragen tot de geschiedenis van de Amsterdamse scheepsbouw', *JA*, 48 (1956): 38.

'De bruidegoms van Amsterdam van 1578 tot 1601', *TvG*, 48 (1933): 337; 49 (1934): 136 and 329; 52 (1937): 144 and 251.

'De zijdenijverheid van Amsterdam historisch geschetst', *TvG*, 45 (1930): 18.

Nijenhuis, W., 'Varianten binnen het Nederlandse calvinisme in de zestiende eeuw', *TvG*, 89 (1976): 358.

Noordegraaf, Leo, *Hollands welvaren? Levensstandaard in Holland 1450–1600*, Bergen (Noord-Holland), 1985.

Noordeloos, P., *Pastoor Maarten Donk*, 2 vols., Utrecht, 1948.

Obser, Karl, 'Aus dem Freiheitskampf der Niederlande. Briefe eines badischen Kriegsmanns', *BMHG*, 47 (1926): 39.

Oldewelt, W. F. H., 'Het aalmoezeniersweeshuis', *JA*, 61 (1969): 126.

Amsterdamsche archiefvondsten, Amsterdam, 1942.

'De Hollandse imposten en ons beeld van de conjunctuur tijdens de Republiek', *JA*, 47, 1955: 48.

Opstall, Margaretha E. van, *De reis van de vloot van Pieter Willemsz. Verhoeff naar Azië 1607–12*, The Hague, 1972.

Ordonnantie der schutterijen ende wachten binnen der stad Delft, 12 May 1580, Delft, 1616.

Oudenhoven, Jacob van, *Oud-Hollant, nu Zuyt-Hollandt*, Dordrecht, 1654.

Overbury, Thomas, *The miscellaneous works in prose and verse*, London, 1856.

Pabon, N. J., 'Bijdragen over het godsdienstig, zedelijk en maatschappelijk level in Den Haag tot het einde der 16e eeuw', *Die Haghe, Jaarboek* (1936): 36.

Parker, Geoffrey, *The Army of Flanders and the Spanish Road 1567–1659*, Cambridge, 1972.

'Francisco de Lixalde and the Spanish Netherlands (1576–1577): some new evidence', *TvG*, 89 (1976): 70.

Petit, Ian François le, *Nederlandsche republycke*, Arnhem, 1615.

Pijnacker, Hordijk, A., *Kerkelijk Naaldwijk*, Nijmegen, 1898.

Plomp, C., 'Het leerlingwezen in den Haag van de 15e tot de 18e eeuw', *Die Haghe, Jaarboek* (1936): 1.

Plomp, N., *Woerden 600 jaar stad*, Woerden, 1972.

Poelhekke, J. J., *Frederik Hendrik*, Nijmegen, 1978.

Geen blijder maer in tachtigh jaer. Verspreide studiën over de crisisperiode 1648–1651, Zutphen, 1973.

Met pen, tongriem en rapier, Amsterdam, 1976.

't Uytgaen van den treves, Groningen, 1960.

Pol, Lotte C. van de, 'Beeld en werkelijkheid van de prostitutie in de zeventiende eeuw', in G. Hekma and H. Roodenburg, *Soete minne en helsche boosheit. Seksuele voorstellingen in Nederland 1300–1850*, Nijmegen, 1988, p. 109.

Polman, OFM, P., *Godsdienst in de gouden eeuw*, Utrecht, 1947.

Pont, J. W., *Geschiedenis van het Lutheranisme in de Nederlanden tot 1618*, Haarlem, 1911.

Post, R. R., *Kerkelijke verhoudingen in Nederland vóór de reformatie van ± 1500 tot ± 1580*, Utrecht, 1954.

Posthumus, N. W., *Bescheiden betreffende de provinciale organisatie der Hollandsche lakenbereiders*, Amsterdam, 1917.

Bronnen tot de geschiedenis van de Leidse textielnijverheid, IV, *1611–1650*, The Hague, 1914.

'Gegevens betreffende landbouwtoestanden in Rijnland in het jaar 1575', *BMHG*, 25 (1914): 169.

De geschiedenis van de Leidsche lakenindustrie, II, The Hague, 1939.

'Kinderarbeid in de 17e eeuw in Delft', *Economisch Historisch Jaarboek*, 22 (1943): 48.

De nationale organisatie der lakenkoopers tijdens de Republiek, Utrecht, 1927.

Poujol, D. F., *Histoire et influence des églises wallonnes dans les Pays-Bas*, Paris, 1902.

Price, J. L., *Culture and society in the Dutch republic during the 17th century*, London, 1974.

Pringsheim, Otto, *Beiträge zur wirtschaftlichen Entwicklungsgeschichte der Vereinigten Niederlande im 17. und 18. Jahrhundert*, Leipzig, 1890.

Prinsen, J., 'Een paar "seltsame trou-gevallen"', *Oud-Holland*, 35 (1917): 181.

Provisionele openinghe van eenige saecken die tzedert ettelijcke jaren herwaerts binnen der stede van der Goude voor-gevallen en gepasseert zijn, door een Gouds liefhebber, 1637.

Quintijn, Gilles Jacobs, *De Hollandsche Lijs, met de Brabandsche Bely: poetischer wyse voorgestelt ende gedicht*, The Hague, 1629.

Ravestyn, Jr, W. van, *Onderzoekingen over de economische en sociale ontwikkeling van Amsterdam gedurende de 16de en het eerste kwartaal der 17de eeuw*, Amsterdam, 1906.

Der reden-ryckers stichtighe aenwijsinghe van des werelts dwael-paden ... op 't ontsluyt der vraghe, waerdoor de werelt meest heyloos en blindich dwaelt, Schiedam, 1616.

Regt, H. W., *Geschied- en aardrijkskundige beschrijving van den Hoekschen Waard*, Zwijndrecht, 1849.

Regtdoorzee Greup-Roldanus, S. C., *Geschiedenis der Haarlemmer bleekerijen*, The Hague, 1936.

Reitsma, J., and S. D. van Veen, *Acta der provinciale en particuliere synoden, gehouden in de Noordelijke Nederlanden gedurende de jaren 1572–1620*, I–III, Groningen, 1892.

Resolutien van Holland 1572–1648.

Reyd, Everhard van, *Historie der Nederlantsche oorlogen begin ende voortganck tot den jaere 1601*, Leeuwaarden, 1650.

Ringoir, J. D. B., *Plattelandschirurgijns in de 17e en 18e eeuw. De rekeningenboeken van de 18-eeuwse Durgerdamse chirurgijn Anthony Egberts*, Bunnik, 1977.

Rogge, H. C., *Brieven van Nicolaes van Reigersberch aan Hugo de Groot*, Amsterdam, 1901.

'Een preek van Jacobus Trigland', *Godgeleerde Bijdragen voor 1865*, Amsterdam, 1905.

Rogier, L. J., *Geschiedenis van katholiek Delfshaven*, Haarlem, 1930.

Geschiedenis van het katholicisme in Noord-Nederland in de 16de en 17de eeuw, 5 vols., third edition, n.p., 1964.

Rollin Couquerque, 'Heksenprocessen te Goedereede', *Tijdschrift voor Strafrecht*, 12 (1897): 116 and 331.

Romein, J., *De lage landen bij de zee*, Utrecht, 1934.

Roorda, D. J., *Partij en factie*, Groningen, 1961.

Royen, P. C. van, *Zeevarenden op de koopvaardijvloot omstreeks 1700*, Amsterdam, 1987.

Rutgers, F. L., *Acta van de Nederlandsche synoden der zestiende eeuw*, Utrecht, 1889.

Het kerkverband der Nederlandsche Gereformeerde kerken, gelijk dat gekend wordt uit de handelingen van den Amsterdamschen kerkeraad in den aanvang der 17e eeuw, Amsterdam, 1882.

Sabbe, Maurits, *Brabant in 't verweer*, Antwerp, 1933.

Salgado, Gamini, *Cony-catchers and bawdy baskets: an anthology of Elizabethan low life*, Harmondsworth, 1972.

Sande, Johan van den, *Nederlandsche historie, dienende voor continuatie van de historie van wijl. Everhard van Reyd*, Leeuwaarden, 1650.

Sangers, W. J., *De ontwikkeling van de Nederlandse tuinbouw (tot het jaar 1930)*, Zwolle, 1952.

Schaïk, R. van, 'Prijs- en levensmiddelenpolitiek in de noordelijke Nederlanden van de 14e tot de 17e eeuw: bronnen en problemen', *TvG*, 91 (1978): 214.

Schakel, M. W., *Geschiedenis van de hoge en vrije heerlijkheden van Noordeloos en Over Slingeland*, Gorinchem, 1955.

Scheltema, Jacobus, *Geschiedenis der heksenprocessen*, Haarlem, 1828.

Volksgebruiken der Nederlanders bij het vrijen en trouwen, Utrecht, 1832.

Schelven, A. A. van, *Omvang en invloed der Zuid-Nederlandsche immigratie van het laatste kwart der 16e eeuw*, The Hague, 1919.

Willem van Oranje, Amsterdam, 1948.

Scheurleer, D. F., *Van varen en vechten*, I, The Hague, 1914.

Scholtens, H. J. J., *Uit het verleden van Midden-Kennemerland*, The Hague, 1947.

Schoorl, H., *Zeshonderd jaar water en land: bijdrage tot de historische geo- en hydrografie van de kop van Noord-Holland in de periode 1150–1750*, Groningen, 1973.

Schotel, G. D. J., *Kerkelijk Dordrecht*, I, Utrecht, 1841.

Geschiedenis der rederijkers in Nederland, 2 vols., Rotterdam, 1871.

De openbare eeredienst der Nederlandsch hervormde kerk in de zestiende, zeventiende en achttiende eeuw, second edition, ed. H. C. Rogge, Leiden, n.d.

Vaderlandsche volksboeken en volkssprookjes, 2 vols., Haarlem, 1873–4.

Schottmüller, Kurt, 'Reise-eindrücke aus Danzig, Lübeck, Hamburg und Holland 1636', *Zeitschrift des Westpreussischen Geschichtsvereins*, 52 (1910): 201.

Schrek, Johanna R., *El sitio de Bredá. Comedia de Don Pedro Calderón de la Barca*, The Hague, 1957.

Schulten, C. M., 'Het beleg van Alkmaar', in *Alkmaar ontzet 1573–1973*, ed. I. Schöffer, Ter Burg, 1973.

Sellin, T., *Pioneering in Penology: the Amsterdam houses of correction in the sixteenth and seventeenth centuries*, Philadelphia, 1944.

Sikesz, G. J., *De schutterijen in Nederland*, Utrecht, 1864.

Slive, Seymour, *Rembrandt and his critics 1630–1730*, The Hague, 1953.

Sloots, OFM, ed., Cunibertus, *De minderbroeders te Leiden*, Rotterdam, 1947.

Smit, J., *Den Haag in den geuzentijd*, n.p., 1922.

'De levensmiddelenpolitiek in Den Haag gedurende de jaren 1572–1574', *BVGO*, fifth series, 6 (1919): 260.

Sneller, Z. W., 'De tijkweverij te Rotterdam en te Schiedam in de eerste helft der 17e eeuw', *TvG*, 45 (1930): 237.

Soetendorp, J., *Ontmoetingen in ballingschap, II: 1250–1700*, Hilversum, 1965.

Souterius, Daniel, *Nuchteren Loth. Dat is, middel om op te staen, uyt de ziel- verderffelijkcke sonde van dronckenschap*, Haarlem, 1623.

Seer uytmuntenden Nederlandtsche victoriën, 2 vols., Haarlem, 1630.

Sprenger van Eijk (Eyck), P. J., *Geschiedenis en merkwaardigheden der stad Vlaardingen*, I, Rotterdam, 1831.

Storm van 's-Gravensande, 'Rotterdam in het begin van april des jaars 1572', *BVGO*, first series, 7 (1850): 10.

Stoye, J. W., *English travellers abroad 1604–1667*, London, 1952.

Tack, Johannes, *Die Hollandsgänger in Hannover und Oldenburg*, Leipzig, 1902.

Tawney, R. H., *Business and politics under James I: Lionel Cranfield as merchant and minister*, Cambridge, 1958.

Tersteeg, J., 'Vijf bange jaren (Gouda 1572–1576)', *BVGO*, fourth series, 5 (1906): 1.

Tex, J. den, *Oldenbarnevelt*, 5 vols., Haarlem, 1960–1970.

Thysius, *Historia navalis*, Leiden, 1657.

Tiele, P. A., 'Documenten voor de geschiedenis der Nederlanders in het Oosten', *BMHG*, 6 (1883): 222.

'Steven van de Haghen's avonturen van 1575 tot 1597 door hem zelven verhaald', *BMHG*, 6 (1883): 377.

Timmer, E. M. A., 'De impost op de pijlbieren', *BVGO*, fifth series, 5 (1916): 360.
Knechtsgilden en knechtsbossen in Nederland. Arbeidsverzekeringen in vroeger tijden, Haarlem, 1913.

Tukker, C. A., *De classis Dordrecht van 1573 tot 1609*, Leiden, 1965.

Udemans, G., *'t Geestelyck roer van 't coopmansschip*, second edition, Dordrecht, 1640.
Practycke, dat is werckelijcke oeffeninge van de christelijcke hooftdeughden, second edition, Dordrecht, 1640.

Uytenbogaert, Joannes, *Kerckelicke historie*, Rotterdam, 1647.

Uytenbogaert, *see also* Wtenbogaert.

Valcooch, Dirrick Adriaensz., *Chronycke van Leeuwenhorn*, Amsterdam, 1740.

Valcoogh, Dirck Adriaensz., *Regel der Duytsche schoolmeesters*, ed. G. D. J. Schotel, The Hague, 1875.

Valk, H. A. van der, *Kerkelijk Oud-Beijerland*, Oud-Beijerland, 1907.

Veenendaal, A. J., *Johan van Oldenbarnevelt. Bescheiden betreffende zijn staatkundig beleid en zijn familie*, II–III, The Hague, 1962–7.

Velius, T., *Chronyk van Hoorn*, fourth edition, Hoorn, 1740.

Veltenaar, C., *Het kerkelijk leven der gereformeerden in Den Briel tot 1816*, Amsterdam, 1915.

Velthuyse, J. I. J. M., *Katholiek Berkel en Rodenrijs in de loop der eeuwen*, Rotterdam, 1948.

Venne, A. van de, *Tafereel van de belacchende werelt*, The Hague, 1635.
Tafereel van sinne-mal, Middelburg, 1623.

Verhey, H. J. W., *Soli Deo Gloria. Geschiedenis van de oud-katholieke parochie van de Heilige Laurentius en Maria Magdalena te Rotterdam sedert de hervorming tot 14 mei 1940*, De Bilt, 1950.

Verhoofstad, K., *Katholiek Purmerend*, Purmerend, 1943.

'Verslag van den ambassadeur in Den Haag, Francesco Michiel, aan doge en senaat, 27 mei 1638', *BMHG*, 7 (1884): 67.

Vervou, Fredrich van, *Enige aenteekeningen van 't gepasseerde in de vergadering van de Staten-Generael anno 1616–1620*, Leeuwaarden, 1874.

Verwer, Willem Janszoon, *Memoriaelbouck. Dagboek van gebeurtenissen te Haarlem van 1572–1581*, ed. J. J. Temminck, Haarlem, 1973.

Visser, J., *Rovenius und seine Werke*, Assen, 1966.

Vloten, J. van, *Het Nederlandsche kluchtspel van de 14e tot de 18e eeuw*, 3 vols., Haarlem, n.d.

Vloten, J. van, *Paschier de Fyne*, 's-Hertogenbosch, 1853.

Vondel, J. van den, *Werken*, ed. J. van Lennep, revised by J. H. W. Unger, I–IV, Leiden, n.d.

Voogd, N. J. J. de, *De doelistenbeweging te Amsterdam in 1748*, Utrecht, 1914.

Vos Azn., G. J., *Voor den spiegel der historie!! Amstels kerkelijk leven van de eerste zestig jaren der vrijheid*, Amsterdam, 1903.

Vosters, S. A., *Spanje in de Nederlandse litteratuur*, Amsterdam, 1955.

Vrankrijker, A. C. J. de, *Geschiedenis van het Gooiland*, II–III, Amsterdam, 1940–1.

Vrankrijker, A. C. J. de, 'De textielindustrie van Naarden', *TvG*, 51 (1936): 152 and 264.

Vries, Jan de, *The Dutch rural economy in the golden age*, New Haven, 1974.

Vries Azn., J. de, 'Adolphus Tectander Venator', *Oud-Holland*, 40 (1922): 124.

Vrijman, L. C., *Kaapvaart en zeeroverij*, Amsterdam, 1938.

Vugt, T. van, *De gehangenen in de turfschuur. Brielse julinacht 1572*, Hilversum, 1972.

Wagenaar, J., *Vaderlandsche historie*, 21 vols., Amsterdam, 1749–59.

Waddington, A., 'Sommaire de la forme du régime des Provinces-Unies des Pays-Bas 1647', *BMHG*, 15 (1894): 153.

Warnsinck, J. C. M., *Drie zeventiende-eeuwse admiraals*, Amsterdam, 1943.
  Reizen van Nicolaus de Graaf naar alle gewesten des werelds 1639–1687, met Oost-Indise Spiegel, The Hague, 1930.
Wassenaer, Claes, *Historisch verhael alder gedenckweerdichste geschiedenissen die hier en daer in Europa … van den beginne des jaers 1621, tot den herfst toe voorgevallen zyn*, Amsterdam, 1622.
Wassenburgh, *Dans-feest der dochteren te Silo: wt den woorde Gods, de oudt-vaders, ende heydensche autheuren met sijn behoorlijcke sauce op-gedischt*, Dordrecht, 1641.
Weber, R. E. J., *De beveiliging van de zee tegen Europeesche en Barbarijsche zeeroovers 1609–1621*, Amsterdam, 1936.
Wessel, J. H., *De leerstellige strijd tusschen Nederlandsche gereformeerden en doopsgezinden in de zestiende eeuw*, Assen, 1945.
Westermannus, A., *Christelijcke zee-vaert*, seventh edition, Amsterdam, 1630.
Wijn, J. W., *Het krijgswezen in den tijd van Maurits*, Utrecht, 1934.
  'Het Noordhollandse regiment in de eerste jaaren van de opstand tegen Spanje', *TvG*, 62 (1949): 235.
Willigen, A. van der, *Les artistes de Harlem*, 1870.
Wiltens, Nikolaas, and Paulus Scheltus, *Kerkelyk Plakaatboek*, 2 vols., The Hague, 1722–35.
Witt Huberts, F. de, 'Een tot nu toe niet gebruikt dagverhaal van Haarlem's beleg, geschreven door een ooggetuige', *BMHG*, 47 (1926): 1.
Woldendorp, J. J., 'Flitsen uit de kerkelijke geschiedenis van Zoetermeer-Zegwaart na de reformatie', *Jaarboekje voor geschiedenis en oudheidkunde van Leiden en omstreken*, 1956: 87.
Wolff, M., 'De eerste vestiging der Joden in Amsterdam, hun politiek, en economische toestand', *BVGO*, fourth series, 9: 365; 10: 134 and 354.
Woltjer, J. J., 'Van katholiek tot protestant', in *Historie van Groningen, Stad en Land*, ed. W. J. Formsma (Groningen, 1976), 207.
Woude, A. M. van der, *Het Noorderkwartier*, 3 vols., Wageningen, 1972.
Woude, C. van der, *Sibrandus Lubbertus*, Kampen, 1963.
Wtenbogaert, Johannes, *Brieven en onuitgegeven stukken verzameld en met aanteekeningen*, ed. H. C. Rogge, I–II, Utrecht, 1868–9.
Zumthor, P., *La vie quotidienne en Hollande au temps de Rembrandt*, Paris, 1959.
Zyll, W. C. van, *Oudewater en omtrek, geologisch, mythologisch en geschiedkundig geschetst*, Oudewater, 1861.

INDEX